ISSUES IN CONTEMPORARY MACROECONOMICS AND DISTRIBUTION

The purpose of this and the companion volume, *Issues in Contemporary Microeconomics and Welfare*, is to capture and convey the spirit, fundamental issues, underlying tensions, rich variety, accomplishments and failures in contemporary economics. The chapters reflect a wide gamut of alternative approaches, in many cases presented and interpreted by those who participated in shaping and advancing the ideas. Many of the contributors are of architectonic stature. Some of them have shaped economics in the last thirty years or more; others are bright new lights.

ISSUES IN CONTEMPORARY MACROECONOMICS AND DISTRIBUTION

Edited by
George R. Feiwel

State University of New York Press
Albany

First published un U.S.A. by
State University of New York Press, Albany

For information, address State University of New York Press
State University Plaza, Albany, NY   12246

Printed in Hong Kong

Library of Congress Cataloging in Publication Data

Main entry under title

Issues in contemporary macroeconomics and distribution

Includes index
1. Macroeconomics Addresses, essays, lectures
2. Distribution (Economic theory) Addresses essays
lectures.   I Feiwel George R.
HB172.5 I87   1985   339   84-8487
ISBN 0-87395-942-6(v. 1)
ISBN 0-87395-943-4(pbk.   v.1)

Contents

v

Notes on the Contributors

Kenneth J. Arrow is Joan Kenney Professor of Economics and Professor of Operations Research, Stanford University. He was formerly James Bryant Conant University Professor of Economics, Harvard University. He has been President of the Econometric Society, the American Economic Association, the Institute of Management Sciences, and the Western Economic Association, and is currently President of the International Society for Inventory Research. He has received the John Bates Clark medal of the American Economic Association and the Nobel Memorial Prize in Economic Science. He is a Member of the National Academy of Sciences and a Corresponding Member of the British Academy. His many contributions include *Social Choice and Individual Values* (1951, 1963), *Essays in the Theory of Risk Bearing* (1971), *Limits to Organization* (1974), and *General Competitive Analysis* (with F. H. Hahn, 1971).

Jean-Pierre Béguelin is Assistant Director, Economic Studies, Swiss National Bank. He was formerly Assistant Professor of Economics, University of Geneva, and Visiting Scholar at MIT and the National Bureau of Economic Research (New York).

Jean-Pascal Benassy is Maître de Recherches at the Centre National de la Recherche Scientifique and Research Associate at the Centre d'Etudes Prospectives d'Economie Mathématique Appliquées à la Planification (CEPREMAP) in Paris. He holds a PhD degree from the University of California–Berkeley (under the direction of Gérard Debreu). He is the author of *The Economics of Market Disequilibrium* (1982) and of numerous articles on the microeconomic foundations of macroeconomics and on non-Walrasian macroeconomic theory.

Michael J. Boskin is Professor of Economics, Stanford University, and Director of the Social Insurance Program, National Bureau of Economic Research. He was a Visiting Professor at Harvard and a member of several of President Reagan's economic policy task forces. He has published extensively in public finance, macroeconomics, and labour economics. He is the editor of *Prices and Social Security* (1977), *Economics and Human Welfare: Essays in Honor of Tibor Scitovsky* (1979), *Federal Tax Reforms* (1978), *The Economy in the 1980s: A Program for Stability and Growth* (1980), and *The Economics of Taxation* (with H. Aaron, 1980).

Martin Bronfenbrenner is Kenan Professor of Economics and Lecturer on Japanese History, Duke University. He has written extensively in many areas of economics. Most closely related of his publications to his contribution in this volume is *Income Distribution Theory* (1971), supplemented by his chapter, 'Ten Issues in Distribution Theory', in *Modern Economic Thought* (ed. Sidney Weintraub, 1977). He is also the editor of *Is the Business Cycle Obsolete?* (1969) and the author of *Macroeconomic Alternatives* (1979). At the end of the academic year 1983–4 he plans to retire from Duke and become Professor of International Economics, School of International Politics, Economics, and Business, Aoyama Gakuin University, Tokyo, Japan.

Edwin Burmeister, formerly Professor of Economics, University of Pennsylvania, and Visiting Professor, University of Chicago, is now Commonwealth Professor of Economics at the University of Virginia. He served as editor of the *International Economic Review* from 1969 to 1975. He has published numerous articles in areas of mathematical economics and economic theory, particularly in the fields of capital theory, economic growth and macroeconomics. He is also the author of *Capital Theory and Dynamics* (1980) and *Mathematical Theories of Economic Growth* (with L. Dobbins, 1970).

Otto Eckstein is Paul M. Warburg Professor of Economics, Harvard University and Chairman of Data Resources Inc. In 1959–60 he was Technical Director of the Joint Economic Committee of the US Congress, in 1964–6 he served as a Member of President Johnson's Council of Economic Advisors. He is the author of various books, including *The Great Recession* (1978), *Core Inflation* (1981), and *The Data Resources Model of the US Economy* (1983). He has also written books and articles on such subjects as economic forecasting and simulation, public finance, employment, and productivity.[1]

George R. Feiwel is Alumni Distinguished Service Professor and Professor of Economics, University of Tennessee. He has been Visiting Professor, University of Stockholm, Harvard University, University of California

(Berkeley and Davis) and on several occasions has been Senior Faculty Visitor, Cambridge University. He is the author of more than ten books, including *The Economics of a Socialist Enterprise* (1965), *The Soviet Quest for Economic Efficiency* (1967, 1972), *Industrialization Policy and Planning Under Polish Socialism*, 2 vols (1971), *The Intellectual Capital of Michal Kalecki* (1975), and *Growth and Reforms in Centrally Planned Economies* (1977). He is also a contributor to and editor of *Samuelson and Neoclassical Economics* (1982).

Benjamin M. Friedman is Professor of Economics, Harvard University, and Director of Financial Markets and Monetary Economics Research, the National Bureau of Economic Research. He was a Marshall Scholar, King's College, Cambridge University. He is the author of *Economic Stabilization Policy* (1975) and *Monetary Policy in the United States* (1981), editor and part author of *New Challenges to the Role of Profit* (1978) and *The Changing Roles of Debt and Equity in Financing US Capital Formation* (1982), and author of many articles on monetary economics, macroeconomics, and economic policy. His principal research interests focus on financial markets and their effect on non-financial economic activity, including especially the effect of monetary policy.

Donald J. Harris was formerly at the University of Wisconsin (Madison) and is currently Professor of Economics, Stanford University. He is the author of many articles on growth theory and economic development and of *Capital Accumulation and Income Distribution* (1978).

Lawrence R. Klein is Benjamin Franklin Professor of Economics, University of Pennsylvania. He was formerly at the University of Chicago, University of Michigan, and the Oxford Institute of Statistics. He is Chairman of the Professional Board, Wharton Econometric Forecasting Associates, Inc.; principal investigator, Project LINK; and a Member of the National Academy of Sciences. He is past president of the American Economic Association, the Econometric Society, and the Eastern Economic Association. In 1976 he served as co-ordinator of Jimmy Carter's Economic Task Force. He was awarded the John Bates Clark medal of the American Economic Association and the Nobel Memorial Prize in Economic Science. His numerous contributions include *The Keynesian Revolution* (1947, 1966), *An Econometric Model of the United States, 1929–1952* (1955), *Essay on the Theory of Economic Prediction* (1968), and *An Introduction to Econometric Forecasting and Forecasting Models* (1980).

Takashi Negishi is Professor of Economics, University of Tokyo. He taught at the universities of New South Wales, Minnesota, and London. He is the author of *General Equilibrium Theory and International Trade* (1972), *Microeconomic Foundations of Keynesian Macroeconomics* (1979), and of numerous articles on economic theory and the history of economic thought.

Yew-Kwang Ng is Reader in Economics, Monash University (Australia). He was a Visiting Fellow at Nuffield College and Visiting Professor at Virginia Polytechnic Institute. He is the author of a number of articles on welfare economics and on macroeconomics under imperfect competition, as well as of *Welfare Economics: Introduction and Development of Basic Concepts* (1979, 1983).

Joan Robinson, who died on 5 August 1983, was Professor Emeritus, University of Cambridge, where she spent her entire academic career. She played a major role in revolutions and controversies in economics of our times. A member of Keynes's inner circle when the *General Theory* was being written, in the postwar period she made considerable contributions to the generalization of the General Theory and to the theory of growth. She made an earlier breakthrough in the theory of imperfect competition. She was a prolific writer of wide-ranging interests and concerns. Her numerous books include *Economics of Imperfect Competition* (1933, 1969), *Introduction to the Theory of Employment* (1937), *Essay on Marxian Economics* (1942, 1966), *The Accumulation of Capital* (1956, 1966), *Essays in the Theory of Economic Growth* (1963), *Economic Philosophy* (1963), *Freedom and Necessity* (1970), *Economic Heresies* (1971), and *Introduction to Modern Economics* (with J. Eatwell, 1973). Most of her articles can be found in *Collected Economic Papers*, vols 1–5, and *Further Contributions to Modern Economics* (1980).

Kurt Schiltknecht, a former researcher at the Institute for Economic Research, the Swiss Institute of Technology in Zurich and Visiting Researcher at the Econometric Research Unit of OECD in Paris and the Economics Research Unit, University of Pennsylvania, is currently with the Swiss National Bank where he serves as Director of the Economic Section (Research, Economics, Banking Studies, and Statistics) and Deputy Head of Department I of the Bank. He lectures at the University of Basle and is a member of the National Research Council of the Swiss National Science Foundation.

Dieter Sondermann is Professor of Economics and Statistics and Director of the Institut für Gesellschafts-und Wirtschaftswissenschaften, Statistische

Abteilung, University of Bonn. He was Visiting Research Professor, Center for Operations Research and Econometrics, Université Catholique de Louvain, Visiting Ford Professor, University of California (Berkeley), and Fellow of the Institute for Advanced Studies, Hebrew University of Jerusalem. He is the author of many articles in mathematical economics and econometrics.

Lawrence H. Summers, previously at MIT, is Professor of Economics, Harvard University, and Domestic Policy Economist at the Council of Economic Advisors to President Reagan. He is the author of a number of articles on taxation, inflation, and labour market problems.

Jan Tinbergen is Professor Emeritus, Erasmus University – the former Netherlands School of Economics where he was Professor of Development Planning until 1973. He was also Claveringa Professor of International Co-operation at Leiden University from 1973 to 1975. He was formerly Director, Central Planning Bureau, Netherlands Government and adviser to various governments and the United Nations on development problems. Together with Ragnar Frisch, he was the first recipient of the Nobel Memorial Prize in Economic Science (1969). He contributed vastly in the areas of econometric business-cycle research, economic policy and welfare economics, development planning, and income distribution. His many books include *Statistical Testing of Business Cycle Theories*, 2 vols (1939, 1968), *Centralization and Decentralization in Economic Policy* (1954), *Economic Policy: Principles and Design* (1956, 1967), *Development Planning* (1967), *Income Distribution: Analysis and Policies* (1975), and *Mathematical Models of Economic Growth* (with H. C. Bos, 1962).

James Tobin is Sterling Professor of Economics, Yale University. During the preparation of his chapter in this volume he was Ford Visiting Professor, University of California (Berkeley). In 1961-2 he was a Member of the Council of Economic Advisors to President Kennedy. He is a recipient of the John Bates Clark medal of the American Economic Association. In 1981 he was awarded the Nobel Memorial Prize in Economic Science. He is a past president of the American Economic Association and the Eastern Economic Association. He is a Member of the National Academy of Sciences. He has contributed vastly to modern macroeconomics, partly reflected in collected volumes entitled *Essays in Economics: Macroeconomics* (1972), *Essays in Economics: Consumption and Econometrics* (1975), and *Essays in Economic Theory and Policy* (1982); and in *National Economic Policy* (1966), *The New Economics One Decade Older* (1974), and *Asset Accumulation and Economic Activity* (1980).

Henry Y. Wan Jr is Professor of Economics, Cornell University, and was previously at the University of California (Davis). He is the author of *Economic Growth* (1970) and of a number of articles on various topics in economics, including differential games, economic stabilization under Knightian uncertainty, and international trade.

NOTE

1. It is painful to record Otto Eckstein's untimely death on 23 March 1984 after a courageous battle with cancer. He had a warm heart and a cool, brilliant and creative mind. We are all the poorer for his passing.

Preface

These two volumes are modest attempts to capture and convey the spirit, essence, controversies, richness, variety, achievements and failures of some major advances in contemporary economics. They make no pretence at being comprehensive surveys of contemporary economics, nor at an encyclopaedic exposition of selected issues. They strive to shed some light on the fundamental issues, underlying tensions, and perennial challenges in contemporary economics. They present the reader with a sampling of the recent and ongoing quest to provide solid, 'hard', scientific foundations for the dismal, yet fascinating subject of economics. This modern quest seeks to define more precisely the limits of economic knowledge and the conditions under which certain theorems hold, to exploit opportunities, and wherever possible to transgress previous limits with an enriched conceptual apparatus and more sophisticated techniques of analysis and measurement.

Modern economists often ask smaller questions than did their predecessors. But whether large or small, old questions are being reiterated not only because of their intrinsic vitality and the fact that the available equipment is more sophisticated and thus may yield different and more precisely formulated answers, but also because the questions are framed somewhat differently, possibly affecting some of the answers. They also focus on new questions that have been attacked more or less (un)successfully with the aid of existing techniques. At the same time these techniques are being refined and amended or new ones invented and tried. In scholarly analysis, as in real life, it is the dynamics of the process that matter.

The state of the art and science of economics depends vitally on its practitioners' ability to identify real problems, to devise means for overcoming apparently insurmountable difficulties, and to take advantage of unexploited opportunities for doing useful and exciting work. Modern economics is characterized by sharp disagreements about some of the fundamentals and large gaping lacunae in our knowledge and understanding. If it is true that a science lives and flourishes on its unsolved problems, economics is one of the most vital, exciting, and promising sciences.

Economic theory is often criticized for its elegant articulation of states that never did and never will exist, for producing models that abstract from the most essential features of reality, and for evolving theory for the sake of theory that is further and further removed from the real world. Ultimately, however, the best of economic theory, no matter how abstract, is concerned with the understanding and improvement of the human condition in the ordinary business of life and with explaining and influencing the forces that govern the dynamics of production, organization, exchange, and distribution of the complex, interdependent, and evolving world around us.

Among the multiplicity of factors that foster or constrain an economy's dynamism, structure, and welfare of its actors, the quality of economic theory and policy really matters. From the perspective of accretion of economic knowledge, the continuing clashes of competing perceptions of economic processes tend to advance, refine, and spread economic knowledge, no matter how futile and retrogressive particular debates seem to be or how little we sometimes appear to have learned from the history of our subject or policy experience.

With a science whose several branches are as interdependent as those of economics, the compartmentalization of subjects is not without its pitfalls. This is particularly true of the conventional and artificial separation into micro and macro, which was undertaken for pragmatic purposes. The problem is further complicated by the fact that a vocal challenge to mainstream pragmatic macroeconomics is in some sense nothing but a microeconomic analysis of macroeconomic phenomena.

In eliciting the contributions to these volumes no effort was spared to offer the reader (within the obvious feasibility constraints) the widest possible gamut of alternative approaches, presented and interpreted often by those who participated in shaping or advancing the ideas. My aim was to have an eclectic and open-minded approach and to learn all that is constructive in different streams of thought. By and large the response to the invitations was gratifying, but understandably and regretably certain important gaps remained. Thus, with some compunction, I undertook the task of expanding the two introductory chapters to these volumes beyond the scope of background material and overview originally envisaged. Recognizing the limits of my own objectivity, I endeavoured to remain in the background in these introductions. It would be wrong and presumptuous of me to steer the reader in the 'right' direction. I point to alternatives; the choice is the reader's.

INTRODUCTION TO TWO VOLUMES

Issues in Contemporary Microeconomics and Welfare

Chapter 1 of this volume offers a perspective for the eloquent analysis in the chapters that follow. The account is perforce selective and an attempt is made to provide a perception of the alternative approaches, achievements, controversies and issues together with the underlying tensions and their sources.

Part I concentrates on resource allocation processes. There is no more fitting way to begin than with a subject that is one of the pivots of economics, sets the stage for the analyses and controversies in both volumes, and is a continuous and increasing source of tensions; that is, the potentials and limits of the market. It is our good fortune to have this analysed by Arrow in Chapter 2. He observes that at this juncture pure economic theory enjoys prestige status, yet there remain widespread doubts about the descriptive power and normative utility of general competitive equilibrium. Indeed, neoclassical microeconomic equilibrium theory, with fully flexible prices, represents a beautiful picture of mutual articulations of a complex structure, with full employment as one of its major elements. But, Arrow asks, what is its relationship to the real world? He calls attention to three major unsolved problems of general competitive equilibrium: (i) the failure to provide a microfoundation for Keynesian macroeconomics, (ii) the failure to take seriously, capture the essence of, and integrate imperfect competition into the system, and (iii) the failure to account for costs of transaction and of obtaining information, thus of running the market resource allocation process itself. He adds that demand and supply for money has not been fully integrated with general competitive equilibrium. Moreover, other objections to neoclassic theory revolve about its neglect of 'non-economic' arguments in the utility function such as power, status, social approval, etc. that also motivate economic actors, and of such constraints as capacity for calculation and social controls. More specifically, in Chapter 2 Arrow examines the relations between competitive equilibrium and Pareto efficiency. He then takes time and uncertainty into account and provides an extension of general equilibrium under uncertainty. A discussion of externalities, market failures, and transaction costs follows. He concludes that though the price system is valuable in many respects, it suffers from serious defects and cannot be left to itself to guide social life. In many situations the market should be supplemented by social decision-making – a subject he explores in Chapter 3 of *Issues in Contemporary Macroeconomics and Distribution*.

In Chapter 3 Hurwicz penetratingly illuminates the designer's point of view — the position of the economist designing the organizational structure. He makes the important, and yet subjective, distinction between what the designer considers as given (the environment) and what he can redesign (the mechanism). Specifically, this chapter deals with some major problems in designing efficient resource allocation systems when there is dispersal of information among the economic agents. It focuses on the minimum of communication that such a system requires, giving consideration to the incentives that condition the agent's behaviour. The channel capacity needed for communication can be measured by the dimension of the message space of the process. Hurwicz warns that the systems thus far obtained by the procedures for simplified situations that he outlines in his chapter should only be considered illustrative: 'We are still a long way off from designing systems for real economies.'

In a somewhat similar vein, Wilson (Chapter 4) points to the organization of trading when the participants have market power and private information (itself a source of market power). The problem is one of designing trading rules that promote efficient transactions while taking into account the effects of strategic behaviour. The purpose is to elaborate precisely how the trading rules and each participant's strategic behaviour (using his private information) combine to determine terms of trade that substantially mirror the dispersed information. Specifically, Wilson concentrates on incomplete information and on multilateral trade in a static environment, which is in addition 'severely restricted' by the absence of a number of other important features. The methods used are relatively new in theoretical economic literature. They serve to illuminate the role of institutionalized trading rules (represented here by the double auction) in promoting gains from trade. Wilson concludes: 'One can rejoice as well that a single trading rule suffices to attain incentive efficiency *uniformly* over a fairly wide class of economic environments: the usefulness of market processes to allocate resources and their persistence as institutionalized forms depend ultimately on their robustness in coping with a variety of circumstances.'

The game theory methodology, into which Aumann offers us valuable insights in Chapter 5, has had a love–hate relationship with economics for many years. Whatever its intrinsic merits, it is of special significance in these volumes because so many of our authors apply (or in some cases specifically reject) it in attempting to solve the problems they pose. Aumann's exposition of the theory of repeated games goes to the heart of the process of co-operation that emerges from repetition. To this extent the theory of repeated games provides a paradigm for bargaining. The fundamental result is the 'Folk Theorem' which suggests that the set of outcomes of repeated play may be very large; restrictions in various directions (e.g. on the information available to agents) yield sharper, more specific results.

Using the repeated game as a basis for co-operation, in the opening chapter (6) of Part II, concerned with duopoly and oligopoly, Kurz develops a theory of oligopolistic behaviour in non-contestable markets and where optimal firm size is not negligible. He suggests that such markets will develop a systematic and stable co-operative behaviour. This will take the form of an implicit contract among firms with respect to the procedures they use to change their output in equilibrium. The chapter focuses on the characterization of this procedure and on the resulting equilibrium. Kurz points out that the co-operative theory that he proposes for a duopoly can be extended to any oligopolistic industry. And his analysis suggests a rather novel connection between co-operation in oligopoly and social allocation of public goods. He shows that the allocation suggested by a 'Lindahl Equilibrium' may have a counterpart in co-operative oligopoly situations giving rise to 'Lindahl Agreements'.

In Chapter 7 Kuenne provides a contrasting view of oligopoly, but one that, like Kurz, seeks to capture the often neglected co-operative aspects of oligopoly. He stresses the concept of 'power structure' in mature industries that contains an amalgam of the competitive and co-operative specific to each industry and that reflects a 'rivalrous consonance of interests' among the firms in the process of decision-making. He suggests that methods and frameworks have to be tailored to the specifics of various industries at various times. Thus the 'institutional' dominates the general as the power structure gains in importance in defining the firms' objectives and conditioning their actions. Kuenne concludes that the concepts of rivalrous consonance and crippled optimization are promising flexible tools for operational analysis of oligopolistic pricing, and uses them in this chapter to analyse target-rate-of-return strategies.

Part III, which presents the new developments in the theory of industry structure, opens with Baumol's analysis of contestable markets (Chapter 8). He suggests that the theory of contestable markets, defined roughly as markets without barriers to entry or exit, constitutes a significant new departure in the analysis of firm and industry structure and provides a standard for public policy that is far broader and more widely applicable than the traditional ideal of perfect competition. Essentially, it challenges some previously held notions about entry barriers; it rejects the notion that economies of scale are an entry barrier, defined as an invariable source of welfare losses, and considers the presence of sunk costs as the prime form of entry barrier. The main features of a perfectly contestable market are: no excessive profits for anyone; absence of any sort of inefficiency in production; no cross subsidy for any product; and the sufficiency of even two firms to ensure that equilibrium prices will satisfy the necessary conditions for Pareto optimality. Thus in a perfectly contestable market the structure that emerges in any particular industry in the long run is the one that produces the output as cheaply as possible. On the theoretical side, contestability theory provides an extensive set of tools for the analysis of multiproduct firms and industries and, albeit for a polar case, yields a unique working model of oligopoly behaviour. In addition, because in such markets their prices must be parametric, the theory promises to permit incorporation of imperfectly competitive and oligopolistic firms into general equilibrium models. On a policy plane, by stressing that market structure is ultimately shaped by market forces, contestability theory points to the difficulties, sometimes failures, and relative undesirability of government's attempts to alter this structure. The implication is that public policy should aim at obtaining industry performance that approximates as much as possible a contestable market, rather than the unattainable goal of perfect competition.

In Chapter 9 Mirman, Tauman, and Zang take up the issue of perfectly contestable markets. In particular, they study the properties of equilibrium in such markets. Their questions revolve about the conditions (taking into account potential entry) that in perfectly contestable markets would result in only one firm producing the entire vector of outputs and operating under sustainable prices. They show that when technology is expressed by a joint subadditive cost function, the notion of a sustainable monopoly can be derived as a result of a Bertrand–Nash equilibrium of an economy consisting of many potential multiproduct firms.

In Chapter 10 Kreps and Spence provide an insightful survey of some interesting recent developments in the area of new industrial organization pertaining to the role of history in industrial competition. Their main theme is that the behaviour and performance of a mature industry are significantly conditioned by that industry's history. They contend that if the basic trichotomy (structure, conduct, performance) were to be extended by variables that are encompassed by the category of history, the power of prediction in mature industries would be considerably enhanced, a position that is also supported by Kuenne's analysis. The role of history can be properly understood by studying the process of industry dynamics. They concentrate on two basic approaches: (i) the rational actors approach which maintains that firms are able to anticipate the future consequences of their current actions, and (ii) the Simon-like approach that denies 'super' rationality, that relies on custom and routine, adaptation to unanticipated events, and evolution of decision-making procedures. In the latter case they focus on the Nelson and Winter framework (which is also outlined in Chapter 1).

This is followed by a chapter (11) by Harris and Townsend who propose a novel approach for the prediction of both the allocation of resources and the resource allocation mechanism in specific environments where before trading the agents are asymmetrically informed. The thrust of their approach is to define the concept of an optimal resource allocation mechanism and to characterize such optimal mechanisms and their associated optimal allocations for given economic environments. Their approach uses the 'Revelation Principle', that is, any equilibrium allocation of any mechanism can be achieved by a truthful, direct mechanism. By using this principle, they can find an optimal mechanism (and its associated equilibrium allocation) by choosing an allocation rule that maximizes some social welfare function, subject to technological feasibility and incentive–compatibility conditions. They argue that to analyse the resource allocation in certain types of environments with asymmetric information, the process of achieving allocations must first be considered. They present a methodology for such analyses and apply this approach to a specific, abstract environment characterized by asymmetry of information between two agents.

In Chapter 12, Goldberg focuses on the New Institutionalism, in particular on two concepts: namely, the production function and transaction costs. He warns about the need for greater care in the use of the former and is strongly critical of the latter. (A contrasting review of the transaction-cost approach can be found in Chapter 1.)

Part IV of this volume deals with welfare economics, social choice (which is also dealt with in Part I of this volume and in Chapter 3 of the companion volume), and consumption. It opens with a far-ranging and insightful survey by Hammond of the contemporary sweeping changes in welfare economics. After a lull of about a decade, the abundant crop of contributions to welfare economics in the 1970s has effectively broken away from both the 'old' and 'new' welfare economics. This modern break-through, still very much in progress, consists of three main parts: (i) the development of optimal tax theory, (ii) the elaboration of the theory of incentives (also dealt with in Chapter 3), and (iii) the emergence of a coherent theory of social choice with interpersonal comparisons. The latter at last permits us to address the classic issues of public finance such as how to redistribute income for economic justice (an issue also dealt with in Chapter 3 of the companion volume) and how to raise taxes equitably for the financing of public goods. Hammond concludes that the major progress is that it allows us to discuss the classic issues of public finance on a sounder basis of theoretical welfare economics than was possible even in the late 1970s.

Taking up some fundamental issues in social welfare, in Chapter 14 Ng defends welfarism and the Pareto principle. He argues that even when non-welfarist principles are accepted and the Pareto principle correspondingly extended, ordinalism is still an insufficient foundation for social welfare judgements and interpersonal comparable cardinal utilities are still essential. He argues that the belief in the sufficiency of ordinalism is inconsistent with the Bergson–Samuelson tradition of individualistic social welfare functions. He defends some methods of measuring cardinal utilities (such as the Neumann–Morgenstern index, some voting and market mechanisms, and the use of just noticeable differences). Though the methods are imperfect, he considers that they can contribute to more informative social welfare judgements.

In Chapter 15 Kemp and Kojima examine the paradox (in contrast to received doctrine) that foreign aid is frequently more harmful than beneficial to the recipient country and is advantageous for exporters in the donor country. Their aim is to rework the economics of foreign aid under relaxed assumptions. In particular, they make allowance for the possibility that aid is either wholly or partly tied in the donor or the recipient. They verify that the donor may gain and the recipient lose and that these outcomes may be compatible with market stability. The formal analysis of the major part of their chapter culminates in a set of necessary and sufficient conditions for perverse outcomes in stable economies.

In the final chapter of this volume (Chapter 16), Lau offers a formal analysis of the common assertion that 'two can live as cheaply as one' which is often backed by casual empiricism. He proposes a novel way of modelling the technology of joint consumption within a household, to allow for potential empirical identification of the nature of economies of scale, if such indeed exist. The crucial idea is one of distinguishing between the quantity of a consumer good bought and the quantities of 'services' that this good renders to each household member. The latter are assumed as produced in accordance with a production function, using the purchased good as an input. The production function must satisfy certain plausible restrictions. Lau characterizes the class of production functions that in fact meet these restrictions. Given the individual utility functions of the members of the household and the rules of allocation and distribution within the household, the production functions can be used to analyse the demand patterns of two-individual households relative to single-individual households.

Issues in Contemporary Macroeconomics and Distribution

Chapter 1 sets the stage by highlighting the alternative approaches to macroeconomics, allowing the various protagonists to speak for themselves, and by pointing to the issues and tensions. In the opening chapter (2) of Part I (concerned with some alternative perspectives on macroeconomics and distribution issues) the lively and sometimes bitter controversies surrounding such a strongly and directly policy-oriented subject as macroeconomics are reviewed by a major and creative veteran of the clashes. Tobin concentrates on the theoretical issues among the contestants — revolutionary and counter-revolutionary alike. Of major interest here is not only his perception of the counter-revolutions, but also of the *General Theory* as elaborated, applied and modified in the postwar period. He uses general equilibrium as a central frame of reference and points to the vulnerability of Keynesian economics to come to terms with this powerful tradition and to the contemporary attempts to reformulate Keynesian economics in order to overcome this failure — if such it is.

Looking at the economy from the normative perspective, in Chapter 3 Arrow makes a powerful case for distributive justice. Though he disagrees on many other points with Rawls, Arrow agrees with the basic thrust: justice values both liberty and equality. Arrow denies that there is any contradiction between these two ideals and asserts the opposite: one is not realizable without the other. He reviews the issues of trade-off between efficiency and equity — the market and distributive justice. He then proceeds to illuminate the role of social choice in guiding income distribution. In making his case for redistribution, Arrow poses the fundamental questions as to whether equality is really the meaning of distributive justice; the essence of the meaning of just or equal distribution of income, power, and other economic goods; the possibility of conflict between other legitimate social goals and justice and how to evaluate the trade-offs; the just intergenerational allocation of goods; and the extent to which the nature, ideology, functioning, and institutional arrangements of capitalism promote or hamper the achievement of justice. Even under assumptions most favourable to decentralization, there is an irreducible need for social choice on distribution. Indeed, there are a number of solutions where replacement of the market by collective action is desirable.

Chapter 4 provides some insights into Joan Robinson's perspective. She starts out with a brief critique of pre-Keynesian economics and proceeds to a challenge of the Keynesian neoclassical synthesis and the unfortunate compartmentalization of economics into micro and macro. She sees this as an attempt to save equilibrium theory from Keynes which has landed it in a number of contradictions. On the analytical plane there is the problem of time: 'Equilibrium, it seems, lies in the future. Why has it not been established already? Jam tomorrow but never jam today.' She also castigates the inequalities stemming from the free play of market forces. She then takes to task capital theory and points to Sraffa's inspiration.

As these volumes were going to press it was with much sadness that we have learned of Joan Robinson's death. In many respects she has made a real difference to the economics of our age. Both those that agree and those that disagree with her will probably miss her challenges. This is not the place to pay tribute to the truly great economist she was, but to record how privileged I am to share with the reader her last contribution. It is presented here in the draft form Joan originally sent me. Because of her prolonged and incapacitating illness she was not able to revise it. Naturally I consider it inappropriate to tamper with her writing. In Chapter 1 of this volume I have attempted to provide some background on the development of her thought.

Part II is concerned with finding an appropriate microeconomic underpinning for Keynesian macroeconomics. It opens with a chapter (4) by Negishi who develops a non-Walrasian microeconomic theory as a basis for the Keynesian fixprice model. His inspiration stems from Menger who pointed out that the price is not the sole important factor in the theory of exchange and stressed the asymmetry between demand and supply. Negishi argues the case for microfoundations based on the theory of kinked demand curves not perceived by oligopolistic but by more competitive firms. He concludes by pointing to the essential differences between Walrasian and non-Walrasian economics.

In a similar vein, in Chapter 6 Benassy presents a two-market model that diverges from the 'standard' fixprice non-Walrasian macro models in the sense that (i) there is upward but not downward price flexibility, (ii) wages are related to the price level, with allowance for situations ranging from no indexation to full indexation. The model is an application of more general concepts of non-Walrasian equilibrium. The study concentrates on the relative efficiency of combating unemployment via Keynesian demand management policies versus 'classical' incomes policies, aimed at reducing the wage level. The model is studied under three different regimes. (Regime A – excess supply of labour and goods; regime B – excess supply of labour with goods market cleared; and regime C – excess demand for labour, with goods market cleared.) While regime A displays standard Keynesian features, it appears in regime B that indexation can reduce considerably the effectiveness of demand management even though involuntary unemployment exists. In the corresponding case, however, incomes policies are effective in reducing unemployment. Benassy concludes that analysis of macroeconomic problems by means of non-Walrasian equilibrium concepts appears to be effective both to predict the policy consequences of various price formation mechanisms and to synthesize hitherto antagonistic models.

Also in the non-Walrasian approach, Sondermann shows in the next chapter (4) that for a three-commodity model there exist equilibrium states with involuntary unemployment. Unemployment equilibria may occur whenever prices (and wages) adjust slower than quantities. The characteristics of equilibria arrived at in his model include: the inequality of demand and supply (non-Walrasian); stability in the sense that neither producers nor consumers find it advantageous to upset the *status quo*; a non-tâtonnement generation process for both quantities and prices; involuntary unemployment; prices that are neither fixed nor set by an auctioneer, but by producers with normal price expectations; wages that are neither fixed, arbitrary, nor inflexible, but depend on the economy's history; and finally the possible inefficiency of the equilibrium at which the economy may arrive, providing room for the types of government intervention suggested by Keynes.

In the final chapter (8) in Part II, Ng outlines a micro–macro method to study the effects of industry-wide and economy-wide changes in demand, costs, expectations, etc. on the average price and aggregate output. He uses the concept of the representative firm but, in contrast to the Marshallian tradition, the response of the representative firm is used to approximate that of a typically non-perfectly competitive industry or the whole economy, with interesting non-traditional results. Ng uses the analysis to show the possibility of real expansion and contraction without affecting the price level in a monopolistically competitive economy (not possible in a perfectly competitive one since no lags, no misinformation or other frictions are assumed). He shows that an increase in nominal aggregate demand may lift the real-wage demand-for-labour function, leading to a real expansion and that the practical possibility of this non-traditional result is increased if some firms are revenue maximizers. In the last section of his chapter, Ng summarizes some further results (on entry/exit of firms, oligopoly, and some applications of his analysis) that he elaborates in a forthcoming book.

The arguments of the new classical macroeconomics (also known as rational expectations or equilibrium business-cycle theory) are expounded in Chapter 1 of this volume. Part III deals with theoretical and policy conceptions and evaluations of this approach. It opens with a chapter (9) by Wan who disputes the claims of the new classical macroeconomics from a game-theoretic perspective. He contends that: (i) any policy evaluation reminds all agents that policies once made can also be remade and unmade later. Rational agents do not confuse the incumbent's present intent with policy rules of the future. Future rules are predicted only in the light of what is said and done by the current government. To influence agents, words and deeds of the current regime play the same roles as those of its predecessors. 'How influential?' is on econometric record. Thus Keynesian econometrics is not fatally flawed. (ii) Any time-inconsistent policy is not 'sub-game perfect' and hence tempts future regimes to renege. Thus, any policy that is credible to rational agents must be time-consistent. (iii) In any world where agents are heterogeneous policy almost surely is effective.

In Chapter 10 Burmeister shows that both rational expectations and perfect foresight models feature a similar indeterminacy problem. This is an important economic problem which if it remains unresolved (as it has thus far) hampers empirical and policy evaluation work. Since most existing rational expectation models postulate convergence, convergent expectations are a crucial assumption that is basic to both the theoretical analysis and empirical estimation of these models. Burmeister conjectures that we would be in a better position to understand the business cycle if we built models that were capable of dynamic instability and/or non-stochastic oscillations instead of ruling them out by assumption as is frequently the case when standard procedures for 'solving' rational expectations models are used.

Benjamin Friedman's chapter (11) concludes this part with further insights into trends in macroeconomics and into the macro problems. He offers the thesis that the experience of the early 1980s — the anticipated, non-surprise disinflationary policy and its aftermath — directly contradicts the central policy conclusions of new classical macroeconomics. It represents at least as powerful a refutation as that which earlier led to disillusionment with the existing macroeconomic orthodoxy. Friedman makes a point for a symbiosis of old and new developments in macroeconomics, to derive policy conclusions in conformity with the perceived functioning of the economy; that is, that money is not neutral, that trade-offs do exist, and that policy influences real economic outcomes.

Part IV on inflation and disinflation opens with Chapter 12 by Klein who defends mainstream macroeconometric models against the charge that they did not anticipate the inflationary surge of the 1970s. He shows that the variances between forecasts and actual outcomes were not as significant as some critics claimed and reveals also how the models were gradually extended to give increasing cognizance to the energy and food sectors. He acknowledges the need for constant model improvement, but rejects radical model reform or abandonment.

In Chapter 13 Eckstein analyses the disinflation process of the early 1980s. He asks the pertinent questions whether the severity of the 1982 recession finally reduced core inflation, whether inflationary expectations have come down as much as actual prices; whether the economy's structure has altered sufficiently to reduce the inflationary bias built-in in the last three decades; whether inflation will return quickly in the recovery; and finally what can be done to ensure that the recovery does not suffer from its predecessors' ills. He attempts to answer these questions by quantitative analysis on the basis of a cohesive theoretical structure.

In Chapter 14 Béguelin and Schiltknecht discuss monetarism and monetary policy from the standpoint of central bankers. They point out, *inter alia*, that central bankers cannot be assumed to have more information than the rest of the world and that they more or less frequently make wrong decisions that destabilize the economy. They contend that the only means of bridging the credibility gap is to control the trend of money supply in the long run. They believe that central banks should lean towards medium-term control of the money supply through a succession of annual rather than quarterly targets, and conclude that, though it is not an ideal solution for all problems, the monetarist approach to monetary policy is the optimal solution.

Part V, concerned with distribution, growth, and policy alternatives, opens with Chapter 15 by Tinbergen who surveys the factors that condition income distribution in developed countries. He illuminates a wide variety of economically relevant factors, including the morphology of markets, production functions, innate or learned abilities, sociological factors such as power and discrimination, and non-productive sources such as households and institutional units (e.g. the military) as well as income transfers primarily from a social security system.

In Chapter 16 Bronfenbrenner presents a modern, temperate defence of marginal productivity as a theory of input demand rather than of wages and takes up some aspects of the capital controversy with Joan Robinson.

In the following chapter (17) Don Harris points to the discord between the historical picture of uneven growth as a persistent phenomenon and growth theory that essentially negates this phenomenon. He presents an overview of some of the theoretical issues involved and proposes the analyses of uneven growth where one of the central analytical problems is understanding the mechanism of mutual interaction and interdependence among the development of various sectors.

The concern with the economy's productive capacity has a long and respectable ancestry. In Chapter 18 Feiwel discusses the driving forces of and constraints to economic growth. He then contrasts basically two approaches to stimulate growth: one that concentrates exclusively on supply and the other that integrates supply and demand, or from a some-what different vantage point, one that uses a microeconomic approach to macroeconomic problems and the other that integrates both macro and micro approaches. Fundamentally the approaches differ in their percep-tions of the dynamics and *modus operandi* of a modern economy, the range and effectiveness of policy options, and the elasticity of response of agents to economic stimuli. Economic models of the first approach essen-tially distort reality if they do not perceive the economy as subject to trend, fluctuations, stochastic disturbances, and major market failures, in contrast to the second approach which does make an attempt to incor-porate those factors in its models .

In Chapter 19 Summers summarizes his recent research on the develop-ment of an asset price approach for analysing capital income taxation. He discusses a number of reasons for focusing on the role of asset prices in analysing public finance problems, including the role of asset prices in determining investment decisions and the role of changes in asset prices as indicators of the horizontal and vertical equity effects of tax reforms. He also reviews recent empirical research that studies asset price information in order to measure the effects of tax reforms on economic behaviour and to distinguish between alternative models of the effects of capital income taxation.

Many of the most important modelling and policy issues in both macroeconomics and income distribution revolve around the emphasis placed on the length of the time horizon, the role of expectations, and the responsiveness of behaviour to incentives. In the final chapter (20) of this volume, Boskin examines these issues by developing several examples. The potential role of fiscal policy in stabilizing the economy is discussed in terms of various perceptions of the role of government debt and the relative importance of short- and long-run perceptions about income in determining spending behaviour. The incidence of various alternative tax policies is also pursued from the perspectives of annual and lifetime income; *ex ante* and *ex post* realizations of income; and presumed time horizons governing consumption and saving behaviour. Boskin demonstrates that the answers to many frequently posed policy questions depend on the modeller's assumptions concerning the above-mentioned three factors and conjectures about them on the basis of available statistical studies. He concludes that the introduction of a longer-term focus in macroeconomics and income distribution debates has been one of the most important developments in economics in the last fifteen years, but that problems such as incomplete markets lead to models that combine emphasis on shorter-run current income and longer-term expected values.

ACKNOWLEDGEMENTS

I am beholden and deeply grateful to all the contributors. They and their selfless co-operation, often in the face of considerable difficulties, have made the real difference. One of the great rewards in seeing this project through the processes of design, gestation, and fruition has been in experiencing the spirit of professionalism and dedication revealed by the contributors. Many of them are of architectonic stature in their fields; some of them have shaped economics in the last thirty years or more, others are bright new lights. As editor I have sought to weave their contributions into designs that reflect the major developments in micro- and macroeconomics of the last two decades or so and to anticipate those of the next, filling in the inevitable gaps in the fabric with my own efforts. All inadequacies are the editor's; all praise goes to the contributors.

I am a bankrupt when it comes to thanking those contributors who unsparingly gave of their time to discuss the various aspects of the project, offered wise counsel, and/or graciously commented on my introductory chapters. Special gratitude is owed to : Arrow, Aumann, Baumol, Benassy, Boskin, Bronfenbrenner, Eckstein, Ben Friedman, Hammond, Milt Harris, Hurwicz, Kemp, Klein, Kreps, Kuenne, Kurz, Lau, Negishi, Tauman, Tinbergen, Tobin, Townsend, Wan, and Wilson.

A large number of people made an imprint on these volumes. I fear that this acknowledgement can hardly do justice to the debt I owe them for their influence, time, patience and good advice. I will spare the reader the major names in the history of economic thought and reluctantly will abstain from enumerating my teachers, colleagues, and students. But I should be remiss not to mention G. Debreu, F. Hahn, D. Jorgenson, E. Kalai, A. Roth, L. Shapley, E. Sheshinsky, and O. Williamson. Thanks are also due for interesting discussions with M. Abramovitz, G. Ackley, I. Adelman, A. Blinder, J. Chipman, P. David, D. Dillard, S. Fischer, F. Fisher, C. Garison, N. Georgescu-Roegen, E. Glustoff, J. Green, R. Hall, H. Jensen, D. Kaserman, J. Kendrick, D. Laidler, H. Leibenstein, J. Letiche, A. Lindbeck, R. Looney, B. McCallum, B. Holmstrom, A. Mas-Colell, E. Maskin, T. Mayer, P. Milgrom, J. R. Moore, M. Morishima, M. Nerlove, N. Rosenberg, T. W. Schultz, J. Stiglitz, and J. Tirole.

My research burden was lightened, and hopefully the coverage broadened, by the kind co-operation of numerous authors who have sent me their writings (often in unpublished form). My thanks to K. Brunner, M. Friedman, R. Gordon, S. Grossman, G. Harcourt, Sir John Hicks, L. Johansen, Lord Kahn, Lord Kaldor, I. Kirzner, R. E. Lucas Jr, J. E. Meade, A. Meltzer,

F. Modigliani, J. Muth, R. Nelson, W. Nordhaus, R. Radner, John Roberts, T. Sargent, A. Sen, C. Sims, G. Stigler, and J. E. Taylor.

Once again I am happy to acknowledge a special debt of gratitude to Robert Bassett (and his assistant Warner Granade) of the reference department of the University of Tennessee library for imagination, initiative, and exertions beyond the call of duty. Thanks are also due to the Greene Library at Stanford, the University of California (Berkeley) libraries and numerous colleagues who graciously lent me their books and materials.

The customary disclaimer applies to all the above mentioned – *mea culpa* all the way, except for my wife, Ida, who shares much greater culpability than she allows me to mention.

Whatever is wrong with economics (and, indeed, there is much), one cannot but feel proud to belong to a profession that numbers among its members someone like Jan Tinbergen – who, as H. C. Bos records in the *International Encyclopedia of the Social Sciences*, would have been as worthy a candidate for the Nobel peace prize as for the one he was awarded in economics. Ida and I feel privileged to respectfully and affectionately dedicate these two volumes to Jan who is 80 years young this year.

G. R. Feiwel

1 Quo Vadis Macroeconomics? Issues, Tensions and Challenges

G. R. FEIWEL

THE KEYNESIAN REVOLUTION AND THE CLASSICS

The 'classical' macroeconomic theory that dominated economic thought before Keynes (and is resurfacing at present in a sophisticated guise) viewed the economy as a more or less self-propelled and self-regulating mechanism, where a tendency to establish full employment prevails. The flexibility of wages, prices, and interest rates ensures the operation of the mechanism. In such a system lapses from full employment are transitory and disequilibria are eliminated rapidly and effectively. Full employment is that which is determined by the factors of supply and demand on the market – whatever it may be. Unemployment is thus considered to be merely an accidental and temporary displacement from such a state (see also Sargent, 1979, pp. 44–5).

Such an oversimplified view generally conforms to the classical writers' propensity to take the long view of the economic process.[1] In some sense it does underrate the breadth of their grasp of the economic process; of the dynamics of transitional states and, indeed, the accompaniment of growth of economic activity by short-term fluctuations however dimly perceived. One of the bones of contention is whether the long-term growth of national production or wealth of nations could be fully understood and usefully separated from the oscillatory movements or the dynamics of the short-run adjustments (no matter how protracted, imperfect and incomplete).

It matters not how novel Keynes's ideas were, nor how appropriate his criticism of the classics or of his contemporaries (like Pigou and Robertson) was. He did succeed in undermining the major orthodox preconception of the presumption of strong forces in the capitalist economy to move, find, and maintain endogenously full employment. Though theoretically unarmed, his basic vision of the capitalist economy could already be discerned in the *Consequences*. This vision was crystallized in a popular 1934 BBC discussion that appeared in the *Listener* (Keynes, 1973, pp. 485–92) of which some excerpts are very enlightening:

> On the one side are those who believe that the existing economic system is, in the long run, a self-adjusting system, though with creaks and groans and jerks, and interrupted by time lags, outside interference and mistakes. . . These authorities do not, of course, believe that the system is automatically or immediately self-adjusting. But they do believe that it has an inherent tendency towards self-adjustment, if it is not interfered with and if the action of change and chance is not too rapid.
>
> On the other side of the gulf are those who reject the idea that the existing economic system is, in any significant sense, self-adjusting. They believe that the failure of effective demand to reach the full potentialities of supply. . . is due to much more fundamental causes [pp. 486–7] . . .
>
> The strength of the self-adjustment school depends on its having behind it almost the whole body or organised economic thinking and doctrine of the last hundred years. This is a formidable power [p. 488] . . .
>
> Now *I* range myself with the heretics. I believe their flair and their instinct move them towards the right conclusion. But I was brought up in the citadel and I recognise its power and might. A large part of the established body of economic doctrine I cannot but accept as broadly correct. I do not doubt it. For me, therefore, it is impossible to rest satisfied until I can put my finger on the flaw in that part of the orthodox reasoning which leads to the conclusions which for various reasons seem to me to be inacceptable. I believe that I am on my way to do so. There is, I am convinced, a fatal flaw in that part of the orthodox reasoning which deals with the theory of what determines the level of effective demand and the volume of aggregate employment; the flaw being largely due to the failure of the classical doctrine to develop a satisfactory theory of the rate of interest [p. 489] . . .
>
> Now the school which believes in self-adjustment is, in fact, assuming that the rate of interest adjusts itself more or less automatically, so

as to encourage just the right amount of production of capital goods to keep our incomes at the maximum level which our energies and our organisation and our knowledge of how to produce efficiently are capable of providing. This is, however, pure assumption. There is no theoretical reason for believing it to be true [p. 490] . . .

Even as things are, there is a strong presumption that a greater equality of incomes would lead to increased employment and greater aggregate income. . . At present, it is important to maintain a careful balance between stimulating consumption and stimulating investment. . . The right course is to get rid of the scarcity of capital goods — which will rid us at the same time of most of the evils of capitalism — whilst also moving in the direction of increasing the share of income falling to those whose economic welfare will gain most by their having the chance to consume more.

None of this, however, will happen by itself or of its own accord. The system is not self-adjusting, and, without purposive direction, it is incapable of translating our actual poverty into our potential plenty [p. 491].

In the book that was the Magna Carta of the Keynesian Revolution (Keynes, 1936, p. 249), Keynes depicted his contemporary capitalist economy:

In particular, it is an outstanding characteristic of the economic system in which we live that, whilst it is subject to severe fluctuations in respect of output and employment, it is not violently unstable. Indeed it seems capable of remaining in a chronic condition of sub-normal activity for a considerable period without any marked tendency either towards recovery or towards complete collapse.

Whatever else needs to be said about the Keynesian revolution in macroeconomics and monetary theory and its various interpretations, it undermined the myth that full employment is the normal state of the economy. It focused on the seriousness of the macroeconomic failures of the system, on the sources of disturbances, on the opportunities for improvement, on effective demand as a central problem, on the possibilities that real output and employment is possible at any level of activity, on the possibilities for economies to get stuck in unsatisfactory equilibrium, on prolonged periods of underemployment equilibrium or persisting disequilibrium, on the persistence of involuntary unemployment which conventional economic analysis found so awkward to accommodate, and on the fallacies of the classical saving–investment–interest rate mechanism and of the doctrine of full employment via flexible wages and prices and of the classical policy prescriptions in general.

One of the perennial sources of tensions between pragmatic macro-economists (such as Tobin in Chapter 2 of this volume) and those who insist on applying the standard rules of neoclassical theory, is whether or not Keynes succeeded in proving the existence of equilibrium with involuntary unemployment. Whatever the verdict of history (and he probably did not), the larger and more fundamental question is whether it really matters, for historically the Great Depression did take place and there still exists the possibility of protracted unemployment which the natural adjustments of a market economy remedy very slowly, if at all.

The Keynesian revolution means different things to different people. In essence it refers to the impact of the theory of determination of the level of aggregate output and employment; it underscores the dependence and impact of the level of effective demand on the degree of utilization of labour and capacity; it provides the analytical innovation of the consumption function; it focuses on expectations in an uncertain world in general and on marginal efficiency of investment and speculative liquidity preference in particular; it cogently distinguishes between the acts of saving and investment and the problems of offsets to saving; and it emphasizes, *inter alia*, the fluctuations in total investment demand (and its dependence on shifts in expected profitability, which in turn depends on fairly unpredictable dynamic factors and subjective psychology and is beneficially influenced by a reduction of uncertainty about the future when the economy is steadily working in high gear) as a source of macroeconomic instability. The policy implicit in the theory assigns a crucial role to deliberate government policy for influencing (if not regulating) effective demand and, in a broader sense, to use whatever policy instruments are most appropriate to influence and co-ordinate both demand and supply and to keep the system reasonably close to a desirable full employment growth path, while minimizing adverse side effects. Subject to qualifications, it appears that Modigliani (1980a, p. 3) captured 'the fundamental practical message of the *General Theory*: that a private enterprise economy using an intangible money *needs* to be stabilized, *can* be stabilized, and therefore *should* be stabilized by appropriate monetary and fiscal policies'.

Keynesian macroeconomics *per se* is neutral with regard to the uses to which it could be put (as, indeed, we are painfully reminded in the preface to the German edition of the *General Theory*). It does not logically lead to a particular position regarding the content of the full- or high-employment economy or the means by which it is to be achieved. Nor does it have a specific position *vis à vis* the relative size of the private and public sectors or the degree of income redistribution and welfare-state measures in general. It enlarges the scope of opportunities for the policy-maker for achieving whatever goals he (or the electorate) set for himself. In the customary mixture of normative and positive, the specific contents of Keynes's proposals made at a particular time and place are surely overshadowed by the general potentials and limits of his approach.

As Joan Robinson (1962, pp. 138-9) — Keynes's young friend and collaborator — with the benefit of hindsight and the tinge of her own strong views about the message of the Keynesian revolution, wrote in a terse passage:

> It is possible to defend our economic system on the grounds that patched up with Keynesian correctives, it is, as he put it, the 'best in sight'. Or at any rate that it is not too bad, and change is painful. In short, that our system is the best system that we have got.
>
> Or it is possible to take the tough-minded line that Schumpeter derived from Marx. The system is cruel, unjust, turbulent, but it does deliver the goods, and, damn it all, it's the goods that you want.
>
> Or, conceding its defects, to defend it on political grounds — that democracy as we know it could not have grown up under any other system and cannot survive without it.
>
> What is not possible, at this time of day, is to defend it, in the neoclassical style, as a delicate self-regulating mechanism, that has only to be left to itself to produce the greatest satisfaction for all.

We should digress at this junction to clarify one important point: the fundamental notion underlying some of the interpretations of the *General Theory* by Keynes's followers and critics alike is that the economy is inherently unstable. Klein (1973, p. 11), however, challenges the contention of the inherent instability of the economy. He allows that the economy is 'oscillatory or subject to fluctuations and that it has a tendency to move about a position of underemployment equilibrium, but this is far different from saying that the economy is unstable'. (See also Fisher, forthcoming.)

As previously alluded, in the eyes of the beholders there was more than one Keynes and he continues to mean different things to different people. There was the Keynes of the *General Theory* (with the perennial disputes over his relationship to the pre-*General Theory* Keynes, in particular to the Keynes of the *Treatise*) storming the citadel of orthodoxy with an analytical apparatus. There was also the Keynes of public policy, concerned with curing the ills of his time. In a true Marshallian fashion, Keynes's many profound observations about the world around him could not be captured in any model. The essentially static *General Theory* is nevertheless rich in dynamic implications.

The interpretations, reinterpretations, and reappraisals of the Keynesian analytical system have been going on for nearly five decades. In the pages that follow we shall touch on some of them.

Like many breakthroughs, the *General Theory* gave rise to different and often conflicting (but also in many respects overlapping) interpretations and spin-offs. Some of them derived strongly clashing implications owing to differences in underlying philosophies and descent from different intellectual family trees (say, Walrasian or Marshallian). In fact, one group may even question whether the other is 'Keynesian' at all.[2] The various groups sometimes even compete among themselves as to who is 'more Keynesian than Keynes'. And, a recurring theme is that perhaps Keynes himself failed to understand his theory. Even among similar versions there is an abundance of variants — and not only for reasons of product differentiation.

Without at this point elaborating on their differences and similarities, some of the most representative variants are: Kalecki's theory of dynamics and fluctuations of national income and its distribution between profit and wages (an antecedent and independent version of the general theory); 'Hicksian–Walrasianism' (IS–LM) prior to his 'reincarnation' as a 'born-again' Keynesian'; American neoclassical Keynesians (including Alvin Hansen, Samuelson, L. R. Klein, Modigliani, James Tobin, and Solow) — proponents of what has come to be known as the mainstream (Samuelsonian) synthesis of neoclassical and Keynesian theory and policy; the formal macroeconomic general disequilibrium and non-Walrasian equilibrium theorists, whose work is also known as the non-market clearing or quantity constrained models (including (a) the 'Americans' — influenced by Patinkin — Clower, Leijonhufvud, the 'young' Barro, and Hershel Grossman, and (b) the 'French–German–Japanese': Benassy, Grandmont, Malinvaud, Negishi, and Sondermann); and last but not least the 'Cambridge Keynesians', the younger collaborators of Keynes (including Richard Kahn, Joan Robinson, and Kaldor) and their disciples as well as their 'cousins' the American post-Keynesians (including Sidney Weintraub, Paul Davidson, Minsky, Eichner, and Kregel). Needless to say, such a listing begs more questions than it answers.

Before proceeding with the various spin-offs, perhaps we should pause here on Harry G. Johnson's (1971, pp. 4-6) provocative speculation about the ingredients that make for a successful revolution in economics specifically the Keynesian revolution, of which Johnson was not a particularly friendly critic. He listed five main characteristics:

(1) An existing orthodoxy whose central theme was the assumption that the economy tended towards full employment.

(2) The thrust of novelty, yet embedded as much as possible in what was valid in pre-existing theory — even if the pre-existing concepts were given new and confusing names, such as the transmogrification of the old 'marginal productivity of capital' into the 'marginal efficiency of capital' and the 'desired ratio of money to income' into a minor element of 'liquidity preference'.

(3) Some sufficient complexity to make for difficulty in and resistance to understanding by older scholars and to challenge the younger ones to grasp it. The latter, according to Johnson (1971, p. 5), jumped on and drove 'the bandwagon, and permitted a whole generation of students. . . to escape from the slow and soul-destroying process of acquiring wisdom by osmosis from their elders and the literature into an intellectual realm in which youthful iconoclasm could quickly earn its just reward (in its own eyes at least) by demolition of the intellectual pretensions of its academic seniors and predecessors'.

(4) A new methodology, which Johnson (1971, p. 5) sees as departing from the orthodox Marshallian partial equilibrium and moving towards the then renaissance of general equilibrium (GE). 'The new methodological challenge was coming from the explicitly mathematical general-equilibrium approach of Hicks and Allen, an approach whose empirically and historically almost empty generality was of little general appeal. The *General Theory* found a middle ground in an aggregated general-equilibrium system which was not too difficult or complicated to work with — though it demanded a substantial step forward in mathematical competence — and which offered a high degree of apparent empirical relevance to those who took the trouble to understand it'.

(5) Important empirical relationships that could provide fodder for the emerging group of econometricians.

MAINSTREAM SYNTHESIS OF NEOCLASSICAL AND KEYNESIAN THEORY

The controversial attempts to reconcile Keynesian and neoclassical streams of thought were undertaken in part by 'converts' to Keynes's message (or by those who, like Pigou, recanted), yet who remained under the influence of the neoclassical teaching on which they were nurtured. There are various versions of the synthesis, some more neoclassical and others more Keynesian. The most influential version, at least in the USA, is Samuelson's who was partly influenced by Hicks. Samuelson was, in fact, largely instrumental in constructing and propagating the so-called 'grand' neoclassical synthesis (see also Modigliani, 1980a; Klein, 1966; Tobin, 1971; Hicks, 1977). In a sense the germ of the synthesis can be found in a controversial passage by Keynes (1936, pp. 378-9):[3]

> If our central controls succeed in establishing an aggregate volume of output corresponding to full employment as nearly as is practicable, the classical theory comes into its own again from this point onwards. If we suppose the volume of output to be given, i.e. to be determined by forces outside the classical scheme of thought, then there is no objection to be raised against the classical analysis of the manner in which private self-interest will determine what in particular is produced, in what proportions the factors of production will be combined to produce it, and how the value of the final product will be distributed between them.

In view of the unsettled nature of the subject, the shifting conceptions in time, and its dominance over postwar US mainstream economics, it is advisable to glean the essence from Samuelson's words. In the early 1950s, he (1966, p. 1581) described the synthesis as something of a 'compromise doctrine' which emerges from the marriage of classical, neoclassical, and Keynesian analysis:

> A legitimate and convenient name for this common core is, I suggest, 'neoclassical'. Neoclassical analysis permits a fully stable *under*employment equilibrium only on the assumption of either frictions or a peculiar concatenation of wealth–liquidity–interest elasticities; and this is in a sense a negation of the more dramatic claims of the Keynesian revolution. On the other hand, this neoclassical doctrine is a far cry from the old notion that unemployment is simply the consequence of imposing too high real wages along a sloping aggregate marginal productivity demand schedule for labor: it goes far beyond the primitive notions that by definition of a Walrasian system, equilibrium must be at full employment; and beyond the view that the same analysis which demonstrates a drop in price will equate supply and demand in any small partial equilibrium market will also suffice to prove that a drop in general wages must clear the labor market. It rejects the question-begging gobbledygook of Say's law of markets.

What is generally perceived as the crux of the neoclassical synthesis was summarized by Samuelson with shifting emphasis in the successive editions of his textbook. The neoclassical synthesis was given great prominence in the third edition where he (1955, p. vi) promised that 'it heals the breach between aggregative macroeconomics and traditional microeconomics and brings them into complementing unity'. In the mid-1960s he (1964, p. 361) still maintained that 'mastery of the modern analysis of income determination genuinely validates the basic classical pricing principles; and the economist is now justified in saying that the broad cleavage between microeconomics and macroeconomics has been closed'. In the later editions the neoclassical synthesis has been fading away. In the eleventh edition it does not appear in the index; it is not called so by name, but its notion is present albeit in much weaker form (Samuelson, 1980, p. 322).

As Tobin (1980a) points out, a central supposition of the synthesis is the separation of long-run supply trends from short-run demand fluctuations (analysable by modern Keynesian tools). Roughly the view is that the trend of production is supply-determined, governed by the steady improvement of labour, capital, and techniques. The trend represents equilibrium that can be explicated by neoclassical theory of intertemporal choices of savers and investors. In the Keynesian fashion it is the task of government to ensure that the augmented savings potential is translated into real investment.

Short-run fluctuations around the trend are mainly traceable to disturbances in aggregate demand. The response of relative prices is too protracted and weak to be relied upon. Movements of quantities are thus intrinsic to the system's response to disturbances. Without stabilization policies, the endogenous mechanism of quantity adjustment can generate cumulative and substantial oscillations. Such short-run disequilibria mirror lagged and costly adjustments, market imperfections, and asymmetries of information and expectations. While disturbances may originate from various sources, they can also be government created.

To recall, from another vantage point, one of the perennial controversies is whether Keynes did, indeed, prove the existence of equilibrium with involuntary unemployment. But surely the larger issue is: if Keynes failed to prove his case, as is widely held, did he really need to do so? As Tobin (1975) has argued, the essential question is not the existence of a long-run static equilibrium with unemployment, but the likelihood of perservering movement that the endogenous mechanism of the market economy cannot cope with or overcome effectively. Thus the phenomena Keynes analysed are perhaps better viewed as disequilibrium dynamics.[4]

THE NEOCLASSICAL-KEYNESIAN SYNTHESIS ON A POLICY PLANE

In the early 1950s, Samuelson (1966, pp. 1271-1330) attempted to formulate certain policy implications of the neoclassical synthesis. Full employment, in his view, should be regarded as only one of many goals and pursued only to the extent that the benefits exceed the costs. With maintained 'high employment' the old questions of scarcity and costs come into their own.

Clearly, efficiency does matter, for a more efficacious husbandry of resources enables the economy to achieve a higher realization of ends. But this is not equivalent to realization of given ends with fewer resources (unemployment). The neoclassical synthesis does not consider waste of resources in unemployment as optimal.

Given alternative ways of yielding a desirable pattern of wants fulfilment, efficient output entails such a combination of available resources for producing the maximum product mix that the various buyers, individuals or interdependent democratic citizens, really want. Scarcity entails choice among opportunities available, reckoning all consequences when weighing alternative actions. At all times public services should be viewed as vying with each other as well as with private demand for consumption and investment for the limited resources available. Undertaking public works cannot be justified by needs of stabilization policy alone. The only justifiable reason for undertaking them (or any other policy) is dictated by individual and social choices.

The implication is that expansion or contraction of each activity of the governmental sector is to be subjected to a cost–benefit analysis in terms of utilizing resources that could be better utilized elsewhere. This does not mean opposition to government expansion that does meet the test.

Theoretically, full employment can be achieved with widely differing compositions of output, patterns of investment and consumption, and mixes of public and private sectors. In the 1950s, Samuelson (1966, p. 13) contended that once near-full employment has been ensured by the appropriate stabilization policies, the 'purely classical' question may be asked: 'How much of current national income ought to be saved, and how fast a rate of progress should be our goal?' Scientific economics cannot resolve the question about the 'desired' rate of capital formation, nor that of the economy's ability to achieve a postulated rate of investment. 'With proper fiscal and monetary policies, our economy can have full employment and whatever rate of capital formation and growth it wants' (Samuelson, 1966, p. 1329).

Understandably, the economists who had vivid memories of the Great Depression tended to underemphasize inflation. At the outset of the Second World War, when the economy shifted from insufficient demand to excess demand, the demand-pull inflation was conspicuous. In the postwar period different sources of inflation began to emerge, with different configurations and force over time. But the problems became really serious only in the latter 1960s and alarming in the 1970s and gave rise to clashing analyses of the nature of inflation and proposed remedies, more about which presently.

The famous '45° Keynes cross' diagram popularized by Samuelson is, of course, a crude approximation. Flexibly interpreted, the 'Keynesian notion' is that the rate of increase of prices depends on the state of the economy and that the degree of resource utilization determines the shape of the aggregate supply curve. Thus, with an increase of effective demand, the primary effect is on output, but as the economy approaches nearer to the difficult-to-define neighbourhood of full employment, the price increases become more steep, and once the threshold of full employment is passed, the effect is primarily on prices. One of the crucial issues is how changes in spending will be distributed between changes in real output and the price level. This depends, *inter alia* 'upon how much or how little labor and capital remains unused to be drawn on, and upon how strong or weak are the cost-push upward pressures that come from the institutional supply conditions of organized labor, or oligopolistic price administrators and more perfectly competitive enterprises' (Samuelson, 1966, p. 1371).

A. W. Phillips's (1958) findings of the inverse relationship between the rate of unemployment (a real magnitude) and the growth rate of wages (a monetary magnitude) over just a century in British industry implied that the lower the level of aggregate economic activity, the weaker are the wage pressures, and that reduced unemployment entails stronger wage demands (with the inference that wage inflation means price inflation; it is wages minus gains in productivity that are among the key determinants of prices).[5]

In 1960 Samuelson and Solow gathered US data in an attempt to analyse to what extent this relationship held for the USA. For earlier periods in their long time series, the results were quite dissimilar, but for 1946–58 the points did cluster along a curve that was not unlike one that could have been derived from Phillips's data. Hence they concluded that for the US economy, a 2 per cent annual wage increase (corresponding to the average productivity growth) would correspond to a 5–6 per cent unemployment rate, and that at the 'desirable goal' of 3 per cent unemployment, inflation would advance by 4–5 per cent annually. Thus these were the derived trade-offs between price stability and unemployment on the one hand, and 'near-full' employment and inflation, on the other (Samuelson, 1966, pp. 1346–51).

Friedman (1977b, p. 469) critically perceives the hypothesis of a stable Phillips curve as filling a gap in Keynesian analysis and appearing to provide a reliable policy tool that could serve to enlighten the policy-maker about his alternatives. It was widely accepted, though with minority dissent (including Friedman). 'But as the '50s turned into the '60s, and the '60s into the '70s, it became increasingly difficult to accept the hypothesis in its simple form. It seemed to take larger and larger doses of inflation to keep down the level of unemployment. Stagflation reared its ugly head.'

Solow (1978b, pp. 11-18) subsequently extended the series and admitted that though the data for 1960-69 were not too far off from their previous findings, those for 1970-7 were quite contrary. He found that for 1970-2 the economy continued to move along a Phillips curve that had deteriorated by about two percentage points. But in 1974-7, when much of the instability was generated by the supply side and 'external and special' factors, the data depicted price-employment relationships that were quite at variance with the simplified view of the two-variable Phillips curve. Solow suggested that aside from unprecedented price shocks, there is an upward bias in the economy, with wages and prices becoming increasingly downward sticky, *inter alia*, because the economic actors expect that the economy will not be subject to extreme booms and busts – and inflation then becomes the price of stabilization.

The controversial Phillips curve (later augmented by expectations and various interpretations of the level of unemployment and potential output) was considered as a convenient portrayal of choice: the price of lower unemployment is higher inflation, and lower inflation can be bought at the cost of higher unemployment. Fundamentally, it made the target of full employment a variable one, with the implication derived by many that the only 'cure' for inflation is contrived deflation and unemployment. But, to repeat, in the early 1970s the trade-offs became increasingly cruel and in the latter 1970s the curve seemed to have disappeared from view. Friedman (1977b, p. 459) suggested that a so-called positively sloping Phillips curve appeared. Those who believed in the existence of a Phillips curve (and in a sense some who did not) were struck by the sharp worsening of the trade-offs and the unsystematic shifts of the curve. Hence the whole question of improving the trade-offs assumed new dimensions (see Klein, 1977).

Friedman (1977b, p. 469) claims that the 'attempts. . . made to patch up the hypothesis by allowing for special factors' ran counter to experience which 'stubbornly refused to conform to the patched-up versions'. At the cost of anticipating the material in a subsequent section, we should digress to what Friedman (1977, pp. 469-70) advocates instead:

A more radical revision was required. It took the form of stressing the importance of surprises. . . It restored the primacy of the distinction between real and nominal magnitudes. There is a natural rate of unemployment at any time determined by real factors. This natural rate will tend to be attained when expectations are on the average realized. The same real situation is consistent with any absolute level of prices and of price changes provided allowance is made for the effect of price change on the real cost of holding money balances. In this respect, money is neutral. On the other hand, unanticipated changes in aggregate nominal demand and in inflation will cause systematic errors of perception on the part of employers and employees alike that will initially lead unemployment to deviate in the opposite direction from its natural rate. In this respect, money is not neutral. However, such deviations are transitory, though it may take a long chronological time before they are reversed and finally eliminated as anticipations adjust.

The natural-rate hypothesis contains the original Phillips curve hypothesis as a special case and rationalizes a far broader range of experience, in particular the phenomenon of stagflation.

Klein's position is of interest here by way of contrast. He negates the need to go back to the drawing boards. Contemporary macroeconomic theory can explain recent events. It is only necessary to use it appropriately to fit the new configuration of circumstances. Klein (1977, p. 411) argues that 'the Phillips curve is being misunderstood and that proper analysis of full system properties can lead to the generating of rising prices and rising unemployment in a model that is based on received doctrine, including acceptance of the hypothesis underlying the Phillips Curve'.

Similarly, Blinder (1979, pp. 20–1) contends that there is a perfectly coherent, mainstream Keynesian explanation of what happened in the sorry 1970s. To grasp why the obituaries of the trade-off were premature and that it is 'alive and well and living', it is necessary to distinguish between the trade-off itself and the Phillips curve as an empirical regularity. The Phillips curve relations work well only as long as macroeconomic fluctuations originate on the demand side. The disintegration of the Phillips curve in the 1970s was primarily due to adverse shifts in aggregate supply as the predominant source of economic instability. Policy-makers can still exploit the trade-off between inflation and real output. Their ability to influence the macroeconomy is largely limited to the demand side, for they do not yet know how to shift the aggregate supply curve:

Regardless of what type of statistical Phillips curve the data for the years 1980–2000 actually produce, the policymakers' trade-off between inflation and unemployment will persist until someone finds a reliable way to manipulate aggregate supply. The limited capability of policy to influence supply poses a particularly vexing problem in a stagflationary world since any stabilization policy adopted in response to stagflation is bound to aggravate one of the problems even as it helps cure the other. Such is the policy dilemma of stagflation.

And this brings us to the 'Keynesian' (as contrasted with the monetarist — about which in a subsequent section) view of various forms and guises and varieties of inflation — a view that may yet pave the way to finding less painful solutions.

There are several varieties and sources of inflation (real, monetary, and institutional). There is no single cause (inordinate money supply, budget deficit, union wage push, oligopolistic pricing, OPEC and so on), nor is there a single cure. The eclectic attitude is not caused by intellectual indecision or uncertainty, but because the multipatterned experience requires a bold mixture of causations.

Inflation is endemic to modern democratic industrial societies. Excess demand is not the only inflation tale. Simultaneous inflation and excess supply battered the world economy through much of the 1970s. One of the major lessons of stagflation is that it has a life of its own in several senses: built-in patterns, bias, and accidents. At any time the economy inherits from the past an internal rate of inflation that is firmly and stubbornly built into its habits, expectations, and wage patterns.

The principal ingredients of inflation are the demand factors, shocks, and the core component. As Eckstein (1981, p. 7) so clearly put it:

> A satisfactory theory of the inflationary process must make room for three kinds of effects. First, the state of demand affects short-term price behavior. Second, shocks, i.e., sudden changes in particular costs, can add to the short-term inflation rate. Third, the succession of short-term demand and shock effects produces a core inflation rate which has a great propensity to persist.
>
> The core rate is the trend increase of the cost of the factors of production. It originates in the long-term expectations of inflation in the minds of households and businesses, in the contractual arrangements which sustain the wage-price momentum, and in the tax system. Core inflation can be made better or worse by the particular circumstances of any short period but it can only be modified gradually because no brief experience will undo the cumulative effects of previous reality.

Whatever its historical origins, once it is consistently entrenched into the system, the self-replicating pattern of wage and price inflation gains its own momentum. In the present world, price escalation in one sector is not usually offset by de-escalation in another; it tends to upset the entire price structure and raise its average level. Existing institutional arrangements are conducive to price–wage and wage–wage leapfrogging in the face of a major microeconomic inflation. The dynamics and transmission mechanism of inflation are conditioned by the strong dependence of current wage and price changes on recent and past movements and expectations of future movements. These factors are reinforced, *inter alia*, by management's desire to have a relatively stable and content workforce and the possibility of passing on cost increases to consumers in sometimes even higher prices than those warranted by high wage settlements.

A difficult dilemma for central bankers is accommodation versus non-accommodation. Inflation, as Tobin (1982) points out, may be symptomatic of certain nagging and real economic, social, and political problems. The central bankers may choose accommodation as the least of the evils. In another, more general sense, monetary expansion is not the cause but the result of sustained general inflation because central bankers are accommodative in order to avoid deteriorating economic activity in the short run. And, if they are not, they face the 'made-in-Washington' recessions of recent vintage. (For the consequences of disinflation see the chapters by Eckstein and B. Friedman in this volume).

Among contemporary economists, Okun has made signal contributions to our understanding of inflation and has pointed the way to compromise solutions (see Nordhaus, 1983, pp. 264–7). Okun (1981, p. 263) stresses that 'the most perplexing problem for macroeconomic policy and social welfare in modern industrial economies is the balancing of the benefits of higher output and employment on the one hand with the costs of inflation on the other'. He (1981, p. 278) considers it a central proposition 'that the social cost of inflation is the main reason to avoid strong pressure of aggregate demand – and the only reason for taking a significant risk of recession or even slack'. But he (1981, p. 356) has quite a different remedy in mind:

> The cost-reducing tools are potentially the great reconciler of employment targets and price level (or nominal GNP) targets. In response to OPEC price increases or wage adaptation, cuts in indirect taxes and tax-based incomes policies provide important opportunities for staying close to the price target without major shortfalls from desirable utilization rates. These options avoid the destructive losses of severe recessions and prolonged slack and also those of the impairment of the value of money. The cost-influencing measures should become part of the standard arsenal of government policies. They are not instruments for fine tuning. However, they should be used as routinely to combat major upward cost disturbances or inflationary adaptation as tax cuts are now used to combat serious recessions.

SOME CRITIQUES OF THE NEOCLASSICAL SYNTHESIS

The neoclassical synthesis has been under attack from 'friends' and 'foes' alike. At this juncture we shall not be concerned with the latter — those like Friedman and Lucas who are not only hostile to the neoclassical synthesis, but also to the central message and the technical apparatus of the *General Theory*. They will get a hearing in subsequent sections. The more 'friendly' critics — if one may call them so — have attacked the neoclassical synthesis not only on the grounds of details of construction, but for its very foundations, and for having deviated too drastically from what 'Keynes was all about'.

First there is the problem of microfoundations for macroeconomics — the subject of the next section. In Chapter 2 of this volume, Tobin defends the architects of the neoclassical synthesis on the grounds that they were too preoccupied with pragmatic macroeconomic concerns to develop formally the many sources of market failures to which there are pointers in the *General Theory* (see also Solow, 1980a).

Be that as it may, it is of some interest to note Samuelson's own ambivalent attitude to neoclassical price theory. As Arrow (1967, p. 733) points out, 'a careful examination of the papers both on theory and on policy yields only the most oblique suggestion that neoclassical price theory is descriptive of the real world. Of course, there is no flat denial, but Samuelson's attitude is clearly guarded and agnostic'. Indeed, the neoclassical synthesis has not provided us with the macro–micro integration that it was purported to have done. In Arrow's (1967, p. 734) words, 'Samuelson has not addressed himself to one of the major scandals of current price theory, the relation between microeconomics and macro-economics'. Arrow (1974, p. 2) strongly stresses that the 'recurrent periods of unemployment which have characterized the history of capitalism' are quite incompatible with the neoclassical market equilibrium model. 'A post-Keynesian world in which unemployment is avoided or kept at tolerable levels by recurrent alterations in fiscal or monetary policy is no more explicable by neoclassical axioms, though the falsification is not as conspicuous'.

Another stream of criticism is that implied in Sir John Hicks's recantation of his former position. 'Hicksian–Walrasianism' and its byproduct IS–LM are classics in more than one sense.[6] This framework was instrumental in teaching so-called Keynesian economics — criticized by Joan Robinson (1978, p. xiv) for confusing and reducing 'the General Theory to a version of static equilibrium'.[7] In his recent change of heart, Hicks admits that his model was a relapse into statics and reduced the *General*

Theory to equilibrium economics. He (1977, p. 148) contends that the *General Theory* 'provides a model on which academic economists can comfortably perform their accustomed tricks. Haven't they just? With ISLM I myself fell into the trap. . . The *General Theory* is a brilliant squeezing of dynamic economics into static habits of thought. The *Treatise* is more genuinely dynamic, and therefore, more human'. Hicks (1979, p. 1452) sees the neoclassical synthesis as 'the colonization of more and more of the *dynamic* territory by "classical" (if Walrasian was classical) methods. At the height of its success, the colonization seemed to be complete: "Keynes" had been pushed right over the edge. The quarry of the hunt had just disappeared'. This situation, of course, led Clower (1975, p. 5) to ask the very pertinent question: 'How is it possible. . . to maintain that developments set in motion by the publication of the *General Theory* can be fully appreciated only by viewing them as part and parcel of a Neo-Walrasian revival?'

The view reappears, ever more frequently, that in the synthesis of Keynesian and pre-Keynesian economics, it is the latter that has been gaining pre-eminence, pre-empting the former. Such views have long been held by the Cambridge Keynesians. We owe a fresh insight into these issues to the painstaking and scholarly study of Leijonhufvud (1968)[8] who, according to Joan Robinson (1969, p. 581), has perceived the neoclassical synthesis as 'the basis of a new orthodoxy which wraps Keynes up again in the very doctrines from which he had "a long struggle to escape".'

Reflecting on his 1968 study, Leijonhufvud (1981, pp. 316–17) points out that he was

> concerned with the problems and conundrums resulting from the collision of Keynesianism with the, by then stronger, 'neoclassical' programme. . . One theme of the book. . . became the distinction drawn between Keynes's theory and the subsequent developing, largely American, school of Keynesian economics. . . The distinction is an important one to make, I contend, because it was this later version of Keynesianism that succumbed so readily to the 'neoclassical synthesis'.

In Joan Robinson's (1969, pp. 581–2) perception, Keynes essentially recognized that wages are paid in money and so are household expenses. He recognized historical time and uncertainty. Monetary policy operates on employment in such a way that a decline in the interest rate, with given long-term expectations of future profits, increases the current value of real assets, thus encouraging further investment and, by bestowing windfall gains on wealth-holders, is also likely to encourage consumption. Keynes also took notice of the behavioural patterns of various individuals (workers, householders, capitalists, financiers, etc.) in the process of production and distribution. Joan Robinson (1969, p. 582) objects to Leijonhufvud (1968) who, in her words:

> finds it necessary to express all this in terms of the 'transactions structure', the 'aggregation structure' and the 'dynamic structure' of Keynes' model. He works it out in great detail, buttressing his argument at every point with an exposition of the logical requirements of Keynes' system. He contrasts it with the neo-neoclassical model, which has eliminated money prices, fails to distinguish between the past and the future, and treats rentiers, workers and entrepreneurs all alike as 'transactors' and 'asset holders'. He patiently disentangles the confusions in the neo-neoclassical scheme and sorts out the cross-purposes in many controversies.[9]

Davidson (1980, p. 151) and other post Keynesians have emphasized that the neoclassical synthesis is merely a restatement of the neoclassical framework, seasoned with some Keynesian terminology. Whereas the flavour of some of Keynes's policy prescriptions was retained, the essential logic of Keynes's economic theory was abandoned. As a result, 'the fundamental Keynesian revolution was aborted'.

Such statements echo what Joan Robinson has been saying for years. She claims that the neoclassical synthesis has opened the way for the neoclassical Keynesians (whom she calls by a less polite name) to pursue 'theorems about an ideal free market economy'. In this way, 'Keynes' work, far from being the starting point for realistic study of the imperfect market economies in which we live, became an excuse for economists to carry on as before' (Robinson and Cripps, 1979, p. 140).

Joan Robinson (1978, pp. 91ff.) militantly attacks what she calls 'pre-Keynesian theory after Keynes'; the treatment of accumulation decisions as governed by the propensity to save of the economy as a whole, and the validity and relevance of neoclassical price and distribution theories. When they formulated the neoclassical synthesis, its architects underrated the seriousness of the problem of insufficiency of effective demand and overrated the ability and willingness of the policy-maker to stabilize the economy so as to utilize its full potential. The neoclassical synthesis suffers from the separation of long-run growth trends from short-run, demand-determined fluctuations — a controversial and perplexing problem in business-cycle theory — a subject to which we shall return later.

One of the differences between the neoclassical Keynesians and Cambridge Keynesians is that the latter assign greater weight to the objective of maintaining full employment and to its content and equity, and a lower weight to efficiency considerations.

Joan Robinson perceives the essence of the Keynesian revolution to lie in placing the analysis in historical time and stressing the pervasive influence of uncertainty — concepts that fell into neglect with the rise of the neo-classical synthesis, but that, as pointed out in the companion volume, are increasingly being taken into account, though the intrinsic difficulties in modelling have yet prevented their effective incorporation into main-stream analysis. In her 1971 Ely Lecture (1978, pp. 4-5) she reiterated eloquently her position:

> Consider what was the point of the Keynesian revolution on the plane of theory and on the plane of policy. On the plane of theory, the main point of the *General Theory* was to break out of the cocoon of equilib-rium and consider the nature of life lived in time — the difference between yesterday and tomorrow. Here and now, the past is irrevoc-able and the future is unknown.

And she again emphasized that uncertainty was the very essence of Keynes's problem. In the neoclassical synthesis

> this point is lost. By one simple device, the whole of Keynes' argument is put to sleep. Work out what saving *would be* at full employment in the present short-period situation, with the present distribution of wealth and the present hierarchy of rates of earnings for different occupations, and arrange to have enough investment to absorb the level of saving that this distribution of income brings about. Then hey presto! We are back in the world of equilibrium where saving governs investment and micro theory can slip into the old grooves again.

MICRO-MACRO: DICHOTOMY OR UNITY?

To many economists Keynesian economics deals with important relevant problems and General Equilibrium theory deals with no relevant prob-lems at all. This view is often the consequence of the ease of learning Keynesian macro-arithmetic compared with reading Debreu. But it also has, alas, an element of truth. This is quite simply that General Equilib-rium theorists have been unable to deliver one half at least of the required story: how does General Equilibrium come to be established? Closely related to this lacuna is the question of what signals are per-ceived and transmitted in a decentralised economy and how? The importance of Keynesian economics to the General Equilibrium theorist is twofold. It seems to be addressed to just these kinds of questions and it is plainly in need of proper theoretical foundations (Hahn, 1977, p. 25).

For about 40 years now, economics has been split between two partial and conflicting representations of the functioning of market economies. The first [is] exemplified by general equilibrium models. . . The second [is] exemplified by macroeconomic models in the Keynesian tradition. . . In spite of numerous attempts at reconciliation, it has become increasingly clear that these two representations correspond to two different classes of economic models with quite different structures (Benassy, 1982, p. 1).[10]

Whatever the strengths and weaknesses and lessons derived from the early work in disequilibrium macroeconomics of Patinkin, Clower, Leijonhufvud, the 'young' Barrow, Hershel Grossman, and others,[11] it was followed by an ongoing flourishing of highly theoretical studies by Hahn, Negishi, Drèze, Benassy, Grandmont, and others (represented in this volume in the chapters by Benassy, Negishi, and Sondermann). These studies have been frequently praised for their technical sophistication, elegance, and rigour, but the question remains whether they are not simply mathematically elegant restatements of generally recognized facts (see Drazen, 1980, p. 283).

For example, in Chapter 2 Tobin argues that essentially these are merely formal models aimed at communicating to GE theorists the Keynesian questions in a language that they readily understand. However, as a contribution to macroeconomics *per se*, these models provide little new real insights and often miss some essential Keynesian arguments (see also Hahn, 1977, p. 26-7).

Malinvaud (1977, p. 35) points to a major and persistent source of tension in economics: the tension between the pragmatic macroeconomists working in the Keynesian framework who have an inherent feeling for involuntary unemployment and the microeconomists. The former suspect the latter of providing a classical explanation of unemployment (i.e. caused by excessively high real wages rather than by insufficient demand for goods). Such suspicion raises the hackles of the microeconomists. Malinvaud sees his purpose as attenuating this tension by reconsidering the Keynesian and GE theories and unifying them so that they no longer appear as fundamentally distinct.

The conflicting appraisals of the achievements can be glimpsed in the conclusions reached in different surveys. For example, Roy Weintraub

(1979, p. 125) claims that 'to be brutal about the matter, any macro-economist who relies on the rock-solid foundations of general equilibrium theory to reconstruct macroeconomics has been misled by the technical sophistication of models which have weak conclusions'. On the other hand, Drazen (1980, p. 304) concludes that

> the recent theoretical developments in non-Walrasian unemployment theory have, in my opinion, advanced our understanding. . . The mathematical rigour which characterizes the newer work is a flaw only if it masks a lack of insight. Furthermore, one can argue that a full integration of monetary and value theory may eventually require such rigour. Prior to Clower, there was a sneaking suspicion that the classical theory was really the general theory and Keynes the special case. Reformulating equilibrium theory à la Clower and Hahn. . . indicates that Keynesian theory may be the more general theory after all, and it may, after all these years, give a sound basis to macroeconomics.

Granted that macroeconomics needs a micro base (a proposition that is by no means generally accepted), the issue then is what kind of micro and how sound or useful the micro theory is. Indeed, there is no, or should not be any, presumption that the micro base is restricted to GE or a particular variant thereof. Be that as it may, the dominant and influential scholars who have been working on this problem have imbibed GE with their mother's milk. They consider it incredible and theoretically unsound to derive the central propositions of the *General Theory* outside the discipline and rigour of rational optimizing behaviour of agents. These younger-generation scholars do not differ from their elders (like Hicks, Samuelson, Tobin, and others) merely in their fascination with a sophisticated technical apparatus, but mainly in their remoteness from the Great Depression and in different social concerns.

In this respect, as in many others, there is Arrow – a towering figure among GE theorists – who stands apart. In Chapter 2 in the companion volume and from another vantage point in Chapter 3 of this volume, Arrow shows the potentials and limitations of GE. Indeed, he calls attention to three major scandals of GE: (i) the failure to provide a microfoundation for Keynesian macroeconomics, (ii) the failure to take seriously, capture the essence of, and integrate imperfect competition into the system, and (iii) the failure to account for costs of transaction and of obtaining information, thus of running the market resource allocation process itself.

As we know, considerable work has been done by GE theorists (some of which is, indeed, reflected in several chapters in both these volumes) to attenuate some of the scandals, improve the models, and relax some of the restrictive assumptions.

In a reflective series of lectures, Malinvaud (1977), drawing on and developing the contributions of his younger French colleagues, attempts to explain the reasons for approaching the study of unemployment via GE. He does so to counter many economists' objections to this idea.

> The objection comes from a misunderstanding of what general equilibrium analysis really is. Economists have been brought up to think that the very notion of equilibrium implies that, for each commodity, supply must equal demand, which of course cannot be the case for labour if some involuntary unemployment remains. But a general equilibrium is an abstract construct that has no logical obligation to assume equality between supply and demand.

> The classical development of economic theory and the dominant role played by the Walrasian system explain why many people are now reluctant to accept that the name 'equilibrium' could be applied outside of this system. Some of these people, often irritated by the highbrow mathematical theory that was built around the concept of competitive equilibrium, claim that such a concept is hopelessly inadequate to any real problem. Others speak as if the Walrasian equilibrium was not an abstraction but almost a real situation that would prevail if no disturbance occurred. They combine, however, in suspecting someone intending to use a general equilibrium approach to the study of unemployment (Malinvaud, 1977, p. 5).

In his (1977, p. 5) view this is the reasoning behind most contemporary economists' reference to 'disequilibrium analysis'; that is, an analysis that accepts the notion that demands can diverge from supplies (see Benassy, 1982 *passim*; Leijonhufvud, 1968 *passim*).

Malinvaud (1977, pp. 7-8) stresses that when the analysis is confined to equilibrium it is implicitly assumed that the speed of adjustment towards equilibrium is rapid enough. Thus such a study is not very helpful when dealing with the phenomenon in question. 'This implicit assumption of course deserves a good deal of attention when one inquires into the significance of the theory that is being applied. But the alternative way of proceeding, i.e. to rely on a true "disequilibrium analysis", would in most cases raise at least as many questions'.

Malinvaud (1977, pp. 8-9) recognizes that modern markets and ever-increasing centralization of production and exchange are in sharp contrast with the Walrasian teaching and the perception of rapid price adjustment to excess demand and supply which are thus increasingly inadequate for short-run macroeconomic analysis (see Hahn, 1978; Grandmont and Laroque, 1976):

> Trained in classical price theory, we are used to thinking of a broad agreement between short-run and long-run equilibrium: the course followed by prices is such that it permits equalization between supply and demand whether we consider the current production and its uses, or whether we turn our attention to the supply of savings and the demand for investment. But as soon as prices are sticky, the whole matter becomes much more complex (Malinvaud, 1977, p. 97).

Yet, Malinvaud (p. 116) believes that properly applied, the GE approach is not only extremely relevant, but also presents intriguing challenges even in a world characterized by rigid or really sticky prices in the short run (see Drazen, 1980, p. 286; Hahn, 1977).

Malinvaud (1977) presents a simplified macro model that relies on the notion of GE under rigid prices and quantity constraints (rationing). This model focuses on quantity adjustments, with nominal wages and prices exogenously determined,[12] or moving only slowly, despite the prevalence of excess supply (involuntary unemployment) or demand in the labour and product markets. Equilibrium is studied at each point of time with fixed prices and to describe dynamics as a varying equilibrium as prices change. The model is derived from Keynes. One of the key conclusions is that, in general, unemployment is of the Keynesian rather than the classical variety.

In a retrospect on earlier developments, Hahn (1977, p. 38) reflects that 'the recent literature for the first time takes seriously the importance of the past and the expected future in Keynesian economics'. He continues:

> the most interesting development is undoubtedly the change in the requirement for short-period equilibrium. In particular, the study of the given money wage case suggested an equilibrium notion as a snapshot of a non-tâtonnement. That is, one abandons the implausible view that agents consider that they can transact what they wish to at going prices when they in fact find that they cannot. . . It has led some enthusiasts to go to the extreme of fixed price equilibrium and to call that Keynesian. But, of course, there is no good prior reason why agents should treat quantity constraints and prices parametrically. When that assumption is dropped things become more interesting and more difficult. Negishi conjectures appear. . .
>
> Keynes deserves the credit for forcing one to look sequence economics in the face. He deserves little credit for the rest since he insisted on

a purely neoclassical micro-theory. At least this is so at a highly theoretical level. On the other hand if one looks at the sum total of his informal insights one may conclude that all one is doing is to give them adequate theoretical form.

Very recently there have been significant developments in the macroeconomic disequilibrium theory on embedding the inflexibility of prices and wages into the system as against having them exogenously determined (see Drazen, 1980, p. 304; Malinvaud, 1980; Negishi, 1979; Benassy, 1982).

Understandably, the reaction is mixed. Those unsympathetic to the GE approach, like Lord Kahn (1977a), claim that the attempt to reconcile GE and Keynesian modes of analysis and perceptions is a *mésalliance*. Even some mainstream neoclassical Keynesians point to the difficulty, if not undesirability, of making macroeconomic models look like the abstract and elegant GE constructs without emptying them of 'the aggregative simplicity, institutional content, and definiteness of conclusion which are their *raison d'être*' (Tobin, 1980b, p. x; see Harcourt, 1977, pp. 372–96). Moreover, one cannot analyse market behaviour and relations without a perception of the macro setting in which they operate. Hence microeconomics also needs a macrofoundation (see Joan Robinson, 1977, p. 1320; Solow, 1979, p. 354).

THE MONETARIST COUNTER-REVOLUTION

The Keynesian revolution has always been under attack from many quarters. In this section I should like to single out the not-always-unified group of economists under the leadership in the USA of the libertarian Chicago school, founded by Henry Simons, led by the famous Frank Knight, who was scornful of the post-New Deal world, and enhanced by the articulate and scintillating Milton Friedman, the high priest of 'capitalism and freedom' and of monetarism (the new form of the quantity theory of money (QTM)).[13] What Friedman called, perhaps over-dramatically, the 'counter-revolution in monetary theory' challenged not only the basic precepts of the *General Theory* and the Keynesian techniques of achieving full employment, but also the fundamental philosophy that such a state and the society to which it gives rise are desirable.

As Friedman (1970a, p. 7) put it, 'a counter-revolution must be preceded by two stages: an initial position from which there was a revolution, and the revolution. . . The initial position I shall call the quantity theory of money. . . The revolution. . . was made by Keynes in the 1930s.'

Friedman (1963, p. 1) sees one of the main features of the Keynesian revolution as

> an attack on the quantity theory of money. By the end of World War II, there was almost as much agreement among economists as there had been in, say, 1930; but agreement on almost exactly opposite views. It was widely agreed that money is of little importance, that it is a minor part of the economic system, and that if one wants to understand the way the economic system works, it is better to concentrate on invest-ment or autonomous expenditures, the consumption function, and similar relations.

Within the next two decades 'there has been something of a counter-revolution in thinking about the behavior of money. . . there has been a revival of interest in monetary theory and in the quantity theory of money' (Friedman, 1963, p. 1). And, speaking of the need for labels, Friedman (1970a, pp. 7–8) points out that

> perhaps the one most widely used in referring to. . . [this counter-revolution] is the 'Chicago School'. More recently, however, it has been given a name which is less lovely but which has become so attached to it that I find it hard to avoid using it. That name is 'monetarism' because of the renewed emphasis on the role of the quantity of money.

This counter-revolution, like many others in history and science, did not restore the *status quo ante*. Its altered position was in Friedman's (1963, p. 1) words, 'very much influenced by Keynesian ideas', and monetarism 'has benefited much from Keynes's work' (Friedman, 1970a, p. 8). He (1970a, p. 8) boldly asserts that 'if Keynes were alive today he would no doubt be at the forefront of the counter-revolution. You must never judge a master by his disciples'.

In a preceding section we have outlined the ingredients about which Harry G. Johnson speculated as essential for the making of a successful revolution. He (1971, pp. 6–11) perceived something of a corollary in the emergence of a successful counter-revolution, in particular the Friedman-led monetarist counter-revolution:

(1) The ossification of the preceding revolution into its own orthodoxy. Johnson (1971, p. 6) perceived that Keynes's followers (i.e. the economic profession at large) 'elaborated his history-bound analysis into a timeless and spaceless set of universal principles, sacrificing in the process much of his subtlety, and so established Keynesianism as an orthodoxy ripe for counter-attack'. In a sense these followers

prevented their juniors from making a mark for themselves, thus paving the way for counter-revolution.

(2) Finding an important social problem that the established orthodoxy is apparently weak in solving. Johnson (1971, p. 7) saw that this problem was inflation which only came to exercise Americans in the 1970s — the era when monetarism flourished. 'The history of the monetarist counter-revolution has, in fact, been characterized by a series of mostly vain efforts to convince the profession and the public (a) that inflation is an important question and (b) that monetarism can provide an explanation and a policy whereas Keynesianism cannot'.

(3) Embedding the counter-revolution in some of the tenets of the preceding revolution; that is, Friedman's generalization of Keynes's theory of liquidity preference. The restatement of QTM afforded sufficient difficulty of understanding to the older scholars and challenge to the younger ones.

(4) The new and attractive methodology was that of positive economics — discussed in Chapter 1 of the companion volume — which essentially allowed the scholar to predict 'something large from something small' (Johnson, 1977, p. 9).

(5) Further fodder for the econometricians — the demand function for money.

Probably the crucial difference between Keynesians (of whatever persuasion) and monetarists (their degree and intensity notwithstanding) is their view of the stability of the economy — a tension to which we have alluded at the beginning of this chapter. While the Keynesians essentially perceive the economy as fairly but not fatally unstable and improvable by stabilization policies, the monetarists perceive the economy as inherently fairly stable and monetary disturbances as the major source of instability. Hence the need to restrict the manipulatory ability of the government.[14]

There are, of course, major differences among the members of the monetarist fraternity about their interpretations of QTM or about Friedman's linkage to the Keynesian theory of liquidity preference. Quantity theorists accord varied significance to the long- and short-term process. Friedman (1970b, p. 27) is often concerned mostly with short-term fluctuations. 'I regard the description of our position as "money is all that matters for changes in *nominal* income and for *short-run* changes in real income" as an exaggeration but one that gives the right flavor of our conclusions'.

Some of the key tenets of monetarism can be briefly summarized as follows:[15]

(1) 'There is a consistent though not precise relation between the rate of growth of the quantity of money and the rate of growth of nominal income' (Friedman, 1970a, p. 22). Variation in money supply is the dominant, if not exclusive, determinant of variation in money income. Aside from the stochastic variables, the path of aggregate nominal demand depends only on the path of the quantity of money, however defined.

(2) But the link between nominal magnitudes and money supply may not be proportional and it may entail lags and leads and stochastic variables. In Friedman's (1970a, p. 22) words, the link 'is not obvious to the naked eye largely because it takes time for changes in monetary growth to affect income and how long it takes is itself variable'.

(3) Another implication of 1. is the emphasis on the stock of money as the target of monetary policy. The focus is of cardinal importance, *inter alia*, because it determines the rate of inflation in the long run and the fluctuations in real output and employment in the short run. 'In the short run, which may be as much as five or ten years, monetary changes affect primarily output. Over decades, on the other hand, the rate of monetary growth affects primarily prices. What happens to output depends on real factors' (Friedman, 1970a, pp. 23-4). The proposition is that monetary policy should be solely governed by the stock (growth rate) of money (a variable over which the monetary authority is supposed to have control), rather than interest rates, bank or total credits, and other indicators such as the unpredictably volatile velocity of monetary aggregates. Monetarism has suffered from the perennial difficulty of identifying the aggregate monetary variable; that is, the exogenously determined stock to which all endogenous monetary variables adapt. Nominal interest rates must be sharply distinguished from real interest rates. The nominal rates are considered unreliable because they are strongly influenced by expectations and thus, with a lag by actual inflation. Initially, the market impact of expansionary monetary policy may entail reducing interest rates, but this is fairly soon reversed when the inflationary premiums augment the interest rates.

(4) Major economic fluctuations are attributed to vagaries of monetary supplies, rather than to exogenous real disturbances. Therefore the major policy recommendation is 'an automatic policy under which the quantity of money would grow at a steady rate' and 'would provide a stable monetary framework for economic growth without itself being a source of instability and disturbance' (Friedman, 1970a, p. 26). Hence the preference is for the controversial fixed and announced rule of monetary policy without feedback. In other words, the policy prescription, reduced to its bare essentials, is to chart an unvarying monetary course, undis-

turbed by either economic conditions or prospects, with the understanding that the economy will adjust itself to this steady course. Where such an adjustment takes place will be the 'best' possible solution, no matter what the rate of unemployment will be.

(5) The argument is that pure fiscal policies (unsupported by changes in quantity of money) cannot have a significant impact on the path of nominal income. Yet fiscal policies do matter as they affect the partition of national income into consumption and capital accumulation and allocation between the private and public sectors. This partition affects the economy's future growth path and capacity to produce. Friedman (1970a, p. 24) stresses that 'fiscal policy is extremely important in determining what fraction of total national income is spent by government and who bears the burden of the expenditure. By itself, it is not important for inflation'.

(6) Inflation is, according to Friedman (1970a, p. 24) *'always and everywhere a monetary phenomenon* in the sense that it is and can be produced only by a more rapid increase in the quantity of money than in output'. Friedman (1975a, p. 176) is adamant that 'the price level and inflation are monetary phenomena, not institutionally determined data to be analyzed by psychologists and industrial relations and industrial organization specialists'. At the cost of belabouring the point, inflation cannot be attributed to social institutions, economic power, and other non-monetary sources. All these, monetarists claim, may affect shifts in relative prices, but they are only ephemerally linked to the price level. They thus reiterate the 'classical dichotomy'; that is, between the relations that determine all relative prices and real magnitudes (which are determined by the real forces of demand and supply) and the set that determines the absolute price level (which is determined by the quantity of money) and is thus a monetary phenomenon.

(7) 'There is no stable Phillips curve trade-off. This is the empirical counterpart of the critical role in monetary theory today of the distinction between "anticipated" and "unanticipated" magnitudes' (Friedman, 1975a, p. 176). Friedman (1977b, p. 458) claims that there is really no long-run policy choice, for we might as well reconcile ourselves to the dismal prospect of having more unemployment now or later. His concept of the 'natural rate of unemployment' – a term he coined to parallel Knut Wicksell's 'natural rate of interest' – is a throwback to pre-Keynesian economics. It rejects the possibility of a permanent trade-off between price stability and full employment; unemployment above the 'natural rate' would decelerate inflation, and below the 'natural rate' would accelerate inflation – but these are only transitory phenomena. The 'natural

rate' deals essentially with the elusive and difficult to model expectations and expectational errors, and relates variations in unemployment rates to incorrect inflationary expectations because 'what matters is not inflation *per se*, but unanticipated inflation; there is no stable tradeoff between inflation and unemployment; there is a "natural rate of unemployment". . . which is consistent with the real forces and with accurate perceptions; unemployment can be kept below that level only by an accelerating inflation; or above it only by accelerating deflation' (Friedman, 1977b, p. 458).

The policy implications are the non-existence of a permanent tradeoff between unemployment and inflation. The unemployment rate deviates from the natural rate only when the economic actors are bamboozled by the rate of inflation. No matter what the time lags (which under adaptive expectations may be quite protracted), as soon as it becomes widely recognized that prices are rising the advantages in terms of higher real output and employment will fade away. Government policy that aims at a rate of unemployment below the natural rate will produce a continuously accelerating inflation. The corollary is a continuously decelerating deflation if the policy aims at a higher than the natural rate of unemployment. The natural (or equilibrium) rate of unemployment can only be lowered by reducing distortions in the labour market, of which the minimum wage is offered as the standard example.

The natural rate hypothesis (NRH) sparked off a good deal of controversy as to its meaning and implications (see Tobin, 1972; Phelps, 1979, pp. 97-107; Friedman, 1975b, pp. 23-5; Gordon, 1976, pp. 191-7). At this juncture, before proceeding further with the Friedman framework, we should digress briefly on the different motivations behind and uses made of NRH by Friedman and Phelps (who, indeed, initially did not use that term). Friedman uses NRH to buttress his fundamental preconception that Keynesian-style policies carry risks that far exceed their potential benefits. On the other hand, Phelps's (1970) interest was primarily theoretical – an attempt to reinforce the neoclassical synthesis by finding a microeconomic foundation for the labour market and product pricing side of the standard models, or what became known as the 'new microeconomics' of inflation and employment theory (see Lucs, 1981a, pp. 282-3; Gordon, 1976, p. 205-7). Recently Phelps (1979, pp. 93-4; see also pp. 299-300) has traced the origin of the idea to the Austrians via his teachers Fellner and Wallich:

What I have sometimes called the *natural rate hypothesis* consists of two propositions. The first states that. . . any disequilibrium in the labor market must eventually vanish and the course of employment must converge to its equilibrium path as long as the rate of change of aggregate demand — we may think here of the growth rate of the money supply — stays within certain bounds outside of which monetary equilibrium ceases to be possible. Subject to that proviso, then, expectations tend to be equilibrating.

The second proposition states that, with regard to any equilibrium scenario, the addition of a fixed number of points to the percentage growth rates of wages and prices will not have any permanent effect upon the equilibrium path of employment. In a model in which there is no overhang of previously set money-wage rates and money prices, there will not result even a temporary alteration of the equilibrium path of employment. In particular, the equilibrium steady-state rate of unemployment to which the equilibrium path of the unemployment rate converges under essentially stationary conditions is invariant to the addition of k points to the steady rate of wage and price inflation. The equilibrium steady state unemployment rate, if inflation-invariant, is called the 'natural' rate. Any stimulus to employment that would otherwise have been produced by the faster growth of aggregate demand generating the faster inflation is offset by the necessarily equal rise of the expected rate of wage inflation prevailing in this equilibrium state.

'It has often been said that Friedman's celebrated essay on the Quantity Theory could just as well have been called "The Theory of Liquidity Preference — a Restatement" ' (Laidler, 1981, p. 3). Harry G. Johnson (1973, p. 26) argues also that Friedman's restatement of QTM is very Keynesian. It should probably be understood as an appropriation of the portfolio-balance analysis. Friedman treats money demand as demand for an asset and via explicit expectations of change injects liquidity. His version of QTM is a theory of the demand for money and not a theory of the price level, nor of income (output) determination. In its final form, Friedman's demand for money function is not substantially different from a modern Keynesian formulation.

> In fact, both the more sophisticated Keynesians and the quantity theorists of contemporary times have absorbed Keynes's basic monetary-theoretic contribution; that money is a form of wealth and that the demand for it is a manifestation of optimum portfolio choice subject to the yields and uncertainties connected with various assets as alternative forms of holding wealth (Johnson, 1974, p. 10).

Friedman (1956) has claimed that his restatement of QTM drew on the 'Chicago oral tradition'. In his 1969 famous and controversial essay on

Friedman and the Chicago tradition, Patinkin (1981, pp. 241-74) documents the 'invalidity' of Friedman's contention. 'As a minimum statement let me say that though I shared with Friedman — albeit, almost a decade later — the teachers at Chicago whom he mentions (namely Knight, Viner, Simons, and Mints), his description of the "flavor of the oral tradition" which they were supposed to have imparted strikes no responsive chord in my memory' (Patinkin, 1981, p. 242). On the contrary, Patinkin (1981, p. 242) claims that Friedman's reformulation of QTM 'is a misleading designation and that what Friedman has actually presented is an elegant exposition of the modern portfolio approach to the demand for money which, though it has some well-known (albeit largely undeveloped) antecedents in the traditional theory, can only be seen as a continuation of the Keynesian theory of liquidity preference'. As we have anticipated, Harry G. Johnson (1971, pp. 10-11) has also stressed this theme. He pointed to Friedman's 'invention of a University of Chicago oral tradition that was alleged to have preserved understanding of the fundamental truth among a small band of the initiated through the dark years of Keynesian despotism'.[16]

Friedman (1970b, p. 158) retorted that Patinkin and Johnson 'criticize me for linking my work to a "Chicago tradition" rather than recognizing that, as they see it, my work is Keynesian. In the course of their criticism, they give a highly misleading impression of the Chicago tradition.' These accusations, Friedman (1970b) admits, 'would indict my perception, or integrity, or scholarship, but it would in no way contradict the existence of an important Chicago tradition in the field of money that had a great influence on subsequent work in monetary economics and on my own work in particular'. Furthermore, he (1970b) asserts: 'My restatement *is* a restatement of the quantity theory and is not Keynesian in any meaningful sense of that term.'

The distinction between real and nominal magnitudes is the pivot of QTM. 'Extreme monetarism' would feature complete independence of monetary from real magnitudes. Milder versions distinguish to a varied yet important degree that the interactions between money supply (velocity changes) and prices and quantities have time dimensions — short, intermediate, and long runs, although such distinctions are open to arbitrariness.

Friedman's disavowal of the imperative to explain the division of monetary impulses between prices and quantities has been subject to severe attacks (see, *inter alia*, Tobin, 1970).

Friedman's restatement of the quantity theory obtained the immediate tactical advantage of freeing it from the Keynesian criticism of assuming an automatic tendency towards full employment in the economy, by making it a theory of the demand for money without commitment to the analysis of prices and employment. The advantage, however, has proved something of an embarrassment subsequently, given the success of the quantity-theory counter-attack on Keynesianism and the rise of the monetarist approach to economic policy, since it apparently leaves the quantity theorist with nothing to say about the relative impact of short-run variations in the money supply, and hence in aggregate demand, on money prices on the one hand and physical output on the other (Johnson, 1973, p. 27).

Reverting to the controversy with Patinkin, Friedman (1970b, p. 158) alleges that it stems from Patinkin's proclivity to understand QTM to mean only one thing 'namely, the long-run proposition that money is neutral, even though he fully recognizes, indeed insists, that the quantity theorists (myself included) were concerned mostly with short-run fluctuations'. Furthermore, Friedman (1970b, p. 172) conjectures that the reason Patinkin labels his framework Keynesian stems from Patinkin's concentration on 'neutrality'.

> For if he interprets my framework as in the 'quantity-theory' tradition, he cannot continue to regard the 'quantity theory' as synonymous with the long-run neutrality of money, since my framework is clearly and obviously not about that — just as I believe the writings of earlier quantity theorists, from Ricardo and Thornton to Keynes, were not about that either. So cut down the forest to let the 'neutrality tree' stand proud and tall.

Indeed, Friedman touches on the most fundamental issue of the long versus the short view in economics. Generally, the classical writers, of which Ricardo was a prime example, were somewhat reluctant to explore the short and intermediate runs. However, they discerned the dynamic transitional states, short-term fluctuations, and the non-neutrality of money in the short run. Keynes's comparative advantages lay in the short-run analysis.

Friedman (1975a, pp. 176–77) traces the roots of his 'rediscovery' of QTM to Hume, emphasizing that he merely restated Hume's insight into the short-run effects of growth in money supply on growth of real output. In particular, he draws a parallel between his position on money, inflation and employment (Phillips curve) and these words of Hume:

> Though the high price of commodities be a necessary consequence of the increase of gold and silver, yet it follows not immediately upon that increase; but some time is required before the money circulates through the whole state. . . At first no alteration is perceived; by degrees the

price rises, first of one commodity, then of another; till the whole at last reaches a just proportion with the new quantity of specie. . . In my opinion, it is only in this interval or intermediate situation, between the acquisition of money and rise of prices, that the increasing quantity of gold and silver is favourable to industry. . . From the whole of this reasoning we may conclude, that it is of no manner of consequence, with regard to the domestic happiness of a state, whether money be in a greater or less quantity. The good policy of the magistrate consists only in keeping it, if possible, still increasing; because, by that means, he keeps alive a spirit of industry in the nation. . . There is always an interval before matters be adjusted to their new situation; and this interval is as pernicious to industry, when gold and silver are diminishing, as it is advantageous when these metals are increasing (quoted after Friedman, 1975a, p. 177).

Friedman (1975a, p. 177) observes that since Hume, progress was only in two respects: (i) a firmer understanding of the quantitative relationships,[17] and (ii) 'we have gone one derivative beyond Hume'. Whereas in Hume's times stable prices were the norm, at present a rising price level has become entrenched in agents' expectations. Thus, in order to produce the effects that Hume attributed to a changing price level one has to resort to a rate of change in monetary growth. Friedman (1975a, pp. 177 and 178) notes that 'we may soon be forced to still higher derivatives'. Furthermore, 'the change in nominal income has been linked now as in the past to the first derivative of money through a relatively stable velocity function. But the division between price and output has been linked to the higher derivatives through their effect on the division of monetary changes between anticipated and unanticipated changes'.

Friedman (1975a, p. 177) sees the need to go to Hume as the key to the analysis of anticipations, in particular of rational expectations (RE).[18] In commenting on a paper by Stanley Fischer (1975), Friedman (1975a, p. 177) made his position clear:

Once we recognize, as Hume did, that only unanticipated changes in the quantity of money will systematically produce a divergence between the actual rate of unemployment and the 'natural' rate, the way anticipations are formed becomes a vital issue in the evaluation of monetary policy. The recent work in this area discussed by Fischer, particularly by R. Lucas and T. Sargent, brings us back to Henry Simons. As Fischer noted, if anticipations are formed rationally, no fixed policy on the part of the monetary authorities will produce a divergence between the actual and 'natural' rates of unemployment. Only continuously 'fooling' the public will do that. Is it not far better, along with Simons, to get instead the co-operation of the public by announcing in advance a policy and sticking to it? Though Lucas and Sargent have stated the point formally far better than it has been stated earlier, this has always been, as I see it, an essential foundation of the preference by Simons and his followers, including myself, for a fixed and announced rule of monetary policy.

We have previously referred to Harry G. Johnson's conception of the necessary ingredients for successful revolutions and counter-revolutions. He was a maverick, conversant with neoclassical Keynesians, Cambridge, and Friedman's Chicago. In Johnson's (1971, pp. 12–13) opinion the monetarist counter-revolution will eventually fade away because it focuses on less important social issues (inflation) versus the much more significant one of unemployment and because of the floundering methodology of positive economics on which it is based. In fact, he (1973, p. 24) castigates Friedman's critics for not taking this methodology sufficiently to task, particularly with reference to Friedman's restatement of QTM. About ten years later, Tobin (1981a) judged this prediction to be premature, simply because inflation seemed to be so persistent and mainly because monetarism of the 'middle-age' vintage, though at loggerheads with the 'young Turks', was propped up by the second wave of monetarism – the subject of the next section – that has built on some of the old and simultaneously breathed new life into it. On the other hand, Klein's (1971, p. 35) assessment still appears to ring true:

> It is my opinion that the rush towards monetarism has been just. . . a fad and that the hard facts behind economic interrelationships are proving sobering to those who think that there has been a revolution (or counter revolution) in economic thought. In the financial columns of newspapers and other popular media there has been at attempt to settle very difficult and intricate problems in a superficial way that suggests that there has been a monetarist revolution, but the real answers are going to be found in serious scholarly studies, and I would ask fellow economists to reserve their judgment at this time.

And more than a decade later, Klein (1982b, pp. 256–60) continues to brand both 'middle-aged' and the new wave of monetarism as fads.

EQUILIBRIUM BUSINESS CYCLE CUM RATIONAL EXPECTATIONS

Whether it be considered a revolutionary turnabout, a mere constructive focus on inadequate treatment of expectations in macroeconomic models, a transient fad, or whatever, the so-called 'rational expectations counter-revolution' has generated much enthusiasm, heat, and strong condemnation. While there are many reasons for the clashing attitudes both on the planes of theory and policy, it is probably its widely (mis)perceived policy-ineffectiveness implication that accounts for its notoriety. Lucas and Sargent (1981, p. xi), two of its principal architects, perceive it as enjoying 'popularity as a slogan or incantation with a variety of uses. It may also suffer some notoriety due to presumed links with conservative political views or with excessive concern over the consequences of money supply changes'.

However analytically innovative and creatively applied, RE alone does not represent the hallmark, nor is it even the dominant component of the novel approach which is more appropriately identified by its proponents as the new classical macroeconomics (NCM), or by Lucas, the chief theoretician of the 'school', as equilibrium business cycle (EBC) models. While recognizing the fine distinctions and nuances, in what follows we shall to some extent use NCM and EBC interchangeably.

Since many of the contributions to this volume take a more or less critical look at NCM, EBC, and RE (see in particular the chapters by Tobin, Klein, Wan, Burmeister, B. Friedman, Béguelin and Schiltknecht, and the last section of Arrow) and regretfully the chapter that was to expound this point of view did not materialize in the last moment, it behoves me to give more comprehensive and as objective as possible a treatment of its tenets in this introductory chapter. In doing so, and within the space limitations allowed, I shall try to stand back and let the chief advocates articulate their own case.

In a nutshell, the differentia specifica of NCM (EBC) resides in *three postulates:* (i) instantaneous and continuous competitive market clearing, with perfectly flexible prices and wages; (ii) optimizing behaviour of individuals, with agents' expectations being rational; and (iii) agents' imperfect information not only about future events, but also about the current state (see Lucas, 1981a, pp. 179–80).[19]

This approach is a very tight version of neoclassical GE applied to macroeconomics. It provides a bolder and analytically sophisticated support for pre-Keynesian classical macroeconomics and monetary theory, though in the sense of economic content it is an impoverished version of the latter. In the stronger super-neutrality form, it resuscitates the 'classical dichotomy', and the 'neutrality of money'. 'The model that we construct is in a fundamental sense a direct descendant of the textbook classical model, being an equilibrium model *and* tending to bear "classical" policy implications' (Sargent, 1979, p. 367).[20]

This approach views departure from equilibrium as due to expectations of future economic events subject to significant errors, which tend to be transient. Money is neutral, and systematic monetary and fiscal counter-cyclical policies tend to have no significant effects on the real economy because the outcomes of the policies are informed predictions of anticipated and understood economic events and will be fully accounted for and offset in decision-makers' rational expectations. Macroeconomic policy can succeed only if policy-makers are able to bamboozle persistently the micro agents. Supposedly, economic actors are fast learners who use and revise efficiently all available information (which renders the policy-makers' behaviour a crucial determinant in forming expectations) and who succeed in eliminating expectational misconceptions. This approach places the foremost stress on unsystematic (i.e. unanticipated) monetary-fiscal shocks (policy surprises, entailing expectational distortions) in the fluctuation-generating mechanism, underrating real economic disturbances that occur in the process of economic growth and change.

NCM runs counter to (i) the Keynesian revolution in general, and the Samuelsonian neoclassical synthesis in particular both on the planes of theory and policy,[21] (ii) Klein-type macroeconometric models, (iii) Friedman's monetarism, and (iv) the neoconservatives like Feldstein and others. Not to mention the NCM proponents' denigration of economics that is not mathematically and statistically sophisticated, and the obvious tension between them and the GE theorists who are so profoundly aware of the limitations of the theory (for the latter's case see Arrow's chapter in the companion volume).

Lucas and Sargent (1978, pp. 49–50) perceive the predictions of neoclassical Keynesian economics as 'wildly incorrect' and the doctrine on which they rest as 'fundamentally flawed'. These they assert, 'are now simple matters of fact, involving no novelties in economic theory. The task which faces contemporary students of the business cycle is that of sorting through the wreckage, determining which features of that remarkable intellectual event called the Keynesian Revolution can be salvaged and put to good use, and which others must be discarded.' The difficulties, they say, are 'fatal' and they (1978, p. 50) see modern macroeconomic models as being 'of *no* value in guiding policy'. Lucas (1980, p. 18) is adamant that 'Keynesian economics is dead (maybe "disappeared" is a better term). I don't know when this happened, but it is true today and it wasn't true ten years ago.' He (1980, p. 19) views the existence of 'a middle ground between these extremes of socialism and *laissez-faire* capitalism' as the 'central message of Keynes'. At the present juncture, according to Lucas (1980, p. 20):

this middle ground is gone — not because people don't like the middle ground anymore, but because its intellectual rationale has eroded to the point where it is no longer serviceable. . . I think that the problem, in a nutshell, was that the Keynes–Samuelson view involved two distinct, mutually inconsistent theoretical explanations of the determination of employment. For a time, we thought we could find a new theory that would unify or reconcile these two explanations, but the more progress we made, the more difficulties came into view, dragging us farther under.

Lucas and Sargent emphasize their fundamental methodological contrast with Keynesian macroeconomics.[22] They (1978, p. 50) stress that 'the Keynesian Revolution was, in the form in which it succeeded in the United States, a revolution in *method*. It was not Keynes's. . . intent, nor is it the view of all of his most eminent followers. Yet if one does not view the revolution in this way, it is impossible to account for some of its most important features.' They (1978, p. 58) perceive that Keynes founded what came to be known as macroeconomics 'because he thought that it was impossible to explain the characteristics of business cycles within the discipline imposed by classical economic theory, a discipline imposed by its insistence on adherence to the two postulates (a) that markets be assumed to clear, and (b) that agents be assumed to act in their own self-interest'.[23] Furthermore, Lucas and Sargent (1978, p. 58) see Keynes as freeing himself from the discipline of classical postulates by adopting such rules of thumb as consumption function and liquidity preference instead of 'decision functions that a classical economist would insist be derived from the theory of choice. And rather than require that wages and prices by determined by the postulate that market clear. . . Keynes took as an unexamined postulate that money wages are "sticky".' This decision to postulate rigid wages, 'on the part of the most prestigious theorist of his day freed a generation of economists from the discipline imposed by equilibrium theory, and. . . this freedom was rapidly and fruitfully exploited by macroeconometricians' (Lucas, 1981a, p. 220).[24]

Lucas and Sargent (1978, p. 59) underline the counter-revolutionary nature of their approach 'for it presupposes that Keynes and his followers were wrong to give up on the possibility that an equilibrium theory could account for the business cycle'. As Sargent and Wallace (1981a, p. 208) point out, 'ordinarily we impose two requirements on an economic model: first, that it be consistent with the theoretical core of economics-optimizing behavior within a coherent general equilibrium framework; and second, that it not be refuted by observations'.

Lucas (1981a, p. 9) recalls his fascination with the pre-Keynesian literature on business cycle theory, which he describes as 'sophisticated' even though it was not buttressed by 'modern theoretical technology'.[25] He found that this literature stressed the recurrent nature of business cycles, that the individual agents' errors in forecasting the future played an important role in this recurrence, and that attempts were made to 'rationalize these mistakes as intelligent responses to movements in nominal "signals" of movements in the underlying "real" events we care about and want to react to. If Wesley Mitchell could view agents as "signal processors" in 1913, then I saw no reason to regard my own adoption of this viewpoint in 1972 as unduly speculative.'

Furthermore, Lucas (1981a, p. 215) cites Hayek's prewar statement that 'the incorporation of cyclical phenomena into the system of [Walrasian] economic equilibrium theory, with which they are in apparent contradiction, remains the crucial problem of Trade Cycle Theory.' Lucas (1981a, p. 216) then claims that 'it is likely that many modern economists would have no difficulty accepting Hayek's statement of the problem as roughly equivalent to their own'. Thus, Lucas (1981a, p. 216) insists that 'the most rapid progress toward a coherent and useful aggregate economic theory will result from the acceptance of the problem statement as advanced by the business cycle theorists, and not from further attempts to refine the jerry-built structures to which Keynesian macroeconomics has led us'. He calls for 'a resumption of the work of pre-Keynesian theorists'.

Interestingly, Lucas (1981a, pp. 274–5) considers Keynes's *Treatise* an important example of pre-Keynesian business cycle theory. He views the contrast with the *General Theory* as useful because it emphasizes that limited technical skills to design explicit theory circumscribe one's ability to visualize phenomena productively. He considers the essence of the *Treatise* to be an attempt to understand fluctuations where real variables are determined by the real considerations of neoclassical price theory and where nominal magnitudes are determined by the quantity theory of money. Lucas perceives that while Keynes dealt intelligently with the fundamental problems of business cycles, his algebra was 'trivial'. Lucas (1981a, p. 275) sees Keynes's difficulty as one of lack of technical apparatus to deal with the problems. 'Though he discusses them verbally about as well as his contemporaries, neither he nor anyone else was well enough equipped technically to move the discussion to a sharper or more productive level.'

In contrast to those economists who search for a microfoundation for Keynesian macroeconomics, the EBC protagonists 'abandon' Keynes's *General Theory* and extend GE microeconomics to business cycle theory.[26] Lucas (1981a, p. 222) argues for the 'practical necessity of accounting' for the cyclical behaviour in quantities and prices 'in equilibrium (that is, non-Keynesian) terms. That is, one would like a theory which accounts for the observed movements in *quantities* (employment, consumption, investment) as an optimizing response to observed movements in *prices*.'

Looking at developments in a historical perspective, Lucas and Sargent (1978, pp. 58-9) point out that

> when Keynes wrote, the terms 'equilibrium' and 'classical' carried certain positive and normative connotations which seemed to rule out either modifier being applied to business cycle theory. . . In recent years the meaning of the term 'equilibrium' has undergone such dramatic development that a theorist of the 1930s would not recognize it. It is now routine to describe an economy following a multivariate stochastic process as being 'in equilibrium'. . . . This development which stemmed mainly from work by K. J. Arrow. . . and G. Debreu. . . implies that simply to look at any economic time series and conclude that it is a 'disequilibrium phenomenon' is a meaningless observation.

They (1978, p. 59) perceive the modern conquests of GE theory as smoothing the way for them to pursue a research line that 'involves the attempt to discover a particular, econometrically testable equilibrium theory of the business cycle, one that can serve as the foundation for quantitative analysis of macroeconomic policy'.

EBC proponents explicitly accept the challenge of providing alternative explanations to the great puzzle of business cycles. Sargent (1981b, p. 522) admits that the static (deterministic, non-random) classical macroeconomic model is flawed because in a most essential way it is so much at variance with empirical time series patterns. Perhaps the most prominent defect of that model was its failure to explain 'the persistence from one business cycle to another of positive output-price and positive money-output correlations, which apparently contradicts the classical neutrality propositions' (Sargent, 1979, p. 366).

Lucas and Sargent (1978, p. 60) claim that they 'now have rigorous theoretical models which illustrate how these correlations can emerge while retaining the classical postulates that markets clear and agents optimize. . . The key step in obtaining such models has been to relax the ancillary postulate used in much classical economic analysis that agents have perfect information.'

Tracing the intellectual development of EBC, Lucas (1981a, pp. 6-7) refers to his work with Rapping and acknowledges his debt to Phelps (1970) for pointing the discussion in GE terms and asking, *inter alia*, whether one agent's misapprehension that relative prices are shifting in his favour is not counteracted by another with the contrary misconception. Lucas then asks the loaded question whether it is possible 'to describe an entire economy operating in a mutually consistent way that is led into large-scale employment fluctuations via informational imperfections alone'. He admits that thus far he has not succeeded in achieving this feat though in most of the papers he wrote on the subject he presupposed that he could do so (see also Barro, 1981a, pp. 42–4).

In his celebrated, highly abstract, and technically innovative 1972 paper,[27] Lucas (see 1981a, pp. 66–89) formalizes and builds on the Phelps argument that he also utilizes and develops in subsequent papers. In the 1972 paper the exchange in the economy studied occurs in two physically separate markets (or islands).[28] In each period the allocation of transactors across the two localized markets is partly stochastic, introducing fluctuations in relative prices between the markets. The system is also subject to stochastic monetary disturbances which in itself entails fluctuations in the nominal price level. Agents are informed about these disturbances only through prices in the markets in which they operate. The rational money-illusion free agents are set in a framework where 'prices convey this information only imperfectly, forcing agents to hedge on whether a particular price movement results from a relative demand shift or a nominal (monetary) one' (Lucas, 1981a, p. 66). The decision problem that individual agents face is made fully explicit. The fact that they only have incomplete information implies that the economy does not solve the 'grand maximum problem'. The modification of the information structure of a model that is in other respects neoclassical in nature leads to a real response to a purely nominal experience.

In a 1979 paper (see Lucas, 1981a, pp. 179–214) production and trade are viewed as taking place in a large number of markets that are neither physically nor informationally perfectly linked. The mechanism that generates business cycles entails unanticipated monetary–fiscal shocks whose effects are spread intertemporally owing to the gradual diffusion of information lags, to capital accumulation and to an accelerator effect (see also Barro, 1981a, pp. 79–104).

In explaining secular movements in the general price level, Lucas (1981a, pp. 232–3) considers it incontestable that they arise primarily from changes in the quantity of money. He argues, however, that paradoxically the weakness in the short-run evidence linking money to economic activity and especially to prices 'is *encouraging* from the point of view of monetary business cycle theory'. This is so because the theoretical link between general price movements and economic activity in EBC rests on the hypothesis 'that the signal processing problem of identifying general price movements from observations of a few individual prices was *too difficult* to be solved perfectly by agents'.

'The postulate that agents optimize means that their supply and demand decisions must be functions of real variables, including perceived relative prices' (Lucas and Sargent, 1978, p. 60). All forms of money illusion are rigorously expurgated. This does not rule out, however, that agents are subject to error; that is, sometimes even rational agents confuse purely nominal with real movements.[29]

Differences notwithstanding, there are several interesting versions of the imperfect-information tale. Explaining his EBC model, Lucas (1981a, p. 232) claims that 'since in a competitive economy, employment and output of various kinds are chosen by agents in response to price movements, it seemed appropriate to begin by rationalizing the observed quantity movements as rational or optimal responses to observed price movements.' A key element of the standard models of Lucas, Sargent and Wallace, and Barro is the response of supply to the movement of relative price variables. Incomplete and dispersed information has been modelled by postulating that agents observe a subset of current prices, but do not have access to contemporaneous information about the state of the economy during the decision period and receive information about the overall price level and some other prices or variables with varied lags. EBC models where information is conveyed about such quantity variables as sales or inventories have not yet been constructed (see Barro, 1981a, p. 50).

In summary, the essential aspects of the problem of the information gap are captured by Lucas and Sargent (1978, p. 60):

On the basis of their limited information − the lists that they have of current and past absolute prices of various goods − agents are assumed to make the best possible estimate of all of the *relative* prices that influence their supply and demand decisions. Because they do not have all of the information that would enable them to compute perfectly the relative prices they care about, agents make errors in estimating the pertinent relative prices, errors that are unavoidable given their limited information. In particular, under certain conditions, agents will tend temporarily to mistake a general increase in all absolute prices as an increase in the *relative* price of the good that they are selling, leading them to increase their supply of that good over what they had previously planned. Since everyone is, on average, making the same mistake, aggregate output will rise above what it would have been. This increase of output ... above what it would have been will occur whenever this period's average economy-wide price level is above what agents had expected this period's average economy-wide price level to be on the basis of previous information. Symmetrically, average output will be decreased whenever the aggregate price turns out to be lower than agents had expected. The hypothesis of 'rational expectations' is being imposed here because agents are supposed to make the best possible use of the limited information they have and are assumed to know the pertinent objective probability distributions. This hypothesis is imposed by way of adhering to the tenets of equilibrium theory.

In the preceding theory, disturbances to aggregate demand lead to a positive correlation between unexpected changes in the aggregate price level and revisions in aggregate output from its previously planned level. Further, it is an easy step to show that the theory implies correlations between revisions to aggregate output and unexpected changes in any variables that help determine aggregate demand. In most macroeconomic models, the money supply is one determinant of aggregate demand. The preceding theory easily can account for positive correlations between revisions to aggregate output and unexpected increases in the money supply.

Lucas and Sargent (1981, p. xi) perceive the very term RE as carrying a significant *charge:* 'In our view this charge is not incidental or uninteresting: Muth's hypothesis *is* a contribution of the most fundamental kind, an idea that compels rethinking on many dimensions, with consequent enthusiasm and resistance.'

Essentially the RE hypothesis states that individual agents use their limited information as best they can; that is, their expectations are the optimal forecasts that they can make using the relevant information they possess or can acquire. These expectations are formed in such a way that they are consistent with the rational agents' perceived self-interest. In Lucas's (1981a, p. 187) words, 'the behavior of each trader is *rational* both in the conventional sense of optimal, given objectives and expectations, and in the Muthian sense. . . that available information is optimally utilized in forming expectations'.

In the above simplest form RE is neither particularly novel nor especially objectionable to mainstream economists, for it is a creative application of the standard neoclassical maxim that agents that maximize their objective function intertemporally under constraints would make the best possible use of all available information and would equate marginal costs and benefits of expectational activities.[30] Whatever the intrinsic merits of RE in focusing on the formation of expectations or within its microeconomic content (see Jordan and Radner, 1982), it is its application to macro models that, expectational phenomena aside, derive the powerful neutrality of money proposition and their most far-reaching policy implications that raises the hackles of the critics and challengers.

Muth (1961) provides a most important analytical building block for EBC. It introduces the RE hypothesis in general arguments and as a corollary of the principles of GE. Essentially what Muth means by RE is that the individual agent's expectations are no worse than the forecasts of economic models. This is equivalent to saying that expectations depend in the proper way on what 'relevant' and 'correct' economic theory says that they should depend (see Sargent, 1981a, p. 160).[31]

Muth (1961, p. 316) suggests that 'expectations, since they are informed predictions of future events, are essentially the same as the predictions of the relevant economic theory. . . At the risk of confusing this purely descriptive hypothesis with a pronouncement as to what firms ought to do, we call such expectations "rational".' Furthermore, referring to Simon, Muth points to the fallacy of arguing 'that the assumption of rationality in economics leads to theories inconsistent with, or inadequate to explain, observed phenomena, especially changes over time. . . Our hypothesis is based on exactly the opposite point of view: that dynamic economic models do not assume enough rationality.' Muth (1961, p. 316) rephrases the RE hypothesis in what he considers to be a more precise fashion: 'Expectations of firms (or more generally, the subjective probability of distribution of outcomes) tend to be distributed, for the same information set, about the prediction of the theory (or the 'objective' probability distributions of outcomes)' (see also Lucas and Sargent, 1981, pp. xvi–iii).

Muth (1961, pp. 316–17) states that the RE hypothesis asserts the following tripod:

(1) Information is scarce, and the economic system generally does not waste it. (2) the way expectations are formed depends specifically on the structure of the relevant system describing the economy. (3) A 'public prediction' in the sense of Grunberg and Modigliani. . . will have no substantial effect on the operation of the economic system (unless it is based on inside information). This is not quite the same thing as stating that the marginal revenue product of economics is zero, because expectations of a single firm may still be subject to greater error than the theory.[32]

In his terse and insightful introduction, Muth (1961, p. 315) notes that recognition of expectational errors is well established in studies of business cycle fluctuations.[33] However, he goes on:

As a systematic theory of fluctuations in markets or in the economy, the approach is limited. . . because it does not include an explanation of the way expectations are formed. To make dynamic economic models complete, various expectations formulas have been used. There is, however, little evidence to suggest that the presumed relations bear a resemblance to the way the economy works.

He (1961, pp. 315–16) then goes on to ask what kind of information is used and how it is processed to predict future conditions. This is important because of the character of dynamic processes that are sensitized to the influence of the actual unfolding of events on the formation of expectations. Moreover, 'it is often necessary to make sensible predictions about the way expectations would change when either the amount of available information or the structure of the system is changed. . . The area is important from a statistical standpoint as well, because parameter estimates are likely to be seriously biased towards zero if the wrong variable is used as the expectation.'

Perhaps we should digress here and point out that Muth (1961) can be traced to Holt, Modigliani, Muth, and Simon (1960). Simon (1982, p. 486) sees Muth's elaboration of RE as in some sense enshrouded in historical irony. In the aforementioned management science study, the co-authors evolved a dynamic programming algorithm for the specific, easily computable, case of quadratic cost functions, where the decision rules are linear and the probability distributions can be supplanted by their expected values, used as certainty equivalents (see also Theil, 1957). As Simon (1982, p. 486) put it:

> Muth imaginatively saw in this special case a paradigm for rational behavior under uncertainty. What to some of us in the HMMS research team was an approximating, satisficing simplification, served for him as a major line of defense for perfect rationality. . . Instead of dealing with uncertainty by elaborating the model of the decision process, he would once and for all — if his hypothesis were correct — make process irrelevant.

In a reflective mood, Lucas (1981a, pp. 223–4) emphasizes that to understand business cycles and the decision problems the agent faces under uncertainty 'one needs to imagine a fairly precise view of the future in the mind of this agent. Where does he get this view, and how can an observer infer what it is?' In this sense Lucas (1981a, p. 224) is assisted by RE:

> Insofar as business cycles can be viewed as repeated instances of essentially similar events, it will be reasonable to treat agents as reacting to

cyclical changes as 'risk', or to assume their expectations are *rational*, that they have fairly stable arrangements for collecting and processing information, and that they *utilize* this information in forecasting the future in a stable way, free of systematic and easily correctable biases.[34]

It is a controversial issue whether the idea of RE implies that the agents are omniscient or 'econometric wizards'.[35] For example, according to McCallum's (1981, p. 49) explicit and clear statement, RE does not imply that agents have perfect foresight or that their expectations are always error-free. It does imply, however, that agents reconsider past errors and generally will attempt to rapidly eradicate sources of errors. Furthermore, it presumes that, despite sizeable expectational errors, the systematic sources of such errors are successfully eradicated. Thus these errors are not systematically related to information available at the time the expectations are formed.

Sargent and Wallace (1981a, pp. 209–10, see also 1981b) suggest four reasons for using the RE hypothesis in their macro models:

(1) The alternatives, such as fixed-weight autoregressive models they find objectionable. The traditional distributed-lag method of accounting for expectations in macroeconometric models results, in their view, in general econometric underidentification of the coefficients of expectations.

(2) 'If expectations are rational and properly take into account the way the policy instruments and other exogenous variables evolve, the coefficients in certain representations of the model (e.g. reduced forms) will change whenever the processes governing those policy instruments and exogenous variables change. A major impetus to work on rational expectations is thus that it offers one reason, but probably not the only reason, that macroeconometric models fail tests for structural change' (Sargent and Wallace, 1981a, p. 209).

(3) RE is in line with the economists' perception of the agents' behaviour as governed by self-interest. 'This is not to deny that some people are irrational and neurotic. But we have no reason to believe that those irrationalities cause *systematic and predictable* deviations from rational behavior that a macroeconomist can model and tell the monetary authority how to compensate for. In this regard, it should be noted that the rational expectations hypothesis does not require that people's expectations equal conditional mathematical expectations, only that they equal conditional mathematical expectations plus what may be a very large random term (random with respect to the conditioning information)' (Sargent and Wallace, 1981a, pp. 209–10).

(4) 'We must specify exactly the horizon over which the expectations

are cast and what variables people are assumed to see and when, things that most macroeconometric models are silent on. In doing policy analysis under rational expectations, we must specify whether a given movement in a policy variable was foreseen beforehand or unforeseen, an old and important distinction in economics, but one that makes no difference in the usual evaluations of policy made with macroeconometric models' (Sargent and Wallace, 1981a, p. 210).

Sargent and Wallace (1981a, pp. 210-11) also call attention to a general dilemma:

> Dynamic models that invoke rational expectations can be solved only by attributing to the agents whose behavior is being described a way of forming views about the dynamic processes governing the policy variables. Might it not be reasonable at times to attribute to them a systematically incorrect view? Thus suppose an economy has been operating under one rule for a long time when secretly a new rule is adopted. It would seem that people would learn the new rule only gradually as they acquired data and that they would for some time make what from the viewpoint of the policymaker are forecastable prediction errors. During this time, a new rule could be affecting real variables.

In a sense the paramount question is how fast a learner and adapter the agent is: to what extent is he a prisoner of the past, governed largely by habit and routine and/or to what extent is he forward looking? The question, of course, hinges not only on the agents' abilities and preferences and motivations, but also on the dispersion, availability, and reliability of information and on the cost of acquiring and processing it.

The dramatically different implications of EBC models, contrasted with the fixed autoregressive or adaptive expectation macro models, are partly derived from the postulates of RE that agents use information (including government policy and their own expectations of future government policy) besides past prices in forming their forecasts of the price level and that the agents are quick learners and thus not prisoners of the past. The implication is that policy alterations will be rapidly deciphered by the agents whose expectations will take such alterations into account.

In a number of papers the EBC protagonists focus on a common substantive policy question: do changes in monetary (fiscal) policy affect real output and employment? Their striking answer is: when they are systematic and anticipated they do not; only the unsystematic and unanticipated surprise policy changes affect real variables. In other words, 'no systematic monetary policy, once anticipated and understood, can have any real effects, because optimizing private agents offset them in order to remain at their preferred positions. . . The general message of such models is that efficiency is best served by avoiding unpredictable monetary injections which can only contaminate observed price signals' (Weiss, 1980, p. 222).

Lucas and Sargent (1978, pp. 60-1) make these policy implications quite explicit:[36]

> While such a theory predicts positive correlations between the inflation rate or money supply, on the one hand, and the level of output on the other, it also asserts that those correlations do not depict 'tradeoffs' that can be exploited by a policy authority. That is, the theory predicts that there is no way that the monetary authority can follow a systematic activist policy and achieve a rate of output that is on average higher over the business cycle than what would occur if it simply adopted a no-feedback, X-percent rule of the kind Friedman. . . and Simons. . . recommended. For the theory predicts that aggregate output is a function of current and past unexpected changes in the money supply. Output will be high only when the money supply is and has been higher than it had been expected to be, i.e., higher than average. There is simply no way that on average over the whole business cycle the money supply can be higher than average. Thus, while the preceding theory is capable of explaining some of the correlations long thought to invalidate classical macroeconomic theory, the theory is classical both in its adherence to the classical theoretical postulates and in the 'nonactivist' flavor of its implications for monetary policy.

As we know, Friedman's brand of monetarism posits that in the long run there is no inflation–unemployment trade-off. Lucas (1981a, p. 104) points to the fallacy of the inference that permanent inflation will induce a permanent economic high: 'As soon as Phelps and others made the first serious attempts to rationalize the apparent trade-off in modern theoretical terms, the zero-degree homogeneity of demand and supply functions was re-discovered in this new context (as Friedman predicted it would be) and re-named the "natural rate hypothesis".' However, contrary to Lucas, the Friedman interpretation contains what by stretching the point could be called a Keynesian connection; that on the policy plane in the short run (which may be long in calendar time) there may be exploitable trade-off variants. Sargent (1977, p. 1) points out that the NRH was introduced as a provocative but somewhat vague statement that in the long run there would be no inflation–unemployment trade-off, for eventually agents' expectations would adjust to eliminate any money illusions. NRH in conjunction with adaptive expectations did not appear to threaten conventional activist Keynesian policy which Sargent (1977, p. 1) perceives as 'incorporating feedback from past economic conditions to current policy settings':

> That was because 'in the long run' could be taken to mean 'in the distant future'. A meaningful tradeoff between inflation and unemployment, one with an interesting dynamic structure, still existed under the natural rate hypothesis with adaptive expectations. The feedback rules that resulted from solving the dynamic optimization problem posed by that tradeoff were of the usual Keynesian form.
>
> It was left for Robert E. Lucas. . . to show that, when combined with the hypothesis of rational expectations, the natural unemployment rate hypothesis has very unconventional policy implications. In particular, there obtains a class of stochastic neutrality propositions that imply severely limited possibilities for engaging in successful activist counter-cyclical policy. These neutrality propositions emerge in models that, potentially at least, seem to be capable of generating the correlations between policy variables and real economic variables that form the empirical basis for Keynesian models. One of the virtues of models like Lucas's is that they do not involve vague concepts such as 'short run' and 'long run'. Instead, the models are equilibrium models that (like Arrow–Debreu state preference models) determine the probability distributions of all the endogenous variables as functions of the probability distributions of the exogenous variables and random shocks. The models restrict data and are thus refutable (pp. 1–2).

Confrontation of the static, non-random, classical model with the observed Phillips curve is a puzzle, for, to recall, inordinate rates of money expansion should leave output and unemployment unaffected. Clearly, observations that imply influence from enlarged aggregate demand to expanded real output and reduced unemployment (instead of increasing prices only) are at loggerheads with the classical model. 'More generally, such evidence seems to contradict any general equilibrium model in which agents' decisions about real economic variables are homogeneous of degree zero in nominal magnitudes, as a large body of economic theory predicts' (Sargent, 1979, p. 324).

Lucas's EBC models embody NRH which in this context is interpreted as merely asserting that the agents' decisions are functions of relative prices only. 'Within the confines of such a hypothesis, if one is to explain why high inflation and high nominal aggregate demand seem to induce high aggregate output, it is necessary to construct an operational model of "money illusion". Lucas, in effect, constructed a simple model of "money illusion", one compatible with rational, optimizing behavior' (Sargent, 1979, p. 325). NRH and the rationality hypothesis are tightly interwoven for, as Sargent (1981a, p. 161) argues, NRH cannot be properly formalized without invoking the rationality hypothesis.

Indeed, Lucas (1981a, p. 283) recalls that the attempts to formalize NRH ran into the defectiveness of the then prevalent ways of modelling expectations. The RE hypothesis turned out to be the sensible way to formalize NRH. 'Subsequent research in macroeconomics has revealed the sweeping implications of this [RE] hypothesis, and the extent to which it proves subversive of the main positive and policy presumptions underlying the neoclassical synthesis.' Put somewhat differently, still in Lucas's (1981a, p. 133) words:

> all formulations of the natural rate theory postulate rational agents, whose decisions depend on *relative* prices only, placed in an economic setting in which they cannot distinguish relative from general price movements. Obviously, there is no limit to the number of models one can construct where agents are placed in this situation of imperfect information; the trick is to find tractable schemes with this feature.

According to Lucas (1981b, p. 562) EBC models

> provide examples of monetary economies in which money has the kind of long-run neutrality that the Friedman–Phelps logic requires, yet retains the capacity to induce short-run disruptions of the sort documented by Friedman and Anna J. Schwartz (1963). These models do, to be sure, carry implications that are stronger than those obtained by Friedman and Phelps, but surely it is the desire to obtain *all* the implications of a set of assumptions which leads us to prefer explicit theoretical models to looser, verbal arguments. They do not, however, succeed in reconciling a Friedman–Phelps long-run with a Keynesian short-run: there is simply nothing Keynesian about them. I will confess that this worried me at first, but I got over it after a while.[37]

Lucas (1981a, pp. 234–5) notes that EBC on a policy plane aims at understanding and explicating policy proposals of the Chicago school:

> By seeking an equilibrium account of business cycles, one accepts *in advance* rather severe limitations on the scope of governmental counter-cyclical policy which might be rationalized by the theory. Insofar as fluctuations are induced by gratuitous monetary instability, serving no social purpose, then increased monetary stability promises to reduce aggregate, real variability and increase welfare. There is no doubt, how-

ever, that *some* real variability would remain even under the smoothest monetary and fiscal policies. There is no *prima facie* case that this residual variability would be better dealt with by centralized, governmental policies than by individual, decentralized responses.

Lucas conceives his theoretical work on EBC as a rationalization for the rules that will eliminate erratic monetary and fiscal shocks as independent sources of instability. He (1981a, pp. 254-5) has gone beyond Friedman:

> research based on the idea of *rational expectations* has played a role in buttressing the case for thinking about policy, as Friedman argued we should, as a problem in selecting stable, predictable policy *rules*. The main argument turns out to be a positive (as opposed to normative) one: our ability as economists to predict the responses of agents rests, in situations where expectations about the future matter, on our understanding of the stochastic environment agents believe themselves to be operating in. In practice, this limits the class of policies the consequences of which we can hope to assess in advance to policies generated by fixed, well understood, relatively permanent rules (or functions relating policy actions taken to the state of the economy).

Thus, in a nutshell, in contrast to the earlier, Friedman-type monetarists, the NCM proponents attribute much stronger perpetual market-clearing properties to our economy and even deny that there is a trade-off to anticipated systematic monetary and fiscal policy in the short run. In fact, essentially in their models the 'ambiguous' distinction between the short and long run is eliminated and long-run results rule universally; that is, they hold in the short run as well.[38]

On the subject of coping with inflation − the disease of the 1970s − one may contrast the 'Keynesian', Friedmanite, and NCM views. The first, to recall, points out that inflation is complex and multidimensional, with an interaction of causations, and with its own momentum (core inflation) that cannot be eliminated by monetary policy alone. The second school sees inflation as a monetary phenomenon, but advocates a 'go slow' policy in view of adverse short-term effects of monetary shocks. The third school denies inherent momentum to the inflationary process and asserts that the government can eliminate inflation very rapidly and with virtually no depressing effects on real variables, thus with virtually no Phillips-curve costs. This would be so if the government made it clear that the policy rules are firm, uncontroversial, and unlikely to be reversed (see Sargent, 1981d).

However, we need to digress here to note that there is a continuous emergence of steadily weakened versions of NCM. In a plethora of articles it has become well established that the policy-ineffectiveness results do not generally hold in RE models if the perfect price flexibility assumption is discarded. These models demonstrate the potentials for even anticipated monetary policy for the stabilization of fluctuations in output and employment (see Taylor, 1980 and 1983; Fischer, 1983).

In a number of papers on the general implications of EBC models for macro policy, their protagonists examine the importance of the treatment of RE in drawing inferences from econometric models and the agents' behaviour from observed time series, including such formidable questions as the alterations of agents' behaviour under a different environment or under one that was altered in some specific way by the hypothetical policy changes. Concurrently, they are highly critical of Keynesian macroeconometrics (see Lucas and Sargent, 1978, pp. 56-7).

A central issue here is whether the strong attack on the conventional use of econometric models for policy analysis should be viewed, as Sims (1982) argues, as a 'cautionary note', or as a deadly blow. 'As in most revolutions, the old regime toppled by the rational expectations revolution was corrupt and in some sense deserved its fate. However, as is often the case, the revolution itself has had its excesses, destroying or discarding much that was valuable in the name of utopian ideology' (Sims, 1982, pp. 7-8). He (p. 8) concludes 'that the rational expectations critique of econometric policy analysis is a cautionary footnote to such analysis rather than a deep objection to its foundations'.

Whatever their other objections against Keynesian models, the EBC protagonists attack them on grounds that they are atheoretical, that they impose several types of *a priori* restrictions, and that they will provide faulty interpretations and predictions about economic behaviour in hypothetically new environments (see Sargent, 1981c; Lucas, 1981a, p. 11; Sims, 1977a). More specifically, Lucas (1981a, p. 221) sees a 'fatal' flaw in 'virtually all sectors of modern macroeconomic models, primarily because of the faulty treatment of expectations in these models'. He (1981a, pp. 220-1) also considers the ability of Klein-type models to imitate the actual behaviour of the economy as having almost nothing to do with ability to make accurate conditional forecasts which he considers as the most important one. Such an ability requires invariance of the structure of the model.[39]

Invariance of parameters in an economic model is not, of course, a property which can be assured in advance, but it seems reasonable to hope that neither tastes nor technology vary systematically with variations in countercyclical policies. In contrast, agents' *decision rules will* in general change with changes in the environment. An equilibrium model is, by definition, constructed so as to predict how agents with stable tastes and technology will *choose* to respond to a new situation.

Clearly, the future needs to be forecast on the basis of the past. The linear forecasting rules are not questioned by Lucas and Sargent (1981, p. xvi):

> The difficulty lies not in postulating forecasts which are linear functions of history but rather in introducing the coefficients in these linear functions as so many additional 'free parameters', unrestricted by theory. That this practice is unnecessary, and in an important way fatal to the purposes of the empirical study of economic time series, is the message of Muth's classic paper.

Thus the EBC protagonists tend to stress that the RE hypothesis is not only the foundation for their models, but that they derive their policy implications from it (or in other versions in combination with NRH). It seems, however, that it is the market-clearing assumption they make that is a *sine qua non* component of their striking policy-ineffectiveness implication, as Tobin stresses in Chapter 2 of this volume.

It needs to be emphasized that market clearing is just an assumption. In EBC models 'prices and quantities are taken to be always in equilibrium. In these models, the concepts of excess demand and supplies play no observational role and are identified with no observed magnitudes' (Lucas, 1981a, p. 287). Lucas (1981a, p. 101) explains his position by pointing out that

> the issue whether to treat observed prices and quantities as market clearing arouses more controversy than it deserves. I prefer thinking of markets as cleared partly because of logical difficulties with the leading alternative view. . . and partly because it leads the theory into the crucial questions of intertemporal substitution and expectations and away from the mechanical 'auctioneer' of the standard dynamics.

The objections to market clearing and optimizing are documented in the companion volume. Only some specific criticisms will be pointed to here. In a witty and trenchant retort, Solow (1978a, p. 204) points out that in some instances Lucas and Sargent firmly underline that EBC is

> based on two terribly important postulates – optimizing behavior and perpetual market clearing. When you read closely, they seem to regard the postulate of optimizing behavior as self-evident and the postulate of market-clearing behavior as essentially meaningless. I think they are

too optimistic, since the one that they think is self-evident I regard as meaningless and the one that they think is meaningless, I regard as false.

Hahn (1982, p. 48), a distinguished contributor to modern GE theory, comments that

> when Lucasians postulate that prices are 'flexible' they seem to mean that we can observe only Walrasian market-clearing prices. There is no nonsense here about the invisible hand doing any noticeable and comprehensible work: its task is accomplished by definition. So right at the centre of the argument there seems to be a gaping void.

He (1982, p. 54) then quips that 'for the Lucasians, prices change to keep Walrasian markets cleared by a mechanism that is entirely secret in the Lucasian mind'. Thus Hahn (1982, p. 49) views prices in the 'Lucasian world' as

> not properly endogenous to the fundamental theory, because there is no theory of the actions of agents that explains how prices come to be such as to clear Walrasian markets. It is an article of faith that they always do so, or, perhaps less pejoratively, an axiom. But I do not find it helpful to have a central problem of economic theory, and indeed of economic policy, treated in this way. (See also Arrow, 1959; Barro, 1981a, pp. 203–4.)

Whatever the analytical merits of the concept of market clearing, it is based on the quixotic assumption of perfect price and wage flexibility and omits some of the most essential properties of the dynamics and *modus operandi* of the mixed capitalist economy.[40] By abstracting from the pervasive phenomenon of disequilibrium, the market-clearing approach empoverishes economic theory in some essential way. Such an approach does not confront the problems of change; that is, upheavals, resistance, and learning. Thus, such an approach considers disequilibrium as promptly and smoothly eliminated by the forces of excess supply or demand. The impediments to the dynamic adjustment process and the difficulties, efforts, and costs involved are underrated or ignored. It is particularly debatable whether the alleged self-stabilizing and self-correcting economic mechanism is sufficiently forceful when the vulnerability of the economic system to external or random disturbances is considered. Usually the dynamic system can be moved towards equilibrium by some forces while others push it away. Nor is any equilibrium of whatever kind necessarily desirable or socially optimal.

In a broader perspective, the differences between the EBC proponents and their critics revolve around diametrically different perceptions of aggregate demand and supply and the morphology of markets. More specifically, underlying changes in demand and supply may not be translated into price changes; adjustments may lag, be incomplete, or costly; industrial prices tend to respond primarily to variations in costs (cost-plus prices) and underutilized capacity influences price movements; markets are asymmetrical; there are market adjustment frictions and persistent rigidities; prices are sticky to a varied degree; the labour market (a heterogeneous entity by itself) is partly guided by the participants' revealed preferences for long-term contracts, these contracts are staggered, featuring leapfrogging and overtaking and different configurations of inertia and anticipation; intensity of monopoly and trade union power; and markets are generally not impersonal — while the personal relationship and trust can be terminated, they often persist, even if not formalized, for both parties seem to perceive benefits from long-term relationships of mutual trust and reliability.[41]

By imposing an inordinately tight concept of rationality and continuous market clearing as well as super-neutrality of money, the EBC models help to focus their critics' attention on the perplexing question as to why the real world does not essentially work as the models postulate. This contribution should not be underrated, for, as Solow (1978a, p. 204) remarked, 'every orthodoxy, including my own, needs to have a kick in the pants frequently, to prevent it from getting self-indulgent, and applying very lax standards to itself'.

And what about this interaction between the EBC proponents and their critics? With his usual astuteness, Solow (1983, p. 284) sees it in his own deflected light:

> It seems to me that equilibrium theorists are saying: the world *must* be like the Walrasian model because that is the model we have. Those who are more in touch with reality seem to say: the world is not like the Walrasian model, but perhaps the resemblance could be made closer. That is real progress. I would like to argue for even a little more imagination: the world might have its reasons for being non-Walrasian.

It is of some interest to note that one of the leading contemporary macro-economists of the 'middle-age' generation, Stanley Fischer (1983, p. 274), sees a tendency towards a consensus — a 'neo-Keynesian–Friedman–Phelps–Lucas synthesis' that features a vertical Phillips curve in the long run and a non-vertical one in the short run:

> The short-run nonverticality arises from several factors, among them nominal contracting, concern about relative wages, and expectational

errors. The proportions in which these factors matter depend heavily on the state of the economy and the types of policy being followed. In normal times prices will be quite sticky, and policy can rely on the type of responses that Keynesian sticky price-wage models suggest. But radical policy changes could reduce stickiness rapidly. Price stickiness is not a structural characteristic of the economy. It can be relied on only so long as policy actions not too different from those of the past are undertaken.

The synthesis Fischer (1983, p. 274) visualizes also features considerable uncertainty about the structure and vitality of the economy in view of policy changes:

Optimal policymaking is best viewed as a cooperative game in which the government maximizes a welfare function that is positively associated with the utilities of private agents. Actual policy may deviate from the optimum, and it is important both to study actual policymaking and to discuss institutional arrangements to improve its performance.

Fischer (1983) views the resistance to such a synthesis as mainly predicated on the lack of theoretical underpinning for price stickiness.[42]

This has long been a bone of contention. As Solow (1980a, p. 7) imaginatively pointed out, many economists believe that it is not possible to conceive of market failures if one has not an acceptable theory for such an occurrence:

That is a remarkable precept when you think about it. I remember reading once that it is still not understood how the giraffe manages to pump and adequate blood supply all the way up to its head; but it is hard to imagine that anyone would therefore conclude that giraffes do not have long necks. At least not anyone who had ever been to a zoo.

If we do not know how the giraffes do it, would it be helpful to theorize that they either have short necks or thin blood? In the same vein, if we observe prevalent price stickiness and cannot satisfactory explain it (at least in theoretical terms), is it helpful to postulate that markets continuously clear?

Classical economics is superior to its present-day version (NCM) in that it perceives competition as part of a growth process and conceives the allocation problem within the context of a dynamic economy with changing endowment of resources, techniques, and tastes. Furthermore, NCM seems to be a retrogression from the classical view and subsequent neoclassical theorizing on the dynamics of transitional states of stable equilibrium and the dynamic modification of the crude static classical system. The resurrected version of classical economics rests on an implausible and distorted conception of economic processes. It abstracts from the salient features of the realities of modern capitalism. It achieves extraordinary analytical rigour and elegance at an extraordinarily high cost to relevance and usefulness to the real world. As Tobin (1980b, p. 46) so aptly remarked, NCM could be 'seriously advanced only by persons with extravagant faith in their own abstract models and with historical amnesia'.

The test of theory is relevance to reality and, whatever NCM's other grave shortcomings, its empirical foundations are flimsy. *Inter alia*, the content of RE is questionable, for it does not explain how these expectations are formed, nor does it show the learning process by which the actors discover, acquire, and interpret the information and the use they make of it (see Simon, 1982, pp. 438–9 and 486; Klein, 1981, pp. 62–5).

Yet this type of criticism might not even dent the hide of the EBC theorist. Lucas emphatically stresses that progress in economics has to be evaluated in terms of advances in the technology of economic analysis. He (1981a, p. 276) points out 'that progress in economic thinking means getting better and better abstract, analogue economic models, not better verbal observations about the world'. Indeed, referring to his 1972 paper, he (1981b, p. 563) admits that 'if ever there was a model rigged, frankly and unapologetically, to fit a limited set of facts, it is this one'.

Lucas (1981a, p. 271) views the tension between model building and reality as follows:

> One of the functions of theoretical economics is to provide fully articulated, artificial economic systems that can serve as laboratories in which policies that would be prohibitively expensive to experiment with in actual economies can be tested out at much lower cost. To serve this function well, it is essential that the artificial 'model' economy be distinguished as sharply as possible in discussion from actual economies. Insofar as there is confusion between statements of opinion as to the way we believe actual economies would react to particular policies and statements of verifiable fact as to how the model will react, the theory is not being effectively used to help us to see which opinions about the behavior of actual economies are accurate and which are not. This is the sense in which insistence on the 'realism' of an economic model subverts its potential usefulness in thinking about reality. Any model that is well enough articulated to give clear answers to the questions we put to it will necessarily be artificial, abstract, patently 'unreal'.

NCM has attracted and continues to attract many bright, technically gifted young economists who have invested their intellectual capital in sophisticated mathematics and statistical techniques and computer technology. It is perhaps to them that the quip (told me by Christopher Bliss) that an economist is someone who when observing real events worries whether they can happen in theory, is most applicable. Their forte lies in equilibrium economics, and, as such, a number of them have little or no interest in the economic realities around them, nor do they have any genuine macro policy concerns or motivations. They are largely microeconomic theorists used to dabbling in a world of GE or statistical probability theory who have applied their (mis)perceived comparative advantages to, or imperialistically invaded, macroeconomics.[43] Often they are impatient and intolerant of those who perceive the complexities of the world and chide NCM for disregarding such complexities and playing with simplistic 'toys'.

THE KALECKIAN ALTERNATIVE

As we have seen, economic theorists approach their subject from different vantage points and with different motivations. As a result quite frequently in the history of economic thought 'theories are being created which may raise problems of great interest but are not very conducive to understanding what actually happened, is happening or should be happening' (Kalecki, 1970, p. 311).

In her review of Leijonhufvud (1968), Joan Robinson (1969, p. 582) acknowledged that 'there is something' to Leijonhufvud's contention 'that we who worked with Keynes were saved from the misunderstandings rife in America because we had the benefit of oral teaching which was not made clear in the book'. But, she continues, 'I think that there are more important explanations. First Kalecki brought to England his own version of the General Theory, which tightened up some loose threads in Keynes' version and brought it into relation with imperfect competition, supplying a missing link in Keynes' theory of prices. To judge by this survey, Kalecki had very little influence on American doctrines.'

Kalecki's influence on and differences with the Cambridge Keynesians are not part of this story, but his ideas are. Kalecki's contributions, even if sometimes not directly identified with him, are especially significant because, as an independent architect of a seemingly overlapping 'general theory', he derived profoundly distinct theoretical and policy implications, which are of particular importance, *inter alia*, because of the modern assaults on the Keynesian revolution and the need to extend and generalize the *General Theory* and also because his ideas are less amenable to the neoclassical synthesis.

Kalecki's theory of dynamics and fluctuations of national income and its partition between profits and wages is more general than Keynes's theory. Kalecki avoided the distinction between micro and macro theories. He constructed his macroeconomic model on the basis of a more realistic theory of the firm that incorporated imperfect competition and income distribution as integral parts of his analysis. He elucidated the dynamic properties of the economic process and dealt with an open economy.[44]

To build a realistic theory, Kalecki explained how industrial prices are formed by mark-ups on costs and distinguished between 'cost-determined' and 'demand-determined' prices. The intensity of the 'degree of monopoly' (together with other distributional factors) is a key for the determination of macrodistribution. The distributional factors are essentially pertinent to effective demand and to fluctuations in aggregate output and utilization of resources. Kalecki's theory of profits is based on the principle that wage-earners do not save, but spend what they get, and that entrepreneurs get what they spend. Thus entrepreneurs' profits are governed by their propensity to invest and consume and not the other way round. Thus, his model not only describes a wider range of economic phenomena, but also presents the economic process in motion (i.e. how one sequence develops from the preceding ones). The model encompasses long-run dynamics, the capacity effects of investments, and some supply considerations. This model provides a starting point for understanding the contemporary problems of simultaneous occurrence of inflation and recession.

Keynes concentrated his attack on the macroeconomic failure of the system, but did not challenge the established value and distribution theories. Tobin (1981b, p. 207) also notes

> Keynes's uncritical acceptance of the neoclassical competitive model. By assuming that firms are price takers in auction markets rather than price setters in monopolistic competition or oligopoly, he made it harder to sustain his vision of persistent disequilibrium, with failures of coordination, communication, and adjustment. Imperfect competition was the other revolution in economics in the 1930s; one of its sites was Keynes's Cambridge, and two of its agents, Joan Robinson and Sraffa, were in his group. Yet for some mysterious reason the two revolutions were never meshed.

Indeed, Keynes appears never to have had a genuine interest in such questions. One of the differences between him and Kalecki is that the latter aimed at providing a macrodistribution theory on firmer foundations of a more plausible theory of the firm; in bringing the strength of the forces of market imperfection, or degree of monopoly (a term he later regretted), in touch not only with the mode of behaviour and pricing policy of the firm and process of price formation in an industry, but in incorporating forces of market imperfection in his model of the economy as a whole; and in demonstrating that the intensity of the degree of monopoly is pertinent to the determination of distributive shares and thus closely tied in with the theory of effective demand and Kalecki's conception about the typical state of underutilization of productive resources in modern capitalist economy.

Kalecki's theory of distribution derives genealogically from the Ricardian tradition. His theory is not merely a deviation or departure from the neoclassical marginal productivity theory (for the latter, see Chapter 16 in this volume). He simply never started from it, but proceeded from a different approach and marginal productivity did not enter into his argument. Kalecki did not simply relax the restrictive assumption of perfect competition. Again, he never started from it. The model of perfect competition is alien to his method of attacking economic problems. He argued that only by dropping the untenable assumption of perfect competition and penetrating the real world of industrial and market structures (imperfect competition and oligopoly) can any plausible propositions about determinants of macrodistribution be advanced.[45]

In building his macrodistribution theory, Kalecki proceed from an unorthodox concept of the theory of the firm. He assumed surplus capacity as a typical phenomenon in manufacturing and perfect competition rather the exception in the economic system as a whole. He then focused attention on the firm's price-*making* opportunities and constraints and the policy decisions that the entrepreneurs actually have to make about prices and other forms of non-price competition and labour contracts under various types of imperfect markets.

At the expense of oversimplification, each firm in an industry fixes the price for its product by 'marking up' its average unit prime cost in order to cover overheads and to achieve profits, that is, prices are formed by adding a proportionate mark-up on to the prime cost.

The major proposition is that the mark-up depends on the process of industrial concentration; on the vigour and weaknesses in competition; on market imperfections; on industrial setting; on the morphology of markets; on the degree of freedom and constraints in price setting; and on income distribution. The mark-up is viewed as governed by a firm's price-fixing policy in relation to price formation in an industry. Its determination is a key to arriving at functional shares of national income, in turn affecting spending propensities and the degree of utilization of resources. True, the margin is a 'catch-all' term, grouping the numerous factors that affect its size. It is *determined* by and *reflects* 'semi-monopolistic and monopolistic influences' resulting from imperfect competition or oligopoly.

Kalecki starts with a definitional equation and manipulates the equation so as to provide a theoretical explanation which, of course, can be proven right or wrong, plausible or logically inconsistent, or can be refuted by economic statistics — but this is a different matter. But once attention shifts to the major factors underlying changes in the 'degree of monopoly', a behavioural relationship is introduced.

Here exists tautology — so to speak — and we enter the field of theorizing where the aim is to explain observable reality. The hypothesis could be verified or disproved by facts. The explanatory value of hypotheses depends on the question raised and propositions advanced that help to illuminate facts and processes. Kalecki offered a hypothesis as to the major causes of change in the degree of monopoly, or rather a framework for the study of chief determinants affecting distribution of national income. True, it might be difficult to quantify the many influences that play on the degree of monopoly.

It is noteworthy that the mark-up is not defined *as* the degree of monopoly, but depends on and is a symptom of the degree of monopoly. This use of mark-up to cover overheads is very important then; though it involves monopoly power, it is not synonymous with it. Kalecki has devised a new way of tackling a formidable problem.

A digression on Kalecki's distinction between cost-determined and demand-determined prices is in order. As contrasted with short-run changes in prices of finished products, which are mainly cost-determined, short-run variations in the prices of primary products are considered largely to reflect variations in demand (demand-determined). The distinction between these two types of price formations arises out of divergent conditions of supply in short periods. The output of finished goods is elastic owing to a prevalence of surplus capacity. A rise in demand is met chiefly by an increase in the rate of production, and the price changes that do occur are caused chiefly by changes in costs of production. While in general prices of finished goods are mainly determined by changes in the cost of production, they are affected, of course, by any demand-determined variations in the price of raw materials; but it is through the medium of costs that the impulses are transmitted. The supply of raw materials is usually inelastic in the short run. Increasing the supply of agricultural products takes considerable time. In a more restricted sense, the same statement applies to mining. In supply-constrained activities, in the short run, a rise in demand causes disinvestment in inventories and consequent rise in price (the initial price movement is frequently accompanied by secondary speculative demand, making it even more difficult in the short period for output to catch up with increased demand). The demand-determined prices of raw materials (inclusive of primary foodstuffs) tend to decline considerably during slumps and to rise considerably during upswings in economic activity.

To recall, then, Kalecki's theory of profits is based on the principle that wage-earners do not save, but spend what they get, and that entrepreneurs get what they spend. Thus, capitalists' profits are governed by their propensity to invest and consume and not the other way around. As a result of the rise in the degree of monopoly, the relative share of profits in income increases only by lowering the relative share of labour. The distribution determinants will affect not the real profits that will remain the same, but rather the real wages and salaries, effective demand, employment and the level of utilization of capacity. A rise in the degree of monopoly entails a rise in the profit/national income ratio, but real total profits do not change, since they continue to be determined by past investment decisions. With constant investment there is the same total amount of profits (saving). While profits remain unyielding, the real wages and real national product will decline purely because of fall in effective demand for wage goods, with a consequent fall in output and employment in the sector producing wage goods. Thus national income will contract just so much that the higher percentage share of profits in output renders an unchanged absolute amount of profits. Here the salient point is that shifts in the distribution of income take place not by way of increase in profits, but through a mechanism of decline in national income. The clue is that with a given level of output and income, an increase in the degree of monopoly and thus a shift from wages to profits will produce a rise in underutilization of productive capacity.

The argument Kalecki advanced in his last article on the modern capitalist economy may seem somewhat startling. We are told that trade unions indeed may affect the distribution of income, but in a much more sophisticated fashion than traditionally expounded. A rise (decline) in trade-union bargaining power leads to a rise (fall) in employment. Redistribution of income in favour of labour's share is feasible only if surplus capacity exists. But if this is not the case, wages in relation to prices of wage goods cannot be increased, for prices are determined by demand. Kalecki (1971, pp. 163–4) argues vehemently that surplus capacity is by and large a typical phenomenon of a developed capitalist economy:

> a wage rise showing an increase in the trade union power leads — contrary to the precepts of classical economics — to an increase in employment. And conversely, a fall in wages showing a weakening in their

bargaining power leads to a decline in employment. The weakness of trade unions in a depression manifested in permitting wage cuts contributes to deepening of unemployment rather than to reviving it.

. . . trade union bargaining may affect the distribution of national income but in a much more sophisticated fashion than expressed by the crude doctrine: when wages are raised, profits fall *pro tanto*. This doctrine proves to be entirely wrong. Such shifts that occur are: (a) connected with widespread imperfect competition and oligopoly in capitalist system; and (b) they are contained in fairly narrow limits. However, the day-by-day bargaining process is an important co-determinant of the distribution of national income.

It should be noted that it is possible to devise other forms of class struggle than wage bargaining, which would affect the distribution of national income in a more direct way. For instance, actions may be undertaken for keeping down the cost of living. The latter might be achieved by price controls which, however, may prove difficult to administer. But there exists an alternative: subsidizing of prices of wage goods which is financed by direct taxation of profits. . . The same is true of the effect of price controls. And, if such measures cannot be carried out by political parties associated with trade unions in the parliament, the power of the trade unions may be used to mobilize supporting strike movements. The classical day-to-day bargaining for wages is not the only way of influencing the distribution of national income to the advantage of the workers.

. . . redistribution of income from profits to wages. . . is feasible only if excess capacity is in existence. Otherwise it is impossible to increase wages in relation to prices of wage goods because prices are determined by demand. Price control of wage goods will lead under the circumstances to scarcities of goods and haphazard distribution. Also subsidizing prices of wage goods (financed by direct taxation of profits) can reduce prices only in the longer run by stimulating investment in wage goods industries.

It should be noted, however, that even contemporary capitalism, where deep depressions are avoided as a result of Government intervention, is in general still fairly remote from such a state of full utilisation of resources. This is best shown by the fact that prices of finished goods *are* fixed on a cost basis rather than determined by demand.

Keynes's *General Theory* was essentially ahistorical. Kalecki was not a historian by predisposition, but he had an inherent perception of the economic process in motion; the present events are the result of preceding development, and they, in turn, condition future development. Kalecki's theory is explicitly dynamic. Thus, by contrast, the *General Theory* dealt not only with a static model, but the argument was explicitly concerned with fundamentally the Marshallian short-run, and thus with short-run determinants of output and employment. Kalecki's model was broader as it took the long run into account. Keynes's assumption of the existing quality and quantity of available plant and equipment and existing techniques is very restrictive. Innovations are of key importance in explaining the process of development. In his analysis of the apparatus of Keynes's *General Theory*, Schumpeter (1954, pp. 1174-5) emphasized:

of all aspects of the investment process, it is only the expenditure effect of new investment which enters the *model* (not the *book*): as Keynes himself rightly emphasized, physical capital (equipment) is assumed to remain constant throughout, both in kind and quantity. This limits the theory to an analysis of the factors that determine the higher or lower degree of utilization of an existing industrial apparatus. Those who look for the essence of capitalism in the phenomena that attend the incessant recreation of this apparatus and the incessant revolution that goes on with it must therefore be excused if they hold that Keynes' theory abstracts from the essence of the capitalist process.

Among the elements in the economic system that Keynes took as given, the assumption of the existing quality and quantity of available equipment and existing techniques is very restrictive. For 'technological change is the essence of the capitalist process and the source of most of its problems, this assumption excludes the salient features of capitalist reality' (Schumpeter, 1954, p. 1144).

Joan Robinson (1955, p. 155) wrote in a review of Harrod's well-known book *Towards a Dynamic Economics:*

No one will disagree with Mr Harrod that modern economic theory lacks, and badly needs, a system of analysis dealing with a dynamic society. Keynes' *General Theory of Employment* broke through the husk of static analysis, but, apart from some *obiter dicta*, scarcely developed any theory of long-run development. Mr. Kalecki's pioneering work has been very little followed up (Mr Harrod makes no reference to him); many others have shot at a venture into the mists, but we have no systematic body of long-run dynamic theory to supplement the short-period analysis of the General Theory and to swallow up, as a special case, the long-run static theory in which the present generation of academic economists was educated.

Indeed, at the time one of the key and often neglected determinants of investment decisions was accumulation of capital. Keynes's own treatment of the capital stock was exceedingly unsatisfactory.

Both Kalecki and Keynes stressed that there does not exist an automatic mechanism that will ensure that what the population tries to save will always be fully invested. The saving-investment problem is an essential element in both approaches. Keynes's approach to the process of determination of national income has now permeated economic textbooks (or is being criticized as the orthodoxy). Kalecki, however, introduced a very different interpretation and analysis of the process by which a rise in investment generates an increase in savings. He did not approach the theory of effective demand by the Kahn–Keynes route of the multiplier which makes his version to some extent less appealing or less rich, but no less forceful. He did go straight to the pure (non-monetary) theory of the business cycle (on which Keynes seems to have been very weak) and his original treatment of the capital-stock adjustment mechanism now constitutes a basis for many business-cycle models. Whatever the relative merits of either approaches, they should not be evaluated independently of the confusion about the equality of savings and investment that arose as Keynesian ideas were integrated into the mainstream.

In his theory of the business cycle, Kalecki introduced interesting fundamental properties, in particular: (i) the clear separation of investment decisions from actual implementation, and (ii) the determinants of the investment decision function. The investment realization lag explains the cumulative character of expansionary and contractionary processes.

If the current rate of investment surpasses that of the preceding period, the level of current profit will rise, profit expectations will improve, investment demand will increase, and more orders will be placed followed by an increased rate of investment activity and enlarged income. The income-generating capacity of investment is the source of prosperity and encourages a further rise in investment. But investment has also a capacity-creating effect; every completed investment adds to productive capacity, competes with the stock of equipment of older vintage, and discourages more investment. Sooner or later investment stops rising and so does the level of current profit. The rate of profit falls. The rise in investment is transitory and the boom cannot endure. A process of cumulative contraction takes place. The growth of national wealth contains the seeds of retardation.

Kalecki modified, reformulated, and improved the business-cycle model many times, seeking to bring it closer to reality. While his earlier writings were clearly influenced by the severity of the experience in the early 1930s, in the subsequent development of the argument, he made allowances for the relative weak impact of the capital destruction effect. He introduced a certain 'corrective' — a trend factor that shifts investment upward as the cycle continues. In a growing economy investment fluctuates along the long-run trend line. Innovations raise the prospects for profit, thus stimulating investment and engendering an ascending trend. Innovation becomes another weighty factor in the determination of the investment function, together with the change in the rate of profit, the rate of change in the stock of capital and the 'internal' gross savings (depreciation and undistributed profits) of firms.

Kalecki aimed at developing a theory integrating growth and cyclical processes. He advanced an original, provocative, but somewhat sketchy theory of long-run development trends, its determinants both of trend and cycle. Innovation plays a cardinal role in transforming the static system subject to fluctuations (cyclical fluctuation around the zero level of capital accumulation) into one subject to growth trend. Kalecki emphasized that he failed to see why the business-cycle approach should be abolished in studying the process of economic development. He now approached the growth rate at a given time as a phenomenon deeply rooted in past economic, social, and technological development of the system (where the current state is the result of the preceding developments and contributes, in turn, to the future long-run development of the economy). The two basic relations in the approach to business cycles: (i) the impact of effective demand generated by investment on profits and national income, and (ii) the determination of investment function by the level and the rate of change in income or expenditures, should be so formulated as to yield the trend *cum* business-cycle phenomenon. Such a task is incomparably more exacting than the pure business-cycle model. But the results of such inquiry are closer to the reality of the process of development. The approach of 'mechanistic' theory is based often on such indefensible assumptions as a constant long-run rate of utilization of capacity. However, the difficulty of the task should not be an excuse for disregarding this approach which seems to be the only one for a realistic analysis of the dynamics of a capitalist economy (see Feiwel, 1975, pp. 156–8).

To Kalecki the key prerequisite for becoming an entrepreneur is the ownership of capital. The outside finance that can be secured is largely restricted by the size of the entrepreneurial capital. Moreover, entrepreneurs tend to be unwilling to use their full borrowing potential because risk increases with the amount invested. In case of bad investment, the higher the ratio of borrowing to the entrepreneur's own capital, the greater is the decrease of the entrepreneur's income, or risk of wiping out his equity.

These considerations cannot be ignored in the theory of investment decisions and in the analysis of factors circumscribing the size of the firm. Such decisions are related to the firm's 'internal' accumulation of gross savings. These savings allow the firm to make new investments without facing the problems of the limited capital market or 'increasing risk'.

At this juncture we should call attention (if only in endnotes) to Kalecki's different treatment of what Keynes considered the three major gaps in the orthodox theory that he had to fill, namely, the analysis of the propensity to consume,[46] the definition of MEC,[47] and the theory of the rate of interest.[48]

Kalecki deals with an open system. He treats the rate of export surplus as a promoter of prosperity and the balance of payments difficulties that tend to accompany an upswing as a factor limiting expansion.

Keynes's *General Theory* was cast in terms of a closed system. Kalecki analysed the rate of export surplus as a promoter of prosperity and how expansionary policy in an open system is impeded by its likely adverse effects on balance of payments. Upswing is usually followed by rising demand for imports but there is no mechanism ensuring that growth of output will be accompanied by appropriate growth of export. In fact, certain forces are in operation preventing correction of the balance of payment disequilibrium. Indeed, stimulated upswing has a limit: aggregate output cannot be allowed to expand to the level where required imports would exceed the maximum imports that could be secured by lowering the value of currency. Thus, upswing (say, engendered by deficit spending) will fail to lead to full utilization of productive capacity because of the deficiency of complementary inputs, particularly raw materials. Budget deficit not always leads to deterioration in foreign exchange position. The point is that budget deficit has a negative effect on foreign exchange only when it has a positive effect on output. There is an important qualification to this rule. If the belief is widely held that there is a direct link between budget deficit and foreign exchange situation, the rise of the budget deficit encourages holding of gold and foreign exchange. This may upset the foreign exchange position of the currency even to a much greater extent than the effect of the budget deficit engendering expansion of output.

Whatever the rationale of the *economics* of full employment, the *political* problems are formidable. Kalecki realized that full-employment policies could be used to reform the capitalist system toward beneficial welfare-oriented growth, whose fruits would be directed to the advancement of living standards of the lower-income groups. He saw the opportunity, but was mindful of the grave political problems and, in 1943, predicted the emergence of the political business cycle. He argued that opposition by the 'leaders of industry' to full employment stimulated by government spending may be expected because of the inherent fear of government interference (in particular opposition, in principle, to government spending generated by budget deficits), opposition to the objects of government spending (particularly to public investments and the subsidizing of consumption), fear of inflationary pressures, opposition to sustained full employment (as against mere prevention of deep depressions), and the dislike of the social and economic changes resulting from the maintenance of full employment (including laxity of workers' discipline). He felt that business cycles in milder form than hitherto would continue and result in some sort of stop-go. These short-lived and relatively moderate cycles would proceed from a situation where the government would stimulate business activity, then withdraw at the early signs of an upswing under the clamour of an 'unsound' financial situation (and even undertake deflationary policies near the peak) only to re-enter as a stimulating agent when unemployment would again rise beyond an 'acceptable level', thus vacillating between combating unemployment and inflation.

In the postwar period there has been a remarkable revival of concern with growth which is now on the wane. The exceedingly practical motivation was, however, in sharp contrast with the rather esoteric nature of the theoretical concerns of the growth model building industry. Sad to say, the research in growth economics was stimulated by logical curiosity rather than by relevance considerations. Though bitter controversy surrounded many issues, the extent of infighting was not really a gauge of the issues' importance (see Sen, 1970, pp. 9–40).

In general, the neoclassical growth model (see Solow, 1970) provides no theory of economic history. 'It is of no help in answering Max Weber's famous question and only of marginal use in understanding, say, the Industrial revolution... There is no class conflict, no "rising middle class", no actual government, no labour unions, no war, no financial panic, no history' (Hahn, 1971, p. vii; see also Chapters 4 and 17 in this volume and Chapter 1 in the companion volume to this book).

In contrast to demand-dominated models, in truly Keynesian persuasion, in the neoclassical growth models that occupy a central place in the voluminous body of recent literature on the theory of economic growth, the rate of growth is usually determined by supply considerations (see Hahn and Matthews, 1964). Contrariwise, the theories of business cycle have been chiefly concerned with causes of fluctuations in *effective demand*, and the supply considerations have often been underrated. The neoclassical growth models assume away the Keynesian question of effective demand and suffer from the absence of the investment function. For example,

although Meade's (1961, p. ix) standard elucidation is 'certainly not classical in the sense of being pre-Keynesian', it rests on the 'assumption of an ideally successful Keynesian policy which at every point of time manages to keep the value of investment at the desired level'.

In his important and rather technical 'Trend and Business Cycles Reconsidered', Kalecki (1971, pp. 165-91) reproved the contemporary theory of growth for tending to consider the problem of trend and business cycles in terms of a moving equilibrium, rather than adopting an approach similar to business-cycle theorizing. He offered an integrated approach.

In his last public lecture given at Cambridge University, Kalecki (1970, pp. 311-12) reflected on the tendency in contemporary economics to build pre-institutional *general* growth theory, fairly remote from the realities of contemporary capitalist, mixed, or socialist economies. He felt that many writers relate, at least by implication, to some sort of idealized *laissez-faire* capitalism:

To my mind the central problem of the *laissez-faire* capitalist system. . . is that of effective demand i.e. that of finding markets for its products at full utilization of resources. It is also this problem that in the fifties was still generally in the centre of interest of Western economists in connexion with the theory of cyclical fluctuations and with the problem of government intervention to counteract them.

But from the time the discussion of economic dynamics has concentrated on problems of *growth* the factor of effective demand was generally disregarded. Either it was simply *assumed* that in the long run the problem of effective demand does not matter because apart from the business cycle it need not be taken into consideration; or more specifically the problem was approached in two alternative fashions: (a) the growth is at an equilibrium (Harrodian) rate, so that the increase in investment is just sufficient to generate effective demand matching the new productive capacities which the level of investment creates. (b) Whatever the rate of growth the productive resources are fully utilized because of long-run price flexibility: prices are pushed in the long run in relation to wages up to the point where the real income of labour and thus its consumption is adequate to cause the absorption of full employment national product.

I do not believe however in justifying the neglect of the problem of finding markets for the national product at full utilization of resources either in (a) or in (b) fashion. It is generally known that the trend represented by the (a) case is unstable: any small fortuitous decline in the rate of growth involves a reduction of investment, and in consequence of the national income, in relation to the stock of equipment, which affects investment adversely and induces a further fall in the rate of growth. The belief that such disturbance creates merely a downswing followed by an upswing in relation to the growth proceeding at an equilibrium rate i.e. that it yields a trend *cum* business cycle is mathematically indefensible: the underlying equations are uncapable of producing a solution corresponding to a combination of an exponential curve with a sine line. Nor do I subscribe to the long-run price flexibility underlying theories of the (b) type. The monopolistic and semi-monopolistic factors involved in fixing prices — deeply rooted in the capitalist system of all times - cannot be characterized as temporary short period price rigidities but affect the relation of prices and wage costs both in the course of the business cycle and in the long run.

JOAN ROBINSON'S CHALLENGE

This is not the place to speculate on where we would be now had alternative versions or interpretations of the Keynesian revolution (other than the neoclassical synthesis) penetrated the mainstream.[49] Many contemporary economists eloquently and brilliantly argue their positions, but none with the special blend of insight, vigour, quasi-religious fervour, tenacity, persuasiveness, polemic brilliance, and 'Cambridge-style' disregard for the niceties of social intercourse that is so typical of Joan Robinson.[50] Her succinct chapter in this volume (Chapter 4) is flavoured with what she stands for and against,[51] and is in a way representative of most of her writing, characterized both by positive contributions in many areas and trenchant criticism of what she considers to be fallacies of modern economics.[52]

A partial glimpse of Joan Robinson's position was already afforded in the preceding sections. Here we can do no more than provide a sketchy background for her chapter in this volume.[53]

In Chapter 1 of the companion volume to this book we have pointed to Joan Robinson's position on ideology in economics and to the dangers of unconscious ideological bias. She is very candid about the fact that her own interest in and contributions to economic theory have been stimulated by her preoccupation with the social, moral, and political aspects of economic issues which makes her a political economist *par excellence*. She labels herself a left-wing Keynesian; in fact, probably one of the first and perhaps one of the rare few to be thus labelled now. She believes, *inter alia*, that a democratic society can control income distribution from property (public ownership of the means of production) and can control the content of investment.

She insists that the existence of considerable unemployed resources should not be viewed as a troublesome problem, but as a splendid exploitable opportunity to do something really useful.

She (1978, p. 8) sees the second crisis in economics as arising 'from a theory that cannot account for the *content* of employment'. Once the first crisis had been resolved, and

> now that we all agree that government expenditure can maintain employment, we should argue about what the expenditure should be for. Keynes did not *want* anyone to dig holes and fill them. He indulged in a pleasant daydream of a world in which, when investment had been kept at the full employment level for thirty years or so, all needs for capital installations would have been met, property income would have been abolished, poverty would have disappeared and civilized life could begin.

But the postwar reality was something quite different. For twenty-five years serious recessions were avoided. 'The most convenient thing for a government to spend on is armaments. The military-industrial complex took charge. I do not think it plausible to suppose that the cold war and several hot wars were invented just to solve the employment problem. . . So it has come about that Keynes's pleasant daydream was turned into a nightmare of terror' (Robinson, 1978, p. 9)

Robinson has creatively adapted the Kaleckian–Keynesian approach to long period problems, concentrating on the processes of accumulation and effective demand, cyclical and secular change, the determinants of income distribution among social classes, the relationship between inflation and the business cycle to go on in the long-term dynamics of capitalism and the institutional-political requirements for maintaining non-inflationary full employment.

She often speaks of her arrival in Cambridge in 1921 as a student when 'Marshall *was* economics'. As she points out in Chapter 4 in this volume (p. 157): 'We used to say in Cambridge "Everything is in Marshall" I added later: the trouble is that everything else is as well.'

> There is a deep-seated conflict in the *Principles*, of which Marshall himself was uneasily aware (especially in connection with 'increasing returns') between the analysis, which is purely static, and the conclusions drawn from it, which apply to an economy developing through

time, with accumulation going on; but somehow we managed to swallow it all (Robinson, 1973a, p. ix).

She goes on to say that when she returned eight years later and began to teach, Cambridge insularity was being penetrated by Piero Sraffa who 'was calmly committing the sacrilege of pointing out inconsistencies in Marshall (Robinson, 1978, p. ix). The 'authorities' continued to defend Marshall, but the 'young Turks' were increasingly aware of the profound inconsistencies between the static base and the dynamic superstructure. Nonetheless Joan Robinson is a Marshallian in the best sense of the term. Her interest in short-period analysis sheds light on her interpretation of Keynes in terms of uncertainty, unattained expectations, and conflicting decisions. For her (1979, p. xi) 'the recognition of uncertainty undermines the traditional concept of equilibrium'. But we anticipate.

Inspired by Sraffa she produced in 1933 her *Economics of Imperfect Competition* of which she takes a dim view in retrospect (see 1978, pp. 166–81). She (1973a, p. x) now sees her aim as having been 'to refute, by means of its own arguments, the doctrine that wages are determined by the marginal productivity of labour'.[54]

She notes that meanwhile an even more powerful attack against equilibrium theory was the nascent Keynesian revolution. As she came under its influence, she realized that her 'Pigovian book' was leading up a blind alley:

It was obvious enough in real life that a free market does not guarantee equilibrium, for the world economy had fallen into the great slump, but it took a long time to find out where the mistake lay in the theory and to sketch out a new approach. Unbeknownst to us, Michal Kalecki, writing in Polish, evinced the same solution, in the main, as Keynes. His version of the General Theory of Employment was less rich than Keynes's but in some respects more coherent. He brought imperfect competition into line with the analysis of effective demand and laid the basis for what is nowadays called the 'Cambridge' theory of distribution (Robinson, 1973a, p. x).

Joan Robinson's subsequent writings reveal the strong influence of Kalecki ('His work was the most original and important of any in the inter-war years', 1978, p. xvi). Generally, in addition to Kalecki, her intellectual exchanges with Kahn, Keynes, and Sraffa have had the most direct impact on her work.

One of Robinson's recurring themes is to 'throw off the incubus of equilibrium'. She is particularly exercised about what she calls the problem of 'getting into equilibrium', and the attempts to infuse GE into the Keynesian system.

During the war she began to read Marx 'as a distraction from the news':

> I began to read *Capital*, just as one reads any book, to see what was in it; I found a great deal that neither its followers nor its opponents had prepared me to expect. Piero Sraffa teased me, saying that I treated Marx as a little-known forerunner of Kalecki. There is a certain sense in which this is not a joke (Robinson, 1966, pp. vi–vii).

She (1973a, p. x) records that to her Marx's central message was that economists had to think in terms of history rather than equilibrium. 'This, of course, was the message of the Keynesian revolution too, but I had applied it only in short-period terms. . . Now I began to catch a glimpse of an approach that would emancipate us from the dominance of equilibrium analysis.'

Essentially for Joan Robinson (1973b, pp. 3 and 5) the theoretical message of the Keynesian revolution is the shift from the conception of equilibrium to that of history and from the principles of rational choice to decisions made on the basis of routine and guesswork. She points out (1973b, p. 5) that 'once we admit that an economy exists in time, that history goes one way, from the irrevocable past into the unknown future, the conception of equilibrium based on the mechanical analogy of a pendulum swinging to and fro in space becomes untenable'. She (1979, pp. xi–xii) elaborates on this further by explaining that the concept of micro-economic equilibrium in a competitive market is self-contradictory since the future cannot be known for certain. 'When a market is in equilibrium, all participants are satisfied that, in the circumstances in which they were placed, they made the best possible choices, but they could not have done so unless they knew, when choices were open, what the outcome was going to be. Equilibrium is conceivable only in a completely traditional economy, where everyone knows what everyone else will do. But in that situation, there are no decisions to be taken or choices to be made.' To her the crucial issue is that of historical time. In a world that would be constantly in equilibrium there would be no difference between the past and the future; there would be no history and no need for Keynes.

One cannot overemphasize Joan Robinson's strong opposition to the micro-macro dichotomy — she considers it as one of the most adverse consequences of the US reprocessing of Keynes:

> Micro questions. . . cannot be discussed in the air without any reference to the structure of the economy in which they exist, and to the process

of cyclical and secular change. Equally, macro theories of accumulation and effective demand are generalizations about micro behaviour: the relation of income to expenditure for consumption, of investment to the pursuit of profit, of the management of placements, in which financial wealth is held, to rates of interest, and of wages to the level of prices results from the reactions of individuals and social groups to the situations in which they find themselves (Robinson, 1977, p. 1320).

Robinson also questions the orthodox doctrine of consumer sovereignty on the grounds that it is the innovators and producers by designing and advertising that shape tastes and transform lifestyles (e.g. cars and television), rather than the consumers by formulating their requirements and aspirations — a view also propounded by Galbraith (see Chapter 1 of the companion volume). For her the crucial aspects of the pattern of consumption is the degree of inequality of distribution of income according to property ownership and the hierarchy of earnings in various occupations — an aspect that is difficult to present as maximizing welfare from a given flow of output.

In the postwar period Joan Robinson set out to 'generalize the General Theory' by dealing with the long run in her *magnum opus, The Accumulation of Capital*, and by tackling the thorny issue of the rate of profit. Her contributions to the theory of growth and distribution were heavily enmeshed in time-consuming and sometimes frustrating controversies. What follows is only one example — perhaps one of the best known.

The notorious and often recondite Cambridge–Cambridge controversy transgresses the theory of capital and involves the whole corpus of economic theory and underlying ideologies. 'It is understandable that strong convictions should lead to strong language, as any reader of the "capital controversies" can document in quantitative detail, author by author' (Samuelson, 1977, p. 141). The last word has not been said on what the shouting is all about, what the principal issues of controversy and central questions of theory are, and what is the appropriate methodology. Clearly the personalities of the chief combatants — (i) the so-called Anglo-Italian offence (led by Joan Robinson, Kaldor, and Pasinetti, and inspired by Sraffa), and (ii) the MIT Institute Professors (Samuelson, Solow, and Modigliani, but also including 'residents' of Cambridge-on-the-Cam, Hahn and Meade) — matter, but much more is at stake. As Samuelson (1977, p. 113) acknowledged: 'Behind an esoteric dispute over "reswitching" or heterogeneity of capital there often lurk contrasting views about fruitful ways of understanding distributional analysis and affecting its content by alternative policy measures.'

In a standard survey of the controversies, Harcourt (1972) (with strong affinities for Cambridge-on-the-Cam) sees the main issues under discussion as those grand themes that preoccupied Ricardo and Marx; the relations between accumulation and income distribution and the origins of profits, their absolute and relative size at any point of time and intertemporally, and similar questions about wages. The debate revolves around value, capital, growth, and distribution theory. The Anglo-Italian criticism is directed against the neoclassical 'apologetic' conception loosely identified under the heading of marginal productivity theory and the neoclassical approach to growth theory, including the neglect of effective demand. Solow (1975, p. 277) considers that the main battle is over the theory of profits and capital. He argues that the Anglo-Italians have 'gone after peripheral aspects of the profit-cum-interest story, and left its center untouched'. In a review article of Harcourt, Stiglitz (1974, pp. 901–2) (another partisan of MIT) focused on what he considers to be the three major issues — the determination of savings and the interest rate, reswitching of techniques, and aggregate capital — where the Anglo-Italians have 'gone astray'. He argues, *inter alia*, that ideology plays a far less important role than Harcourt suggests. He claims that 'there is a well-known propensity of individuals to dislike what they don't or can't understand', implying that his opponents 'do not understand neoclassical capital theory'. To him it appears that 'it is the confused attempt to discredit the marginal-productivity interpretation of the interest rate which imbues the topics of capital theory with their ideological interest to the devotees of Cambridge (U.K.) doctrine'.

The voluminous literature, including the growing industry of commentators, defies brief synopsis. As so much misunderstanding enshrouds the controversy, and since it might be illusory that the participants are actually communicating with each other, it might be wise to call attention here to some of the statements by the chief contestants themselves to convey an impression of their own perceptions of their positions and those of their opponents.[55]

> The controversies over so-called capital theory arose out of the search for a model appropriate to a modern western economy, which would allow for an analysis of accumulation and of the distribution of the net product of industry between wages and profits (Robinson, 1978, p. 114).

Joan Robinson reminisces about the early stages of the discussion on long-run growth in the Keynesian tradition which was spurred by the publication in 1949 of Harrod's *Towards a Dynamic Economics*. Whatever the shortcomings of the latter, 'he also lacked a rate of profit'. She acknowledges that it was not till she found the 'corn economy in Sraffa's *Introduction* to Ricardo's *Principles* that I saw a gleam of light on the question of the rate of profit on capital' (1978, pp. xvi–xvii). She (1978, pp. 76 and 90) fired the first round of the capital controversy in 1953 by stating:

> The dominance in neo-classical economic teaching of the concept of a production function. . . has had an enervating effect upon the development of the subject, for by concentrating upon the question of the proportions of factors it has distracted attention from the more difficult but more rewarding questions of the influences governing the supplies of the factors and of the causes and consequences of changes in technical knowledge.

And, further:

> When presented with the task of determining the distribution of the product of industry between labour and capital, the neo-classical production function comes to grief (even in the most perfect tranquillity) on the failure to distinguish between 'capital' in the sense of means of production with particular technical characteristics and 'capital' in the sense of a command over finance.
>
> When presented with the task of analysing a process of accumulation the production function comes to grief on the failure to distinguish between comparisons of equilibrium positions and movements from one to another.

Twenty years later she (1978, p. xvii) quipped that in this first round she was 'innocently remarking that the Emperor had no clothes'.

In the further development of the controversy, Joan Robinson (1982a, p. 91)

> set about to dismantle the neoclassical production function by introducing what I called a book of blueprints showing the concrete stock of means of production required for each level of output with a given labour force. From this developed what Professor Solow called a pseudo-production function. . . I do not think I ever misused it as Professor Samuelson does nowadays, but it certainly took me a long time to understand its meaning and its limitations.
>
> A pseudo-production function represents a list of mutually non-superior techniques with a flow of homogeneous final output and given employment of labor, each in a self-reproducing state with its appropriate stock of means of production. Each technique is eligible at at least one rate of profits (with the corresponding share of wages in the

value of net output). Between each pair is a switch point at which both yield the same rate of profits.

After much water had passed under the bridge and some sensibilities had been exacerbated, Joan Robinson (1978, pp. 122-3) pointed out that Samuelson accepted 'after some hesitation', the logic of the pseudo-production function and

> he even referred to a 'general blueprint technology model of Joan Robinson and MIT type' but his interpretation of it was (and still is) very different from mine. He recognized that each point on a pseudo function is supposed to represent an economy in a steady state, in which inputs arc being reproduced in unchanged physical form, and yet he supposed that saving could raise an economy from one point to the position at another. He envisages a process of accumulation creeping up the pseudo-production function from lower to higher shares of wages, and higher to lower rates of profit. But an increase in gross investment above the rate required to maintain a steady state would entail an enlargement of investment industries (which would have to shrink again when a new steady state was reached). The former pattern of prices would be upset. Inputs appropriate to one technique would have to be scrapped and replaced by those appropriate to another. And how are we to imagine that the prospect of a lower rate of profit in the future induces these changes to be made?

In 1975 Joan Robinson (1982a, p. 91) stressed that the pseudo-production function 'permits only of comparisons of imaginary equilibrium positions already in existence, not a process of accumulation going on through time'. From Samuelson's rebuttal (1977, pp. 134-41) it appeared that with respect to accumulation 'he is still a completely unreconstructed pre-Keynesian neoclassic. He expects to find the rate of interest (which is what he calls what Sraffa calls the rate of profits) lowered by successful saving-investment abstaining from consumption' (Robinson, 1982a, p. 91).

'The furore about "reswitching" raged around the conception of a pseudo-production function' (Robinson, 1978, p. 121). As Joan Robinson (1982a, p. 92) sees Samuelson's interpretation:

> Evidently, we are in an era when a slow secular fall in the rate of profits is going on. Each time it passes a switch point (whether towards a technique which requires a higher or a lower value of capital than the last) there must be a certain period of investment and disinvestment installing the stock required for the latest technique and clearing away

the debris of the former one. We are not told anything about what goes on in these interludes, which seem to pass as though in a dream.

The whole process may take centuries but all the while there is no technical progress or learning by doing. The specifications of all the techniques were available in the original book of blueprints.

And she (1982a, p. 43) claims to have shattered the pseudo-production function again in 1974:

Obviously, stocks of equipment appropriate to different techniques cannot co-exist both in time and space. It should never have been drawn in a plane diagram in the first place. Different techniques are not isolated from each other on 'islands'. They succeed each other through time as new discoveries and inventions become operational. Normally, a new technique is *superior* to the one in use and does not have to wait for a change in the rate of profit to be installed.

Pseudo-production functions flourished again independently after the appearance in 1960 of Sraffa's classic *Production of Commodities by Means of Commodities*. In this model

one of the ingredients among the inputs exists in two versions or brands. The difference between them is in the time pattern of reproduction, not any physical characteristic. Sraffa did not intend this for a pseudo-production function. His purpose was to refute marginalism by showing that the least conceivable difference alters the whole system (Robinson, 1982a, p. 93).

According to Joan Robinson (1982a, p. 94) Samuelson's initial reaction to Sraffa was

to produce a form of pseudo-production function in which, beyond each switch point, a higher rate of interest is associated with a lower ratio of value of capital to output so that backward switching cannot occur. This was countered by the construction of a spate of pseudo-production functions exhibiting switches of all kinds. They are now so elaborate, elegant and beautiful and their designers have become so fond of them, that it seems cruel to point out that they are unable to say anything without falling into Samuelson's fallacy.

Looking over the controversy, Joan Robinson (1979, p. xv) mused:

The participants in the controversy, on both sides, failed to observe that it had nothing whatever to do with the analysis of the choice of technique or the determination of the rate of profit in a process of accumulation going on through historical time.

Perhaps I am partly to blame for introducing the expression 'a book of blueprints' for an imaginary list of mutually non-superior techniques all available at once, but at least I did insist that my pseudo-production function could be used only for comparing stocks of capital each already in existence.

In his numerous writings on the subject, Samuelson has reformulated his conceptions, admitted to some failings, but upheld the essence of his position:

Repeatedly. . . I have insisted that capital theory can be rigorously developed without using any Clark-like concept of aggregate 'capital', instead relying upon a complete analysis of a great variety of heterogeneous physical capital goods and processes through time. Such an analysis leans heavily on the tools of modern linear and more general programming and might therefore be called neo-neo-classical. It takes the view that if we are to understand the trends in how incomes are distributed among different kinds of labor and different kinds of property owners, both in the aggregate and in the detailed composition, then studies of changing technologies, human and natural resources availabilities, taste patterns, and all the other matters of *micro*economics are likely to be very important. . .

But must there always be a need for mutually exclusive choice? Cannot each in its place be useful? What I propose to do here is to show that a new concept, the 'Surrogate Production Function', can provide *some* rationalization for the validity of the simple J. B. Clark parables which pretend there is a single thing called 'capital' that can be put into a single production function and along with labor will produce total output (of a homogeneous good or of some desired market-basket of goods) (Samuelson, 1966, pp. 325-6).

Until the laws of thermodynamics are repealed, I shall continue to relate outputs to inputs — i.e. to believe in production functions. Until factors cease to have their rewards determined by bidding in quasi-competitive markets, I shall adhere to (generalized) neoclassical approximations in which relative factor supplies are important in explaining their market remunerations (Samuelson, 1972, p. 174).

And, referring to his 1966 summary of the debate, where he clearly differentiates his position from that of his opponents (1972, pp. 230-5) and the shots fired for another decade, Samuelson reports that his '1966 discussion seems to stand up very well, and it would be hypocritical of me to give it other than a clean bill of health as a representation of my 1975 views' (Samuelson, 1977, pp. 134–5).

Joan Robinson (1978, p. xix) complains that she and her colleagues were never answered and the mainstream flows on as before. In a typical Robinsonian fashion she adds: 'I was delighted to find in a dictionary the word mumpsimus, which meàns stubborn persistence in an error after it has been exposed.'

Perhaps there is no more fitting conclusion than to let Joan Robinson (1978, p. xxii) evaluate her contributions which she sees as bringing 'theoretical analysis nearer the actual problems of economic life instead of further away from them'. In another passage she (1973a, p. xii) states:

I have been trying for the last twenty years to trace the confusions and sophistries of current neo-neoclassical doctrines to their origin in the neglect of historic time in the static equilibrium theory of the neo-classics and at the same time to find a more hopeful alternative in the classical tradition, revived by Sraffa, which flows from Ricardo through Marx, diluted by Marshall and enriched by the analysis of effective demand of Keynes and Kalecki.

Joan Robinson (1980, pp. 227–8) sees the challenge to the new generation of economists in these terms:

We must throw out concepts and theorems that are logically self-contradictory, such as the general equilibrium of supply and demand, the long-run production function, the marginal productivity of capital and the equilibrium size of firms. . .

Swings of activity must be seen, not as starting up from cold, but as overlaying slow long-run changes in productive capacity produced by accumulation, technical change (including changes in methods of operation of the labour force) and alterations in the composition of output. The interaction between the long-run and the short-run consequences of technical innovations is a complicated subject which requires more study.

The evolution of business activity and trade-union policy should be approached in the spirit of natural-history observation of the behaviour of classes and groups.

The analysis of international trade should be preceded by an inquiry into the meaning of a 'nation' in the relevant respects — a question which nowadays is not so simple as used to be supposed.

All this, and much more, indicates work to be done, provided that we give up the search for grand general laws and are content to try to enquire how things happen.

Her (1978, p. 75) typical advice to students of economics is: Any theory that we follow blindly will lead us astray. To make good use of an economic theory we must first sort out the relations of the propagandist and the scientific elements in it, then by checking with experience, see how far the scientific element appears convincing, and finally recombine it with our own political views. The purpose of studying economics is not to acquire a set of ready-made answers to economic questions, but to learn how to avoid being deceived by economists.

A CONCLUDING NOTE

Much could be said about the major themes and philosophical perceptions that reappear periodically in the history of economic ideas and condition the vision and conceptions of the economic process and mechanism. As we have seen in the preceding sections, and shall see in the chapters that follow, one can single out in broad contours: (i) the tendency to focus on the beneficial effects of competitive *laissez-faire* and defects of government intervention, and (ii) the tendency to focus on market failures and on the need for 'something more' than the market. Economists evincing either of these tendencies fall into two distinct groups, but even within a group they differ sharply on many aspects of the discipline.

The extraordinarily remarkable, but often seriously underperforming, and at times conspicuously failing, and in a fundamental sense improvable by sensible public policy, modern industrialized market ('mixed') economy' is a dynamic, creatively destructive, evolving, but inertia-bound, complex and interdependent system. This system is subject to the interaction of long-term trends, overall cyclical fluctuations, shifts in supply or demand conditions specific to individual activities (markets); macroeconomic stochastic (random) disturbances; institutional and human imperfections; bounded rationality of economic actors operating in an uncertain world; market failures; and informational flaws and rigidities.

A partial identification of the driving forces behind the long-term rise in the capacity to produce and of the shifts in production structure and ability to supply a larger volume, diversity and improved quality of goods and services includes physical capital formation and investment in education and research, technological (product and process) innovation, 'learning by doing', distribution of income, working arrangements or economic mechanisms for the generation, diffusion, and application of useful knowledge and incentives to spur creativity, entrepreneurship and willingness to produce, and good workmanship. The weight assigned to the various, if indeed separable, sources of growth is subject to bitter controversies, which periodically feature fluctuating fascination with capital accumulation (technical dynamism) as a principal determinant and at other times and in other places the focus shifts to the role of long-term demand (or 'realization'). Not only is evidence relating to the relative significance of the various factors fostering growth (productivity, technological innovation, etc.) tenuous, but our knowledge about how to affect these factors is limited.

Cyclical fluctuations are traceable to a plethora of real, monetary, expectational (misperceptions), and institutional factors and the interaction of exogenous and endogenous forces. They cannot be reduced to monistic explanations (e.g. monetary business cycle). Nor can the cycles be understood independently of the growth process. The most promising avenue for the study of the mixed economy still appears to be one that would involve trend cum cycle (with an endogenous policy-maker) and that would perceive the economy's *modus operandi* and patterns of behaviour of economic actors within and dependent on the macroeconomic setting.

When all is said and done, one cannot help but agree with Arrow (Chapter 3, p. 155): 'Increase in economic knowledge leads to a greater realization of the potentials and limitations of social mechanisms (market) and of social action which extends the domain of individual rationality.' He (pp. 155–6) concludes:

An economist, of whatever school, necessarily recognizes limits. Whether he defends the present mixture of private and public controls or argues for a closer approximation to *laissez-faire*, the economist should never claim to advocate a utopia. In a world of limited resources and imperfect understanding, all that can be asked for is the reduction of flaws. Like political democracy, to which it is so closely linked, the mixed economy has much to answer for; it is merely less bad than its alternatives.

NOTES

1. 'The economists of my generation and earlier were trained to concentrate on so-called long-run analysis in their pure theorizing. When they ventured into the discussion of questions of public policy, they accord-

ingly tended to be preoccupied with the long view, with the effects which a given action would have on the more distant future, and to disregard or to weigh lightly its more immediate effects' (Viner, 1958, p. 106).

2. Hicks (1957, p. 289) has pointed out that Patinkin's work (which I have not included in my listing) is largely classical in spirit: 'The theory which Patinkin sets out, though it owes much to Keynes, is not Keynesian; it is a modernised version of the theory which Keynes called "classical".'

3. As is well known, Keynes refers to 'classical' economics in connection with the problem of neglect of effective demand. He groups under that heading economists from Ricardo to Pigou who are conventionally classified into either the classical or neoclassical schools.

4. The idea that Keynes is really focusing on an economy in disequilibrium, or in a sequence of constrained temporary equilibria, employs skilfully comparative statics apparatus, has a vast tradition. It should be noted here, however, that in a number of influential publications, Patinkin (1956, ch. 13) and others have stressed that the *General Theory* should be interpreted not as a static theory of unemployment equilibrium, but as a dynamic theory of unemployment disequilibrium. See also Clower, 1965; Leijonhufvud, 1968; Barro and Grossman, 1976; Benassy, 1982; Glustoff, 1968; Fisher (forthcoming).

5. As Solow (1978c, p. 147) argues, there is little specifically Keynesian (historically or analytically) about the Phillips curve. The monetarists criticized it at an early stage. 'Once upon a time economists had believed that there was no durable (I will not insist on permanent) gearing between real things and monetary things. Keynes had disagreed and apparently carried the day. Now it was argued that there could be no durable gearing between real things and the rate of change of monetary things, and some of the arguments sounded very much like the earlier ones.'

6. Clower (1975, p. 7) speaks of 'the links that Hicks forged to connect Keynes's ideas with Neo-Walrasian theory. . . As a consequence, what is now called "Keynesian Economics" owes as much or more to the author of *Value and Capital* and 'Mr Keynes and the Classics' as to the author of the *General Theory of Employment, Interest and Money*!' In Clower's (1975, p. 3) opinion, 'the history of the Keynesian Revolution — more particularly, the reasons why it effectively fizzled out — can be fully appreciated, therefore, only by viewing it as an episode within a broader and ultimately more influential series of doctrinal developments which. . . I shall refer to as the *Neo-Walrasian Revolution*.' Clower (1965, p. 103) sees Hicks as launching in 1937 a 'Keynesian Counterrevolution' which is 'now being carried forward with such vigour by Patinkin and other general equilibrium theorists. . . The elegance and generality of this literature makes it most alluring. At the same time, one can hardly fail to be impressed — and disturbed — by the close resemblance that some of its central doctrines bear to those of orthodox economics.'

7. 'Soon after the *General Theory* was published Hicks produced an

attempt to reconcile Keynes and the "Classics" by means of his *LM* and *IS* diagram. Of course, this had nothing whatever to do with the "Classics" (as Keynes called them), that is with the neoclassical orthodoxy based on Marshall and Pigou. They treated the rate of interest as equilibrating the supply and demand of real investible resources — man-power and means of production. Hicks's formulation is purely monetary. On the *IS* curve income grows as the interest rate falls, because a fall in the rate of interest stimulates investment (according to Keynes's propensity to invest) and investment increases income (according to Keynes's multiplier). On the *LM* curve the rate of interest rises with income (according to Keynes's demand for liquidity) because the quantity of money is assumed to be fixed. This is nothing but a simplified version of the monetary theory of the rate of interest which Keynes was substituting for the "real" one (Robinson, 1969, p. 581).

8. As he has himself warned, Leijonhufvud's 1968 account defies a brief summary without doing him great injustice. However, Johnson (1973, pp. 71-6) has attempted such a résumé. (See also Leijonhufvud, 1969.)

9. Joan Robinson (1969, p. 582) also objects to Leijonhufvud's treatment of the Cambridge Keynesians as some peculiar sect of 'believers' who have preserved traditions that the neoclassical synthesis had lost. It is also worth noting here that in her (1982b, p. 295) review of Leijonhufvud (1981) she criticizes him for expostulating on a monetary theory that is 'both confused and confusing'. She adds: 'When I reviewed the earlier book I purported to find some sense in it (which surprised some of my colleagues) but this time I am quite defeated.'

10. Benassy (1982, p. 2) sees the 'Keynesian puzzle' in these terms: 'Even a quick examination of macroeconomic models in the Keynesian tradition shows us that they do indeed violate the main characteristics of equilibrium economics: (i) since the labor market shows some unemployment, at least one market is not in equilibrium, (ii) some adjustments are not brought about by price movements alone, e.g. the goods market is equilibrated through movements in the level of income, and (iii) finally, agents do not react only to price signals, e.g. the Keynesian consumption function depends on the level of income.' See also Hahn, 1977, pp. 25-39; Clower, 1965; Drazen, 1980, p. 285.

11. In evaluating the contributions of the earlier work, Drazen (1980, pp. 286-7) points out that, for example, many of Leijonhufvud's arguments are interesting or merely suggestive of points, rather than offering a rigorous analysis of making key concepts operational. 'What looks promising often fails to be convincing on slightly closer examination, and we are left, once again, with exogenous price inflexibility.' And, despite Clower's major contribution, 'the early work failed to really explain causes of unemployment, and much of it ends up sounding like early interpretations of Keynes. We are still left with the question: is exogenous wage rigidity necessary for the existence of unemployment equilibrium and will removing this inflexibility "return" us to full employment?'

12. The prevalence of quantity over price adjustments in the short run is seen by Malinvaud (1977, pp. 10–11) as a crucial institutional fact that must be reckoned with when constructing a theory of short-term equilibrium. However, it is more than that; it is seen as following from the theory of rational behaviour under uncertainty. (See also Phelps, 1970 and 1981; and Radner, 1982.) For an illuminating discussion of the implications of taking the money wage or price as given for new or refined equilibrium concepts and forgotten misinterpretations of Keynesian economics, see Hahn, 1977; Patinkin, 1983; Meltzer, 1983. See also Solow, 1980b; Wallace, 1980; and Hall, 1980, p. 237.

13. In this section, unless otherwise stated, we shall concentrate on the Friedman brand of monetarism, recognizing, of course, that monetarism appears in many shades and varieties. Some of them take a much stronger stand than Friedman; that is, they are further removed from the Keynesian view. In this category the work of Brunner and Meltzer stands out. There is also Patinkin's real balance approach to the quantity theory which aroused its own share of controversy. Interestingly, Laidler (1981) and Mayer (1978) deny that Patinkin could be regarded as a monetarist. Neither, according to Hicks, is he a Keynesian (see note 2 above). The British monetarists (Laidler and others) are yet another branch. Of course, there is also the St Louis Bank approach. For an informative survey, see Mayer, 1978. See also Stein, 1976.

14. Laidler (1981, p. 8) makes this point explicitly. Monetarists have long been 'asserting a belief in the "inherent stability" of the private sector in the absence of policy induced monetary disturbances, by which they have usually meant nothing more complex than that the system tends in and of itself to operate at or near "full employment", regardless of the inflation rate, if policy makers do not upset matters'.

15. For Friedman's statement of these propositions see 1970a, pp. 22–5. Mayer (1978, p. 2), though he warns that his listing is quite arbitrary, lists the monetarists propositions as follows: '1. The quantity theory of money, in the sense of the predominance of the impact of monetary factors on nominal income. 2. The monetarist model of the transmission process. 3. Belief in the inherent stability of the private sector. 4. Irrelevance of allocative detail for the explanation of short-run changes in money income, and belief in a fluid capital market. 5. Focus on the price level as a whole rather than on individual prices. 6. Reliance on small rather than large econometric models. 7. Use of the reserve base or similar measure as the indicator of monetary policy. 8. Use of the money stock as the proper target of monetary policy. 9. Acceptance of a monetary growth rule. 10. Rejection of an unemployment-inflation trade-off in favor of a real *Phillips*-curve. 11. A relatively greater concern about inflation than about unemployment compared to other economists. 12. Dislike of government intervention.' For Friedman's critics' views of these propositions, see Gordon, 1970.

16. Harry G. Johnson (1973, p. 23) speculates that 'as a result of his studies of the Marshallian demand curve and his year as a visitor in Cambridge, Friedman became enamoured of the "Cambridge oral tradition" as a concept permitting the attribution to an institution of a

wisdom exceeding that displayed in its published work, and unconsciously stole a leaf from Cambridge's book for the benefit of his own institution'.

17. In a discussion with Modigliani, Friedman (1977a, p. 12) agreed 'that the differences that separate so-called monetarists. . . from non-monetarists are entirely empirical rather than theoretical'. On the distinction between the empirical and theoretical propositions, see B. Friedman, 1978a.

18. For Friedman's somewhat critical views of RE, see 1975b, pp. 26–8.

19. To account for business cycles as equilibrium phenomena, Barro (1981a, p. 41) extends these postulates by specifying the following characteristics: a variant of the 'Lucas supply function', which allows nominal shocks to have temporary effects on real variables, and some version of the NRH which rules out real effects of perceived nominal variables, like money stock.

20. At least this is the more extreme version pursued by Sargent as a more or less general case.

21. For a comprehensive critical survey of the neoclassical synthesis, see Sargent, 1979 *passim* and Lucas, 1981a, pp. 277–81.

22. The issue of methodological distinction, B. Friedman (1978b, pp. 74–5) notes, does not withstand careful appraisal. He quotes Klein to show that neoclassical Keynesian models are derived from optimizing behaviour.

23. 'Keynes chose to begin the *General Theory* with the declaration (for Chapter II is no more than this) that an equilibrium theory was unattainable: that unemployment was not explainable as a consequence of individual choices and that the failure of wages to move as predicted by the classical theory was to be treated as due to forces beyond the power of economic theory to illuminate' (Lucas, 1981a, pp. 219–20).

24. For a revealing contrast between Keynes and Lucas on the prerequisites for successful model building, see Chapter 1 of the companion volume to this book.

25. Lucas (1981a, p. 9) points out that it would be a mistake to conclude that his 'abstract "toy models" are a step that can be dispensed with, or that one can go directly to the formulation of useful, simple linear models or to reading Mitchell with new understanding without their assistance. It is, at least for me, the working out of these highly abstract but explicit models that is the *source* of ideas for constructing new econometric models, criticizing old ones, or reading the classics from a fresh viewpoint.'

26. For Lucas's innovative utilization of the concept of GE, see Lucas, 1981a, pp. 67–81. See also Lucas and Prescott, 1981.

27. Lucas started by locating some Lucas–Rapping households in a monetary economy subject to stochastic disturbances in the quantity of money, and then to trace the consequences. Samuelson's 'exact consumption-loan model' provided a convenient framework. As in his work with Prescott in 1971 (Lucas and Prescott, 1981), Lucas defined equilibrium as a point in a space of functions of a few 'state variables',

leading to greater precision about terms such as 'information' and 'expectations', and to a formulation and utilization of Muth's RE hypothesis. Thus, Lucas (1981a, p. 7) claims that 'the needed ingredients for a general-equilibrium formulation seemed to be readily at hand'.

28. Lucas (1981a, pp. 7–8) sees the Phelps concept of island economies (with traders locally dispersed and short on useful economy-wide information) as an analytically helpful device, for it allows all transactors at the same time to conceive that relative to others they have benefited from a monetary shock. Lucas (1981a, p. 8) acknowledges that it is analytically difficult to incorporate this feature into a GE system, but 'the "fit" between the workings of the completed model and the conjecture of Friedman, Phelps, Rapping and me, and others turned out to be perfect'.

29. Sargent (1981b) and Barro (1981b) test time series observations with models that postulate that individual agents' expectational mistakes are the only mechanism via which movements in aggregate demand provide impulses for business fluctuations. These models assert that anticipated variations in aggregate demand influence only nominal prices and do not contribute to real business activity fluctuations. Thus only unanticipated movements in money are posited to generate fluctuations in real economic variables. For a discussion of the formidable problems of statistically representing and testing the hypothesis of neutrality, see Sims, 1977b.

30. An agent might discriminate against costly information required for minor local or routine decisions where it might be imprudent to incur considerable costs, in contrast with key decisions or where significant variations in the economy or its major segments are perceived.

31. Sargent (1979) emphasizes stochastics and statistical decision theory.

32. Essentially the problem posed by Grunberg and Modigliani concerns the possibility of making correct public predictions in view of the fact that those whose behaviour is being predicted react to the prediction. The problem was answered by means of Brower's fixed point theorem. See Modigliani, 1980b, pp. 461–74.

33. For a view of RE in historical perspective, the Austrian influence and the contrast with other important approaches to expectational phenomena, see Kantor, 1979, pp. 1426–38. See also Hirshleifer and Riley, 1979, pp. 1411–14, Kirzner, 1982. As always, 'it is all in Marshall'. For an informative exploration of Marshall's concept of expectations and linkage to RE, see Grossman, 1981, p. 542.

34. Sargent (1981c, pp. 215–16) asks why would anyone want to 'interpret time series data as representing the results of interactions of private agents optimizing choices? The answer is not that this way of modeling is aesthetically pleasing, although it is, nor that modeling in this way guarantees an analysis that implies no role for government intervention, which it does not. The reason for interpreting time series in this way is practical: potentially it offers the analyst the ability to predict how agents' behavior and the random behavior of market-determined variables will each change when there are policy interven-

tions or other changes in the environment that alter some of the agents' dynamic constraints. There is a general presumption that private agents' behavior and the random behavior of market outcomes both will change whenever agents' constraints change, as when policy intervention or other changes in the environment occur. The most that can be hoped for is that the parameters of agents' preferences and technologies will not change in the face of such changes in the environment. If the dynamic econometric model is formulated explicitly in terms of the parameters of preferences, technologies, and constraints, it will in principle be possible for the analyst to predict the effect on observed behavior of changes in the stochastic environment'.

35. Among the critics, Kaldor (1982, p. 30) claims that this is merely perfect foresight in disguise. Omniscience is implied by many others. See Hirshleifer and Riley, 1979, p. 1413; Simon, 1982, p. 445.

36. As McCallum (1981b, p. 277) put it, 'the Lucas–Sargent Proposition. . . may be stated as follows: if aggregate-supply fluctuations are initiated by informational errors. . . and if economic agents' expectations are formed rationally, then countercyclical monetary policy will be entirely ineffective'.

37. In a revealing passage, Lucas (1981a, p. 16) points out that unsurprisingly the basic source for his facts turned out to be Friedman and Schwartz (1963):
'As·a student, I had thought this monograph was made unduly difficult by its failure to use any explicit, general theoretical framework, to give structure to the complicated history of US economic tie series, and therefore I had paid it only casual attention. Now, thoroughly disillusioned with standard macroeconomic theory, I appreciated the book's relative atheoretical approach. From Friedman and Schwartz, it is a short and direct step back to the work of Wesley Mitchell. . . These connections were not pursued from genealogical interest, but because they are helpful in organizing one's thinking about the implications of the evidence. It is the similarity from cycle to cycle of comovements among scrics, as documented by Mitchell, that leads one to a single-shock view of business cycles. *Given* this, Friedman and Schwartz have no alternative but to identify this single shock with monetary instability. What are the other candidates?'

38. Whether or not macroeconometric models' policy implications are correct depend on whether or not the models are structural (invariant with respect to policy) and not at all on whether the models can be successfully caricatured by terms such as 'long' and 'short' run (Lucas and Sargent, 1978, p. 69).

39. Following Hurwicz and Koopmans, Sims (1977a, p. 21) defines *structure* as something that remains fixed when a policy change is undertaken and the structure is identified if it can be estimated from the given data. See also Lucas and Sargent, 1978, p. 69.

40. 'I find this assumption of continuous market clearing so unlike what goes on in most markets in our sort of developed economies that I would reject these Non-Keynesian models as being of no serious use in analysing our macroeconomic behaviour. In fact through trade

union and customary conventions workers set and insist on the rate for the job; and our theories of what is needed to offset the monopsonistic powers of small number of employers facing a large number of workers in imperfect markets provide a very good explanation of such behaviour. Similarly the existence of oligopolistic markets for the sale of products which make it impossible to calculate at all precisely the price elasticity of demand for a single manufacturer's output provides a well-known explanation of the practice of setting selling prices for manufactured products on the basis of a conventional mark-up of the variable cost of production' (Meade, 1981, p. 49).

41. Many of these features gain clarity and sharpness in Okun's (1981) contrast between auction and customers' markets, whatever reservations one might have about the choice of labels. See also Okun (1980) for a perceptive criticism of NCM.

42. Robert Hall (1982) points out that the synthesis that Fischer visualizes is somewhat exaggerated for many reasons. He points to the underlying tension between Friedman-type monetarism and NCM. Klein (1982a, p. 13), on the other hand, suggests that 'when all is said and done, the arguments by the proponents of rational expectations have led us to consider, more or less carefully, the structure of lags in mainstream models and also to consider other elements in the information set besides own history of a given variable. It has also encouraged model builders to take a more serious look at expectation variables from sample surveys to integrate them more fully in mainstream models.'

43. It is interesting to note that in another context, Douglas Gale (1978, pp. 847–8) has accused sophisticated GE theorists of letting rigour go overboard when they tackle macroeconomic problems. In his view 'they have taken a holiday from the standard they would have had to apply' in microtheory. 'Some of them are clearly capable of better things, as their past work testifies, but "macroeconomics" seems to have brought out the worst in them.' In his opinion 'macroeconomics seems to be more and more just microeconomics without the rigour or generality now required in general equilibrium theory'.

44. For a more comprehensive analysis of the Kaleckian system see Feiwel, 1975, pt I. But, of course, there is no substitute for the original. See, *inter alia*, Kalecki, 1971.

45. Kalecki's theory of distribution 'is important both because his theory is important in its own right and because it focuses attention on an aspect of distribution theory which had hitherto been neglected because of the preoccupation of earlier writers with the production function and perfect competition' (Hahn, 1972, p. 37).

46. On the other hand, Kalecki's analysis is based on social classes, rather than on a 'fundamental psychological law'.

47. In a nutshell, Keynes argued that the actual rate of current investment will be pushed to the point where the marginal efficiency of capital is equal to the market rate of interest. As there exists at any time a variety of investment projects which can be arranged in descending order of their expected rate of return over cost (excluding interest but

allowing for risk) the actual rate of investment will be pushed at any time to the point where the spread between the prospective yield and rate of interest is reduced to nought. Kalecki, on the other hand, asked the fitting question: If there are investment opportunities offering positive yields in excess of cost of financing, why wouldn't each entrepreneur undertake the indefinitely large volume of investment and exploit the opportunities of reaping extra profits? He differed from Keynes in the reply. He argued that the supposition of a rising supply curve in production of investment goods is unrealistic, at least for a considerable range of production. But even if costs do rise sufficiently, the rise takes place as a result of investment plans actually implemented. MEC is defined in terms of expectation of returns and the current supply price of the capital asset. In providing the answer Kalecki's basic distinction between investment decisions and realization is cardinal and provides a framework for modern business-cycle theory and econometric research. Furthermore, Kalecki brought into the argument the problem of availability of finance for entrepreneurial capital as going to the heart of the capitalist system, as we have alluded to above.

48. As we know, the place of interest rates in the economic process is highly controversial. The role of liquidity preference theory in Keynes's system as well as its peculiar features have been and continue to be subject to searching scrutiny (see Klein, 1966; Patinkin, 1956, Leijonhufvud, 1968). For instance, Shackle (1965) argued that the liquidity theory itself, though intimately necessary to the *General Theory* can be considered in isolation, and stands as Keynes's most inalienable piece of original economic thought. It is remarkable that in his original formulation, Kalecki did not treat liquidity preference and the interest rate. But shortly after the publication of his original model, he introduced a theory of interest, suggesting that the velocity of circulation of cash balances in fact closely depends on the short rate of interest. According to Kalecki, this rate cannot be determined as in traditional theory because investment automatically generates an equal amount of saving. If investment 'finances itself', irrespective of the level of the rate of interest, the rate of interest itself is determined by the interplay of other factors. Kalecki proposed that the short-term rate of interest is determined by the value of transactions and the supply of money by the banking system. In turn, the long-term rate is determined by anticipations of the short-term rate based on past experience and by estimates of the risk involved in the possible capital loss of holding long-term assets. Velocity of circulation is not a constant, but depends on the movements of the interest rate. Short-term rate of interest is closely connected with marginal convenience of holding cash. With a given turnover of cash balances, the smaller the volume of cash balances possessed the greater the convenience derived from holding the marginal unit of cash for transaction purposes. But after the volume of cash holdings drops below a certain level, its further reduction involves a very strong rising marginal inconvenience. If, however, cash is abundant with given turnover, the marginal

convenience declines to zero at this level if the supply of cash increases further. Thus, subject to qualification, the marginal convenience of holding cash is an increasing function of the velocity of circulation. If the short-term rate of interest exceeds this marginal convenience, the opportunity cost provides stimuli for lending extra cash; if the interest rate is lower, it becomes beneficial to withdraw from short-term assets and get cash. Thus equilibrium is reached when the short-term rate of interest equals the marginal convenience of holding cash. This theory set forth by Kalecki is an alternative way of looking at the Keynesian theory of liquidity preference. Both theories are alike in assuming that velocity is not a constant and is affected by interest rate movements.

49. Even less is this the place to contemplate the possible conquest of orthodoxy by radical or Marxist streams — whatever their inherent merits or limitations. For a review of recent thought in this area, see McFarlane, 1982.

50. Harcourt (1979), where an informative and sympathetic biographical sketch of Joan Robinson can be found, cites the not-so-sympathetic Harry G. Johnson's reminiscences: 'Once she came to Chicago to talk to my students there; they looked at her and decided, "Well, we'll certainly show this old grandmother where she gets off". . . They picked their heads up off the floor, having been ticked off with a few well-chosen blunt squelches' (quoted after Harcourt, 1979, p. 663). For an interesting and critical evaluation of Joan Robinson's position see Tobin, 1973. As this volume was going to press there appeared the sympathetic survey of Robinson's contributions by Gram and Walsh (1983). See also the forthcoming issue of the *Cambridge Journal of Economics* which was originally planned to celebrate her 80th birthday.

51. Unfortunately the state of her health at the time this volume was being completed did not allow her to elaborate on and polish the original draft.

52. Samuelson (1966, p. 1593) aptly noted: 'Cambridge economists, God bless them, also deserve justice; and since they cannot always be counted on to pour it on each other in buckets, it is up to us barbarians to join in the rituals.' In this spirit, he (1970, p. 397) went on to extol his most faithful and severe critic (in a passage that Joan Robinson told me she considers patronizing):

'If an ignoramus in economics says that the current economic system cannot be interpreted as a rational scheme, that is nothing. But if one of the greatest analytical economists of our era says this, she is worth listening to. Joan Robinson. . . won fame young as one of the inventors of the theory of imperfect competition. She consolidated her world-wide reputation by becoming one of the leading contributors to the Keynesian macroeconomic literature. . . In recent decades Mrs Robinson has been an important pioneer and critic of growth models. For any of these accomplishments she might well be awarded the Nobel Prize in Economics.'

Another reluctant 'admirer', Bronfenbrenner (1979, p. 446), comments:

'Voltaire is supposed to have said "I do not agree with a word you say, but shall defend to the death your right to say it". May I paraphrase him, speaking as a "bastard Keynesian" purveyor of "rubbish" and "stinking fish"? I do not agree with most of what Joan Robonson has been saying these past forty years, but hope she wins a Nobel Prize for saying it". Mrs Robinson has done more than any other contemporary economist (Milton Friedman being her only rival) to save our discipline from ossified cut-and-driedness; also it occasionally occurs to me that she may be right about some matters in dispute, or that some of my favourite fish may be getting a trifle over-ripe with age.'

53. Regretfully this is not the place to review the important contributions of other members of the Cambridge school, such as Kahn, Kaldor, Sraffa, and Pasinetti. Neither can we give justice to the contributions of the American post-Keynesians. For a survey of the latter, see Eichner, 1979.

54. 'A few months before *Imperfect Competition* was published, Edward Chamberlin's *Monopolistic Competition* appeared. He was upset by the coincidence and all the rest of his work was devoted to showing that my theory was quite different from his. During his reign at Harvard, it used to be said that you could always get a good degree by abusing Mrs Robinson. I recognized that several of the questions that he raised. . . were more interesting than mine but obviously there was a very large overlap between the two books. I suppose that Chamberlin was annoyed at having to share all his footnotes and reviews with me. . . but there was a deeper reason. I had been very well pleased to refute the orthodox theory of wages, which had stuck in my gizzard as a student, while Chamberlin refused to admit that his argument damaged the image of the market producing the optimum allocation of given resources between alternative uses. This ideological difference underlay an otherwise unnecessary controversy' (Robinson, 1978, p. x).

55. For a more comprehensive review of Samuelson and in general the 'MIT professors' position, see the authoritative reflections of Solow, 1983b. See also Feiwel, 1982; Burmeister, 1980.

REFERENCES

Abramovitz, M. (1981) 'Welfare Quandaries and Productivity Concerns', *American Economic Review*, 71 (March): 1–17.

Ackley, G. (1983) 'Commodities and Capital: Prices and Quantities', *American Economic Review*, 72 (March): 1–16.

Alternative Policies to Combat Inflation (1979) St Louis: Center for the Study of American Business.

Arrow, K. J. (1959) 'Toward a Theory of Price Adjustment', in M. Abramovitz *et al.*, *The Allocation of Economic Resources*, Stanford: Stanford University Press, pp. 41–51.

Arrow, K. J. (1967) 'Samuelson Collected', *Journal of Political Economy*, 75: 730–7.

Arrow, K. J. (1974) 'Limited Knowledge and Economic Ideas', *American Economic Review*, 64 (March): 1–10.

Barro, R. J. (1981a) *Money, Expectations, and Business Cycles*, New York: Academic Press.

Barro, R. J. (1981b) 'Unanticipated Money Growth and Unemployment in the United States', in R. E. Lucas and T. J. Sargent (eds), *Rational Expectations and Econometric Practice*, pp. 563–84.

Barro, R. J. and H. I. Grossman (1976) *Money, Employment and Inflation*, Cambridge: Cambridge University Press.

Benassy, J.-P. (1982) *The Economics of Market Disequilibrium*, New York: Academic Press.

Blinder, A. (1979) *Economic Policy and the Great Stagflation*, New York: Academic Press.

Bronfenbrenner, M. (1979) 'Review of Joan Robinson, *Contributions to Modern Economics*', *Economic Journal*, 89 (June): 446–7.

Brunner, K. (1981) 'The Case Against Monetary Activism', *Lloyds Bank Review*, 139 (1): 20–39.

Burmeister, E. (1980) *Capital Theory and Dynamics*, Cambridge: Cambridge University Press.

Clower, R. (1965) 'The Keynesian Counterrevolution: A Theoretical Appraisal', in F. H. Hahn and F. P. R. Brechling (eds), *The Theory of Interest Rates*, London: Macmillan, pp. 102–25.

Clower, R. (1975) 'Reflections on the Keynesian Perplex', *Zeitschrift für Nationalökonomie*, 35: 1–24.

Colloquium on Alternatives for Economic Policy (1981) New York: The Conference Board.

Davidson, P. (1980) 'Post Keynesian Economics', *Public Interest*, (special edn): 151–73.

Denison, E. F. (1979) *Accounting for Slower Growth*, Washington: Brookings.

Drazen, A. (1980) 'Recent Developments in Macroeconomic Disequilibrium Theory', *Econometrica*, 48 (March): 283–306.

Eckstein, O. (1981) *Core Inflation*, Englewood Cliffs, N.J.: Prentice-Hall.

Eichner, A. S. (ed) (1979) *A Guide to Post Keynesian Economics*, New York: Sharp.

Feiwel, G. R. (1975) *The Intellectual Capital of Michal Kalecki*, Knoxville: University of Tennessee Press.

Feiwel, G. R. (1982) 'Samuelson and Contemporary Economics', in G. R. Feiwel (ed), *Samuelson and Neoclassical Economics*, Boston: Kluwer-Nijhoff, pp. 1–28.

Feldstein, M. (1982) 'The Fiscal Framework of Monetary Policy', NBER, Working Paper no. 986 (mimeo).

Feldstein, M. (ed.) (1980) *The American Economy in Transition*, Chicago: Chicago University Press.

Fischer, S. (1975) 'Recent Developments in Monetary Theory', *American Economic Review*, 65 (May): 157–66.

Fischer, S. (1983) 'Comment' in J. Tobin (ed.), *Macroeconomics Prices, and Quantities: Essays in Memory of Arthur M. Okun*, Washington: Brookings, pp. 267–76.

Fisher, F. M. (forthcoming) *On Disequilibrium Foundations of Equilibrium Economy*, Cambridge: Cambridge University Press.
Friedman, B. (1978a) 'A Theoretical Nondebate about Monetarism', in T. Mayer *et al., The Structure of Monetarism*, New York: Norton, pp. 94–112.
Friedman, B. (1978b) 'Discussion', in *After the Phillips Curve*, Boston: Federal Reserve Bank of Boston, pp. 73–80.
Friedman, M. (1956) 'The Quantity Theory of Money – A Restatement', in M. Friedman (ed.), *Studies in the Quantity Theory of Money*, Chicago: University of Chicago Press, pp. 3–21.
Friedman, M. (1963) 'The Present State of Economic Theory', *Economic Studies Quarterly*, 14 (September): 1–15.
Friedman, M. (1970a) *The Counter-Revolution in Monetary Theory*, London: Institute of Economic Affairs.
Friedman, M. (1970b) 'A Theoretical Framework for Economic Analysis' and 'Comments on the Critics', in R. J. Gordon (ed.), *Milton Friedman's Monetary Framework*, Chicago: University of Chicago Press, pp. 1–62 and 132–85.
Friedman, M. (1975a) 'Discussion', *American Economic Review*, 65 (May): 176–81.
Friedman, M. (1975b) *Unemployment and Inflation: An Evaluation of the Phillips Curve*, London: Institute of Economic Affairs.
Friedman, M. (1977a) 'Discussion', in 'The Monetarist Controversy', *Federal Reserve Bank of San Francisco Economic Review* (Spring Supplement): 12–22.
Friedman, M. (1977b) 'Nobel Lecture: Inflation and Unemployment', *Journal of Political Economy*, 85 (3): 451–72.
Friedman, M. and A. J. Schwartz (1963) *A Monetary History of the United States, 1867–1960*, Princeton: Princeton University Press.
Gale, D. (1978) 'Review of G. Schwödiauer, *Equilibrium and Disequilibrium in Economic Theory*', *Economic Journal*, 88 (December): 845–8.
Glustoff, E. (1968) 'On the Existence of a Keynesian Equilibrium', *Review of Economic Studies*, 35 (July): 327–34.
Gordon, R. J. (ed.) (1970) *Milton Friedman's Monetary Framework*, Chicago: University of Chicago Press.
Gordon, R. J. (1976) 'Recent Developments in the Theory of Inflation and Employment', *Journal of Monetary Economics*, 2: 185–219.
Gram, H. and V. Walsh (1983) 'Joan Robinson's Economics in Retrospect', *Journal of Economic Literature*, 21 (June): 518–50.
Grandmont, J.-M., and G. Laroque (1976) 'On Keynesian Temporary Equilibria', *Review of Economic Studies*, 43: 53–67.
Grossman, S. J. (1981) 'An Introduction to the Theory of Rational Expectations Under Asymmetric Information', *Review of Economic Studies*, 48: 541–59.
Hahn, F. H. (ed.) (1971) *Readings in the Theory of Growth*, London: Macmillan.
Hahn, F. H. (1972) *The Share of Wages in National Income*, London: Weidenfeld & Nicolson.
Hahn, F. H. (1977) 'Keynesian Economics and General Equilibrium

Theory: Reflections on Some Current Debates', in G. C. Harcourt (ed.), *The Microeconomic Foundations for Macroeconomics*, pp. 25–40.

Hahn, F. H. (1978) 'On Non-Walrasian Equilibria', *Review of Economic Studies*, 45: 1–17.

Hahn, F. H. (1982) *Money and Inflation*, Oxford: Blackwell.

Hahn, F. H. and R. C. O. Matthews (1964) 'The Theory of Economic Growth: A Survey', *Economic Journal*, 74 (December): 779–902.

Hall, R. E. (1980) 'Comment', in S. Fischer (ed.), *Rational Expectations and Economic Policy*, Chicago: University of Chicago Press, pp. 235–8.

Hall, R. E. (1982) *'Monetary Trends in the United States and the United Kingdom:* A Review from the Perspective of New Developments in Monetary Economics', *Journal of Economic Literature*, 20 (December): 1552–6.

Harcourt, G. C. (1972) *Some Cambridge Controversies in the Theory of Capital*, Cambridge: Cambridge University Press.

Harcourt, G. C. (1979) 'Joan Robinson', in *International Encyclopedia of the Social Sciences*, vol. 18: *Biographical Supplement*, New York: Free Press, pp. 663–71.

Harcourt, G. C. (ed.) (1977) *The Microeconomic Foundations of Macroeconomics*, London: Macmillan.

Hicks, J. R. (1957) 'A Rehabilitation of 'Classical' Economics?' *Economic Journal*, 67: 286–8.

Hicks, J. R. (1977) *Economic Perspectives*, Oxford: Clarendon Press.

Hicks, J. R. (1979) 'Review of Weintraub's *Microfoundations*', *Journal of Economic Literature*, 17 (December): 1451–4.

Hirshleifer, J., and J. G. Riley (1979) 'The Analytics of Uncertainty and Information – An Expository Survey', *Journal of Economic Literature*, 17 (December): 1375–1421.

Holt, C. C., F. Modigliani, J. F. Muth, and H. A. Simon (1960) *Planning Production, Inventories and Work Force*, Englewood Cliffs, N.J.: Prentice-Hall.

Jensen, H. E. (1983) 'J.M. Keynes as a Marshallian', *Journal of Economic Issues*, 17 (March): 67–94.

Johansen, L. (1977) *Lectures on Macroeconomic Planning*, Amsterdam: North-Holland.

Johnson, H. G. (1971) 'The Keynesian Revolution and the Monetarist Counter-Revolution', *American Economic Review*, 61 (May): 1–14.

Johnson, H. G. (1973) *Further Essays in Monetary Economics*, Cambridge, Mass.: Harvard University Press.

Johnson, H. G. (1974) 'The Current and Prospective State of Economics', *Australian Economic Papers*, 13 (June): 1–27.

Jordan, J. S., and R. Radner (1982) 'Rational Expectations in Microeconomic Models: An Overview', *Journal of Economic Theory*, 26 (April): 201–23.

Kahn, R. (1974) *On Re-reading Keynes*, London: Oxford University Press.

Kahn, R. (1976) 'A Keynesian View', (mimeo).

Kahn, R. (1977a) 'Malinvaud on Keynes', *Cambridge Journal of Economics*, 1 (December): 375–88.

Kahn, R. (1977b) 'Mr Eltis and the Keynesians', *Lloyds Bank Review*, 124 (April): 1–13.

Kaldor, N. (1982) *The Scourge of Monetarism*, Oxford: Oxford University Press.

Kalecki, M. (1970) 'Theories of Growth in Different Social Systems', *Scientia*, 105 (May–June): 311–16.

Kalecki, M. (1971) *Selected Essays on the Dynamics of the Capitalist Economy*, Cambridge: Cambridge University Press.

Kantor, B. (1979) 'Rational Expectations and Economic Thought', *Journal of Economic Literature*, 17 (December): 1422–41.

Kendrick, J. W. (1979) 'Productivity Trends and the Recent Slowdown', in W. Fellner (ed.), *Contemporary Economic Problems*, Washington: American Enterprise Institute.

Keynes, J. M. (1919) *The Economic Consequences of the Peace*, London: Harcourt Brace.

Keynes, J. M. (1930) *A Treatise on Money*, 2 vols, London: Macmillan.

Keynes, J. M. (1936) *The General Theory of Employment, Interest and Money*, London: Macmillan.

Keynes, J. M. (1973) *The Collected Writings of John Maynard Keynes*, ed. D. Moggridge, vol. 13, London: Macmillan.

Kirzner, I. M. (ed.) (1982) *Method, Process, and Austrian Economics*, Lexington, Mass.: Heath.

Klein, L. R. (1966) *The Keynesian Revolution*, London: Macmillan.

Klein, L. R. (1971) 'Empirical Evidence on Fiscal and Monetary Models', in J. J. Diamond (ed.), *Issues in Fiscal and Monetary Policy*, Chicago: De Paul University Press.

Klein, L. R. (1973) 'Commentary on "The State of the Monetarist Debate" ', *Federal Reserve Bank of St Louis Review*, 55 (September): 9–12.

Klein, L. R. (1977) 'The Longevity of Economic Theory', in *Quantitative Wirtschaftsforschung*, Tubingen: Mohr, pp. 411–19.

Klein, L. R. (1981) 'Statement', in US Congress, Joint Economic Committee, *Expectations and the Economy*, Washington: GPO, pp. 62–5.

Klein, L. R. (1982a) *The Present Debate about Macro Economics and Econometric Model Specification*, Nankang, Taipei, Taiwan: Institute of Economics, Academia Sinica.

Klein, L. R. (1982b) 'The Neoclassical Tradition of Keynesian Economics and the Generalized Model', in G. R. Feiwel (ed.), *Samuelson and Neoclassical Economics*, Boston: Kluwer-Nijhoff, pp. 244–62.

Kuznets, S. (1973) *Population, Capital, and Growth*, New York: Norton.

Laidler, D. (1981) 'Monetarism: An Interpretation and an Assessment', *Economic Journal*, 91 (March): 1–28.

Laidler, D. and M. Parkin (1975) 'Inflation: A Survey', *Economic Journal*, 85 (December): 741–809.

Leijonhufvud, A. (1968) *On Keynesian Economics and the Economics of Keynes*, New York: Oxford University Press.

Leijonhufvud, A. (1969) *Keynes and the Classics*, London: Institute of Economic Affairs.

Leijonhufvud, A. (1981) *Information and Coordination: Essays in Macroeconomic Theory*, New York: Oxford University Press.

Lindbeck, A. (1980) *Inflation*, Leuven: Leuven University Press.

Lucas, R. E. Jr (1980) 'The Death of Keynesian Economics', *Issues and Ideas*, University of Chicago: Graduate School of Business.

Lucas, R. E. Jr (1981a) *Studies in Business Cycle Theory*, Cambridge, Mass.: Harvard University Press.

Lucas, R. E. Jr (1981b) 'Tobin and Monetarism: A Review Article', *Journal of Economic Literature*, 19 (June): 558–67.

Lucas, R. E. Jr, and E. C. Prescott (1981) 'Optimal Investment with Rational Expectations', in R. E. Lucas and T. J. Sargent (eds), *Rational Expectations and Econometric Practice*, pp. 67–90.

Lucas, R. E. Jr, and T. J. Sargent (1978) 'After Keynesian Economics', in *After the Phillips Curve*, Boston: Federal Reserve Bank of Boston.

Lucas, R. E. Jr, and T. J. Sargent (eds) (1981) *Rational Expectations and Econometric Practice*, Minneapolis: University of Minnesota Press.

Lundberg, E. (1957) *Business Cycles and Economic Policy*, London: Allen & Unwin.

Lundberg, E. (1977) *Inflation and Anti-Inflation Policy*, Boulder: Westview Press.

McCallum, B. T. (1981a) 'The Role of Expectations in Economics', in US Congress, Joint Economic Committee, *Expectations and the Economy*, Washington: GPO, pp. 48–53.

McCallum, B. T. (1981b) 'Price-Level Stickiness and the Feasibility of Monetary Stabilization Policy with Rational Expectations', in R. E. Lucas and T. J. Sargent (eds), *Rational Expectations and Econometric Practice*, pp. 277–84.

McFarlane, B. (1982) *Radical Economics*, New York: St Martin's Press.

Malinvaud, E. (1977) *The Theory of Unemployment Reconsidered*, Oxford: Blackwell.

Malinvaud, E. (1980) *Profitability and Unemployment*, Cambridge: Cambridge University Press.

Mayer, T. *et al.* (1978) *The Structure of Monetarism*, New York: Norton.

Meade, J. E. (1961) *A Neo-Classical Theory of Economic Growth*, London: Allen & Unwin.

Meade, J. E. (1976) *The Just Economy*, London: Allen & Unwin.

Meade, J. E. (1981) 'Comment on the Papers by Professors Laidler and Tobin', *Economic Journal*, 91 (March): 49–55.

Meltzer, A. (1983) 'Interpreting Keynes', *Journal of Economic Literature*, 21 (March): 66–78.

Modigliani, F. (1980a) *The Collected Papers of Franco Modigliani*, vol. 1: *Essays in Macroeconomics*, ed. A. Abel, Cambridge, Mass;: MIT Press.

Modigliani, F. (1980b) *The Collected Papers of Franco Modigliani*, vol. 3: *The Theory of Finance and Other Essays*, ed. A. Abel, Cambridge, Mass.: MIT Press.

Monetary Policy Issues in the 1980s (1982) Kansas City: Federal Reserve Bank of Kansas City.

Muth, J. F. (1961) 'Rational Expectations and the Theory of Price Movements', *Econometrica*, 29 (July): 315–35.

Negishi, T. (1979) *Microfoundations of Keynesian Macroeconomics*, Amsterdam: North-Holland.

Nordhaus, W. D. (1983) 'Macroconfusion: The Dilemmas of Economic

Policy', in J. Tobin (ed.), *Macroeconomics, Prices, and Quantities: Essays in Memory of Arthur M. Okun*, Washington: Brookings, pp. 247–67.

Okun, A. M. (1980) 'Rational-Expectations-with-Misperceptions as a Theory of the Business Cycle', *Journal of Money, Credit and Banking*, 12 (November), pt 2: 817–25.

Okun, A. M. (1981) *Prices and Quantities: A Macroeconomic Analysis*, Washington: Brookings.

Patinkin, D. (1956) (new edn 1965) *Money, Interest, and Prices*, New York: Harper & Row.

Patinkin, D. (1981) *Essays on and in the Chicago Tradition*, Durham: Duke University Press.

Patinkin, D. (1983) 'New Perspectives or Old Pitfalls? Some Comments on Meltzer's Interpretation of the *General Theory*', *Journal of Economic Literature*, 21 (March): 47–51.

Phelps, E. S. *et al.* (1970) *Microeconomic Foundations of Employment and Inflation*, New York: Norton.

Phelps, E. S. (1979) *Studies in Macroeconomic Theory*, vol 1: *Employment and Inflation*, New York: Academic Press.

Phelps, E. S. (1981) 'Okun's Micro-Macro System: A Review Article', *Journal of Economic Literature*, 19 (September): 1065–73.

Phillips, A. W. (1958) 'The Relations between Unemployment and the Rate of Change of Wage Rates in the United Kingdom, 1861–1957', *Economica*, 25: 283–99.

Radner, R. (1982) 'Equilibrium Under Uncertainty', in K. J. Arrow and M. D. Intriligator (eds), *Handbook of Mathematical Economics*, vol. 2, Amsterdam: North-Holland, pp. 921–1006.

Robbins, L. (1952) (new edn 1978) *The Theory of Economic Policy in English Classical Political Economy*, Philadelphia: Porcupine.

Robinson, Joan (1955) *Collected Economic Papers*, vol. 1, Oxford: Blackwell.

Robinson, Joan (1962) *Economic Philosophy*, Chicago: Aldine.

Robinson, Joan (1966) *An Essay on Marxian Economics*, 2nd edn, London: Macmillan.

Robinson, Joan (1969) 'A Review of Leijonhufvud's *On Keynesian Economics and the Economics of Keynes*', *Economic Journal*, 79 (September): 581–3.

Robinson, Joan (1973a) Foreword to J. Kregel, *The Reconstruction of Political Economy*, New York: Wiley, pp. ix–xiii.

Robinson, Joan (1973b) *After Keynes*, Oxford: Blackwell.

Robinson, Joan (1977) 'What are the Questions?' *Journal of Economic Literature*, 15 (December): 1318–39.

Robinson, Joan (1978) *Contributions to Modern Economics*, New York: Academic Press.

Robinson, Joan (1979) Foreword to *A Guide to Post Keynesian Economics*, ed. A. S. Eichner, New York: Sharp.

Robinson, Joan (1980) 'Time in Economic Theory', *Kyklos*, 33 (2): 219–29.

Robinson, Joan (1982a) 'Misunderstandings in the Theory of Production', in G. R. Feiwel (ed.), *Samuelson and Neoclassical Economics*, Boston: Kluwer-Nijhoff, pp. 90–6.

Robinson, Joan (1982b) 'Shedding Darkness', *Cambridge Journal of Economics*, 6: 295–6.

Robinson, Joan, and F. Cripps (1979) 'Keynes Today', *Journal of Post Keynesian Economics*, 2: 139–44.

Rosenberg, N. (1982) *Inside the Black Box: Technology and Economics*, Cambridge: Cambridge University Press.

Samuelson, P. A. (1955) *Economics*, 3rd edn, New York: McGraw-Hill.

Samuelson, P. A. (1964) *Economics*, 6th edn, New York: McGraw-Hill.

Samuelson, P. A. (1966) *The Collected Scientific Papers of Paul A. Samuelson*, ed. J. E. Stiglitz, 2 vols, Cambridge, Mass.: MIT Press.

Samuelson, P. A. (1970) *Readings in Economics*, New York: McGraw-Hill.

Samuelson, P. A. (1972) *The Collected Scientific Papers of Paul A. Samuelson*, vol. 3, ed. R. C. Merton, Cambridge, Mass.: MIT Press.

Samuelson, P. A. (1977) *The Collected Scientific Papers of Paul A. Samuelson*, vol. 4, ed. H. Nagatani and K. Crowley, Cambridge, Mass.: MIT Press.

Samuelson, P. A. (1980) *Economics*, 11th edn, New York: McGraw-Hill.

Sargent, T. J. (1977) 'Testing for Neutrality and Rationality', in T. J. Sargent and N. Wallace (eds), *Rational Expectations and the Theory of Economic Policy*, Minneapolis: Federal Reserve Bank of Minneapolis, pp. 1–21.

Sargent, T. J. (1979) *Macroeconomic Theory*, New York: Academic Press.

Sargent, T. J. (1981a) 'Rational Expectation, the Real Rate of Interest, and the Natural Rate of Unemployment', in R. E. Lucas and T. J. Sargent (eds), *Rational Expectations and Econometric Practice*, pp. 159–98.

Sargent, T. J. (1981b) 'A Classical Macroeconometric Model for the United States', in R. E. Lucas and T. J. Sargent (eds), *Rational Expectations and Econometric Practice*, pp. 521–51.

Sargent, T. J. (1981c) 'Interpreting Economic Time Series', *Journal of Political Economy*, 89 (April): 213–48.

Sargent, T. J. (1981d) 'Stopping Moderate Inflations: The Methods of Poincaré and Thatcher' (May) (mimeo).

Sargent, T. J. and N. Wallace (1981a) 'Rational Expectations and the Theory of Economic Policy', in R. E. Lucas and T. J. Sargent (eds), *Rational Expectations and Econometric Practice*, pp. 199–213.

Sargent, T. J. and N. Wallace (1981b) ' "Rational" Expectations, the Optimal Monetary Instrument and the Optimal Money Supply Rule', in R. E. Lucas and T. J. Sargent (eds), *Rational Expectations and Econometric Practice*, pp. 215–28.

Schumpeter, J. A. (1934) *The Theory of Economic Development*, trans. from the German 1926, 2nd edn, Cambridge, Mass.: Harvard University Press.

Schumpeter, J. A. (1954) *History of Economic Analysis*, New York: Oxford University Press.

Sen, A. (ed.) (1970) *Growth Economics*, Harmondsworth: Penguin.

Shackle, G. L. S. (1965) 'Recent Theories Concerning the Nature and Role of Interest', in *Surveys of Economic Theory*, vol 1: *Money Interest and Welfare*, London: Macmillan, pp. 108–53.

Simon, H. A. (1982) *Models of Bounded Rationality*, vol. 2: *Behavioral Economics and Business Organization*, Cambridge, Mass.: MIT Press.

Sims, C. A. (1977a) 'Macro-Economics and Reality', Discussion Paper no. 77-91 (December), University of Minnesota, Center for Economic Research (mimeo).

Sims, C. A. (ed.) (1977b) *New Methods in Business Cycle Research*, Minneapolis: Federal Reserve Bank of Minneapolis.

Sims, C. A. (1982) 'Policy Analysis with Econometric Models', *Brookings Papers on Economic Activity*, 1: 107–64.

Solow, R. M. (1970) *Growth Theory*, New York: Oxford University Press.

Solow, R. M. (1975) 'Cambridge and the Real World', *Times Literary Supplement*, 14 March, pp. 277–8.

Solow, R. M. (1978a) 'Summary and Evaluation', in *After the Phillips Curve*, Boston: Federal Reserve Bank of Boston, pp. 203–9.

Solow, R. M. (1978b) 'What We Know and Don't Know About Inflation', *Technology Review*, 81 (3): 2–18.

Solow, R. M. (1978c) 'Down the Phillips Curve with Gun and Camera', in R. L. Teigen (ed.), *Readings in Money, National Income, and Stabilization Policy*, Homewood, Ill.: Irwin.

Solow, R. M. (1979) 'Alternative Approaches to Macroeconomic Theory: A Partial View', *Canadian Journal of Economics*, 12: 339–54.

Solow, R. M. (1980a) 'On Theories of Unemployment', *American Economic Review*, 70 (March): 1–11.

Solow, R. M. (1980b) 'What to Do (Macroeconomically) when OPEC Comes?' in S. Fischer (ed.), *Rational Expectations and Economic Policy*, Chicago: University of Chicago Press, pp. 249–64.

Solow, R. M. (1983a) 'Comment', in J. Tobin (ed.), *Macroeconomics, Prices, and Quantities: Essays in Memory of Arthur M. Okun*, Washington: Brookings, pp. 279–84.

Solow, R. M. (1983b) 'Modern Capital Theory', in E. C. Brown and R. M. Solow (eds), *Paul Samuelson and Modern Economic Theory*, New York: McGraw-Hill, pp. 169–87.

Stein, J. (ed.) (1976) *Monetarism*, Amsterdam: North-Holland.

Stiglitz, J. E. (1974) 'The Cambridge–Cambridge Controversy in the Theory of Capital: A View from New Haven', *Journal of Political Economy*, 82 (4): 893–903.

Taylor, J. B. (1980) 'Recent Developments in the Theory of Stabilization Policy', in *Stabilization Policies: Lessons from the 70s and Implications for the 80s*, St Louis: Federal Reserve Bank of St Louis, pp. 1–40.

Taylor, J. B. (1983) 'Rational Expectations and the Invisible Handshake', in J. Tobin (ed.), *Macroeconomics, Prices, and Quantities: Essays in Memory of Arthur M. Okun*, Washington: Brookings, pp. 63–82.

Theil, H. (1957) 'A Note on Certainty Equivalence in Dynamic Planning', *Econometrica*, 25 (April): 346–9.

Tobin, J. (1970) 'Friedman's Theoretical Framework', in R. J. Gordon (ed.), *Milton Friedman's Monetary Framework*, Chicago, University of Chicago Press, pp. 77–89.

Tobin, J. (1971) *Essays in Economics*, vol. 1: *Macroeconomics*, Amsterdam: North-Holland.
Tobin, J. (1972) 'Inflation and Unemployment', *American Economic Review*, 72 (March): 1–18.
Tobin, J. (1973) 'Cambridge (UK) v. Cambridge (Mass.)', *Public Interest*, 31 (Spring): 102–9.
Tobin, J. (1975) 'Keynesian Models of Recession and Depression', *American Economic Review*, 65 (May): 195–202.
Tobin, J. (1980a) 'Stabilization Policy Ten Years After', *Brookings Papers on Economic Activity*, 1 (Tenth Anniversary Issue): 19–72.
Tobin, J. (1980b) *Asset Accumulation and Economic Activity*, Chicago: Chicago University Press.
Tobin, J. (1981a) 'The Monetarist Counter-Revolution – An Appraisal', *Economic Journal*, 91 (March): 29–42.
Tobin, J. (1981b) 'Review of Patinkin, *Keynes' Monetary Thought*', *Journal of Political Economy*, 89 (1): 204–7.
Tobin, J. (1982) 'Inflation', in D. Greenwald (ed.), *Encyclopedia of Economics*, New York: McGraw-Hill.
Viner, J. (1958) *The Long View and the Short*, Glencoe, Ill.: Free Press.
Wallace, N. (1980) 'Comment', in S. Fischer (ed.), *Rational Expectations and Economic Policy*, Chicago: University of Chicago Press, pp. 264–8.
Weintraub, E. R. (1979) *Microfoundations: The Compatibility of Microeconomics and Macroeconomics*, Cambridge: Cambridge University Press.
Weiss, L. (1980) 'The Role of Active Monetary Policy in a Rational Expectations Model', *Journal of Political Economy*, 88 (April): 221–33.

Part I
Alternative Perspectives on Macroeconomics and Distribution

2 Theoretical Issues in Macroeconomics

JAMES TOBIN

Economics has always derived inspiration and energy from the burning issues of the day. Economists have shared the concerns of their fellow citizens and have addressed them as analysts, teachers, and advocates. Their own controversies have mirrored the ideological and political debates of their societies and epochs. From these encounters have developed principles and methods that outlasted their practical origins and gave our subject the cumulative continuity and internal dynamics of a discipline. Adam Smith's challenge to mercantilism, Ricardo's attack on the Corn Laws, and the Austrian School's response to Marxism are examples.

Reaganomics is a political counter-revolution against the economic ideas alleged to have motivated policies over the past half century. Thatcherism is a similar reaction in the UK. Throughout the non-communist developed world the spirit of the times reflects disillusionment with past policies; their intellectual foundations are rejected in favour of opposing theories old and new. Within our profession, the same counter-revolutionary war is waged – in journals, classrooms, and conferences rather than in popular media, political debate, and elections. The parallelism is not accidental. The great inflation and stagflation of the 1970s were the common inspiration. Economists' ideas spill easily and rapidly into wider currency, frequently propagated by economists themselves. In a memorable passage Keynes observed that men of affairs and crusading zealots unconsciously echo the theories of bygone academics (1936, pp. 383–4). Today the lags are short, the academics are not even bygone, and the debts are not always unconscious.

In Reaganomics we economists have no trouble discerning the presence, albeit in distorted and exaggerated forms, of several fashionable strands of professional opinion. Their common thread is one of the Great Ideas of

103

intellectual history: the miraculous efficiency and optimality of decentralized market processes free of government intervention. The overriding goal
is to reduce the economic size, burden, and activity of government.

Monetarism, especially in its more recent form, the new classical
macroeconomics, extends to macroeconomic policy the grasp of these
central principles. The new vogue is to forswear counter-cyclical measures,
scornfully called 'fine-tuning', in favour of firm steadiness in the policy
instruments themselves. Market processes will then, it is argued, take the
economy to its best equilibrium.

Supply-side economics has been identified with some ludicrous claims
and forecasts. Qualitatively, however, it is new emphasis on an old theme:
the importance of incentives and rewards for thrift, work, enterprise, and
risk-taking. The corollaries are de-emphasis of redistribution via taxes and
transfers and devaluation of public consumption and investment.

Finally, traditional financial and fiscal orthodoxy, always opposed to
manipulation of fiscal and monetary powers for macroeconomic objectives,
has gained renewed respect and influence in the counter-revolutionary
climate.

However, the several branches of conservative economics are not fully
consistent with one another. Though they are all represented in government, their ideological messages and policy counsels are frequently not
harmonious.

The common target of the counter-revolutions in macroeconomic
theory and policy is Keynesian economics, the ideas of the *General Theory*
as elaborated, modified, and applied since the Second World War. The
Keynesian revolution itself was inspired by real world events, the Great
Depression, and by the patent incapacity of the existing economic orthodoxy to provide either explanation or remedy. Four decades later the
Great Inflation evoked the monetarist and classical revivals and discredited
Keynesian orthodoxy. In both cases intellectual history was obviously
shaped by events external to our discipline and by the political, ideological,
and analytical vacuums and opportunities they created.

But that is by no means the whole story. The discipline itself imposes
an internal logic on its developments, as the revolution and counter-
revolutions in macroeconomics also exemplify. In discussing 'macroeconomics under debate' today, I shall emphasize the internal debate and
describe the theoretical issues among the contestants, revolutionary and
counter-revolutionary. A good place to begin, a good frame of reference, I
think, is Walrasian general equilibrium theory — the basic paradigm of our
discipline and, as it happens, the scientific counterpart of the common
central theme of the conservative counter-revolutions, the Invisible Hand.

Within the profession the vulnerability of Keynesian economics, even as modified in the 'neoclassical synthesis' of the two postwar decades, to recent challenges, is its long-standing failure to come to terms with this powerful theoretical tradition. In discussing the debate in this framework, I shall also be led to comment on contemporary attempts to reformulate Keynesian economics to overcome this failure.

THE INVISIBLE HAND AND THE NEOCLASSICAL PARADIGM

The 'invisible hand' *is* one of the Great Ideas of intellectual history. According to Adam Smith, market competition transmutes selfish and myopic individual actions into the wealth of nations (1776, p. 400). Central direction is not necessary. The system demands of its participants neither altruism nor omniscience. Natural self-interest is enough motivation; everyday local observation is enough information. All that is required of the participants is respect for property rights and contractual obligations. All that is required of government is to establish and enforce those laws and to defend the society against internal and external enemies. Government interferences in markets are generally inefficient because they prevent individuals from making mutually and socially beneficial trades and contracts.

This momentous idea has flourished for two centuries. As political ideology it provided the economic content of nineteenth-century liberalism and of twentieth-century conservatism. In both phases it has been the weapon of bourgeois business and capital against rival interests and movements — landed aristocracies, labour unions, bureaucrats, populists, socialists. Simultaneously, economic theory developed and refined Smith's insight. The task of giving rigour and precision to the relation of individual actions and aggregate outcomes has engaged the best minds of our profession, including Walras, Pareto, Hicks, Samuelson, Debreu, and Arrow. The propositions that survived this process are more sophisticated and more limited than the conjectures of earlier writers and the extravagent claims of the ideology.

Modern general equilibrium theory describes an economy with two principal features, individual optimization and price-cleared competitive markets. Each individual agent, given her endowments of productive resources and other commodities and given their market prices, buys and sells and produces so as to maximize her utility, a function of the quantities she consumes of the several commodities. Firms maximize the wealth of the agents who own them. These choices imply aggregate schedules relating demands for and supplies of all commodities to all their prices. Market prices, equating demands and supplies and governing quantities produced, bought, and sold by all agents, are determined simultaneously for all commodities and resources. Under certain assumptions the system of simultaneous equations has at least one solution, a 'competitive equilibrium' of the economy, and may have many solutions. Each competitive equilibrium is 'Pareto-optimal', that is, no reallocations of goods among agents could fail to make at least one agent worse off. Moreover, any feasible allocation that is Pareto-optimal corresponds to some competitive equilibrium based on some initial distribution of endowments. The model encompasses intertemporal choices, time-consuming production technologies, and uncertainties about the future by a simple ingenious expedient, extending the list of commodities, prices, and markets by distinguishing the dates and contingencies in which commodities are to be delivered.

Where does the modern version of the theory leave the Invisible Hand? Two quite opposite responses are conceivable. On the one hand there is the good news: the intuitions of Adam Smith and many later writers can indeed be rigorously formulated and proved. The bad news is that the theorems depend on a host of conditions, many of dubious realism. Restrictions on preferences and technologies are stringent. The concept of social optimality, the Pareto criterion, is weak. The theory does not describe a process in real time by which the economy reaches an equilibrium solution. When commodities are multiplied to cover future and contingent deliveries, the possibility that competitive markets do or could exist for all of them is remote. The modern version might be taken to refute, not to support, the applicability of invisible hand propositions to real-world economies.

Wiser economic theorists have always been cautious. Joseph Schumpeter called the Walrasian system the *magna charta* of economics because it showed that the central problem of allocation of resources and final goods was in principle solvable. (In fact the formal proof came not from Walras (1874), who only showed that there were as many equations as unknowns, but three-quarters of a century later from Arrow (1953) and Debreu (1959).) Schumpeter's own description of economic progress under capitalism, however, relied on wholly different mechanisms. A common view — shared for example by Walras, Wicksell, Fisher, Marshall, and Pigou — was that neoclassical analysis disclosed important and ultimately decisive tendencies but did not literally describe how observed prices and quantities were determined. Anglo-Saxon economics in the nineteenth and early twentieth centuries, less mathematical and more pragmatic than on the continent, was especially characterized by loose adherence to the *magna charta*.

Neoclassical theory itself developed an 'anatomy of market failure', a catalogue of ways in which departures from the conditions under which markets theoretically deliver optimal outcomes might occur and conceivably call for government interventions. These include: monopolies and other deviations from pure competition; public goods and bads and other externalities, that is, extra-market ways in which one individual's actions give utility or disutility to others; absence of markets, in particular for future and contingent deliveries; inadequacies of information. The categories overlap. A standard mode of argument and analysis regarding any actual or proposed government intervention developed. The first question is why the market does not solve the problem, if it is solvable at all. The answer must be to identify one or more of the recognized market failures and to show that the intervention remedies it. The presumption is that the market works. The burden of proof is on the advocate of intervention.

Of course interventions can be advocated on grounds of distributional equity, whether or not there is a market failure. Long ago neoclassical economics washed its hands of such messy questions by saying there is no way to compare the utility of one person with that of another. Pareto-optimality is no help. Redistributions always make someone worse off. Interventions that make everyone better off are virtually impossible to find. The best the neoclassical paradigm can do is to point out that if a given redistribution is to be made there are more and less efficient ways of accomplishing it. The more efficient ways, not surprisingly, generally rely on market processes, and so far as possible on redistributions of initial endowments rather than of final outputs.

Many of the ablest minds attracted into professional economics find their exposure to general equilibrium theory the most exciting intellectual experience of their lives. Elegant, rigorous, mathematically powerful, the theory reaches far from obvious results. It gives economics a theoretical core that 'softer' social sciences lack and often envy. It 'is the only game in town'. It especially enchants those who were drawn into the profession more because it challenges their mathematical and logical skills than because it might help to solve real-world puzzles and problems. They are particularly disposed to regard general equilibrium propositions as reference points, and to assign burdens of proof to anyone who consciously or unconsciously alleges otherwise. Supporting this attitude is the 'methodology of positive economics' (Friedman, 1953, pp. 3–43). The patent and admitted unrealism of assumptions does not matter. The question is whether the outcomes of the system as a whole are *as if* they were solutions of the postulated system. Since the system in its full generality generates precious little in the way of propositions refutable by observations, it is not very vulnerable to tests of 'as if' methodology (Sonnenschein, 1973).

MONEY AND GENERAL EQUILIBRIUM

Money has always been an awkward puzzle for neoclassical general equilibrium theory (Kareken and Wallace, 1980). The use of a conventional unit of account, Walras's *numeraire*, is no problem; any arbitrary commodity or package of commodities will serve this purpose, and the results do not depend on the choice. But the holdings of intrinsically useless paper as stores of value is a puzzle. How can fiat monies command any value in terms of the goods and services that enter utility and production functions? Even commodity monies raise the question, because they acquire more value from their monetary status than they would otherwise have.

The question is not answerable in the standard general equilibrium framework. With frictionless, costless, simultaneously cleared auction markets for all commodities, there is no need for money holdings to bridge gaps between sales and purchases or to mitigate costly searches for advantageous barters. Common sense tells us that money is held and has value because, absent the super-computer of the Walrasian multi-market auctioneer, the use of money facilitates exchanges.

It is not easy to incorporate this common-sense observation in the standard paradigm, for two main reasons. First, transactions technologies do not fit the formulations of input–output relations needed to solve the system. Second, money has attributes of a public good; the standard paradigm has well-known difficulties handling externalities occurring when the utility or productivity of a commodity to any one agent depends on how many others use it.

The makeshift compromise in neoclassical theory has been the alleged *neutrality* of fiat money. The idea is simple: whatever functions money may perform, whatever holdings agents may therefore desire, the *real* equilibrium must be independent of the stock of money as measured in its own nominal units. After all, it cannot matter whether the unit of account is a dollar or a dime. If a unit's change multiplies the nominal quantity by ten, the system will remain in equilibrium with all prices multiplied by ten, future and contingent prices as well as spot. All relative prices, including real interest rates, and all quantities will be the same as before.

Buttressed by this reasoning, older neoclassical economists and their reincarnations in new classical macroeconomics assert that money is just a veil. Anyone who looks through it can see that the real economy is the same as if the veil were not there. In extreme form the proposition is clearly false. If money performs real functions for individuals and for society, the equilibrium of a monetary economy cannot be the same as that of a barter economy. Indeed that of a barter economy, given the costs of search and barter, could not be the Walrasian solution (Hahn, 1982). But the extreme proposition is not needed. Monetary exchange can yield a solution different from barter, presumably a superior one because money compensates at least in part for the absence of the Walrasian auctioneer. But the altered and improved solution could be independent of the size of the stock of nominal money.

Money neutrality in this sense is the basis for the 'classical dichotomy' (Patinkin, 1955) separating the determination of real variables and relative prices from the determination of the absolute price level, the reciprocal of the value of money. The dichotomy is the fundamental rationale of the quantity theory of money, the proposition that absolute prices are proportional to the stock.

However, the analogy of money stock variations to units changes requires extreme caution in application. A thorough change of units would rescale proportionately the nominal quantities of all individual holdings of all existing assets and debts denominated in the monetary unit of account, and of all expectations of future quantities of money and of promises to pay money in every future contingency. The operations by which governments and central banks alter stocks of money involve issuing currency or its equivalent to make transfer payments or to buy goods and services or to buy outstanding promises to pay currency in future. These operations obviously do not alter all nominal stocks, present and future, individual and aggregate, proportionately. They leave unchanged the aggregates and the distributions of most pre-existing assets and debts. The application of the neutrality proposition to actual real-world monetary policies is a prime example of the fallacy of misplaced concreteness. Those who attribute real consequences to monetary policies and events are not *per se* guilty of attributing irrational 'money illusion' to households and business managers.

As previously observed, wise neoclassical economists have been circumspect in application of general equilibrium results. This caution has embraced the implications of neutrality and dichotomy. Quantity theorists from David Hume to Irving Fisher to Milton Friedman expected to see plenty of important real consequences of monetary policies and events for long short runs. It is only recently that neutrality has been more sweepingly and indiscriminately applied.

In logic, non-neutralities are not confined to any short run. For example, a permanent change in the growth rates of government-issued currency and promises to pay currency in future is not an operation that can be assimilated to a units change, because it would not alter all present and future nominal stocks in the same proportion. Variations of money growth and inflation rates alter the *real* rate of return on monetary assets that carry a nominal interest rate fixed at zero or any other number, and therefore have further real consequences (Tobin, 1965). More generally, if an economy approaches a steady state, its constellation of real variables is bound to be influenced by the monetary events occurring along the path (Hahn, 1982).

KEYNES AND THE NEOCLASSICAL PARADIGM

In the *General Theory*, John Maynard Keynes had the audacity to claim discovery of massive, endemic, possibly chronic market failure, not just one of the minor exceptions to market performance in the usual canonical list. Keynes was quite explicit in this contention, opposing his 'general' theory to what he called 'classical' theory, which he relegated to the status of a special case. (He clearly meant theory that would now be called 'neoclassical' to distinguish it from the classical economics of Britain before the advent of marginalism and subjective utility circa 1870.) The market failure is the unemployment of labour and other productive resources whose owners would gladly accept employment for remuneration no greater than their prevailing marginal productivities and would gladly purchase the output the employment would produce.

Ever since 1936, today more than ever, this claim has been received with incredulity by theorists whose trained instincts lead them to use general competitive equilibrium as a presumptive point of reference. Keynes did not help them understand his point. In keeping with the ethnocentrism of English economics, especially in Cambridge, he paid little attention to continental writers. His main 'classical' target was another Cambridge economist, Professor A. C. Pigou. He attacked F. A. von Hayek, who had moved from Austria to London, and he briefly cited Walras as an exemplar of 'classical' interest theory (Keynes, 1936, pp. 19, 32, 56, 59-60, 176-7). Keynes used only simple mathematics, and that sparingly. His language, terminology, and style of argument were pragmatic and worldly like Alfred Marshall's rather than rigorous and abstract like Walras's. Although he did in fact set forth a system of simultaneous equations, he did not present it with formal clarity. Most students owe their understanding of it to elucidations by Hicks and others. Anyway, his structural and behaviour equations differ from those of full-blown neoclassical general equilibrium models by their heroic aggregation. The consumption function, for example, represents the economy as a whole; its derivation from the consumption choices of individual agents is loose and informal.

For years general equilibrium theorists have said they 'simply don't understand' Keynes, or for that matter any macroeconomics, which owes its identification as a distinguishable branch of economics to the Keynesian revolution. Frequently, not always, this is a polite way of saying they believe or suspect it is wrong. That in turn means that Keynesian theory must assume somewhere, implicitly or explicitly, irrational, non-optimizing behaviour by individual agents. 'Money illusion' is the most frequent example, that is, imputing to individuals as workers or consumers behaviour motivated by the monetary outcomes rather than those real outcomes that can be the only ultimate source of utility. Or Keynes must assume that for some unexplained reasons markets do not clear, for example, because nominal wages and prices are rigid or sticky.

Keynes contributed to the sources of these disbeliefs by insisting that his conclusions applied to the *equilibrium* of a *competitive* system. He attacked the classicals on their own ground. He appeared to charge that though the classicals had the right pieces of the puzzle they had not assembled them correctly. He was not content to regard the Great Depression as an especially slow and painful example of the time it takes neoclassical equilibrium tendencies to win out. Nor did he attribute the difficulties of the system to imperfections and monopolistic elements ignored in the competitive model, even though at the very time he was writing, microeconomic theories stressing these phenomena were flourishing in his Cambridge as well as in Cambridge, Massachusetts (Chamberlin, 1933; Robinson, 1933; Shove, 1930; Sraffa, 1926; Young, 1930).

Despite these obstacles to communication, the *General Theory* is clear enough about the sources of macroeconomic market failure to enable careful and open-minded readers to grasp the points. Ultimately the basic reason for incredulity is the presumption against so enormous a market failure: surely rational individuals would find ways to conclude bargains that make all parties better off and thus to escape the Keynesian impasse. This viewpoint leaves the sceptics with the uncomfortable task of reconciling observed unemployment, both in the Great Depression and in other business cycles, with the presumptions of neoclassical faith. This task was pretty much finessed until the recent ambitious attempts at reconciliation by the new classical macroeconomics, discussed below.

In Keynesian theory there are several interrelated sources of the macroeconomic market failure. First, Keynes was explicit about the incompleteness of markets, particularly the absence of future and contingent markets. He observed that savers abstaining from present consumption do not simultaneously place specific orders either for future consumption or for capital goods. Instead they acquire generalized stores of value, which they can spend when they please on what they please. Savers and investors, lenders and borrowers, are not the same individuals. Convenient and efficient as it is, the divorce of saving from specific future consumption and from contemporaneous investment imposes on capital and commodity markets an immense burden of co-ordination. The spot market signals from reduced consumption do not guide producers to make inventory and fixed investments to prepare for future consumption demands; the signals may even elicit perverse behaviour (Keynes, 1936, pp. 210–12). Intrinsically unreliable expectations and information have to fill the market gaps. The tests that investment projects must pass can easily be the wrong hurdles, especially when capital-building projects have to compete with returns expected on monetary assets (Keynes, 1936, pp. 210–44).

Second, Keynes emphasized the essential unpredictability, even in a probabilistic sense, of the returns to real and monetary assets. They depend on what future buyers will be prepared to pay for them, and that in turn depends on what those buyers' expectations will be about what future buyers. The indeterminacy is both cause and effect of the absence of markets for future and contingent deliveries. For this reason, Keynes regarded the 'state of long-term expectations' as an autonomous determinant of investment and aggregate demand, not as an endogenous variable (Keynes, 1936, pp. 147–64).

Third, Keynes observed that prices, including wages, are quoted and set in the monetary unit of account. The practice is socially and individually convenient, but it does have real consequences. It is difficult for agents, especially workers, to make effective their true demands and supplies at real, relative prices (Keynes, 1936, pp. 4–22). He did not note, perhaps because he regarded it as self-evident, that the use of nominal numeraire would make no difference if a Walrasian auctioneer continuously cleared and recleared all markets simultaneously, knowing at each moment everyone's demands and supplies as functions of all prices. Keynes was probably thinking implicitly of more realistic wage- and price-setting mechanisms, in which specific prices are set locally and subsequently adjusted only with delay and cost. Consequently his point was misunderstood and seemed vulnerable to the 'money illusion' accusation. Now in the context of contract theory and other models of non-Walrasian price-setting, his intuitions — including the importance of wage comparisons in local wage bargains — are being formally modelled.

Fourth, Keynes's principle of effective demand is a clear statement of the role of quantity variation, as well as price variation, in clearing markets. Individuals' demands are constrained by what they actually sell at prevailing prices, and this may be less than what they would like to sell at those prices given their endowments. Unemployed workers consume less than they would like because they sell less labour than they would like (Keynes, 1936, pp. 23-36). That, not failure to understand that supply of labour can be an endogenous decision, is the reason income is a principle argument in a Keynesian consumption function. Quantity equilibration becomes a key process whenever relative prices, including interest rates, are slow to move. This can happen even when nominal prices are quite flexible, as Keynes observed in his story wherein goods prices follow money wages down and workers are unable to lower their real wages (Keynes, 1936, pp. 257-79). In this story the price stickiness is elsewhere in the economy, in the determination of interest rates. One interpretation of the 'general' in General Theory is allowance for quantity as well as price variation in clearing markets.

Fifth, Keynes rejected neutrality of money. Money competes with other assets, including real capital, as a vehicle for holding wealth. The yield on money, its implicit advantages in liquidity and safety included, influences the returns savers and investors require of other assets. Consequently real interest rates are not independent of monetary phenomena. Keynes was particularly concerned, writing in the Great Depression, that the advantages of holding monies and near-monies would prevent interest rates from falling low enough to induce real investment sufficient to match the economy's potential saving (Keynes, 1936, pp. 222-44). Curiously, unlike Irving Fisher, Keynes did not note that price inflation was a way to lower the real return on money, probably because he saw that actual events were bringing deflation, moving the real return on money in the wrong direction.

SYNTHESES OF NEOCLASSICAL AND KEYNESIAN ECONOMICS

Two developments in macroeconomics subsequent to Keynes derived their impetus in large measure to the gap in understanding, language, and credibility between Keynesian theory and general equilibrium theory. These are first, the neoclassical synthesis, the mainstream macroeconomics of the quarter-century after the Second World War, and second, more recently, formal disequilibrium theory.

The first might better be called the neoclassical neo-Keynesian synthesis.

Several of its architects, notably Hicks (1946) and Samuelson (1947), were in the 1930s and 1940s active participants in the development and refinement of pure neoclassical theory. They were among the writers who were bringing at long last Walras, Pareto, and the continental tradition into English-speaking economics. At the same time, living through the Great Depression, they were impressed by the realism and relevance of Keynes. In the cautious vein of older neoclassicals, they found the neoclassical paradigm useful for long-run trends but saw nothing problematic in departures from those trends for a variety of reasons, for example, market imperfections, adjustment costs, information lags. These departures need not imply any irrationality or any permanent failure of markets to clear; the properties of full general equilibrium should not be expected to hold every day or every year.

Keynes's analysis looked like a good model of lapses from full employment equilibrium. Its long-run stagnationist pessimism could be dropped. It was empirically and theoretically unsound, the more so if Keynesian stabilization policies themselves reinforced the mechanisms that return the economy to its long-run growth track. The debate over Keynes's pretension to a permanent equilibrium with involuntary unemployment could be declared a draw; it was largely semantic and anyway operationally irrelevant. Keynes's comparative statics methodology worked well enough in the short run. Dynamics could be added. The structural equations could be both improved theoretically and tested and estimated empirically. Principles of neoclassical welfare economics could be applied to macroeconomic policy choices, correcting Keynes's intimations that wasteful make-work projects have zero opportunity cost when resources are idle and providing criteria for choices among the several instruments of macroeconomic stabilization available.

This 'synthesis', however, did not still the complaints that macroeconomics could not be understood or believed because it had no firm 'microfoundations'. Its authors and practitioners were too busy with pragmatic macroeconomics to develop formally the several sources of market failure described by Keynes.

The second development, formal disequilibrium macroeconomics, presented Keynes's ideas in a manner designed to communicate them to general equilibrium theorists, though not necessarily to make them more acceptable.[1]

In these models the vector of prices is, for reasons not explained, stuck at values other than the Walrasian general equilibrium solution. Agents — consumers, workers, employers — are constrained in their demands and supplies by the actual transactions they are able to consummate at these wrong prices. They cannot effectuate their 'notional' demands and supplies — the transactions they would choose to make at these prices if constrained only by their endowments — because those will not clear the markets except at the 'right' prices of the Walrasian solution. But the markets may nonetheless clear at some vector of quantities, which replace prices as the equilibrating variables. Finding this disequilibrium, with agents solving their constrained optimization problems, is a task engaging the same mathematical techniques and analytical talents as standard general equilibrium theory. That is one reason why it seems to enable some theorists to understand what Keynes meant. The approach holds considerable promise. Perhaps some day it will fulfil Keynes's vision of a 'general' theory, of which both his own and Walrasian equilibrium will be special cases.

As a contribution to macroeconomics, however, these models have so far added little new. Recall the 'principle of effective demand' in Keynes, his stress on output variation as equilibrator of saving and investment, his concern that prices, specifically real wages and interest rates, are wrong. Why these points, clear enough in Keynes and in many subsequent expositions, suddenly become revelations when repeated in somewhat different language is a mystery. Nor have the repetitions altered or improved the substance of standard macroeconomic analyses of underemployment. Indeed they are in many ways more primitive, neglecting monetary and financial markets, fiscal institutions and policies, intertemporal phenomena, and the dynamics of prices and wages. They also miss a basic point of Keynesian logic: there could be an underemployment equilibrium or disequilibrium even if prices happened to be the 'right' ones for full Walrasian equilibrium.

The new models are, it is true, in some ways more general. They call attention to the possibilities and properties of outcomes neither Keynesian nor Walrasian, for example, classical unemployment and over-full employment. They apply the fixed-price variable-quantity calculus to larger numbers of markets simultaneously.

In contrast to these two developments, a school of self-styled post-Keynesians regard any synthesis or reconciliation, in substance or in language, of Keynes and neoclassical economics as a betrayal of the revolution. They reject equilibrium analysis altogether, stress the historical, institutional, and evolutionary aspects of economic development, and emphasize the macroeconomic implications of the non-competitive structures of modern economies. Their valid points do not add up to a coherent theory, but many of them will have to be tackled in eclectic work in macroeconomics in the future. Many mainstream Keynesian economists have long agreed that Keynesian macroeconomics cannot be grounded on pure or perfect competition in product and labour markets. As increasing numbers of them have come to the conclusion that wage and price controls or other incomes policies are at least occasionally necessary to prevent inflation at full employment, the practical gap between them and post-Keynesians has narrowed.

THE MONETARIST COUNTER-REVOLUTION

The quantity theory of money, the central propostion of monetarism, has two guises. One is the fundamental neutrality proposition discussed above. As there noted, the axiom that paper money is not held or valued for its own sake is unexceptionable but offers limited mileage in application to real-world monetary operations. The other quantity theory is a brand of pragmatic macroeconomics, methodologically similar to Keynesian theory and no less a specialized deviation from full-blown neoclassical general equilibrium. It too has a long history. For example, Irving Fisher breathed life into his famous identity, the Equation of Exchange $MV = PQ$, by analysing and studying empirically the behaviours and institutions that determine the velocity V of the supply of transactions media M, and the properties of the economy that determine the division of MV impulses between price level P and quantity Q in short and long runs (Fisher, 1911). The influential monetarist resurgence under Milton Friedman this past quarter-century follows the same tradition, though emphasizing subjective factors in money demand as well as transactions mechanics (Friedman, 1956). This movement I call Monetarism I to distinguish it from the later and theoretically purer Monetarism II, also known as the new classical macroeconomics. Though Monetarism I borrows credence from the neutrality proposition, that proposition neither implies Monetarism I nor limits its applicability.

The debates of the last quarter-century between Keynesians and Monetarists I concerned matters of substantial importance in macroeconomic policy, but from a theoretical standpoint they were internal to standard macroeconomics. They concerned: the theoretical plausibility and empirical validity of alternative specifications of aggregative equations and models; the relative usefulness of alternative languages, one based on the national income = expenditure identity, the other on the Equation of Exchange; the plausibility of differing estimates of parameters, notably the interest-elasticity of money demand and the speeds of price and output adjustments in response to variations in aggregate nominal demand, MV; the reliability and stability of crucial behavioural equations, money demand

and aggregate expenditure; the relative importance of money supply shocks and real demand and supply shocks in generating business-cycle fluctuations; the role of expectations of monetary policies in generating inflation expectations affecting interest rates; and the empirical constancy of real interest rates. These are all important questions, with decisive implications for policy. Monetarists' answers to them led them to assign minor macroeconomic importance to fiscal policy, to oppose activist 'stabilization' policies of any kind, and to advocate central bank policies focused on steady growth of money supplies unmodified by concern for interest rates or any other variables. But they do not raise fundamental issues of theory and method. They are in principle, if not in practice, resolvable by established techniques of theoretical and econometric research in macroeconomics.

Inflation in the late 1960s and 1970s brought widespread support to Monetarism I, both inside and outside the economics profession. Keynesian theory was perceived to be incapable of explaining or foreseeing the inflation, and Keynesian policies to be incapable of arresting it. More and more people agreed with the monetarists that Keynesian economics actually promoted inflation.

The *General Theory* provides no theory of persisting inflation except in cases when real aggregate demand chronically exceeds the full employment output potential of the economy. For the usual case of underemployment, the theory explains why prices will be positively related to employment but not why they might continue to rise with employment stable or even falling. Postwar periods of inflation at times when the economy did not appear to be at full employment underscored the gap. As a practical matter, it was filled by the Phillips curve, interpreted to offer a policy trade-off between unemployment and inflation. Statistical findings that rates of wage and price inflation varied inversely to the unemployment rate were elevated into a structural equation of the model. As the economy approached full employment, the curve became very steep, approaching the vertical. While thoughtful devotees of the Phillips curve were aware that longer-run inflationary consequences of increases in employment would be greater than short-run impacts because of feedbacks from actual inflation on to expectations and patterns of wage settlement and price-settings, they were encouraged by initial empirical indications that such feedbacks were slow and incomplete. At the same time, they never believed that unemployment could be pushed indefinitely low without running into classic excess-demand inflation, as Keynesian theory itself envisaged when aggregate real demand exceeded full employment output. Indeed there was a long-standing belief among Keynesian economists that price stability could not be maintained at full employment without some form of wage and price controls or incomes policies. The empirical question, important for policy, was to identify the unemployment rate that indicated 'full employment'.

Milton Friedman's 1967 Presidential Address (1968) argued, as Phelps had independently argued shortly before (1967), that there could be no permanent trade-off of unemployment and inflation. Full employment, re-named the natural rate of unemployment, was the point of inflation stability, at whatever rate was consistent with the growth of money stocks. At higher unemployment rates, prices would be decelerating, and at lower rates accelerating. The moral for policy was not to aim at any unemployment rate, or at any other real variable. Follow a stable monetary growth policy, preferably one consistent with price stability, and unemployment will gravitate to its natural rate, that is, whatever it gravitates to will be the natural rate. Though not denying that monetary policies have real consequences in short runs, Friedman was now stressing more fundamental neoclassical propositions, the neutrality of money, than in the earlier monetarist–Keynesian debates. He had already moved in this direction when he tried to conclude the controversy over the relevance of the interest-elasticity of money demand to the efficacies of fiscal and monetary policies by saying in effect that it was irrelevant if prices were flexible and the economy was in full employment equilibrium (Friedman, 1966). In any case his presidential address was the bridge from old monetarism to new.

Robert Lucas followed up and went further. He offered an interpretation of Phillips-curve statistical correlations that deprived them of indicating any trade-off possibility exploitable by policy even in the short run (Lucas, 1972). That price increases are associated with gains in employment and production indicates only that workers and business managers were temporarily confused between relative prices and absolute prices. They mistook a general price increase due to a monetary shock for a favourable improvement in their real terms of trade. But the monetary authority cannot fool them for long. Markets clear at prices reflecting the best information, including anticipations and perceptions of policy, that agents have. This was the beginning of the most fundamental counter-revolution.

STAGFLATION AS A TEST OF MACROECONOMIC THEORIES

Was the stagflation of the 1970s a prima facie refutation of Keynesian macroeconomics? Economic theories and the policies based upon them stand or fall in professional esteem by their perceived congruence with large and long-lasting events. Gross and simple historical tests are much more persuasive than sophisticated econometrics. What Keynes called classical orthodoxy, exemplified by Pigou's theory of unemployment and by the famous or notorious 'Treasury View', was discredited by the Great Depression, for which it appeared to have neither explanation nor remedy. Mainstream Keynesian macroeconomics itself gained credibility and converts over the first two decades after the Second World War from the prosperity and growth to which its policies were perceived to have contributed. But the Great Inflation and Stagflation of the 1970s, it is commonly asserted and believed, refuted this brand of macroeconomics as decisively as the Great Depression undermined the classical target of the Keynesian revolution forty years earlier. Monetarism and the new classical macroeconomics were the counter-revolutions that benefited from the turn of events. They in turn are in danger of flunking the latest test, the disinflation of the early 1980s, though it is too early to be sure or to identify the intellectual beneficiaries of the latest economic disappointments.

Is a verdict against Keynesian macroeconomics justified by the evidence of the 1970s? New Classical macroeconomics argues that the verdict is self-evident.[2] Neo-Keynesian theory of the 1950s and 1960s was just incapable of envisaging the combination of high and rising unemployment with high and rising inflation observed in the 1970s. The Phillips curve, embraced by Keynesians in the preceding decades, predicted not positive but negative correlation of inflation and unemployment. Nor was the 180-degree mistake, in their indictment, a harmless academic error. Keynesian policies, recommended and adopted in order to lower unemployment by riding up the Phillips curve, generated much more inflation than bargained for, while *raising* unemployment at the same time. In the review of my book cited above, Lucas expressed astonishment that an accomplice to such monumental error still speaks or writes about such matters in public.

What did Keynesian economists think in the 1960s about the relation of unemployment and inflation and about the dependence of both outcomes on macroeconomic policies? How and why did a curve through A. W. Phillips's scatter diagram (Phillips, 1958) become a structural equation in theoretical and textbook models and in large macroeconometric models? Such a structural equation was needed to 'explain' the inflation of the mid-1950s; that inflation, which peaked below 5 per cent, may seem trivial in retrospect, but it caused considerable alarm at the time. It occurred at rates of unemployment, 4 per cent plus, then regarded as too high to correspond to 'full employment'. Standard macroeconomic theory of that day did not envisage continuing, persistent inflation in an underemployed economy. Wage and price *levels* were supposed to be positively associated with employment, for reasons given in chapter 21 of the *General*

Theory. This relation implied that prices would be rising in cyclical up-swings but would settle down if output and employment were stabilized. Continuing inflation, a wage–price spiral, would occur in response to an 'inflationary gap', an excess of aggregate real demand over full employment output.

The disturbing observation of the 1950s was a wage–price spiral in the apparent absence of excess demand. This species of inflation was dubbed 'cost-push' in distinction to the classic variety 'demand-pull'. Just naming the phenomenon and treating it as an unexplained exogenous event was intellectually unsatisfying. The Phillips curve came along to fill the gap, attributing inflation to both cost and demand pressures simultaneously and avoiding the dubious knife-edge discontinuity of the 'inflationary gap' model.

However, incorporation of the Phillips curve into the standard macro-economic model did *not* imply that demand expansion could increase employment and production without limit, and always with definite and limited inflationary cost. There remained the notion of full employment, beyond which demand expansion would unleash wage-spiral inflation qualitatively different from Phillips curve inflation, engendered by excess demand not removed by price rises. There had long been a Keynesian theory of this kind of inflation, of its mechanics and its speed, provided by Keynes himself and subsequent contributions (Keynes, 1940; Holtzman, 1950; Koopmans, 1942; Smithies, 1942).

Indeed Keynes himself and others had for a long time recognized that prices and their rates of increase were essentially indeterminate at levels of demand greater than or equal to full employment output. A common formula around Harvard in the late 1940s when I was a graduate student was that a modern mixed economy could not enjoy more than two of three desiderata: full employment, price stability, and freedom from wage and price controls.

The Samuelson–Solow article 'Analytical Aspects of Anti-Inflation Policy' (1960) is frequently cited as a notorious example of the naivety with which Keynesians embraced the notion of a Phillips trade-off exploitable in both long and short run by demand management policies. In truth, the authors were quite agnostic about the long run, and canvassed various possible ways that policy-induced movements along the short-run curve might shift the curve itself:

> [It] might be that. . . low-pressure demand would so act upon wage and other expectations as to shift the curve downward in the longer run — so that over a decade, the economy might enjoy higher employment

with price stability than our present-day estimate would indicate. But also the opposite is conceivable. A low-pressure economy might build up within itself over the years larger and larger amounts of structural unemployment. . . The result would be an upward shift of our menu of choice, with more and more unemployment being needed just to keep prices stable.

Subsequent history suggests that these were both reasonable concerns.

Even before the 'natural rate' articles of Phelps and Friedman, some Keynesians were quite aware of the feedbacks from actually realized price and wage inflation via expectations and emulative or catch-up patterns on to subsequent inflation, of the implication that the Phillips curve is steeper and the trade-off less favourable in the long run than in the short, and of the possibility that the long-run Phillips curve is vertical and allows no trade-off at all. Let me quote Tobin writing in 1966 (Tobin, 1967):

> Nor do we know the answer to the even more basic question whether continuation of 4 per cent unemployment would, so long as it generates any inflation, generate an accelerating inflation. This would be the orthodox prediction: Wages and other incomes rise because people want real gains, and the bargaining power of individuals and groups depends on the real situation. If they find that they are cheated by price increases they will simply escalate their money claims accordingly. On this view the Phillips curve would blow up if growth at a steady utilization rate were maintained. Only cyclical interruptions in the learning process have saved us from accelerating inflation. On this interpretation, the only true equilibrium full employment is the degree of unemployment that corresponds to zero inflation − any higher rate of utilization can be called excess demand. This is a dismal conclusion if true, because it appears to take a socially explosive rate of unemployment − more than 6 per cent in the USA − to keep the price level stable.

What Keynesians of that day were not prepared to do was to identify as full employment equilibrium the point of price or inflation stability on the Phillips curve, or to believe that inflation or acceleration and deflation or deceleration are symmetrical consequences of deviations up or down from that point, or to accept the 'natural rate' as a Phillips curve as an empirical aggregate summary of imperfectly competitive wage- and price-setting institutions and of disequilibrium adjustments rather than a description of the workings of Walrasian auction markets.

Was the combination of higher inflation with higher unemployment something that could never have been foreseen by the macroeconomic theories and models of the 1960s? The world-wide 'wage explosion' of 1970–1 occurred during a recession. It could not be explained either by unemployment, which was rising, or by contemporaneous or recent price increases, which the wage gains overshot. But it was no surprise to Samuelson, Solow, and others who thought 'cost-push' shocks could occur at any time. A 'cost-push' shock, it was well understood, causes simultaneously more inflation and more unemployment, in proportions depending on the degree of policy accommodation. Thus a positive correlation of the two outcomes was not a complete novelty either in theory or in practice. No one in the 1960s foresaw the commodity price and oil shocks later in the 1970s or thought about the macroeconomic consequences of such shocks. The failure of foresight and imagination does no one credit, but it does make it difficult to speculate how an economist in the 1960s would have analysed the case had it been presented to him.

The relevant question is not the one Lucas would hypothetically present. His question would be as follows: observe as of 1969 the prospective true paths of money supplies during the succeeding ten years and say on this information alone what outcomes in inflation and unemployment you would anticipate. This formulation conceals the reasons for the monetary expansions. They did not come out of the blue. They did not occur because central bankers wanted to ride up Phillips curves and to lower unemployment at some inflationary cost. They were accommodations, grudging and partial, of commodity price increases external in origin. These were prototypical stagflationary shocks, reducing aggregate demand and raising costs and prices simultaneously. They increased unemployment as well, the more so because they were incompletely accommodated. Had the monetary authorities not accommodated them at all, unemployment would have risen even more, at the same time that prices were rising faster. Nothing in this story is inconsistent with Keynesian analysis or warrants filing for intellectual bankruptcy.

As I understand Lucas and Sargent, they should not have expected a rise in unemployment in the 1970s had they been told in advance only the rates of money growth. Their best guess of the equilibrium unemployment rate in the 1970s would have been the average actual unemployment rate of the 1960s. They would logically have guessed that all the extra money creation would go into prices. Had they been told in advance of the supply shocks, they — unlike Keynesians — would have or should have expected shifts in terms of trade between oil and other goods to have no more than very transient effects on overall price indexes.

The 1970s caught us all, Keynesians and monetarists and new classicals, unprepared. But the decade is no decisive evidence for or against any school of macroeconomics.

THE NEW CLASSICAL MACROECONOMICS

Monetarism II (also known as the New Classical Macroeconomics/Equilibrium Business Cycle Theory) is not just a revival of pre-Keynesian neoclassical or 'classical' macroeconomics. It is a more literal and sweeping affirmation of its assumptions. What theorists of those older times were content to regard as long-run tendencies their contemporary successors take to apply every day. Agents optimize continuously. Flexible prices clear all markets. The mythical Walrasian auctioneer functions perfectly. In the latter two respects the new classicals are at the opposite pole from the new disequilibrium school discussed above.

However, their models differ from those of full general equilibrium theory in two important and related ways, which I suppose qualifies them as macroeconomic models. Like Keynes they assume a monetary economy; money would have no place in an Arrow–Debreu world. Like Keynes, they assume the absence of most of the futures and contingent futures markets which complete the Arrow–Debreu version of general equilibrium.

Also as in Keynes, expectations play an important role in an economy where markets do not provide contractual insurance against all contingencies. Here the resemblance stops. Keynes thought for reasons recounted above that savers and investors could not have fully rational expectations of the future variables that would determine the outcomes of their decisions, because those outcomes will depend on the behaviour and thus the expectations of others. In contrast, the new classicals take expectations to be unbiased forecasts, not themselves sources of shocks. In their models, expectations of the variables, both their mean values and other moments of probability distributions, are those that the models themselves would generate. The actors all calculate them from the same model, the one known to the author. Disturbances to the system come chiefly from surprises in government policies. Rational expectations take the place of the missing Arrow–Debreu markets and enable the full general equilibrium to be realized.

New classical macroeconomic models rely heavily, even more uncritically than Monetarism I, on the neutrality of money. Though explicitly justified by the 'units change' analogy (Lucas, 1981, p. 558-67), the proposition is applied to real world money supply operations and to short runs as well as long. Indeed in models designed to illuminate effects of policies, or rather their lack of real effects, M's are altered exogenously without specification of the transactions by which governments and central banks bring the changes about. The primitive way in which monetary and financial markets are modelled could be remedied, but not without peril to the more striking policy conclusions of the school.

An implication of money neutrality is a purely monetary theory of inflation. Friedman has told the world that inflation is everywhere and at all times a monetary phenomenon. Both brands of monetarism have ridiculed attributions of inflation to trade unions, OPEC shocks, taxes, and other non-monetary institutions and events. Paradoxically, the 'classical dichotomy' they thus embrace as explanation of inflation also implies that inflation is costless and painless. Yet the main appeal of monetarism is that, in contrast to Keynesian economics, it provides an explanation and remedy for inflation.

The methodology of new classical macroeconomics, like that of neo-classical general equilibrium theory, stresses the requirement that the behaviour assumed of economic agents be rooted explicitly in individual optimizations. This is an especially rigorous requirement, because the new classicals regard the entire path of the economy as one of continuous, continuously changing, equilibrium. What less ambitious theorists might regard as lagged adjustment behaviour, which economic theory neither can nor need explain, the new classicals propose to bring within the tent of optimization. That is not easy, to say the least. Moreover, as I mentioned above, neoclassical general equilibrium theory is too general to yield conclusions, even as to the direction of effects, in macroeconomics or elsewhere. How can the new classicals, seeking even greater generality, do better? There are no free lunches for them either. When new classical models give definite conclusions about the effects of policies or other variations, they obtain them by simplifications. One short cut is to assume all agents are alike in preferences, endowments, or both; in advanced analyses two or three types of agents are assumed, with emphasis on their differences in age. Another short cut is to attribute to the agents special preference or utility functions of mathematical form tractable in carrying out the obligatory optimizations. These expedients enable the theorist to claim that their behaviour equations have the microfoundations that are fatally missing from Keynesian and Monetarist I models. But what you gain on the swings you lose on the roundabouts.

Empirically the main challenge to new classical macroeconomics is how to explain as moving *equilibrium* the fluctuations in general economic activity we actually observe. The theory implies that labour 'markets', for example, are in the same equilibrium, cleared by wages and prices, at 11 per cent or 25 per cent unemployment as at 3 per cent or 5 per cent unemployment, with the same balance of supply and demand. On the surface this seems to be refuted by all kinds of evidence, on vacancies, quits, layoffs, hours of work, and wage movements. Moreover, the theory has trouble accounting for the persistence of slumps and booms, rather than serially uncorrelated noisy wobbles around smooth trends (Okun, 1980; Tobin, 1980). The two types of business-cycle theory offered by the school seem equally implausible. One is a completely real model, explaining fluctuations in employment and production as swings in tastes and technologies, evoking decisions to shift the timing of work and leisure. The other, building on Lucas's interpretation of Phillips curve statistics recounted above, finds the origins of fluctuations in unanticipated money supply policies. But these have real consequences only because of inadequacies and asymmetries of information arbitrarily assigned to market participants, and they have cyclical consequences only with the help of further arbitrary assumptions. Whether these are more or less objectionable, more or less *ad hoc*, than the much-criticized Keynesian assumptions of wage and price inertia seems a question more of taste than of principle.

The emphasis of new classical theories on expectations, especially expectations of policy, rather than on inertia, made many economists and policy-makers optimistic about 'credible threat' policies for disinflation (Fellner, 1980). The idea was that government should make clear its determination relentlessly to diminish monetary growth to non-inflationary rates, whatever the consequences for employment and production. If this was understood, it was argued, wage and price inflation would decline much more quickly than in the past, when workers and business managers expected counter-cyclical monetary and fiscal policies to restore their markets. Both Prime Minister Thatcher in the UK and Federal Reserve Chairman Volcker in the USA recently followed this policy. Disinflation occurred all right, but it was no less fraught with painful real consequences than in recessions under prior policy regimes. The 1980s may be as difficult for monetarism as the 1970s were for Keynesianism and the 1930s for old-style neoclassical orthodoxy.

SUPPLY-SIDE ECONOMICS AND FISCAL ORTHODOXY

I turn finally to two other trends in current macroeconomic debate, important both within the profession and without, so-called 'supply-side' economics and old-fashioned fiscal and financial orthodoxy. These are less novel in methodology and more diffuse in content than the identifiable counter-revolutions discussed above. They are renewed emphases of long-standing neoclassical themes, allegedly ignored or underrated in Keynesian and neo-Keynesian macroeconomics.

'Supply-side' economics is not a coherent theory. It has no great book or prophet, no Walras or Keynes or Friedman or Lucas. Its identification as a distinct counter-revolution comes from media enthusiasm for its simplistic label, which suggests that Keynesian macroeconomics went wrong in theory and practice by exclusive attention to the 'demand side'. In the policy debates of the late 1970s and early 1980s, the supply-siders' diagnosis was that government spending, taxes, and regulations were retarding economic growth. Their prescription was to reduce drastically government presence in the economy in all these dimensions. In these conclusions supply-siders agreed with other conservative counter-revolutionaries. However, they disagreed sharply on tactics. While traditional orthodoxy argued for lowering public expenditures and receipts in step, supply-siders proposed to lower taxes first, recognizing that lowering expenditures is more difficult politically and administratively. Sometimes this tactic was rationalized by the judgement that politicians will spend less if they have smaller tax receipts and face large deficits. But more typically supply-siders argued that deficits do not matter very much — a point of view that ironically allied them with Keynesians — and would in any case be removed by the economic growth the tax reductions would stimulate (Ture, 1980; Wanniski, 1975 and 1978).

This claim took the form of the famous Laffer curve, employed to assert that in our overtaxed society lowering tax rates will actually raise revenues. A slightly more modest claim was that the lower rates would evoke enough extra saving to make up for any net loss of tax receipts, so that public sector borrowing requirements would not be greater. These propositions are reminiscent of the more extravagant claims of demand-side pump-primers, not generally accepted in Keynesian analyses of fiscal policy. The supply-siders were, however, relying not on the re-employment of idle resources, but rather on additional economic activity and productivity in full employment equilibrium. The distinction has become blurred in fiscal policy debates in 1982 and 1983, when the economy has been depressed.

Although monetarists generally share supply-siders' aversion to government, supply-siders perceived that monetarist anti-inflation policies could hamper their scenario for economic growth. Specially, recession and high real interest rates could nullify the incentives of 'supply-side' tax cuts for investment, enterprise, risk taking, and work. As this actually happened in 1981–3, supply-siders found further affinity to their Keynesian enemies.

As for disinflation, however, the supply-side alternative to unadulterated monetarism clearly could not be the incomes policies favoured by some Keynesians. Instead, some supply-siders offered the hope that productivity growth stimulated by their tax cuts would do the job, a prospect even less likely than Laffer curve miracles. Their monetary solution was to return to the gold standard, a discipline that was supposed to have the same salutary self-fulfilling effect on expectations as the 'credible threats' of relentless monetary restriction advocated by new classical rational expectations theorists (Mundell, 1981).

Stripped of its more ludicrous cocktail-napkin extravagances, supply-side economics simply emphasizes the familiar incentive and substitution effects dear to standard neoclassical economics and attacks the distortions or dilutions of these effects by taxes, transfer payments, and regulations. Its more sober protagonists describe it as simply 'good microeconomics' (Penner, 1981). Since theorists of all persuasions acknowledge incentive and substitution effects, the main issues are quantitative: are these effects empirically as large as the supply-siders' estimates?

The more sophisticated practitioners of supply-side economics regard it as the application of neoclassical public finance theory. Given the government's programmatic requirements, there is no way to avoid some distortions of price signals. There is no way to collect taxes or make transfers in 'lump sums', that is, in ways that would not give households and businesses some inducements to inefficient tax-avoiding or transfer-increasing behaviour. The problem is to find the 'second-best' welfare economic solution. Some ways of collecting revenues and making transfers and other outlays create fewer distortions than others.

Of course a final judgement cannot be reached without considering distributional effects too. Supply-siders, sometimes explicitly but often implicitly, feel that in the past redistribution has been overemphasized with blind disregard of allocational distortions. Furthermore, they call specific attention to the possibly inadvertent extra distortions caused in the 1970s by the interaction of inflation with tax codes written in nominal dollar terms (Feldstein, 1983).

It is fair to say that Keynesian and neo-Keynesian macroeconomics, in its focus on the massive market failure it attributed to inadequate aggregate demand and to involuntary unemployment of labour and existing capital, underplayed the allocational effects of relative prices, as distorted by taxes and transfers, on labour supply, unemployment, saving, investment, and portfolio choice. But these matters were certainly not entirely ignored (Hall and Tobin, 1955). In the neo-Keynesian neoclassical synthesis, they arose in the context of long-run growth and therefore in the choice of instruments for short-run demand stabilization. It was, after all, the Kennedy administration, in the hey-day of neo-Keynesian influence on policy, which introduced the investment tax credit and lowered top-bracket marginal income tax rates. Likewise neo-Keynesian theorists advocated a mix of fiscal and monetary policies combining tax disincentives to consumption with monetary low-interest incentives to investment, as a means of allocating more resources to capital formation in order to promote long-run growth.

Prior to the coining of the 'supply-side' slogan, revisionist thinking in the same spirit had substantial influence in macroeconomic policy debate. A central issue throughout the 1970s was the upward drift of actual unemployment rates and of the rates apparently consistent with stable inflation. How much unemployment was involuntary and 'Keynesian', how much was voluntary or frictional? A new view arose, which attributed increasing amounts of unemployment to voluntary search or personal choice, influenced by unemployment compensation and other transfer programmes, and by minimum wages and other regulations. In its strongest form, this new view alleged that most unemployment was of short duration, caused little discomfort to the unemployed, and was neither a social problem nor a condition remediable by macroeconomic demand management (Feldstein, 1978, pp. 155–8).

Another revisionist argument challenged the policy-mix recommendation of the mainstream synthesis, and this too stressed the importance of tax distortions magnified by inflation. Residential investment, it was argued, was heavily subsidized by the deductibility of nominal mortgage interest and the freedom from taxation of implicit rental incomes on owner-occupied homes. On the other hand, non-residential investment, much more strategic for economic growth, was penalized by the inadequacy of depreciation allowances and the taxation of purely nominal capital gains on inventories and other assets. Consequently the recommendation was for a tight money policy to control inflation and to deter overinvestment in housing via high real interest rates, accompanied by tax concessions to stimulate saving and fixed business investment (Feldstein, 1980, pp. 182–6).

This recipe was consistent with another proposal, advanced under the supply-side banner. The idea was to pursue a high-interest-rate tight monetary policy in order to appreciate the exchange rate, gaining counter-inflationary headway by lowering the domestic prices of internationally traded goods. This would reduce the country's trade surplus or increase its trade deficit. The compensating increase in demand would be obtained by an 'easy' fiscal policy, achieved by supply-side tax cuts (Mundell, 1975). The troubles with this recipe are several: it is not a game that every country can play; one country's lower prices of traded goods are another country's higher prices. Anyway, the price advantage occurs only once; continuing counter-inflationary help requires continuing appreciation of the currency resulting from an ever-wider interest differential above the rest of the world. Finally, since this policy mix crowds out foreign investment in favour of domestic uses of resources, its effect on the growth of future consumption opportunities is not necessarily favourable.

Fiscal and financial orthodoxy has been a durable opponent of Keynesian theory and policy. It has received a new lease of life in the contemporary climate of disillusionment with government. The focus is on two major points, limiting the size and growth of government and balancing the government budget. Government, it is alleged, tends to become too big because of a bias in the politics of representative democracy. The gains from specific public expenditures, purchases of goods and services or transfers, are concentrated on minorities with intense special interests. The costs are widely diffused, and therefore have inadequate weight in the budgetary process. In legislatures the organized interest groups prevail over the unorganized taxpayers. The costs may be further diffused and disguised by deficit financing, postponing the taxes to future years and future generations or substituting inflation for taxes honestly and explicitly enacted. For these reasons, the orthodox view condemns Keynesian economics for attempting, with considerable success, to eliminate the discipline of the norm of balancing the budget (Buchanan and Wagner, 1977). To restore and solidify the balanced budget norm and to overcome the alleged political bias towards large and growing government are the purposes of constitutional amendments recently proposed, favoured by more than thirty state legislatures and by the US Senate.

A macroeconomic argument against deficit financing is that it 'crowds out' private investment in favour of public and private consumption. This is also an argument against pay-as-you-go social retirement insurance – it replaces private saving without substituting any public saving (Feldstein, 1976). The synthesis agrees that crowding out can be a problem at full employment. Indeed this is the basis for its recommendation of an easy-money-tight-budget policy mix. The orthodox view, however, is not so discriminating as between situations of underemployment and full employment. Keynesians would not worry about 'crowding out' in situations where idle resources are available both for government and private use, and where their re-employment would generate the saving to finance both government deficits and private investment. This is an ancient controversy. During the Great Depression the orthodox economists of the UK Treasury opposed Keynes's public works proposals on the grounds that they would simply substitute public employment for more productive private employment (HM Treasury, 1928-9). The famous 'Treasury View' was echoed in the USA at the time, and it has recurred in every recession, including that of 1981-2.

In this respect fiscal orthodoxy differs from some other strands of contemporary conservative economics. Supply-siders, as already noted, are not so worried about deficits and advocate a bold tax-cutting strategy for stimulating investment. For a different reason, some new classical rational expectations theorists are not at all worried about crowding out. They argue that rational taxpayers will save enough to pay postponed taxes, so that the macroeconomic effect of government expenditures is the same whether they are financed by contemporaneous taxes or by borrowing (Barro, 1974).

OPTIMISTIC CONCLUSION: A NEW SYNTHESIS?

The present disarray of world economies, macroeconomic policies, and macroeconomics itself is certainly disheartening. But I am an optimist at heart, and I feel that the worst is over. The unprecedented shocks that generated economic turmoil in 1966-80 are not likely to be a recurrent feature of the economic environment. In a more benign climate public opinion will not support ideological extremes and simplistic nostrums. Policies will be more pragmatic and more respectful of hard-learned lessons of the past.

Within professional macroeconomics, the slow but trustworthy internal discipline of our science will prevail over our methodological and doctrinal conflicts. The developments I have reviewed here, revolutionary and counter-revolutionary as many of them are, have already inspired serious theoretical and empirical research transcending those divisions. The objectives, common to scholars across the whole spectrum, are to understand and model more satisfactorily the roles of expectations and inertia; the reasons for explicit and implicit contracts and for their absence, and for the inclusion of some contingencies and the neglect of others; the setting of prices and the processes of search in the absence of Walrasian auction markets, and the role of quantity variations in balancing demands and supplies. Eventually, I should think in the 1990s, a new synthesis will replace the present disarray of macroeconomics.

NOTES

1. The seminal article is by Clower (1965); Leijonhufvud (1968); Grossman (1971) and Barro and Grossman (1971) developed the theme. It has been the focus of a group of French theorists, whose prolific work is well summarized in Malinvaud (1978).
2. Notably in two well-read polemics, one by Lucas and Sargent (1978), the other Lucas's review of a book of my own (Lucas, 1981, pp. 558–67).

REFERENCES

Arrow, K. J. (1953) 'Le rôle des valeurs boursières pour la répartition la meilleure des risques', *Econométrie*, Paris. Centre National de la Recherche Scientifique, 41–8.

Barro, R. J. (1974) 'Are Government Bonds Net Wealth?' *Journal of Political Economy*, 82 (November/December): 1095–1117.

Barro, R. J., and H. I. Grossman (1971) 'A General Disequilibrium Model of Income and Employment', *American Economic Review*, 61 (March): 82–93.

Buchanan, J. M., and R. E. Wagner (1977) *Democracy in Deficit*, New York: Academic Press.

Chamberlin, E. M. (1933) *The Theory of Monopolistic Competition*, London: Oxford University Press.

Clower, R. (1965) 'The Keynesian Counter-Revolution: A Theoretical Appraisal', in F. H. Hahn and F. P. R. Brechling (eds), *The Theory of Interest Rates*, London: Macmillan.

Debreu, G. (1959) *The Theory of Value*, New York: John Wiley.

Feldstein, M. (1976) 'Social Security and Savings in the Extended Life-Cycle Theory', *American Economic Review*, 66 (May): 77–86.

Feldstein, M. (1978) 'The Private and Social Costs of Unemployment', *American Economic Review*, 68 (May): 155–8.

Feldstein, M. (1980) 'Tax Rules and the Mismanagement of Monetary Policy', *American Economic Review*, 70 (May): 182–6.

Feldstein, M. (1983) *Inflation, Tax Rules, and Capital Formation*, Chicago: University of Chicago Press.

Fellner, W. (1980) 'The Valid Core of Rationality Hypothesis in the Theory of Expectations', *Journal of Money, Credit, and Banking*, 12 (4) pt 2 (November): 763–87.

Fisher, I. (1911) *The Purchasing Power of Money*, New York: Macmillan.

Friedman, M. (1953) 'The Methodology of Positive Economics', *Essays in Positive Economics*, Chicago: University of Chicago Press, pp. 3–42.

Friedman, M. (1956) 'The Quantity Theory of Money – A Restatement', *Studies in the Quantity Theory of Money*, Chicago: University of Chicago Press, pp. 3–24.

Friedman, M. (1966) 'Interest Rates and the Demand for Money', *Journal of Law and Economics*, 9 (October): 71–86.
Friedman, M. (1968) 'The Role of Monetary Policy', *American Economic Review*, 59 (March): 1–17.
Grossman, H. I. (1971) 'Money, Interest, and Prices in Market Disequilibrium', *Journal of Political Economy*, 79 (September–October): 269–73.
Hahn, F. (1982) *Money and Inflation*, Oxford: Blackwell.
Hall, C. A., and J. Tobin (1955) 'Income Taxation, Output, and Prices', *Economia Internazionale*, 8 (August): 522–38.
Hicks, J. R. (1946) *Value and Capital*, 2nd edn, Oxford: Oxford University Press.
HM Treasury (1928–9). *Memoranda on Certain Proposals Relating to Unemployment*, reports of the Minister of Labour and of the Treasury, Command Paper no. 3331, Parliamentary Accounts and Papers, 1928–9, vol. XVI, pp. 1–15 and 43–54.
Holtzman, F. D. (1950) 'Income Determination in Open Inflation', *Review of Economics and Statistics*, 32 (May): 150–8.
Kareken, J. H., and N. Wallace (eds), (1980) *Money of Monetary Economics*, Federal Reserve Bank of Minneapolis.
Keynes, J. M. (1936) *The General Theory of Employment, Interest, and Money*, London: Macmillan.
Keynes, J. M. (1940) *How to Pay for the War*, New York: Harcourt, Brace.
Koopmans, T. (1942) 'The Dynamics of Inflation', *Review of Economics and Statistics*, 24 (May): 53–65.
Leijonhufvud, A. (1968) *On Keynesian Economics and the Economics of Keynes: A Study in Monetary Theory*, Oxford: Oxford University Press.
Lucas, R. E. (1972) 'Econometric Testing of the Natural Rate Hypothesis', in O. Eckstein (ed.), *The Econometrics of Price Determination: Conference, October 30-31, 1970*, Washington: Board of Governors of the Federal Reserve System, pp. 50–9.
Lucas, R. E. (1981) 'Tobin and Monetarism: A Review Article', *Journal of Economic Literature*, 19 (June): 558–67.
Lucas, R. E., and T. Sargent (1978) 'After Keynesian Macroeconomics', in *After the Phillips Curve: The Persistence of High Unemployment and High Inflation*, Boston: Federal Reserve Bank of Boston.
Malinvaud, E. (1978) *The Theory of Unemployment Reconsidered*, Oxford: Oxford University Press.
Mundell, R. A. (1975) 'Inflation from an International Viewpoint', in D. I. Meiselman and A. B. Laffer (eds), *The Phenomenon of Worldwide Inflation*, Washington: American Enterprise Institute, pp. 141–52.
Mundell, R. A. (1981) 'Gold Would Serve into the 21st Century', *Wall Street Journal*, 198 (30 September): 28.
Okun, A. (1980) 'Rational-Expectations-with-Misperceptions as a Theory of the Business Cycle', *Journal of Money, Credit, and Banking*, 12 (4) pt 2 (November): 817–25.
Patinkin, D. (1955) *Money, Interest, and Prices: An Integration of Monetary and Value Theory*, Evanston, Ill.: Row, Peterson.
Penner, R. (1981) 'Policies Affecting Savings and Investment', in *Proceedings of the Colloquium on Alternatives for Economic Policy*, New York: Conference Board.

Phelps, E. (1967) 'Phillips Curves, Expectations of Inflation, and Optimal Unemployment over Time', *Economica*, 34 (August): 254–81.

Phillips, A. W. (1958) 'The Relations between Unemployment and the Rate of Change of Money Wage Rates in the United Kingdom, 1861–1957', *Economica*, 25 (November): 283–99.

Robinson, J. (1933) *The Economics of Imperfect Competition*, London: Macmillan.

Samuelson, P. A. (1947) *Foundations of Economic Analysis*, Cambridge, Mass.: Harvard University Press.

Samuelson, P. A., and R. M. Solow (1960) 'Analytical Aspects of Anti-Inflation Policy', *American Economic Review*, 50 (May): 177–94.

Shove, G. F. (1930) 'The Representative Firm and Increasing Returns', *Economic Journal*, 40 (March): 94–116.

Smith, A. (1776) *The Wealth of Nations*, New York: E. P. Dutton.

Smithies, A. (1942) 'The Behavior of Money National Income under Inflationary Conditions', *Quarterly Journal of Economics*, 57 (November): 113–28.

Sonnenschein, H. (1973) 'The Utility Hypothesis and Market Demand Theory', *Western Economic Journal*, 11 (December): 404–10.

Sraffa, P. (1926) 'The Laws of Returns under Competitive Conditions', *Economic Journal*, 36 (December): 535–50.

Tobin, J. (1965) 'Money and Economic Growth', *Econometrica*, 33 (October): 671–84.

Tobin, J. (1967) 'The Cruel Dilemma', in A. Phillips (ed.), *Price Issues in Theory, Practice, and Policy*, Philadelphia: University of Pennsylvania Press.

Tobin, J. (1980) 'Are New Classical Models Plausible Enough to Guide Policy?' *Journal of Money, Credit, and Banking*, 12 (4) pt 2 (November): 788–99.

Ture, N. (1980) Testimony before the US Congress, Joint Economic Committee, 21 May 1980.

Walras, L. (1874) *Eléments d'économie politique pure*, Lausanne: Corbaz.

Wanniski, J. (1975) 'The Mundell–Laffer Hypothesis', *The Public Interest*, 39 (Spring): 31–52.

Wanniski, J. (1978) *The Way the World Works: How Economies Fail and Succeed*, New York: Basic Books.

Young, A. A. (1930) in R. T. Ely (ed.), *Outlines of Economics*, New York: Macmillan, pp. 562–3.

3 Distributive Justice and Desirable Ends of Economic Activity

KENNETH J. ARROW

JUSTICE, EQUALITY, AND FREEDOM

It is no part of economics, certainly not of modern post-1870 economics, to argue the purpose of the economy's production.[1] The purpose of the economy is the welfare of the consumers, public and private. In no sense is mere production as such a proper measure, rather, it has to be production for the ends that people want. Output, income, and consumption are important aims and preconditions for achieving other goals of individuals; that is, they are only a part of what people live for.

The multifarious goals of economic policy are drawn from both inside and outside the economic sphere (some of the latter are national security, quality of urban life, health, and internal order and personal security). The so-called endogenous goals (perhaps defined as those for which the market is or could be used as a detailed allocative instrument) also range over a wide gamut. However, most of them can be classified under three broad headings: (i) economic stability, (ii) efficient resource allocation, and (iii) distribution; though, of course, these three have many points of interaction and overlap.

By economic stability, I mean the problems associated with unemployment and inflation, with maintaining the utilization of labour and other resources at a high level, and keeping prices fairly steady.

Efficient resource allocation is designed to insure that the resources utilized are used most productively, taking account of all social and private uses; in particular, this includes an appropriate growth policy, balancing present against future needs.

There are at least two aspects of the distribution that are of special concern. One is distribution by use; that is, private and public consumption and accumulation (capital formation). The other is the distribution of income by size — the fact that some people receive more goods than others. This is the outcome of the economic system that is judged by the criterion of equality. If existing distribution is for some reason or another considered to be inequitable, the problems of redistribution are those of increasing the income of some groups and decreasing that of others on the basis of poverty, age, occupation, or other criteria.

The use of taxing power to achieve a redistribution of income has been increasing over time in a marked way. Popular support of this doctrine has also tended to increase, though with much ebb and flow. The philosophical and ethical foundations of redistribution have come under sharp debate in intellectual and academic circles as well. Economists, after much neglect, have revived their interest in the axioms that underlie the distribution and redistribution of income. Arguments I find convincing imply that the desirable income distribution will be more nearly equal than that which would be yielded by the natural workings of the market system. I regard equality of income as desirable, other things being equal. It can be objected that the drive for equality may dull incentives, and the net result will be a reduction in everyone's real income. This is a legitimate instrumental objection, but not an objection to the value presumption in favour of equality as such.

Economists have tended to evaluate the performance of the economy in terms of efficiency and much less so in terms of distributive justice, not surprisingly since here the deepest philosophical issues are at stake.

Every advanced and dynamic society needs a concept of justice, by which I mean what Aristotle termed distributive justice, more specifically justice in the allocation of goods and services. In a static world, when things are as they have always been, questions about justice are not raised in people's minds. In other cultures, religion attempts to provide an explanation.

However successful religion may be at times in supplying a rationalization for the existing distribution of goods in the broadest sense of the term, it is not adequate to a world in which changes occur as a result of human design. For one thing, the religious scheme of rewards and punishments does not distinguish between the effects of nature and those of society.

The modern world owes its greatest successes to rational thought and precision of observation which distinguish different causal factors for different kinds of events. The benefits and costs yielded by the economic system are rather plainly the outcomes of human and social actions. Not only are the immediate givers of rewards other human beings, but, more importantly, the institutions and rules that govern the allocation of goods are themselves clearly of human origin.

When the rules of the social game are a matter of human choice they are open to criticism. As such, it is surprising that the political process in democratic countries has not thrown up sharper attacks on the distribution of income. Power in one form or another is part of the explanation but cannot be the whole story. There is also still a belief that the operations of the economic and political system must of necessity be more or less right and just, a belief that I take to derive from a fundamentally religious attitude, at once a hangover from the past and an expression of man's continued need to find comfort and security in a world made increasingly alienated and disenchanted by the increase of knowledge.

Justice now appears as a problem. What happens in the economic world can be judged and possibly found wanting. In the modern world, we no longer say, 'what is must necessarily be right'. But what are the standards of justice? And, what are the social mechanisms for bringing it about?

Since justice became an issue recognised as subject to debate, we have had the benefit of consideration by the best of minds, with no strong consensus emerging. To consider the European tradition only, Plato, Aristotle, Thomas Aquinas, Moses Maimonides, Immanuel Kant, and John Stuart Mill have expressed their widely varying views. Perhaps the most important recent intellectual event in the area of distributive justice has been the publication of John Rawls's *A Theory of Justice*, which has drawn together many threads into a grand synthesis and was followed by attacks on Rawls and on the desirability of equality in general by Irving Kristol, Robert Nisbet, and others and by the elaboration by Robert Nozick of the entitlement theory of justice which is designed in particular to undermine the view that the state or something like it is needed to ensure redistribution of property in the name of justice.

Though I disagree with many specific parts of Rawls's analysis, I find myself in strong agreement with his broad thrust and basic presuppositions. One basic element in his analysis is that justice values both liberty and equality. It is often held that these two ideals are basically in contradiction. But in fact the opposite is true. Neither aim is realizable without the other. For liberty to be an aim that is justifiable on broad philosophical grounds, it must mean liberty for all and in all the relevant dimensions. In particular, one of the most powerful constraints on an individual's freedom of action and choice is the size of his budget. His income determines his freedom to choose his consumption pattern or to shift to jobs that are pleasanter or more rewarding personally. Inequality of income implies that for many the freedom to choose consumption and jobs is restricted while a few enjoy broad freedom. The limitations of liberty without equality have been expressed with keen irony by the French writer, Anatole France: 'The law in its majestic equality forbids the rich as well as the poor from sleeping on park benches.'

The price system does not provide within itself any defensible income distribution, and this is a key drawback. In fact, the price system tends to obscure the fact that low income is a restriction on freedom. The individual consumer does, in fact, have the freedom of choosing his consumption within the limitations of his budget, and I would agree that this freedom is far from trivial. But the average consumer and the observer of the allocation process are apt to exaggerate this freedom and ignore the fundamental restriction on the consumer's opportunities implied by poverty.

Income inequality also constrains freedom in dimensions other than economic. Political freedom, the freedom to express one's views meaningfully and to reach others, depends on the availability of goods. Especially in large political systems, the diffusion of ideas is costly in terms of resources. Thus, political ideas acceptable to the rich have a greater chance of success. Further, a market develops in which the wealthy supply funds for political operations and receive specific favours in addition to general political agreement. Hence, even in societies where formal guarantees of political freedom are in force, an equalization of income will increase the political freedom of the lower-income groups.

In every social system individuals can achieve satisfactions for themselves by other than economic means. Among these are power relations of one kind or another. Certainly if equality of income is important for the achievement of liberty, equality of power is even more so. Indeed, the exercise of power is by definition a limitation on the liberty of others. Absence of freedom for some usually means greater concentration of power in the hands of others. Certainly China and Cuba do not represent ideal egalitarian societies though they have to some extent achieved considerable equalization of income and material goods. But clearly all the basic decisions of the society are made in very small self-perpetuating circles. Sophisticated qualifications, important as they are, should not draw attention away from the simple basic idea that inequalities of income and of power are in and of themselves constraints on the achievement of freedom for all.

THE MARKET AND INCOME DISTRIBUTION: THE TRADE-OFF
BETWEEN EFFICIENCY AND EQUITY

There is indeed a strong argument for competitive price-setting and for
freedom of entry into business as a contribution to efficiency in the
allocation of resources. But while a market economy excels in generating
productive efficiency, no social institution has ever felt justified solely by
material product. Moreover, the inequalities in the distribution of this
material wealth and in the power and control over the activities by which
it is created constitute a steady indictment. As noted, the market in no
way prescribes a just distribution of income and the idealization of freedom through the market fully disregards that for many relatively poor
people this freedom is circumscribed indeed.

Take the extreme, but nevertheless realistic, case of famines in underdeveloped countries, or of hunger associated with poverty. In a free-
enterprise economy every good or service has a price, and each economic
agent starts out by owning some goods or services. The rice farmer owns
some land, used for producing rice, which can then be sold on the market
at the going price or reserved for use by the farmer and his family. The
receipts from sales can be spent on other goods — different goods, spices,
clothing, and so forth. The agricultural labourer has only his or her labour
to sell; the proceeds can be spent on rice or other goods. Similarly, the
cities contain workers who sell labour for money to buy food, shelter, and
clothing, and entrepreneurs who buy goods and labour, produce other
goods, sell them, and have the proceeds for personal consumption and
investment in business expansion. People will starve, then, when their
entitlement is not sufficient to buy the food necessary to keep them alive.
The food available to them, in short, is a question of income distribution
and, more fundamentally, of their ability to provide services that others in
the economy are willing to pay for.

Modern neoclassical general equilibrium theory provides a rigorous
statement of the usefulness and limitations of the market as a mechanism
for efficient allocation of resources and, to some extent, can be used to
argue that the goals of efficiency and equity can be separated, that any
distribution deemed equitable can be achieved without loss of efficiency.

It is useful to review the problems of reconciling efficiency and equity
in intratemporal and intertemporal contexts. Here we concentrate on the
former while relegating the latter to a later section of this chapter. Doubtless the answers to the conceptual questions of what is meant by efficiency
and what is meant by equity will always be controversial as long as tensions
between the demands of individuals and society will prevail.

Efficiency and equity are both judgements, statements of preference about allocations of resources. The allocation as a whole must be feasible, that is, there must be a balance between commodities used and commodities available, and it must be consistent with the available technological knowledge. There are in general many possible feasible allocations of resources. Allocations to different uses may be inefficient; that is, it may be that by shifting resources among different uses more of every commodity can be produced.

Another aspect of efficiency is the full employment of resources, and particularly, of course, the full employment of labour. If there are idle people, or idle machines for that matter, there is prima facie evidence of inefficiency in the system. Full employment is one of the goals where equity and efficiency do not generally conflict. Because income is usually tied to employment and it is typically the poorest part of the working population that is unemployed, full employment, by increasing their income, reduces inequality.

A more subtle sense of efficiency is the definition by Pareto. Assume each individual to be a competent judge of his needs and wants; then he wants to achieve as high a level of satisfaction as possible. An allocation is said to be dominated in the sense of Pareto if there is another feasible allocation which will make everybody better off. An allocation then is said to be Pareto efficient if it is not dominated by any feasible allocation. To be Pareto efficient, an allocation must clearly be efficient in the production of commodities, but it must also be true that among the commodities that are produced there can be no further exchange among the individuals in the economy which will make them all better off. The only ambiguity in this definition, is the meaning of 'better off'. I will confine myself to the individualistic interpretation: each individual is to be the judge of when he or she is better off, so that we respect individual decisions in the market and in voting.

As can be seen in my chapter in the companion volume to this book (Chapter 2), modern general equilibrium theory teaches the extent to which a social allocation of resources can be achieved by independent private decisions co-ordinated through the market, provided that some significant conditions are met. We are assured indeed that not only can an allocation be achieved, but the result will be Pareto efficient. But there is nothing in the process that guarantees that the distribution be just.

Given the way resources are distributed initially, including primarily human resources, abilities, training and the like, and also property, the system prescribes, through some very elaborate and indirect methods, how they are to be valued. There is no simple argument, and there are few economists who would defend the proposition that there is a simple argument, which states that the resulting distribution of income has any special claim to be called just. Pareto efficiency in no way implies distributive justice. An allocation of resources could be efficient in a Pareto sense and yet yield enormous riches to some and dire poverty to others.

Indeed, the theory teaches us that the final allocation will depend on the distribution of initial supplies and of ownership of firms. If we want to rely on the virtues of the market but also to achieve a more just distribution, the theory suggests the strategy of changing the initial distribution rather than interfering with the allocation process at some later stage.

Pareto optimality is a very useful concept in clearing away a whole realm of possible decisions that are not compatible with any reasonable distributional judgements. It has turned out also be be useful in characterizing sharply the types of institutional arrangements that lead to efficient solutions, making it possible to isolate the debate on distributive problems that it cannot solve.

DISTRIBUTIVE IMPLICATIONS OF SOCIAL CHOICE

In the prescription of economic policy normative questions of distributive justice inevitably arise. The implicit ethical basis of economic policy judgement is some version of utilitarianism. At the same time, descriptive economics has relied heavily on a utilitarian psychology in explaining the choices made by consumers and other economic agents. The above-mentioned basic theorem of welfare economics: that, under certain conditions, the competitive economic system yields an outcome that is optimal or efficient (in a sense which requires careful definition), depends on the identification of the utility structures that motivate the choices made by economic agents with the utility structures used in judging the optimality of the outcome of the competitive system. As a result, the utility concepts which, in one form or another, underlie welfare judgements in economics have been subjected to an intensive scrutiny. There has been more emphasis on their operational meaning, but perhaps less on their specific content. Philosophers have been more prone to analyse what individuals should want, where economists have been content to identify 'should' with 'is' for the individual (not for society).

The hedonistic psychology essential to Jeremy Bentham's utilitarianism has dominated modern economic analysis, especially in the form of neoclassical and Austrian economic thinking, as originated by W. Stanley Jevons, Carl Menger, and Léon Walras between 1871 and 1874. In this doctrine, the act of choice becomes entwined with evaluation and judgement. What is chosen must have been preferred; and what is preferred must be in some sense better. These simple remarks have given rise to a vast literature on the structure of decision and value, both individual and social, and on their relations. Though we have been taught to distinguish sharply between the 'is' and 'should', the logical analysis of decisions tends to blur the lines between them. The distinction can, and in my judgement should, be kept, but it requires great clarity of thought to do so. Needless to say, matters are not made easier by the analyst's being also a human being who is being analysed.

The problem of social choice is the aggregation of the multiplicity of individual preference scales about alternative social actions. The individual plays a central role in social choice as the judge of alternative social actions according to his own standards. We presume that each individual has some way of ranking social actions according to his preferences for the consequences. These preferences constitute his value system. They are assumed to reflect already in full measure altruistic or egoistic motivations, as the case may be.

The aim of the theory of social choice is to provide a normative rationale for making social decisions when the individual members of the society have varying opinions about or interests in the alternatives available. Any kind of decision, social or individual, can be regarded as the interaction of the preferences or desires of the decision-maker with the range of alternative decisions actually available to him — the opportunity set. The latter may vary from time to time because of changes in the wealth or technology of the community. The usual formalism of social welfare theory, derived from economic theory, is that preferences (or tastes or values) are first expressed for all logically possible alternatives. Then the most preferred is chosen from any given opportunity set. There is a serious and unresolved dispute about the strength of the statements that it is appropriate to make about preferences.

The theory of social choice, as it has developed in the last thirty years, but with earlier history reaching back into the eighteenth century, seeks to analyse the concept of rational choice as it extends from the individual to a collectivity.

Narrowly construed, the scope of the theory is the analysis of the conditions under which some mechanism or rule can be found that permits a collectivity (government, social organization, labour union, business) to arrive at decisions which, in some way or another, reflect the decisions desired by its members. It is therefore a normative theory of elections and legislative choices.

More broadly, it can be interpreted to provide one aspect of any normative judgement about interpersonal relations which is based, in some measure, on the satisfaction of individual needs. A theory of justice, such as Rawls's, in which the truth-value of a proposition of the form 'state x is just' or, still more in the spirit of the theory, 'state x is more just than state y', depends on the truth-values of propositions of the form 'state x is better for individual i than state y', or 'state x is fairer to individual i than state y', for each individual i, is an example of social choice falling within the purview of the general theory.

Unfortunately, the search for some kind of objective criterion can surely be said to have been inconclusive for reasons intrinsic to the logic of the subject. The root facts here are the incommensurability and incomplete communicability of human wants and values. The social optimum, as in the determination of a just income distribution, is an abstraction of some kind from the individual values of the members of society. But this abstraction can only be based on interpersonally observed behaviour, as in market purchases or voting, not on the full range of an individual's feelings. As is by now well known, attempts to form social judgements by aggregating individual expressed preferences always lead to the possibility of paradox.

To recapitulate, each individual may be assumed to have a preference ordering over all possible social states. This ordering expresses not only his desire for his own consumption but also social attitudes, his views on justice in distribution or on benefits to others from collective decisions. The ordinalist viewpoint forbids us from ascribing a definite quantitative expression to this preference, at least a quantitative expression that would have any interpersonal validity.

Classical utilitarianism specifies that alternative actions be judged in terms of their consequences for people, or, in our terminology, in terms of the individual preference scales for social choices. This by itself does not supply a sufficient basis for action in view of the multiplicity and divergence of individual preference scales. It is therefore at least implicit in classical utilitarianism that there is a second level at which the individual judgements are themselves evaluated (explicitly recognized in Bergson's 1938 paper), called a welfare judgement; it is an evaluation of the consequences to all individuals based on their evaluations.

The process of formation of welfare judgements is logically equivalent to a social decision process or constitution. Specifically, a constitution is a rule that associates to each possible set of individual orderings a social choice function, that is, a rule for selecting a preferred action out of every possible environment. That a welfare judgement is a constitution indeed follows immediately from the assumption that a welfare judgement can be formed given any set of individual preference systems for social actions. The classification of welfare judgements as consitutions is at this stage a tautology, but what makes it more than that is a specification of reasonable conditions to be imposed on constitutions, and it is here that any dispute must lie.

The following four conditions are suggested as reasonable to impose on any constitution: (i) collective rationality – for any given set of orderings, the social choice function is derivable from an ordering; that is, the social choice system has the same structure as that assumed for individual value systems, (ii) Pareto principle – if alternative x is preferred to alternative y by every single individual according to his ordering, then the social ordering also ranks x above y, (iii) independence of irrelevant alternatives – the social choice made from any environment depends only on the orderings of individuals with respect to the alternatives in that environment; and (iv) non-dictatorship – there is no individual whose preferences are automatically society's preferences independent of the preferences of all other individuals, probably the least controversial of all the conditions.

There is a difference between the first two conditions and the last two that is worth noting. The assumptions of (i) and (ii) are statements that apply to any fixed set of individual orderings. They do not involve comparisons between social orderings based on different sets of individual orderings. On the contrary, (iii) and (iv) are assertions about the responsiveness of the social ordering to variations in individual orderings.

As I have shown in *Social Choice and Individual Values*, these four reasonable-sounding requirements are contradictory. That is, if we devise any constitution, then it is always possible to find a set of individual orderings that will cause the constitution to violate one of these conditions. In one special form, this paradox is old. The method of majority voting is an appealing method of social choice. Like any other voting method, it satisfies (iii), (ii), and (iv). But, as Condorcet pointed out as far back as 1785, majority voting may not lead to an ordering. More specifically, intransitivity is possible. Consider the following example. There are three alternatives, x, y, and z, among which choice is to be made. One-third of the voters have the ranking x, y, z; one-third, the ranking y, z, x; and one-third, the ranking z, x, y. Then a majority of the voters prefer x to y, a majority prefer y to z, and a majority prefer z to x. Unfortunately, this result is not due to a removable imperfection in the method of majority voting.

Thus the main results of the theory so far have been negative. That is, if we impose some reasonable-sounding conditions on the process of forming social choices from individual preferences, it can be demonstrated that there are no processes that will always satisfy those conditions. Most recent research has been devoted to seeking ways of overcoming this difficulty. Although there is no thoroughly satisfactory resolution, and there probably can never be a truly all-embracing one, some of the recent contributions are illuminating and very likely hopeful.

THE CASE FOR REDISTRIBUTION

Whatever the state of theory, the issue of income redistribution faces some fundamental questions:

(1) Is equality in some appropriate sense the meaning of distributive justice?

(2) What is meant by just or equal distribution of income, power, and other economic goods?

(3) Are there other legitimate and important social aims that might conflict with justice and how are the trade-offs to be evaluated?

(4) What is a just allocation of goods among individuals of different generations?

(5) To what extent does the nature of capitalism, its institutions, its functioning, or its ideology facilitate or inhibit the achievement of justice?

These five very large questions cannot be answered with any degree of definitiveness and precision. Let me state my position bluntly. I believe strongly in the fundamental desirability of equality and even a fairly rigid version of it with regard to income. But I must confess that I cannot define the exact meaning of equality. But this lack of definiteness need not prevent discussion of the broad issues.

(1) A recurrent theme of conservative opinion over the centuries has been a denial that equality is a significant attribute of justice or a desirable end of policy. In making the case for equality, a brief explicit statement of some of the arguments implied in the previous section is in order. Any society, democratic or not, must have as a root element some degree of mutual obligation and some sense of respect for every individual, however low he may wind up in the hierarchy. A principle of justice or morality is, by its nature, universalizable; an individual cannot defend an allocation of goods to himself unless others benefit similarly from this policy. This is the essence of Kant's categorical imperative.

The argument has been given modern form in the notion of the 'original position' as developed by William Vickerey and John Harsanyi and the philosopher John Rawls. To make concrete the concept of an impersonal judgement, they introduce the fiction of an 'original position', in which each individual knows all the possible conditions he or she can be in the society but does not know which particular condition he himself will have. The term 'condition' refers to both inherent personal endowment, the individual's capacities and values, and to the social rewards to be received. In the original position, we may imagine the members of the society considering alternative social arrangements for resource allocation. Because of the symmetry of their positions, all would agree in their preferences; hence, they would arrive at a mutually beneficial contract.

The contract would be in effect an arrangement for mutual insurance and have the same advantages. If a group of individuals have the same uncertain prospects, they will each prefer a situation in which beforehand they agree to share their fortunes; those who gain relatively will give up some of their winnings to those who lose relatively. This argument, to be sure, presupposes that individuals may be presumed averse to the bearing of risks; but this is surely a safe assumption.

The insurance contract thus leads to an equalization of income. This contract and its outcome are purely questions of prudence. We may similarly presume that in the original position, where the uncertainties are the whole outcomes of a life, the individuals would find it prudent and desirable to enter into a mutual insurance agreement, to redistribute the incomes they would subsequently receive to make them more nearly equal.

The fiction of the original position is designed to bring out the ethical judgements. What would be a question of prudence, of the self-interest of each in an original position, is interpreted in the actual world as a moral judgement, as the content of justice. Thus, the original-position argument shows that the impersonality that characterizes moral judgement implies that the content of that judgement is an equalization of outcomes. There is considerable room for differences in the precise interpretation of equality. Vickery and Harsanyi have tended to a view close to that of classical utilitarianism, a position from which Rawls has sought to distinguish himself. But I would judge that the similarities are much more important than the differences; all tend to lead to the moral obligation to redistribute income and other goods more equally.

There is one very important implication of any view that starts from the impersonality and symmetry of welfare judgements. The assets of the society, its productive wealth, are to be thought of as a common pool available to achieve the ends of individuals in society, including the ends of justice. The holding of property cannot be regarded as an absolute. It may be defended on instrumental grounds, as a useful device for creating incentives, but redistribution of existing property is also a legitimate procedure if it serves the ends of justice.

Clearly the argument for equality of outcome does not depend on any assumption that individuals have equal ability or even the assumption that they would have roughly equal abilities if environmental conditions were equalized.

(2) Basically there seem to be two versions of equality: the productivity principle (that an individual is entitled to what he creates) and the redistributionist principle (that even natural advantages and superiorities do not in themselves create any claims to greater rewards). In practice these versions are not completely incompatible.

It will be usually accepted that the competitive system does not work perfectly and therefore individuals do not receive their marginal productivities; in that case some degree of redistribution would be called for in theory even under the productivity principle. But a redistributionist position would not permit accepting an inegalitarian outcome of the market even if it perfectly reflected marginal productivity. An impersonal criterion leads naturally to a redistributionist principle. In the original position, productivities are not known; therefore, rational insurance calls for rewards independent of productivity. In any case, the marginal productivity reward system can never be strictly maintained. The most significant redistributive system in any society is the family. Another is recognition of classes of individuals incapable of earning an income and therefore entitled to support by others, either through private charity or through the government.

I would further argue that the productivity principle is not just even among members of the labour force, for two reasons: (i) the marginal product of an individual or of his or her talents or property depends usually on the quantities of complementary or substitute factors, hence, on a context for which the individual is in no way responsible. (ii) Even one's natural talents cannot be regarded as deserved, certainly not to the extent that they are genetic or acquired as a result of particular familial or educational influences.

The first argument appears to me to be uncontroversial. It is part of the general principle that the social context always plays an important role in productivity or indeed in any accomplishment and the individual is always formed by the society. Hence, an individual never has a clearly just claim to any outcome. The second is admittedly less clear-cut. Nevertheless, it is my strong view that inequality in the possession of natural productive assets simply creates a moral obligation on the part of the better endowed to use their talents for the common good.

(3) The conflict between incentive and equity occurs in a utilitarian framework and was already noted by Edgeworth who took the utilitarian philosophy very seriously and developed its implications at considerable length. It is perfectly obvious in his writings that he was very conservative and did not like equality at all, but he found himself driven by his logic to deducing egalitarian concepts of income distribution that were quite unpleasant to him. He then proceeded to blunt his implication on the matter by inventing all sorts of ingenious counter-arguments. But he was an honest man and did not suppress these results.

Rawls is inexplicit about the incentive effects of redistribution. I share his view that equality of outcome is a condition of justice, but I depart from him on efficiency which I believe is also worth achieving. Making everyone better off is good even if some are made better off than others. Even making the great majority better off is desirable if sufficiently few are hurt.

Efficiency is used as a justification for some inequality to the extent that it is necessary to offer incentives to elicit superior performance. To some extent this justifies rewarding talents. But one must distinguish between rentals and necessary incentives. A talent that the individual will wish to supply in any case need not be rewarded. It is not necessary to reward the extraordinarily able scholar or artist more than the mediocre one. But it may be necessary to compensate them for the income they have lost during the educational process. Thus the incentive considerations do have the effect of moving the income distribution somewhat in the direction of productivity but not entirely, and the inequalities created by the needs for incentives are by no means identical with those implied by the productivity principle.

In the actual capitalist world it is surely true that not all incomes represent necessary incentive payments. Particularly, most very high incomes do not reflect productivity at all or are rents. How can the capitalist system yield payments not justified by productivity? Competition is supposed to wipe such payments out. Monopolistic elements are one possible answer and uncertainty is another.

(4) As noted before, the efficiency and equity trade-off has both intratemporal and intertemporal implications. One of the most difficult questions in allocative justice is the distribution of wealth over generations. To what extent is one generation obligated to save so as to increase the welfare of the next generation? The traditional economic problem has been the general act of investment in productive land, machines, and buildings which produce goods in the future; more recently, we have become especially concerned with preservation of undisturbed environments and natural resources. The most straightforward utilitarian answer

is that the utilities of future generations enter equally with those of the present. But since the present generation is a very small part of the total number of individuals over a horizon easily measurable in thousands of years, the policy conclusion would be that virtually everything should be saved and very little consumed, a conclusion that seems offensive to common sense.

Initially we assume that growth basically results from capital accumulation. Then, the greater the capital accumulation, the faster is the rate of growth. Clearly this process cannot continue indefinitely; eventually the rate of growth is constrained by labour and other fixed factors. But an increase in capital accumulation can increase growth for a relatively long period.

The conflicts between equity and efficiency in intertemporal and intratemporal redistributions differ in one important aspect. Usually we think of the latter as reducing total product by reducing incentives. Redistribution from the present to the future, however, is typically productive, so that a transfer from an earlier to a later generation means, in general, that the later generation receives more (measured in commodity units) than the earlier generation gave up. In this case our egalitarian presuppositions are somewhat upset; clearly if we have any regard at all for the future generations (as justice demands) and if the gain from waiting is sufficiently great, then we will want to sacrifice some for the benefit of future individuals even if they are, to begin with, somewhat better off than we are.

There are, however, two offsetting considerations: (i) Since present investments tend to make future individuals better off than present ones, the redistribution is from the present poor to the future rich. To minimize this adverse redistribution, the rate of return required on investments for the future should be higher, the higher is the rate of growth. (ii) The assertion of a criterion of maximizing a sum of discounted utilities, in which the utilities of future generations are given successively smaller weights. The foundations of such a criterion seem arbitrary, though the implications of such policies seem to be more in accordance with common sense and practice.

No individual living today can really regard individuals living in the distant future as being equivalent to himself. Indeed, if benefits for all future generations were counted equally, the value of the present would dwindle into insignificance. If we consistently refuse to discount the future, then a current generation should reduce itself to subsistence levels if there is any positive return on investment, no matter how small.

Thus a rough consensus is that a future investment ought to be made if and only if the productivity of the investment is at least as great as the sum of two countervailing effects: the pure futurity or discount effect and an allowance for the greater income of future generations. I will call this statement the Investment Criterion.

Here we relax the initial assumption that capital accumulation is the basic engine of growth. In fact, much of modern economic growth results from technological advances that are largely independent of the usual form of capital accumulation. Hence the future generations may well be richer even if no investment were made today and the argument for restricting redistribution to the future is strengthened.

Typically we argue that public investment should be governed by the Investment Criterion. But actual public investments are not necessarily so governed and neither are private investments. Indeed, if concern for the future is considered social rather than individual in nature, we would expect individuals to save and invest less than the Investment Criterion requires.

Our simple model is further complicated by the fact that individuals live over time and are concerned about the futures of their families. Hence individuals as well as society have some reason to save or invest for the future. Their behaviour in this regard is indeed parallel to that of the social sector, and they may come up with a rather similar criterion. To the extent that this is true, we may suppose that the market will lead to something like a just and efficient intertemporal allocation. The theoretical argument might suggest some underinvestment in the future: optimal investment might be more than would be sustained by the preferences of individuals for their own future and for that of their children. And a more serious question may be that of imperfections of the capital market. In a world of uncertainty, borrowing cannot necessarily reach the optimal levels. In particular, borrowing for human capital formation, as in education or for development of new technologies, is likely to be restricted, and the government intervention for these purposes has been well argued.

Classical redistributive policy through the tax system affects efficiency and growth. The first, and perhaps most important, negative effect is the reduced efficiency of the economic system which also affects growth. The loss of potential income means both that there is less available for capital accumulation and that the capital accumulated is used less efficiently. Hence the economy is on a permanently lower level, and perhaps the growth rate is lowered.

A second problem arises out of the redistribution itself. It appears that savings by individuals are likely to rise more than proportionately with income. Hence total personal savings will fall as a result of redistribution. Further, to the extent that redistributive taxes fall on the business institutions that form such a large part of the saving mechanism, there may again be a reduction in saving. The income, concentrated in fewer places and therefore easier to use for saving, is now scattered. In a world of perfect capital markets, this redistribution from firms to individuals would make no difference, but internal financing by firms is to a large extent precisely a compensation for imperfect capital markets. Hence the aggregate volume of capital formation may fall as a result of redistribution. However, there are compensating factors in the form of recipients of the redistributed income who now have greater incentives to save and better access to capital markets and in the form of increased ability of lower-income individuals to engage in types of capital formation not handled well through the market, in particular human capital formation.

On the whole, taxation-financed redistribution will probably lower aggregate saving, but it might redirect part of it into higher-return activities. However, such a policy will in general have a positive effect in reducing the future inequality of income. On the high-income side, taxation will reduce the concentration of wealth. If they are taxed the rich will in general reduce both consumption and saving. Hence to the extent that income inequality is perpetuated by inheritance, the same policies that redistribute wealth today will reduce inequality tomorrow. On the low-income side, inheritance can make no significant contribution to improving the income of the next generation of poor. But the subsidies will be used for human capital formation — in the sense of improved household environment and education — thus affecting income tomorrow.

Different types of taxes can be used to finance redistribution. The ordinary income tax, despite its merits, distorts the choice between labour and leisure, but this is probably unavoidable in any tax system. It imposes a double taxation on saving by taxing both saved income and the return on that saving. The seriousness of the resulting distortion might be considerable. It can be avoided by shifting to progressive taxes on total consumption which, in addition, from the redistributionist point of view, will have the virtue of taxing consumption derived from gifts and inheritances, which are effectively taxed at much lower rates. However, annual taxes on wealth will still be necessary to prevent a concentration of wealth among the thrifty rich. The rate can be low enough to minimize disincentives to save for the purpose of future consumption, while the annual repetition of the tax over a long period will be a disincentive to wealth accumulation for the sake of power.

On the whole, though income redistribution through taxes and transfers does involve a risk of intratemporal and intertemporal efficiency losses, redistribution within a single generation tends to have some positive effect toward equality in the future.

Redistribution should largely concentrate on social capital formation of a kind that will raise the productivity of the poor. The negative income tax will allow the poor the right to choose their own consumption patterns, for example. But I think that it is fairly clear that many kinds of capital formation that will benefit them cannot be carried out at all, or at least cannot be carried out efficiently, on an individual level and must rely on social capital formation.

In addition to concentrating on schooling, especially technical education, health-care, and improved housing, the government should assume an enlarged role in the development of basic civilian technology. In a competitive world, where patent rights protect only a limited range of innovations, a firm's incentives to innovate will be limited if the innovation will become everyone's property. Government addition to the supply of innovative effort will, therefore, improve efficiency. Government development of civilian technology will also contribute to equality. In the absence of markets to achieve sufficient risk bearing, the resources for technological development come from those already wealthy, and hence technical progress on the whole reinforces the existing distribution of income. If the supply of new technologies comes from the government and is freely available to all newcomers, there is likely to be greater opportunity for equalization of wealth through competition.

(5) In answering the last question we shall briefly examine how the capitalist system enhances or impedes the achievement of justice and other desiderata. The ideology, and to a considerable extent the practice, of the capitalist system do encourage equality of opportunity. But since the opportunities have a strong element of uncertainty about them, this very equality of opportunity is apt to lead to inequality of outcomes. As stressed earlier, inequalities of present possessions in turn impede equality of opportunity; wealth achieved from earlier success increases opportunities for oneself and one's children both directly and through family influences and connections.

Even to the extent that equality of opportunity is well served by the present system, it must be recognized that these are opportunities to do what is rewarded in the market. They are not opportunities to achieve the egalitarian ideal. In fact, the individualistic ideology of capitalism, though favourable to equality of opportunity, is antagonistic to deliberate redistribution. Indeed, it is opposed to co-operation among the members of the society, to the ideal of reciprocity. The emphasis is throughout on self-help, not on mutual assistance. And, for a variety of other reasons as well, would conclude that reliance on the free operation of the market will not end to equality.

Income and property are certainly the instruments of an individual's freedom. Clearly the domain of choice is enhanced by increases in those dimensions. It is true not merely in the sense of expanded consumer choice but also in broader contexts of career and opportunity to pursue one's own aims and to develop one's own potential.

A great deal of intellectual confusion comes, in my view, from thinking of property rights as basic and axiomatic. The forms of private property are indeed capable of mystification. Many current thinkers object to distributive equality on principle, on the grounds that it contradicts freedom of property. But property is itself a social contrivance and cannot be taken as an ultimate value; indeed institutions that lead to gross inequalities are affronts to the equal dignity of humans and can only be accepted as necessary evils.

Clearly one needs to distinguish between personal assets (labour, skills, and the like) and material assets. The problem of original acquisition and the difficulties of the Lockean proviso disappear or at least are greatly attenuated when reference is made to personal assets. These do unmistakably and clearly belong to an individual. Both Rawlsian and utilitarian views imply that personal assets are available for redistribution. The extent to which they can be used may be limited by privacy considerations. It may be difficult to know the extent of an individual's talents and therefore it may be better to induce their use by rewards than to require it. I would be tempted to say that an individual with unusual talents has something of an obligation to the world to use these talents; but even apart from that, I see no argument against saying that if he is highly rewarded for applying his talent, those rewards should in part be devoted to the less fortunately endowed.

The three concepts of private property, property income, and profit are interchangeable for some problems but for others they must be clearly distinguished. Profits can be used as a measuring device in a society where asset private property is absent. However, the ability to own property is closely related to any kind of profit system, and associated with it is the concept of property income. Profit is only one form of property income; the others include rental and interest.

It is obvious, empirically at any rate, that profits certainly add to the inequality of income, and therefore a demand for equality does involve, among other things, an attack on profits and, in fact, on property income in general. While we now understand that most inequality in income is due to inequality of so-called labour incomes, it is certainly true that the ability to acquire profits increases inequality. Therefore, an egalitarian policy will tend to hit, to a rather considerable extent, at property income

Profits in the residual sense are rather harder to justify on efficiency grounds than property income in general. The very fact that they are residual and the assumption that there is a considerable amount of randomness in the return imply precisely that the incentive effects are blunted in many ways as compared with the incentive effects of a sure return on the income. Probably the strongest argument for profits in the strict sense of the term as improving the efficiency of the economic system is Schumpeter's argument that the possibility of profits is the incentive to innovate and therefore that the role of profits is to encourage the development of new ideas and new uses for property.

The case against assumption of social responsibility by corporations often makes the normative assertion that firms ought to maximize profits; that they practically have a social obligation to do so. This well-known argument breaks down for a variety of reasons that can roughly be grouped under the headings of indivisibilities, inappropriability, and uncertainty (discussed in my chapter (2) in the companion volume to this book). However serious the limits on the theoretical validity of the price system, the actual market differs substantially from the competitive model, and is particularly flawed by monopoly distortions and by recurring and costly failures of reaching full employment − a very conspicuous kind of misallocation indeed.

At least one distributional implication of a capitalist system intrinsically marked by uncertainty and risk is the creation of opportunities for speculation and for the exploitation of differential information. Hence there is room for profits by outguessing others. These profits need not correspond to any net social productivity, but only to a redistribution of rewards, thoroughly analogous to betting on horse races. Though speculation has some social value, a great deal of speculative profits are unrelated to productivity. Hence, they are to a considerable extent a suitable subject for planned redistribution to help achieve justice, instead of the chaotic redistribution of the market.

The vast inequalities of income generated by the private economic system weaken a society's sense of mutual concern. Profit maximization tends to point away from the expression of altruistic motives. Altruistic motives are motives whose gratification is just as legitimate as selfish motives, and the expression of those motives is something we probably wish to encourage. A profit-maximizing, self-centred form of economic behaviour does not provide any room for the expression of such motives.

In a world of any complexity, there must necessarily be both antagonistic and co-operative elements. The model *laissez-faire* world of total self-interest would not survive for ten minutes; its actual working depends upon an intricate network of reciprocal obligations, even among competing firms and individuals.

MARKET FAILURES AND COLLECTIVE RESPONSIBILITY

Thus even under assumptions most favourable to decentralization of decision-making, there is an irreducible need for a social or collective choice on distribution. In point of fact there are a great many other situations in which the replacement of market by collective decision-making is necessary or at least desirable.

A case in point is the business cycle, which has been a recurring and fundamental property of the capitalist system almost since its inception. Certainly since the extensive observations of Clément Juglar in 1859, it has been accepted that there are fluctuations in economic activity, with positive but imperfect correlation of the different sectors of the economy, which show distinct persistence in time. The fluctuations are certainly not periodic in any strict sense of that term but rather are like irregular waves of varying amplitude and varying time intervals from peak to peak (or trough to trough). We still lack a systematic theory, but we do have a general understanding: these cycles are characterized at least at their lower levels by what certainly appear to be disequilibria: failures to equate supply and demand. Some labour and some capital goods stand idle while other, apparently identical, workers and tools are used.

In textbook theories of the smoothly working economy as well as in such theories as rational expectations, prices and wages fall whenever supply exceeds demand, and rise in the opposite case. In fact, they are rigid or only slowly moving, so that unemployment, for example, is not immediately followed by sharp drops in wages. There is too much pressure to maintain them.

In fact, at any moment of time there are really disequilibria; individuals are not able to carry out all the transactions they want to at the current set of prices. Most strikingly, workers are unable to sell in the market all the labour they would like to sell at the going wage. Hence, the income on which they base their purchasing decisions is not the income they will receive by selling all the labour they want, as it would be in Walrasian or Marshallian equilibrium theory, but rather by selling the labour for which there is an effective demand.

In view of the serious macroeconomic failures of the system, Keynes and others before and after him have urged a more active role for the government. It is better to stimulate an insufficient demand by government intervention than to let valuable resources remain idle. Various government policies have been used increasingly in the postwar period. Both in the USA, and in other countries following similar policies, the period of active government intervention was the most stable ever. Indeed, despite the current disillusionment with Keynesian economics, the policies of alteration of effective demand have served their purpose well. At this juncture the problem is that the wage and price rigidities, accompanied by exogenous shocks, have set off an inflationary spiral. This policy dilemma – that a stable full-employment economy has a built-in inflationary bias, foreseen by the early advocates of Keynesian policies – does not imply that government stabilization policy is a mistake. Inflation is an evil, but not comparable to the wastage and cruelty of repeated unemployment.

Increase in economic knowledge leads to a greater realization of the potentials and limitations of social mechanisms (market) and of social action that extends the domain of individual rationality. It is possible to have a mixed economy that retains the essentials of the capitalist drive and initiative, and yet makes room for the government or other social institutions to intervene with the aim of avoiding the worst inefficiences of unemployment and the idling of other resources, of dealing with the many other imperfections of the market system, and of redistributing incomes more equitably.

Jan Tinbergen has stated as a general principle of policy that in trying to achieve economic goals, the number of instruments has to equal the number of goals. These instruments do indeed include private decisions to buy and sell and to set prices, but they also include the instruments in the hands of government and of other social organizations (including such invisible institutions as the principles of ethics and morality).

It may be worth emphasizing that the current mixed economy, with its high but not dominant proportion of government activity, did not emerge by accident or by the wilful design of corrupt politicians. It arose as a series of responses to felt needs. This condition does not mean that the specifics of the mixed economy must be regarded as ideal. On the contrary, just as in the private sector, particular commodities may always be found wanting or be replaced by superior alternatives. But the needs met by the government sector must be recognized. To argue for drastic reduction is to say that their desirability is illusory or that the private sector will rush in with alternatives.

An economist, of whatever school, necessarily recognizes limits. Whether he defends the present mixture of private and public controls or argues for a closer approximation to *laissez-faire*, the economist should never claim to advocate a utopia. In a world of limited resources and imperfect under-standing, all that can be asked for is the reduction of flaws. Like political democracy, to which it is so closely linked, the mixed economy has much to answer for; it is merely less bad than its alternatives.

NOTE

1. This chapter focuses on and synthesizes arguments that are elaborated at length in, *inter alia*, Arrow, 1951 (new edn 1963), 1967, 1973a, 1973b, 1974, 1976, 1978, 1979, and 1981, where the reader will also find comprehensive references to the literature.

REFERENCES

Arrow, K. J. (1951) (new edn 1963) *Social Choice and Individual Values*, New York: John Wiley.

Arrow, K. J. (1967) 'Values and Collective Decision-Making', in P. Laslett and W. G. Runciman (eds), *Philosophy, Politics and Society, Third Series*, Oxford: Blackwell, pp. 215–32.

Arrow, K. J. (1973a) 'Some Ordinalist-Utilitarian Notes on Rawls's Theory of Justice', *Journal of Philosophy*, 70 (May): 245–63.

Arrow, K. J. (1973b) 'Rawls's Principle of Just Saving', *Swedish Journal of Economics*, 75: 323–35.

Arrow, K. J. (1974) 'General Economic Equilibrium: Purpose, Analytic Techniques, Collective Choice', *American Economic Review*, 64 (June): 253–72.

Arrow, K. J. (1976) *The Viability and Equity of Capitalism*, E. S. Woodward Lectures in Economics, Vancouver: University of British Columbia.

Arrow, K. J. (1978) 'Nozick's Entitlement Theory of Justice', *Philosophia*, 7 (June): 265–79.

Arrow, K. J. (1979) 'The Trade-off Between Growth and Equity', in H. I. Greenfield (ed.) *Theory for Economic Efficiency: Essays in Honor of Abba P. Lerner*, Cambridge, Mass.: MIT Press, pp. 1–11.

Arrow, K. J. (1981) 'Introduction: The Social Choice Perspective', 'Symposium: The Implications of Social Choice Theory for Legal Decision-making', *Hofstra Law Review*, 9 (Summer): 1373–80.

4 The Theory of Normal Prices and Reconstruction of Economic Theory

JOAN ROBINSON

1

I am one of the few survivors of the generation that learned economic theory before the Keynesian revolution. Alfred Marshall was the over-mastering influence on teaching in the English-speaking world. There were many disputed points within the Marshallian canon, such as the meaning of the 'representative firm', but other schools — Walras, Pareto, the Austrians — were dismissed in footnotes. We used to say in Cambridge: 'Everything is in Marshall'. I added later: 'The trouble is that everything else is as well'.

The general practical moral of Marshallian teaching was the defence of *laissez-faire*. Interference with the 'free play of market forces', however well meant, will do more harm than good. Thus the devastating unemployment of the 1930s and Keynes's plea to do something about it created a confrontation.

Everything is in Marshall. The most coherent and usable part of Marshall's theory is the analysis of the 'short period'. The short period is not a length of time, but a situation at a moment of time when equipment and stocks of inputs in existence and the available labour force provide for a potential supply of output that may be less or more fully utilized. Marshall, using his one-at-a-time method, analysed this question in terms of the fishing industry. Keynes adapted it to deal with changes in the general level of effective demand in an industrial economy.

The coverage of the *General Theory* is narrow. It says very little about

157

international trade. The influence of the flow of investment on employment is a central topic but accumulation as a historical process is very scrappily dealt with; the distribution of the flow of gross income between wages and profits is discussed but the formation of an overall rate of profit is left hazy. Much remained to be discussed, but the complacent equilibrium theory was deeply shaken.

After the Second World War, the baton of leadership in teaching economics, along with leadership in the capitalist world, passed to the USA. Instead of meeting the challenge of the Keynesian revolution head on, the profession in the USA split the subject into two parts, macro and micro. In the macro section it was permissible to contemplate fluctuations in employment and even to hint at remedies for a deficiency in effective demand, while micro theory returned to the analysis of equilibrium established by the free play of market forces. Keynesian ideas were allowed a certain sphere of operation while the central doctrine was safely walled off from them. Professor Heilbroner ('The New Economics', *New York Review of Books*, 21 February 1980) describes the result:

> Microeconomics is concerned with aspects of the economy that are centred in the act of choice, allocation, decision-making. Macro economics is devoted to the performance of the economy as a whole, especially with regard to employment and output and inflation. This seems, on the surface, like a very convenient way of examining the economy from two different vantage points, micro yielding a worm's eye view, macro a bird's eye view. But what is strange is that there is no way of going from one view to the other. One would think that by opening up the worm's eye lens one would eventually take in the entire flow of output or employment that originates in the 'micro' acts of individuals or firms — but no such comprehensive view emerges, only a blur. Conversely, it would appear that by closing down the macro lens we could bring into sharp focus the individual actions that are the constituent elements of the flow of output or the rise in prices, but again no such picture emerges: the macro lens simply cannot distinguish the individual actors. Thus macro and micro are not the complementary slides of a stereopticon giving us a single complete picture from two incomplete ones. They are, rather, two quite different pictures that cannot be combined.

The position in what is sometimes called main-line teaching is even more unsatisfactory than Heilbroner allows, for micro theory in turn is split into two sections — a theory of exchange and a theory of production. Exchange and the *relative* prices of particular commodities are treated in terms of auctions of ready-made goods, as elaborated by Walras, while production is treated in terms of 'supply curves' derived from Marshall by Pigou and elaborated by the early Joan Robinson. The two types of analysis are essentially incompatible because the underlying models have completely different time schemes. In Walrasian markets, prices are varying from day to day to reconcile demand to supply while, in the Pigovian scheme, prices are governed by costs of production 'in the long run'. In the textbook the two theories generally lie side by side without any attempt being made to reconcile them. There is also a long-period macro theory in terms of 'factors of production'; this has run into trouble over the meaning and measurement of a 'quantity of capital' regarded as a 'factor'.

The attempt (whether deliberate or instinctive) to save equilibrium theory from Keynes has landed it in a number of contradictions.

First of all, on the analytical plane, there is the problem about time. *When* is the date when equilibrium is going to rule? It is usually said that, at any moment, markets are *tending* towards equilibrium, or that demand governs supply *in the long run*. Equilibrium, it seems, lies in the future. Why has it not been established already? Jam tomorrow but never jam today.

There is a contradiction also on the plane of ideology. The burden of the equilibrium theory is still the same as in Marshall's day — the presumption in favour of *laissez-faire*, of the beneficial effects of the 'free play of market forces', which brings about the maximization of the flow of 'utilities' to be got from 'given resources'. The free play of market forces necessarily brings about inequality. If it did not, it would have no effect. It operates by rewarding success and penalizing failure. This freedom necessarily produces inequality not only in the 'rewards' to be earned in each generation but in the distribution of handicaps — inherited wealth and education — from one generation to the next. This comes into conflict with the claim that the market system is efficient, for a flow of output cannot be measured just in tons of stuff — it is supposed to be measured by its power to offer 'satisfaction' or *'utilities'*. Because of the principle of diminishing marginal utility of additional consumption, a given flow of goods produces less total utility for a given population if it is very unequally distributed. Some individuals are near starvation while others are destroying their livers by overeating. It has to be admitted that inequality in the distribution of consuming power among a given number of human beings reduces the amount of satisfaction to be got from a given flow of consumption.

At one time the neoclassics (particularly the Austrian branch of the school) tried to get out of this by appealing to the principle of 'no bridge' between subjective consciousnesses so that a comparison of quantities of utility has no meaning. In that case, comparisons of quantities of products has no meaning either.

The whole subject is so embarrassing that in fact it is scarcely mentioned. There is no treatment at all of the determination of the distribution of income in orthodox teaching, and precious little about its consequences. What to the general public appears one of the most interesting of all questions in economics is simply left out of the syllabus.

In its general influence on educated public opinion, orthodox teaching has been not merely feeble and confused but positively pernicious. It gives support to the view that expenditure by a government that is beneficial to the inhabitants of its territory is 'socialism' and must be prevented at all costs. This reconciles an otherwise more or less sane and benevolent public opinion to the arms race which seems to be dragging us all to destruction. But that is another story.

2

It seems to me that the whole complex of theories and models in the textbooks is in need of a thorough spring cleaning. We should throw out all self-contradictory propositions, unmeasurable quantities and indefinable concepts and reconstruct a logical basis for analysis with what, if anything, remains.

The first notion to be discarded, in such a process, must be 'equilibrium in the long run'. It is possible to conceive of a particular market being in equilibrium in the very short run in the sense that the prices of commodities and the flows of receipts being experienced today are setting up expectations that they will be the same next week, provided that no relevant 'change in the news' occurs meanwhile, so that the same situation will be experienced again next week. This conception needs to be handled with care; when accumulation or depletion of stocks is going on, the mere fact that next week follows this week causes the situation in the market to have changed, but there may be periods in history when it is not unreasonable to form fairly clear expectations about the very short run. It is strange that the concept of 'rational expectations' over the long run has come into fashion among economists just at a moment when prospects for the capitalist world are more uncertain and more threatening than they have been ever since capitalism came into existence.

The given position in an economy is a purely logical structure — an elaborate thought experiment. There is no causation and no change. At each moment, in any one system, the stock of inputs required for its technology and its growth rate has already come into existence, which implies that in the past, when stocks were being replaced, there must have been correct foresight of what 'today' would be like, so that the profit-maximizing variety of technology has been installed — in short, the distinction between the future and the past, as viewed from 'today', has been abolished.

For this reason, the characteristics of a technological system can be described only in terms of imaginary comparisons — what would be different if. . . There is no room here for short-period 'Keynesian' movements in the level of utilization of stocks of inputs or employment of labour. The language of change may be used, for it is difficult to describe a map without using the language of moving about on it, but essentially the argument is conducted strictly in terms of comparisons of logically possible positions.

'Keynesian' analysis, by contrast, is developed by making predictions about the consequences of change — what would follow if. . . For this reason, Keynesian analysis has proved more fruitful than long-period theory. It proceeds by making predictions of what consequences can be expected to follow from events now taking place. When the expected consequences do not follow, the analysis is proved to be mistaken and can be corrected.

Keynesian analysis starts ever afresh from the short-period situation that past history has brought into existence 'today' and attempts to understand what consequences will follow from recent changes in it. The Keynesians may not get them right but they can learn from their own and each other's mistakes so that it is at least possible gradually to gain more insight as time goes by, while long-run theory must remain in a perpetual fog.

The most troublesome point to clear up has been the concept of 'capital' as a 'factor of production' because of the problem of 'normal prices'. *When* are normal prices going to obtain? Marshall was very much troubled by this. In a rare burst of candour, in appendix H in the *Principles*, he admitted that it had beaten him but in the main text he tried to bluff his way through the problem as usual. At a low level of abstraction, he described profit as the 'reward' 'of business ability in command of capital'. Here, if we take 'capital' to mean finance that can be used to acquire productive equipment and pay out wages, this is merely a description of how an industrial economy works. At a more philosophical level, *interest* (identified with the rate of profit) is described as the reward of *waiting*, but *waiting* only means owning property and refraining from selling out and consuming it. The 'reward' of owning property is the advantage of having it, in which its power to earn interest is only one element. All this remained in an impenetrable fog during the reign of Alfred Marshall and, for the most part, it still does so today.

Keynes was somewhat troubled by the lack of a coherent theory of the rate of profit on capital[1] but he could get on well enough without it, for his main concern was with forward-looking expectations of the rate of return on investment and the flows of current profits being received at a moment of time.

On this basis, some progress has been made in interpreting current events and the effects of national policies under the slogan 'history versus equilibrium'.

3

Piero Sraffa had a programme of spring cleaning of his own. He tells in the preface to *Production of Commodities by Means of Commodities* that he tried to discuss it with Keynes in 1928 but it was not published until 1960. Meanwhile he kept his ideas very much to himself though some leaked out in his Introduction to *Ricardo's Principles*.

His main attack was upon 'marginal products' and supply curves based on proportions of 'factors of production':

No changes in output and (at any rate in Parts I and II) no changes in the proportions in which different means of production are used by an industry are considered, so that no question arises as to the variation or constancy of returns. The investigation is concerned exclusively with such properties of an economic system as do not depend on changes in the scale of production or in the proportions of 'factors'.

This standpoint, which is that of the old classical economists from Adam Smith to Ricardo, has been submerged and forgotten since the advent of the 'marginal' method. The reason is obvious. The marginal approach requires attention to be focused on change, for without change either in the scale of an industry or in the 'proportions of the factors of production' there can be neither marginal product nor marginal cost. In a system in which, day after day, production continued unchanged in those respects, the marginal product of a factor (or alternatively the marginal cost of a product) would not merely be hard to find – it just would not be there to be found (Sraffa, 1960).

Sraffa approaches the problem by setting up the input–output table for an integrated industrial economy in physical terms. Of course, in reality it would not be possible to describe in full detail the technology for a whelk

stall, let alone for a complex industrial economy. The argument is conducted at the level of abstract principles, far above that of operational
analysis.

Now if the necessary real wage per man-year is given in physical terms
(as the classical economists were inclined to assume) then the prices of all
commodities in money-wage units and the overall rate of profit uniform
throughout the system are determined. Sraffa breaks out of this straitjacket
by allowing the wage to be a *share* in net output. Then he traces the
behaviour of prices and the uniform rate of profit (for the given technical
system) for every value of the share from unity to zero (or to the minimum that will support life).

This ingenious and elegant analysis forms the core of the argument.
Here is a solution for the much vexed problem of what is meant by a
'quantity of capital'. For a given technique and rate of net output, the
physical quantity of capital is a list of specific inputs required to implement the technique. When the share of wages in net output is known,
Sraffa shows that the prices of commodities and inputs that will correspond to a rate of profit uniform throughout the system are determined.
This is illustrated by a diagram in which the *x* axis represents the rate of
profits, uniform throughout the economy and the *y* axis the flow of net
output in physical terms measured in units of the standard commodity.

The definition of the standard commodity takes up a great part of
Sraffa's argument but personally I have never found it worth the candle.
Each technical system has its own standard commodity so that one quantity cannot be compared with another. This is not the unit of value like a
unit of length or of weight that Ricardo was looking for. It is simpler to
take the money-wage bill as the numeraire and allow the level of money
prices to represent the share of profits (the ratio of exploitation).

There are some further puzzles in the exposition. To define *net* output
it is necessary to suppose that inputs are replaced in kind as they are used
up whereas Sraffa seems to permit them to be replaced, as they might be
in reality, by something physically different. When part of profit may be
consumed by capitalists it would be natural to suppose that physical output is influenced by distribution so that it varies with the rate of profit.
These are puzzles and complications in Sraffa's analysis but they do not
give any help or comfort to marginal productivity.

The main difficulty is that suddenly, without warning (apart from the
hint in the preface quoted above), the question is changed. In part III we
are to consider the choice of technique by 'a producer who builds a new
plant' (p. 81).

Choice depends upon profitability and the producer is conceived to 'switch' from one technique to another with changes in the rate of profits.

Now, we can imagine a variety of techniques for producing a single flow output set up in a 'book of blueprints' but we cannot imagine switching from one to another at an instant of time. A switch would require availability of the appropriate stocks of inputs already in existence. Moreover, differences in techniques are introduced successively through time as research and development goes on responding to historical changes not merely to shifts in the rate of profit.

To put the point in methodological terms, it is not correct to draw two or more wage-profit curves in the same axes, for the y axis represents the flow of net output in only one particular technique.

It seems that its own author has been puzzled by the exposition of this enigmatic book, but that does not mean that we cannot make use of it in reconstructing analysis after the spring cleaning has been completed.

4

To reconcile the two parts of Sraffa's analysis we may treat it as follows. The 'system' of production in use in an economy at a moment of time, and the stocks of inputs required to implement it, are set out in terms of a physical input–output table. It does not represent a stationary state or a equilibrium position. It is simply the position that has been reached, 'today', as a result of accumulation of stocks and of technical knowledge over the past history.

At a moment of time there can be no change but if accumulation or decumulation is going on, say from week to week or from year to year, there must be technical change to accommodate changes in the relations of inputs to employment of labour and even when the total stock is in some sense constant choices are required about the form in which replacements are being made of items used up. Thus, as history marches on, there is slow gradual change. There may also be bouts of important changes from time to time, following major discoveries, and 'Keynesian' swings of effective demand run to and fro over the long-term evolution.

The control of production may in principle be appropriate to any social and political system — socialist, co-operative or capitalist. Where the land and stocks are owned by a class of capitalists they are paying a certain wage bill per annum in terms of dollars. Dollar prices then determine the real wage rate per man-year of employment and the share of gross and net profits in proceeds. The ratio of net profit in dollars to the wage bill is the ratio of exploitation. According to Sraffa, the prices of commodities are such as to make the rate of profits on the dollar value of capital uniform and constant through time, but in real life this condition is not exactly fulfilled.

The rate of exploitation (with the corresponding level of the rate of profits) may, in principle, be anything between zero (which permits only enough gross profit to keep stocks intact) and the maximum that permits the labour force just to exist and reproduce itself.

There does not seem to be much point in making further systematic generalizations. We have here a broad frame within which detailed studies of actual history can be carried out.

This is where Sraffa leaves us and hands us over to Keynes.

NOTE

1. See M. Milgate, 'Keynes on the "Classical" Theory of Interest', *Cambridge Journal of Economics*, September 1977.

REFERENCE

Sraffa, P. (1960) Preface, *Production of Commodities by Means of Commodities*, Cambridge: Cambridge University Press.

Part II
Non-Walrasian
Macroeconomics

5 Non-Walrasian Foundations of Macroeconomics*

TAKASHI NEGISHI

MICROECONOMICS OF ALTERNATIVE MACROAPPROACHES

The aim of macroeconomics is, particularly after Keynes's *General Theory*, to explain changes in the aggregate output or employment as well as those in the price level.

The explanation of these changes in the macroeconomics of the so-called monetarism is well founded on the traditional Walrasian microeconomics, that is, the determination of the price by the equilibrium of demand and supply. Friedman (1968) describes the effects of an increase in the rate of growth of money supply at the long-run equilibrium where prices have been stable. Because prices of products typically respond to an unanticipated rise in nominal demand faster than the prices of factors of production, real wages received go down – though real wages anticipated by employees go up since at first they are likely to evaluate the wages offered at the unchanged price level, with the result that in the short-run equilibrium both demand and supply of factors of production are equally larger than those in the long-run equilibrium. This 'simultaneous fall *ex post* in real wages to employers and rise *ex ante* in real wages to employees is what enables employment to increase'. But soon employees begin to realize that prices are rising and they demand higher nominal wages. To keep the supply of labour larger than the equilibrium long-run supply, real wages

*The author is grateful to Professors Shigeo Akashi, Shozaburo Fujino, Kotaro Suzumura, Kiichiro Yagi, and Messrs Asaji Hirayama and Takashi Oginuma for their comments on the earlier versions, though they are not responsible for any remaining flaws.

169

now have to be higher than the long-run equilibrium ones. Any rise in real wages, however, decreases the demand for labour and tends to return employment to its former long-run equilibrium level.

'Temporary increase in employment comes not from inflation *per se*, but from unanticipated inflation', and exists only so far as inflation is not fully anticipated even though the rate of money growth and price rise continue to be higher than the initial long-run equilibrium rate.

This is quite a contrast to the quantity theory of money before Keynes. Even in the discussion of transition period, Fisher (1918) admitted that

> the amount of trade is dependent, almost entirely, on other things than the quantity of currency, so that an increase of currency cannot, even temporarily, very greatly increase trade. In ordinarily good times practically the whole community is engaged in labor, producing, trans- porting, and exchanging goods. The increase of currency of a boom period cannot, of itself, increase the population, extend invention, or increase the efficiency of labor. These factors pretty definitely limit the amount of trade which can be reasonably carried on.

In other words, pre-Keynesian quantity theory of money considered that any changes in the supply of money are absorbed in changes in the price level, with the level of employment unchanged even in the short-run.[1] The hard core of Walrasian paradigm or research programme, that is, the deter- mination of short-run equilibrium by the equality of demand and supply, is shared by both pre-Keynesian and post-Keynesian quantity theories of money. The former cannot explain the changes in the level of employment in the short run whereas the latter, equipped with a new protective belt, does so by means of the discrepancy between anticipated and realized changes in real wages that changes both demand and supply of factors of production in the same direction.[2]

In the so-called fixprice model of macroeconomics considered by Barro and Grossman (1976), Benassy (1982), Malinvaud (1977), and others, on the other hand, demand and supply do not have to be equalized by changes in prices and the level of output or that of employment is determined by the short-side principle that either demand or supply, whichever is smaller, is realized. Fixprice implies that prices are independent of the relation between demand and supply. Since prices rise naturally in the face of excess demand unless they are controlled institutionally, we are mainly concerned with the fixprice model in the Keynesian case where prices are not reduced in the face of excess supply rather than in the case of suppres- sed inflation where prices cannot rise in the face of excess demand. The Keynesian case in the fixprice model is more Keynesian than the *General Theory*, since excess supplies exist not only in the labour market but also in the goods market. In other words, the first postulate of classical economics, that is, the equality of price and marginal cost, is also discarded so that firms wish to sell more, if they can, at the current price or even at a price slightly lower. In a depression, certainly, it is more realistic to suppose excess or idle capacities and unintended inventories as well as involuntary unemployment rather than to assume away, as in the *General Theory*, the former and to concentrate the analyses on the latter.

Keynesian or fixprice macroeconomics, however, has not been so well founded on microeconomic theory. Unlike the macroeconomics of the quantity theory of money, it cannot be founded on traditional Walrasian microeconomic theory, since we have to explain why price is not reduced in the face of excess supply or why price changes so slowly that it remains practically unchanged in the short run. We have to, therefore, develop a non-Walrasian microeconomic theory. In the next section, we argue that Carl Menger, who shared with Walras the honour of being one of the founding fathers of the marginal revolution, is the earliest and the greatest non-Walrasian economist. We can start our consideration of non-Walrasian economics from the microeconomics of Menger who pointed out that the price or the ratio of exchange is not the only important factor in the theory of exchange and emphasized the asymmetry between demand (offer of money, the most liquid commodity) and supply (offer of other commodities), that is, the former is easily realized while the latter is not. As a matter of fact, Fujino (1982a) pointed out (based on his (1978, 1980 and 1982b)), referring to Menger, that such an asymmetry always exists in a monetary economy, irrespective of the existence of excess supply or excess demand, because money is superior in liquidity to goods. In the next section however, our argument is more limited and is confined only to the Keynesian case of excess supply. Then in the third section, we summarize our own argument on the microeconomic foundations of Keynesian macroeconomics, based on the theory of kinked demand curves that are perceived, not by oligopolistic firms as in Sweezy (1939), but by more competitive firms. The final section is devoted to arguing that traditional Walrasian theory of perfect competition does not need to be based on the theory of the large economy and to examine the essential difference between Walrasian and non-Walrasian economics.

MENGERIAN MARKETS AND EXCESS SUPPLY

Unlike Walras who considered ideally well-organized markets, Menger is mainly interested in more realistic markets where we observe 'that it does not lie within our power, when we have bought an article for a certain price, to sell it again forthwith at that same price. . . The price at which anyone can at pleasure buy a commodity at given market and a given point of time, and the price at which he can dispose of the same at pleasure, are two essentially different magnitudes' (Menger, 1892). To explain these market-phenomena, Menger introduces the concept of *Absatzfaehigkeit der Waaren*, that is, saleability or marketability of commodities, and considers that the smaller the difference between the higher buying price and lower selling price, the more marketable the commodity usually is.

We must note, at first, that Menger distinguishes the commodity from the goods and has a separate chapter on the theory of commodity in his *Grundsaetz* (1871). He defines 'commodities as (economic) goods of any kind that are intended for sale', and explains as follows the relation between goods and commodities:

Commodity-character is therefore not only not property of goods but usually only a transitory relationship between goods and economizing individuals. Certain goods are intended by their owners to be exchanged for the goods of other economizing individuals. During their passage, sometimes through several hands, from the possession of the first into the possession of the last owner, we call them commodities, but as soon as they have reached their economic destination (that is, as soon as they are in the hands of the ultimate consumer) they obviously cease to be commodities and become consumption goods in the narrow sense in which this term is opposed to the concept of commodity. But where this does not happen, as in the case very frequently, for example, with gold, silver, etc., especially in the form of coins, they naturally continue to be commodity as long as they continue in the relationship responsible for the commodity-character.[3]

But why do some goods cease to be commodities quickly while coins never cease to be commodities? In other words, why can little metal discs, apparently useless as such, be commodities and exchanged against useful things that can become consumption goods? This is because of the different degrees of saleability or marketability of commodities. Money is the most saleable or marketable of all commodities. 'The theory of money necessarily presupposes a theory of saleableness of goods'.[4] Degree of saleability or marketability is defined by Menger as 'the greater or less facility with which commodities can be disposed of at a market at any convenient time at current purchasing prices, or with less or more diminution of the same' (Menger, 1892).

Although Menger described in detail the circumstances upon which the degree of saleability or marketability of commodities depends, from our point of view the interesting fact is that it depends on whether the relevant market is well organized or poorly organized.

If the competition for one commodity is poorly organized and there is danger therefore that the owners will be unable to sell their holdings of the commodity at economic prices, at a time when this danger does not exist at all, or not in the same degree, for the owners of other commodities, it is clear that this circumstance will be responsible for a very important difference between the marketability of that commodity and all others. . . Commodities for which an organized market exists can be sold without difficulty by their owners at prices corresponding to the general economic situation. But commodities for which there are poorly organized markets change hands at inconsistent prices, and sometimes cannot be disposed of at all (Menger, 1871, pp. 248-9).

Since the Walrasian model concentrates on a well-organized market, Menger's theory of commodity for which the market is poorly organized and whose marketability is not high suggests to us a non-Walrasian theory of the market. Menger's criticism of pre-Mengerian economics that 'investigation into the phenomena of price has been directed almost exclusively to the quantities of the commodities exchanged, and not as well to the greater or less facility with which wares may be disposed of at normal prices' (Menger, 1871, p. 242; see also Menger, 1892), can also be applied to Walrasian economics. In other words, Menger's theory of marketability of commodities is a first attempt of non-Walrasian economics.

Fixprice models of recent studies of macroeconomics are based on the short-side principle that in disequilibrium, transaction realized equals the minimum of supply and demand. From the point of view of Menger's marketability, the short-side principle can be interpreted to imply that commodities are highly marketable when their suppliers are on the short-side of the relevant market and not so marketable when they are on the long-side of the market. We can argue, however, that in the type of markets considered by Menger suppliers of commodities other than money are generally likely to be on the long-side of the market in the sense that they wish, if they can — that is, if there is enough demand — to sell more at the current price. This is so because, unlike the Walrasian markets where all the commodities are as marketable as money is, in Mengerian markets there is asymmetry between demand that is to offer money, the most marketable commodity, and supply that is to offer less marketable commodities.

In Figure 5.1, we consider the case of a typical supplier of a commodity,

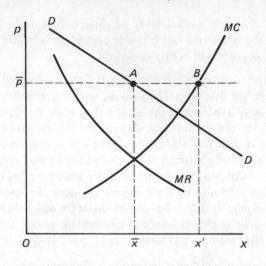

FIGURE 5.1

that is, a firm that produces it, and the level of output x is measured horizontally, and price p and cost vertically. A downwardly sloping demand curve DD is perceived by this firm, not especially because it is a monopolist, nor because its product is differentiated, but more fundamentally because the market in which the commodity is exchanged for money is poorly organized, so that the larger amount of the commodity can be disposed of in the market only at a less favourable ratio of exchange. The equilibrium of the firm is shown to be at A, or $(\overline{p}, \overline{x})$, with the marginal revenue MR equalized with marginal cost MC at $\overline{x}$. At the current price $\overline{p}$, the firm wishes to sell as much as x', but is quantitatively constrained at $\overline{x}$, since there is not enough demand. There exists an implicit excess supply AB or $x' - \overline{x}$, and the commodity is less marketable than the money.

There are two kinds of demand and supply, that is, regular, stable demand and supply and irregular, casual demand and supply. For example, the demand curve in Figure 5.1 is concerned with regular demand that is perceived by a regular supplier. When A and B do not coincide and the regular suppliers possess excess supply, casual demand will be easily satisfied by regular suppliers at the current price $\overline{p}$. Casual supply has to compete with regular excess supply to catch casual demand and will not be easily satisfied, unless the price is reduced. The marketability of the relevant commodity is low and the resale price of those casual suppliers who want to get rid of the commodity they have just bought will be much lower than the price at which they bought as regular demanders.

PRICE RIGIDITY AND KINKED DEMAND CURVES

As we saw in the preceding section, Menger's theory of commodity suggests that demand and supply are asymmetric and competitive suppliers perceive downwardly sloping demand curves in non-Walrasian markets. In our arguments on microeconomic foundations of Keynesian economics, however, we have been insisting that in a Keynesian situation competitive suppliers perceive demand curves that are not only downwardly sloping, but also flatter to the left than to the right, having an upward-pointing kink in the middle. Such a kinked demand curve was used by Sweezy (1939) to explain observed price rigidity in oligopolistic industries.[5] Although the reasons for the existence of a kink in the demand curve perceived in a Keynesian situation is different from the one given by Sweezy in the case of oligopoly, our explanation of why the price is not reduced in the face of excess supply is, at least in formal aspects, very similar to Sweezy's explanation of oligopolistic price rigidity.

Sweezy insisted that the perceived demand curve, which he called the imagined demand curve, can only be thought of with reference to a given starting point, that is, a price-output combination that depends upon the history of the case. In Figure 5.2, where the quantity q is measured horizontally and the price p vertically, the point P is such a starting point, that is, the point of currently realized price and the sale of output of an oligopolistic firm. The firm perceives a subjective demand curve from this

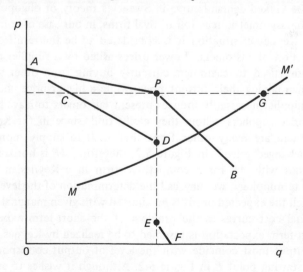

FIGURE 5.2

starting point. Sweezy pointed out that rival firms react asymmetrically according to whether a price change is upward or downward. If the firm raises its price it must expect to lose business to its rivals who will not raise their price, while if the firm cuts its price it has no reason to believe it will succeed in taking business away from its rivals who will retaliate by cutting their prices so as to avoid the loss. The perceived demand curve tends to be elastic going up and inelastic going down from the starting point P. In other words, it has a corner or a kink at P, like APB in Figure 5.2.

The marginal revenue curve derived from APB is $CDEF$, which has a discontinuity at the level of output where the perceived demand curve has a kink. If the marginal cost curve MM' passes, as in Figure 5.2, between the two parts of the discontinuous marginal revenue curve, the starting point P is also the point of profit maximization. Sweezy pointed out that any disturbance that affects only the position of the marginal cost curve may leave the equilibrium price and output entirely unaffected. More important for oligopolistic price rigidity is, however, the fact that, as Sweezy stated, any shift in demand will clearly first make itself felt in a change in the quantity sold at the current price. In other words, a shift in demand changes the position of the starting point P at which the kink occurs to the right or left without affecting the price. If the marginal cost is not increasing rapidly, the equilibrium price remains unchanged while shifts in demand are absorbed by changes in the level of output.

While the kinked demand curve in Sweezy's theory of oligopoly is the result of the asymmetric reaction of rival firms, in our case of competitive firms in a Keynesian situation it is considered to be the result of asymmetric reaction of customers. 'Lower prices asked by a supplier may not be fully advertised to customers currently buying from other suppliers who are maintaining their current price, while a higher price charged by the same supplier necessarily induces present customers to leave in search of lower price suppliers' whom they easily find, since in the Keynesian situation there are many other firms that wish to supply more at the current unchanged price.[6] In Figure 5.2, therefore, AP is horizontal and CD coincides with AP for a competitive firm in a Keynesian case. In Keynesian terminology, we may call the determination of the level of output at which the expected profit is maximized with given marginal revenue and marginal cost curves as the problem of the short-term expectation. Since short-term expectation is assumed to be realized by Keynes,[7] such a level of output must coincide with the level of output corresponding to the given starting point P in Figure 5.2. Although it wishes to supply at the current price up to the level of output corresponding to point G where the current price and the marginal cost are equalized, the firm is trapped at the level of output corresponding to P, with no incentive to reduce price to increase demand. There exists an implicit excess supply or idle capacity GP owing to the deficiency of the aggregate effective demand. Any shift in the aggregate effective demand changes the position of P horizontally, with price unchanged. If the marginal cost is not increasing rapidly, shifts in the aggregate demand are entirely absorbed by changes in the level of output.[8]

It is encouraging that Scitovsky (1978) also emphasized the possibility of asymmetric behaviour of customers which renders results in a kinked demand curve:

A price increase causes those who have previously bought to buy less or stop buying altogether; a price reduction prompts previous buyers to buy more and some people who previously bought nothing to start buying. Now that last group of people are in a very different position from all the others, in that most of them learn about the price change only if the producer goes to the trouble and expense of advertising it. The others are already established customers, who learn about the price change automatically, in the course of their routine purchases and at no cost to the seller. In other words, the whole market responds to a price increase but only part of it responds to a price reduction, unless the seller advertises it.[9]

THE LARGE ECONOMY AND MARKET IMPERFECTIONS

We argue in our non-Walrasian microeconomics that even a perfectly competitive supplier cannot perceive an infinitely elastic demand curve for his product and has to admit that to increase sales the price must be reduced. By perfect competition we mean that suppliers are supplying a homogeneous good (the product is not differentiated) and they perceive infinitely elastic demand curves only in a well-organized market where the information is perfect. The most often raised objection to this argument is that even in non-Walrasian situations a single supplier can perceive an infinitely elastic demand curve, since his size is infinitesimally small relative to the market, and a relatively infinitely large market can absorb any changes in the supply of a single supplier without any change in the price. In a Walrasian tâtonnement market, the number of suppliers can be finite and a not infinitesimally small supplier can safely assume an infinitely elastic demand curve since his assumption is justified and he can sell the amount of his product that he wished to sell at the price cried by the auctioneer when the tâtonnement is finished, while no actual trade is carried out until the tâtonnement is finished. Certainly, however, there are other non-Walrasian justifications of infinitely elastic demand curves, which presuppose the existence of infinitely many suppliers whose size is infinitesimally small.

An example is Cournot's theory of oligopoly without product differentiation, in which oligopolistic firms non-co-operatively compete with each other under the assumption that other firms do not change their level of output.[10] Suppose, for the sake of simplicity, that the demand function for the industry as a whole is linear and is given in its inverse form as

$$p = A - B \sum_{i=1}^{i=n} X_i \qquad (5.1)$$

where A and B are positive constants and X_i is the level of output of the i-th firm, $i = 1, \ldots, n$. The inverse demand function for a single firm, say the first firm, is also perceived as linear, that is:

$$p = A - B \sum_{i \neq 1} X_i - B X_1 \qquad (5.2)$$

since X_i's, $i \neq 1$, are regarded as constants by the first firm. The condition for the equilibrium of the first firm, that is, the equality of the marginal revenue and the marginal cost is:

$$A - B \sum_{i \neq 1} X_i - 2 B X_1 = C \qquad (5.3)$$

where the positive constant C denotes the marginal cost. If we suppose all the firms are identical, $X_1 = X_2 = \ldots = X_i = \ldots = X_n$, at the equilibrium, we can see from (5.3) that:

$$X_i = (A - C)/B (n + 1), \text{ for all } i. \qquad (5.4)$$

Then by substituting (5.4) into (5.1), we have:

$$p = (A + n C)/(n + 1). \qquad (5.5)$$

If the number of firms, n, get infinitely larger, we can see from (5.5) that the price p converges to the marginal cost C, which is equal to the marginal revenue. In other words, an infinitesimally small firm perceives an infinitely elastic demand curve.

We have to admit, therefore, that the existence of infinitely many firms is a sufficient condition for the perfect competition in which a single firm perceives an infinitely elastic demand curve. It is, however, by no means a necessary condition. Even for the case of $n = 2$, that is, a duopoly, Bertrand

and Fellner argued that the price will be equalized to the marginal cost if each duopolist assumes that the other will keep his price (not output) unchanged and average as well as marginal costs are constant.[11] If the price is higher, each firm will undercut its rival by a very small margin because it will obtain maximum profits by undercutting infinitesimally. In other words, a Bertrand-type duopolist behaves as if he perceived an infinitely elastic demand curve. Bertrand's assumption can be critized, of course, since duopolists will know, when they are out of equilibrium or when they decide to test their assumption, that their assumptions are incorrect; their rivals do not keep their prices constant. But Cournot's assumption is also subject to the same criticism, and we cannot accept Cournot and at the same time reject Bertrand.[12]

We can slightly generalize the case for Bertrand when the number of firms are increased. Suppose the marginal cost function, though still identical for all firms, is not constant but is increasing, though not continuously but stepwisely. When n is large but still finite, there is an equilibrium where the price is equalized with the marginal costs, and no oligopolists have the incentive to reduce the price to increase the sale, assuming that others keep their price unchanged. Under the same assumption, there is also no incentive to raise the price, since in general other firms can increase their sales without increasing marginal costs. At least at equilibrium, therefore, each oligopolist perceives an infinitely elastic demand curve. In this case, unlike that of constant marginal cost, the equilibrium profit can be positive for each identical firm.

Another example is Edgeworth's demonstration that the only stable outcome of a pure exchange economy is the perfectly competitive equilibrium and all the other allocations are blocked by traders co-operatively when the number of traders is infinitely large. Figure 5.3 is an Edgeworth box diagram, where the quantity of the first good is measured horizontally, that of the second good, vertically, the quantities of goods given to trader A are measured with the origin at A, those given to trader B, with the origin at B, curve DEF is the contract curve which is a locus of points where indifference curves of two traders are tangent, point C denotes the initial allocation of goods before trade, and point E is the perfectly competitive equilibrium with the common tangent to indifference curves at E passing through point C. It is shown that all the points on the contract curve between D and F are stable outcomes if there are only two traders A and B, while Edgeworth insists that all the points except E can be blocked by a coalition of some traders if there are infinitely many identical (in taste and initial holdings) traders A and infinitely many identical traders B.[13]

Since an identical amount of goods must be allocated to the identical

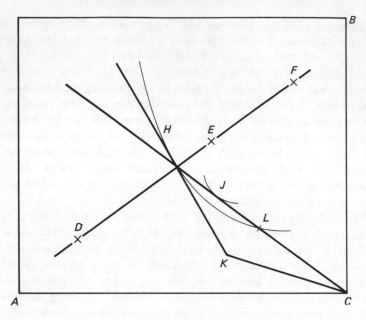

FIGURE 5.3

traders after trade, the Edgeworth box diagram can still be used to consider exchanges among infinitely many traders. Consider point H. This allocation can be blocked by a coalition formed by all the A traders and more than half but less than all of the B traders. In the coalition some traders A still continue to trade with B traders and are located at H, while the rest of the A traders who have no trade partners are located at C. By increasing the number of B traders that join the coalition sufficiently, therefore increasing the number of A traders located at H, we can make the average allocation of A traders (some at H, some at C) J located on CH between L and H. By reallocation among themselves, therefore, all the A traders are better off than they were at the allocation H. With some side-payments to B traders in the coalition, all the traders joining the coalition can be better off than they were at H, and the allocation H is blocked by such a coalition. Obviously only the point E belongs to the core, that is, the set of allocations that are not blocked by such a coalition.

If the number of traders is infinite, therefore, stable outcome of a pure exchange economy with perfect information and no friction (no restriction of trade, no cost of trade, no cost of organizing coalitions, etc.) can be derived as an equilibrium of perfect competition in which each trader is behaving as if he were taking the price ratio (the slope of *EC*) as constant. In this sense, the existence of infinitely many traders is a sufficient condition for perfect competition. But again it is not necessary, since, as we argued elsewhere, only *E* belongs to the core when there are only two *A* traders and two *B* traders if we rule out lump-sum transaction, assume the divisibility of transaction and take arbitrages leading to the law of indifference into consideration.[14]

Consider point *H* in Figure 5.3, which cannot be blocked by a coalition of two *A* traders and one *B* trader in a way suggested by Edgeworth, since *L* is located nearer to *H* than to *C*. We note that there must be at least two successive transactions like *CK* and *KH* and the ratio of exchange should vary in the course of exchange between *C* and *H*, if allocation *H* can ever be reached by exchange starting from *C*. Otherwise, that is, if there is only a single transaction and the exchange ratio remains unchanged throughout the exchange process, it must be equal to the slope of *CH* and exchange must proceed on *CH*, starting from *C* and towards *H*. Such an exchange process has to, however, be terminated at *J*, since it is unfavourable for *A* to go beyond. Suppose, therefore, A_1 trader exchanges with B_1 trader, firstly along with *CK* and then along with *KH*, and A_2 trader exchanges with B_2 trader similarly. Then the allocation *H* can be blocked by arbitrages of different exchange ratios. B_1 proposes to A_2 some new *CK* transaction or a slightly less favourable (to B_1) one, so that B_1 can be better off than at *H*. On the other hand, A_2 accepts this proposal of B_1 by cancelling a part of his *CK* transaction with B_2, so that A_2 is indifferent to or better off than at *H*. Since B_2 is not the only supplier of the second good, A_2 expects that the rest of his transaction with B_2 would not be cancelled by B_2. Not only B_1, but also B_2, A_1, and A_2 will do similarly to take advantage of different exchange ratios. The only allocation that can be blocked neither by Edgeworth coalitions nor by arbitrages is point *E*, even if there are only two *A* traders and two *B* traders.

In view of the arguments in this section, it is now clear that the difference between Walrasian economics and non-Walrasian economics lies not in whether the number of traders is assumed to be infinite or finite but in whether or not the market is perfect in the sense that the information is free and perfect, there is no cost to organize coalitions, and so on.

NOTES

1. See Fisher, 1918, pp. 55–73. Discussion with Professor Hirotaka Kato was highly useful and appreciated.

2. For the concepts of research programmes, hard core, and protective belt, see Lakatos, 1970.
3. See Menger, 1871, pp. 239, 240–1 (page numbers refer to English translation).
4. See Menger, 1892, where *Absatzfaehigkeit* is translated into saleableness. See also Menger, 1871, p. 242, where *Absatzfaehig* translated into liquid and *Absatzfaehigkeit* into marketability.
5. For the significance of the theory of kinked demand curve, see Reid, 1981, and Negishi, 1979, pp. 79–81.
6. See Negishi, 1979, pp. 36, 87.
7. See Negishi, 1979, pp. 28–9, 90. It is interesting, on the other hand, to note that short-term expectations are assumed not to be realized in the modern quantity theory as was shown in the first section of this chapter.
8. See Negishi, 1979, pp. 89–90, and Reid, 1981, pp. 65–6.
9. See also Reid, 1981, p. 97.
10. See Cournot, 1838, pp. 79–98 (page numbers refer to English translation). See also Fellner, 1965, pp. 56–69.
11. See Bertrand, 1883, and Fellner, 1965, pp. 77–86. Discussion with Professor Yoshihiko Otani was highly useful and appreciated.
12. Edgeworth, 1925, pp. 111–42, and Fellner, 1965, pp. 79–82, introduced different cost functions for different firms and/or upper limits on the amount firms produce, and argued that price oscillation appears. We disregard, however, these complications, since we are considering the possibility of perfect competition with a finite number of firms and different costs and capacity limits imply essentially the imperfectness of the competition.
13. See Edgeworth, 1881, pp. 34–42, and Negishi, 1982.
14. See Negishi, 1982, for details, and see also Akashi, 1981, for a closely related and more rigorous demonstration.

REFERENCES

Akashi, S. (1981) 'Price Competition and Competitive Equilibrium in an Economy with a Finite Number of Agents', Hitotsubashi University (mimeo).

Barro, R. J., and H. I. Grossman (1976) *Money, Employment and Inflation*, Cambridge: Cambridge University Press.

Benassy, J. P. (1982) *The Economics of Market Disequilibrium*, London: Academic Press.

Bertrand, J. (1883) 'Review of Théorie mathematique de la richesse sociale and Recherches sur les principes mathematiques de la théorie des richesses', *Journal des Savants*, 499–508.

Cournot, A. (1838) *Recherches sur les principes mathematiques de la théorie des rechesses*, Hachette, (*Researches into the Mathematical Principles of the Theory of Wealth*, trans. Bacon, London: Macmillan, 1897).

Edgeworth, F. Y. (1881) *Mathematical Psychics*, London: Kegan Paul.
Edgeworth, F. Y. (1925) *Papers Relating to Political Economy*, vol. I, London: Macmillan.
Fellner, W. (1965) *Competition Among the Few*, New York: Kelley.
Fisher, I. (1918) *The Purchasing Power of Money*, London: Macmillan.
Friedman, M. (1968) 'The Role of Monetary Policy', *American Economic Review*, 58: 1–17.
Fujino, S. (1978) 'Keynes Keizaigaku no Saikochiku (A Reconstruction of Keynesian Economics)', *Contemporary Economics*, 32 (Autumn): 50–67.
Fujino, S. (1980) 'A Microeconomic Reconstruction of Keynesian Economics: A Theory of Effective Demand-Supply and Involuntary Unemployment', Discussion Paper Series, 28, Institute of Economic Research, Hitotsubashi University, March.
Fujino, S. (1982a) Book Review of T. Negishi's *Microeconomic Foundations of Keynesian Macroeconomics*, *Economic Review*, 33: 94–6.
Fujino, S. (1982b) 'Kahei Keizai no Ronritekikozo (The Logical Structure of a Monetary Economy)', Discussion Paper Series, 52, Institute of Economic Research, Hitotsubashi University, February.
Lakatos, I. (1970) 'Falsification and the Methodology of Scientific Research Programmes', in I. Lakatos and R. Musgrave (eds), *Criticism and the Growth of Knowledge*, Cambridge: Cambridge University Press.
Malinvaud, E. (1977) *The Theory of Unemployment Reconsidered*, Oxford: Blackwell.
Menger, C. (1871) *Grunsaetze der Volkswirthschaftslehre*, Braumeller, (*Principles of Economics*, trans. Dingwall and Hoselitz, New York: Free Press, 1950).
Menger, C. (1892) 'On the Origin of Money', *Economic Journal*, 2: 239–55.
Negishi, T. (1979) *Microeconomic Foundations of Keynesian Macroeconomics*, Amsterdam: North-Holland.
Negishi, T. (1982) 'A Note on Jevons's Law of Indifference and Competitive Equilibrium', *Manchester School of Economics and Social Studies*, 50: 220–30.
Reid, G. C. (1981) *The Kinked Demand Curve Analysis of Oligopoly*, Edinburgh: Edinburgh University Press.
Scitovsky, T. (1978) 'Asymmetries in Economics', *Scottish Journal of Political Economy*, 25: 227–37.
Sweezy, P. M. (1939) 'Demand Under Conditions of Oligopoly', *Journal of Political Economy*, 47: 568–73.

6 A Non-Walrasian Model of Employment with Partial Price Flexibility and Indexation

JEAN-PASCAL BENASSY

INTRODUCTION

In recent years some theories have developed that formalize in various ways the basic Keynesian idea that prices may not clear markets at all times, and thus that economic adjustments take place by quantities as much as by prices, a point that had been emphasized notably by Clower (1965) and Leijonhufvud (1968). These theories have been developed both in a microeconomic and in a macroeconomic framework.[1]

On one hand, at the microeconomic level, a wide variety of non-Walrasian equilibrium concepts have been constructed: Benassy (1975; 1976b; 1977b; 1982), Drèze (1975), Hahn (1978), Negishi (1961; 1979), and Younès (1975). These have the characteristics of being able to accommodate numerous price mechanisms: besides the usual market clearing 'auctioneer' mechanism, they can handle rigid prices, monopolistic competition, and many other schemes. An important feature of these models is that they generate endogenously multiple regimes.

On the other hand, a number of macroeconomic models have been built along the same line. They also display a multiplicity of regimes where prices and quantities are determined by different sets of equations. Many of these models have been concerned with studying the determination of employment, and the impact of employment policies according to the regime of the model. The 'standard' model in this area, found in the seminal work of Barro and Grossman (1971; 1976), had a rigid price and

184

wage in the short run, and three regimes[2] displaying quite different properties. It was followed by a number of contributions.[3] Unfortunately most of these works, following in that respect the initial model of Barro and Grossman, assumed also a fully rigid price and wage in the short run, even though the underlying microeconomic models admit much more possibilities. Such an extreme assumption of complete nominal rigidity presents a number of shortcomings: first all these models displayed rationing of goods demand in two of the three regimes obtained, a somewhat undesirable feature as such rationing is not often observed on a macroeconomic scale in capitalist economies. Second, the models, by considering explicitly nominal rigidity only, did not allow the study of phenomena of full or partial indexation which are of very great importance in assessing the efficiency of employment policies.[4]

So we shall study in this chapter a two-market model that differs from the 'usual' non-Walrasian macroeconomic model in the following ways: first, the price level is flexible upwards (though it remains rigid downwards) so that consumer rationing on the goods market disappears. Second, the wage is linked to the price level; the formulation we shall adopt will allow all situations from nominal wage rigidity (no indexation) to real wage rigidity (full indexation). The model is a particular case of more general concepts of non Walrasian equilibrium (Benassy, 1975, 1976b, 1982; Drèze, 1975). Within this model we shall particularly study the relative efficiency against unemployment of Keynesian demand management policies (via government spending or taxes) versus 'classical' incomes policies, aimed notably at reducing the level of wages.[5]

THE MODEL

We shall consider here a very simple aggregate monetary economy. There are three representative economic agents, a household, a firm and the government, and three commodities: a consumption good (output), labour and money. Accordingly there are two current markets, on which labour is exchanged for money at the wage w, and output for money at the price p. Quantities exchanged are denoted respectively l and y. Whenever demand and supply do not match, transactions are equal to the minimum of the two.

Price and Wage

As we indicated above, we shall assume that the price is flexible upwards, but rigid downwards with a minimum value $\bar{p}$ so that:

$$p \geqslant \bar{p}$$

As for the wage, we shall describe its link to prices by the following relation:

$$w = \theta\phi(p) \quad \phi' > 0$$

The multiplicative parameter θ is put here to reflect in the simplest manner the effects that incomes policies may have on wage formation. A 'classical' policy of wage restraint, for example, will be represented by a decrease in θ. The link of wages to prices, represented by the function ϕ, may be more or less strong depending on the elasticity of ϕ that we shall call;

$$\epsilon = \frac{p\phi'(p)}{\phi(p)}$$

We shall assume that ϵ is positive, but always between zero and one. So at one extreme ($\epsilon = 0$) we have nominal wage rigidity, while at the other extreme ($\epsilon = 1$) real wage rigidity.

The Firm

The representative firm has a short-run production function $F(l)$ with the traditional properties:

$$F(0) = 0 \qquad F'(l) > 0 \qquad F''(l) < 0$$

The firm does not use or build up inventories in the period considered, so that in equilibrium production is equal to output sales y. The firm attempts to maximize profits $\pi = py - wl$. These profits are entirely distributed to the household, whose real income is thus equal to y.

The Household

The household has an initial quantity of money m and an endowment of labour l_0. We assume that the household has no utility for leisure, so that its supply of labour is constant and equal to l_0. Actual employment, however, may be smaller than l_0. The household's effective demand for goods is described by a consumption function $C(y, p, m, \tau)$, where τ is the level of taxes in real terms. In general we shall assume:[6]

$$0 < C_y < 1 \qquad C_p < 0 \qquad C_m > 0 \qquad C_\tau < 0$$

As an example one may think of a function linear in real disposable income and in real money balances:

$$C(y, p, m, \tau) = \alpha(y - \tau) + \beta \, \frac{m}{p}$$

Government

The government collects taxes at the level τ (in real terms) and expresses an effective demand for output g. Because the price is flexible upwards, this demand will always be satisfied if an equilibrium exists.

Walrasian Equilibrium

The temporary Walrasian equilibrium price and wage p_0 and w_0 are determined by the conditions of equilibrium of supply and demand on the goods and labour market. This yields:

$$C(y_0, p_0, m, \tau) + g = y_0$$

$$\frac{w_0}{p_0} = F'(l_0)$$

Note that p_0 and w_0 depend on m, g and τ. We shall assume in what follows that the values of these parameters are such that the first equation has a solution, which guarantees the existence of the Walrasian equilibrium.

The Aggregate Demand Function

For the computations that follow, it will be convenient to use the solution in y to the equation:

$$y = C(y, p, m, \tau) + g$$

which we shall denote by $K(p, m, g, \tau)$. The partial derivatives are easily computed as:

$$K_g = \frac{1}{1 - C_y} > 1 \qquad K_\tau = \frac{C_\tau}{1 - C_y} < 0$$

$$K_m = \frac{C_m}{1 - C_y} > 0 \qquad K_p = \frac{C_p}{1 - C_y} < 0$$

We shall name this function the aggregate demand function, by an evident analogy with the traditional aggregate demand function of Keynesian models.

THE THREE REGIMES

As we shall see below, this model will have three different regimes:

Excess supply on both markets (regime A)
Excess supply of labour, goods market cleared (regime B)
Excess demand for labour, goods market cleared (regime C)

A fourth potential regime, with excess demand for labour and excess supply of goods, turns out to be a degenerate one, as is usual in such models in the absence of inventories, and will thus not be considered.

We shall describe in detail the above three regimes. In each case we shall compute the values p^*, w^*, y^*, and l^* of price, wage, output sales and employment associated to the basic parameters $\bar{p}$, θ, m, τ and g, and study which policy measures are effective in curing an eventual unemployment.

Before going on to the study of each specific case, we may remark that two equations will remain the same in all regimes: first the wage equation is the same throughout:

$$w = \theta\phi(p)$$

Second, because the price is flexible upwards, demand of goods will never be rationed, and the sales of goods will be equal to total demand:

$$y = C(y, p, m, \tau) + g$$

Or equivalently:

$$y = K(p, m, g, \tau)$$

which will hold in all situations. We shall now turn to the study of the other equations in each regime, and derive the policy implications.

Regime A: Excess Supply on Both Markets

With excess supply on the goods market the price is blocked at its minimum value:

$$p = \bar{p}$$

With excess supply on the labour market, employment is equal to the demand for labour. But because there is excess supply on the goods market the demand for labour is equal to $F^{-1}(y)$, that is, the level of employment just necessary to produce the quantity demanded y:

$$l = F^{-1}(y)$$

The equilibrium values of the variables are thus given by the following system:

$$\begin{cases} p^* = \bar{p} \\ w^* = \theta\phi(p^*) \\ y^* = K(p^*, m, g, \tau) \\ l^* = F^{-1}(y^*) \end{cases}$$

We see immediately that in this region we find the traditional Keynesian effects: an increase in government spending g or a reduction in taxes τ will increase production and reduce unemployment:

$$\begin{cases} \dfrac{\partial y^*}{\partial g} = K_g = \dfrac{1}{1 - C_y} > 0 \\ \dfrac{\partial y^*}{\partial \tau} = K_\tau = \dfrac{C_\tau}{1 - C_y} < 0 \end{cases}$$

In the contrary, a 'classical' incomes policy such as a reduction in wages through θ, will have no effect on production. We may remark that a diminution of the minimum price $\bar{p}$ will increase production and employment:

$$\frac{\partial y^*}{\partial \bar{p}} = K_p < 0$$

For regime A to obtain, the parameters $\bar{p}, \theta, g, m, \tau$ must be such that the equilibrium values that we found correspond actually to an excess supply on the two markets. This yields:

$$\begin{cases} y^* \leqslant F[F'^{-1}(w^*/p^*)] \\ l^* \leqslant l_0 \end{cases}$$

which, by inserting the equilibrium values, gives the following conditions:

$$\begin{cases} K(\bar{p}, m, g, \tau) \leqslant F[F'^{-1}\{\theta\phi(\bar{p})/\bar{p}\}] \\ K(\bar{p}, m, g, \tau) \leqslant y_0 \end{cases}$$

Regime B: Excess Supply on the Labour Market, Goods Market Cleared

As the goods market is cleared, transactions must be equal to the firm's effective supply of goods. Since the firm is unconstrained on the labour market, this supply is the neoclassical supply, that is:

$$y = F[F'^{-1}(w/p)]$$

Since there is excess supply of labour, employment is demand determined. As the firm is unconstrained on the goods market the demand for labour has the neoclassical form, so that:

$$l = F'^{-1}(w/p)$$

Combining these with the two other equations already seen, we obtain the equilibrium values as solutions to the following system:

$$
\begin{cases}
y^* = K(p^*, m, g, \tau) \\
y^* = F[F'^{-1}(w^*/p^*)] \\
w^* = \theta\phi(p^*) \\
l^* = F'^{-1}(w^*/p^*)
\end{cases}
$$

We may note already that the minimum price $\overline{p}$ no longer exerts any influence, an expected result since the goods market clears. To express the effects of policy parameters on production and employment, let us define the following elasticities:

σ: elasticity of the 'neoclassical' supply function $F[F'^{-1}(w/p)]$ with respect to w/p

κ: partial elasticity of $K(p, m, g, \tau)$ with respect to p

Note that $\sigma < 0, \kappa < 0$. Solving the system above we can first compute the effect of Keynesian policies:

$$\frac{\partial y^*}{\partial g} = \frac{\sigma(1-\epsilon)}{\sigma(1-\epsilon)+\kappa} \cdot K_g = \frac{\sigma(1-\epsilon)}{\sigma(1-\epsilon)+\kappa} \; \frac{1}{1-C_y} \geqslant 0$$

$$\frac{\partial y^*}{\partial \tau} = \frac{\sigma(1-\epsilon)}{\sigma(1-\epsilon)+\kappa} \cdot K_\tau = \frac{\sigma(1-\epsilon)}{\sigma(1-\epsilon)+\kappa} \cdot \frac{C_\tau}{1-C_y} \leqslant 0$$

We see that Keynesian policies are still effective, but less effective than in region A, even without any indexation ($\epsilon = 0$). Moreover, the efficiency of Keynesian policies decreases with the degree of indexation ϵ. With full indexation ($\epsilon = 1$) Keynesian policies become completely ineffective. We thus see that the issue of wage indexation is fundamental in assessing the efficiency of Keynesian policies in this region.

Now, contrarily to the case of region A, incomes policies become efficient in region B. Indeed we can compute the effect of variations in θ (in percentages for reasons of homogeneity):

$$\frac{\partial y^*/y^*}{\partial \theta/\theta} = \frac{\sigma\kappa}{\sigma(1-\epsilon)+\kappa} < 0$$

We see actually that a given percentage change in θ will have a greater effect, the higher the degree of indexation ϵ. This is quite intuitive since with a high degree of indexation a variation in θ acts more directly on the real wage, and we are on the supply curve in this region. Now the set of parameters such that region B obtains must be such that the equilibrium price p^* is higher than its minimum value, and that there is excess supply of labour, that is:

$$p^* \geqslant \bar{p}$$
$$l^* \leqslant l_0$$

Helping ourselves with the graphical representation of the solution (Figure 6.1 on p. 193) we see that these are respectively equivalent to the two following conditions:

$$\begin{cases} K(\bar{p}, m, g, \tau) \geqslant F[F'^{-1}\{\theta\phi(\bar{p})/\bar{p}\}] \\ K[\hat{p}(\theta), m, g, \tau] \leqslant y_0 \end{cases}$$

where $\hat{p}(\theta)$ is defined by (cf. Figure 6.1):

$$F[F'^{-1}\{\theta\phi(\hat{p})/\hat{p}\}] = y_0$$

Regime C: Excess Demand on the Labour Market, Goods Market Cleared

Since there is excess demand on the labour market, the level of employment is determined by the supply:

$$l = l_0$$

As for the goods market, the transaction is equal to both the supply and demand. Because the quantity of labour available to the firm is limited to l_0, the supply of goods by the firm is blocked at $y_0 = F(l_0)$. Hence:

$$y = y_0$$

The equilibrium values are thus determined by the following system:

$$\begin{cases} y^* = K(p^*, m, g, \tau) \\ y^* = y_0 \\ l^* = l_0 \\ w^* = \theta\phi(p^*) \end{cases}$$

We see immediately that neither Keynesian policies nor policies of wage restraint will have an effect on the level of employment, which is blocked at its maximum. They will, however, have an effect on the level of wages and prices. These effects are computed directly through the two relations:

$$\begin{cases} y_0 = K(p^*, m, g, \tau) \\ w^* = \theta\phi(p^*) \end{cases}$$

For region C to obtain, the parameters must be such that the equilibrium price is higher than its minimum, and such that there is excess demand on the labour market, that is:

$$\begin{cases} p^* \geqslant \bar{p} \\ l^* \leqslant F'^{-1}(w^*/p^*) \end{cases}$$

These conditions are respectively equivalent to (cf. Figure 6.1).

$$\begin{cases} K(\bar{p}, m, g, \tau) \geqslant y_0 \\ K[\hat{p}(\theta), m, g, \tau] \geqslant y_0 \end{cases}$$

A Graphical Solution

Looking at the above systems of equations, one sees that the equilibrium values p^* and y^* can be found at the intersection in (p, y) space of two curves: the 'aggregate demand curve':

$$y = K(p, m, g, \tau)$$

and a 'supply curve' $S(p)$ which consists of three parts (Figure 6.1): A vertical part (section A) corresponding to $p = \bar{p}$; a horizontal part (section C) corresponding to $y = y_0$; and a positively sloping part (section B) having as equation:

$$y = F[F'^{-1}\{\theta\phi(p)/p\}]$$

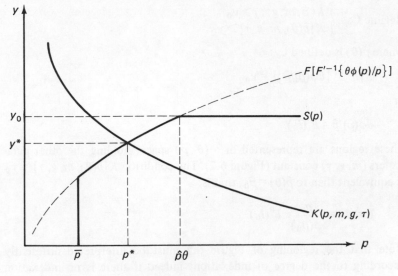

FIGURE 6.1

Note that section B may become horizontal if there is full indexation ($\epsilon = 1$). Moreover, it will actually be part of the 'supply curve' only if:

$$\theta\phi(\overline{p})/\overline{p} > F'(l_0)$$

We see immediately that the resulting equilibrium will be of type A if the two curves cut in section A of the 'supply curve', of type B if they cut in section B, of type C if they cut in section C. Case B has been represented in Figure 6.1.

Delimitation of the Regions

The conditions seen above showing for which subset of parameters one will be in each of the three regimes are found particularly easily by using Figure 6.1 and the corresponding figures for cases A and C, and checking there in which section the curves will cut each other. These conditions are respectively:

Regime A: $\begin{cases} K(\overline{p}, m, g, \tau) \leqslant F[F'^{-1}\{\theta\phi(\overline{p})/\overline{p}\}] \\ K(\overline{p}, m, g, \tau) \leqslant y_0 \end{cases}$

Regime B: $\begin{cases} K(\overline{p}, m, g, \tau) \geqslant F[F'^{-1}\{\theta\phi(\overline{p})/\overline{p}\}] \\ K[\hat{p}(\theta), m, g, \tau] \leqslant y_0 \end{cases}$

Regime C: $\begin{cases} K(\overline{p}, m, g, \tau) \geqslant y_0 \\ \dot{K}[\hat{p}(\theta), m, g, \tau] \geqslant y_0 \end{cases}$

where $\hat{p}(\theta)$ is defined by:

$$F[F'^{-1}\{\theta\phi(\hat{p})/\hat{p}\}] = y_0$$

or

$$\theta\phi(\hat{p})/\hat{p} = F'(l_0)$$

These regions are represented in a $(\theta, \overline{p})$ space, holding the other parameters (m, g, τ) constant (Figure 6.2). The condition $K[\hat{p}(\theta), m, g, \tau] = y_0$ is equivalent then to $\hat{p}(\theta) = p_0$, that is:

$$\theta = \theta_0 = \frac{p_0}{\phi(p_0)} F'(l_0)$$

Note that the regioning of Figure 6.2 must be interpreted differently according to the degree of indexation: indeed if there is no indexation ($\epsilon = 0$), θ has the dimension of a wage, while if there is full indexation ($\epsilon = 1$), θ has the dimension of a real wage.

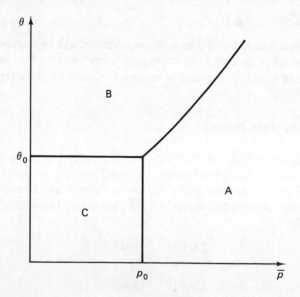

FIGURE 6.2

CONCLUSION

The simple model of this chapter has suppressed a few undesirable features of the standard non-Walrasian model of employment, eliminating notably demand rationing on the goods market, and introducing the possibility of wage indexation. Even though the demand for goods is satisfied in all circumstances, we still found that the efficiency of employment policies was quite different depending on the prevailing regime: in regime A we obtained the results traditionally associated with the Keynesian fixprice models where demand management policies are fully effective. In regime C at the opposite we found that demand management policies resulted only in price increases, as in the usual neoclassical full employment models. Finally, regime B gave a number of results that have been emphasized recently in policy discussions, notably that indexation can reduce considerably the effectiveness of demand management policies, even in the presence of involuntary unemployment. In the corresponding case, however, incomes policies are effective in reducing unemployment. The use of non-Walrasian equilibrium concepts in the study of macroeconomic problems appears thus as an efficient tool both to determine the policy consequences of different price formation mechanisms on the various markets, and to synthesize hitherto antagonistic theories within a single multiregime model.

NOTES

1. These two lines are developed extensively in Benassy, 1982.
2. Four regimes if inventories are added.
3. See, for example, the various adaptations in Benassy, 1976a, 1977a; Malinvaud, 1977; Muellbauer-Portes, 1978; and many others since.
4. See notably Branson and Rotemberg, 1980, on the efficiency of fiscal policies in an international context.
5. The 'Keynesian-classical' terminology is that of Malinvaud, 1977.
6. Subscripts to a function refer to a partial derivative, e.g. $C_y = \partial C/\partial y$.

REFERENCES

Barro, R. J., and H. I. Grossman (1971) 'A General Disequilibrium Model of Income and Employment', *American Economic Review*, 61: 82–93.
Barro, R. J., and H. I. Grossman (1976) *Money, Employment and Inflation*, Cambridge: Cambridge University Press.

Benassy, J.-P. (1975) 'Neo-Keynesian Disequilibrium Theory in a Monetary Economy', *Review of Economic Studies*, 42: 503–23.

Benassy, J.-P. (1976a) 'Théorie néokeynésienne du déséquilibre dans une économie monétaire', *Cahiers du Séminaire d'Econométrie*, 17: 81–113.

Benassy, J.-P. (1976b) 'The Disequilibrium Approach to Monopolistic Price Setting and General Monopolistic Equilibrium', *Review of Economic Studies*, 43: 69–81.

Benassy, J.-P. (1977a) 'A Neokeynesian Model of Price and Quantity Determination in Disequilibrium', in G. Schwödiauer (ed.), *Equilibrium and Disequilibrium in Economic Theory*, Boston: D. Reidel.

Benassy, J.-P. (1977b) 'On Quantity Signals and the Foundations of Effective Demand Theory', *Scandinavian Journal of Economics*, 79: 147–68.

Benassy, J.-P. (1982) *The Economics of Market Disequilibrium*, New York: Academic Press.

Branson, W. H., and J. J. Rotemberg 'International Adjustment with Wage Rigidity', *European Economic Review*, 13: 309–32.

Clower, R. W. (1965) 'The Keynesian Counterrevolution: A Theoretical Appraisal', in F. H. Hahn and F. P. R. Brechling (eds), *The Theory of Interest Rates*, London: Macmillan.

Drèze, J. (1975) 'Existence of an Equilibrium under Price Rigidity and Quantity Rationing', *International Economic Review*, 16: 301–20.

Hahn, F. H. (1978) 'On Non-Walrasian Equilibria', *Review of Economic Studies*, 45: 1–17.

Leijonhufvud, A. (1968) *On Keynesian Economics and the Economics of Keynes*, Oxford: Oxford University Press.

Malinvaud, E. (1977) *The Theory of Unemployment Reconsidered*, Oxford: Blackwell.

Muellbauer, J., and R. Portes (1978) 'Macroeconomic Models with Quantity Rationing', *Economic Journal*, 88: 788–821.

Negishi, T. (1961) 'Monopolistic Competition and General Equilibrium', *Review of Economic Studies*, 28: 196–201.

Negishi, T. (1979) *Microeconomic Foundations of Keynesian Macroeconomics*, Amsterdam: North-Holland.

Younès, Y. (1975) 'On the Role of Money in the Process of Exchange and the Existence of a Non-Walrasian Equilibrium', *Review of Economic Studies*, 42: 489–501.

7 Keynesian Unemployment as Non-Walrasian Equilibria*

DIETER SONDERMANN

INTRODUCTION

One of the fundamental insights that we owe to the work of Clower (1965) and Leijonhufvud (1968) is that the basic difference between the economics of the classics and the economics of Keynes lies in the assumptions made about the adjustment behaviour of the two systems: 'in the short run, the "Classical" system adjusts to changes in money expenditures by means of price-level movements; the Keynesian adjusts primarily by way of real income movements' (Leijonhufvud, 1968, p. 51). 'In the Keynesian macrosystem the Marshallian ranking of price- and quantity adjustments speeds is reversed. . . The "revolutionary" element of the General Theory can perhaps not be stated in simpler terms' (Leijonhufvud, 1968, p. 52).

As is well known, there are two extreme cases among all possible assumptions about the adjustment behaviour of an economic system (i) prices adjust infinitely fast (price-tâtonnement process), (ii) quantities adjust infinitely fast (quantity-tâtonnement process). These two cases lead

*The ideas of this chapter were first presented at the meeting of the Subcommittee for Economic Theory of the Verein für Socialpolitik, September 1978, in Hamburg.

I want to thank the members of the subcommittee for many helpful suggestions. I also profited from many discussions at various places where I presented this chapter in its original form as a paper. In particular, I wish to thank the participants of the seminars in Bonn, at CEPREMAP and MIT-Harvard.

The ideas were also presented as a contributed paper at the fourth World Congress of the Econometric Society, August 1980, in Aix-en-Provence.

to classical or Walrasian analysis at one end, and to fixprice analysis on the other. Both have been studied intensively, although the latter only quite recently (cf. e.g. Barro and Grossman, 1971; Benassy, 1975; Drèze, 1975; Grandmont and Laroque, 1976; Malinvaud, 1977). No doubt, the 'real world' lies somewhere in the whole spectrum of possible price-quantity adjustment processes in between these two extreme cases (cf. Leijonhufvud, 1968, p. 59). Also without doubt we can agree with Leijonhufvud that, in contrast to the classics, Keynes depicted, the 'real world' closer to the second extreme of the spectrum, and therefore concentrated his analysis on the real income (= quantity) adjustment process. This does not mean that Keynes considered prices as fixed (also not in the so-called 'short-run'), nor, in particular, that he merely explained unemployment by downward rigidity of money wages, as has been claimed by the neo-classical interpreters of the *General Theory*. But he was aware that 'income-constrained processes result not only when the price-level velocity is zero, but whenever it is short of infinite' (Leijonhufvud, 1968, p. 67). However, adjustment processes involving both price and income effects simultaneously on all markets are extremely difficult to handle and were beyond the analytical scope of Keynes's times. Keynes's merit was to cut the knot by going to the polar extreme of the classics.

Recent developments in the theory of differential and difference equations, called 'qualitative dynamics',[1] provide a tool to attack, at least partially, the complex problem of simultaneous price-quantity adjustment processes. Qualitative dynamics allows one to study the (qualitative) behaviour of a complex dynamic system without explicit quantitative specification of the adjustment speeds. It is sufficient to specify what part of the dynamic system is considered as 'fast' and which one as 'slow'. No numerical specification is made between 'fast' and 'slow'. The analysis is carried out under the *qualitative* assumption that 'fast' is of a different order of magnitude than 'slow'. How much faster 'fast' is than 'slow' needs no explicit specification. In particular, 'fast' does not mean *infinite* and 'slow' *zero* velocity. This is exactly the situation one meets in the adjustment behaviour of an economic system. Depending on which view we adopt — either the classical or the Keynesian — we believe that prices adjust faster than quantities or vice versa, without being able to give a precise numerical specification for our beliefs.

The present chapter can be considered as an exercise in qualitative dynamics. The results of this simple exercise are surprisingly rich. The exercise consists of starting with a temporary equilibrium model with production and adaptive expectations as developed earlier by the author (1974). Then this general equilibrium model is specialized to a three-commodity-world. As usual in the recent fixprice macroeconomic models, these commodities are consumption, labour and money. Under the qualitative assumption that quantities adjust faster than prices, the simple model thus obtained is analysed by means of the above-mentioned techniques. The result is that there exist equilibrium points, that is, stationary points of the simultaneous price-quantity adjustment process, where unemployment prevails, and, since the economic forces at such an equilibrium have come to a rest, without outside shocks, also *persists*. These unemployment equilibria are not a short-run phenomenon as a result of price rigidities. They may occur even when prices and wages are flexible, but not *perfectly* flexible (i.e. of infinite adjustment speed as the classics assumed). This kind of unemployment at equilibrium passes Keynes's test of 'involuntary unemployment' of Chapter 2 of the *General Theory*. It is therefore called 'Keynesian'. The term 'Keynesian unemployment' is also in accordance with Malinvaud's (1977) regime classification, since at such equilibria producers are constrained on the goods market and consumers on the labour market.

Furthermore, in the adjustment process the model deviates from most of the existing fixprice models in the treatment of the production sector. Instead of assuming an instantaneous neoclassical production function, firms are modelled as in my earlier work (1974) and thus their production decisions are also put into the uncertain environment of a temporary equilibrium. Consequently production decisions cannot be guided by perfect knowledge but must be based on expectations. Whereas Walras sensed 'there is still another complication . . . production . . . requires a certain lapse of time' and decided to 'resolve the second difficulty purely and simply by ignoring the time element at this point' (1954, p. 242), Keynes devoted all of Chapter 5 of the *General Theory* to this 'complication': 'The actual realized results of production and sale of output will only be relevant to employment in so far as they cause a modification of subsequent expectations. Meanwhile the entrepreneur. . . has to form the best expectations he can. . .; he has no choice but to be guided by these expectations, if he has to produce at all by processes which occupy time' (1936, pp. 47, 46). Another consequence of the time element is that monetary considerations enter production decisions. Not only consumers but also firms face a budget constraint. This fact has important consequences for the level of employment, although these effects may have come out too strongly in the present study owing to the absence of a bond market. In addition, the possibility to produce for inventories[2] also influences the level of employment in two ways: first, inventories influence the adjustment process directly by serving as a kind of buffer stock; second, increasing stocks have a downward pressure on the price level, and through adaptive price expectations, an indirect influence on employment. Finally, it is assumed that prices are set by firms in accordance with fluctuations in inventories as proposed by Kaldor (1939) that is, short-run fluctuations in demand do not change the price policy of the firm, but are met by selling out of or producing for inventories. Only when demand declines for several periods, and consequently inventories increase, will the entrepreneur lower his price, and vice versa. This price-setting behaviour is most compatible with a monopolistic competition environment (cf., e.g., Benassy, 1976; Chamberlin, 1956; Grandmont and Laroque, 1976; Negishi, 1960). However, this does not mean that monopolistic practices are responsible for the occurrence of unemployment. It is sufficient that markets are not 'perfectly competitive' and hence price level velocity falls short of infinite. Leijonhufvud has proposed the term 'atomistic' for such markets (1968, ch. 21, p. 2).[3]

The most serious limitations of the model are the absence of a bond market and the assumption of fixed capital stock. These limitations are shared with most of the existing fixprice models. The introduction of government activities and dividend payments is *ad hoc*, but it closes the model and makes it consistent with national accounting. For working with a representative consumer and a representative firm a general equilibrium theorist can only say a 'Pater peccavi'. At least the consumption sector could easily be modelled in a more satisfactory way as was done by Hildenbrand and Hildenbrand (1978). Furthermore, in this chapter, we only study the 'Keynesian regime'. There are three other regimes still to be analysed. Finally, although working with a dynamic equilibrium concept, our study remains purely static, that is, we only study the equilibrium points, but not the paths leading to them.

THE MODEL

The underlying model is the two-period temporary equilibrium under uncertainty model with production of my earlier work (1974). The characteristic feature of this model is that, since production takes time, firms face both uncertainty and a budget constraint. The present model is derived from this general model in a straightforward way by making the following three specifications:

(1) There exists only one input ('labour') and one output ('good') in the economy.

(2) There is only one asset ('money').
(3) Quantities adjust faster than prices.

For the three commodities of the model the following variables are used:
(i) the good can serve three purposes. First, it can be consumed by the consumers or by the government. Private consumption is denoted by c, public consumption by g. Second, it is used as an input for production, denoted by q. Third, it can be produced by firms. Production output and sales are denoted by y. (ii) Labour is offered by consumers, denoted by l, and used by producers as input, denoted by z. (iii) Money, whether held by consumers or producers or printed by the government, is denoted by m. Its price is normalized by one. Prices of the good and labour are denoted respectively by p and w. These notations are summarized in Table 7.1.

TABLE 7.1

Commodities	Quantities*	Prices
'Good'	c, g, q, y	p
'Labour'	l, z	w
'Money'	m	1

*All quantities are measured per capita.

CONSUMERS

It is assumed that consumers have price expectations conditioned by present (and past) prices and wages and that they maximize their expected utility of consumption and hours worked over two periods as follows:

$$E_{p_t} \; [u\,(c_t, c_{t+1}, l_t, l_{t+1})] = \text{Max}$$

$$\text{S.T.} \quad p_t\,c_t + m_t = w_{t-1}\,l_{t-1} + m_{t-1}$$

$$p_{t+1}\,c_{t+1} = w_t\,l_t + m_t$$

$$l_t = l_{t+1}, m_t \geqslant 0$$

Note the time lag in wage income, which means that wages are contracted at the beginning but paid at the end of the period considered. A particular consumer may be employed or unemployed at the beginning of period 1.

If he was unemployed in the past $(l_{t-1} = 0)$ he plans future consumption c_{t+1} under the assumption of finding the desired employment level l_t and keeping it on that level also during the next period $t + 1$. Hence whether or not the consumer was employed in the past or whether or not he finds employment in period t, c_t will be his *effective* demand of consumption. Clower's dual decision hypothesis (1965) is automatically fulfilled owing to the time lag in the income stream.

PRODUCERS

Since there are only two real commodities in the economy, one of which is labour which cannot be stored, the intertemporal technology of the firm (cf. Sondermann, 1974, ch. 8) is of the general form:

$$(q_t, z_t) \overset{F}{\to} \omega_{t+1}$$

where ω_{t+1} is the *net* production available in period $t + 1$, given the good input q_t and labour input z_t in period t. We will assume that F is of the special form:

$$F(q_t, z_t) = q_t + f(z_t)$$

where f is a classical production function with $f' > 0$ and $f'' < 0$. The firm is constrained in its transactions by its wealth which in the present model consists of its market value, that is, the market value of its output plus its money holding. Assuming as in my earlier work (1974) that the objective of the firm is to maximize its market value in the next period, allowing for the possibility that the management may be risk-averse, the firm faces the following decision problem:

Maximize $E_{p_t} [u(p_{t+1} F(q_t, z_t) + m_t)]$

S.T. $p_t q_t + w_t z_t + t^f + d + m_t = p_t \omega_t + m_{t-1}$

             $q_t, z_t, m_t \geqslant 0$

Here E_{p_t} denotes the conditional (subjective) expectation of p_{t+1}, given p_t. Furthermore:

   t^f = corporate taxes

   d = dividend payments

are considered here as exogenous respectively predetermined variables, meaning that:

$$FC = t^f + d$$

is considered by the firm as the fixed cost bloc.

Assuming furthermore that the management of the firm has point expectations, that is, $P(p_t) = p_{t+1}$, and assuming the special form of F, the objective function reduces to:

$$p_{t+1} (q_t + f(z_t)) + m_t$$

which is the expected market value at the beginning of period $t + 1$. If the firm sells the amount y_t at the beginning of period t, its liquidity is:

$$\widetilde{m}_t (y_t) = p_t y_t + m_{t-1} - FC$$

The decision variables of the firm are q_t and z_t which then determine the remaining endogenous variables y_t and m_t. The optimal decisions are given by:

Case A: $p_{t+1} \leqslant p_t$

$$(*) \quad z_t = \text{Min} \left\{ f'^{-1} \left(\frac{w_t}{p_{t+1}} \right), \frac{\widetilde{m}_t (y_t)}{w_t} \right\}$$

$$y_t = \omega_t$$

$$q_t = \omega_t - y_t$$

$$m_t = \widetilde{m}_t (y_t) - w_t z_t$$

Case B: $p_{t+1} > p_t$

$$z_t = \text{Min} \left\{ f'^{-1} \left(\frac{w_t}{p_t} \right), \frac{\widetilde{m}_t (\omega_t)}{w_t} \right\}$$

$$q_t = \frac{1}{p_t} (\widetilde{m}_t (\omega_t) - w_t z_t)$$

$$y_t = \omega_t - q_t$$

$$m_t = 0$$

Here y_t and z_t are the Walrasian supply and demand functions of the firm, that is, y_t are *planned* sales and z_t is *planned* labour input. Observe that the firm may not be able to realize its production optimum owing to lack of liquidity. However, at the beginning of period t the firm may find out that it is rationed on the goods market and that its realized sales $\bar{y}_t$ are less than its planned sales y_t. Then, according to the dual decision hypothesis of Clower, the firm has to revise its demand and supply schedule as follows:

Case A: replace everywhere y_t by $\bar{y}_t$

Case B: replace everywhere $\tilde{m}_t\,(\omega_t)$ by $\tilde{m}_t\,(\bar{y}_t)$

Leaving all other formulas unchanged, this gives, then, the *effective* demand and supply schedule of the firm.

THE GOVERNMENT

The government raises corporate taxes t^f from firms and income taxes t^h from employed consumers. On the other hand, it pays transfer payments z^u to unemployed consumers and has public consumption g. All these variables are treated as exogenous to the model. The budget of the government need not be balanced. Budget deficits are financed by printing money.

JOINT QUANTITY/PRICE ADJUSTMENT UNDER THE KEYNESIAN REGIME

There are four possible regimes in the economy depending on whether the good and the labour market are buyer's or seller's markets.[5] In this chapter we shall confine ourselves to the case of 'Keynesian unemployment', that is, the regime in which consumers are rationed on the labour market, whereas producers are rationed on the goods market. At the beginning of period t the history of the economy is summarized by an unemployment rate u_{t-1}, a money distribution m^e_{t-1} and m^u_{t-1} respectively for employed and unemployed consumers, and a money distribution m^f_{t-1} over firms. For simplicity we assume that these distributions are uniform.

Let $c^e\,(p_t,\,w_t,\,m^e_{t-1})$ denote the demand of an employed and $c^u\,(p_t,\,w_t,\,m^u_{t-1})$ be the (effective) demand of an unemployed consumer. Then the effective demand of consumption goods is given by:

$$y_t = g + (1 - u_{t-1})\,c^e\,(p_t,\,w_t,\,m^e_{t-1}) + u_{t-1}\,c^u\,(p_t,\,w_t,\,m^u_{t-1}) \quad (7.1)$$

Since producers are rationed by the effective demand on the goods market, y_t is also equal to realized sales. Then under Case A and the dual decision hypothesis the effective demand for labour is:

$$z_t = \text{Min} \left\{ f'^{-1} \left(\frac{w_t}{p_{t+1}} \right), \frac{\tilde{m}_t(y_t)}{w_t} \right\} = h\left(p_t, w_t, y_t, m_{t-1}^f\right) \qquad (7.2)$$

The Walrasian supply of labour is given by:

$$l_t = (1 - u_{t-1}) \, l \, (p_t, w_t, m_{t-1}^e) + u_{t-1} \, l \, (p_t, w_t, m_{t-1}^u) \qquad (7.3)$$

which in the Keynesian regime exceeds z_t. Hence the new unemployment rate u_t is determined by

$$l_t \, (1 - u_t) = z_t \qquad (7.4)$$

The four equations (7.1)–(7.4) describe a non-tâtonnement discrete-time quantity adjustment process. For the price/wage adjustment process we assume:

$$\Delta p_t = - K_t \, \Delta q_t \qquad (7.5)$$

where

$$\Delta q_t = q_{t+1} - q_t = f(z_t) - y_t$$

is the change in inventories and $K_t > 0$ an adjustment speed that may depend on t, but is bounded away from zero. Finally, wages are changed according to:

$$\Delta w_t = - \eta_{z,w} \, (z_t - l_t) \qquad (7.6)$$

where $\eta_{z,w}$ is the elasticity of the effective labour demand with respect to the (nominal) wage rate w.

Equations (7.1)–(7.6) define a joint non-tâtonnement quantity/price/wage adjustment process in discrete time. A stationary point of this process is called an 'equilibrium' of the economy. In equilibrium the dynamic forces are at rest. This is a *dynamic* equilibrium concept, in contrast to the static concept of an equilibrium as a state where demand equals supply.

The basic assumption under which the equilibrium points of the adjustment process defined by equations (7.1)–(7.6) are studied is the following assumption common in quantitative dynamics:

> (*QDA*) Although quantities and prices (including wages) adjust jointly, *quantities adjust faster than prices.*

This is in our view the crucial assumption that accounts for most, if not all, of the differences between Walrasian and Keynesian analysis. Whereas the Walrasian equilibrium concept requires that prices adjust faster than quantities,[6] Keynes's study of the real part of the economy rests on the opposite assumption. This does not mean that Keynesian analysis requires that prices and wages be considered as fixed or as rigid downward, as frequently suggested by interpreters of Keynes. It is all a question of the different adjustment speeds. Qualitative dynamics allows one to study the effects of different adjustment speeds without specifying numerically the difference. In analogy to Orwell: *all variables are flexible, but some are more flexible than others.*

QUANTITY ADJUSTMENT – THE 'SLOW MANIFOLD'

The procedure to study the equilibrium points of a fast/slow dynamic process in qualitative dynamics consists of two steps:

(1) Neglecting the slow dynamics, compute the stationary points of the fast dynamics. This defines the so-called 'slow manifold'.
(2) Study the slow dynamics on the slow manifold.

In the present context the fast dynamics is the quantity adjustment process defined by (7.1)–(7.4). The variables of this process are y, u, z, m^e, m^u and m^f. A stationary point is a point such that:

$$y_t = y_{t+1} = \bar{y}$$

$$u_t = u_{t+1} = \bar{u}$$

etc.

Since we restrict ourselves here to the Keynesian regime, we assume that:

$$\bar{z} < z^* \, (p, w) := f'^{-1} \left(\frac{w}{p} \right) \tag{7.7}$$

that is, firms do not reach their production optimum (otherwise the cause of unemployment would be 'classical', cf. Malinvaud, 1977).

Now (7.7) and $m_t^f = m_{t+1}^f = \bar{m}^f$ immediately imply:

$$\bar{m}^f = 0 \tag{7.8}$$

and

$$\bar{z} = \frac{\tilde{m}(\bar{y})}{w} = \frac{1}{w} \, (p \, \bar{y} - FC) \tag{7.9}$$

Since the firm is rationed on the goods market, inventories grow by the constant amount:

$$q_{t+1} - q_t = F(q_t, \bar{z}) - \bar{y} - q_t = f(\bar{z}) - \bar{y} = \Delta \bar{q} \tag{7.10}$$

From (7.9) it follows:

$$p \, \overline{y} = w \, \overline{z} + FC$$

This means that sales just cover the wage bill and the fixed costs. The difference between the value of the output and sales is involuntary inventory investment, since from (7.10):

$$p f(\overline{z}) - p \, \overline{y} = p \, \Delta \overline{q} = : s^f$$

We can now use equations (7.1)–(7.4) to determine y and u by solving the following equations:

$$\overline{y} = g + (1 - \overline{u}) \, c^e \, (p, w, \overline{m}^e) + \overline{u} \, c^u \, (p, w, \overline{m}^u) \tag{7.11}$$

$$(1 - \overline{u}) \, l \, (p, w, \overline{u}) = h \, (p, w, \overline{y}, \overline{m}^f) = $$
$$= \text{Min} \left\{ \frac{1}{w} \, (p \, \overline{y} - FC), z^* \, (p, w) \right\} \tag{7.12a}$$

In the $(\overline{u}, \overline{y})$-plane equation (7.11) is a straight line. For $\overline{z} < z^*$ (or $\overline{u}$ greater than the classical unemployment level $u^* = 1 - z^*/l$) equation (7.12a) can be approximated by the straight line:

$$\overline{y} = \frac{FC}{p} + (1 - \overline{u}) \, \frac{wl}{p} \tag{7.12b}$$

This approximation is exact if l, the (Walrasian!) labour supply, is independent of u. This is the case if the amount of money holdings has negligible influence on the demand for leisure.

(7.11) and (7.12b) can be easily solved graphically (see Figure 7.1).

Theorem 1:
A solution $(\overline{y}, \overline{u})$ exists iff:

$$t^f - z^u \leqslant p \, g \leqslant t^f + t^h \tag{7.13}$$

Theorem 2:
For any level of public consumption g satisfying (7.13) the government's budget will be balanced at the corresponding stationary state $(\overline{y}, \overline{u})$.

The proofs of these two theorems following from the budget equations. If we include taxes, dividends and transfer payments, they are at $(\overline{y}, \overline{u})$:

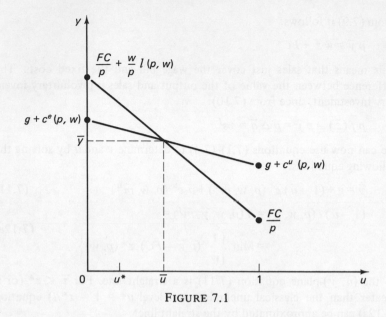

FIGURE 7.1

Consumers: employed $p\,c^e + t^h + \bar{m}^e = w\,z + d + \bar{m}^e$

  unemployed $p\,c^u + \bar{m}^u = z^u + d + \bar{m}^u$

Firms: $\dot{w}\,z + t^f + d = p\,\bar{y} = p\,c + pg$

Government: $p\,g + \bar{u}\,z^u + s^G = (1 - \bar{u})\,t^h + t^f$

PRICE ADJUSTMENT – THE 'SLOW DYNAMICS'

On the slow manifold we can now study the price adjustment process. The equilibrium points are those points on the slow manifold that are stationary with respect to the slow dynamics. By assumption:

$$\Delta p_t = - K_t\,\Delta q_t$$

with

$$K_t \geqslant \alpha > 0$$

Hence for an equilibrium price $\bar{p}$ it follows:

$$\Delta \bar{p} = 0 \text{ iff } \Delta \bar{q} = 0 \text{ iff } f(\bar{z}) = \bar{y}$$

Since in the Keynesian regime $\bar{z} < z^*$, this amounts to:

$$f(\overline{z}) = \overline{y} \quad \text{iff} \quad f\left(\frac{1}{w}\left(\overline{p}\,\overline{y} - FC\right)\right) = \overline{y}$$

$$\text{iff} \quad \overline{p}\,\overline{y} = w f^{-1}\,(\overline{y}) + FC$$

$$\text{iff} \quad \overline{p} = \frac{w f^{-1}\,(\overline{y}) + FC}{\overline{y}} = AC$$

Hence the equilibrium price $\overline{p}$ equals average costs, and there are no profits in equilibrium besides the exogenously fixed dividend payment d, which can then be interpreted as the 'normal' rate of profit. Since in our model firms set prices, this result is consistent with an industry operating under the conditions of monopolistic competition.

Given the wage rate w, an equilibrium is thus characterized by a triple $(\overline{y}, \overline{u}, \overline{p})$ satisfying the following three equations:

(i) $\overline{y} = g + c\,(\overline{p}, w, \overline{u})$

(ii) $(1 - \overline{u})\,l\,(\overline{p}, w) = \text{Min}\left\{\dfrac{1}{w}\,(\overline{p}\,\overline{y} - FC), z^*\,(\overline{p}, w)\right\}$

(iii) $\overline{y} = f\,((1 - \overline{u})\,l\,(\overline{p}, w))$

Hence in equilibrium we have the diagram given in Figure 7.2.

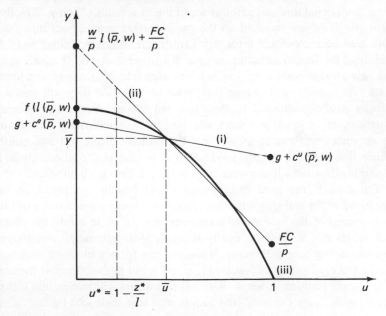

FIGURE 7.2

The solution $(\bar{y}, \bar{u})$ falls into the Keynesian regime if $\bar{u} > u^*$, where

$$u^* = 1 - \frac{z^* (\bar{p}, w)}{l (\bar{p}, w)}$$

is the classical unemployment level.

WAGE ADJUSTMENT

By assumption:

$$\Delta w = \eta_{z, w} (l (\bar{p}, w) - \bar{z})$$

where $\eta_{z, w}$ is the elasticity of the *effective* demand for labour.

In the Keynesian regime one has $\bar{z} < z^* (\bar{p}, w) = f'^{-1} (w/\bar{p})$. Since $f'' < 0$, this implies $f' (\bar{z}) > w/\bar{p}$ that is, real wage is less than its marginal product.[7] But since $\eta_{z, w}$ is non-negative, wages cannot rise. On the contrary, one would expect a downward pressure on wages since there is excess supply of labour. We will explain why in the Keynesian case wages will not fall, if both consumers and producers are 'rational'.

Assume that in the state $(\bar{y}, \bar{u}, \bar{p})$ the wage rate w would be lowered. Then firms could hire more labour according to formula (*) on p. 203. But since the firms are rationed on the goods market more labour input will only lead to involuntary inventory investment, which according to (7.5) will drive the former equilibrium price $\bar{p}$ further down till it equals again the new average costs *w.r.t.* to the lower wage rate. If, however, at a lower wage rate firms do not change their scale of operation they will realize a positive profit (additional to their long-run average dividend payments). Furthermore, output and sales will remain in equilibrium, stocks and hence prices will remain stable, and the positive profit will not vanish. Hence it is rational for the producers not to change the labour input, if labour is offered at a lower wage, that is, $\eta_{z, w}$ is zero in equilibrium.

But even if the total employment would remain unchanged, an unemployed individual may offer his labour at a lower wage in order to find employment at the expense of somebody else. In other words, the allocation seems not to be individually rational. More generally, unemployed consumers together with some producers can form a blocking coalition. Hence the equilibrium allocation $(\bar{y}, \bar{u}, \bar{p})$ is not in the core. But the core is a myopic solution concept. Rational consumers will realize that if they get a job by wage dumping, the people who lose their jobs by this dumping will drive wages still further down, so that workers can only lose by this strategy. Hence also individual rationality, combined with 'rational foresight', would require blocking only if the new allocation cannot be blocked by others. But, as is well known, this kind of rationality leads to the Neumann–Morgenstern-solution. In the case of Keynesian unemployment it is rational for the workers, whether employed or unemployed, to form a labour union that prevents wages from falling. Consequently, it is not the existence of labour unions that keeps wages downward rigid, which in turn leads to unemployment; rather, the logical chain runs in the opposite direction.

Similar rationality arguments apply to the producer side concerning price adjustment. For them it would be rational to form a cartel to prevent prices from falling to the equilibrium price level $\bar{p}$. Indeed, that is what they do if such cartels are allowed.

But in western economies, where labour unions are allowed and price cartels are controlled or prohibited, the equilibrium situation $(\bar{y}, \bar{u}, \bar{p})$ at the wage rate w is stable both in a dynamic and a game 'theoretic sense'.[8] Whereas $\bar{y}$, $\bar{u}$ and $\bar{p}$ are determined by equilibrium conditions only, the wage rate will depend upon the path on which the economy reaches equilibrium. But the path depends on the adjustment speeds of the dynamic process. In determining the other variables of the economy the use of qualitative dynamics dispenses us from the need of specifying exactly these adjustment speeds. But the wage in equilibrium depends on them. At least in the Keynesian regime there is no such thing as an 'equilibrium wage'. Hence the need for wage bargaining. And it is not surprising that an essential part of wage bargaining is concerned with these adjustment speeds.

CONDITIONS FOR FULL EMPLOYMENT

If there is full employment in the economy all three curves in Figure 7.2 will intersect on the y-axis. This means that one has:

$$f(l(p, w)) = \frac{w}{p} l(p, w) + \frac{FC}{p} = g + c^e (p, w)$$

The equality on the left-hand side is equivalent to:

$$p = \frac{w l + FC}{f(l)} = AC$$

This conditions is satisfied for $p = \bar{p}$. The second equality is equivalent to

$$w l + FC = p g + p c^e \tag{7.14}$$

From the budget constraint of an employed consumer it follows that in equilibrium:

$$p c^e = w l + d - t^h$$

Inserting into (7.14) yields:

$$p g = FC - d + t^h = t^u + t^h \tag{7.15}$$

But $t^u + t^h$ is the tax revenue of the government if there is no unemployment. Hence, if the government in the presence of unemployment chooses public consumption according to (7.15) the deficit spending will lead in our model to a full employment equilibrium with balanced budget.

Note: This result only holds if there is no basic level of classical unemployment in the economy, more precisely, if:

$$l (\bar{p}, w) \leqslant z^* (\bar{p}, w) = f'^{-1} \left(\frac{w}{\bar{p}} \right)$$

which is equivalent to $u^* \leqslant 0$

What are the characteristics of the equilibria arrived at in this model?

(1) They are non-Walrasian. Demand does not equal supply.

(2) They are stable in the sense that at these states the economic driving forces have come to a rest. Neither consumers nor producers find it advantageous to deviate from them.[9]

(3) They are the result of a non-tâtonnement process both in quantities and prices.

(4) There is 'involuntary unemployment' in the original sense as Keynes defined it. 'Men are involuntarily unemployed if, in the event of a small rise in the price of wage-goods relatively to the money-wage, both the aggregate supply of labour willing to work for the current money-wage and the aggregate demand for it at that wage would be greater than the existing volume of employment' (1936, ch. 2/iv). Note that Keynes asked for a double test for unemployment being truly of involuntary nature, and it is not difficult to see that in the Keynesian regime the unemployment equilibria pass both tests. *No blame can be assigned to any specific group.* We also remark that what has been called 'Keynesian unemployment' in the fixed price

literature (cf., e.g., Malinvaud, 1977) does not pass the second half of Keynes's test, and probably Mr Keynes would have refuted this terminology (cf. also Leijonhufvud, 1968, p. 93).

(5) Prices are neither fixed nor set by an auctioneer. They are set by producers with normal price expectations in the sense used by Kaldor (1939).

(6) Wages are neither fixed nor arbitrary nor inflexible. Unlike the other economic variables they are not determined by equilibrium conditions, but depend on the history of the economy.[10] In equilibrium they remain what they are since no agent finds it advantageous to change them.

(7) The dynamics of the economy may arrive at an equilibrium 'which we do not like' (quotation from Hahn, 1976). The decisions of the economic agents may be co-ordinated in such a way that the resulting outcome is inefficient. *There is something for the government left to do, namely, what Keynes suggested.*

NOTES

1. A special field of qualitative dynamics, known as 'catastrophe theory', has already found several applications in economics (see, e.g., Zeeman, 1974).

2. The effect of inventories have been studied by, among others, Böhm (1980), Honkapohja and Ito (1980), and Muellbauer and Portes (1978).

3. For other models with endogenous price-setting we refer to the excellent survey of Drazen (1980).

4. For alternative approaches to the theory of decisions by business firms in situations of uncertainty, see the excellent survey of Drèze (1982).

5. For a discussion of three of these regimes in a fixed price model – called respectively 'Keynesian unemployment', 'classical unemployment', and 'repressed inflation' – see, for example, Malinvaud, 1977. In the presence of inventories, as in the present model, a fourth regime, in which producers are rationed both on the goods and the labour market, may also occur (cf., e.g., Böhm, 1980; Muellbauer and Portes, 1978).

6. Walras's tâtonnement-process is just an extreme form of this qualitative assumption, since it requires that prices adjust infinitely faster than quantities.

7. If the real wage exceeds its marginal product then, according to equation (*), firms would not be constrained by their liquidity in their labour demand, but would choose $\bar{z}$ such that $f'(\bar{z}) = w/\bar{p}$. In this case the reason for insufficient labour demand is not the lack of liquidity (caused by insufficient sales) but too high a real wage. Of

course, in this case $\eta_{z,w}$ is negative and there is a downward pressure on wages. This is the regime called by Malinvaud (1977) and others 'classical unemployment'.

8. Clearly, the indicated game theoretic arguments still require further elaboration; in particular, the precise definition of the underlying game.

9. Such states have been called by Hahn (1978) 'Conjectural Equilibria'. This is, however, a rather vague concept. As John (1980) has shown recently, every fixed-price equilibrium can, in a rather trivial way, be sustained by conjectures that make it a conjectural equilibrium in Hahn's definition. And there are not many states in an economy that cannot be described as a fixed-price equilibrium.

10. In a slight modification of Hahn (1976) one could say: 'The wage is today what it is because the past was what it was'.

REFERENCES

Barrow, R. J., and H. I. Grossman (1971) 'A General Disequilibrium Model of Income and Employment', *American Economic Review*, 61: 82–93.

Benassy, J. P. (1975) 'Neo-Keynesian Disequilibrium Theory in a Monetary Economy', *Review of Economic Studies*, XLII: 503–24.

Benassy, J. P. (1976) 'The Disequilibrium Approach to Monopolistic Price Setting and General Monopolistic Equilibrium', *Review of Economic Studies*, XLIII: 69–81.

Böhm, V. (1980) *Preise, Löhne und Beschäftigung*, Tübingen: J.C.B. Mohr Verlag.

Chamberlin, E. H. (1956) *The Theory of Monopolistic Competition*, Cambridge, Mass.: Harvard University Press.

Clower, R. W. (1965) 'The Keynesian Counter-Revolution: A Theoretical Appraisal' in F. M. Hahn and F. P. R. Brechling (eds), *The Theory of Interest Rates*, London: Macmillan.

Drazen, Allan (1980) 'Recent Developments in Macroeconomic Disequilibrium Theory', *Econometrica*, 48: 283–306.

Drèze, J. H. (1975) 'Existence of an Exchange Equilibrium under Price Rigidities', *International Economic Review*, 16: 301–20.

Drèze, J. H. (1982) 'Decision Criteria for Business Firms', CORE Discussion paper no. 8211.

Grandmont, J. M., and G. Laroque (1976) 'On Temporary Keynesian Equilibria', *Review of Economic Studies*, XLIII: 53–67.

Hahn, F. H. (1976) 'Keynesian Economics and General Equilibrium Theory: Reflections on some Current Debates', Stanford University, Economics series, Technical Report 219.

Hahn, F. H. (1978) 'On Non-Walrasian Equilibria', *Review of Economic Studies*, 45: 1–17.

Hildenbrand, K., and W. Hildenbrand (1978) 'On Keynesian Equilibria with Unemployment and Quantity Rationing', *Journal of Economic Theory*, 18: 255–77.

Honkapohja, S., and T. Ito (1980) 'Inventory Dynamics in a Simple Disequilibrium Macroeconomic Model', *Scandinavian Journal of Economics,* 82: 184–98.

John, R. (1980) 'A Remark on Conjectural Equilibria', CORE Discussion paper no. 8009.

Kaldor, N. (1939) 'Speculation and Economic Stability', *Review of Economic Studies*, 7: 1–27.

Keynes, J. M. (1936) *The General Theory of Employment, Interest, and Money*, London: Macmillan.

Leijonhufvud, A. (1968) *On Keynesian Economics and the Economics of Keynes*, New York: Oxford University Press.

Malinvaud, E. (1977) *The Theory of Unemployment Reconsidered*, Oxford: Blackwell.

Muellbauer, J., and R. Portes (1978) 'Macroeconomic Models with Quantity Rationing', *Economic Journal*, 88: 788–821.

Negishi, T. (1960) 'Monopolistic Competition and General Equilibrium', *Review of Economic Studies*, 28: 196–201.

Sondermann, D. (1974) 'Temporary Competitive Equilibrium under Uncertainty', in J. H. Drèze (ed.), *Allocation under Uncertainty: Equilibrium and Optimality*, New York: Wiley, ch. 13.

Walras, L. (1954) *Elements of Pure Economics*, trans. W. Jaffé, Homewood, Ill.: Irwin.

Zeeman, E. C. (1974) 'On the Unstable Behaviour of Stock Exchange, *Journal of Economic Theory*, 1 (1).

8 A Micro-Macroeconomic Analysis Based on a Representative Firm: Progress Report*

YEW-KWANG NG

I developed in Ng (1982), referred to below as the first paper, a method of economic analysis incorporating elements of micro, macro, and general equilibrium to examine the effects of industry-wide or economy-wide changes in demand, costs, expectation, etc. on the average price and aggregate output (denoted mesoeconomics for ease of reference). The analysis is to be extended and applied in a number of directions in Ng (forthcoming, referred to below as the further study). This chapter outlines the main elements and some results of the basic model (the first section) and extensions (the third section) in non-mathematical terms, as well as illustrating a non-traditional result (possibility of real expansion/contraction with no effect on the price level in an equilibrium framework with realized expectations, no lags, no misinformation, etc.) in terms of the (real-wage) demand curve for labour (the second section). A remarkable aspect is that, with the conditions for the non-traditional result prevailing, the classical dichotomy between the real and monetary sectors is broken and we have: (i) aggregate demand curve for labour is lifted by an increase in nominal aggregate demand, or alternatively interpreted, (ii) the aggregate demand curve for labour is not the horizontal summation of the individual firm's demand curves. The practical possibility of this non-traditional result is increased if some firms are profit-constrained revenue-maximizers (see section entitled 'Profit-constrained Revenue-

*I am grateful to my colleague, Lachie McGregor, for his helpful comments.

216

maximizing firms on p. 227) and/or if (with the addition of a government sector) the possibility of changing tax-rates is considered (Ng and McGregor, 1983).

INTRODUCTION AND BASIC ANALYSIS

The concept of a representative firm was first used by Marshall (as far as I know). However, he used it to determine the normal supply price of a perfectly competitive industry. Here, the response of the representative firm is used to approximate the response of a typically non-perfectly competitive industry or the whole economy. More importantly, the effects of macroeconomic variables and secondary disturbances are included in our analysis.

Our non-perfectly competitive aspect resembles the analysis of imperfect competition in some respects. But the theory of imperfect competition greatly needs to be cast in general equilibrium terms, as emphasized by Triffin (1940) who himself has not gone much further than delineating specific cases (pure monopoly, circular and atomistic homeopoly and heteropoly, etc.). On the other hand, modern studies of monopolistic general equilibrium have been based, understandably, on some highly simplistic assumptions (not to mention the loss of comparative statics results).[1]

Our analysis may be particularly reminiscent of Chamberlin's (1933) analysis of monopolistic competition with his use of the pair of *dd* and *DD* demand curves. However, our analysis is used mainly for the whole economy while Chamberlin's analysis is exclusively for an industry. Second, while not attempting to downgrade the historical contribution of Chamberlin, his analysis yields few comparative statics results as emphasized by Archibald (1961). The use of the representative-firm methodology to an economy (and also an industry) allows us to derive definite comparative static results both for the short run and for the long run, both for aggregate output and for individual output (of the representative firm),[2] etc. Without adequately imposing the characteristics required by a representative firm, the behaviour of an individual firm (in the presence of economy-wide or industry-wide changes) is largely unpredictable (lack of comparative static results). But the whole group of firms and hence the representative firm is fairly predictable. I cannot resist the temptation of noting the similarity in thermodynamics and quantum physics where an individual event (e.g. movement of a particular molecule, radiation of a specific particle, etc.) is unpredictable, but a large number of events conform to fairly strict laws (e.g. half-life).

For many purposes, we are interested mainly in the responses of the whole economy or an industry to certain changes, not so much in the responses of a specific firm. For these purposes, a representative-firm analysis is adequate.

A question arises as to why concentrate on a representative *firm* and not a representative *consumer* instead. The simple reason is that price and output decisions are made and changed by firms. Since we want to model changes in prices and output, it is most fruitful to concentrate on the firm. Consumers do exert important influences on the decisions of firms through the demand functions for firms' products and through the input supply functions that affect the cost functions of firms. These influences of consumers are mainly modelled in our analysis through demand and cost functions.

A most straightforward case where a representative-firm analysis is acceptable is the case of a number of identical firms. Apart from changes in the number of firms, each firm is representative of the whole economy. Even if firms are not identical, one may still use a representative firm to approximate the whole economy if we define the representative firm appropriately.

Consider the marginal cost curve (*MCC*) illustrated in Figure 8.1. Start-

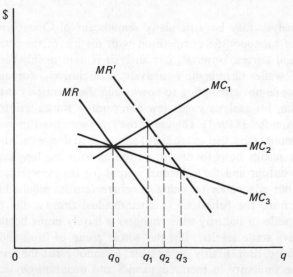

FIGURE 8.1

ing from an initial profit-maximizing equilibrium A, suppose the marginal revenue curve (MRC) moves from MR to MR': output will expand (abstracting from any possible movement in MCC to be discussed below) to q_1, q_2, q_3 respectively if the MCC is MC_1, MC_2, MC_3. Thus for the case of three firms of similar size with MC_1, MC_2 and MC_3, we may take MC_2 as the MCC of the representative firm. Somewhat unexpectedly (but certainly not counter-intuitively), a better way to define the elasticity of MCC is to take the weighted average of the corresponding elasticities of all firms (in practice of course only a sample can be used), using as weight not just the share of the individual firm in total production, but rather the product of this share and the income elasticity of demand for the firm's output (Ng, forthcoming). This is so since, with different income elasticities of demand, the MRC of different firms will move differently with respect to aggregate demand.

Some readers may have reservations about our analysis owing to its preoccupation with only a single (even though representative) firm. It may be thought that the interaction of a large number of firms is too complicated to be modelled by a single firm even as a first approximation. A single-firm analysis may fail to capture some essential elements of the interaction which are cumulative such that the firm completely misrepresents the economy. To dispel such scepticism, a general-equilibrium analysis of N firms is used to show that: (i) for any given exogenous change in cost or demand, there exists (in a hypothetical sense) a representative firm whose response to the change *accurately* (no approximation needed) represents the response of the whole economy in aggregate output and the average price, (ii) a representative firm defined by a simple method of weighted average can be used as a good approximation of the response of the whole economy to *any* economy-wide changes in demand and/or costs. This second question arises despite the theoretical existence of an *exact* representative firm since the latter is usually difficult to pin down in practice and only applies to a *given* change.

Obviously, the price and output of a single firm cannot represent the *structure* of prices or output levels of individual firms. It is the aggregate output and the average price that can be represented. Since inter-firm changes are ignored, mesoeconomics is designed to handle economy-wide (or industry-wide) changes in aggregate output and the average price of the whole economy (industry).

The representative firm is taken to face a demand function for its product which is non-increasing in its price. Thus perfect competition, monopolostic competition, and monopoly can all be allowed. But each firm is taken as small relative to the whole economy and the complication of oligopolistic interdependence has been abstracted away in the first paper but will be analysed in the further study. While recognizing that all prices, in general, affect the demand for the product of a firm, mesoeconomics is marked by the simplification of taking account of just the price of the product (p), the average price for the whole economy (P), (nominal) aggregate demand (α) and the number of firms (N). It is thus something like a convex combination of micro, macro, and general equilibrium.[3] In the first paper, the number of firms is also taken as given. Changes in this are analysed in the further study, which also allows for changes in demand elasticity as aggregate demand changes (assumed to cause isoelastic changes in demand in the first paper).

The cost of the firm is taken to be a function of its own output (q), the average price, the aggregate output (Q) and some exogenous factors (ϵ). Some commentators have been puzzled by the absence of wages. But the effects of wages are allowed through P, Q, and ϵ. An endogenous change in wages caused by higher prices or higher employment is allowed through π or Q. An exogenous change (including greater union militancy) enters through ϵ. Wages and a labour supply function can be explicitly introduced without affecting the analysis as done in Ng (1980).[4]

The firm is assumed to maximize its profits (constrained revenue maximization is analysed in the further study) with the corresponding first-order condition: marginal revenue (μ) = marginal cost (c). The comparative statics results are derived by the total differentiation of this condition as well as the requirement of aggregate equilibrium $\alpha = PQ = pq\bar{N}$ and the determination of aggregate demand by $\alpha = \alpha\,(P, Q, X)$ where X is some exogenous factor probably including the money supply. A number of propositions are derived, including the following (notation $\eta^{xy} \equiv \partial x/\partial y.\ y/x$).

Proposition 1. The primary effects of an exogenous increase/decrease in marginal costs are to increase/decrease prices and reduce/expand output less than/exactly/more than proportionately if *MCC* (the marginal cost curve of the representative firm) is upward-sloping/horizontal/downward-sloping. The second effects, through endogenous shifts in *MCC*, reinforce/offset the primary effects if $(1 - \eta^{\alpha P})\eta^{cQ} - (1 - \eta^{cQ})\eta^{cP} - (n^{\alpha P} - \eta^{\alpha Q})$ is negative/positive. The total effects are larger the larger/smaller are the (proportionate) responses of marginal cost to price/output changes and the less/more upward/downward sloping is *MCC*.

The primary effects in the borderline case of a horizontal *MCC* are illustrated in Figure 8.2, where the initial demand curve $D°$ is drawn as linear

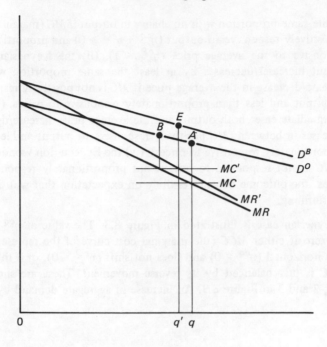

FIGURE 8.2

(not required for our results) for ease of drawing. A 10 per cent increase in
MC to *MC'* increases the price by less than 5 per cent (from *A* to *B*) before
the effect of a higher *P* on the demand curve is taken into account. However, as the exogenous cost increase is not confined only to this one firm
but is economy-wide, *P* increases as *p* increases, shifting the demand curve
upward. (As *P* increases, the same increase in *p* causes less decrease in *q*
than if only *p* increases; see the first paper for details.) This leads to a
further increase in *p* and hence *P*, and so on (but successively by smaller
and smaller amounts). A final equilibrium *E* is reached when both *p* and
P have increased by 10 per cent and output *q* has fallen by 10 per cent to
q' (if firms foresee this, the full adjustment may be instantaneous). It is
not difficult to see that, if *MCC* is upward/downward sloping, the changes
in *p* and *q* will be smaller/larger.

Proposition 2. The effects of an exogenous increase/decrease in aggregate demand (excluding the price and income-multiplier effects, which
reinforce the following responses) may be classified into the following
cases: (i) the quantity theory case: the average price increases/decreases

by the same proportion with no change in output if MC (marginal cost) is positively responsive to output ($\eta^{cq} + \eta^{cQ} > 0$) and proportionately responsive to the average price ($\eta^{cP} = 1$), (ii) the Keynesian case: output increases/decreases by at least the same proportion with no increase/decrease in the average price if MC is not positively responsive to output and less than proportionately responsive to prices, (iii) the intermediate case: both output and the average price increase/decrease for cases in between (MC positively responsive to output and less than proportionately responsive to prices), (iv) the Expectation Wonderland: if MC is not responsive to output but proportionately responsive to prices, the outcome depends entirely on expectation that will then be self-fulfilling.

The Keynesian case is illustrated in Figure 8.3. The value of $\eta^{cq} + \eta^{cQ}$ equals zero if either MCC (the marginal cost curve of the representative firm) is horizontal ($\eta^{cq} = 0$) and does not shift ($\eta^{cQ} = 0$), or if the slope of MCC is just balanced by its reverse movement. These are shown as cases 1, 2 and 3 in Figure 8.3. An increase in aggregate demand by x per

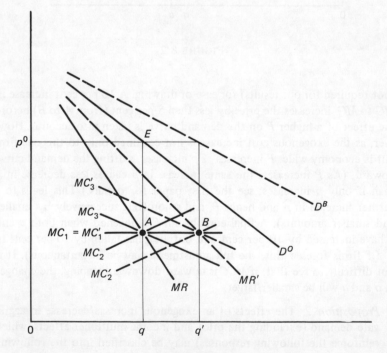

FIGURE 8.3

cent moves the demand curves and hence MRC (marginal revenue curve) rightward by x per cent if P is unchanged. The new MRC (i.e. MR') intersects the new MCC (MC'_1, MC'_2 or MC'_3 as the case may be) at an output level x per cent higher, with the profit-maximizing price remaining unchanged, confirming the original expectation of no price changes. If $1 - \eta^{cP} > 0$, it can be shown that this is the only expectation that will be realized in the present case of $\eta^{cq} + \eta^{cQ} = 0$.

The above result is based on the simplification that a change in real aggregate demand shifts the demand curve isoelastically or equiproportionately at each price, hence leaving the marginal revenue unchanged at any given price. If this assumption is relaxed, an additional term is needed on the effect of real aggregate demand on marginal revenue

$$\left(D \equiv \frac{\partial \mu}{\partial \alpha/P} \cdot \frac{\alpha/P}{\mu} \mid p, p, N \mid \right)$$

This does not completely invalidate the above results. It just means that $\eta^{cq} + \eta^{cQ}$ has to be replaced by $\eta^{cq} + \eta^{cQ} - D$.

THE NON-TRADITIONAL RESULT IN TERMS OF THE LIFTING OF THE DEMAND CURVES FOR LABOUR

The possibility of a real expansion/contraction without changing the price level (the Keynesian case and the Expectation Wonderland) in our model of no lags, no misinformation, etc. is a non-traditional result. This result may also be illustrated in terms of the (real-wage) demand curve for labour. This is interesting since, in the case where the non-traditional result prevails, the aggregate demand curve for labour is lifted by an increase in nominal aggregate demand, or, alternatively interpreted, the aggregate demand curve for labour is *not* a horizontal summation of the individual firms' (or micro) demand curves, as in the traditional case.

The condition for the non-traditional result is that the slope of MCC (the marginal cost curve of the representative firm) is offset by its shift as aggregate output changes. In a one-variable input (labour) model, this condition will be satisfied if (but only only if) the labour supply function and MCC are both horizontal. (Cumulative real effects are likely if the labour supply function is horizontal and MCC is downward sloping; see Ng, 1980, pp. 607-8.) In addition to this 'technical' condition, an expectation of no price effect is necessary if costs are proportionately responsive to prices (i.e. no lags, no money illusion). But the expectation, if held, will in fact be realized.

To have a horizontal *MCC* in a model of one-variable input (labour), the marginal physical product of labour is constant (over the relevant range). But the micro demand curve for labour is still downward-sloping as *MRC* is downward-sloping, making marginal-revenue-product curve downward-sloping. Each firm's demand curve for labour is downward-sloping because as it (the firm alone) expands employment and output, its marginal revenue falls, making marginal revenue product of labour fall despite a constant marginal physical product. Real marginal revenue product (*MRP*/price level) also falls since the price level is not appreciably affected by the firm's own expansion which reduces its own price and its own *MR*. But if all firms expand employment and output, real aggregate output and income increases, raising aggregate demand and hence raising the demand curve for each firm's product and *MRC* faced by each (or at least by the representative) firm. Under conditions where real expansion can take place without increasing prices, as in the case of Figure 8.3, marginal revenue remains unchanged ($q'B = qA$).

In terms of the micro demand curve for labour in Figure 8.4(a), the downward-sloping *dd* curve is lifted to $d'd'$, with the locus of equilibrium points *AB* as a horizontal line over the relevant range. (See the appendix for a more formal demonstration.) Thus the macro employment locus over the relevant range is the horizontal segment of the labour supply curve *SS* in Figure 8.4(b).

However, while there may be a continuum of equilibria between *C* and *G*, th economy may be caught at a particular equilibrium point, say A'

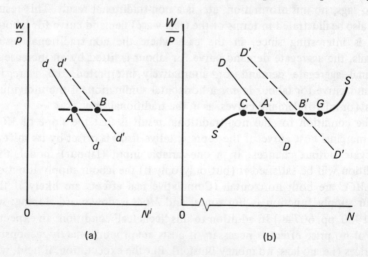

(a)   (b)

FIGURE 8.4

(corresponding to A at the firm level). This is so since each firm may be stuck at a point like A (Figure 8.3 and Figure 8.4(a)). If all firms expand simultaneously, they can all expand from A to B and the economy from A' to B', with expanded aggregate output and employment (and also profits, since average cost curves are downward-sloping). But each firm on its own cannot profitably expand. In using the representative firm analysis, one must not only be careful not to commit the fallacy of composition, one must also avoid the reverse one, the fallacy of attribution. It is wrong to attribute what all firms can do together to a single firm, even if representative. If a representative firm (which may not actually exist) knows that it is representative (in a model of a number of identical firms,[5] each may know precisely that), it knows that, if it charges a certain price (or expands output by a certain percentage) according to its profit-maximizing calculation, it will turn out to equal the average price of the economy (aggregate output of the economy will expand by the same percentage). Nevertheless, it cannot then assume that, whatever price it charges or whatever output expansion it undertakes, that will also be the result for the whole economy. This would be the case only if there were complete implicit collusion (not assumed in my model). In the absence of collusion, each firm has to maximize with respect to the variable under its own control. In fact, once a firm (but not all firms) does not follow this rule and acts as if the aggregate outcome will conform to whatever action it undertakes, it is no longer a representative firm. It may have representative cost and demand functions but its behaviour is no longer representative. Hence the aggregate outcome is *not* represented by its action.

With this understanding of the fallacy of attribution, one can then see that, though the marginal physical product of labour may be constant, the micro demand curve for labour is downward-sloping even if we stick to the realization of expectation, that the expected average price should equal the actual price of the representative firm. The whole demand curve D^O (Figure 8.3) and the micro demand curve for labour dd (Figure 8.4(a)) (and also D^B and $d'd'$) are consistent with the average price being equal to P^9. One cannot say that all points on the demand curve D^O except E are irrelevant since they do not equal the average price. The firm consults the whole relevant section of its demand curve to work out its marginal revenue. Even though no point other than E can be the equilibrium one, one cannot disregard all other points on the demand curve. The same is true for the micro demand curve for labour dd.

While the firm is stuck at A and the economy at A', an increase in money supply (or any other thing that causes the aggregate demand to increase) may initiate a real expansion by lifting the demand curve to D^B

(Figure 8.3) and the micro demand curve for labour to $d'd'$ (Figure 8.4(a)). This lifting is due to, at the risk of repetition, an increase in aggregate demand (both in nominal and in real terms), not to an increase in the price level. In fact, for the non-traditional case under discussion, the price level does not change. With the 'technical' condition prevailing, an increase in money supply (if not expected to increase the price level) increases only real output and employment. The representative firm moves from A to B and the economy from A' to B'. The lifting of the micro demand curve for labour from dd to $d'd'$ moves the economy from A' to B'. What about the aggregate demand curve for labour? Is it being lifted from DD to $D'D'$ (Ng, 1980) or is it just the locus $A'B'$ (Hillier, Lambert and Turner, 1982) in Figure 8.4(b)? The answer should be the former, at least if we take the conventional interpretation of the aggregate demand curve for labour.

According to the conventional interpretation, the aggregate demand curve for labour (DD and $D'D'$ in Figure 8.4(b) 'is merely the horizontal summation of all the firms' demand curves' (Crouch, 1971, p. 42). 'In general, the economy's (aggregate) demand curve for labour is found by horizontally aggregating all the firms' demand curves. Thus the economy's demand curve (for labour) behaves exactly as the average firm's demand curve does' (Hadjimichalakis, 1982, p. 49). This horizontal summation is taken to be the case even if monopolistic elements are introduced. 'In an economy with a mixture of monopolistic and competitive elements, the aggregate demand for labour will be a horizontal sum of many individual demand curves' (Branson, 1979, p. 100). With this conventional interpretation, the aggregate demand curve for labour is obviously being lifted from DD to $D'D'$, with $A'B'$ being merely the equilibrium employment locus.

However, one may argue, as Hillier, Lambert and Turner (1982) seem to, that the demand curve DD is based on a certain expectation about prices and aggregate demand. That expectation is realized only at the point A'. Similarly, the expectation consistent with $D'D'$ is only realized at B'. Thus, if we are confined to the realization of expectation, the aggregate demand curve is $A'B'$. It seems to me that this definition is better termed 'the equilibrium employment locus'. Even for a simple market demand curve for milk, only a single point on that curve is consistent with realized expectation in the general equilibrium system.

Nevertheless, even if we accept the definition of aggregate demand curve for labour by Hillier, Lambert and Turner, our non-traditional result (which is of course independent of semantics) is still remarkable with respect to the aggregate demand curve for labour since the latter is then not the horizontal sum of the individual firms' demand curves for labour as universally taken to be the case.[6]

SOME EXTENSIONS

Profit-constrained Revenue-maximizing Firms

The probability of the non-traditional result (real expansion/contraction with no change in the price level) prevailing is significantly increased if firms are profit-constrained revenue maximizers. The profit constraint is assumed to be effective as otherwise the firm will use the excess profit to engage in revenue-raising activities such as advertising (Baumol, 1958). The equilibrium of the firm is then marked by the intersection of the demand curve and the minimum-profit-inclusive average cost curve. Then, as shown in Figure 8.5, even if an upward-sloping input supply curve

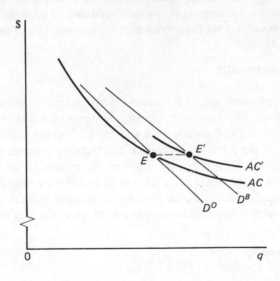

FIGURE 8.5

pushes the *AC* curve to *AC'*, an expansion from *E* to *E'* may yet involve no increase in prices. This case is more likely to prevail than case 3 in Figure 8.3 since it is more likely for *ACC* than for *MCC* to be downward-sloping.

The extension to the case of revenue maximization leaves all propositions in the first paper (including the ones reproduced above) unchanged except that all references to marginal cost should be replaced by average cost.

Long-run Analysis

The long-run analysis is marked by allowing the number of firms to be a variable and allowing for changes in demand elasticity at a given price as real aggregate demand changes. Apart from analysing the effects of entry/exit, the important specific case of free entry/exit is examined in some detail. In addition to expectation, the slope of the marginal cost curve (of the representative firm), the response of marginal cost to prices and output, important factors determining how output and prices will be affected by exogenous changes in cost, demand, etc., are: the degree of competition, the responses of total costs to prices and output, the effects of the number of firms and real aggregate demand on the demand elasticity. Both the quantity theory and the Keynesian theory are still special cases. A pure price expectational change (i.e. one not validated by changes in nominal aggregate demand, say via the money supply) may still be self-fulfilling.

The Case of an Industry

An explicit industrial demand function is introduced. The short-run and long-run effects of exogenous changes in costs, demand, etc. can be examined both for the general case and for the specific case of a 'small' industry where the price and output of the industry does not appreciably affect the costs of firms in the industry. In particular, an increase in marginal costs increases the price of a small industry by roughly the same proportion in the short run, an increase in demand *reduces* the average price of a small monopolistic-competitive industry in the long run.

Size and Oligopoly

Despite the generalization to account of oligopolistic elements, all propositions for an economy and for a 'small' industry remain valid, though the standard deviation of the probability distribution of the error of approximation becomes larger. In particular, despite the possible existence of kinks in the demand curves, a change in marginal costs leads to a roughly proportionate change in prices, contrary to the popular explanation of price rigidity by the kinky demand curve hypothesis. The empirical evidence of Stigler (1947), Simon (1969), Primeaux and Bomball (1974), etc. (see Reid, 1981 for a survey) on flexible oligopoly prices is thus consistent with our results. The generalization also subsumes pure monopoly, monopolistic and perfect competition as special cases.

Some Applications

Among other things, the analysis will be used to show that (i) mark-up pricing may be much more consistent with profit-maximizing marginalism than the traditional analysis suggests, (ii) it is the *industrial* demand elasticity rather than the concentration ratio (related to demand elasticities at the firm level) that is important with respect to the industrial power of the union, (iii) a contributing factor to the explanation of business cycles may be found in the (approximate) prevalence of the Expectation Wonderland, (iv) the analysis of the expectation-augmented Phillips curve, being implicitly based on perfect competition, may be misleading, since even if the expected rate of inflation is realized, output need not be at the 'natural' level, (v) indirect taxes may be fully, or even more than fully, passed on to consumers.

APPENDIX 8.1

Can the Micro, Real-Wage Demand-for Labour Function with Realized Price Expectations be Lifted?

The (inverse) demand-for-labour function of the representative firm is given by its real marginal revenue product of labour:

$$\mu f_{Ni}/P \tag{8.1}$$

where μ = marginal revenue, f_{Ni} = marginal product of employment of this i^{th} firm, N^i, and P = price level. To see whether the function can be lifted by an increase in money supply (M), differentiate (8.1) with respect to M at given N^i):

$$\frac{d\mu f_{Ni}/P}{dM} = \frac{\mu f_{Ni}}{P}\left(\frac{d\mu/dM}{\mu} - \frac{dP/dM}{P}\right) \tag{8.2}$$

In the special case of perfect competition, $\mu = P$ and $d\mu = dP$. The right-hand side of (8.2) thus equals zero. With perfect competition, an increase in money supply cannot lift the micro (or macro for that matter) demand-for-labour function. With non-perfect competition, as shown in Figure 8.3 in the text (and in more detail in Ng, 1980, especially appendix II), marginal revenue can increase proportionately more than price at given N^i (hence q^i). The right-hand side of (8.2) may thus be positive indicating that the micro demand for money function can be lifted. Price expectation is realized as shown in the text.

On the other hand, the macro demand-for-labour function is determined by the actual equilibrium points at the firm level. While marginal revenue increases proportionately more than price at given q^i, it increases by the same proportion as P (both remain unchanged) between the two equilibria A and B. Thus, the macro demand-for-money function does not shift.

For the case when real effects are absent (when the 'technical' condition does not prevail or when expectation is for a price change), the demand curve faced by the representative firm shifts vertically upward by the same proportion, leading to a equiproportional increase in marginal revenue even at given q^i (and N^i). In this case, both the micro and macro demand-for-labour functions remain unchanged, despite the fact that prices do increase.

NOTES

1. See Kuenne (1967, p. 219n) on some restrictive aspects of Negishi's (1961) pioneering analysis of general monopolistic equilibrium. Arrow (1971) also noted the use of the rather contrived condition of 'visibility'. Nikaido (1975) works with objective demand functions (this is what he means by 'effective' demand which is not aggregate demand in the macroeconomic sense as in our analysis) and hence represents an improvement over Negishi's analysis based on perceived demand functions. However, Nikaido has to adopt the very restrictive Leontief system. For some recent studies in the area of general monopolistic competition, see Hart, 1979; Novshek and Sonnenschein, 1978; Roberts and Postlewaite, 1976; and Roberts and Sonnenschein, 1977.
2. The response of aggregate output may differ from that of the individual output in the presence of changes in the number of firms.
3. If strict convexity of preferences, as assumed by economists, applies here, mesoeconomics must be superior to micro, macro, and general-equilibrium analysis, taking them to be of similar merit.
4. More traditionally, we may write the cost function as $C(q, P, w, \epsilon)$ where w is the (nominal) wage-rate. But since w may be written as a function of P, ϵ and L (labour), where L is itself a function of P and Q, we have our cost function that avoids the explicit introduction of w.
5. Identical in the sense of having similar cost and demand functions and behaviour but they may be producing differentiated (monopolistic competition) or completely different (monopoly) products.
6. See McGregor and Ng (forthcoming) for a more detailed treatment of the aggregate demand curve for labour.

REFERENCES

Archibald, G. C. (1961) 'Chamberlin versus Chicago', *Review of Economic Studies*, 24: pp. 9–28.

Arrow, K. J. (1971) 'The Firm in General Equilibrium Theory', in R. Marris and A. Wood (eds), *The Corporate Economy*, Cambridge, Mass.: Harvard University Press.

Baumol, W. J. (1958) 'On the Theory of Oligopoly, *Economica*, 25: 187–98.

Branson, W. H. (1979) *Macroeconomic Theory and Policy*, 2nd edn, New York: Harper & Row.

Chamberlin, E. H. (1933) *The Theory of Monopolistic Competition*, Oxford: Oxford University Press.

Crouch, R. L. (1971) *Macroeconomics*, New York: Harcourt Brace Jovanovich.

Hadjimichalakis, M. G. (1982) *Modern Macroeconomics: An Intermediate Text*, Englewood Cliffs, N.J.: Prentice-Hall.

Hart, O. D. (1979) 'Monopolistic Competition in a Large Economy with Differentiated Commodities', *Review of Economic Studies*, 46: 1–30.

Hillier, B., P. Lambert, and R. Turner (1982) 'Macroeconomics with Non-perfect Competition: Comment, *Economic Journal*, 92.

Kuenne, R. E. (ed.) (1967) *Monopolistic Competition Theory; Studies in Impact*, New York: John Wiley.

McGregor, L., and Y-K Ng (forthcoming) 'Can Aggregate Demand Affect the Demand Function for Labour? Different Results under Conditions of Perfect and Non-perfect Competition', (mimeo).

Negishi, T. (1961) 'Monopolistic Competition and General Equilibrium', *Review of Economic Studies*, 28: 196–201.

Ng, Y-K (1980) 'Macroeconomics with Non-perfect Competition', *Economic Journal*, 90 (September): 598–610.

Ng, Y-K (1982) 'A Micro–Macroeconomic Analysis Based on a Representative Firm', *Economica*, 49 (May): 121–39.

Ng, Y-K (forthcoming) *Mesoeconomics: A Micro–Macroeconomic Analysis*, London: Harvester Press.

Ng, Y-K and L. McGregor (1983) 'Macroeconomics with Non-perfect Competition: Tax-cuts and Wage Increases', *Australian Economic Papers* (December).

Nikaido, H. (1975) *Monopolistic Competition and Effective Demand*, Princeton: Princeton University Press.

Novshek, W. and H. Sonnenschein (1978) 'Cournot and Walras Equilibrium', *Journal of Economic Theory*, 19: 223–66.

Primeaux, W. J. Jr, and M. R. Bomball (1974) 'A Re-examination of the Kinky Oligopoly Demand Curve', *Journal of Political Economy*, 82 (July/August): 851–62.

Reid, G. (1981) *The Kinked Demand Curve Analysis of Oligopoly*, Edinburgh: Edinburgh University Press.

Roberts, D. J., and A. Postlewaite (1976) 'The Incentives for Price Taking Behavior in Large Exchange Economies', *Econometrica*, 44: 115–27.

Roberts, D. J., and H. Sonnenschein (1977) 'On the Foundations of the Theory of Monopolistic Competition', *Econometrica*, 45: 101–13.

Simon, J. L. (1969) 'A Further Test of the Kinky Oligopoly Demand Curve', *American Economic Review*, 59: 971–5.

Stigler, G. J. (1947) 'The Kinky Oligopoly Demand Curve and Rigid Prices', *Journal of Political Economy*, 55: 432–49.
Triffin, R. (1940) *Monopolistic Competition and General Equilibrium Theory*, Cambridge, Mass.: Harvard University Press.

Part III
Interpretation and Assessments of New Classical Macroeconomics: Theoretical and Policy Views

9 The New Classical Economics–A Game-theoretic Critique*

HENRY Y. WAN, JR

INTRODUCTION

From the game-theoretic perspective, the 'new classical economics' has elevated macroeconomic debates to a new peak of sophistication. Discussions are conducted in such terms as rational agents, equilibrium strategies, information structures and agent-government interactions. None the less, in any analytic treatment of an applied problem, neither the sophistication of problem formulation, nor the rigour of reasoning is sufficient to validate the conclusions. Specifically, whether the assumptions postulated are appropriate to the substantive issues must be weighed with methodical care. In this context simplifying assumptions may be harmless, but the omission of some essential mechanism is a completely different matter. In this study, we shall explore the conceptual foundations underlying the 'new classical economics'.

To begin with, the 'new classical economics' is at the confluence of two major streams of macroeconomic theory. Methodologically, it is one of several recent efforts to anchor macroeconomic theory to microeconomic foundations. To be specific, agents act rationally on their best available

*This chapter originated from my visit to the Board of Governors, the Federal Reserve Bank as a visiting scholar, in 1979. I benefited much from talks with M. Canzonieri, D. Henderson and G. Stevens. Subsequently, R. Radner encouraged me to continue this project. My colleagues, K. Burdett, R. Chirinko, S. Clemhout, D. Easley, and U. Possen offered comments to an earlier draft. I, alone, am responsible for all the opinions and shortcomings in this chapter.

235

information, while the interaction between the policy-maker and the agents play a central role in such analyses. Ideologically, it is the latest counter-attack by the 'conservative' economists against the Keynesian position. In fact, the 'new classical' school devotes little time to proclaiming their favourite policy — the same *laissez-faire* doctrine that goes back to the days of Adam Smith. Their basic mission is to rebut the Keynesian view, either with general, methodological discourses, or with elegantly constructed analytical parables.[1]

To recapitulate, a decade ago the Keynesian advocacy of macroeconomic stabilization could be summarized in a pseudo-chemical formula:

$$\text{Econometric models} + \text{Control theory} \rightarrow \text{Anti-cyclical policy}$$

Each of these three components has come under heavy fire from the 'new classical' school. From the methodological point of view, according to Lucas (1976), (Keynesian) econometric models are *useless* for policy evaluation, and according to Kydland and Prescott (1977), control theory is *inapplicable* to macroeconomics. Using carefully crafted parables, Lucas (1972), as well as Sargent and Wallace (1975), suggest that macroeconomic policy may be irrelevant for the systematic alleviation of cyclical economic fluctuations. In defence of the relevance of these parables, Lucas (1981a) cites as evidence (i) that their detractors care to criticize them, and (ii) they are so hard to construct.[2]

Such strong opinions have not gone unchallenged.[3] Some critics emphasize that presently available micro theory may not supply a suitable basis for macro economics. Others focus attention on econometric evidence. Still other economists question the robustness of specific parables by debating the realism of each, on an equation-by-equation basis. We shall concentrate on a somewhat different angle, that is, the appropriateness of the postulates of the new classical economics. Of course, almost inevitably, quite a few of the points raised here have been mentioned by other economists. Inasmuch as exhaustive cross-reference is impossible, I shall disclaim originality on any argument with which the readers happen to agree.

In the second section we shall outline the major postulates adopted in most of the new classical school literature, and comment upon them. In the third section we review the claim that (Keynesian) econometrics is useless for policy evaluation. It appears that not only the concept of policy revision is ambiguous but the alleged misspecification of (Keynesian) econometric models is a moot point. In the fourth section, we examine the claim that control theory is inapplicable to macroeconomics. Again we find the validity of that assertion questionable, if government policy is supposed to be credible, and hence 'sub-game perfect'. In the fifth section, we scrutinize the claim that anticipated government policies must be neutral and it turns out that once the 'homogeneous agent' assumption is relaxed, policy may have systematic effect. The sixth section supplies some concluding remarks.

THE BASIC POSTULATES

We shall outline five postulates for easy reference. While to our knowledge, these have not been formally presented in one place in this form, we do believe that we are not guilty of gross misrepresentation:

P1 (Rational Expectations)

All individuals have subjective probability distributions over future events that agree with the conditional objective probability distribution, corresponding to their respective information. This latter includes:

(a) The *economic structure* that implies that given (i) the 'past history', (ii) the 'government policy', (iii) the 'general environment', then a known 'outcome' follows.
(b) *Government policy* that is anticipated.
(c) *Past history*.
(d) 'Local environment'.
(e) The statistical association between the local and the general environments.

Remarks:
(1) The 'past history' is a sequence of 'states', one for each past period, where the state description includes the economic conditions, for example, output, agents' actions, government measure and 'environments', for example, weather and prices.
(2) 'Government policy' is a contingent plan prescribing government measures, for example, 10 per cent increase of money supply, to particular configurations of 'past history', for example, 10 per cent unemployment for ten months.
(3) The general environment is not instantly known to all individuals, but the local environment is. From past experience, individuals can forecast the general environment in probability terms from the local environment.

(4) Outcome of the economic structure includes the economic conditions, agents' actions and the government actions, for the present.

P2 (Individual Rationality)

Individuals maximize their expected objectives, which means expected utility for households and expected profits for firms.

P3 (The Natural Rate Hypothesis)

Macroeconomic policy matters if it affects the *local environment* and causes unanticipated shifts in the estimated general environment.

P4 (Continued Market Clearance)

At any positive market price, the demand and supply of the good in question must match.

P5 (The Absence of Market Failure)

Neither monopoly power, nor externalities, nor any similar factors, prevent perfect competition or Pareto optimality from prevailing.

P1 and P2 together are used in the methodological attacks against (Keynesian) econometrics and the application of control theory. All five postulates are needed to show that macroeconomic stabilization policies are futile means to dubious ends: futile, because systematic policy will be anticipated and therefore ineffective; dubious, because government intervention is unwarranted if Pareto efficiency already prevails.

Before analysing the specific claims of the 'new classical school', we offer some general comments regarding the realism of the postulates and their impact.

(1) *Risk or uncertainty.* According to the trichotomy of Frank Knight, uncertainty is a situation where one cannot assign known, meaningful objective probabilities to specific outcomes. In a laboratory, one can assign subjective probabilities to an agent when he has taken certain choices among various lotteries. But one cannot describe his expectations as rational nor is there a logical basis for another person to predict his action beforehand. This may create difficulties for a researcher to predict the action of this second person as well, on the basis of his rationality. Such a difficulty is well known to Lucas (1977), who essentially hopes

this problem will go away. It also lurks behind Keynes's view that investment depends on 'animal spirit'. The same phenomenon is perhaps at the bottom of the 'co-ordination failure', emphasized by Clower and Leijonhufvud (1975) as the cause for economic crises. The presence of uncertainty will render P1 and P2 undefined. The 'new classical' claim against control theory will become meaningless, even though traditional control theory must be substituted by some other approach (e.g. Leitmann and Wan, 1977). Moreover, the 'new classical' claim against macroeconomic policy also becomes tenuous; P3 and P5 hardly apply under uncertainty.

(2) *Uniqueness.* P1 assumes a unique outcome, that is, the natural rate in P3. If multiple equilibria coexist, conceivably the government can influence the likelihood for some equilibrium to happen. For instance, the declaration of a Bank Holiday by Roosevelt probably affected the outcome of the economy in a crisis situation. This invalidates P3. Cass and Shell (1980) note that in a monetary economy multiple equilibria may coexist, offering opportunities for intervention. We may recall that in general equilibrium theory, there is no palatable condition that may be imposed on agents to assure uniqueness (see Arrow and Hahn, 1971). One might classify equilibria as 'stable' or 'unstable' by some criterion. However, there may be multiple stable equilibria. One consequence of this is that there is no natural way to estimate the odds at which equilibrium will materialize. This is a genuine cause for Knightian uncertainty. One needs novel approaches to analyse such issues (e.g. Wan, 1979; Gertler and Wan, 1981).

(3) *Rational expectations.* In the absence of random shocks and imperfect information, rational expectations reduce to perfect foresight. The 'new classical school' postulates randomness, in order to accommodate imperfect information. The purpose of postulating imperfect information is to prepare the way for policy-by-surprise. Thus, the *laissez-faire* ideology can coexist happily with the Phillips-curve phenomenon. But, for our purpose, we can concentrate on the simpler concept of perfect foresight.

In their professional life, presumably most economists are believers in free will and not predestination. Perfect foresight does not imply the inspired divination of the manifested destiny, but the self-fulfilling prophecy. But if the successful accomplishment of a task is self-fulfilling, so must be its complement: failure at that task. Hence, inherent in the definition of rational expectations, multiple probabilistic relations must prevail. An example of this sort is found in a theatre on fire: orderly evacuation and chaotic disaster are both self-fulfilling events! Yet this example suggests a further dilemma, if self-fulfilling events involve group interaction, the infinite-regress arrives with 'I expect that you expect that I expect. . .' One might claim that this is not necessarily a problem: consider the prisoners' dilemma as a Nash equilibrium. Yet the case of a single Nash equilibrium (e.g. prisoners' dilemma) can never be guaranteed. Multiple Nash equilibria (e.g. the battle of the sexes) are well known to exist. Here, the final horror raises its head. Without pre-play communication, the presence of multiple equilibria invalidates the descriptive value of any equilibrium: one never can foretell which equilibrium strategy the other player(s) will choose. Hence, the scenario of rational expectations almost guarantees Keynes's view of 'animal spirit', the Clower–Leijonhufvud concern for 'co-ordination failure' – and the natural benefit of intervention!

One might argue that learning may gravitate the economy to one equilibrium. This is not true.[4]

(4) *Aggregation*. In most examples of the 'new classical' literature, the uniqueness of outcome comes serendipitously from aggregation. In general, a model with identical consumers will have a unique equilibrium (i.e. the 'Hicksian' economy in Arrow and Hahn, 1971). However, with 'localized' events, two identical twins, one luckier than the other, may trade at two equilibria, as long as Engel's curves are non-linear (see Wan, 1979). The 'new classical' literature often adds additional assumptions to rule out multiplicity. However, the fact that all agents are *ex ante* identical has additional implications (again favouring the conservative cause!).

In olden days, even advocates of conservative economics had to face the efficiency-equity trade-off. Life turns out to be simpler these days. In microeconomics, the study of incomplete markets (e.g. Hart, 1975; and Grossman, 1977) shows that competitive equilibrium may no longer guarantee Pareto efficiency. In macroeconomics, the assumption of one single type of agent has removed the equity issue by aggregation!

The more important point for a less aggregated model is that in such a case, macroeconomic policy may gain leverage through the redistribution of purchasing power among groups with differential behaviour patterns. In fact, in the English tradition of 'capitalists save all and workers spend all', there is built-in leverage for the government by redistribution (see Kaldor, 1955-6).

(5) *Market clearance*. Lucas (1978) regards Keynes's distinction between voluntary and involuntary unemployment as evasive and wordplay. However, it is possible to construct microeconomic models that will allow for involuntary unemployment (e.g. Solow, 1980). In fact, this can be done through the imperfect information phenomenon (see Foster and Wan, 1983).

THE POLICY-DEPENDENT ECONOMIC STRUCTURE: LUCAS

Macroeconomics arose to answer policy needs. It is its relevance to policy-making that justifies the 'heroic aggregation' that bypasses all details. Central to all macroanalysis is the role of the government. It is Lucas's perception of the government's role that transforms the rational expectations concept overnight: from the estimation tool of Muth (1961) to the central instrument against the Keynesian theory.

We shall first recapitulate Lucas's framework:

The government selects its *policy*, which is a sequence of periodic *decision rules*, one for each period, extending over the entire horizon of the future. Each decision rule prescribes the complex of *government measures* taken at a period, according to the available *information*, that is, the entire *historical series*, up to that date. Such series include for each period, the *state of the economy*, the *government measures*, and *individual actions*.

Individuals supposedly experience *government measures* prevailing in the present, and perceive the *government policy* relevant for the future. They act according to their own best interest. The evolution of the system is thus decided.

Under the same policy, different measures may be taken over time. Under different policies, the same measure may be taken in some situations. Individuals are presumed to perceive readily the distinction between a change of measure and a change of policy. They adjust to both.

Thus the economic system may be affected by the government through two distinctly different channels: *directly* through the impact of *government measures* and *indirectly* through the modification of individuals' behaviour (i.e. *how* to act under *what* available information), in relation to changes in the perceived *government policy*.

Lucas (1976) claims that econometric models, up to that date, described the system's performance under the past *government policy*. The effectiveness of government measures, deduced from past observations under the same policy, can never portray the impact of a contemplated policy change. 'Fatally' misspecified by neglecting such structural discontinuities, these econometric models can lend no support to the Keynesian counter-thrust against his position (e.g. as in Modigliani, 1977).

This same view of Lucas also underlies the conceptual structure of the entire new classical economics literature, including, in particular, both the Kydland–Prescott view and the Sargent–Wallace position on macro-economic policy, quite apart from the fact that the former claims that control theory leads to suboptimal policies but the latter concludes that no policy can matter systematically.

In turn, the validity of Lucas's position hinges upon the appropriateness of his interpretations of one single concept, namely, 'government policy'. Inasmuch as this term carries quite different connotations in its common usage, its role in the traditional macroeconomic literature, and in decision science (i.e. control theory and game theory), we must approach this term with as much pedantic care as we can.

Taken literally, the justification of the Lucas view depends on the following four conditions:

(1) The government *can* formulate such a policy.
(3) The government *will* formulate such a policy.
(3) The (private) agents *understand* such a policy.
(4) The (private) agents *believe* such a policy.

None of these is a simple matter. We shall consider each in turn.

(1) According to Lucas, a policy is distinctly different from the *current* government measures taken under it, precisely because it foretells what 'the government' might do in *future* contingencies. Yet 'the government' is a sequence of regimes, none of which can commit its successor which displaces it at the ballot box or by means a good deal stronger. President Carter could not have bound President Reagan after the latter's inauguration. Reza Shah Pahlavi could not dictate what Ayatollah Khomeini should do in ruling the Islamic Republic. The length of tenure of any regime is always probabilistic, at any rate, providence wills it! The most the current regime can do is to limit the room for action of its successor, as is treated in the models of Phelps and Pollak (1968), as well as Peleg and Yaari (1973). Still, the private agents must play a multi-stage game, with the 'attributes' of the government-player stochastically distributed in each separate future stage.

(2) Granted that (private) agents presume the indefinite permanence of the incumbent regime, that regime probably will never formulate policies, as theorized by Lucas, but make *piecemeal* decisions, as observed by Sims (1980). In fact, governments have good reasons for their *piecemeal* decision-making. That mode of operation, in turn, will matter greatly in assessing the realism of Lucas's view.

In principle, real-life agents may set up the full complement of Arrow–Debreu markets for contingent claims, each promising the delivery of some commodity in a particular event. Event specification should cover exhaustively various details, for example, am I in a 'working mood' this morning, or how many agents of what characteristics will be born on which future date. Since (i) the setting up of markets and the specification of contingent claims are costly, (ii) agents' ability to solve problems of astronomically large dimensions is limited, (iii) the verification of some event (e.g. *my* 'working mood') is difficult, and (iv) most Arrow–Debreu markets may be too 'thin' to be competitive, the real world almost surely would never operate in this fashion. Even if they lead lives of Diogenesian simplicity, agents would make piecemeal plans and trade on spot markets in a sequence of dates.[5] It is beyond comprehension how any economist can seriously postulate that governments will formulate exhaustively comprehensive plans for their infinitely more complex affairs.

(3) Even granted that a government formulates such a *policy*, there is no evident reason why it will make public such details of the policy that are of interest to the agents. Casual empiricism shows that there are types of government plans usually announced to the public, for instance, the Humphrey–Hawkins Full Employment Act and the constitutional amendment for balancing the federal budget, advocated in some circles. Other plans related to the reservation prices in the competitive sales of public properties are sometimes held secret. The same holds for the guidelines for government interventions in foreign exchange markets, under a 'dirty-float'.

(4) Finally and most importantly, even if the government proclaims the current comprehensive policy, the private agents probably will doubt that such a policy can remain 'on course' throughout their planning horizons.

It must be emphasized that the above discussion is not a matter of mere 'descriptive accuracy', If the answer is 'no' to either point (1) or point (2), there is no policy to be evaluated. If the answer is 'no' to either point (3) or point (4), agents continue to respond as if the old policy had continued, so that no misspecification will arise, and the (Keynesian) econometric procedure is the right one to choose.

But even if the answers are 'yes' to points (1), (2), and (3), a deeper issue exists, casting doubts on the Lucas formulation altogether. It almost surely implies that the answer to point (4) is a partial 'no'. As we shall see, that is enough to blunt Lucas's critique. Consider the following example.

During the policy evaluation in period t_1, the available econometric data come from periods t_0 to $t_1 - 1$ inclusive, under the current policy P'. Any meaningful policy evaluation must encompass at least two options: *both* the continuation of P', *and* the supersession of P' by some other policy P'', starting from period t_1 or a later date. The adoption of P'' must inevitably prove to the agents that their faith in P' was *mis*placed. Once burnt, twice wary, the agents must then suspect that the arrival of still another policy at some unknown future date $t_2 > t_1$ would render P''

itself *null and void*, from period t_2 on. After all, in recent US history, what was done under the 18th Constitutional Amendment was undone under the 21st.

All the arguments raised above point to one direction: real-life agents act upon their observed government measures for the present and their probabilistic beliefs of the periodic government decision rules in the future. Such beliefs themselves are derived from the observed government measures, as well as other 'incoming messages', for example, institutional reforms. Like the current prices in the temporary equilibrium models (see Grandmont, 1977), present government measures affect the economic system in their dual roles: *both* directly *and* as 'incoming messages' that modify agents' behaviour by serving as predictors for future government actions. Such dual roles are played by present government measures in exactly the same manner as they were played by past government measures. These presumably can be captured by well-specified econometric models. Other 'incoming messages' about future government decisions such as official statements, institutional changes, etc. will be best accommodated through 'dummy variables' and 'judgemental model revisions' as econometricians have always been doing.[6]

The upshot is, discrete policy revisions are undefined, if policy is to be interpreted in the Lucas sense. In their place in real life' is a continuous stream of Bayesian iterations on the part of private agents who use periodic observations of government measures for successive updating. In practice, this does not mean that conventional econometric models are less fallible than we have always known them to be. In methodology, however, econometric procedures are never guilty of Lucas's charge.

One might question, why does the same simplifying assumption — that decision-makers make comprehensive contingent plans — prove so fruitful in game theory, decision theory and many microeconomic contexts, yet become objectionable in the macrorational expectations literature. The best answer can be found in Friedman (1953): the choice of an assumption must depend upon the specific context. In Friedman's example, to assume that all the mass of the earth concentrates at its centre is satisfactory for Newtonian dynamics but 'as wrong as one can ever be' for explaining plate tectonics. The assumption that decision-makers plan exhaustively becomes wrong only in conjunction with another postulate: such plans are instantly and perfectly understood by other decision-makers, throughout their continuous interactions. Again in Friedman's terms, what is wrong is not merely its lack of descriptive realism but the fact that what is unrealistic happens to be analytically relevant. Citing Friedman still again, to assign putative telepathic powers to private agents is like to assume tree-leaves migrating in seeking sunlight. What begins as a *deceptively simple* parable ends up as a *simply deceptive* fallacy.

As game theoretic traditions go, one might illuminate matters further with the analogy of a parlour game. Consider a chess game where the black is played by a single player, but the white is played by members drawn randomly from a team for each move. The random scheme may be state-dependent, for example, when in-check, the player of the last move is excluded from being drawn for the next move. Clearly, the black (the private agent) cannot hope to understand the strategy of '*the* particular player' for the white (the government). Neither a unique opponent, nor a comprehensive strategy for the opponent, exists, in any event. Nor is there any chance that he will be informed of a trustworthy, genuine strategy for the white, even had such a strategy existed. The likelihood of the opponent's subsequent moves may be assessed from the white's current moves, as well as from other information on the board. The one playing black should use his information optimally and play optimally in the Bayesian way. It is not possible for him to know or to explore the entire contingent plan of the next player for the next move, outside that single response to the black's current move. There is never any sense in trying to divine the changes in the opponent's strategy, more than there is sense in counting the colours of the threads on the emperor's invisible robe!

Convinced that it is to his advantage, a white player might try to trick the black into the belief that his move has more profound influence over his successors' moves than is truly the case. He might even succeed, either because the black player fails to respond optimally, or, because, with imperfect information, even a Bayesian player cannot always call his opponent's every bluff. But what is said above should be true for the *past*, no more or less than it is for the *present*. Both the *past* attempts and successes of such tricks, if any, are on record, within the transcript of the play. That transcript can be judged as *fatally misspecified* for evaluating the current white's move, only if the plaintiff can establish, beyond reasonable doubt, that the present player of the white enjoys such significantly superior ingenuity to trick, compared with his predecessors, as to make a real difference to his choice. Wishful thinking of the current white, over successsive contingent moves, beyond his own tenure, is admittedly entertaining, but regrettably irrelevant, and hardly worthy of evaluation. On this point, we rest our case.

It is time to speculate why those macroeconometric models performed so poorly during the 1970s, if they are not 'fatally flawed' as Lucas claims. The truth may be simpler than most of us have imagined, even though no easy solution might be in sight. The 1970s was the first period in US history when a 'creeping' inflation transformed itself to double-digit price rises during peacetime. Any success in predicting such an occurrence requires the extrapolation of some empirical relationship outside the usual range of observations. Extrapolation is a challenging task requiring care, insight and good luck.[7] Consequently, erroneous prediction of inflation in the 1970s does not imply that some methodological mistake has been committed.

THE TIME-INCONSISTENCY OF THE OPTIMAL POLICY: KYDLAND AND PRESCOTT

Following Lucas's view on government policy, Kydland and Prescott (1977) concluded that in macroeconomic applications, both dynamic programming and control theory yield sub-optimal solutions. Hence, most Keynesian studies of macroeconomic stabilization must be faulty. The crux of their view is that optimal policies must be 'time-inconsistent'. Since both dynamic programming and optimal control satisfy Bellman's 'principle of optimality', their solutions must exhibit 'time-consistency', and therefore cannot be optimal. We shall first digress into a few relevant concepts, before assessing the merits of the Kydland–Prescott case. The theory of 'dynamic games' supplies the framework.

In the description of the macroeconomic system (as in the beginning of the last section), it is generally assumed that:

(1) The objectives of both the government and private agents are sums (or integrals) of expressions that may depend upon:
(a) the *state* (vector) of the economy,
(b) the *government measures*, and
(c) *agents' actions* pertaining to the particular instant, and
(2) The evolution of the state may depend upon items (a), (b) and (c) in (1), but not upon how the *present* state comes into being (history is irrelevant).

Factors that affect the system but are not affected by it (e.g. solar output) may be summarized as the effect of 'calendar time' which is a component of the state of the economy.

In the usual Keynesian models, attention is focused on the decision-making of the government, and no explicit recognition is given to private agents who also optimize intertemporally. For Kydland and Prescott, the government is surrounded by private agents who take the government policy as given.

Let us divide the entire time horizon into two arbitrary, successive phases. Bellman's *principle of optimality*, roughly translated, states that: 'A policy which is optimal for the entire horizon, must be *optimal in each phase*'. To make this precise, one must define a 'sub-problem', and a class of 'sub-policies', so that *optimal in the final phase* (that is, among alternative 'sub-policies' for that 'sub-problem') has its obvious meaning.

Consider, for example, the *original problem* of causing the state to evolve from $\underline{x}$ at $\underline{t}$, to $\overline{x}$ at $\overline{t} > \underline{t}$, with the least welfare loss from cyclicalities between $\underline{t}$ and $\overline{t}$. A programme proposes an evolution path that has the state equal to x_0 at some t_0, $\underline{t} < t_0 < \overline{t}$. Then one can unambiguously define a *sub-problem*: how to steer the state to evolve from x_0 at t_0 to $\overline{x}$ at $\overline{t}$, causing the least welfare loss, between t_0 and $\overline{t}$. Bellman's *principle of optimality* states that the optimal *policy* for this *optimal problem* prescribes the same government measures at (x_0, t_0), as would an optimal (sub-) policy for the *sub-problem*, at the same (x_0, t_0).

Write the optimal policy for the original problem in its sequence form:

$$(d_{\underline{t}}(\cdot), d_{\underline{t}+1}(\cdot), \ldots, d_{t_0}(\cdot), d_{t_0+1}(\cdot), \ldots, d_{\overline{t}}(\cdot))$$

then the subsequence,

$$(d_{t_0}(\cdot), d_{t_0+1}(\cdot), \ldots, d_{\overline{t}}(\cdot))$$

remains optimal for the sub-problem, for each t_0 between $\underline{t}$ and $\overline{t}$, as long as the state evolves under the optimal policy. This aspect is referred to as 'time-consistency'.

In an intertemporal game (i.e. 'multi-stage game' or 'differential game', depending on whether time is discrete or continuous), one may define a 'Nash non-cooperative equilibrium' in terms of a list of 'strategies', one for each player, in the following manner: Suppose each player regards the strategies of all *other* players as given, he can seek an *optimal policy* for himself, called the *best reply* to the other players' strategies. In so doing, he treats the other players' strategies as if they were part of 'nature'. A merchant operating in bi-metalist days, with his government guaranteeing unlimited convertibility between silver and gold, can assume that the government is no different from a chemical (or alchemical?) process, transforming one metal into another in an automatic fashion. A Nash non-co-operative equilibrium of strategies is a list of strategies, one per player, and each is a 'best reply' for the collection of all the others. Here Bellman's *principle of optimality* is generalized by Selten (1975) as 'sub-game perfectness'.

In the static analogue of oligopoly, the Nash non-co-operative equilibrium corresponds to the Cournot–Nash solution. Suppose that one player assumes that all other players will use their 'best replies', whatever his choice, and he does not limit himself to using a 'best reply', *relative to the other players*, then in principle he might do better: optimizing with fewer restrictions could never make one worse-off. In fact, in the oligopolist case, Stackelberg showed that one would do better. The so-called 'best reply' is *best* only to answer a *fixed* message, and the fact that other players use *best replies*, means their messages are *variable*, and *not fixed*, so that there is no point in responding to them by such 'best reply' of one's own.

The application of such an idea in dynamic games led to the Stackelberg differential game of Chen and Cruz (1972). The adaptation of such an idea to macroeconomics is the principal thrust in Kydland and Prescott. They further deduced the time-inconsistency property of their (Stackelberg) optimal policy for the government. This can be illustrated as follows.

Example

A *principal* may desire the change of the state of the world, say, a pile of snow, which may be affected by the (unobservable) 'action' of the *agent*, e.g. snow-removal, a feat incurring 'disutility' to the latter. Thus the principal may proclaim a 'contract' for the agent: a reward will automatically go to the agent if the 'outcome' of a desired state, say, *all* snow is gone, happens. The granting of this reward is costly to the principal. There is a known upper limit of the agent's performance, per unit of time, say, how much he can remove, per hour.

Imagine that events happen in the following sequence:

Date 1	*Intermediate period*	*Date D*
Contract awarded	The agent *may* work and other natural forces, e.g. natural melting, also operate, beyond the principal's observations	Outcome inspected and reward paid

Clearly, the closer is the date of verification, the *less* the principal is likely to agree to pay: within the time-span left, the effort of the agent is not likely to be able to affect the outcome very much, anyway. The important fact is that the *announcement* of the contract should precede the date of inspection with a sufficient time-span, in order to induce the agent to work. This is a clear example for time-inconsistency.

In assessing the macroeconomic significance of the Kydland–Prescott view, four points should be made:

First, Kydland and Prescott argued against the use of control theory in macroeconomics by showing that the optimal Stackelberg policy must have the time-inconsistence property. Actually, their case against control theory can be reached even if no optimal Stackelberg policy exists and hence there is no test for time-inconsistency. Recognizing private agents who adopt their 'best replies' to any government policy, the application of control theory by the government implies a Nash non-co-operative equilibrium for a dynamic game, in which the government policy must also be a 'best reply' to the strategies of private agents. Let:

P be a government policy

$B(P) = Q$ be the agents' best reply, which
                is assumed to be unique, here

$W(P, Q)$ be the government's objective function,

then the government's Nash policy, P^N, solves:

Problem N Max $W(P, B(P))$
subject to: P is a best reply to $B(P)$,   (*)

while the government's optimal Stackelberg policy. P^S, solves:

Problem S Max $W(P, B(P))$

Even if Problem S has no optimal solution, it must have a feasible solution no worse than P^N (since P^N itself is feasible for Problem S), and possibly some superior feasible solution P^f such that $W(P^f, B(P^f)) > W(P^N, B(P^N))$. All this is due to the relaxation of requirement: (*).

Second, sometimes the optimal Stackelberg policy is ill-defined, if the agents have more than one 'best replies' to a particular government policy. Consider the following example where the government has only two policies: P^1 and P^2, and for the agent, $B(P^1) = Q^1$ but $B(P^2) = \{Q^2, Q^3\}$. The government's objective function is such that:

$$W(P^2, Q^2) > W(P^1, Q^1) > W(P^2, Q^3)$$

In this case, the government might hesitate to adopt P^2, since it is completely up to the agent to use Q^2 or Q^3 against P^2, and the adoption of Q^3 may be quite unfavourable to the government.

The same dilemma can also arise for the Nash policy.

How relevant is this consideration depends upon whether the government can modify the rule of the game, adding to P_2, by providing some modicum of inducement to encourage agents to adopt Q^2 rather than Q^3 in response.

Third, more seriously, the Stackelberg formulation may become unrealistic, if some private agents, single or *in coalition*, would challenge the government policy rather than accept it as given and seek their self-interest accordingly. Unionized labour, or self-employed operators, may carry out direct challenges, for example, the English General Strike of 1926, the Chilean truckers' strike against Allende and the defiance of the Polish Solidarity Union against the 'leadership role' of the Communist Party. A more complex issue is the parliamentary lobbying by special interest groups.

Fourth, the most crucial assumption for the Stackelberg policy is that the private agents believe that those policy proclamations of the current regime will remain in force over their own planning horizon. This has been extensively discussed in the previous section, so that we shall concentrate on a single issue below: the 'credibility' of the policy proclamations.

Any *time-inconsistent* policy contains the inherent temptation for the policy-maker to renege. History is replete with repudiated public debts and suspended convertibility clauses for paper currencies. If legal provisions can be declared as 'inoperative' by pleading *'force majeure'*, there is even less hesitation for regimes to alter 'doctrines', 'traditions', or 'usages' that the private agents are *led to believe* is the government policy. For, in reality, macroeconomic policy in the sense of Lucas exists only in the hearts and minds of private agents. When one regime succeeds another, whether to continue the policy of the *ancien régime* is completely at the pleasure of those displacing it. It may be argued, therefore, that any *credible* macroeconomic policy must be 'subgame perfect', and hence 'time-consistent'. This is a Nash equilibrium strategy of the government when private agents are explicitly taken account of. If one then subsumes all activities of the private sector into an aggregate equilibrium response towards the government, and considers that as the 'environment', then the government's policy becomes an optimal solution of control theory.

In the context of American macroeconomic policy, Tobin (1977) has discussed the difficulty of implementing such a Stackelberg strategy, as advocated by Fellner. In a micro context, Radner (1980) prefers subgame perfect strategies. Thus, the Kydland–Prescott view is moot.

THE NEUTRALITY OF GOVERNMENT POLICY: SARGENT AND WALLACE

Among all positions taken by the advocates of the Macro-Rational Expectations Hypothesis, the one that attracts the most attention is the view that *policies do not matter*. This view was set forth by Sargent and Wallace (1975) at two different levels, by literal argument and through a demonstration with a simple, and admittedly *ad hoc*, example. The latter has been much debated equation by equation, variant by variant. We shall instead step back and take a *game*-theoretic view, asking what properties a model must have, for the Sargent–Wallace position to be valid. After all, the weakness or strength of a single illustrative model should not be decisive for the validity of a general macroeconomic position.

We should state at the outset that *game theory* is a formulation that does not rule out the possible coincidence of interest among all players. At worst, it reduces to the special cases of 'the theory of teams' or 'the theory of mathematical programming', depending respectively upon whether relevant information can or cannot be costlessly pooled among all individuals. Specifically, the interaction between a democratically elected government and its constituents can be cast as a game, at the potential danger of a redundant formulation, but nothing worse.

We shall assume, as Sargent and Wallace apparently did, that the government can be modelled as a single player, formulating policies that cover the entire planning horizon. By definition, an anticipated policy is instantly known to every agent, down to the last specifics. Having discussed the realism of all these in previous sections, we turn to ask what more might be needed to prove the Sargent–Wallace results. For this purpose, we shall need some notations.

Let P be government policy; $B(P)$ the set of 'best replies' of the private agents to P, which may or may not be unique; A the class of all strategy pairs (P, Q) with the agent's contingent plan Q belonging to $B(P)$, that is, when the agent uses his *best reply*. Then we can state:

The Sargent–Wallace proposition:
The pay-offs for either the government, or the private agent are exactly the same over the entire class, A. If we can represent A schematically, then all 'points', that is, strategy pair (P, Q), in A belong to the same indifference class for both the government, and the private agent. Included in A is the subset A^* of pairs (P^*, Q^*), with Q^* in $B(P^*)$, where P^* represents *laissez-faire*, and $B(P^*)$ is the set of 'best replies' of the private agents to it.

Following the Sargent–Wallace proposition, no anticipated interventionist macropolicy can do better than the *laissez-faire* policy, but nor can it ever be worse.

On the other hand, for unanticipated policy, agents can only use their imperfect knowledge to hedge against it. This will have a Phillips curve effect. Agents cannot be fooled for ever; the systematic alleviation of business cycles requires an anticipated policy.

What conditions one must impose to obtain such unusually strong results remain to be seen. In the context of monetary policy, the Sargent–Wallace argument may be reduced to the following components:

(1) Only the real balance and the relative prices matter in macroeconomics and nothing else.

(2) Real balance and relative prices take unique equilibrium values in the absence of government interventions.

(3) Government interventions *would* be 'offset' by private agents, so long as the latter have the information and capacity to do so.

(4) Private agents *can* and *do* fully 'offset' the government policy in that the choice of government policy has no effect on the pay-offs of all parties.

With regard to point (1), Cass and Shell (1980) have shown that even such things as 'sunspots' and placebos that people are misled to believe as important will matter. With regard to point (2), Cass and Shell (1980) indicated that in overlapping generation models with money, an infinity of equilibria may coexist. Hence, there is no reason for a system to return to a position before the perturbation. With regard to (4), B. Friedman (1970) and Fischer (1977) raised objections due to both the agents' ability to learn and the restriction of long contracts. Point (3) remains to be considered:

We note that by and large, money is created by open-market operations and not through the proverbial helicopter drop. Open-market operations allow banks to expand their credit, granting more loans to investors than they receive as deposits from the savers. Investors and savers differ in their propensities to spend. The redistribution of purchasing power among these two groups inevitably exercises a leverage effect. It is an effect that will not be offset. The investors who gain from it would not and the savers who lose out cannot. Hence, monetary policy is likely to matter, in a systematic and predictable way. The argument here is analogous to the analysis of Tobin (1980) against the 'Ricardian' doctrine.

It is time to recall that Friedman (1968) as well as the 'new classical' school never claimed that *micro*economic policy and institutional reforms have no effect on the 'natural rates'. The *deus ex machina* in their position is that government policies can be neatly partitioned into a macro–micro dichotomy, or equivalently what they regarded as the macroeconomic policy would not have 'side-effects' indistinguishable from what they regarded as the microeconomic policy. The public works programme in Roosevelt days must have had undeniable micro-effects. The analysis of debt-finance by Tobin (1980) points out the micro-effects of substituting tax by debt issues. The financing of public expenditure by monetary expansion, or the monetization of debts, raised for counter-cyclical public expenditures, brings in micro-effects of the monetary policy as well.

All in all, based upon the existing arguments of the 'new classical' school, the view that 'anticipated policies are ineffective' is less than convincing.

SOME CONCLUDING REMARKS

Several of the points made above have appeared in the voluminous literature. In fact, advocates of the new classical view have time and again stated that real-life government policies are often piecemeal, and the understanding of the government policy is often imperfect. However, these observations and remarks are not usually set in such a perspective and context. It is in that respect that we hope our discussion can help to achieve a balanced assessment of the 'new classical' view.

In a nutshell, the new classical school has set forth a logical framework that is based upon 'very strong' assumptions. They are *strong* in the sense that their validity appears unlikely and counter-intuitive. Whether such apparently unrealistic conditions are none-the-less fruitful approximations of reality must be decided by empirical evidence, which lies beyond our present scope.

It is important to emphasize that the evidential assessment must proceed with care. The current resurgence of 'monetarism' in its new classical form owes much to the aftermath of the inflationary episodes since the latter part of the Lyndon Johnson administration. One interpretation of this sequence of events is that the Keynesian policies of the Kennedy–Johnson era succeeded by *fooling* a public that was money-illusion-prone. But quite a different interpretation would be to recognize that monetary and fiscal measures for expansion have their 'genuine' stimulating effects, through such channels as the disparate spending propensities of debtors and creditors, etc. By 'genuine', we mean that such effects do not depend upon the imperfect information of the public about government intentions. This does not contradict the fact that continued use of such expansionary measures beyond certain limits would cause long run deleterious effects. As analogies, the frequent application of the footbrake by a driver against the down hill slide may wear out the brake. The injudicious prescription of antibiotics against minor infections may usher in either an allergic reaction of the patient, or even the emergence of antibiotics-immune strains of bacteria in the environment. It may be an effective expedient to warn drivers and physicians, by saying that the braking mechanism and the antibiotics would matter only when car tyres and bacteria are temporarily 'fooled' by 'surprises', and in the longer run, such 'surprises' are bound to wear off. However, such explanations neither help in the search for the full scientific truth, nor contribute to designing the optimal responses of the drivers and doctors on the scene. Such explanations are on the level of 'migrating tree-leaves thesis' à la Friedman, or 'creation myths', well known to all ancient cultures and modern folklorists. Their connection to botany and scientific cosmology must be said to be somewhat 'unclear', at the moment.

In our subjective assessment, most of the alleged defects of Keynesian economics, alluded to in the first section, are 'not proven'. The new classical literature has mainly contributed in stimulating all economists to enrich macroeconomic discussions with microeconomic analysis.

A methodological note is apropos at this juncture. Game theorists are usually most cautious in staking claims for the descriptive value of any single 'solution concept' (e.g. Shubik, 1982). Leading microeconomists, without exception, are keenly aware of the fact that many real-life issues lie beyond the present state of the art. What distinguishes macroeconomics from microeconomics is perhaps a matter of context and hence approach. In microeconomics, researchers select research topics among the relatively researchable, namely, where simple and tractable equilibrium concepts capture the essence of the real-life problems. In macroeconomics, researchers batter against a single problem of predominant importance to society: the current paucity of neat, appropriate models provides insufficient cause to suspend the effort. Consequently, we should be sympathetic to efforts to bring an ever-wider range of analytic artillery to bear on this all-important problem of macroeconomic stabilization; at the same time we should be ready to recognize all the inherent difficulties in various approaches.

NOTES

1. For example, only a single chapter in Lucas (1981b) is a policy paper, the only such paper he ever wrote, according to himself. In that article he rests his defence for the Friedman programme upon the 'presumption of ignorance'. The 'new classical' literature endeavours to show that the Keynesian theory has not narrowed down our ignorance of the nature of business cycles.
2. It is intrinsically difficult to say how relevant is a parable. However, the two points (i) and (ii) strike us as rather unusual grounds to defend a parable. If (i) is taken seriously, then *any* denial of *any* assertion seems to grant the latter stature. If (ii) is to be stressed, one might develop the suspicion that the difficulty in its construction suggests that it is an artificial curiosum. More persuasive defence should be sought.

3. As a *random* example, Modigliani (1977), Shiller (1978), Buiter (1980), Chow (1981), Grossman (1980), Hahn (1980), and Tobin (1980). Quite a few others are cited in the text.
4. Blume and Easley (1982) showed that depending on the initial beliefs, learning process may lead to different limits. Sometimes, prices reveal the true information; sometimes, this is not so.
5. Radner (1970) provides a penetrating discussion on this topic. The survey of Grandmont (1977) contains an extensive list of relevant references. Arrow (1982) offers a non-technical discussion as to why it is that the market economy does not guarantee efficiency in such a framework. Intriguingly, having echoed Hayek's call for explaining business cycles in the framework of the Lausanne School (see Lucas, 1977), the 'new classical' literature made little attempt to relate its work to the aforementioned contributions in the modern Walrasian tradition.
6. Compare the third section, Lucas (1976).
7. It is perhaps appropriate to compare the task of the 'economic adviser' with either the operations analyst in war-time or the physician diagnosing the confounding symptoms of a patient. To err is human. Due professional care, after all, is all that can be taken.

REFERENCES

Arrow, K. J. (1982) 'A Cautious Case for Socialism', in I. Howe (ed.), *Beyond the Welfare State*, New York: Schocken Books, pp. 261–76.
Arrow, K. J. and F. H. Hahn (1971) *General Competitive Analysis*, San Francisco: Holden-Day.
Blume, L. E., and D. Easley (1982) 'Learning to be Rational', *Journal of Economic Theory*, 26(2): 340–51.
Buiter, W. H. (1980) 'The Macro-economics of Dr. Pangloss', *Economic Journal*, 90: 34–50.
Cass, D., and K. Shell (1980) 'In Defense of a Basic Approach', in J. A. Kareken and N. Wallace (eds), *Models of Monetary Economics*, Minneapolis: Federal Reserve Bank of Minneapolis, pp. 251–60.
Chen, C. I., and J. Cruz (1972) 'Stackelberg Solution for Two-person Games and Biased Information Patterns', *IEEE Transactions on Automatic Control*: AC-17: 6.
Chow, G. (1981) *Econometric Analysis by Control Methods*, New York: Wiley Interscience.
Clower, R., and A. Leijonhufvud (1975) 'The Co-ordination of Economic Activities: A Keynesian Perspective', *American Economic Review*, 65 (2): 182–8.
Fischer, S. (1977) 'Long-term Contracts, Rational Expectations, and the Optimal Money Supply Rule', *Journal of Political Economy*, 85 (1): 191–205.
Foster, J. E., and H. Wan Jr (1984) '"Involuntary" Unemployment as a

Principal-Agent Equilibrium', *American Economic Review*, forthcoming.

Friedman, B. (1979) 'Optimal Expectations and the Extreme Information Assumptions of Rational Expectations Macro-models', *Journal of Monetary Economics*, 5 (January): 23–42.

Friedman, M. (1953) *Essays in Positive Economics*, Chicago: University of Chicago Press.

Friedman, M. (1968) 'The Role of Monetary Policy', *American Economic Review*, 58 (1): 1–17.

Gertler, M., and H. Wan Jr (1981) 'Fluctuations in Output and Inflation in an Uncertain Environment, SSRI Workshop Series 8105, Madison: University of Wisconsin.

Grandmont, J. M. (1977) 'Temporary General Equilibrium Theory', *Econometrica*, 45: 535–72.

Grossman, H. (1980) 'Rational Expectations, Business Cycles, and Government Behavior', in S. Fischer (ed.), *Rational Expectations and Economic Policy*, Chicago: University of Chicago Press.

Grossman, S. (1977) 'A Characterization of the Optimality of Equilibrium in Incomplete Markets', *Journal of Economic Theory*, 15 (1): 1–15.

Hahn, F. H. (1980) 'Discussion', in J. A. Kareken and N. Wallace (eds), *Models of Monetary Economics*, Minneapolis: Federal Reserve Bank of Minneapolis, 161–5.

Hart, O. D. (1975) 'On the Optimality of Equilibrium when the Market Structure is Incomplete', *Journal of Economic Theory*, 11 (3): 418–43.

Kaldor, N. (1955–6) 'Alternative Theories of Distribution', *Review of Economic Studies*, 23 (2): 83–100.

Kydland, F. E., and E. C. Prescott (1977) 'Rules rather than Discretion: The Inconsistency of Optimal Plans', *Journal of Political Economy*, 85 (3): 473–93.

Leitmann, G., and H. Y. Wan, Jr (1977) 'Macro-economic Stabilization for an Uncertain Dynamic Economy', in A. Mazzolo (ed.), *New Trends In Dynamic Systems Theory and Economics*, New York: Springer Verlag.

Lucas, R. E. Jr (1972) 'Expectations and the Neutrality of Money', *Journal of Economic Theory*, 4: 103–24.

Lucas, R. E. Jr (1976) 'Econometric Policy Evaluation: A Critique', in K. Brunner and A. Meltzer (eds), *The Phillips Curves and Labor Markets*, Amsterdam: North-Holland, pp. 19–46.

Lucas, R. E. Jr (1977) 'Understanding Business Cycles', in K. Brunner, and A. Meltzer (eds), *Stabilization of the Domestic and International Economy*, Amsterdam: North-Holland, pp. 7–29.

Lucas, R. E. Jr (1978) 'Unemployment Policy', *American Economic Review*, 68 (2): 353–7.

Lucas, R. E. Jr (1981a) 'Tobin and Monetarism: A Review Article', *Journal of Economic Literature*, 19: 558–67.

Lucas, R. E. Jr (1981b) *Studies in Business Cycle Theory*, Cambridge, Mass.: MIT Press.

Modigliani, F. (1977) 'The Monetary Controversy, or Should We Foresake Stabilization Policies', *American Economic Review*, 67 (1): 1–19.

Muth, J. F. (1961) 'Rational Expectations and the Theory of Price Movements', *Econometrica*, 29: 315–35.

Peleg, B., and M. E. Yaari (1973) 'On the Existence of a Consistent Course of Action when Tastes are Changing', *Review of Economic Studies*, 40: 391–401.

Phelps, E. S., and R. A. Pollak (1968) 'On Second-best National Saving and Game-equilibrium Growth, *Review of Economic Studies*, 35: 185–99.

Radner, R. (1970) 'Problems in the Theory of Markets under Uncertainty', *American Economic Review*, 60: 454–60.

Radner, R. (1980) 'Collusive Behavior in Non-co-operative Epsilon Equilibria of Oligopolies with Long but Finite Lives', *Journal of Economic Theory*, 22: 136–54.

Sargent, T. J., and N. Wallace (1975) ' "Rational" Expectations, the Optimal Monetary Instrument and the Optimal Monetary Supply Rule', *Journal of Political Economy*, 83 (2): 241–54.

Selten, R. (1975) 'Re-examination of the Perfectness Concept for Equilibrium Points in Extensive Games', *International Journal of Game Theory*, 4: 25–55.

Shiller, R. (1978) 'Rational Expectations and the Dynamic Structure of Macro-economic Models', *Journal of Monetary Economics*, 3: 1–44.

Shubik, M. (1982) *Game Theory in the Social Sciences*, Cambridge, Mass.: MIT Press.

Sims, C. (1980) 'Macro-economics and Reality', *Econometrica*, 48: 1–48.

Solow, R. M. (1980) 'On Theories of Unemployment', *American Economic Review*, 70 (1): 1–10.

Tobin, J. (1977) 'How Dead is Keynes?' *Economic Inquiry*, 16: 459–68.

Tobin, J. (1980) *Asset Accumulation and Economic Activity: Reflections on Contemporary Macro-economic Theory*, Chicago: Chicago University Press.

Wan, H. Y. Jr (1979) 'Causally Indeterminate Models via Multi-valued Differential Equations', in O. Gurel and O. E. Rossler (eds), *Bifurcation Theory and Applications in Scientific Disciplines*, New York: New York Academy of Sciences, 530–44.

10 On the Assumption of Convergent Rational Expectations

EDWIN BURMEISTER*

INTRODUCTION

Both rational expectations and perfect foresight models are featured by the following indeterminacy problem: for given initial values of predetermined state variables, there may exist more than one dynamic equilibrium path. This type of indeterminacy arises because there are non-state variables whose initial values must be determined using criteria outside of the formal model. In general 'the model' can be expanded to include restrictions that uniquely determine these non-state variables. However, if there are many equally plausible sets of restrictions, the uniqueness issue remains unresolved.

Such indeterminacy is obviously an important economic problem: unless it can be satisfactorily resolved, no empirical work or policy evaluations can proceed. It is, therefore, necessary to understand that most existing work in the rational expectations literature proceeds by *postulating* that rationally formed expectations are always convergent. Convergent expectations represent a crucial assumption in the sense that both the theoretical analysis and empirical estimation of rational expectations models depend upon it.[1] Often progress in a science depends upon dropping a crucial assumption in favour of a more general formulation, and the

*Parts of this chapter are based on 'Indeterminacy and the Dynamic Properties of Both Rational Expectations and Perfect Foresight Models' which I presented at the Summer Meetings of the Econometric Society, San Diego, California, 24–27 June 1981. Research support from the National Science Foundation (SES-8218229) is gratefully acknowledged.

common methods for obtaining unique solutions to rational expectations models may be in this category. Moreover, once the link to dynamic properties is understood, it becomes possible to empirically test the crucial assumptions. Some work in this direction has been done by Burmeister and Wall (1982) and Flood and Garber (1980), who, however, reach contradictory conclusions.

To many, one of the most fundamental unresolved economic problems is an explanation of the business cycle. It is reasonable to conjecture that our understanding would be enhanced if we built models that were *capable* of dynamic instability and/or non-stochastic oscillations, instead of ruling out instability and/or non-stochastic oscillations by assumption, as is often the case when the standard procedures for 'solving' rational expectations models are used. An important ingredient of more general theories is likely to involve the diffusion of private information. These and related matters are discussed in more detail elsewhere (Burmeister, 1980a), and the purpose of mentioning them here is only to alert the reader that what is at stake in the subsequent discussion involves more than technical quibbles.

SOME PRELIMINARIES

It must be recognized that initial condition indeterminacy is in no way a 'defect' peculiar to rational expectations formulations, for consider a conventional adaptive expectations specification in which:

π = the expected value of the rate of inflation,
g = the actual rate of inflation,
α = the speed-of-adaptation coefficient,

and it is hypothesized that:

$\pi = \alpha(g - \pi).^2$

For simplicity assume $g = 0$ so that:

$\pi(t) = \pi(0)e^{-\alpha t}.$

Clearly the path of the expectations $\pi(t)$, which presumably influences the path of observed variables, depends upon the arbitrary initial condition $\pi(0)$. Hence adaptive expectations formulations exhibit initial condition indeterminacy because there is nothing in the model to predetermine $\pi(0)$.

However, the fact that other expectations hypotheses exhibit the same difficulty is not a justification for neglect. The purpose of this chapter is to explore the problem of initial condition indeterminacy for linear rational expectations models that encompass a large number of alternative structural specifications. In particular, we shall show how the assumption of convergence – which can be justified in particular formulations by transversality conditions – may resolve the problem in some (but not all) instances.

Two red herrings must be dispensed with: First, the problems discussed here in a continuous time framework also arise in discrete time specifications, and continuous time has been selected simply because it is more convenient.[3] Second, the issues to be discussed here arise both in perfect foresight and in rational expectations models, and for our purposes the mathematical structures of these two cases are *identical*. In perfect foresight models the time path of each variable is by assumption known, while in rational expectations models the time path must be interpreted in terms of expected values. This exact equivalence arises because the stochastic error terms entering the structural equations are all assumed to have zero expected values when calculated forward from any point in time using all the then available information. Thus consider a perfect foresight model $\dot{x} = Ax$ and a stochastic model $\dot{x} = Ax + \epsilon$, where ϵ is a white noise process. Letting x^* denote rationally formed expectation of x, the dynamic behaviour of rational expectations *forward* in time is simply $x^* = Ax^*$, which has dynamic properties identical to the perfect foresight case.

There is another simple economic reason why it suffices to consider the dynamic stability properties of deterministic systems. Since the expected future values of the stochastic terms are all zero, taking rational expectations at any time s (conditional upon all the then available information) results in a deterministic dynamic system. But every variable has rationally formed expectations, and therefore the difference between any actual value $x(t)$ and its rationally formed expectation formed at time $s \leqslant t$, say $x^*(t, s)$, is a stochastic term $\xi(t)$ with the property that $E_s\, \xi(t) = 0$:

$$x(t) - x^*(t, s) = \xi(t)$$

Thus the *stochastic stability* properties of the actual values $x(t)$ depend upon the dynamic stability properties of the rational expectations $x^*(t, s)$, as well as on the stochastic stability properties of $\xi(t)$. For example, the actual random variable $x(t)$ can be stochastically stable in various common senses only if $x^*(t, s)$ is asymptotically stable and $\lim_{t \to \infty} x^*(t, s) = \overline{x}^*$ for all $s \leqslant t$.[4]

We shall consider systems of the form:

$$\begin{bmatrix} \dot{y} \\ \dot{z} \end{bmatrix} = M \begin{bmatrix} y \\ z \end{bmatrix}$$

where y is an $n \times 1$ column vector, z is an $m \times 1$ column vector, and M is an $(n + m) \times (n + m)$ matrix. This framework allows us to establish extremely general results that are valid for all linear rational expectations models having the stated error properties.[5]

THE BASIC FRAMEWORK AND THE ROLE OF THE STABILITY ASSUMPTION

Consider a dynamic system in the $n + m$ dimensions:

$$\begin{bmatrix} \dot{z} \\ \dot{y} \end{bmatrix} = M \begin{bmatrix} z \\ y \end{bmatrix} \begin{bmatrix} A & B \\ C & D \end{bmatrix} \begin{bmatrix} z \\ y \end{bmatrix} \tag{10.1}$$

where the column vectors z and y measure deviations from a dynamic equilibrium value, z is $n \times 1$, y is $m \times 1$, and the matrix M is $(n + m) \times (n + m)$. Assume that M has $n + m$ distinct characteristic roots with non-zero real parts. The solution to (10.1) then is:

$$\begin{bmatrix} z(t) \\ y(t) \end{bmatrix} = \begin{bmatrix} \beta_{11} & \beta_{12} \\ \beta_{21} & \beta_{22} \end{bmatrix} \begin{bmatrix} e^{\lambda_1 t} & 0 \\ 0 & e^{\lambda_2 t} \end{bmatrix} \begin{bmatrix} c_1 \\ c_2 \end{bmatrix} \tag{10.2}$$

where: $\lambda_1 = \text{diag}(\lambda^1, \ldots, \lambda^n)$, $\lambda_2 = \text{diag}(\lambda^{n+1}, \ldots, \lambda^{n+m})$; the $n + m$ characteristic roots satisfy $\det[M - \lambda 1] = 0$; $\begin{bmatrix} \beta_{1i} \\ \beta_{2i} \end{bmatrix}$ is the eigenvector associated with λ^i ($i = 1, 2, \ldots, n + m$); $\begin{bmatrix} e^{\lambda_1 t} & 0 \\ 0 & e^{\lambda_2 t} \end{bmatrix} = \begin{bmatrix} e^{\lambda^1 t} & & & & \\ & e^{\lambda^n t} & & & \\ & & e^{\lambda^{n+1} t} & & \\ & & & e^{\lambda^{n+m} t} \\ 0 & & & \end{bmatrix}$;

and c_1, c_2 are $n \times 1$ and $m \times 1$, respectively, column vectors of arbitrary constants. Since the characteristic roots are distinct and non-zero, the matrix of eigenvectors, namely:

$$\beta \equiv \begin{bmatrix} \beta_{11} & \beta_{12} \\ \beta_{21} & \beta_{22} \end{bmatrix}, \text{ is non-singular.}$$

If $z(0)$, $y(0)$ are both fixed initial conditions, the dynamic behaviour of $z(t)$, $y(t)$ is completely determined by (10.2) since the arbitrary constants then must satisfy:

$$\begin{bmatrix} c_1 \\ c_2 \end{bmatrix} = \beta^{-1} \begin{bmatrix} z(0) \\ y(0) \end{bmatrix} \tag{10.3}$$

Suppose, on the contrary, that the z's are state variables whose initial values are fixed at a known value $z(0)$, but that the y's are not state variables. Thus consider cases for which $y(0)$ is open to choice, although it may be determined by other economic considerations as yet not explicitly stated.

The issue of *initial condition determinacy* clearly hinges upon whether or not the complete model — including all economic considerations — determines a *unique* $y(0)$, say $y^*(0)$. Given $z(0)$, the dynamic behaviour of the system is then given uniquely by:

$$\begin{bmatrix} z(t) \\ y(t) \end{bmatrix} = \begin{bmatrix} \beta_{11} & \beta_{12} \\ \beta_{21} & \beta_{22} \end{bmatrix} \begin{bmatrix} e^{\lambda_1 t} & 0 \\ 0 & e^{\lambda_2 t} \end{bmatrix} \begin{bmatrix} \beta_{11} & \beta_{12} \\ \beta_{21} & \beta_{22} \end{bmatrix}^{-1} \begin{bmatrix} z(0) \\ y^*(0) \end{bmatrix} \quad (10.4)$$

for all $t \in [0, +\infty)$. If, on the other hand, $y^{**}(0) \neq y^*(0)$ is also a legitimate initial condition for the non-state variables, then it will generate a dynamic path which differs from (10.3), and both $y(0)$ and hence the dynamic behaviour of the system become indeterminate.

Since the matrix M has $n + m$ distinct characteristic roots with non-zero real parts, and since the initial $n \times 1$ vector $z(0)$ is predetermined, in general a solution path $\begin{bmatrix} z(t) \\ y(t) \end{bmatrix}$ will converge, as $t \to +\infty$, to the dynamic equilibrium point $\begin{bmatrix} 0 \\ 0 \end{bmatrix}$ only for certain choices of $y(0)$. More precisely, let N designate the number of characteristic roots with negative real parts. If $N = 0$, the origin is completely unstable, and all paths that do not start at the dynamic equilibrium $z(0) = 0$, $y(0) = 0$ will diverge. If $0 < N < n$, there will exist *some* values of $z(0)$ for which there corresponds a unique $y(0)$ that implies convergence, that is, with certain particular pairs of $z(0)$ and $y(0)$,

$$\lim_{t \to +\infty} \begin{bmatrix} z(t) \\ y(t) \end{bmatrix} = \begin{bmatrix} 0 \\ 0 \end{bmatrix} \quad (10.5)$$

However, if we are to be assured that (10.5) holds for *all* values of $z(0)$, it is necessary that $N \geq n$. If $N = n$, and if the assumption stated below holds, then for any given value $z(0)$, there exists a *unique* $y(0)$ for which (10.5) holds.[6] If $N > n$, there may exist more than one initial value $y(0)$ that is consistent with convergence.[7] And finally, if $N = n + m$, the system is completely stable, and (10.5) holds for *all* initial values of $z(0)$ and $y(0)$.

The most economically interesting cases are those for which stability is possible starting from any initial value $z(0)$; consequently, we now restrict our attention to the cases where $N \geqslant n$. The following two theorems prove the results asserted above.

Theorem 1 (N = n)

Let $N = n$; under the assumption of the Lemma below, the dynamic model (10.1) has a unique dynamic path exhibiting the stability property:

$$\lim_{t \to +\infty} \begin{bmatrix} z(t) \\ y(t) \end{bmatrix} = \begin{bmatrix} 0 \\ 0 \end{bmatrix}$$

starting from an arbitrary initial state vector $z(0)$ *if, and only if,* the initial non-state vector is:

$$y(0) = \beta_{21} \beta_{11}^{-1} z(0)$$

Moreover, setting $y(0) = \beta_{21} \beta_{11}^{-1} z(0)$ *is equivalent* to setting $c_2 = 0$ in (10.2).

Proof:

Without loss of generality the characteristic roots of M may be ordered so that $Re\ \lambda^i < 0$ for $i = 1, \ldots, n = N$ and $Re\ \lambda^i > 0$ for $i = n+1, \ldots, n+m$. Thus from the solution (10.2) it is evident that we must have $c_2 = 0$ if (10.5) is to hold, for otherwise the solution $\begin{bmatrix} z(t) \\ y(t) \end{bmatrix}$ will contain a term involving an exponential with a positive real part, at least for some $z(0)$. Hence from (10.2) with $t = 0$ and $c_2 = 0$, we have that:

$$z(0) = \beta_{11} c_1$$

and

$$y(0) = \beta_{21} c_1$$

We shall assume that β_{11}^{-1} exists, and hence:

$$c_1 = \beta_{11}^{-1} z(0) \tag{10.6}$$

and

$$y(0) = \beta_{21} \beta_{11}^{-1} z(0) \tag{10.7}$$

Thus the unique stable solution is given by:

$$z(t) = \beta_{11} (e^{\lambda_1 t}) \beta_{11}^{-1} z(0) \tag{10.8}$$

and

$$y(t) = \beta_{21}(e^{\lambda_1 t})\beta_{11}^{-1} z(0) \tag{10.9}$$

To prove that this choice of $y(0)$ is equivalent to setting $c_2 = 0$, note that:

$$z(0) = \beta_{11}c_1 + \beta_{12}c_2$$

and

$$y(0) = \beta_{21}c_1 + \beta_{22}c_2$$

Hence

$$\beta_{21}\beta_{11}^{-1}[\beta_{11}c_1 + \beta_{12}c_2] = \beta_{21}c_1 + \beta_{22}c_2$$

or

$$[\beta_{21}\beta_{11}^{-1}\beta_{12} - \beta_{22}]c_2 = 0 \tag{10.10}$$

The latter holds for $c_2 \neq 0$ if, and only if, $\det[\beta_{21}\beta_{11}^{-1}\beta_{12} - \beta_{22}] = 0$; but since $\det \beta = \det \beta_{11} \cdot \det[\beta_{22} - \beta_{12}\beta_{11}^{-1}\beta_{21}] \neq 0, c_2 \neq 0$ is impossible.

QED

The economic significance of Theorem 1 is that when $N = n$, the *assumption* of dynamic stability implies that there is (at most) one path starting from an arbitrary initial state vector. In these circumstances the system is determinate. The force of the assumption that β_{11}^{-1} exists is to insure existence of this unique stable path starting from *any* $z(0)$; when β_{11} is singular, there may exist values of $z(0)$ for which convergence is impossible, that is, for which no stable path exists.

Theorem 2 (n < N < n + m)

Let $n < N < n + m$. Starting from an arbitrary initial state vector $z(0)$, up to $C_n^N = \dfrac{N!}{n!(N-n)!}$ stable paths exist for which

$$\lim_{t \to +\infty} \begin{bmatrix} z(t) \\ y(t) \end{bmatrix} = \begin{bmatrix} 0 \\ 0 \end{bmatrix}$$

and for which, setting $c_2 = 0$, $y(0)$ is uniquely determined by $z(0)$.

Proof:

There are $N > n$ characteristic roots with negative real parts, and there exist

$$C_n^N = \frac{N!}{n!(N-n)!}$$

ways of selecting n of these N roots to construct the diagonal matrix λ_1. Thus setting $c_2 = 0$, it follows from the proof of Theorem 1 that there exist C_n^N different stable paths, provided that β_{11}^{-1} exists for each choice of λ_1. QED

It follows that *the assumption of stability does not imply determinacy* unless $n = N$. Moreover, Theorem 2 does not exhaust the number of stable paths that exist when $N > n$. Rather than setting $c_2 = 0$, stability requires only that $m - (N - n)$ elements of c_2 be zero, thereby eliminating the contribution of every characteristic root with a positive real part in the solution (2). Suppose, for example, that $N = n + 1$, and we order the roots so that $Re\ \lambda^i < 0$ for $i = 1, 2, \ldots, n + 1$. Stability obtains if we set the last $m - 1$ elements of c_2 at zero. Now, however, $y(0)$ will not necessarily be uniquely determined by $z(0)$; in general one element of $y(0)$ may be picked arbitrarily, and there then exists a unique choice of the remaining $m - 1$ elements consistent with stability. Thus under these circumstances there exist an infinity of stable paths, all starting from the same initial state $z(0)$. *Accordingly, even if stability is assumed, without additional restrictions the dynamic evolution of the model is indeterminate when $N > n$.*

CONCLUDING REMARKS

The hypothesis of intertemporal maximization may result in models that do not have the initial condition indeterminacy problem, but this trick begs the real question at issue since all maximization problems that are concave in an appropriate space necessarily have a unique solution. The important economic question is under what circumstances individual maximizing agents, *each having heterogeneous tastes, information, and expectations,* will make decisions that imply aggregate macroeconomic behaviour qualitatively similar to the solution of some maximization problem. To date, the only available evidence is negative for this approach.[8]

We are left, therefore, with the conclusion that currently we have no justifiable theoretical reasons in support of the hypothesis that rational expectations models are determinate. I do not find this particular result surprising; indeed, it is known to be a possibility from the earlier work of Burmeister, Caton, Dobell, and Ross (1973) and Taylor (1977). Conventional rational expectations modelling, at least in most applications, presupposes that economic agents have observed the system long enough to know its structure and its relevant parameter values. The unmodelled learning process by which this knowledge is acquired carries with it a history of $z(t)$ and $y(t)$ for $t \leqslant 0$, and it seems to me that the economically significant question concerns how or under what circumstances $y(0)$, given by history, is consistent with convergence. Similarly, if an economy should for whatever reason find itself on a divergent path, we should like to know what mechanisms might come into play to get it back on to a convergent track. To *assume* that convergence always prevails is to prejudge as unnecessary some possible roles for government policy, and this strategy is unlikely to convince the proponents of interventionism. Until these issues are more definitely resolved, the appropriate scientific research strategy is to specify models that are free of stability *assumptions* and to test empirically whether or not the dynamic evolution of realized paths justifies assuming convergent rational expectations.

NOTES

1. Lucas (1972a, 1972b) explicitly recognized that his solution procedure entailed strong restricteds implying convergent rational expectations; see note 8 in Lucas, 1972a, and note 10 in Lucas, 1972b. Subsequent authors have sometimes been careless in not explicitly stating the restrictive nature of their assumptions.
2. It is proved in Burmeister and Turnovsky (1976) that this specification for rates of change is valid in continuous time; see, especially, p. 890.
3. Every continuous time system can be approximated as closely as desired by a discrete time system of the same order, but the converse is false. This follows from the fact that a discrete time model of order n is capable of generating a richer variety of dynamic behaviour than an n-th order continuous time model. For example, consider $x(t + h) - x(t) = -2hx(t)$, $h \geqslant 0$. For $h = 1$ the solution is $x(t) = \dot{x}(0) \, (-1)^t$ which oscillates, but as $h \to 0^+$ the differential equations $x(t) = -2x(t)$ has a monotonic solution $x(t) = x(0)e^{-2t}$; moreover, no first-order differential equation generates oscillations.
4. As readers familiar with stochastic calculus will recognize, the conversion of a discrete time process with a time period of length $h > 0$ to a continuous time process by letting $h \to 0$ often involves treacherous

technicalities. For example, one may obtain a model in which the actual variables are generated by the stochastic process:

$$\dot{x}(t) = Ax(t) + \epsilon(t)$$

where $\epsilon(t)$ is white noise. In this case the path $x(t)$ is differentiable and $\dot{x}(t)$ is continuous but not differentiable. The mathematical requirement for obtaining a solution is that $\epsilon(t)$ be integrable, which it will be almost surely if $\epsilon(t)$ is a white noise process.

However, one may obtain systems of the form:

$$dx(t) = \alpha x(t) + \sigma z(t) \sqrt{dt}$$

where $dx(t)$ is an Ito stochastic differential and $z(t)$ is a standard normal variable for each t.

These technical details, which involve how the *actual* variables are generated, are not central for our purposes here. The point is that for *all* economically meaningful specifications, the solution to the expectation equations will enter the equations generating the actual variables, and the expectation equations, derived by taking expectations of the structural equations at time t conditional upon the information available then, will be ordinary non-stochastic differential equations. Accordingly, in this chapter we shall be concerned only with the dynamic properties of expectations, with actual variables being determined by the equation stated previously in the text: $x(t) - x^*(t, s) = \xi(t)$.

5. In some cases models may include forcing function, for example, in the scalar case we may have:

$$x(t) = ax(t) + f(t), \quad a > 0$$

Provided $f(t)$ is integrable, the forward-looking solution is of the form:

$$x(t) = ce^{at} - e^{at} \int_{\theta=t}^{\infty} e^{-a\theta} f(\theta) \, d\theta$$

which, since $a > 0$, is convergent if, and only if, $c = 0$.

In the vector case the general solution of:

$$\dot{x}(t) = Ax(t) + f(t)$$

is of the form

$$x(t) = ze^{\lambda t} c + zv(t)e^{\lambda t}$$

where x is $(n \times 1)$, z is an $(n \times n)$ matrix of eigenvectors, $e^{\lambda t}$ is diagonal, and $v(t)$ is $(n \times 1)$. If the system is to converge, it is necessary that $ze^{\lambda t} c$ converge; likewise, the system diverges if $ze^{\lambda t} c$ diverges. Thus in all cases the stability of the homogeneous part is crucial for the stability of the general solution, and we lose no insights by restricting our attention to deterministic systems of the form:

$$\dot{x}(t) = Ax(t)$$

Stochastic cases arise in rational expectations models when $f(t)$ is an autocorrelated stochastic term, that is, when $E[f(s) \mid I(t)] \neq 0$ for

$s \geqslant t$ and the set $I(t)$ includes $f(s)$ for $s < t$. By 'differencing' the data and considering the system:

$$\dot{z}(t) = az(t) + \epsilon(t)$$

where $\dot{z}(t) \equiv \ddot{x}(t)$, $z(t) \equiv \dot{x}(t)$, $\epsilon(t) \equiv \ddot{f}(t)$, we may end up with a system in our original form where $\epsilon(t)$ is white noise. This will be true, for example, if $f(t)$ is a Wiener process; see Arnold, 1974, p. 53. Thus as a practical matter we lose no generality by restricting our attention in this chapter to stochastic systems of the form:

$$\dot{x}(t) = Ax(t) + \epsilon(t)$$

where $\epsilon(t)$ is white noise.

We also note that non-linear systems are also covered by this chapter provided we interpret:

$$\dot{x}(t) = Ax(t)$$

as the linearization around a dynamic equilibrium point, in which case all our stability results are local. For stochastic cases we must then interpret expected variables as linear least squares predictions.

Finally, note that even though we deal with first-order systems, standard procedures enable one to handle derivatives of any order. Hence the scalar second-order system:

$$a\ddot{x} + b\dot{x} + cx = 0$$

can be transformed by defining:

$$x_1 \equiv \dot{x}, \quad \dot{x}_1 \equiv \ddot{x}, \quad x_2 \equiv x$$

to give:

$$a\dot{x}_1 + bx_1 + cx_2 = 0$$
$$\dot{x}_2 = x_1$$

or

$$\begin{bmatrix} \dot{x}_1 \\ \dot{x}_2 \end{bmatrix} \quad \begin{bmatrix} -\dfrac{b}{a} & -\dfrac{c}{a} \\ 1 & 0 \end{bmatrix} \begin{bmatrix} x_1 \\ x_2 \end{bmatrix}$$

Similarly, structural specifications which include different derivatives in the same equation (e.g. structural equations such as $\dot{m} = \rho_0 + \rho_1 \dot{p} - m$) can be transformed into the canonical form $\dot{x} = Ax$.

6. If in addition $N = n = m$, the dynamic equilibrium point $\begin{bmatrix} 0 \\ 0 \end{bmatrix}$ is termed a *regular saddlepoint*.

7. One of the first examples of such non-uniqueness is contained in Burmeister, Caton, Dobell, and Ross (1973).

8. See Burmeister, 1980b, ch. 6.

REFERENCES

Arnold, L. (1974) *Stochastic Differential Equations: Theory and Applications*, New York: John Wiley.

Burmeister, E. (1980a) 'On Some Conceptual Issues in Rational Expectations Modelling', *Journal of Money, Credit, and Banking*, 12 (4) pt 2 (November): 800–17.

Burmeister, E. (1980b) *Capital Theory and Dynamics*, New York: Cambridge University Press.

Burmeister, E., C. Caton, A. R. Dobell and S. Ross (1973) 'The "Saddlepoint Property" and the Structure of Dynamic Heterogeneous Capital Good Models', *Econometrica*, 41 (January): 79–95.

Burmeister, E., and S. J. Turnovsky (1976) 'The Specification of Adaptive Expectations in Continuous Economic Models', *Econometrica*, 44 (5) (September): 879–905.

Burmeister, E., and S. J. Turnovsky (1978) 'Price Expectations, Disequilibrium Adjustments, and Macroeconomic Price Stability', *Journal of Economic Theory*, 17 (April): 287–311.

Burmeister, E., and K. D. Wall (1982) 'Kalman Filtering Estimation of Unobserved Rational Expectations with an Application to the German Hyperinflation', *Journal of Econometrics*, 20 (November): 255–84.

Flood, R. P., and P. M. Garber (1980) 'Market Fundamentals vs. Price Level Bubbles: The First Tests', *Journal of Political Economy*, (August): 741–71.

Lucas, R. E. Jr (1972a) 'Expectations and the Neutrality of Money', *Journal of Economic Theory*, 4 (April): 103–24.

Lucas, R. E. Jr (1972b) 'Econometric Testing of the Natural Rate Hypothesis', in O. Eckstein, (ed.), *Econometrics of Price Determination Conference*, Washington, D.C.: Board of Governors of the Federal Reserve System.

Taylor, J. B. (1977) 'Conditions for Unique Solutions in Stochastic Macroeconomic Models with Rational Expectations', *Econometrica*, 45 (6) (September): 1377–87.

11 Recent Perspectives in and on Macroeconomics

BENJAMIN M. FRIEDMAN

For a would-be science with no laboratory, whatever experiments nature provides carry great weight. For economics, and especially for macroeconomics, the experience of actual economies not only motivates ideas but also sometimes disconfirms them. When actual economic events are sufficiently compelling, they can even change long-established thinking or reverse the momentum of newer approaches just establishing themselves.

The economic experience of the early 1980s in the industrialized Western countries, and in the USA in particular, may well be having just that effect. Real economic activity abated sharply during this period, bringing record levels of both unemployment and idle industrial capacity. Restrictive monetary policy aimed at slowing price inflation was a key element, probably *the* key element, in producing this decline. Moreover, at least in the USA after 1980, disinflationary monetary policy was hardly a surprise.

This combination of circumstances has had, and should have a powerful influence on macroeconomic thinking, in large part because it directly contradicts the predominant new line of macroeconomic research developed in the 1970s — the 'new classical macroeconomics'. The central policy conclusion of the new classical macroeconomics is that real economic activity is invariant to monetary policy actions that are anticipated in advance. The corollary of this principle with special relevance to the leading economic policy debate of the past decade is that disinflation produced by tight monetary policy need not be costly. The apparent contradiction between the primary policy message of the new classical macroeconomics and the actual economic experience of the early 1980s has already dulled the appeal of this direction of thinking to a noticeable extent.

The thesis of this chapter is that the contradiction between recent economic experience and the new classical macroeconomics is not just apparent but real, and that it represents a disconfirmation at least as compelling as the set of events that led to disillusionment with the previously prevailing macroeconomic consensus and thereby provided the attraction of the new classical macroeconomics in the first place. The implication that follows for macroeconomic research is not, of course, to return without modification to that earlier set of views. Instead, it is that still further approaches, of which some are already at hand, offer the best vehicle to retain what remains attractive about the methodology of the new classical macroeconomics yet derive policy conclusions consistent with the apparent working of actual economies in any but the longest time horizons – specifically, that money is not neutral, that trade-offs exist, and that policy matters for real economic outcomes.

The first section re-emphasizes the connection between macroeconomic thinking and actual economic experience, and in particular relates the rise of the new classical macroeconomics to the experience of price inflation in the 1960s and 1970s. The second section reviews the main assumptions and conclusions of the new classical macroeconomics, and compares these conclusions to the observed results of the disinflation policy pursued in the early 1980s. The third section summarizes the implications of this comparison, and calls attention to several new directions in macroeconomic thinking – each bearing different policy conclusions than the new classical macroeconomics – that have already emerged.

THE NEW CLASSICAL MACROECONOMICS IN THE CONTEXT OF MACROECONOMIC EXPERIENCE

Major developments in economic thinking often owe as much to the influence of actual economic events as to the internal momentum of scientific discovery building on itself. The attitudes that economic theories embody towards the role of government are a particular case in point. For example, a society's live experience of the consequences of uncontrolled negative externalities like air pollution or unsafe driving often spawns an era of fertile thinking about the benefits of authoritative intervention. Conversely, realized disappointment over ineffective or even counter-productive government correctives typically renews interest, at the abstract level as well as the practical, in the power of the market mechanism.

Macroeconomics has always displayed a special responsiveness to the tide of prevailing economic circumstances. One cause of this sensitivity, of course, is simply that the goal of so much of macroeconomic analysis is to address the potential role (or lack thereof) for government policy. Another factor, often overlooked but of substantial importance non-the-less, is the commonality of the macroeconomic experience in the modern economy. Specific industries and geographic regions display great hetero-geneity, to be sure, but the major macroeconomic events — prosperity or contraction, stability or volatility, inflation or steady prices — emerge, recede, and re-emerge in importance at roughly the same time to almost everyone in the society, including its economists. Moreover, increasing interdependence among nations' economies in the modern world has kept pace with the erosion of international impediments to scientific exchange, so that much of the commonality of experience that matters in this con-text also extends well beyond the economists of any one country.

As a result, the history of macroeconomics is in many respects a mirror of macroeconomic history. As early as the first decades of the nineteenth century, problems of wartime finance and its aftermath stimulated interest in price inflation and the role of money, and not much later the evolution of the modern banking system fostered new and different thinking on closely related issues. The continuing clash of agrarian and industrial interests, virtually throughout the nineteenth century, powerfully set the stage for the development of new fundamental ideas on free trade versus protection. The worldwide depression of the 1930s, perhaps the most striking example of this kind of influence, led to whole new concepts based on sticky prices and realized excess demands in place of the earlier progressive refinement of neoclassical ideas appropriate to a fully employ-ed economy with flexible prices. Since the second World War macro-economists have focused — again, not just in recognizable attempts to be 'practical', but in basic theoretical work as well — on a series of emerging conditions in the actual economic environment, including irregularly periodic business contractions, persistent and accelerating price inflation, disappointing productivity trends and, most recently, external shocks imposed via prices of cartelized raw materials.

Probably the most interesting development at the fundamental level of macroeconomics in recent years, and certainly the most challenging along several dimensions, has been the emergence of the 'new classical macro-economics'. This line of research, as the label in part suggests, uses a combination of theoretical insights and specific assumptions, often along with modern mathematical and statistical tools, to establish in a more dramatic way the policy ineffectiveness propositions previously associated with an earlier analysis.

Several distinguishing features of this line of thinking have importantly enhanced its attractiveness. The rigour of the explicit optimizing framework it imposes, for example, creates a proliferation of research opportunities at the theoretical level, including potentially important new avenues for the integration of macro- with microeconomics. In addition, the set of restrictions it delivers on observable outcomes presents both challenges to and opportunities for research on the methodology of statistical inference. As a corollary, of course, it also presents an entire agenda for applied empirical research. Still, even these substantial implications of this new line of thinking cannot fully account – indeed, nor should they – for its proven attractiveness among macroeconomists.

The main reason why the new classical macroeconomics has proved so broadly compelling is that it connects in a direct way to specific questions and problems that macroeconomists have addressed, often with sharply diverging answers, since at least the mid-1960s: Does monetary policy affect real economic outcomes? Is there scope for macroeconomic choice in the usual sense of policy trade-offs? Are whatever trade-offs the economy presents exploitable? Does the framework defining monetary policy decisions and actions matter? Is disinflation costly?

The principal innovators in the new classical macroeconomics, Robert Lucas and Thomas Sargent, have both written delineating the emergence of this line of thinking as a scientific phenomenon (Lucas, 1980; Sargent, 1982). Lucas's account places this development in the context of the evolution of general equilibrium theory broadly construed, embracing the flow of ideas both in economics and in related disciplines, while Sargent's emphasizes prior steps in statistical methodology. Both convey a useful sense of the axiomatic dimension of the cumulative process characteristic of scientific inquiry.

Nevertheless, macroeconomic ideas rarely develop in isolation from the unfolding of actual economic events, and in this case too what has doubtless provided the real thrust behind the advance of the new classical macroeconomics has been the power and relevance of its conclusions about economic behaviour in the context of currently pressing questions about economic policy. As Lucas and Sargent writing together have emphasized, the new classical economics is intended as a replacement for a previously prevailing consensus paradigm that bore implications which, in their view, economic experience plainly falsified (Lucas and Sargent, 1978). As is clear in their joint paper as well as throughout Lucas's earlier writings,[1] the central economic 'event' motivating this development was the acceleration of price inflation during the 1960s and 1970s.

More precisely, the central motivating factor has been the apparent contradiction between, on the one hand, the observation of upward drift in the inflation rate over time and, on the other, the 'Keynesian' conclusion that macroeconomic policy could indefinitely maintain higher trend levels of output and employment at the cost of a higher, but none-the-less stable, inflation rate. In their joint paper Lucas and Sargent highlight this experience as a 'decisive test' of the earlier views, as embodied in the macroeconometric models of the time, and label the contradiction between these views and the observed outcome 'spectacular' and 'wildly incorrect' – an 'econometric failure on a grand scale'. More recently Lucas has argued, on the basis of this same contradiction, that the earlier approach was 'in deep trouble, the deepest kind of trouble in which an applied body of theory can find itself: It appears to be giving seriously wrong answers to the most basic questions of macroeconomic policy' (Lucas, 1981).

That the experience of two decades apparently contrasted with such an important policy implication of Keynesian macroeconomic thinking (actually, a post-Keynesian synthesis of Keynesian and neoclassical ideas) clearly testified to the need for substantial modification at a minimum, and perhaps wholesale replacement. That the aspect of economic behaviour most obviously at issue in accounting for the apparent inconsistency between actual experience and the earlier macroeconomic paradigm – the dynamic interaction between expectations and labour supply decisions – was also the principal focus of the new paradigm, immediately drew the latter way of thinking into the vacuum created by rejecting the former.

The link between the new classical macroeconomics and the debate over the stability of the inflation–unemployment trade-off – or, put the other way around, the 'accelerationist' debate – is clear enough. As Phelps and Friedman had pointed out early on, the stability of the 'Phillips curve' summarizing wage- (and hence price-) setting behaviour rested on the assumed failure of workers or their agents to recognize, and respond to, the implications of inflation for their real wages.[2] In addition, as an early contribution by Lucas showed (Lucas, 1970), and as Sargent's recent paper emphasizes, this important aspect of economic behaviour had a close parallel in the problem of statistically modelling expectations and slow adjustments. Through an evolution that is now familiar history, the solution proposed by Lucas, drawing on Muth's earlier work,[3] in time became the new classical macroeconomics.

What is striking in all this – though hardly surprising, in the light of the history of macroeconomics – is the importance of a specific economic 'event' both in motivating a new line of analysis and in making it attractive to large numbers of researchers. The 'great inflation' of the 1960s and 1970s was hardly as shocking an event as the 'great depression' of the 1930s, but each in its turn profoundly affected economic thinking just as it realigned political priorities and allegiances. In response to persistent inflation, macroeconomists have chosen new questions and looked for new answers. For many, the way of seeking those answers has been the new classical macroeconomics.

What one economic 'event' can do, however, another can undo – at least in some respects. Because empirical evidence can disconfirm a theory but, strictly speaking, can never confirm one, scientifically operational hypotheses are like Humpty-Dumpties. To the extent that the experience of the 1960s and 1970s really disproved the then-prevailing macroeconomic consensus, no subsequent experience can restore it. By contrast, further experience *can* equally damage the new classical economics. An important question that macroeconomics faces today is whether the experience of the early 1980s has already done so.

THE NEW CLASSICAL MACROECONOMICS AND RECENT MACROECONOMIC EXPERIENCE

Has the economic experience of the early 1980s provided yet another major economic 'event' to change the course of macroeconomic thinking? In order to decide even whether a test of the new classical economics has occurred, it is first necessary to determine the chief implications of that line of thinking for observable economic behaviour.

The proposition of the new classical macroeconomics that most closely corresponds to the earlier promise of a stable inflation–unemployment trade-off, which Lucas and Sargent take to provide the basis for the 'decisive test' of the earlier 'Keynesian' thinking, is the promise of costless disinflation. These two policy conclusions, offered respectively by two lines of thinking, share important parallels. Each addressed that aspect of the macroeconomic condition widely identified as the primary public policy problem of the time – unemployment in the 1960s, and inflation in the 1970s. Most importantly, each offered the prospect of solving the policy problem it addressed with*out* incurring the perceived cost that both economists and the general public feared would accompany the most obvious remedies. Certainly by the 1960s, the idea that government policy could reduce unemployment was hardly new; what was novel was the promise of doing so, permanently, without significantly inducing inflation. Similarly, in the 1970s the idea that government policy could slow inflation was not new either; the novelty was the promise of doing so without significantly raising unemployment, or reducing output and incomes, even in the short run.

For a would-be science eager to avoid value judgements, the promise of costless disinflation had special appeal. In place of the earlier discussion of trade-offs between percentage points of inflation and point-years of unemployment, policy analysis could now focus strictly on the inflation problem without considering the consequences of disinflation for the real economy.

Moreover, analysing away any real costs was of particular importance in mounting practical arguments for a disinflationary policy. On the one side, as Okun and others emphasized,[4] most conventional estimates of those costs were large, ranging from 2 to 6 point-years of unemployment for every one-point reduction in inflation, with a median just over 3-for-1. Further, if each 1 per cent change in unemployment corresponded to some 3 per cent in the economy's real growth, then that median estimate implied that slowing inflation from, say, 10 per cent to 5 per cent per annum would ultimately cost half a year's output — hardly a small sum. On the other side, economists were frustrated by their failure to provide any persuasive analysis indicating comparable real costs of inflation itself. Apparently the public's aversion to inflation, if it was not simply misguided, stemmed more from hard-to-quantify concerns about the fragility of societal relationships than from the kinds of costs that comfortably suit economic analysis.

At least in its formal evolution, the new classical macroeconomics did not start out with the proposition of costless disinflation any more than the earlier analysis had begun from the idea of a stable long-run inflation-unemployment trade-off. As is well known, the two basic building blocks of this line of research are the assumptions that expectations are 'rational' and that supply decisions lead to 'full employment' output and employment except in the context of specific kinds of surprises.[5] As is also well known, both of these propositions depend in turn on still more elementary assumptions, including the ideas of individual optimizing behaviour and market clearing that Lucas and Sargent have emphasized, and others as well.[6] The required 'rationality' of expectations, for example, depends on individuals' not only using efficiently whatever information they have but also having enough information to know, both qualitatively and quantitatively, how the economy works. Similarly, the 'Lucas supply function' depends not only on the flexibility of prices and wages but also on suppliers' observing their output prices before observing their input prices.

The achievement of the new classical macroeconomics was to combine this set of assumptions not just to show that disinflation is costless but to derive the more general conclusion that anticipated monetary policy actions do not affect real economic activity, and hence that no trade-off exists between inflation (or, for that matter, any other nominal magnitude) and employment or output (or any other real magnitude). Costless disinflation follows simply as a specific application of the general result.

In a completely atemporal context, it is difficult to know how to react to these propositions. Indeed, the oxymoron 'new classical' itself suggests this tension. Notwithstanding the 1960s view of a 'permanent' inflation-unemployment trade-off, there is nothing either new or surprising in monetary neutrality propositions that obtain under appropriate conditions in some sufficiently long run. Apart from Tobin effects,[7] which are likely to be quantitatively small, few economists would argue that the average rate of money growth maintained over a century would much influence the level of real economic activity at the century's end, while most would expect an effect on the average inflation rate over that time. By contrast, what is new and striking — as well as of great practical importance, if it is true — is the conclusion of the new classical macroeconomics that these familiar neutrality propositions obtain in the short run too.

How, then, has the new classical macroeconomics met the 'decisive test' provided by the quest for costless disinflation in the early 1980s? In 1980 the US economy entered a period of protracted weakness involving in record short order, two successive business recessions (as identified in the standard NBER chronology). The economies of other industrialized Western nations exhibited similar, if not even more severe, weakness. In the USA the utilization of both labour and capital resources fell to post Second World War record lows by the year ending 1982, with 10.8 per cent of the labour force unemployed and 32.7 per cent of industrial capacity idle. While neither the 1980 recession (the shortest on record) nor the 1981-2 recession (the longest since the Second World War) was extraordinary individually, the effect of the two together represented as great an impact on the real economy as any business-cycle experience in the post-war era. It also dramatically slowed inflation.

What makes this 'event' so immediately relevant to evaluating the new classical macroeconomics is the important role of monetary policy, especially after 1980, in bringing it about. Business-cycle historians will no doubt continue for some time to debate the causes of the brief recession in the spring of 1980. The new 'monetarist' monetary policy adopted in October 1979 was a factor, to be sure, but so were the imposition of credit controls in March 1980, the movement of the federal budget into surplus on a high-employment basis in 1979, and the doubling of world oil prices in 1979-80.

By contrast, restrictive monetary policy stands out as the primary force halting the recovery that began in mid-1980. Whether measured by money growth or by interest rate levels, monetary policy was tight during this period. After declining from 8.2 per cent in 1978 to 7.4 per cent in 1979 and 7.2 per cent in 1980, the growth of the M1 money stock fell to 5.2 per cent in 1981 — or only 2.5 per cent after the Federal Reserve Board's suggested adjustment to reflect the nationwide authorization of NOW accounts at the year's outset. Both short- and long-term nominal interest rates moved to new record highs at year-end 1980 and remained at those levels until late in 1981. Moreover, even when nominal interest rates finally declined, they remained (and, through the time of writing, continue) at unprecedently high levels in relation to the economy's ongoing rate of price inflation. The primacy of this tight monetary policy stance in bringing about the recession that began in mid-1981 is all the clearer in that the high-employment federal budget was moving progressively into deficit, and real oil prices were falling, throughout this period.

What implications, for price inflation and for real economic activity, does the new classical macroeconomics suggest as a consequence of this monetary policy? It is always possible to argue, of course, that that analysis carries no implications at all for the outcome of any such policy because it is impossible to know whether the policy was anticipated or not. This response is not satisfactory, however. Although the initial change in monetary policy in October 1979 may well have caught the public unaware, the continuation of that policy from late 1980 onward was hardly a surprise. Especially in the context of the 1980 general election, the tight monetary policy during this period was probably about as well anticipated as such a policy is ever likely to be. Because expectations are unobservable, of course, it is impossible ever to establish definitively what was and what was not anticipated in advance. Even so, if the new classical macroeconomics analysis of anticipated monetary policy is not relevant to US monetary policy during this period, then it is not clear when — or if ever — that analysis is likely to be relevant.

Table 11.1 summarizes some basic dimensions of US macroeconomic experience in 1980–2, including not only the slowing of price inflation but also the decline in real economic activity. For purposes of establishing some minimal historical context, the table also traces the re-acceleration of inflation during the years after the 1973–5 recession. The rise in the inflation rate in 1976–80 was gradual at first, then more rapid as the business expansion carried the economy to higher utilization levels and finally as international oil prices rose sharply in 1979–80. The subsequent drop in the inflation rate was somewhat sharper, halving it in two years, and thereby more than reversing the entire rise since 1975 and bringing inflation to its slowest pace since 1972.

What about the behaviour of real economic activity that accompanied

TABLE 11.1 Inflation, growth and employment of resources: 1976-82

	Inflation		Growth		Employment of resources	
	Total GNP deflator %	Consumption deflator %	Real GNP %	Industrial production %	Unemployment rate %	Capacity utilization %
1976	4.7[1]	5.1[1]	4.4[1]	7.4[2]	7.8[3]	80.0[4]
1977	6.1	5.8	5.7	5.2	6.4	82.6
1978	8.5	7.0	5.8	8.0	6.0	86.4
1979	8.2	9.0	1.4	0.5	6.0	84.4
1980	10.2	10.3	−0.6	−1.4	7.3	79.1
1981	8.9	8.6	0.7	−4.7	8.8	74.8
1982	4.4	5.1	−1.1	−2.5	10.8	67.6

NOTES   1 Fourth quarter growth from previous year's fourth quarter.
2 December growth from previous year's December.
3 December level.
4 Fourth quarter level.

SOURCE   US Department of Commerce, US Department of Labor, Board of Governors of the Federal Reserve System.

this disinflation? Was this experience consistent with the central propositions of the new classical macroeconomics? Did the performance of the
real economy bear out the prediction of costless disinflation?

The economic events documented in Table 11.1 suggest anything but
costless disinflation. Instead, they are strikingly in line with the conventional estimates of the cost of disinflation surveyed by Okun some years
before the fact.

The slowing of inflation from 10 per cent per annum in 1980 to 5 per
cent in 1982 had, just by year-end 1982, required an average unemployment rate of $7\frac{1}{2}$ per cent during the three years 1980, 1981, and 1982. If
the economy was approximately at full employment in 1978-9, when the
unemployment rate was 6 per cent on average, then the cost through
1982 of about five points of disinflation was about five point-years of
unemployment. Stopping the accounts at year-end 1982 makes no sense,
however. The calculation is incomplete without tallying the continuing
point-years of unemployment that accrue until the economy returns to
full employment. The current federal government projection as of the time
of writing, for example, places the return to 6 per cent (actually $6\frac{1}{2}$ per
cent) unemployment in 1988, with an average of $8\frac{1}{2}$ per cent of the labour
force unemployed in 1983-8 (and no further slowing of inflation).[8] This
outlook therefore implies an additional fifteen point-years of unemployment, bringing to twenty point-years the total associated with five points
of disinflation, for a final trade-off of 4-to-1 — towards the pessimistic end
of Okun's range.

It is also possible to construct a more favourable picture on the basis of
more optimistic assumptions, of course. For example, if the post-recession
business expansion were sufficient to reduce unemployment to $9\frac{1}{2}$ per cent
in 1983, $7\frac{1}{2}$ per cent in 1984, and then 6 per cent in 1985 and thereafter —
and all that without any re-acceleration of inflation — then the relevant
total would have been 'only' ten point-years of unemployment, implying a
final trade-off of 'only' 2-for-1 — about at the optimistic end of Okun's
range.

Whether the correct number summarizing the unemployment cost of
disinflation ultimately turns out to be somewhat above or somewhat
below Okun's median estimate is beside the point. What matters is that
the disinflation already has not been, and will not turn out to be, costless.
Experience has belied the most significant policy implication of the new
classical macroeconomics, the implication that, at an important level, gave
this new line of thinking its appeal.

Does this event constitute 'a decisive test'? Was the prediction of cost
less disinflation 'wildly incorrect'? Was the inconsistency between it and

the economy's observed behaviour 'spectacular', representing 'econometric failure on a grand scale'? Did the analysis that concluded that disinflation was costless give 'seriously wrong answers to the most basic questions of macroeconomic policy'? Is the new classical macroeconomics therefore now in 'the deepest kind of trouble in which an applied body of theory can find itself'?

Such terms are difficult to assess, much less to apply. What does seem clear is that the decline of real economic activity that accompanied the disinflation of the early 1980s has contradicted the chief policy implication of the new classical macroeconomics just as surely, and just as greatly, as the overall upward trend in inflation during the 1960s and 1970s contradicted the chief policy implication of an earlier macroeconomic analysis.

FUTURE DIRECTIONS FOR MACROECONOMICS

Where does macroeconomics go from here? To be sure, the wrong lesson to draw from the recent experience would be that thinking on the subject should simply return to its prevailing state of a decade or two ago, rejecting as a whole all developments associated with the new classical macroeconomics. In the first instance, the disconfirmation of the costless disinflation proposition does not eliminate from the empirical record the earlier disconfirmation of the stable inflation–unemployment trade-off proposition. Breaking a new eggshell today does not restore to integrity another eggshell broken yesterday.

More importantly, it is both unncessary and wrong to reject every new element introduced by the new classical macroeconomics just because the specific combination of elements used in that line of research has led to falsified conclusions. As the discussion above has already emphasized, the assumptions that people behave in their own self-interest and that markets clear (in some broad sense) are not by themselves sufficient to deliver the key results of short-run policy neutrality and costless disinflation. Those more ambitious results follow only from additional, more far-reaching assumptions including the availability of sufficient information, the absence of transactions costs (again in a very broad sense) and the flexibility of wages and prices.

Moreover, the series of methodological developments initially associated with the new classical macroeconomics bears little if any relation to the ultimate behavioural conclusions associated with this line of research. The emphasis on microeconomic foundations, including in particular the effort to derive macroeconomic relationships from explicit models of individual behaviour, is one example. This approach to macroeconomics is not without costs, of course, including (at least to date) the need to assume away aggregation issues as well as to ignore valid aspects of the individual behavioural environment, like transactions costs, that would render formal analysis intractable. Nevertheless, in many contexts these costs may well be worth incurring in order to exploit the power of the available microeconomic theory. Another example is the use of empirical estimation methods that exploit the theory underlying a multi-equation model to impose cross-equation restrictions on the admissible parameter values. Here too there are costs, but in many contexts they may be justified by the resulting advantages in terms of more rigorous hypothesis testing or, under a maintained hypothesis, better quantitative estimates.

The important point is to distinguish these and other methodological developments in macroeconomic thinking from the context of the policy conclusions derived by the new classical macroeconomics under quite specific, and in some cases implausible, assumptions. Genuine methodological advances are applicable more broadly. The current direction of macroeconomic research is not abandoning these developments, nor is the future direction of research in the field likely to do so.

At the same time, if macroeconomics is not simply to continue to focus on a framework that delivers falsified conclusions, important departures from the new classical macroeconomics are clearly necessary. In part those departures are already in progress. At least to date, two major themes – one based on the costs of decisions and transactions, and the other based on informational limitations and asymmetries – have predominated. These themes have appeared separately and also in conjunction.

Early on in the debate over the then emerging new classical macroeconomics, Phelps and Taylor (1977) as well as Fischer (1977) pointed out the necessity of the price flexibility assumption for the policy neutrality conclusion. The specific context of this and the ensuing literature was the existence of fixed nominal wage contracts, perhaps the most obvious violation of the flexibility assumption in modern Western economies, but the point at issue really applies to sticky wages and prices of any kind, anywhere within the system. As economists have known for decades, stickiness of wages and/or prices matters importantly, and the associated implications are no less striking in the context of the methods and other assumptions typical of the new classical macroeconomics. Indeed, wages or prices set for fixed but overlapping time periods are sufficient, even within this framework of analysis, to generate persistent inflation and real activity effects that last well beyond the length of the longest contract, as well as business cycles in the sense of policy or other effects on real economic activity that first build before subsiding.[9]

Moreover, price and wage inflexibility is itself just an instance of the broader theme of decision and transactions costs. In the spirit of the new classical macroeconomics, it is helpful not just to accept sticky wages and prices as a fact but to seek additional insights from trying to understand the reasons behind their existence. Some economic rationale often underlies the form of society's institutional arrangements. In this case the prevalence of arrangements setting inflexible wages or prices for either fixed or indefinite periods of time no doubt reflects the costs of making decisions, including the costs of gathering the information needed for decision-making. In the presence of such costs, even an economy made up entirely of people who optimize their own interests within optimally chosen arrangements will fail to exhibit the central properties claimed by the new classical macroeconomics.[10]

Issues of information availability not only provide a basis for wage and price stickiness but also constitute yet a further potential avenue for using the methods of the new classical macroeconomics without proceeding to its empirically falsified conclusions. Even under the maintained assumption that only deviations of outcomes from the associated prior expectations affect real economic activity, an important question is the basis on which those prior expectations are formed. What especially matters in the context of the potential role of monetary policy is whether the central bank, and the people whose behaviour more proximately matters for decisions affecting output, share the same basis for forming expectations.[11] If not, then even systematic monetary policy is not neutral with respect to real economic activity.

Moreover, if the respective information differential between the central bank and the relevant parts of the economy's private sector is such as to favour (in a minimum-variance sense) the central bank, then monetary policy will be able to exploit the resulting non-neutrality. Especially since the presumed sign of the effect of surprises on output decisions in this analysis makes sense primarily in the context of the decisions of households, rather than of businesses or of traders in financial markets, an information differential in the required direction is hardly implausible. Once again, much of the method and analytical body of the new classical macroeconomics can still obtain (here even including the price flexibility assumption), yet the end result of the analysis is an altogether different set of policy conclusions.

Finally, the transactions cost theme and the information availability theme blend in other ways as well. A third direction for subsequent macroeconomic research is to emphasize the actual process of making and co-ordinating decisions in the modern, large-scale market economy. One way to view wages or price stickiness, for example, is simply as the result of the private sector's being able to take and implement price and output decisions at less frequent intervals than the central bank can take and implement monetary policy decisions. Another element in this line of thinking is to recognize the impossibility of fully simultaneous decision-making among all relevant actors throughout the market economy. Blanchard, for example, has shown that the lack of synchronization of price and production decisions is itself sufficient to lead to different policy conclusions, even within a remaining context drawn entirely from the new classical macroeconomics.[12]

What has already emerged from recent research, therefore, is the extreme fragility of the central policy conclusions of the new classical macroeconomics. Under even small and apparently reasonable modifications in the underlying assumptions, a fully corresponding analysis indicates that money is not neutral, that systematic policy affects real output and employment, and that trade-offs exist — and that disinflation is not costless. If the objective of the analysis were to defend the specific policy conclusions of the new classical macroeconomics, recent trends in macroeconomic research would be as distressing at the theoretical level as the actual experience of disinflation in the early 1980s has been at the empirical level.

If the objective is instead to gain an even better understanding of how the macroeconomy works, however, these new directions are likely to prove constructive. They show that it is possible to exploit what is useful from the advances of the previous decade without following an inevitable path to empirically falsified results.

In the light of how macroeconomics has always developed, all this is not surprising. The respective disappointments over the economy's failure to recover quickly from the depression of the 1930s and then to avoid inflation in the 1960s and 1970s in both cases led to substantial rethinking, and now so too has the failure to achieve costless disinflation in the early 1980s. It is this responsiveness to actual economic events, just as much as the cumulative nature of scientific thinking in the abstract, that gives macroeconomics its vitality.

NOTES

1. See, even more recently, Lucas, 1981.
2. See Phelps, 1967; and Friedman, 1968.
3. Muth, 1960, 1961.

4. Okun, 1978. See also, for example, Gordon, 1975; and Cagan, 1978.
5. Gordon, 1976; and Shiller, 1978, are useful surveys.
6. See, for example, Taylor, 1975; Friedman, 1978, 1979; and Simon, 1979.
7. Tobin, 1965. See also Sidrauski, 1969.
8. US Government, 1983.
9. See Taylor, 1980, 1982.
10. See, for example, Grossman and Weiss, 1982.
11. See again, Taylor, 1975; and Friedman, 1979; as well as, for example, Weiss, 1980; and Siegel, 1982.
12. Blanchard, 1983.

REFERENCES

Blanchard, O. J. (1983) 'Rigid Relative Prices and Price Level Inertia', Harvard University (mimeo).
Cagan, P. (1978) 'The Reduction of Inflation by Slack Demand', in W. Fellner (ed.), *Contemporary Economic Problems 1978*, Washington: American Enterprise Institute.
Fischer, S. (1977) 'Long-Term Contracts, Rational Expectations, and the Optimal Money Supply Rule', *Journal of Political Economy*, 85 (February): 191–206.
Friedman, B. M. (1978) 'Discussion', in *After the Phillips Curve: Persistence of High Inflation and High Unemployment*, Boston: Federal Reserve Bank of Boston.
Friedman, B. M. (1979) 'Optimal Expectations and the Extreme Information Assumptions of "Rational Expectations" Macromodels', *Journal of Monetary Economics*, 5 (January): 23–41.
Friedman, M. (1968) 'The Role of Monetary Policy', *American Economic Review*, 58 (March): 1–17.
Gordon, R. J. (1975) 'The Impact of Aggregate Demand on Prices', *Brookings Papers on Economic Activity*, no. 3: 613–62.
Gordon, R. J. (1976) 'Recent Developments in the Theory of Inflation and Unemployment', *Journal of Monetary Economics*, 2 (April): 185–210.
Grossman, S., and L. Weiss (1982) 'A Transaction Based Model of the Monetary Transmission Mechanism: Parts I and II', National Bureau of Economic Research (mimeo).
Lucas, R. E. (1970) 'Econometric Testing of the Natural Rate Hypothesis', in O. Eckstein (ed.), *The Econometrics of Price Determination*, Washington: Board of Governors of the Federal Reserve System.
Lucas, R. E. (1980) 'Methods and Problems in Business Cycle Theory', *Journal of Money, Credit and Banking*, 12 (November) pt II: 696–715.
Lucas, R. E. (1981) 'Tobin and Monetarism: A Review Article', *Journal of Economic Literature*, 19 (June): 558–67.
Lucas, R. E., and T. J. Sargent (1978) 'After Keynesian Macroeconomics', in *After the Phillips Curve: Persistence of High Inflation and High Unemployment*, Boston: Federal Reserve Bank of Boston.

Muth, J. F. (1960) 'Optimal Properties of Exponentially Weighted Forecasts', *Journal of the American Statistical Association*, 55 (June): 299–306.

Muth, J. F. (1961) 'Rational Expectations and the Theory of Price Movements', *Econometrica*, 29 (July): 315–35.

Okun, A. M. (1978) 'Efficient Disinflationary Policies', *American Economic Review*, 68 (May): 348–52.

Phelps, E. S. (1967) 'Phillips Curves, Expectations of Inflation, and Optimal Unemployment over Time', *Economica*, 34 (August): 254–81.

Phelps, E. S., and Taylor, J. B. (1977) 'Stabilizing Powers of Monetary Policy under Rational Expectations', *Journal of Political Economy*, 85 (February): 163–90.

Sargent, T. J. (1982) 'Beyond Demand and Supply Curves in Macroeconomics', *American Economic Review*, 72 (May): 382–9.

Shiller, R. J. (1978) 'Rational Expectations and the Dynamic Structure of Macroeconomic Models: A Critical Review', *Journal of Monetary Economics*, 4 (January): 1–44.

Sidrauski, M. (1969) 'Rational Choice and Patterns of Growth', *Journal of Political Economy*, 77 (July/August, Part II): 575–85.

Siegel, J. J. (1982) 'Monetary Stabilization and the Informational Value of Monetary Aggregates', *Journal of Political Economy*, 90 (February): 176–80.

Simon, H. A. (1979) 'Rational Decision Making in Business Organizations', *American Economic Review*, 69 (September): 493–513.

Taylor, J. B. (1975) 'Monetary Policy During a Transition to Rational Expectations', *Journal of Political Economy*, 83 (October): 1009–21.

Taylor, J. B. (1980) 'Aggregate Dynamics and Staggered Contracts', *Journal of Political Economy*, 88 (February): 1–23.

Taylor, J. B. (1982) 'Union wage Settlements During a Disinflation', mimeo, National Bureau of Economic Research.

Tobin, J. J. (1965) 'Money and Economic Growth', *Econometrica*, 33 (October): 671–84.

US Government (1983) *The Budget of the United States Government – Fiscal Year 1984*, Washington: US Government Printing Office.

Weiss, L. (1980) 'The Role for Active Monetary Policy in a Rational Expectations Model', *Journal of Political Economy*, 88 (April): 221–33.

Part IV
Inflation and Disinflation

12 Did Mainstream Econometric Models Fail to Anticipate the Inflationary Surge?

LAWRENCE R. KLEIN

The critics of the neoclassical–Keynesian synthesis of macroeconomics usually cite a failure of such models to anticipate the great surge of inflation during the 1970s.[1]

That appears to be a major factor motivating the angry young men into developing new models:

empirical models without theory;
rational expectations models;
new classical models;
monetarist models

I have not seen their numbers, which would be indicative of whether or not they have something better, but I do know more about the actual anticipation of the inflation surge and would like to present a different side of the story.

The critical period is the early part of the 1970s when many unusual inflationary pressures were present. First there was dollar devaluation and the Soviet grain purchases of 1972; and finally there was the oil embargo of 1973–4, followed by OPEC pricing at values never before thought possible by most people. The annual rate of growth of the GNP deflator, from the end of the 1960s, is presented in Table 12.1.

At the time, in the early 1970s, 5 per cent was considered to be very serious, but after some years of higher inflation, it appeared to be a low rate. Nevertheless, econometric model forecasts, from mainstream models,

TABLE 12.1   *Inflation rate–GNP deflator, 1969–76*

Years	Per cent
1969	5.0
1970	5.4
1971	5.1
1972	4.1
1973	5.8
1974	10.0
1975	9.3
1976	5.1

were not badly flawed in this period. In Table 12.2 we have a tabulation of median forecasts, one year ahead, from four models — all in the category under attack by the angry young men — and the consensus report of the American Statistical Association forecasters, many of whom were consulting the same, or their own, models at the time.

Guidance to interpretation of the inflationary situation was provided by the models up to an error of about one or, at most, two percentage points until late 1973 when oil prices started to rise. A period of significant underestimation continued for two years (for eight quarterly forecasts) and was followed by a period that was quite normal with moderate forecast error.

Many people failed to realize how important energy or oil, in particular, was for the economy because it represented only a tiny share of total GNP. It was necessary to model the energy system in some detail in order to trace through the economic process and find different stages at which oil and other energy forms were important. Also, there was a shift to restructuring the economy in order to gain in conservation and put more efficient (in an energy sense) capital into place. This process, together with an intensive exploration for new sources, was expensive and contributed to the run up of inflation.

I shall argue that the mainstream model had to be restructured by introducing more of the 'neoclassical side' in the neoclassical Keynesian synthesis in order to capture a proper assessment of the energy impact. It called for an extension of the mainstream model in a direction that it was already taking and not an overhaul or replacement by something entirely new. Improvements in performance were made, but they were not at all related to the criticism from the side of rational expectations, monetarism, or time series analysis.

TABLE 12.2 *Median forecast error 1971.1–1979.2 one year ahead, inflation rate five forecasters*

Year and quarter	Per cent
71.1	−1.3
71.2	−1.6
71.3	−1.6
71.4	−1.1
72.1	−0.8
72.2	0.1
72.3	−0.7
72.4	−0.4
73.1	−0.7
73.2	−1.7
73.3	−2.8
73.4	−3.7
74.1	−4.1
74.2	−4.0
74.3	−5.4
74.4	−4.5
75.1	−4.6
75.2	−2.4
75.3	0.2
75.4	0.8
76.1	0.1
76.2	0.5
76.3	1.4
76.4	1.1
77.1	0.5
77.2	−0.3
77.3	−0.6
77.4	−0.6
78.1	0.0
78.2	−1.0
78.3	−1.7
78.4	−2.1
79.1	−2.2
79.2	−1.9

SOURCE S. McNees, 'The Forecasting Record for the 1970s', *New England Economic Review* (September/October 1979): 50.

Let us focus attention on 1973. This is the year of take-off into the inflation surge. In fact, inspection of Table 12.1 does not suggest that inflation was policy induced, certainly not from the policies that were coming from the neoclassical–Keynesian model. They were purely exaggerated by the food and oil shocks. A simple univariate time series obviously does not carry all the information that we need to look at, but these figures are so unusual and so closely related to the timing of the disturbance factors that it is not plausible to deny that this is the main effect at work here.

On 19 December 1973 there was a meeting in the office of the Secretary of the Treasury to assess the situation, and I have a summary of the discussion together with a tabulation of forecasts made there. At the time, the inflation rate for the whole of 1973 was not known, but it was evidently moving upward from the figure of 4.1 per cent in 1972 and had been rising throughout 1973. The forecast from the Wharton model, representative among those based on the neoclassical Keynesian synthesis, was for 7.2 per cent in 1974. This was the second highest reported at the meeting; and was associated with an unemployment rate that was predicted to rise to 5.5 per cent. The 1973 figure was 4.9 per cent.

This does look to me like the breakdown of a theory or model. The conventional view from past experience had been one of a trade-off between inflation and unemployment, and here we had a break with the past in which the economy was expected, well in advance, to be going into a period of rising inflation and rising unemployment.

The correct inflation forecast for that meeting would have been 10 per cent instead of 7.2 per cent, but it is my conviction that a forecast of 9 or 10 per cent would not have been accepted as credible. The models with which we were working did not have explicit energy sectors, and we had to estimate energy effects indirectly. Also, we were not sure yet how high oil prices would rise. It seems to me that we were estimating nearly as high a value of inflation acceleration as policy-makers could have been able to accept and act upon. Considering the doctrinal make-up of participants at the meeting, the mainstream model provided nearly the best base for policy guidance.

By studying the way that energy fits into a larger model of the economy as a whole, from both the supply and demand sides, we were able to overcome a lack of information from this area of economic activity and have an amplified model that was able to handle the inflation problem more realistically by mid-1975, when inflation was still strong.

There were at least two very different approaches to follow, at that time, in macroeconometric model building. We could have reacted as the angry young men did and try to construct an entirely new model specification, with a new method of estimation too. Or we could have reacted by building in more food and fuel detail in order to be able to interpret these events better.

In connection with research on the Wharton model, we did precisely what would be suggested by the second approach. We built a great deal of agricultural and energy detail into the system. For agriculture we (through Dr Dean Chen) built an entire, large system of supply and demand for nineteen products. For energy we built an entire detailed sector into our large input–output system and added much detail to our quarterly macro model. All three models – the annual model with input–output detail, the agricultural model, and the quarterly macro model – were always projected together consistently so that a careful monitoring of the contributions to inflation from food and fuel could be estimated quantitatively.

In this process, I can see need for model improvement; that is always important, but I cannot see grounds for radical model reform or abandonment. Any model is an approximation to reality, and the approximations were clearly not strong enough in the food and fuel sectors; so this was a time for research improvement in those areas. After a spate of such research, the model approximation improved.

The mainstream model did forecast an increase in inflation together with an increase in unemployment; that is clearly important for those of us who place much weight on predictive testing. There is yet another way to look at the mainstream model from this point of view, namely to study its simulation properties.

As recent as 1970 there was a conference on the Econometrics of Price Determination, at which results were presented for different mainstream models to show their trade-off properties. The existence of realistic trade-off relationships was accepted as supportive evidence that the models were appropriately interpreting the economy.[2]

In a paper written in 1976, I showed that the Wharton model, if given a conventional fiscal shock, would generate the usual trade-off relationship, but if given a food or fuel price shock would generate a situation of rising unemployment and rising inflation.[3] This is just the opposite of a trade-off relationship but is implied by the model and is realistic.

In a recent paper, using the BEA (Bureau of Economic Analysis of the US Department of Commerce) Model, A. Hirsch obtains similar results by simulation of various price shocks.[4] He finds that a 21 per cent increase in oil prices puts the GNP deflator between 1.5 and 2.0 per cent above a base line case with the unemployment rate rising from 0.1 to 1.0 points above the baseline in five years. This exercise also generates a rise in the rate of inflation over the base case. For a 20 per cent increase in farm prices, the effect on the GNP deflator is slightly stronger for the general price effect, bringing it to a level position 2.7 per cent above the baseline in five years, but is slightly weaker in its effect on unemployment. That measure exceeds the baseline value by only 0.7 percentage points after five years.

The point is clear, none-the-less. Different mainstream models have simulation properties that are quite in line with unusual developments in the economy. They are capable of showing either a trade-off relationship when that is appropriate or in showing rising inflation and rising unemployment, together, when that is appropriate.

Some points of the inflation during the 1970s and the early years of this decade have been due to exchange rate depreciation; some to price shocks; some to general demand/cost pressures. It is hard to see where mainstream models were particularly deficient in any of these lines of influence, and we have yet to see the established records of any alternative approach that is decisively (or even suggestively) better. There are many assertions but no evidence that something better is available.

Much of the focus has been on price shocks; these were not anticipated years or even months in advance. I doubt that we will ever have models with such power, but we do have systems that tell us the expected consequences of such events when they do occur. The next events of unusual macroeconomic importance after the price shocks of the 1970s, were the oil glut, grain surpluses, high deficits (3 digit levels), and high interest rates (2 digits).

The worldwide surpluses of food and fuel, in relation to demand, have predictable effects. They bring inflation rates down. That is what happened; that is what the mainstream models say should happen. Also, the rise in unemployment, all over the world, should, by a Phillips curve analysis, bring down wage increases. Many mainstream models have Phillips curves as structural equations of the labour market. In spite of much thinking to the contrary, careful estimates of these relationships have stood the test of time very well and predictably provided estimates of reduced wage pressure which, in turn, led to down drift of inflation. Thus the models again seem to be right in step with reality. They are producing simultaneous reductions in wage increases and in price increases. That does not seem to be a problem in their interpretation of inflation.

In looking at the combined fiscal and monetary policies of the new administration in the USA in early 1981, mainstream models were unanimous in projecting large budget deficits, moving upwards in absolute value. Model projections were not the only source of such forecasts, but they did not misinterpret the situation. They factored the high interest rates into high public borrowing costs and the combinations of tax cuts with defence spending increases (with some decreases in other areas, too) to get the rises in the budget deficit. This was another critical hurdle that they had to deal with and were successful.

Announced policy changes and known movements in world commodity prices have been handled. These are the problems of the recent past, but where will the next large surprises occur? As long as the macro Keynesian component is embedded in an increasingly sophisticated neoclassical system of more detail, we can hope to be ready for the next big event in the sense that there should be a group of equations that deal effectively with the area in question. There will always be a need to act as we did in the energy shocks of the 1970s and build up detail for a new sector of importance, but as we expand the detail in our systems, the chances are greater that we shall be able to accommodate the analysis of major new developments.

At the international level, project LINK had fortunately split off trade in mineral fuels as a separate item for analysis and data detail as early as 1968. When the energy shock occurred, we were ready to handle the trading portion in some detail, and this contributed to our success in foreseeing (at the Treasury Meeting of December 1973) that a worldwide recession was in the making.[5]

The next major events at the beginning of the 1980s, were, in fact, international financial and trade adjustments. By having networks of trading systems with endogenous exchange rates and some information on capital flows we have been more ready than in 1973 to cope with major new developments. But regardless whether we are ready with the requisite detail to proceed directly to analysis of new situations or whether we have to modify and adopt existing systems, it seems better to try to be constructive by improving existing models rather than to declare immediate need for something radically different and new.

It is better to have continuity of development by building on the cumulative knowledge of the past.

NOTES

1. 'We begin by reviewing the econometric framework by means of which Keynesian theory evolved from disconnected, qualitative "talk" about economic activity into a system of equations which could be compared to data in a systematic way, and provide an operational guide in the necessarily quantitative task of formulating monetary and fiscal policy. Next we identify those aspects of this framework which were central to its failure in the seventies. In so doing, one intent will be to establish that the difficulties are *fatal*, that modern macroeconomic models are of *no* value in guiding policy, and that this condition will not be remedied by modification along any line which is currently being pursued' (R. E. Lucas and T. J. Sargent, ' "New" Explanations of the Persistence of

Inflation and Unemployment', in *After the Phillips Curve: Persistence of High Inflation and High Unemployment*, Boston: Federal Reserve Bank, 1978, p. 500.

2. *The Econometrics of Price Determination*, Washington, D.C.: Board of Governors of the Federal Reserve System and Social Science Research Council, 1972.

3. L. R. Klein, 'The Longevity of Economic Theory', *Quantitative Wirtschaftsforschung*, ed. H. Albach *et al.*, Tubingen: J.C.B. Mohr, 1977, 411–19. This paper was read to E. Malinvaud's seminar in Paris, November, 1976.

4. A. A. Hirsch, 'Macroeconomic Effects of Price Shocks: A Simulation Study', *Survey of Current Business*, 63 (February 1983): 30–43.

5. 'Klein noted that the macro models of Project LINK countries are showing that 1 to 2 percentage points will be shaved off their 1974 real growth rates due to the oil shortage. He posed a danger of worldwide recession because when models of each country are exogenously shocked by lowering real growth by 1 per cent, the international trading system effect is to amplify the reduction by another one-half percent' (Treasury Meeting summary).

13 Disinflation

OTTO ECKSTEIN

The years 1982–4 will enter the economic history books as the period of disinflation. The postwar boom ended in 1973 and had inevitably driven up the prices of goods and resources. But it took nearly another decade, including two bouts of double-digit inflation, before disinflation took over to set the stage for another phase of world development.[1]

This chapter analyses the disinflation process of these years. How did it happen? Was it the severity of the 1982 recession that finally brought down core inflation? Have inflationary expectations improved as much as actual price performance? Has the structure of the economy improved to reduce the inflationary bias that was so evident in the preceding three decades? Will inflation return quickly in the recovery? And what can be done to assure that the next upswing remains free of the problems of its predecessors? Only a quantitative analysis employing a cohesive theoretical structure can provide meaningful answers to these questions. Causal empiricism or non-factual theorizing are not without value, but are hardly likely to provide conclusions concrete enough to be of much help in policy formation.

The study focuses on the experience of the USA, but the world economy has become so integrated through common dependence on oil and the growth of international trade that our own economy cannot be analysed in isolation. Nor would the conclusions be dramatically different for other industrial countries. Experiences were generally common, although variations in detail grow out of the differences in wage-price setting mechanisms, industrial strategies, and macroeconomic policy responses.

The analytical device for this study is the taxonomy of core inflation. Following a reconnaissance of the record, the disinflationary process is decomposed into demand inflation, shock inflation, and core inflation. This analysis sets the stage for an examination of our prospects and the needs of policy.

The demand factor is the traditional response of the price level to the degree of resource utilization in the macro economy. It has most commonly been analysed in terms of the augmented Phillips curve, the curve linking the rate of inflation to the national unemployment rate. What role did the weakening of worldwide and domestic demands play? Has the mechanism underlying the augmented Phillips curves changed, perhaps in the direction of more rapid learning and a more rational formation of the inflation expectations underlying wage and price decisions?

Shock inflation is the temporary upward shift in costs, created by non-recurring events, such as changes in world oil prices, government policies such as higher payroll and excise taxes, and changes in the import costs that may be created by a lower exchange rate. The disinflation process was aided by shock disinflation, particularly the decline of world oil prices. These forces temporarily lowered the curve portraying the aggregate supply price.

Core inflation is the trend rate of increase of the aggregate supply price. It is the rate of increase of unit labour and capital costs, normalized for the equilibrium rate of resource utilization. It is a comprehensive measure of the 'underlying' or 'inertial' inflation rate, the rate that would prevail if there were no shocks and if the aggregate level of activity were consistent with the equilibrium resource utilization rate, that is, were operating at the natural rate of unemployment.

As a first approximation, both shock and core inflation are supply-side phenomena. Indeed, the sum of shocks, capital and labour costs is equal to the aggregate supply price. But in a comprehensive analysis it must be recognized that the shocks may, in fact, be highly responsive to aggregate demand, and therefore a full evaluation of the role of worldwide recession in the disinflation cannot take the shocks as given. Similarly, core inflation is the result of previous shock and demand inflations, so that a period of weak demand will, after delay, lower the core rate.

FACTUAL RECONNAISANCE: THE EXTENT OF DISINFLATION AND ITS COMPOSITION

In 1979 and 1980, the consumer price index rose by 12.4 per cent a year and the producer price index of finished goods rose 12.3 per cent. In the first quarter of 1983, both indexes actually declined. Wage increases averaged 9.1 per cent in 1980 and 1981, but have retreated to 4.9 per cent. This really is disinflation!

The composition of the reductions in the consumer price inflation can be seen in Table 13.1.

TABLE 13.1 *Sources of improvement in the CPI for urban wage-earners and clerical workers*

	Weight	Annual % change		Contribution to slowdown (percentage points)
		Dec 1978– Dec 1980	Mar 1982– Mar 1983	
CPIW – all items	100.0	12.9	3.8	9.2
Food and beverages	19.0	10.4	2.7	1.5
Housing	42.7	14.6	4.3	4.4
Homeownership	23.2	18.7	3.3	3.6
Home purchase	8.7	13.8	11.9	0.2
Financing, taxes, insurance	11.3	26.1	−3.0	3.3
Residential rent	4.9	8.5	6.4	0.1
Energy	11.5	27.9	−2.2	3.5
Motor fuel	6.1	35.2	−9.1	2.7
Electricity and gas	4.0	15.2	11.4	0.2
Apparel and upkeep	4.5	5.9	1.8	0.2
New cars	3.1	7.6	3.3	0.1
Used cars	4.5	8.6	10.2	−0.1
Medical care	4.7	10.4	10.3	0.0
Entertainment	3.4	7.8	4.9	0.1
Other goods and services	4.3	8.8	12.3	−0.2
All other				−0.3

Two components dominate the figures. Home ownership, which has a weight of 23.2 percentage points of the consumer price index, accounted for 39 per cent of the inflation improvement.[2] This reduction was due to the reversal of the interest rate trends. In the high-inflation period, new home mortgage rates rose from 9 per cent to 13 per cent; in the most recent three months, mortgage rates were down to 13 per cent from 15.5 per cent a year earlier. This treatment of home ownership in the index is now considered to have been an exaggeration because house prices contain an investment element and few mortgages were issued during the period of peak rates. The new consumer price index, which uses a rental cost concept, would not have shown the enormous increase in home ownership prices, and its increase over the two peak years would have been lower. But, the extraordinary CPI figures published at the time helped to determine inflation expectations and produced extraordinarily large escalator costs under collective bargaining agreements and federal benefit programmes.

The second major numerical contributor to the reduction of inflation is the energy sector. The composite price of energy in the consumer price index was rising at a 27.9 per cent rate in the high inflation period; in the first quarter of 1983 energy prices came down at a 18.9 per cent rate. This turnaround is largely associated with the end of the second round of the OPEC price explosion and the collapse of the world oil price structure.

Food prices also played a significant, though lesser, role in the inflation turnaround. While food prices were a major factor in the double-digit inflation of the mid-1970s, they did not rise particularly dramatically in the later period of high inflation. However, their recent decline at wholesale and their stability at retail have contributed importantly to the current extraordinarily favourable price performance.

The rest of the consumer price index showed lesser changes. On the high side, some of the consumer services, particularly medical costs, continued at near double-digit rates. Other prices, such as clothing, shoes and furniture, were not rising particularly rapidly before, and now are rising less than 3 per cent. New automobiles, where there are some measurement problems because of the government's attempts to identify quality changes, were up 7.6 per cent over the high inflation years, and more recently were nearly stable.

The price experience of the USA was not unique. Table 13.2 shows the behaviour of consumer prices in other advanced countries, grouping them into the traditional low-, medium- and high-inflation categories. The other low-inflation countries, West Germany, Japan, and Switzerland, avoided the double-digit experience, principally because their governments were more conservative in their fiscal and monetary policies following the 1975 recession. They also had somewhat more slack when the second OPEC price explosion struck their economies, and consequently their energy prices were not converted fully into higher price levels. Also, during the peak inflation period their exchange rates were strengthening, while the US dollar was declining.

In recent months, the price performance of the low-inflation countries was good. The USA has rejoined the ranks of the low-inflation economies, though this is partly an artifice created by the overrepresentation of home ownership costs. US price performance has also been aided by the strengthening of the dollar, though the declines of the yen and the mark do not seem to have done much damage to the price performance of those countries. Their principal imports are materials, including oil, and the deflation in these prices blunted the impact of the declines in their currencies. The UK, South Korea and Taiwan have also entered the low-inflation group.

Other medium-inflation countries also showed substantial improvement,

TABLE 13.2 *Inflation rates around the world*

	Dec 78–Dec 80	*Last 12 months*	*Ending*
Low inflation			
Germany	5.4	3.3	April
Japan	6.6	2.3	March
Switzerland	4.8	4.4	April
Moderate inflation			
Canada	10.5	7.2	March
France	12.7	9.2	April
United Kingdom	16.2	4.6	March
United States	12.9	3.6	March
High inflation			
Chile	35.0	24.9	March
Italy	20.0	16.1	February
S. Korea	27.7	4.7	March
Spain	15.4	12.6	March
Taiwan	17.2	5.1	April
Very high inflation			
Argentina	112.1	287.6	April
Brazil	81.1	118.3	April
Israel	121.9	131.9	January
Mexico	24.8	110.1	January

though it certainly could not be said that their disinflation process was near complete. Some of the medium- and higher-inflation countries, for example, Italy, France, and Spain, largely missed the disinflation experience. While they participated in the world recession and are suffering from much higher unemployment than in the boom years, the policies of their governments and their economic structures seem to have precluded the conversion of the weak demands and lower world oil prices into moderate inflation performance. For one reason or another, their governments missed the opportunity to rid their people of inflation.

The major very-high-inflation countries, such as Brazil, Argentina, Mexico and Israel, are continuing to show worsening performance. Their incredible inflation records must be explained by circumstances specific to their particular domestic economies, and not by worldwide forces. For example, in the case of Israel, the necessity for an enormous military budget, the rush to settle the West Bank territories, and the social expenditures to assimilate a large immigrant population, are at the root of her economic troubles. In the South American countries, political instability, corruption, over-ambitious development plans and structural deficiencies combine to produce the very high inflation rates.

The reconnaissance of the data confirms what is generally believed to be the pattern of disinflation: much of the improvement is the result of lower world oil prices, ample food supplies and, in the case of the USA, the reversal of mortgage interest costs. But these facts are not the whole story: how much of the improvement was due to temporary, non-recurring factors and therefore likely to be lost? How significant was the role of the worldwide recession? To address these questions we must turn to a more formal econometric and theoretical analysis.

CORE INFLATION ANALYSIS

As indicated above, inflation can be divided into three components according to the formula:

Inflation = core inflation + shock inflation + demand inflation + residual

This taxonomy presupposes that there is an inertial element in inflation that gives it a persistence character. If the economy really behaved according to the hypotheses of the neoclassical school, with its emphasis on instant market clearing, there would be no room for core inflation, as aggregate supply and demand would respond instantaneously to disequilibria in aggregate resource utilization.

Figure 13.1 shows core, shock, and demand inflation from 1960 to 1984. This figure is constructed according to the core inflation method outlined in my recent book.[3] Application of the analysis to the years of disinflation shows that the inertial element continues to be important despite the dramatic improvement that has occurred.

THE EFFECTS OF A CHANGING SHOCK INFLATION RATE

Food and energy shocks played a major role in the development of the high inflation rate of the mid- and late-1970s, and are now important in explaining the extraordinary slowdown. Energy prices added 2.9 per cent to the inflation rate of 1974 and 2.3 per cent for 1980, with lesser increases in the surrounding years. In 1983, energy prices are providing a helpful negative shock of 0.2 per cent as a result of the collapse of OPEC. If OPEC alone were the determinant of energy prices, the helpful shock would be much larger, of course. However, natural gas prices and electricity prices

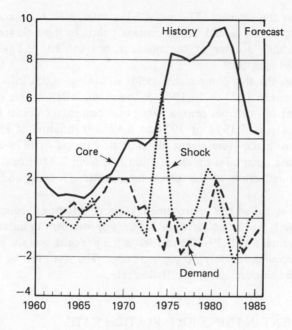

FIGURE 13.1

rose during the disinflation period. Thus the composite producer price index for fuels and power, which rose by 55 per cent in 1974 and 41 per cent in 1980, is only falling by a 6 per cent rate in 1983. While energy is helpful in the current situation and is producing a few dramatic months of improvement in the consumer price index, the overall effect is quite moderate.

The effects of farm prices on inflation are similar. In 1973 the wholesale prices of farm products rose by 41 per cent, adding 2.0 per cent to the inflation rate. In 1982 farm prices were falling by 4.9 per cent, reducing the inflation rate by 0.2 per cent. Distribution costs are cutting the consumer benefits of the price reductions at the wholesale stage.

A significant role in shock inflation was also played by the foreign exchange rate of the dollar. In 1973, after the collapse of the fixed exchange rate regime, the decline of the dollar added 0.2 per cent to the shock inflation rate. In 1982, the dramatic improvement of the exchange rate subtracted 0.5 per cent from the inflation rate, and is reducing the inflation rate of 1983 by another 0.2 percentage points.

The other measurable shock factors played minor roles. The minimum wage added 0.1 per cent in some of the earlier years, but is edging lower in real terms at the moment. The payroll tax rates used to finance social security programmes added 0.2 percentage points to the inflation rate in 1973, are adding nothing at the moment, but will add 0.1 percentage points in 1984 and 1985.

Adding up the five components yields an average shock inflation rate of 3.4 per cent in 1973–4. In 1982–3, the shock inflation rate is helpful to the extent of −0.6 per cent, a swing of 4 percentage points from the high inflation period 1973 or 1974 to the lower inflation of 1982–3. A comparison with the more recent high inflation period of 1979–80 shows a swing in the composite shock inflation rate from 2.3 per cent to −0.6 per cent, a reduction of 2.9 percentage points. (See Appendix Table A13.2.)

It can be seen that the improvement in shock inflation accounted for a significant part, but by no means all, of the improvement in inflation. The total improvement in 1979–80 and 1983 is 9.3 per cent, and the reduction in shocks accounts for only 30 per cent of it. The rest must be found in changes in the core and demand inflation rates.

IMPROVEMENT IN THE CORE INFLATION RATE

In 1981–2 the core inflation rate averaged 9.2 per cent. In 1983 it will be 6.0 per cent, and in 1984 it should be down to 4.9 per cent, given actual data and some extrapolation. The improvement of core inflation is quite predictable, since it is largely based on trend values that are already heavily determined. Even if the next twenty-one months were to contain some minor surprises, the impact on the core inflation rate would be small: most of the projected decline is already built into the data that determine the component trend values.

Sixty-five per cent of the core inflation rate is the unit labour cost trend, the increase in equilibrium wage gains corrected for the productivity trend, where equilibrium is defined at the natural rate of unemployment. Thus the difference between the equilibrium and the actual rates of wage increase is assigned to the demand factor rather than the core inflation rate.

Equilibrium wages have been slowing from 9+ per cent during the peak period to 5.5 per cent in the last four quarters. This reduction in the equilibrium wage gain is due to the gradual reduction in the actual price performance which has lowered price expectations.

Wages will remain on a moderate path over the next several years. Organized workers, many of whom are paid according to three-year contracts, have reached very diverse settlements in the last few months, with some industries, such as steel, granting no increases for the next few years to be followed by relatively small gains near the end of the contract. Other industries are continuing to commit to large contractual wage increases. For unorganized workers, the typical frequency of wage adjustment is one year, with only an occasionally prosperous industry switching to a six-month wage period during periods of high inflation. Since the record of prices was coming down very rapidly in the opening months of 1983, the wage adjustments likely to be granted to unorganized workers over the next twelve months will be substantially smaller than the 1982 results. On the other hand, as the recovery sets in, there will be a tendency for employers to become somewhat more generous and to bid somewhat more aggressively for new workers.

Figure 13.2 shows the historical pattern and the forecast prospects of wages, corrected for industry mix and overtime, both on an actual and

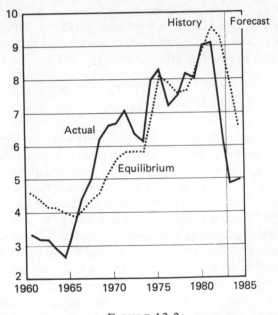

FIGURE 13.2

equilibrium basis. The correction for unemployment is very sizeable just now, but this is a temporary condition. The recovery will gradually move unemployment towards its natural or equilibrium rate as the wage reductions and slowdowns caused by recession disappear.

The labour productivity trend averaged 2.0 per cent from 1960 to

1973, but in the succeeding nine years slowed to 1.2 per cent. The actual productivity figures were considerably more volatile, declining with the onset of recession in 1979 and showing only small gains in 1981 and 1982. Actual productivity was no higher in 1982 than in 1977. However, the core inflation analysis focuses on trend productivity, corrected for the cyclical losses created by high unemployment and low utilization of industrial capacity. On this trend basis, productivity has been less volatile, and it is difficult to find a slowdown in this trend since the apparent downshifting of 1973. As recovery sets in, actual productivity will show large increases, but the productivity trend will not accelerate. The growth of the capital stock was pushed down by the recession, and consequently capital per worker has not been improving. The benefits of the tax incentives of President Reagan's 1981 tax programme will not be felt until the late 1980s.

Combining wage and productivity trends yields the trend in unit labour costs. It shows a 2.3 per cent improvement, from an 8.2 per cent average in the years 1980 and 1981 to 5.9 per cent in 1983–4. With its weight of 0.65 in the core inflation calculation, it creates an improvement of 1.5 percentage points in the core inflation rate.

IMPROVEMENT IN CAPITAL COSTS

The improvement in the trend of capital costs was even more dramatic. The years 1975–81 saw an unparalleled increase in capital costs, averaging 10.8 per cent a year. When weighted by the Cobb–Douglas factor of 0.35, this represented a contribution to the core inflation rate of 3.8 per cent.

Beginning with the year 1981, the capital cost trend improved dramatically. By 1984, when the improvements will have fully worked their way into capital cost calculations, this trend will be only 3.7 per cent, a 7.1 per cent improvement. When weighted by the capital cost factor of 0.35, this represents a reduction in the core inflation rate of 2.5 per cent.

There are several reasons for the extraordinary movements in capital cost trends in recent years. The period of surging capital costs was partly due to the extraordinary increase in capital goods prices. The deflator for non-residential fixed investment rose by an average of 12.9 per cent in the peak years 1974–5, and by 8.6 per cent in the second peak period, 1979–81. The prospects for 1982–4 are for a 3.3 per cent rate of increase in capital goods prices, a big reduction.

Even more important has been the pattern of interest rate changes. Bond yields on top-quality securities ranged between 7 and $8\frac{1}{2}$ per cent in the early 1970s, and jumped to 9 per cent in 1974-5. But the big increases began with the adoption of a more rigid monetarism in late 1979. Bond yields gradually moved up to over 15 per cent for the year 1981, and were still averaging nearly 14 per cent in 1982. Short-term interest rates followed a similar pattern, showing even larger short-run changes. The interest rate on prime bank loans more than doubled between 1977 and 1981 and remained very high until 1982. Both long- and short-term interest rates have fallen quite sharply and are hardly likely to change dramatically over the next year.

The stock market, which determines the price of externally raised equity capital and is a guide to the value of internally generated equity funds, reinforced the trends in financial capital costs. The stock market did poorly in the years of accelerating core inflation, but began to improve sharply once interest rates turned down.

The depreciation reforms, liberalized investment tax, and leasing provisions of President Reagan's 1981 tax programme lowered the after-tax cost of capital quite substantially. While nearly half of the ERTA 1981 reforms were undone by the TEFRA 1982 tax legislation, the benefits remain major and are substantially lowering the rental price of capital.

Combining all of the factors yields a change in the actual rental price of capital from 11.6 per cent in the years 1976-80 to −0.7 per cent for 1981-3. Because business investment can hardly respond instantaneously to changes in the rental price of capital, the core inflation rate smoothes the short-term rental price changes into a trend. The change in the capital cost trend is still dramatic, from 11.1 per cent in the years 1976-81 to 4.6 per cent in 1983-4.

Combining the trends in unit labour costs and capital costs yields the core inflation rate. Its improvement is from a peak rate of 9.0 per cent for the years 1979-81 to 4.9 per cent by 1984. Of the 4.1 per cent improvement, 2.6 per cent is due to the enormous changes in capital cost trends, 1.5 per cent is due to the reduction in unit labour costs.

THE DIRECT ROLE OF DEMAND INFLATION

The effect of the weak demands created by the recession can also be assessed through the core inflation analysis. The equation linking the inflation rate to the level of demand accounts for most of the variation that remains after allowing for the core and shock rates. This equation explains demand inflation by the unemployment rate and the capacity utilization rate of manufacturing. The effects are not instantaneous: it seems to take a full seven quarters before the effect of weak demand on inflation is completed.

There are several reasons for this delay. The principal one is probably the lag in the adjustment of wages to labour market conditions and price expectations. Because of the prevalence of three-year contracts in the unionized sector and of annual wage setting in the unorganized sector, there is considerable delay between objective economic conditions and the resultant wage changes. Even on the price side it takes some time before typical price-setters decide to react to changing economic conditions. Indeed, the biggest increases typically come late in the boom, and the biggest reductions after the bottom of the recession is past. To be sure, there is a large sector of the economy where prices are set through auctions or auction-like mechanisms, and these sensitive prices move much more quickly. But the influence of these markets on the price level is relatively weak both because they constitute a rather small percentage of the total economy and because the affected goods tend to be raw commodities whose costs take considerable time to work their way into finished goods prices.

Because of this gradualness of the effect of demand on prices, the swings created by this factor are not as extreme as one might otherwise expect. Demand inflation was at its worst during the Vietnam War, averaging 1.8 per cent a year for the interval 1966-70. The factor was negative in the early 1960s, and again in the 1970 recession. A brief positive burst was associated with the worldwide boom of 1973-4, but the severe recession of the mid-1970s had the demand factor lower inflation once more. It turned slightly positive in 1979-80, mainly reflecting lagged effects of the brief period of strong activity in 1978. Once the recessions of 1980-3 set in, the demand factor reduced the inflation rate quite substantially, averaging −1.8 per cent for the interval 1981-4. The unemployment rate is high in all of these years, and the utilization rate of industry is at a persistently depressed level.

ADDING UP THE THREE SOURCES OF DISINFLATION

Table 13.3 summarizes the disinflation between the peak years 1979-81 and the trough years 1983-4. The total inflation rate improved from 11.7 per cent to 4.0 per cent, using the DRI forecast for the missing data in the later period. The improvement in the shock inflation rate accounts for 1.9 percentage points out of the total improvement of 7.7 per cent. The

TABLE 13.3 *The inflation improvement: summary of core analysis*[1]

	1979–81 average	1983–4[2] average	Contribution to disinflation
Core inflation rate	9.0	5.5	−3.5
Unit Labour Cost Trend	7.9	5.9	
Capital Cost Trend	11.1	4.6	
Shock inflation rate	2.0	0.1	−1.9
Demand inflation rate	−0.1	−2.4	−2.3
Consumer price index	11.7	4.0	−7.7
(Unexplained residual)	(0.8)	(0.8)	(0.0)

[1] See Appendix Table A13.1 for fuller details.
[2] DRI forecast.

decline in the core inflation rate accounts for another 3.5 per cent. The change in the level of demand produces an improvement of 2.3 per cent.

THE DEMAND FACTOR AND THE REDUCTION OF SHOCK AND CORE INFLATION

While the taxonomy of the inflation analysis into shock, core and demand factors is useful, it hides the relationship between demand and shocks. The shocks are assumed to be exogenous, defined to be forces beyond the control of general economic policy. Yet experience shows that both agricultural and energy prices are not exogenous but are partially controlled by general economic conditions. Thus, to measure the full weight of the demand factor in the disinflation, one has to make allowance for the impact of weak demand on energy and food prices.

The collapse of OPEC is attributable to three factors: first, the two waves of OPEC world oil price increases set loose a worldwide drive for conservation, as families, businesses and governments devised various ways to reduce their energy consumption. Second, natural gas, coal and nuclear energy were substituted for oil. Finally, the worldwide recession lowered energy demands. A DRI analysis of world oil prices suggests that about two-thirds of the downward pressure in prices came from conservation and substitution, and about one-third from the worldwide recession. Applying this conclusion to the path of fuel prices during this period, the actual reduction of the real composite fuel price of 11.2 per cent would have been cut to 7.5 per cent if aggregate demand had not been held down by recession. This would have added 0.3 per cent to the shock inflation rate.

An analysis of food prices suggests a similar pattern of results. In the peak inflation of 1973, farm products rose 41 per cent, contributing 2.0 per cent to the inflation rate. In the peak inflation of 1979–80, food prices played a rather minor role, adding just 0.5 percentage points to the inflation rate. In the disinflation years 1982–3, food prices are subtracting 0.1 per cent from the price level.

The world recession is a significant factor in the declines in farm prices. The real volume of food consumption would be about 3 per cent higher if income growth were normal, and this increase in the quantity demanded would be associated with fram prices that would be higher by a somewhat larger percentage. The impact of weakened food prices on shock inflation is a reduction of about 0.4 per cent.

The high international value of the dollar, which was damaging to US exports but helpful to the domestic price level, must also be attributed to monetary policies of demand restraint. The extraordinarily high interest rates since 1979 are the underpinning of the strong dollar, and if more normal monetary policies had been pursued, its value would probably have changed rather little in these years. Thus, another 0.5 per cent of the reduction in the shock inflation rate can be traced back to demand management policies.

Adding up the several demand influences on shock inflation, one can see that about 1.3 percentage points of the 1.9 per cent improvement in the shock inflation rate can be traced back to the demand factor. Applying these data to the conclusions and periods summarized in Table 13.3, the sum of the demand effects, both direct and via lessened shocks, is boosted from 2.3 to 3.6 per cent, leaving 0.6 per cent for pure shock effects and 3.5 per cent for core inflation. Even the latter figure is gradually affected by demand conditions, of course.

THE UNEXPLAINED RESIDUAL AND ITS IMPLICATIONS FOR ECONOMIC THEORY

The field of macroeconomic theory has been divided by a bitter quarrel between the rational expectations school, with its emphasis on instant market clearing and rationality of expectations, and the traditional school with its emphasis on slow adjustment processes and persistent disequilibria. The rational expectations school emphasizes that a change in the approach to economic policy will produce a change in the structure of the economy.

In particular, the adoption of a tough monetarist regime in 1979 should have produced, according to this theory, an extraordinarily large change in the public's expectations of inflation, which should improve the actual record. Given the change in the inflation rate from 13 per cent at its peak to near zero in recent months, a superficial look at the data would suggest that the rational expectations view must be correct, that a change in regime has been accomplished and that expectations have been improved dramatically.

However, the core inflation analysis does not accept this conclusion. The improvement in the inflation rate can be fully explained by the gradual decrease in the core inflation rate, the reversal of the shock factors from large plusses to small minuses, and the weakness of demand created by the deep recession. There seems to be no need for new, *deus ex machina*, explanations.

Figure 13.3 shows the residual that is not accounted for by the three factors from 1961-83. The residual is generally small, with an average absolute error of 0.56 per cent, and a downward bias of 0.13 per cent. The errors of 1981-2 are no larger than the average for the preceding twenty years and are actually in the wrong direction for the rational expectations theory: the inflation improvement was somewhat less than the historical relationship would suggest. If the date associated with the change in

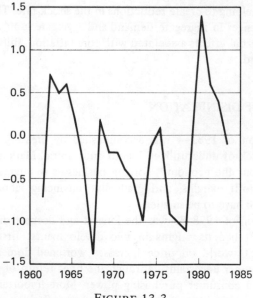

FIGURE 13.3

regime is moved back from the inauguration of President Reagan to the date of the adoption of the new monetarist policy in October 1979, these conclusions become even stronger: the error in 1980 is among the largest of the interval, but again of the wrong direction, with a lesser inflation improvement than historical relationships would suggest. Extrapolating the figures for the full year 1983 shows an exceptionally small error for that year, near zero.

Other tests will be performed to test whether the disinflation involved a change in economic structure. The rational expectations school will argue that expectations did change, or else that the adoption of monetarism under the Reagan economic programme was not sufficiently complete to represent a change in regime. The tests conducted here have one particular advantage: the supply-side changes, whether non-recurring (shock) or more permanent shifts in the aggregate supply price (core inflation), are estimated by an elaborate technique. The remaining inflation is a carefully defined measure of the demand factor and the unexplained residual. This is a more powerful test than the reduced form, single-equation tests that have swept the academic literature. That the core inflation analysis can account for the full extent of the historical disinflation suggests that there are no mysteries to the process and that there is no need to have recourse to such theories as rational expectations. The impact of low aggregate demand was very great, both in directly lowering prices and wages and in helping to create reductions in the shock rate. The traditional analysis of changes in aggregate demand and aggregate supply, after allowing for the inertial effects associated with core inflation, fully explains the historical record.

THE PRICE OF DISINFLATION

The disinflation of 1982–4 was accomplished by creating an enormous amount of slack of underutilized labour and capital. Markets were weakened throughout the economy, forcing businesses to charge lower prices and shrink profit margins, and gradually convincing labour that wage increases would have to be smaller.

The recession of 1978–83 was the longest and deepest since the Great Depression.[4] It had its origins in two developments: first, the second round of OPEC world oil price increases worsened domestic inflation, increased consumer uncertainty through the brief return of gasoline lines, and diminished consumer purchasing power. More important, the public became frightened by the return to double-digit inflation, and forced the government to change its demand management policies in a conservative direction. Thus, President Carter had little choice but to appoint a conservative to head the Federal Reserve System, and in Paul Volcker he found an individual who was both able and willing to manage a monetary policy of disinflation dressed in the garb of monetarism. With inflation driving up the transactions demand for money, introduction of a tough monetarist target rule meant that interest rates would far exceed previous historical peaks, thereby slashing the spending on interest-sensitive categories such as housing and automobiles, and ultimately disappointing business expectations so drastically that spending commitments for new employees, inventories, and capital projects were cut, producing a massive recession. High interest rates also had the incidental effect of raising the value of the dollar to a level where export markets suffered acutely. The record rates also spread to other countries, helping to trigger recessions around the world.

While most serious observers expected that the monetary policy would create a recession of some severity, the ultimate depth of the decline was worse than anyone anticipated. Various reasons can be advanced for this surprise: interest rates stayed near their peaks about six months longer than most people expected, with the prime rate remaining above 15 per cent until August 1982. In previous episodes, the Federal Reserve may have lagged slightly behind actual developments in its counter-cyclical policies, but it never kept interest rates near their peak for a full year into a recession. Second, as the recession deepened in the spring and summer of 1982, household and business expectations went through a second round of downgrading, as fears of a possible depression entered expectations and the uncertainties about jobs and profits became increasingly alarming. As a result, the large personal tax cut of the summer of 1982 was fully offset by a jump in the savings rate and failed to produce the upturn that would ordinarily have been expected. The recession finally came to an end in December 1982, after interest rates had been down by 400 basis points for four months to produce a recovery in housing starts and stabilization of consumer outlays. Once the rate of decline of aggregate demand was no longer so precipitous, the inventory correction ran its course and set the stage for the 1983 recovery.

President Reagan's economic programme of 1981 bore little direct relationship to the development of recession. The programme did endorse the Federal Reserve's monetarist policy, thereby encouraging the Fed to move its policy another major notch towards tightness. Also, the development of the enormous budget deficits created by the incongruous tax reductions and military spending increases cast some clouds over the recovery because it virtually assured the persistence of very high real interest rates. Inadvertently, the administration is helping to prolong the disinflation process by preventing a normal cyclical recovery through its incredible budget policies.

No serious analyst expected the disinflation process to proceed without cost. A major recession was believed to be an unavoidable ingredient. Unemployment in excess of 10 per cent imposed major social costs on the 12 million immediately affected individuals each month, destroying, for many families, a sense of economic security, lowering worker self-esteem, and making it virtually impossible for the young entrants into the labour force to find employment opportunities worthy of their education.

In essence, the disinflation was accomplished by engineering a massive recession. Was the cost of the recession larger or smaller than one would have expected from previous experience? Several scholars have produced estimates of the recession price that has to be paid. Arthur Okun (1978) estimated that it would take a 10 per cent reduction in GNP for one year to produce a 1 percentage point reduction in the inflation rate, with the possible range of this 'output–sacrifice ratio' defined between 6 and 18. Gordon and King (1982) estimate lower sacrifice ratios depending on the particular model, obtaining figures from 3.0 to 8.4. The lower estimates are due to a fuller modelling of repercussions through the exchange rate and import prices which substantially improve the output–inflation trade-offs. Their 'preferred' estimate for an undiscounted sacrifice ratio is 4.8, produced by a model that assumes import prices to be exogenous.

A similar exercise can be carried out with the core inflation model to determine the output–sacrifice ratio. The results are quite similar to the Gordon conclusions. Assuming a non-linear effect of unemployment on wage changes of the sort usually embodied in Phillips curves leads to a dependence of the sacrifice ratio on the range of unemployment in which the sacrifice is being exercised. The output–sacrifice ratio averages 4.71 over the full interval of unemployment ranging from 6 per cent to 11 per cent. In raising unemployment from 6 per cent to 8 per cent, a smaller deviation from the 'natural' unemployment rate, the sacrifice ratio is 3.41. In going from 8 per cent to 11 per cent the ratio rises to 6.30. However, it should be noted that the experience of the last year in finally breaking the pattern bargaining of several heavy industries may imply that the Phillips curve is not of the hyperbola-like curvature usually assumed, but may be closer to a straight line, or perhaps even 'S' shaped. In that event the ratio would be more uniform, presumably near 4.7 per cent over the full range.

The output–sacrifice ratio for the core inflation rate is substantially smaller, of course. Only those demand effects that gradually work their way into the equilibrium aggregate supply price are counted, and the temporary recession gains on inflation are not considered among the accomplishments since they are lost in a return to a normal rate of utilization. Because it takes considerable time for weaker demands to work their way into the core inflation rate, it is necessary to calculate the sacrifice ratio for an interval of at least four years. Over the range actually experienced since 1979, the output–sacrifice ratio for core inflation was 9.0, with an output loss of 40 per cent of a year's potential aggregate supply (aggregated over the six years 1979–84) producing a reduction in the core inflation rate of 4.4 per cent.

Could the sacrifice have been avoided? No doubt it could have been limited by easing interest rates six months earlier so that the recession would not have been quite as deep. Further, if the federal budget were not so grossly mismanaged, recovery might be somewhat stronger, also reducing the output loss.

To an extent, the conclusion depends on the shape of the Phillips curve. If it is near-flat when unemployment exceeds 9 per cent, the extra inflation that would have remained in the system after a milder recession would not have been significantly worse. The new reality for wages in the depressed 'smoke-stack' industries might have set in anyway, since their troubles are more structural than cyclical. But with a linear or 'S'-shaped Phillips curve, the extra depth of the recession would have bought extra disinflation.

Obviously, there were other ways to reduce the total sacrifice required. If the budgets of the 1970s had not been quite so expansive, if monetary policy had not allowed real interest rates to go negative in some years, and if a stronger approach had been taken to energy conservation, the inflation problem never would have become quite as acute, and so the disinflation would not have had to be quite so painful. But these are all matters of the past. It is time to consider ways to avoid the necessity for recurrence of the need to take the disinflation cure in the future.

POLICIES TO ASSURE CONTINUED DISINFLATION

The disinflation of 1979–84 was a painful episode in US and world economic history. In the USA, unemployment was driven to more than 10 per cent, or nearly 12 million people, inflicting a human cost that was disguised by the political impotence of the unemployed. Families whose economic security was blasted out of existence, young people entering the working age with no opportunities to get jobs with a future, industries with profits so depressed that their modernization programmes were scuttled, and erosion of our infrastructure will be long-standing testimonials to the price the USA has paid for disinflation. Other industrial countries suffered comparable unemployment rates, and the less developed countries were forced to slash their development plans.

It is generally recognized that, while the recession was overdone, a major correction had become inevitable after thirty years of worldwide expansion and worsening inflation. Budget and monetary policies were, on average, too stimulative, and financial policies of major lending institutions were seriously flawed. Inflation helped produce the overexpansion of credit, and the excess in values of natural resources, agricultural land, homes and other physical assets. Private decision-making had become seriously twisted by the expectation of continuing inflation. The price had to be paid and we paid it. But now common sense dictates that we turn our minds to devising policies that will avoid a recurrence.

Inflation is a barometer of many of the imperfections of public and private policies. Consequently a full-policy agenda would be an endless list of potential improvements of individual markets, reforms of numerous microeconomic government policies that boost costs, corrections of inadequacies in management and in labour relations, improved information for consumer markets, revision of international trade policies to foster competition, as well as reform in the international monetary system. To lend concreteness to such a list is beyond the scope of this chapter and so I shall confine myself to a few general comments, principally at the macroeconomic end of the policy spectrum.

The first priority for economic policy must be to manage an orderly recovery that is free of inflationary surges in demand. Unemployment should be reduced, but we must recognize that with current labour market policies, the natural unemployment rate (the non-inflationary unemployment rate in the absence of shocks) is of the order of 6–7 per cent. John F. Kennedy's interim target of 4 per cent was lost long ago when policies did not keep pace with changes in the demographic composition of the labour force and structural shifts among industries. If we wish to aim at unemployment rates below 6 per cent, we will need a new set of manpower policies that will improve the functioning of the labour market to reduce frictional and structural unemployment.

How can an orderly reduction of unemployment to the 6–7 per cent range be accomplished effectively? We have learned quite a bit from our past mistakes and so it is possible, at least in general terms, to prescribe some general rules for monetary and budget policies. On the monetary side, the policy must aim at a reasonable combination of growth of the money and credit aggregates and of real interest rate levels. The negative real interest rates created by excessive monetary expansion in some past years were ultimately very destructive. On the other hand, real interest rates of 7 per cent, where they are at the time of writing, will retard capital formation and productivity growth, and thereby will worsen core inflation.

On the budget side of macro policy, the immediate problems are severe because of the excessive tax reductions of 1981 and the enormity of the military spending increases. An enduring orderly recovery cannot be achieved with budget deficits exceeding 5 per cent of GNP, which is what current statutes call for. One way or another, most likely through another financial disturbance, the deficits will bring expansion to an end, destroy a reasonable process of capital formation, further impair the ability of US industry to compete, and create a new wave of human costs associated with recession. If the Federal Reserve does not accommodate the budget deficit by excessive monetization of the debt, interest rates will go back to double-digit spikes that will create an early recession. If the Federal Reserve accommodates the budget deficits, will provide an excessive increase in the money supply, making possible an excessive use of credit, and leading to a later but worse boom-bust cycle. The elimination of the budget deficits must be the top priority of macroeconomic policy, and is a key ingredient of a continuing policy of disinflation.

While the double-digit inflation of the mid- and late-1970s can hardly be blamed on inflationary biases in our wage and price-setting processes, these structural problems remained beneath the turbulent surface. Prices in industrial markets rise too soon and too much in a recovery, long before there is a balance of supply and demand. There is remaining market power, despite the foreign competition, and the short-term incentives on US managements push them into attempts to achieve excessive early earnings gains through ultimately counter-productive higher prices. On the wage side, the lessons of the 1970s have only been learned under disaster conditions. The basic procedures and attitudes in collective bargaining have not changed, and participants still dream of a return to bargaining-as-usual.

While the experience with incomes policies and wage–price controls of the 1970s showed only mixed results, policy cannot wash its hands permanently of the wage–price problem. Government will have to lead, both by example and by use of various consultative arrangements. There is also a continuing potential in setting numerical goals for wage–price behaviour, as demonstrated by the successful results obtained both in West Germany and in Japan. As government policy becomes more concerned with the continued survival and growth of US manufacturing industries, the use of wage–price standards may well become a significant ingredient of such policies.

Finally, the revival of the productivity trend of the US economy is an essential ingredient of a permanent policy of holding down core inflation. Productivity offsets rising wage and capital costs, and is the underpinning of rising living standards.

The decline of the competitive position of our manufacturing industries is a key element in the deteriorated productivity performance. On the one hand, stagnant productivity has hurt our international competitive position; on the other hand, the loss of international market shares has hurt the growth of demand for US products and deprived us of the means to accomplish productivity improvements. A successful industrial policy to overcome our current industrial problems must be part of a permanent programme to prevent renewed inflation.

NOTES

1. For an analysis of the development of double-digit inflation, see O. Eckstein, *Core Inflation*, Englewood Cliffs, N.J.: Prentice-Hall, 1981, p. 121.
2. The changed treatment of home ownership in the CPI makes comparisons of CPI-U difficult. But CPI-W has not been changed yet, so its comparisons have consistency over time.
3. O. Eckstein, *Core Inflation*, Englewood Cliffs, N.J.: Prentice-Hall, 1981, p. 120. The empirical parameters of the model have been re-estimated. The core inflation rate continues to be a weighted average of the equilibrium unit labour cost trend and the capital cost trend, with the weights derived from a Cobb–Douglas production function. The shock inflation rate is derived from model simulations of the 800-equation DRI macro model of the US economy. The simulations change five shock factors and trace their impact on the price level through the structure of the large model. The five elements of shock that are defined are farm prices, aggregate energy prices, the social security tax rate, the minimum wage, and the exchange rate.
4. According to the official National Bureau reference cycle definitions, there were two recessions, a very brief one in 1980, and a second recession beginning in the summer of 1981. However, from an analytical point of view, it really was one recession, created by a major policy commitment to bring the inflation to an end. The oddity of timing was due to the brief but stringent use of consumer credit controls in the second quarter of 1980, which slashed demands at the retail stage and created considerable uncertainty about the future use of credit. However, the government quickly relented and the Federal Reserve let the

money supply surge in the succeeding months, making a second round of even more severe monetary tightening necessary to achieve the desired disinflation result.

REFERENCES

Gordon, R. J., and S. R. King (1982) 'The Output Costs of Disinflation in Traditional and Vector Autoregressive Models', *Brookings Papers on Economic Activity*, 1: 205–44.

Okun, A. M. (1978) 'Efficient Disinflationary Policies', *American Economic Review*, 68 (May) (Papers and Proceedings): 348–52.

APPENDIX 13.1

TABLE A13.1 *The composition of inflation*

	1960	1961	1962	1963	1964	1965	1966	1967	1968	19
Core inflation rate	3.0	2.6	1.7	1.5	1.1	0.7	1.0	1.7	2.0	
Unit labour cost trend (eight 0.65)	3.6	3.7	2.6	2.1	1.6	1.2	1.2	1.5	1.9	
'Equilibrium' wage gains	4.6	4.4	4.2	4.1	4.0	3.9	4.0	4.4	4.6	
Actual wage gains	3.3	3.2	3.2	2.9	2.6	3.4	4.4	5.0	6.2	
Price expectations	2.1	2.0	1.7	1.6	1.6	1.5	1.7	2.0	2.3	
Unemployment rate (level)	5.5	6.7	5.6	5.6	5.2	4.5	3.8	3.8	3.6	
Productivity trend	0.9	0.7	1.5	2.0	2.4	2.7	2.8	2.8	2.7	
Actual productivity gains	0.8	3.0	3.5	3.3	3.9	3.1	2.5	1.9	3.2	–
Capital cost trend (weight 0.35)	1.8	0.5	0.0	0.3	0.3	0.0	0.8	1.9	2.3	
Actual rental price of capital	NA	−5.6	3.7	0.4	−2.3	1.9	6.4	−0.2	9.0	1
Aftertax cost of capital	1.7	−8.6	11.5	2.7	3.1	5.2	3.8	−6.2	1.7	–
Prime rate (level)	4.82	4.50	4.50	4.50	4.50	4.54	5.63	5.63	6.28	7
New High-Grade Corp. Bond Rate (level)	4.68	4.42	4.23	4.25	4.40	4.54	5.44	5.77	6.48	7
Prime expectations	2.1	1.9	1.6	1.5	1.5	1.5	1.8	2.2	2.6	
Dividend-price ratio–S&P 500 (level)	3.5	3.0	3.4	3.2	3.0	3.0	3.3	3.2	3.1	
Price deflator–nonres. investment	0.3	−0.6	0.6	0.8	1.0	1.3	2.9	3.3	4.1	
Shock inflation rate	0.1	0.0	0.1	−0.1	−0.2	0.3	0.7	0.0	0.2	
WPI – farm products	−0.3	−1.0	1.8	−2.1	−1.5	4.4	7.3	−5.6	2.5	
WPI – fuels	1.0	1.1	−0.5	−0.4	−2.7	1.8	2.5	2.3	−1.1	
Trade-weighted exchange rate	0.4	0.9	1.9	0.4	0.0	0.0	0.0	−0.1	−1.3	–
Social security tax rate (diff.)	0.007	0.001	0.003	0.005	−0.002	−0.002	0.014	0.003	0.001	0
Minimum wage ($/hour)	1.00	1.05	1.15	1.18	1.25	1.25	1.25	1.39	1.58	
Demand inflation rate	−0.7	−0.8	−1.3	−0.7	−0.2	0.4	1.6	2.5	1.8	
Capacity utilization in manufacturing (level)	0.801	0.773	0.814	0.835	0.857	0.895	0.911	0.869	0.870	0
Unemployment rate (level)	5.5	6.7	5.6	5.6	5.2	4.5	3.8	3.8	3.6	
Consumer price index	1.5	1.1	1.2	1.2	1.3	1.6	3.0	2.8	4.2	

(% change)

1970	1971	1972	1973	1974	1975	1976	1977	1978	1979	1980	1981	1982	1983	1984
4.2	4.1	3.9	4.4	6.3	7.7	7.6	7.9	8.2	8.7	9.3	9.0	7.8	6.0	4.9
3.5	3.6	3.9	4.3	5.7	6.4	6.1	6.3	6.6	7.2	8.1	8.3	7.6	6.3	5.5
5.6	5.8	5.8	5.8	6.9	8.1	7.9	7.6	7.6	8.1	8.9	9.6	9.3	8.2	7.2
6.7	7.1	6.4	6.1	8.0	8.3	7.2	7.5	8.2	8.0	9.0	9.1	6.9	5.2	5.3
3.4	3.8	3.9	4.1	5.0	6.3	6.6	6.4	6.3	6.7	7.5	8.2	8.2	7.4	6.5
5.0	6.0	5.6	4.9	5.6	8.5	7.7	7.0	6.1	5.9	7.2	7.6	9.7	10.2	9.2
2.1	2.2	1.9	1.4	1.0	1.5	1.7	1.2	1.0	0.9	0.8	1.2	1.6	1.8	1.6
0.3	3.3	3.7	2.4	−2.5	2.0	3.2	2.3	0.6	−1.3	−0.9	1.4	0.1	2.0	2.3
5.7	4.9	3.9	4.6	7.3	10.0	10.6	10.8	11.2	11.4	11.6	10.2	8.1	5.4	3.7
2.2	−0.4	4.6	13.6	19.8	7.9	11.4	11.8	11.8	11.3	11.7	−1.9	3.1	−3.4	6.8
−2.8	−1.1	2.5	12.7	11.3	−5.2	7.2	6.8	6.7	7.1	1.1	4.0	−1.5	−7.4	2.6
7.91	5.70	5.25	8.02	10.80	7.86	6.84	6.82	9.06	12.67	15.27	18.87	14.86	10.43	10.85
8.50	7.36	7.16	7.65	8.96	9.01	8.33	8.06	8.88	9.86	12.47	15.01	13.89	10.42	9.74
3.9	4.2	4.1	4.2	5.7	7.3	7.1	6.4	6.2	6.9	8.1	8.8	8.3	6.9	5.7
3.8	3.1	2.8	3.0	4.3	4.3	3.8	4.5	5.2	5.3		5.1	5.7	4.5	4.4
5.4	5.3	4.0	3.8	11.3	14.4	4.8	5.5	7.4	8.7	9.0	8.1	4.4	1.7	3.9
0.4	0.7	0.8	2.9	3.8	1.1	0.6	0.8	1.1	2.2	2.4	1.5	−0.6	−0.5	0.6
1.7	1.7	10.7	41.0	6.5	−0.5	2.3	0.8	10.4	13.6	3.3	2.2	−4.9	0.0	3.8
5.3	8.5	3.0	13.2	55.0	17.7	8.4	13.8	6.7	26.6	40.6	21.0	−0.2	−6.4	2.9
−2.5	−2.9	−6.1	−5.9	1.2	0.7	2.8	0.8	−6.0	−1.0	−0.1	8.9	9.4	−0.4	−3.8
.001	0.004	0.005	0.014	0.004	−0.001	0.003	0.001	0.003	0.005	−0.001	0.008	0.002	0.002	0.010
.60	1.60	1.60	1.60	1.87	21.0	2.30	2.30	2.65	2.90	3.10	3.35	3.35	3.35	3.35
1.5	−0.2	−0.9	−0.1	1.0	0.2	−1.6	−1.2	−0.6	0.1	0.4	−0.8	−1.4	−2.3	−2.5
.794	0.784	0.835	0.876	0.383	0.729	0.795	0.819	0.844	0.856	0.791	0.784	0.698	0.698	0.746
5.0	6.0	5.6	4.9	5.6	8.5	7.7	7.0	6.1	5.9	7.2	7.6	9.7	10.2	9.2
5.9	4.2	3.3	6.2	11.0	9.1	5.7	6.5	7.6	11.3	13.5	10.3	6.2	3.1	4.8

TABLE A13.2   *The components of shock inflation (percentage points)*

	1960	1961	1962	1963	1964	1965	1966	1967
WPI – farm products	0.0	0.0	0.1	−0.1	−0.1	0.2	0.4	−0.2
WPI – fuels and power	0.0	0.1	0.0	0.0	−0.1	0.1	0.1	0.1
Trade-weighted exchange rate	0.0	0.0	−0.1	0.0	0.0	0.0	0.0	0.0
Minimum wage	0.0	0.0	0.1	0.0	0.0	0.0	0.0	0.1
Social security tax rate	0.1	0.0	0.0	0.1	0.0	0.0	0.2	0.0
Shock inflation rate	0.1	0.0	0.1	−0.1	−0.2	0.3	0.7	0.0
Core inflation rate	3.0	2.6	1.7	1.5	1.1	0.7	1.0	1.7
0.65*labour cost trend	2.4	2.4	1.7	1.4	1.0	0.8	0.8	1.0
0.35*capital cost trend	0.6	0.2	0.0	0.1	0.1	0.0	0.3	0.7

The components of shock inflation (percentage points

	1980	1981	1982	1983	1984
WPI – farm products	0.2	0.3	−0.2	0.0	0.2
WPI – fuels and power	2.3	1.1	0.0	−0.2	0.1
Trade-weighted exchange rate	0.0	−0.1	−0.5	−0.2	0.1
Minimum wage	0.0	0.1	0.0	0.0	0.0
Social security tax rate	0.0	0.1	0.0	0.0	0.1
Shock inflation rate	2.4	1.5	−0.6	−0.5	0.6
Core inflation rate	9.3	9.0	7.8	6.0	4.9
0.65*labour cost trend	5.2	5.4	4.9	4.1	3.6
0.35*capital cost trend	4.1	3.6	2.8	1.9	1.3

1968	1969	1970	1971	1972	1973	1974	1975	1976	1977	1978	1979
0.1	0.3	0.1	0.1	0.5	2.0	0.6	0.1	0.2	0.1	0.5	0.7
-0.1	0.1	0.2	0.5	0.1	0.6	2.9	1.0	0.4	0.7	0.3	1.2
0.0	0.0	0.0	0.1	0.2	0.2	0.1	-0.1	-0.1	0.0	0.1	0.2
0.1	0.0	0.0	0.0	0.0	0.0	0.1	0.1	0.1	0.0	0.1	0.1
0.0	0.0	0.0	0.0	0.1	0.2	0.0	0.0	0.0	0.0	0.0	0.1
0.2	0.5	0.4	0.7	0.8	2.9	3.8	1.1	0.6	0.8	1.1	2.2
2.0	3.3	4.2	4.1	3.9	4.4	6.3	7.7	7.6	7.9	8.2	8.7
1.2	1.9	2.2	2.3	2.5	2.8	3.7	4.2	3.9	4.1	4.3	4.7
0.8	1.4	2.0	1.7	1.4	1.6	2.5	3.5	3.7	3.8	3.9	4.0

14 Monetarism–A View from a Central Bank

JEAN-PIERRE BÉGUELIN and KURT SCHILTKNECHT

Monetarism, and particularly monetarism as a guide to monetary policy, is a controversial issue. Some economists, to quote Lord Kaldor (1981) regard 'monetarism as a terrible curse, as a visitation of evil spirits', For others it is the answer to the current economic malaise in general and inflation in particular. Both monetarists and Keynesians are in full agreement on the ultimate goal of economic policy – full employment, economic growth and stable prices; they disagree, however, on the role of monetary policy in achieving these objectives. Monetarists argue that monetary policy should primarily be used to control inflation. In their view, central bankers should abstain from fine-tuning the economy. For Keynesians, on the other hand, an activist mix of monetary and fiscal policy is necessary to achieve stable economic growth. The controversy over the role of monetary policy is largely the reflection of different opinions about the working of economies, although the two schools of thought are separated by a continuous spectrum of opinions rather than a sharp dividing line. Starting at one extreme, let us say the left, we first meet the 'neo-Keynesians' who deny the existence of a unique Walrasian equilibrium.[1] Next are those who favour a fixprice or temporary disequilibrium approach in which the economy, if left on its own, will move continuously and erratically around its long-term equilibrium.[2] Then we run into the postwar economic mainstream, the so-called neoclassical synthesis. Further to the right, we enter the world of the monetarists where the private sector is considered to be essentially stable unless it is disturbed by inappropriate macroeconomic policies.[3] Finally, we encounter the adherents of the super-neutrality of money for whom monetary and fiscal policy actions have no influence on

324

macroeconomic performance.[4] While monetarists generally believe that, confronted with exogenous shocks, the private sector will return to its steady equilibrium path, Keynesians dispute the inherent stability of the system; or at least they consider the adjustment process to be so slow and painful that it calls for activist stabilization policies.

We will not attempt to outline all the propositions that characterize monetarists and Keynesians here.[5] Instead we will limit ourselves to discussing a few monetarist positions that we think are crucial for the conduct of monetary policy. The assumption of a stable private sector is the logical consequence of the hypothesis that economic agents act rationally.[6] Therefore it is not surprising that monetarists consider the major macroeconomic relationships, and especially the demand for money, as stable, at least in the long run. Inflation is then primarily viewed as a monetary phenomenon for which central bankers are responsible.

THE BASIC MONETARIST APPROACH TO MONETARY POLICY

Basically the monetarists approach monetary policy by assuming that too much money will sooner or later result in inflation. Therefore, in order to avoid inflation,[7] a central bank must prevent the money stock from growing[8] faster (on the average and in the long run) than the potential output.[9] Most economists can agree on such a broad principle, but for monetary authorities the central issue is rather how to allocate the desired amount of growth for the money supply over a long period of time. Confronted with shocks that destabilize the economy, policy-makers have to decide whether to follow an activist policy or stick to their long-term targets.

Activists strongly emphasize the counter-cyclical responsibilities of the authorities and believe that a central bank should tighten its policy during a boom and relax it when the economy slows down. To implement such an approach, a central bank would have to have a great deal of skill and information, perhaps much more than can reasonably be expected. Even in the simplest case of a world with fixed expectations, monetary action takes time to influence real output and the rate of inflation. This time lag results mainly from market frictions arising from government regulations, imperfect competition and long-term contracts.

The situation becomes, of course, even more complicated when changes in expectations are taken into consideration. Economic policy decisions and expectations are obviously not independent of each other. Thus, in order to stabilize the economy, a policy-maker must know how expectations will change in reaction to his actions. This task is very intricate. As

Lucas (1976) has pointed out, the structure of the adjustment process depends on how the new policy decisions are perceived by the markets. In particular, the form and the length of the reaction lags are unstable and almost unidentifiable. At one stage or another, the policy-maker will probably lose control of the policy unless he can outperform all the other economic agents by virtue of his better knowledge about the future. But experience has shown that we cannot assume that central bankers have more information or use it more efficiently than the rest of the world, whatever some of their governors may say in their various speeches.

In the presence of such uncertainties, monetary authorities may more or less frequently make wrong decisions that may destabilize the economy even further. This is the main argument in favour of the non-activist approach advocated by the monetarists. Almost all of them are willing to admit that their policy recommendations do not always keep the economy on its potential output path. But at the same time they stress that, if their suggestions are followed, the deviations from potential output will remain small and the various costs that arise from policy mistakes can thus be avoided. At first sight, the policy guideline would seem to contradict the monetarists' assumption about the stability of the demand for money. If central banks were to know precisely the public's liquidity preference, they would be able to reach rather quickly their monetary objectives. Monetarists, however, consider that stability is assured only when the public's expectations converge to their 'true' values.

They agree that because of incomplete and diffuse information, expectations may very well be mistaken in the short run.[10] Thus the failure up to now to discover empirically constant parameters for short-term money demand is not surprising. Even if the short-term liquidity preference were stable — which is doubtful — its stability would be almost unidentifiable because of the impossibility of observing the right-hand side variables that are heavily dependent on expectations. Most monetarists claim that the overall stability of the demand for money would be clearly enhanced if central banks were to focus on long-term price stability, thus helping to anchor and not to trigger off inflationary expectations. This has resulted in Milton Friedman's famous constant monetary growth rule.[11]

Even if a central banker is ready to adopt a non-activist position, the best tactics for reducing and stabilizing inflationary expectations still have to be found. The choice will obviously depend on the central bank's credibility. Those monetary authorities who have repeatedly shown that they mean business in their fight against inflation and who have more or less succeeded in the past will have almost no problems. Even if the money stock target is missed for a while, economic agents will not revise their long-term inflationary expectations.[12] If its long-term credibility is established, a central bank can even take some mild counter-cyclical actions without running the risk of destabilizing the economy. In this case, long-term interest rates will fluctuate substantially less than short-term rates, portfolio shifts will be rather harmless, and the real impact (due mainly to changes in inventories) will be moderately stabilizing. If, on the other hand, monetary authorities lack credibility, they will have a difficult time carrying out their policies. Financial market participants will then tend to confuse temporary changes — even if they are purely random — with those that are permanent. In this case, the term structure of interest rates will be more volatile and, as there will be large portfolio realignment, the real adjustment process will be more burdensome.[13]

The only medicine for curing a credibility gap is in controlling the trend of the money supply in the long run. How to achieve this can vary from place to place and from one period to another, but there are some general principles for optimizing the control of monetary aggregates, which are always valid.

THE CONTROL OF MONETARY AGGREGATES

After adopting a money stock target, a central bank has to choose how to implement its policy. This will depend on how the central bank's measures act on the monetary aggregate selected as the target. This relationship, which is a behavioural function of the term structure of interest rates, is heavily influenced by regulations governing monetary and financial matters. The unfortunate tendency of monetary authorities to attempt to regulate the monetary sector down to the smallest detail — by changing reserve requirements, pegging some interest rates, or constantly modifying other regulations — has blurred the link between the instruments and targets of many central banks. An optimal control of the monetary aggregates requires stable and as few as possible regulations for the financial and banking sectors.

The attention paid in the USA to the weekly release of M_1 has at times nourished the belief that the success of a monetary policy can be judged within a very brief period of time. But efforts to fine-tune M_1 may well be counterproductive if they raise the volatility of interest rates and that of the different money velocities. Most of the short-term changes in the monetary aggregates are purely random. While it might be possible to distinguish a stochastic change from a systematic one after a certain period of time, it is almost impossible to do this when the data have just been published. If a central bank tries to correct every departure from its targets it may succeed, but only at the cost of greater fluctuations in the monetary base and, in particular, in the banking system's reserves.

Faced with a high degree of instability in their reserves, banks try to distinguish permanent from temporary changes. Their perception of the nature of this shock will determine how they reallocate their portfolio. If the central bank's action is perceived as permanent, a commercial bank has no reason to alter the ratio of its loans to reserves and will expand its lending accordingly. In the case of a temporary shock, the situation is quite different. By definition a temporary change will be reversed some-day, but no one can know exactly when the offsetting move will take place. In a competitive market, banks want to maintain a certain stability in the level of their credits, because granting new loans and losing old customers is very costly. When banks believe that the marginal rise of their reserves will be short-lived, they are prepared to hold on to more high-powered money than usual for a time or to invest part of these supplementary funds in very liquid assets. And, similarly, if confronted with a temporary drop in their reserves, they will not immediately cut back their lendings, but will either risk being temporarily less liquid or will sell some of their securities.[15] Whatever the bank's reactions are, the base multiplier varies more than in the permanent case and offsets to a large extent the initial change in the base.[16] This dampens the short-term efficiency of those actions of the central bank that are perceived as being temporary. Theoretically a stable stochastic solution can always be found. In practice, however, if the base multiplier truly depends so much on expectations in the short run, central banks will be virtually powerless to fine-tune the money stock.

It is not always easy to decide whether to attempt to fine-tune or not. The advantages of very smooth growth of the money stock are clear.The monetary policy will be correctly comprehended, and both inflationary expectations and long-term interest rates will be stabilized. From this point of view a central bank should try to reduce the volatility of the monetary aggregates as much as possible. The dangers of fine-tuning are less apparent but all the more acute. Because of the multiplier's behaviour, fine-tuning results in sharp fluctuations in the money market rates which in turn blur the relationship among nominal income, interest rates and the money stock. The short-term target will most certainly be overshot. Even a central bank with a good anti-inflationary record cannot afford to miss hitting its short-term objectives too often if it wants to maintain its credibility. On the whole, we believe that central banks should favour medium-term control of the money supply through a succession of annual targets, and that they should abstain from setting quarterly objectives.

Basically two methods are applied for controlling the money stock. The more common one operates by changing short-term interest rates. However, because of the link between expectations and the central bank's actions, it is difficult to identify a relationship between short-term interest and the money stock. We, therefore, favour the monetary base approach to controlling the money stock. Though not always valid in the very short run, the correlation between the base and larger monetary aggregates is so strong[17] that a central bank that follows this approach will always be able to keep the trend of the money stock under control.

SOME PRACTICAL CONSIDERATIONS

Controlling the rate of growth of one monetary aggregate[18] would appear in theory to be a sound policy, although in practice central banks encounter many difficulties in trying to implement this. Two problems are especially tricky to solve: persistent high inflation and real exchange rate instability.

In order to bring down a rate of inflation that has been too high for too long, a central bank can either give the economy a shock treatment or it can act more gradually.[19] In many countries this dilemma does not exist as the first alternative is out of the question for political and social reasons. The second solution will work smoothly only if inflationary expectations shrink hand-in-hand with the rate of growth of the money stock. Expectations generally do not decrease continuously but in stages. When one of these drops is steep, the following fall in the long-term interest rate generates a relative decline in the velocity of money. If the monetary authorities do not take notice of this last change, they will tend to become too restrictive and thus worsen the slowdown that is required to restore price stability. There is no easy way to find the right moment and the magnitude for the action to be taken to offset a velocity change. Too early and too strong a reaction can very well give birth to a new wave of inflationary fears and thus destroy the work already accomplished. The risk of this happening is limited if the monetary authorities are persuasive enough to convince the public of their commitment to stable monetary growth in the medium and long run. In this case, and in this case only, the actions taken to offset the drop in velocity are perceived as being temporary and will not push up long-term interest rates again.

Most central banks are deeply concerned with large fluctuations in real exchange rates. Many people argue that in order to reduce the deviations of exchange rates from their purchasing power parities, the monetary authorities should temporarily depart from their money stock target and tighten their policy in the case of a weak currency or relax it when it is strong. But central banks that regularly attempt to follow this strategy have been unsuccessful in their efforts to 'lean against the wind'. Changes in the monetary base that result from systematic foreign exchange interventions are easily recognized as being purely temporary. Because such operations do not alter inflationary expectations and long-term interest rates, they are for the most part absorbed by the money market without their having any effect on the relative earnings from foreign and domestic non-monetary assets. Thus such a policy does not result in a significant change in the exchange rate. Only a policy action that is regarded as permanent can influence the exchange rate. In this case, however, the central bank must accept that its domestic inflation rate will move closer to the worldwide rate. There is no easy way out of this dilemma in the case of a small economy. As long as the fluctuations are not excessive, a central bank should be reluctant to abandon its domestic target in favour of pegging the exchange rate.[20] The real exchange rates would of course be more stable if monetary authorities, especially those of the larger countries, were to adopt a policy that clarified their long-term intentions.

In conclusion, we believe that the monetarist approach to monetary policy is the optimal solution. We are aware of the fact that this approach does not provide the ideal solution for all problems. However, the adoption of such a framework should insure that future policy mistakes will be smaller than those we have made in the past.

NOTES

1. For a presentation of this view, see, for example, Hahn, 1982.
2. There is a large literature illustrating this approach; see, for example, Malinvaud, 1977.
3. See, for example, M. Friedman, 1971.
4. See, for example, Sargent and Wallace, 1975.
5. For such a discussion, see Mayer, 1978; Stein, 1976, 1982.
6. Rationality is understood as maximizing objective functions over time by efficiently using all the available information.
7. The theoretical justification for eradicating inflation is not so clear. For example, in a model where price increases are fully anticipated, the only cost of inflation is the tax on money holdings (see Bailey, 1956). In real life, however, inflation has obviously more negative impact than the 'leather-shoe' effect. Undesirable consequences such

as the redistribution of wealth between debtors and creditors or the difficulties faced by economic agents in differentiating relative from absolute price changes justify the fight against inflation.

8. The size of the rate of increase depends *inter alia* on the long-run trend of the velocity of money which in turn is determined by institutional and technical changes in the monetary sector.

9. One can object that potential output and money supply are not independent of each other, or, to put things differently, that a long-term downward sloping Phillips curve exists. This was hotly debated during the first half of the 1970s, but today more and more people dismiss the idea of a long-term trade-off between unemployment and inflation.

10. One of the main factors that confuses the public is an unstable monetary policy.

11. We will not discuss here the problem of choosing an intermediate target, otherwise known as the indicator problem (on this point see B. Friedman, 1975). A nominal interest rate is obviously a misleading target because it results in an accommodative policy when inflationary expectations change. Other proposals such as targeting a price index or the real interest rate suffer from a confusion between ultimate and intermediate targets. These variables are generally too far removed from the central bank's influence to be considered.

12. The central bank's task is of course facilitated when there are no huge and persistent budget deficits as these always trigger off the fear that they will in the end be financed through money creation.

13. These considerations explain why, despite the fact that the German and Swiss monetary aggregates are much more volatile than their US counterparts, the German and Swiss long-term interest rates fluctuate less than the American. Because of their good record in the fight against inflation, the German and Swiss central banks can depart significantly from their intermediate targets without jeopardizing their anti-inflationary reputations.

15. For a more detailed description of this, see Büttler and Schiltknecht, 1982.

16. In Switzerland, where the money base fluctuates sharply but most of these changes are considered to be of a transitory nature, a 1 per cent increase in the base leads to a 0.85 per cent drop in the multiplier. See Büttler *et al.*, 1979.

17. For empirical evidence, see Johannes and Rasche, 1981; and Fratianni and Nabli, 1979.

18. We do not understand the rationale for selecting multiple targets. Either all targets are consistent − but then there is no need to choose more than one − or they are inconsistent. In the latter case, one target only is deemed to be relevant.

19. On this point, see Fellner, 1981.

20. In 1978 the Swiss National Bank abandoned its money stock target in favour of an exchange rate target. This decision was taken because it was felt that the foreign exchange market was no longer able to develop clear expectations. On this point, see Rich and Béguelin, 1982.

REFERENCES

Bailey, M. (1956) 'The Welfare Cost of Inflationary Finance', *Journal of Political Economy*, 64 (2) (April): 93–110.

Büttler, H.-J., and Schiltknecht, K. (1982) 'Transitory Changes in Monetary Policy and their Implications on Money-Stock Control', unpublished paper presented at the Carnegie–Rochester Conference on Public Policy (November).

Büttler, H.-J., Gorgerat, J.-F., Schiltknecht, H., and Schiltknecht, K. (1979) 'A Multiplier Model of Controlling the Money Stock', *Journal of Monetary Economics*, 5: 327–41.

Fellner, W. (1981) 'On the Merit of Gradualism and on Fall-back Position if it Should Nevertheless Fail: Introductory Remarks', in *Essays in Contemporary Economic Problems*, Washington: American Enterprise Institute.

Fratianni, M., and Nabli, M. (1979) 'Money Stock Control in the EEC Countries', *Weltwirtschaftliches Archiv*, 115: 401–24.

Friedman, B. M. (1975) 'Targets, Instruments and Indicators of Monetary Policy, *Journal of Monetary Economics*, 1 (October): 443–74.

Friedman, M. (1971) 'A Theoretical Framework for Monetary Analysis', Occasional Paper 112, New York: NBER.

Hahn, F. (1982) *Money and Inflation*, Oxford: Blackwell.

Johannes, J. M., and Rasche, R. H. (1981) 'Can the Reserves Approval to Monetary Control Really Work?' *Journal of Money, Credit and Banking*, 13 (August): 298–313.

Kaldor, N. (1981) 'Fallacies on Monetarism', *Kredit and Kapital*, 4: 451–62.

Lucas, R. E. Jr (1976) 'Econometric Policy Evaluation: A Critique', in K. Brunner and A. H. Meltzer (eds), *The Phillips curve and labor markets*, Carnegie–Rochester Conference Series on Public Policy, vol. 1, Amsterdam: North-Holland.

Malinvaud, E. (1977) *The Theory of Unemployment Reconsidered*, New York: John Wiley.

Mayer, T. (1978) *The Structure of Monetarism*, New York: W. W. Norton.

Rich, G., and Béguelin, J.-P. (1982) 'Swiss Monetary Policy in The 1970s and 1980s. An Experiment in Pragmatic Monetarism' (unpublished mimeo).

Sargent, T. J., and Wallace, N. (1975) ' "Rational" Expectations, the Optimal Monetary Instrument, and the Optimal Money Supply Rule', *Journal of Political Economy*, 83 (April): 241–54.

Stein, J. L. (ed.) (1976) *Monetarism*, Studies in Monetary Economics, vol. 1, Amsterdam: North-Holland.

Stein, J. L. (1982) *Monetarist, Keynesian and New Classical Economics*, Oxford: Blackwell.

Part V
Distribution, Growth, and Policy Alternatives

15 Theories of Income Distribution in Developed Countries

JAN TINBERGEN

In this chapter a number of theories of income distribution will be discussed so as to provide the reader with a bird's eye view of the state of the art. In order to keep this survey within manageable proportions some types of theories will be excluded, however. One type to be excluded is normative theories: theories on how income distribution ought to be according to some ethical principles. Another type to be excluded is purely stochastic theories. Every theory recognizes that incomes are subject to a large number of minor unidentified factors. But at least some factors can be identified. A purely stochastic theory can only be considered as an intermediary stage to be followed by the identification of important factors. We consider a lack of such identification a *testimonium paupertatis*: that is, a lack to draw attention to reality, where not all factors can be assumed to be of a random character. The third type to be excluded consists of theories insufficiently tested empirically. It is especially in the field of income distribution that a large number of theories are held by people who are influenced by some belief or ideology and who do not make even a modest attempt to verify their content with observed facts and figures.

The presentation of the theories will not be arranged according to authors, but according to their location within one general scheme. This scheme has been constructed so as to contain the elements emphasized by the authors, but implies an attempt at an integration of their theories.

335

A SURVEY OF THE FACTORS CONSIDERED IN THE PRESENT CHAPTER

Income distribution theory has to be based on a theory of income formation. Incomes have a source from which they flow. A first distinction may be made between productive and non-productive sources (cf. Figure 15.1). Production income is determined largely by economic factors, but to some

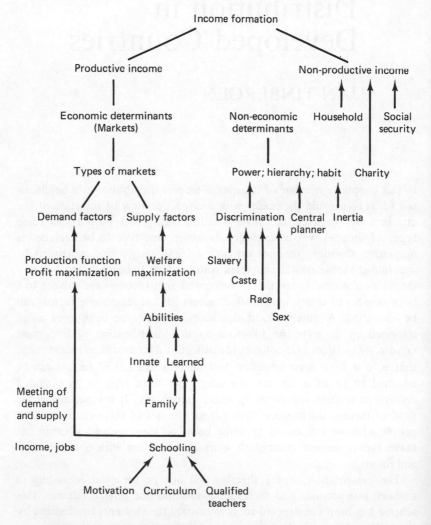

FIGURE 15.1 *Income formation*

extent also by non-economic sociological factors. Non-productive incomes are mainly determined by non-economic forces, and only indirectly by economic ones. Economic factors are grouped around markets, where prices and quantities transacted are determined. There are various types of markets: those where free competition prevails and those where competition is limited, with monopolies as an extreme case. Those who act (the actors) do so either on the demand or on the supply side. Actors on either side may be price-setters or price-takers, as will be discussed in the third section.

Demand for production factors (labour, capital, natural resources) will be exerted by the organizers of production ('entrepreneurs'), who may be private or public. Production should be understood in its broadest sense, including also the production of services, such as transportation, trade, etc. Demand for labour, capital, etc. will depend on the technicalities and psychology of production, as expressed by production functions, whose role will be examined in considerable detail.

The supply of production factors by those who own them is determined by their utility function, reflecting their welfare or satisfaction. The level of satisfaction will be maximized by the choice of a job, given the income that is derived from it, and the individual's abilities and needs (for instance, determined by his or her health and the size of the family).

Abilities, to be discussed in the fifth section, may be innate or learned or both. Both aspects are dependent on a number of characteristics of the individual's family (inherited abilities, early learning process and the environment) and on the formal schooling process completed. This process will be discussed in the sixth section, where such issues as motivation, school level and nature, curriculum and quality of teachers enter the picture.

The confrontation of demand and supply will result in a system of prices of the productive factors, including wages and salaries for various types of jobs or occupations and the quantities employed.

Non-economic sociological factors are the subject of the eighth section. Sociologists are interested in power structures and in habits, to mention two areas. Habits may be seen as a form of inertia in the operation of other factors. Power is partially of an economic nature and these components are implied in the third section through to the seventh. But power structures also involve various forms of discrimination, all the way from slavery to caste, race and sex discrimination. To a varying extent discrimination is economically determined, but sometimes large non-economic components exist.

Non-productive sources of income are still less economically determined. One such source is dependent on family relationships. Households are the wider concept, from institutional households to natural ones: military and hospital units being examples of the former and extended and nuclear families of the latter. Thus, household incomes are divided up into individual incomes for military, ill or otherwise handicapped individuals, children or aged people (cf. the ninth section).

A small part of income transfers derives from charity, and an increasing portion (in the course of an economy's development) from a system of social security, to be discussed in the tenth section.

ECONOMIC FORCES: MARKETS

Economies may be centrally planned or market economies. The pure form of a centrally planned economy may also be called a command economy and is applied within an army or other military unit. Every act or activity in a pure command system would be based on an order and all actors involved are part of a hierarchy. Even during a war this picture is not correct and some acts are spontaneous. The economies known as centrally planned constitute a macroframe of a command hierarchy. But even the strictest forms of centrally planned economies require personal initiatives and decisions inside production units as well as in the activities linking such units. Command hierarchies will be briefly discussed in the eighth section; the commands will reflect to a certain extent, however, forces similar to those operating in market economies. The latter's essential structure will be discussed in the third section through to the seventh.

In a market economy a number of actors are operating: some are individuals and most others are combinations of individuals, called institutions. Institutions range from families and firms to consumer or trade unions, production sectors, parliaments (from local to central), governments and intergovernmental and supranational organizations.

Markets are meeting places – concrete or figurative – where actors engage in transactions, that is exchanges: sales and purchases. We shall use these expressions also for labour markets, where agreements are concluded concerning employment of workers. Alongside the volume of transactions they are characterized by a price; on the labour market the price is the wage or the salary.

Our main interest is concentrated on markets of production factors: labour of various kinds, natural resources and capital (goods).

Each market has its demand and its supply side. On markets for production factors demand is exerted by the organizers of production, private or public. Production should be understood in its broadest sense, including not only the production of goods but also of services such as transportation or education. Sometimes we make a subdivision into primary, secondary and tertiary production. Production is a process with inputs of production factors and intermediary products and outputs of products.

Supply on factor markets is offered by workers and the owners of natural resources and capital (goods).

Markets are characterized by various market forms. These forms depend on the numbers of independent actors on the demand and on the supply side. If that number is large we say there is competition; if it is small we speak of an oligopoly; and if it is one, we speak of a monopoly. The latter two refer to the supply side and the corresponding expressions for the demand side are oligopsony and monopsony. It is possible to refer to oligopoly and monopoly for the demand side as well.

Since the market has two sides each with three possible numbers of actors, there are nine market forms in the sense given to that concept here.

Oligopoly and monopoly may be natural, that is, due to natural causes, or purposely organized.

The behaviour of actors on a market may be price-taking or price-setting. A price-taker considers the price as given; something he cannot change. Competitive markets are price-takers' markets. A monopolist and, to a lesser degree, an oligopolist, are price-setters. A monopolist sets his price at the level at which he hopes to maximize his profits, taking into account the quantity demanded at that price.

Income formation of the factors used (say, labour and capital) by an entrepreneur who is acting in competition with other employers has often been explained with the aid of a simple model in which a distinction is made between market-determined and residual incomes (cf. Tinbergen and Kol, 1980). Labour and capital are supposed to be demanded at the prices (wages, and interest rates) of the market and the product sold on the product market. Depending on the production function for the commodities at stake a residual income called profits may remain for the entrepreneur. Profits may be shared with the employees, according to some agreed key. The entrepreneur may also own the capital or part of it and profits are then the income of risk capital and not predetermined, as is that from loan capital. The latter receives interest whereas risk capital receives dividend. In other cases losses instead of profits may result.

In large enterprises the entrepreneur may be replaced by one or a larger number of managers, who may be hired by the owners of the risk capital and may receive a compensation which constitutes a market-determined income. A large part of total profits is then diverted to managers' compensation, reducing the residual income category. As a limiting case all profit may be transformed into market-determined manager income.

For small as well as for large enterprises there will be no residual if there are no returns to scale. The shares received by the various categories of production factors will add up to the net revenue from the sales. The word net is used to remind the reader of the possibility that capital goods have a finite life span and that their replacement requires the deduction of depreciation allowances from gross receipts.

Markets are said to be in equilibrium, if the quantity demanded equals the quantity supplied. This quantity is, then, the quantity transacted; that is, quantity of capital lent and borrowed in the case of the capital market, or the number of workers employed in the case of the labour market. Especially the latter has to be subdivided into a number of compartments for various types of labour, a subject to be discussed in considerable detail in what follows. Since by far the largest part of national income in developed countries constitutes labour income of some type, this subdivision is essential for any study of income distribution.

Of course markets will often not be in equilibrium. We assume that in such a disequilibrium forces to restore equilibrium are at work. This process is not always a short one. Depending on the actors' demand and supply behaviour the process may be quick and a succession of equilibria is a good approximation of reality; it may also be a lengthy process, sometimes one of fluctuations around an equilibrium path. In later sections, especially the seventh section, more details of these processes will be discussed.

DEMAND FACTORS

In the preceding section a simple model of the behaviour of entrepreneurs, or, more generally, of the organizers of production has been offered. In a large part of the economy they exert demand for various types of workers and it is often assumed that they do so in competition with each other. If so, they are price-takers and will try to maximize profits Z. Indicating the production function by $y = F(x_1, x_2, \ldots, x_I)$ and the prices by p for the product and $w_1, w_2, \ldots$, etc. for the I types of labour, whose quantities to be employed are $x_1, x_2, \ldots, x_I$, profits are:

$$Z = py - x_1 w_1 - x_2 w_2 - \ldots x_I w_I \tag{15.1}$$

Since all prices are supposed given, a maximum of profits will be attained if:

$$\frac{\partial Z}{\partial x_1} = \frac{\partial Z}{\partial x_2} = \ldots \frac{\partial Z}{\partial x_I} = 0 \tag{15.2}$$

or

$$p \, \frac{\partial y}{\partial x_1} = p \, \frac{\partial F}{\partial x_1} = w_1 \qquad (15.3)$$

$$p \, \frac{\partial y}{\partial x_2} = p \, \frac{\partial F}{\partial x_2} = w_2 \qquad (15.4)$$

etc.

Here $\partial F/\partial x_1$ etc. stand for marginal productivity of labour type 1, etc. and the quantity of labour of type $1, x_1$, will be such that the value of its marginal product equals the wage rate of type 1 labour. Similarly, x_2 will be such that the value of its marginal product will be equal to w_2, the wage rate of type 2 labour, and so on.

This simple model will be used to clarify the connection between demand for production factors and the production function. As we shall see, there are a number of complications to be discussed in this section. Most of the section will be devoted to production functions. Before discussing these in a more systematic way, a few remarks are in order.

First, some types of workers may themselves not compete, but act through unions who, within limits, are price-setters. This does not invalidate the statement that, as long as the organizers of production compete for that type of labour, they will employ a number whose marginal productivity value equals the wage rate.

Second, the upper limit set on the price-setting workers will be higher the closer is the type of worker considered to the sociological group of the organizers of production who tend to favour those workers to whom they can relate.

Third, the production function for the individual firm (in microeconomic theory) in fact constitutes an *ex ante*, or expected production function, which need not coincide with observed *ex post* production functions. Later we will discuss some empirical results where this remark has to be kept in mind (cf. subsection on pp. 345-9).

Fourth, in microeconomic theories we may follow Sattinger (1980) and consider the allocation, within a firm, of individual workers to individual machines. One worker may have comparative advantages with regard to another worker in using machines of different types.

Returning to the discussion of production functions we will make a distinction between two categories, to be called long-term and short-term. The same distinction may also be called one of the causal direction. For short-term decisions a category of relations is used where the quantities

x_1 are derived from a value of y; they may be called 'recipe relations'. Their number equals the number I of production factors. For long-term decisions and for macro decisions we often consider the x_i as given (as we did so far) and y as the effect: $y = F(x_1, x_2 \ldots)$.

Some of the simplest production functions are:

(i) The *Cobb–Douglas* production function: $ln \, y = \sum_1^I \lambda_i \, ln \, x_i$ (15.5)

As is well known, here the share of total production value paid to each factor i is λ_i, irrespective of the values x_i.

(ii) The *translog* production function:

$$ln \, y = \sum_1^I \lambda_{oi} \, ln \, x_i + \tfrac{1}{2} \sum_1^I \sum_1^I \lambda_{ij} \, ln \, x_i \, ln \, x_j$$ (15.6)

This function can be seen as a generalization of (15.5). If the organizers of production are competing for the factors of production i the latter's rate of pay (w_i: wages, salaries or interest rates) are $\partial y / \partial x_i$ and their shares in total product are $x_i/y \, w_i = \partial ln \, y / \partial ln \, x_i$. We find these shares from (15.6):

$$\partial ln \, y / \partial ln \, x_i = \lambda_{oi} + \sum_j \lambda_{ij} \, ln \, x_j$$ (15.7)

Clearly the shares are no longer constant.

(iii) The CES or *constant elasticity of substitution* production function is:

$$y^{-\rho} = \sum a_i x_i^{-\rho}$$ (15.8)

in the simplest form it may assume. We do not intend to discuss in this chapter the more complicated forms.

The Allen elasticity of substitution $\sigma = 1(1 + \rho)$ (15.9)

will assume a value depending on the parameters ρ. It can be shown that for $\rho = 0$ (15.8) reduces to (15.5), the Cobb–Douglas function, whose substitution elasticity between factors is unity. For competitive factor markets, rates of pay w_i will be equal to:

$$w_i = \frac{\partial y}{\partial x_i} = a_i \left(\frac{y}{x_i} \right)^{\rho+1} = a_i \left(\frac{y}{x_i} \right)^{1/\sigma}$$ (15.10)

(iv) *Two-level production functions*

This concept may be useful if production factors can be grouped. Thus, labour and capital may be grouped. Various types of labour x_i ($i = 1, \ldots$, *h*) may be combined into one concept labour X_1 and various types of capital goods X_{h+1}, x_{h+2} into one concept X_2, where x_{h+1} may be buildings and x_{h+2} equipment. The values of X_1 and X_2 may be expressed in terms of their components:

$$X_1 = F_1 (x_1, \ldots, x_h) \tag{15.11}$$

$$X_2 = F_2 (x_{h+1}, x_{h+2}) \tag{15.12}$$

and total production *y* may be determined by:

$$y = F (X_1, X_2) \tag{15.13}$$

Each of the F introduced here may be one of the types of production functions (or other types still) discussed in the preceding paragraphs.

As observed in the last paragraph on p. 341, short-run relationships between the quantities of factors used and the quantity of product may sometimes be better approached by an inverted causal relationship we called recipe relations. Here:

$$x_i = f_i (y) \quad i = 1, \ldots, I \tag{15.14}$$

The simplest example is provided by input–output analysis where

$$x_i = a_i y \quad i = 1, \ldots, I \tag{15.15}$$

More complicated relations are more realistic if (i) we analyse time series, and (ii) substitution between inputs is considered. Fluctuations in *y* need not lead to proportional fluctuations in labour employed, since the firing and subsequent hiring of workers may result in higher costs than if a reserve of labour had been maintained.

Production functions must reflect technological development, one of the main determinants of long-term socioeconomic development. The simplest way to do so is to assume disembodied technogical development that simultaneously raises the productivity of all production factors. Another is to assume changes in one or more of the coefficients or parameters of the production function. Thus, in the Cobb–Douglas or the translog function the shares of labour types or capital may be subject to change. The long-term fall in the share of (physical) capital may be the result of changes in the coefficients in (15.5) or (15.7). In the CES function a reduction in the a_i for capital will have a similar result. The same is true for a_i in (15.15), but (15.15) doesn't provide information about the price of capital. Increased demand for some types of services (education, research, government) may imply an increasing share of human capital, that is, higher education (cf. Wolfson, 1979).

Some factor characteristics exert considerable influence on the constraints on production functions.

One is the difference between essential and non-essential production factors. An essential production factor is one whose absence makes production impossible. If its quantity $x = 0$ also $y = 0$. The absence of a non-essential factor does not imply $y = 0$. The terminology is slightly misleading since a non-essential factor may be quite useful. A simple illustration may be borrowed from a distinction between the required and available capabilities of some groups of factors, especially labour. This distinction may be applied to the level of schooling, that is of the formal training level obtained. It seems appropriate to characterize such groups by two indices, for instance h for required and h' for actual level of schooling. Our symbol x_i will now be changed into $x_{hh'}$; if, moreover, quantities of labour are measured as proportions of the total labour force we will use the symbol $\varphi_{hh'}$. It follows that:

$$\sum_h \sum_{h'} \varphi_{hh'} = 1 \qquad (15.16)$$

Required and actual capabilities may also refer to innate capabilities. It is often believed that creativity or leadership and hence managerial quality are innate or at least to a considerable degree so. The proposition that also IQ constitutes an inherited variable has been the subject of intensive debate. In principle any capability, including physical strength, has an innate component.

Since most if not all jobs require a combination of levels of various capabilities and for each of these the distinction between level required for a proper execution of a task and level available makes sense, our input variables x or φ should preferably carry a higher (even) number of indices. Whenever the required and actual level are different we propose to speak of a 'mixed' group. As long as a situation of scarcity of capabilities prevails, production will have to be organized with the help of such 'mixed' (or 'not fully qualified') groups. As far as education is concerned, we may define the situation where only groups exist for which $h = h'$ as one of educational equilibrium.

From each production function we can derive a corresponding set of demand functions for the production factors considered, supposing there is free competition between the organizers of production. Indicating the rate of pay by w_i, we have

$$w_i = \frac{\partial y}{\partial x_i}$$

and hence for the

(i) Cobb–Douglas production function:

$$\frac{x_i}{y} w_i = \lambda_i \quad \text{or} \quad x_i = \lambda_i y / w_i \tag{15.17}$$

(ii) Translog function:

$$x_i w_i / y = \lambda_{oi} + \Sigma_j \lambda_{ij} ln x_j \quad \text{or}$$

$$x_i = (\lambda_{oi} + \Sigma_j \lambda_{ii} ln x_i) \, y / w_i \tag{15.18}$$

(iii) CES function the previously mentioned formula:

$$w_i = a_i \, (y/x_i)^{1/\sigma} \quad \text{or} \quad x_i = y \, (a_i/w_i)^{\sigma} \tag{15.10}$$

We see from these formulae that, because of the appearance of y on the right-hand side, the demand functions for the various factors considered are a set of I relations in I unknown x_i ($i = 1, \ldots, I$).

Since neither the two-level nor the recipe functions have so far been used in empirical work with more than a few types of labour we do not discuss the corresponding demand equations. We mentioned these production functions since they have been used to tackle other interesting problems (such as the demand for energy) and may, in future research, be useful for our subject, income distribution.

Some empirical research results may now be recorded that throw some light on income distribution. Two main types are research based on time series and research based on cross-section data. Whereas the former may supply evidence of short-term and long-term relations, the latter mainly supply evidence of long-term relations. The methods of estimation may vary from the primitive method where the number of unknown parameters equals the number of observations (no degrees of freedom) to the method where the number of observations greatly surpasses the number of unknowns and the reliability intervals can be estimated.

A basic finding is Kuznets's on the share of income from assets (hence, capital income) in the course of the century between, roughly, 1850 and 1950. For the UK and France this share fell from 40 per cent to 20 per cent. A similar rate of change was found for the USA between 1900 and 1950 (Kuznets, 1966, pp. 168-9). For 1970-2 Kuznets arrives at a figure of 17.5 per cent for the USA (in a personal letter to the author dated 20 March 1980). For North-Western European countries the figure is considerably lower, around 10 per cent. These are pre-tax figures; after-tax they are about one-half of pre-tax. Of the remaining 5 per cent a non-negligible portion accrues to pension funds and similar institutions.

Thurow (1968) estimated a Cobb–Douglas production function with capital and labour as the production factors and found that capital was paid more than its marginal productivity as estimated with the help of a Cobb–Douglas production function.

Tinbergen (1979) applied the method without degrees of freedom in order to estimate a number of translog functions. Consequently the results are very crude. For six industrial countries Kuznets's figures were used (table 14.7) in order to estimate the length of the period needed, from 1949 onwards, to reduce to one-half the share of capital income existing in 1949. For some countries two sets of observations were available yielding nine estimates in total. They ranged from six years to eighty-one, with a median of thirty-two. Also in Tinbergen (1979) a translog production function for the USA was estimated (with the aid of the same method) in which three types of labour were being used. Type 1 consisted of professionals and technicians, type 2 of managers, administrators, etc. and type 3 of all other labour. For the purpose of this chapter it seems interesting to show relative figures for 1949 and 1969 for groups 1 and 2, taking group 3 as equal to unity (see Table 15.1).

TABLE 15.1

Group	1949		1969	
	Number	Earnings	Number	Earnings
1. professionals, technicians	0.086	1.84	0.216	1.59
2. managers, administrators	0.122	1.94	0.177	1.60

The figures show that a relative rise in the numbers of both groups was accompanied by a relative fall in their earnings. Assuming that the numbers are supplied by the educational process, and hence in the short run supply is inelastic, the figures reflect the demand relation, but they do not necessarily show the long-run demand relation.

Presented in the form of the left-hand side equation of (15.18) the demand equations are (cf. Tinbergen, 1979, equations (14.12) through (14.14)):

$$\lambda_1 = 0.3748 + 0.1041 \ln x_1 + 0.0028 \ln x_2 - 0.1069 \ln x_3$$

$$\lambda_2 = 0.1764 + 0.0028 \ln x_1 + 0.0001 \ln x_2 - 0.0029 \ln x_3$$

$$\lambda_3 = 0.4488 - 0.1069 \ln x_1 - 0.0029 \ln x_2 + 0.1098 \ln x_3$$

where the shares are λ_i, which add up to unity.

Tinbergen and Kol (1980) estimated, from cross-section data for the USA (1959) and Japan (1975), a Cobb–Douglas production function with a proxy for capital and five types of labour. The observations refer to states for the USA and to prefectures for Japan, supplying about fifty observations for each country. With coefficients of determination $\bar{R}^2$ (corrected for degrees of freedom) > 0.7 for the USA and > 0.5 for Japan, only the regression coefficients λ_i (as used in equation (15.5) above) for white-collar workers in the USA and for workers (white- and blue-collar combined) in Japan are positive and significant at the 1 per cent level. The coefficients for professional workers and technicians are positive but hardly significant. Those for managers and for capital are not significantly different from zero; those for farmers and farm workers, and small entrepreneurs (available for Japan only) are negative, for farmers significantly so. Presumably, these results are less odd than they seem to be at first sight. Small entrepreneurs and most farmers derive psychic income from their independence or from living in a rural environment. Moreover, they often do not calculate correctly their costs of production by underestimating their own labour and capital costs. Blue-collar workers are kept in reserve by most enterprises as has been elaborated by Hart and Robb (1980) and various other authors mentioned in that article.

The *ex post* marginal social productivity of managers and sales workers must be low since to a considerable degree their tasks are counterproductive (cf. Tinbergen, 1981); they must counteract their competitors' activities. Viewed from their own firm's interests their productivity is based on an *ex ante* production function. Viewed from society's interests their productivity consists of maintaining competition (cf. Tinbergen, 1982).

All this is brought out more clearly if we combine the results with those obtained by Gottschalk (1978), Gottschalk and Tinbergen (1982) and Tinbergen (1981a, 1982a). Gottschalk found a way to reduce the unreliability owing to the large number of production factors involved. He did so in an attempt to estimate marginal productivity of the various types of labour in order to compare their earnings with their marginal productivity. The essence of Gottschalk's method consists of viewing a production process characterizing an industry or even a state as a combination of more than one process. The simplest case of two processes may be illustrated by his example of a technical production activity and its administration. Only one factor is used by both sub-processes, the 'common factor'. All other factors are 'specific', that is, used in only one sub-process. Thus, the number of factors used in each sub-process is about half the total number. The method was applied to the Tinbergen–Kol material for the USA and the two relations were expressed in two regression equations:

348   *Theories of Income Distribution in Developed Countries*

Technical production
process: $y = 0.48\,x_1 - 0.53\,x_4 - 0.11\,f + 0.17\,k,\ \bar{R}^2 = 0.69$
     (0.16)   (0.23)   (0.03)   (0.07)

Administration process: $y = 0.40\,x_1 - 0.05\,x_2 + 0.97\,x_3,\ \bar{R}^2 = 0.72$
     (0.18)   (0.14)   (0.19)

Here, the figures in parentheses indicate standard deviations of the regression coefficients. From these two relations Gottschalk (1978) derived a method (to be called I) to estimate the combined production function. This appeared to contain an implicit assumption which may be, however, avoided, as in Tinbergen (1980) (Method II) and the improved version (Tinbergen, 1982a) (Method IV). These methods, together with the Tinbergen-Kol results, are shown in Table 15.2,

TABLE 15.2   *Cobb–Douglas coefficients and their total* Σ *obtained for the USA cross section (state observations) 1959*

Method	x_1	x_2	x_3	x_4	f	k	Σ
T/Kol	0.24 (0.19)	0.01 (0.15)	0.74 (0.22)	− 0.31 (0.23)	− 0.07 (0.16)	0.10	0.71
I G	0.22	− 0.02	0.54	− 0.24	− 0.05	0.07	0.51
II T	0.33	− 0.03	0.83	− 0.18	− 0.04	0.05	0.96
IV T	0.30	− 0.03	0.87	− 0.20	− 0.04	0.06	0.95

x_1 Professional and technical workers.
x_2 Managers, administrators, etc.
x_3 White-collar workers.
x_4 Blue-collar workers.
f Farmers and farm workers.
k Proxy for capital.

In this case, Gottschalk's method appears to be only minimally biased. This makes it worthwhile to have a closer look at the results he obtained with the aid of 267 observations of single industries in single states, with an adjusted R^2 of 0.89 for technical production and one of 0.98 for administration. He computed the ratios between median earnings and marginal product value and found the following figures (see Tinbergen, 1982b):

Managers, etc.	2.03	Operatives	0.44
Sales workers	2.64	Clerical workers	0.63
Professionals, technicians	1.12	Labourers	0.54
Craftsmen	0.35	Service workers	0.49

For managers, etc. and sales workers there is 'over-payment' in comparison to their marginal product values, for professional workers and technicans only slightly so, but there is considerable 'under-payment' in comparison to their marginal productivity, in particular, for small entrepreneurs (craftsmen) but also for other manual workers and white-collar (clerical) workers. In the preceding text we have offered a partial explanation, which incidentally calls for a cautious interpretation of the word over-payment.

The interesting results obtained may, of course, change if other production functions are assumed to be valid. Hence, similar research using other production functions constitutes a highly interesting programme.

SUPPLY FACTORS

Turning now to the supply side of factor markets — and in particular labour market compartments — we have to look to utility, satisfaction, or welfare functions of individuals in order to identify the driving forces. For a long time the role labour plays in the attempt to maximize satisfaction has been dealt with in a rather one-sided way. In particular the emphasis was on the quantitative aspect of the problem, that is, the number of hours worked v. the number of leisure hours. Although for some aspects of labour economics, in particular the very long-term reduction in working hours, this has some relevance, the qualitative aspect, namely the choice of an occupation or a job, is much more relevant to the characterization of society, including its income distribution. For a large part of the labour force and in a normal cyclical position the length of the working week is given.

Economists differ much more in their opinions about utility functions than they do about production functions. Utility or satisfaction is considered by many economists to be non-measurable, and they have gone to great lengths to develop theories circumventing such measurement. Although impressive intellectual achievements have been made one may doubt whether as a scientific strategy this attitude is optimal. In this chapter measurability will be assumed and the choice of a job will be considered as the result of an optimum problem, namely the maximization of utility ω under the restriction(s) imposed by the labour market. As I have set out elsewhere, three elements are supposed to enter into a utility or welfare function, to be called variables, parameters and constants or coefficients (Tinbergen, 1975, p. 58). Variables are elements changing over time and among individuals. Some of them can be chosen by the individual or the household considered, others cannot. A job can be chosen, but its remuneration is determined by the labour market. This restriction may either be a relationship between the job and the remuneration, or it may also be a relationship into which the personality traits of the individual enter. Parameters are supposed to be constants for the individual, but to vary among individuals. They characterize the individual or household, or even groups of households studied. There are two groups of parameters, those characterizing productive abilities and those characterizing needs or tastes. The latter have been studied much more than the former, especially with a view to understanding and measuring consumption demand. The former will be taken up below. Coefficients characterize the utility function and are supposed to be the same for all individuals or households in the community studied. If some coefficients are not found to be the same for all households, a parameter is hidden in them and the research programme is adapted accordingly.

Jobs are usually described in terms of abilities for a proper execution of the tasks pertaining to each job. They are the subject of job classification. For the USA an immense quantity of such information is stored in the *Dictionary of Occupational Titles* (DOT). Each individual will be endowed with a number of abilities up to some level of intensity and hence be capable of doing a range of jobs. The choice of job that maximizes satisfaction depends on the earnings scale.

Examples of productive abilities are manual dexterity (the ability to handle things), intelligence (the ability to handle data) and social intelligence (the ability to deal with people). In the DOT these are indicated for a very large number of occupations, and the level (or intensity or degree) of each ability required is added. This illustrates that a distinction must be made between the qualitative and the quantitative aspects. Apart from these 'three-digit code' abilities, five 'worker trait components' are defined and quantified. A helpful overview is given by Hartog (1981, pp. 102-8). All the preceding definitions are taken from the American DOT. Many countries, and within them, industries, have their own system of job classification and an enormous diversity of terms is being used. There is a clear need to arrive at more uniformity and much has been done already. But apart from a more uniform terminology the question arises whether there is not much overlapping and whether the number of mutually independent abilities is not much smaller than the number of terms used. Hartog (1981, pp. 117-25) applies factor analysis in order to arrive at a (provisional) answer and finds that two factors stand out, which may be thought of as the intellectual and the manual abilities. It is interesting that even social intelligence or the ability to deal with people does not show up as an independent factor in this analysis.

A particularly interesting aspect of abilities is their degree of inheritability. In other words are the abilities which in the present society are rewarded by high incomes innate and hence bound to remain scarce so that these high incomes cannot be avoided? Or can they be developed by a learning process also accessible to less gifted individuals so that income differences can be reduced?

This question of inheritability is relevant in particular to intelligence and to what has been called social intelligence, but may also be described as leadership or in a variety of other terms. Intelligence has often been measured by the IQ and a famous discussion about its degree of inheritance stimulated Goldberger to devote himself for years to this subject. One way of posing the problem is to find whether a relation exists between the IQ of a child and the IQs of its parents. The differences of opinion centre around the question as to what other variables codetermine the child's IQ. We come back to the problem later and in the sixth section of this chapter. Clever attempts have also been made to use data on (monozygotic and dizygotic) twins educated in different environments (cf. Taubman, in Behrmann *et al.*, 1980).

The relevance of a high degree of inheritance and correspondingly low degree of learnability is that in such a situation an imposed learning process does not make much sense. The organization of the schooling system and especially the choice of curricula should, as much as possible, be based on information concerning learnability.

Let us now discuss some of the empirical work done on utility or welfare functions. An important general contribution has been made by Levy and Guttman (1975) who, in 1973 in Israel's four largest cities, conducted an inquiry among about 1,900 adult Jews (20 years and over). The answers to their questionnaire enabled them to measure the intensity of the impact of more than twenty variables on the level of 'well-being'. The main lesson to be learned from this inquiry is the relatively small part of welfare variations originating from economic variables, including income.

An important contribution to the measurement of the impact of income on welfare has been made by Van Praag (1971 and later) and his collaborators, who applied a similar method not only to individuals (or households) but also to communities such as municipalities. Essentially both groups of authors assume a rigid relationship between words (for levels from 'very bad' to 'very good') and figures. Since important decisions by parliaments and governments are based on verbal expressions, the relevance of this method should not be underestimated.

A central point in this method of measurement is that the statement made by an interviewee that, for instance, some income higher than his present income would make him feel 'very well' need not be identical with the feelings expressed later, when that income is attained. An alternative method of collecting information is to restrict it to observed behaviour. As a *quid pro quo* additional assumptions are then needed. Examples have been elaborated by Tinbergen (1975, 1980), and others are in preparation.

Abilities play a central role in the empirical work by Hartog (1981) who, among other results, also found that earnings can be considered as the total of the money value of the quantities (or intensities) of abilities transacted in the labour contract. He also found that the relative price of manual abilities in comparison with intelligence increased considerably between 1949 and 1959 in the USA. For later years lack of comparability of the data available made it impossible to verify this result.

SCHOOLING

At an early stage of individual as well as social development the process of learning becomes important as part of the supply side of the markets of production factors, especially labour. Learning starts with birth and, in the early years of life, the learning process takes place in the family and the immediate neighbourhood in which the family lives. A more formal learning process, organized in a special institution, the school system, is now generally recognized to be necessary and for that reason is imposed by law, as far as the first phase is concerned. A next phase, not obligatory for all, but necessary to have access to an increasing part of the labour market, has also been formalized. After it, learning is continued by training on the job, hence inside production units. In a way it never ends, and for some more complicated occupations the element called 'experience' is of major significance to the productive abilities required.

This section deals with the formal learning process, that is, schooling. Two main types of schooling are general versus vocational schooling. Three main levels of educational attainment refer to consecutive phases and are called primary, secondary and tertiary. The dividing lines are somewhat different in different countries; moreover, they are shifting, so far upward. Partly this is a consequence of the development of science and knowledge and the resulting technogical development. Lately, psychological factors have tended to oppose these tendencies, in order to reorganize the production process towards one yielding more satisfaction from work to as many workers as possible.

With its formalization the schooling process has become another branch of industry, alongside production branches of the conventional type and a sociology of schooling as well as an economics of it have come into existence.

Production functions such as those discussed in the fourth section hardly exist for this 'industry'. One difficulty of estimating such functions lies in identification of the industry's product. This product is multidimensional and its components are not easy to measure. Generally speaking they may be characterized as increases in knowledge, understanding and behaviour, as far as they are attributable to the school. Another set of difficulties springs from the identification of the factors of production. They may be said to be the teachers, the student and the curriculum, but such an answer relies on the identification of the abilities of both the relevant teachers and student and of the elements of the curriculum. Beginnings have been made to measure the product, for instance by the scores attained in some tests. Discussions on the quality of teachers and the usefulness of a number of subjects contained in the curriculum are numerous and increasing in number and depth, but often mainly qualitative.

Education, and more particularly schooling and on-the-job training, require efforts — of both the student and the teachers — and additional costs. The total of these costs are indicated by the phrase 'human capital', and its formation has been studied in the way investments in physical capital were dealt with in economic science. Important representatives of the 'human capital school' are Mincer (1957), Becker (1964), Schultz (1963), Chiswick (1974) and Mrs Ullman Chiswick (1972). Roughly speaking, an individual will continue his or her schooling process as long as the costs are covered by the return. If both costs and returns are restricted to the money costs and income increases, such simple relations can be derived as:

$$ln\, y_s = ln\, y_o + rs \tag{15.19}$$

where y_s is earnings obtained with a level of schooling s, y_o earnings at schooling level zero (which may be the obligatory level) and r is the interest rate. Sattinger (1980) sees this as the simplest interpretation of Mincer's theory and considers it equivalent to a situation in which all (lifetime discounted) earnings have been equalized. The corresponding earnings distribution would be one of complete equalization. Basic assumptions implied are the equality, for all individuals, of the interest rate at which they can borrow and the equality of efforts needed to attain a given level of schooling, or at least their joint effect on years of schooling supplied. Adherents to the human capital 'school' of the economics of education are, however, aware of differences between individuals. Sattinger adds another inequality contributing to inequality of productivity, namely the unequal quantity of physical capital with which individuals of different abilities are combined. Finally, we have so far neglected non-money income; that is, either income in kind or, more important perhaps, psychic income or satisfaction derived from the type of occupation corresponding to various years of schooling attained.

In the early phases of the economics of education the tacit assumption was made that schooling supplies as its final product graduates of all types, able to take up the jobs or occupations needed for the production process proper. Gradually the gap between graduation and job performance has been discovered and with it the existence of the cost of training on the job as well as the true character of the schooling level attained. That character has been indicated as a screening device, that is, a first piece of information needed to sort out the individuals applying for some job. Although vocational schooling makes a start with training for particular sets of jobs, the last part can only be done in the production process. Again the first few years of training inside the factory or office have been more formalized in some countries than in others, especially in Germany; and perhaps since Karl Marx was a German, in all of the communist countries. In many German enterprises training contracts are being concluded with prospective employees with a chance to obtain a job. In most other countries the frequency of such contracts is much lower.

A considerable volume of empirical research illustrates and up to a point quantifies the links set out in the preceding subsections between family, school and society. The type of research done is known as path analysis, started a few decades before econometric model building, and very similar to it. Path analysis may be said to result in models, that is a set of direct relations between a number of independent variables whose variations exert an effect on the variations in a dependent variable. A simple and clear example may be taken from Psacharopoulos (1977):

$$A = 0.237\,F \qquad\qquad\qquad\qquad\qquad\qquad R^2 = 0.056$$
$$ (0.012)$$
$$S = 0.172\,F + 0.511\,A \qquad\qquad\qquad\qquad R^2 = 0.333$$
$$ (0.010)\quad(0.010)$$
$$O = 0.124\,F + 0.191\,A + 0.325\,S \qquad\qquad R^2 = 0.261$$
$$ (0.011)\quad(0.012)\quad(0.013)$$
$$Y = 0.025\,F + 0.132\,A + 0.137\,S + 0.392\,O \qquad R^2 = 0.310$$
$$ (0.011)\quad(0.012)\quad(0.013)\quad(0.012)$$

derived from a sample of 6873 individuals in the UK.

In path analysis it is customary to standardize variables, that is, making their average equal to zero and their standard deviation equal to 1. In the model shown A stands for ability (according to a simple test), F for father's occupation, S for schooling level attained, O for occupation, and Y for annual earnings. For our purpose the last relation is the most relevant one. From it we see that by far the largest direct impact on income is from O. From the other relations we may derive, for instance, the indirect impact of father's occupation by substituting these other relations into the Y-equation; this yields 0.088 F, hence considerably more than the direct impact. Even so the total impact of F on Y becomes 0.113 F, so still less than any of the direct influences of the other variables: A, S and O.

Similar models have been constructed for the USA by Jencks *et al.* (1972), for a Wisconsin sample by Sewell and Hauser (1975), for a Swedish group by Bulcock, Fägerlind and Emanuelson (1924), and for a Dutch group by Dronkers and de Jong (1979).

The models differ in that in several of them more variables have been included; sometimes they restrict themselves to the educational attainment or even to the question whether or not some intermediate level has been attained. We can only show a small selection of results illustrating these differences. One of the more complicated models is Sewell's and Hauser's for a Wisconsin sample of 2069 individuals where the earnings equation reads (in standardized form):

$$Y = -0.017\, V + 0.007\, M - 0.020\, X + 0.136\, I + 0.066\, Q + 0.063\, U + 0.131\, W$$

with $R^2 = 0.074$.

where V stands for father's education, M for mother's education, X for father's occupation, I for income of parents, Q for ability, U for son's education, and W for son's occupation. The reader may compare the coefficients. The negative regression coefficients are significant at the 0.05 level. The significance of the coefficients of the British sample is much higher, perhaps because of the smaller number of independent variables. Sample size may also have improved significance.

As mentioned by Dronkers and de Jong, there is a remarkable difference in the coefficients of determination; from the very low figures for the USA (also Jenck's), to values of 0.65 for the Netherlands.

The way in which inherited characteristics are treated in the models discussed so far tends to substantially underestimate the innate element. This will be immediately clear if we realize that the same combination of variables is supposed to apply to all children of one couple. No differences between these children can be explained in this way. In this respect the research based on data of monozygotic twins holds much more promise (Taubman, in Behrmann *et al.*, 1980). In order to estimate reliably various other variables' influences the variance in these other variables must be considerable, however; data must be available on considerably different schooling and environment if the latter's impact is what we want to know. Taubman's main result is that the impact of schooling proper is about half of what other studies yield. The implication may be that learnability is a restriction on attempts at reducing income inequality. The results that I obtained (Tinbergen, 1975), using very crude data and estimates, showing that income inequality may be almost eliminated if the number of university graduates could be doubled or trebled in comparison to the modest level of 3 per cent attained in 1962 in the Netherlands, may perhaps be useful to stimulate a large volume of more accurate research needed to obtain more reliable insight.

MEETING OF SUPPLY AND DEMAND

The meeting of supply and demand is assumed to result in an equilibrium where price and quantity transacted (for labour: employed) are determined. Disregarding time lags, to begin with, the well-known simplest model may be written:

Demand function: $x^D = a^D y + b^D d$ (15.20)

Supply function: $x^S = a^S y + b^S s$ (15.21)

where x^D is quantity demanded, x^S quantity supplied, y price, d a combination of demand factors, and s a combination of supply factors, all expressed as deviations from their means. In equilibrium $x^D = x^S = x^E$; the resulting price y^E results from

$$a^D y^E + b^D d = a^S y^E + b^S s$$ (15.22)

from which follows:

$$y^E = (b^S s - b^D d)/(a^D - a^S)$$ (15.23)

The quantity transacted:

$$x^E = a^D y^E + b^D d = a^S y^E + b^S s$$

$$x^E = (a^D b^S s - a^S b^D d)/(a^D - a^S)$$ (15.24)

The symbols x, y, s and d may also be logarithms.

As a rule the coefficient $a^D < 0$, and a^S, b^D and $b^S > 0$. This implies that y^E depends positively on d and negatively on s, whereas x^E depends positively on both d and s.

So far we treated a and b as coefficients. They may be operators, for instance functions of the variables in front of which they appear.

A simple illustration may be taken from Tinbergen (1982a), where $s = ln\ \varphi_{h'}$ and $d = ln\ \varphi_{h'}$, and $b^S = b^D$. Here $\varphi_{h'}$ stands for the promillage of the labour force with education h' and φ_h for the promillage of the labour force with required education h, on which figures have been calculated by Rumberger (1981). We consider the compartments of the labour market where $h = h'$ and assumes all feasible values.

Equation (15.23) for earnings now becomes:

$$y = b\ ln\ (\varphi_h/\varphi_{h'}) = f\ (\varphi_h/\varphi_{h'}) \tag{15.25}$$

where $b = b^S/(a^D - a^S)$ and f a rising function of $\varphi_h/\varphi_{h'}$; the latter ratio may be called the scarcity of labour with an education h.

The simplicity of the example lies in the assumption that only one ability, schooling, characterizes the quality differences among individuals. This choice can be defended by Hartog's finding (1981) that intelligence constitutes the most important single ability. In addition it is only for this characteristic that, thanks to Rumberger's achievement, the required intensity distribution is available alongside the actual distribution. For this one-dimensional ability case we may construct a matrix $\Phi_{hh'}$ indicating the data available for all combinations of h and h'. This matrix, or two-entry table, can be used to clarify the variety of definitions that can be chosen for a market compartment. Since a one-dimensional ability is considered, these compartments as a set have to be one-dimensional too, but that implies that the cells of the matrix have to be combined. Special cases are rows or columns, corresponding with one value of h or of h'; but more generally we may take a combination of cells for which $\alpha h + \alpha' h' =$ constant, thus a weighted sum or average. In one compartment one equilibrium wage rate will exist. Using the earnings of the eleven main occupational groups of the 1970 US Census we find:

$$y = -0.069\ h + 1.573\ h' \tag{15.26}$$
$$(0.386)\quad (0.476)$$

hence $\alpha = 0$ and the compartments are defined by the values of h'.

Factor price markets often show time lags either in the supply or in the demand equation or in both. This implies that the time series of prices (incomes) and employment cannot be considered as a chain of equilibrium points, but parts of equilibrium searching paths. Depending on the time paths of determinants and the coefficients in the demand and supply relations, a variety of adaptation paths may occur, well known from some commodity markets. Thus, for some university graduates Freeman (1976) finds cyclical movements of the cobweb type, due to the length of the schooling process after the last decision the student has to take: some four years.

In other markets we may observe a persistence of disequilibria, if both demand and supply are inelastic with respect to price. As discussed on p. 344, jobs may be performed by individuals whose actual schooling does not coincide with the schooling required. But otherwise, schooling is not necessarily exactly determined by the nature of the job.

A considerable literature supplies us with a number of far more complicated 'earnings equations' of the type of equation (15.23), where s and d are algebraic functions of a large number of personality traits or job requirements. A selection of results obtained by many scholars is shown in Tinbergen (1977). Taubman (1974) is one of the authors who have included large numbers of independent variables, such as region of origin, religious affiliation, intelligence, spatial perception etc., where it is not even always clear whether some of these variables are meant to be supply or demand factors.

In the study of income distribution a distinction should be made between research on observable factual information and research on the possibility of changes as a consequence of changes in determinants. Then, factual information may be collected on the changes over time or on the differences between nations or other communities at a given time.

Some well-known results are those obtained by Kuznets (1966) and Paukert (1973), showing that over long periods of development, or for a set of countries at different levels of development, inequality increases until a certain level has been attained and subsequently decreases. Part of the explanation of that decrease may be the decline of the income from assets (or 'capital') mentioned on p. 345.

Figures about the reduction in inequality of incomes over time have been shown by Pen and Tinbergen (1977) for the Netherlands over the period 1938–76. Income inequality decreased by one-quarter before tax and by one-half after tax. Several authors maintain that income inequality in the USA hardly changed over that period. Kuznets (1974), however, shows that inequality did go down if a correction is made for some demographic changes, namely the increase in families without a head in the labour force. Tinbergen (1975) shows that the relative income of intellectuals to that of other groups after 1900 decreased in both the USA and the Netherlands. Burck (1976) shows that between 1952 and 1976 the real compensation of top managers hardly changed, whereas the average income per employee rose by some 30 per cent. Hartog (1981) shows that between 1949 and 1959 income from manual abilities increased relative to that from intelligence.

Coming to some cross-section data, the ratios of earnings between a high-school graduate and a university graduate are (at the age of 25-34 years) in the USA 0.70 and (at the age of 55-64) 0.50. In Japan at similar ages these ratios are 0.95 and 0.91 respectively. (The Japanese figures are from the 1979 Income Survey Report of the Institute of Labour Administrative Research; those for the USA are from the 1970 Census of Population.)

Smolensky *et al.* (1979) estimate that factor income inequality in the USA is considerably higher than in West Germany (Gini coefficients being 0.446 and 0.364 respectively).

Fiegehen and Reddaway (1981) provide data about top manager compensations in the UK and other countries. These are considerably lower in the UK than elsewhere, but no difference in performance could be shown. This study indicates, as does Burck's, that top managers derive considerable psychic income and that in a number of countries they are overpaid.

NON-ECONOMIC SOCIOLOGICAL DETERMINANTS

Sociologists look at society in a broader way than do economists, although there is a general tendency for sciences to expand their objects of research and the methods used. This tendency induces economists to cover a larger area of sociology than they did previously. Among the phenomena studied by sociologists, power structures and their consequences rank high, and they sometimes accuse economists of neglecting that aspect of society. Up to a point this is correct, but not in all respects. Some power elements are given attention by economists, but they use a different terminology from the sociologist's. Scarcity is typically an economic concept and simultaneously a source of income differences; these differences could also be said to be derived from the power of the owners of scarce elements. In the preceding sections we dealt with scarcity and even with two types, which may be called natural scarcity and organized scarcity. An example of the former is a high intensity of intelligence and one of the latter is monopoly. In this section some other power elements that also may cause income differences will be discussed.

Power can be exerted also with the aid of physical violence and the groups often called the 'ruling class(es)' are able to use the violence of police and the military in order to impose their ideology. The ruling class may be feudal, that is the landowners, capitalist, that is the owners of capital, fascist (a combination of capitalist and nationalist) or communist, whose ideology is that of the proletariat, perhaps also combined with nationalist elements. Each of these ruling groups may have preconceived ideas about the incomes of various groups in society, often attached to a hierarchy. Incomes then depend on an individual's position in the hierarchy. Examples of such position theories are given by Lydall (1968), Drucker (1977), Wegner (1981) and others. Such theories may, but need not, be economic theories, in the latter case they may be using the scarcity concept discussed in sections three through to seven, whether natural or (partly) organized. Economic factors may occasionally be strong enough to make the rulers' ideology change in the direction of market forces.

Another element of power is the 'power of habit', sometimes the power of tradition. For lack of another source of inspiration, tradition to many populations is the basis of their juridical order. A sophisticated scientist may judge that habit or tradition is nothing but inertia, or a very slow operation of logical or ethical forces. This element of power may also be the basis of what the ruling classes impose on their citizens.

Some economists seem to be influenced by the power of tradition, if they tacitly assume that the income ratios of different occupations should be maintained or if they use the term 'overeducation'. They may do so if the education attained coincides with the education required – neglecting, then, the possibility of changes in such a requirement. While it has to be admitted that sometimes the education required may be inflated in comparison to what a careful analysis of an occupation actually requires, other developments are possible where more creativity would add to performance and increased creativity may be attained by a better educational process.

Power of various types may show up in numerous types of discrimination, some of them ethically objectionable. This has now been generally accepted for slavery, the first and most outspoken form of discrimination. A second form is caste discrimination, unacceptable to a large part of the world population. A third form is racial discrimination, practised in many countries by a non-negligible part of the population. Thus, in the USA in 1969, a white male aged 25-34 with four years of high school and working 50-52 weeks earned, on the average, $8 766 a year, whereas for the non-white the mean earnings were $6 863. While discrepancies may partly be the result of job differences, we find the respective figures for truck drivers to be $8 738 and $6 797, thus not a large difference from the general averages.

The fourth form of income discrimination is the one against women, hence sex discrimination. For example, in 1969 a male elementary school teacher aged 25-34, with four years of college earned $8 206, and a female $6 621. Some of the differences may be explained by rational arguments. No attempt will be made to go into a detailed discussion, however, since most analyses are indeed left with a good deal of discrimination.

NON-PRODUCTIVE INCOME WITHIN HOUSEHOLDS

So far we discussed productive income, in the traditional sense of income received from productive contributions made through a market. Traditional, that is, because it is assumed that only paid labour is productive, which is incorrect for household work. In this section we shall discuss incomes spent on behalf of non-productive members of households. The concept of household will be used in its widest sense, covering single persons who live by themselves at one extreme and hospitals, army divisions or other similar institutions at the other. By far the largest part of households are, however, families, nuclear or extended. Nuclear families will consist of one or more adults and may also have one or more children below working age. Again, most frequently there are two parents and one or more children. The extended family may embrace other relatives.

The main subject of this section is to discuss various definitions of income, whose distributions are sometimes quite different, leading to confusion and misunderstandings in discussions about such distributions. If in a household there is one income earner his or her income is relevant for a discussion of the factor (for instance, labour) market. For a discussion of welfare, however, the income per person is more relevant. Still better is the income per consumer unit, implying that children and non-earning adults are counted as part of or multiples of an adult of working age. There are various ways of carrying out this transformation.

If there are more income earners in a household, three different concepts of income are needed for a clear definition: income per earner, income per household and income per capita or per consumer unit. Taking simply per capita household income, Thurow (1980, pp. 156, 160) shows the difference (Table 15.3).

TABLE 15.3 *Shares in national income, USA (%)*

	Family income		Per capita household income	
	1947	*1977*	*1948*	*1977*
Lowest 20%	5.0	5.2	4.1	5.6
Highest 20%	43.0	41.5	45.9	38.1

The second dimension of the set of income definitions originates from the interference of transfer payments. Taxes are levied and subsidies lower the cost of a number of goods and services consumed by households. Accordingly, a distinction has to be made between incomes before direct taxes are paid, incomes after these taxes have been paid and incomes after complete redistribution. An estimation of the third concept is complicated by the possibility that the way the authorities spend their revenue changes prices and incomes. One such change is due to the schooling required for the occupations of civil servants: it is, on the average, higher than the mean for the private sector. In the estimates made so far, these price and income changes have often been neglected, as pointed out by Wolfson (1979).

Before discussing, in the last section, the most important category of non-productive income, a few words may be added on voluntary income transfers between households that existed before obligatory transfers were organized by social security systems as they now exist in developed countries. These voluntary transfers, or charity transfers, have never been of much importance. This is another example why a satisfactory income distribution can hardly be expected from the 'free forces of society'.

SOCIAL SECURITY SYSTEMS

In developed countries the most important type of income not derived from simultaneous participation in the production process is income from social security systems. This income is the best example of how, among the determinants of income, alongside the economic determinants, power structures may also be changed. In order to give an idea of the order of magnitude of this income category before the stagflation of the 1970s, the percentage of national income transferred in 1970 for some Western industrial countries may be cited. The figures shown by Huppes (1977, p. 81) vary from 10.5 per cent for the USA to 20.0 per cent for the Netherlands. Among the European countries mentioned, the UK transferred 14.0 per cent, the FRG 17.6 per cent and Sweden 19.1 per cent. The differences reflect some differences in ideology – the US figure compared with the European, or the Dutch figure compared with the German. They also reflect differences in per capita income; this explains the rather low figure of the UK.

When social security started in Europe – about a century ago – it was called social insurance and the insurance element was clearer than today. Increasingly the transfer element from higher to lower income groups became more important, as is illustrated in Tinbergen (1975, pp. 20-1). Of course there is hardly a clear frontier here between the operation of the tax system and that of social security. A difference can be made between (i) systems applying to the population as a whole, (ii) systems applying to employees, and (iii) systems applying to small entrepreneurs. Examples of

(i) are old-age provisions and regulations for children; examples of (ii) are sickness and unemployment insurance; examples of (iii) the previous form of assistance to farmers as it existed in Britain and the Netherlands. This system gave assistance to individual farmers, whose income was below a certain level. Unfortunately in the European Community it has been replaced by the system that keeps agricultural prices at some desired level which implies larger assistance to rich farmers than to poor. This system was chosen because it can be more easily administrated in countries with a weak administration. It is not satisfactory, however, and subject to much criticism.

Income inequality among countries is much larger than within a single country. From a worldwide point of view this is an explosive situation. The problem of theories of these differences is outside the scope of this chapter, however.

In recent years stagnation has given rise to widespread unemployment and an enormous increase in social security expenditures. A number of politicians and economists have expressed doubts about the future of the 'welfare state'. No doubt there is an urgent need for a revision of some scales of unemployment benefits; but even more urgent is the organization of a recovery. This important problem can only be mentioned in passing. One general remark should be stressed in many discussions about reduction of income differences the fear that incentives would be affected seems exaggerated. This exaggeration is the result of the neglect of psychic income. A considerable number of high incomes may be reduced without much danger of a reduction of incentives because these incomes are paid for jobs with a considerable psychic income. Jobs providing a high degree of satisfaction should be distinguished from jobs providing dissatisfaction and irritation. The latter indeed have to be well rewarded, whereas the rewards for the former do not necessarily have to be supported by incentives.

REFERENCES

Becker, G. S. (1964) *Human Capital*, National Bureau of Economic Research, New York: Columbia University Press.

Behrmann, J. R. *et al.* (1980) *Socioeconomic Success*, Amsterdam/New York/Oxford: North-Holland.

Bulcock, J. W., I. Fägerlind and I. Emanuelson (1974) *Education and the Socioeconomic Career*, Institutionen för Internationell Pedagogik, Stockholms Universitet, no. 6.

Burck, C. G. (1976) 'A Group Profile of the Fortune 500 Chief Executives', *Fortune* (May): 173.

Chiswick, B. R. (1974) *Income Equality*, National Bureau of Economic Research, New York: Columbia University Press.

Dronkers, J., and U. de Jong (1979) 'Jencks and Fägerlind in a Dutch Way', *Social Science Information* 18 (4/5): 761–81.

Drucker, P. F. (1977) 'Is Executive Pay Excessive?' *Wall Street Journal* (23 May).

Fiegehen, G. C., and W. B. Reddaway (1981) *Companies, Incentives and Senior Managers*, Oxford: Oxford University Press.

Freeman, R. B. (1976) *The Over-educated American*, New York/San Francisco/London: Academic Press.

Gottschalk, P. T. (1978) 'A Comparison of Marginal Productivity and Earnings by Occupation', *Industrial and Labor Review*, 31: 368–78.

Gottschalk, P. T., and J. Tinbergen (1982) 'Methodological Issues in Testing the Marginal Productivity Theory', *De Economist*, 130.

Hart, R. A., and A. L. Robb (1980) 'Production and Labour Demand Functions with Endogenous Fixed Worker Costs', IIM/80–11, Publication Series of the International Institute of Management, Wissenschaftszentrum Berlin.

Hartog, J. (1981) *Personal Income Distribution. A Multicapability Theory*, Boston/The Hague/London: Martinus Nijhoff.

Huppes, T. (1977) *Inkomensverdeling en institutionele structuur*, Leiden: H. E. Stenfert Kroese.

Jencks, C. *et al.* (1972) *Inequality*, New York: Basic Books.

Kuznets, S. (1966) *Modern Economic Growth*, New Haven/London: Yale University Press.

Kuznets, S. (1974) 'Demographic Aspects of the Distribution of Income among Families: Recent Trends in the United States', in W. Sellekaerts (ed.), *Essays in Honour of Jan Tinbergen*, London and Basingstoke: Macmillan.

Levy, S., and L. Guttman (1975) 'On the Multivariate Structure of Wellbeing', *Social Indicators Research 2:* 361–88.

Lydall, H. F. (1968) *The Structure of Earnings*, Oxford: Oxford University Press.

Mincer, J. (1957) 'A Study of Personal Income Distribution', Ph.D. dissertation, Columbia University.

Moroney, J. R. (ed.) (1979) *Income Inequality*, Lexington/Toronto: D. C. Heath.

Paukert, F. (1973) 'Income Distribution Levels of Development: A Survey of Evidence', *International Labour Review*, 108: 97.

Pen, J., and J. Tinbergen (1977) *Naar een rechtvaardiger inkomensverdeling*, Amsterdam/Brussels: Elsevier.

Psacharopoulos, G. (1977) 'Family Background, Education and Achievement', *British Journal of Sociology*, 28: 321–35.

Rumberger, R. W. (1981) 'The Changing Skill Requirements of Jobs in the US Economy', *Industrial and Labor Relations Review*, 34: 578–90.

Sattinger, M. (1980) *Capital and Distribution of Labor Earnings*, Amsterdam/New York/Oxford: North-Holland.

Schultz, T. W. (1963) *The Economic Value of Education*, New York/London: Columbia University Press.

Sewell, W. H., and R. M. Hauser (1975) *Education, Occupation and Earnings*, New York/San Francisco/London: Academic Press.

Smolensky, E. *et al.* (1979) 'Post-Fisc Income Inequality: A Comparison of the United States and West Germany', in J. R. Moroney (ed.), *Income Inequality*, Lexington/Toronto: D. C. Heath.

Taubman, P., and T. Wales (1974) *Higher Education and Earnings*, New York: McGraw-Hill.

Thurow, L. C. (1968) 'Disequilibrium and the Marginal Productivity of Capital and Labor', *Review of Economics and Statistics*, 50: 23-31.

Thurow, L. C. (1980) *The Zero-sum Society*, Harmondsworth/New York: Penguin Books.

Tinbergen, J. (1975) *Income Distribution*, Amsterdam/Oxford: North-Holland.

Tinbergen, J. (1977) 'Income Distribution: Second Thoughts', *De Economist*, 125: 315-39.

Tinbergen, J. (1979) 'Changing Factor Shares and the Translog Production Function', in H. I. Greenfield *et al.* (ed.), *Theory for Economic Efficiency: Essays in Honor of Abba P. Lerner*, Cambridge, Mass./London: MIT Press, pp. 195-216.

Tinbergen, J. (1980) 'Two Approaches to Quantify the Concept of Equitable Income Distribution', *Kyklos*, 33: 3-15.

Tinbergen, J. (1981a) 'Contraproduktie', in P. J. Eijgelshoven and L. J. van Gemerden (eds), *Inkomensverdeling en openbare financiën: Opstellen voor Jan Pen*, Utrecht/Antwerpen: Het Spectrum, pp. 288-97.

Tinbergen, J. (1981b) 'Fonctions de production contenant plusieurs catégories de travail', *Revue européenne des sciences sociales*, 19: 5-15.

Tinbergen, J. (1982a) 'The Scarcity Earnings Theory Illustrated by Rumberger's Skill Requirements Study', Institute for Economic Research Discussion Paper 8202/G, Rotterdam: Erasmus University.

Tinbergen, J. (1982b) 'Deviations between Earnings and Marginal Productivity', in G. R. Feiwel (ed.), *Samuelson and Neoclassical Economics*, Boston: Kluwer-Nijhoff, pp. 107-18.

Tinbergen, J., and J. Kol (1980) 'Market-determined and Residual Incomes – Some Dilemmas', *Economie Appliquée*, 33: 285-301.

Ullman Chiswick, C. J. (1972) 'The Growth of Professional Occupations in the American Labor Force: 1900-1963', World Bank Paper based on Columbia University dissertation.

Van Praag, B. M. S. (1971) 'The Welfare Function of Income in Belgium: An Empirical Investigation', *European Economic Review*, 2: 337-69.

Wegner, E. (1981) *Die personelle Verteilung der Arbeitseinkommen*, Frankfurt am Main: Campus Verlag.

Wolfson, D. J. (1979) 'Pen and Tinbergen on Income Distribution: A Review Article', *De Economist*, 127: 446-58.

16 Marginal Productivity, a Rehabilitation

MARTIN BRONFENBRENNER

And on the pedestal these words appear,
"My name is Ozymandias, King of Kings!
Look on my works, ye Mighty and despair!"
Nothing beside remains. Round the decay
Of that colossal wreck, boundless and bare,
The lone and level sands stretch far away.
(Shelley, 'Ozymandias in Egypt'.)

Not long ago — well within the memory of living man — the sun never set on the British Empire. But colonies and dependencies have graduated to self-governing dominions, commonwealth members, even republics boasting complete independence. Little is left beyond Shakespeare's 'precious stone set in a silver sea'. Even there, Irish and Scottish and Welsh nationalists would reduce its extent, though not its population, below that of Shakespeare's time. But even should such termites succeed beyond all present probability, 'There'll always be an England.'

Over approximately the same time period, something similar has happened in the realms of intellect to many a leading principle of the natural sciences, not to mention the laggard social ones. Marginal productivity, our present case in point, is merely a minor one among many. Witness the indivisible atom of Newton and the mutationless evolution of Darwin. The question before the house is whether marginal-productivity analysis still retains, and can expect to retain, like England, some measure of existential validity, or whether it will vanish 'into air, into thin air' like phlogiston or the lost Atlantis. By speaking of rehabilitation, I range myself on the side of England, however attenuated, rather than the side of Atlantis, however vast.

At its greatest extent and proudest moment, which we may identify with John Bates Clark's *Distribution of Wealth* (1899, and coincidentally at the end of the Victorian era), marginal productivity professed to be the guiding and unifying principle of income distribution in economics. It applied with equal force to wages, interest, and rent. It was professedly based on physical (i.e. natural) considerations. It claimed dominion, not precisely over Rudyard Kipling's 'palm and pine', but over both the positive and the normative domains – over both 'who gets what?' and 'who deserves what?' Following on hints in my own *Income Distribution Theory* (Bronfenbrenner, 1971)[1] along with later work (Bronfenbrenner, 1977), I propose to examine what is left, beyond King Ozymandias' lone and level sands stretching far away.

Some early revolts and victories against marginal productivity, or at least against Clark's exposition thereof, were on the normative or ethical front. An obvious retort might repeat Jonathan Swift's 'Mankind may judge what Heaven thinks of riches by observing those upon whom it has been pleased to bestow them.' The basic argument, later and more analytical, points out the broad gap or hiatus between the economic productivity of an individual's stocks of either physical or human capital and his ethical merit however defined. (The physical capital may be largely inherited, and the human capital result from public or philanthropic expenditures upon his education and training. Bronfenbrenner, 1971, pp. 185–8, spells these and allied arguments at possibly undue length.) As early as the mid-1930s Jacob Viner, then at Chicago and my own first teacher of formal distribution theory, was claiming that no economist of standing took Clark's ethical justification of the existing order on marginal-productivity grounds at all seriously any longer. (Viner's proposed divorce of the positive from the ethical in marginal-productivity theory may have been premature. At least, I have subsequently found several economists who did take Clark seriously in ethical matters, and who had standing at least on their own campuses or similar air-raid shelters against heterodoxy.)

With almost equal rapidity evaporated any marginal-productivity explanation of the personal distribution of family income by size classes, as distinguished from the functional distribution by income types. No immediate or direct connection between the marginal productivity of inputs and the personal distribution could have been made legitimately for the large agricultural sector of Clark's America, for the incomes of family farmers depended proximately upon the quantities and the farm prices of one or a few farm crops or outputs, and not on input prices at all. But as years passed, and agriculture declined in relative importance to the national income, the non-agricultural phenomena of the multiple-input income (to the property-owning worker or the salaried capitalist), the multiple-earner family, the part-time or overtime employee, combined to take the place of independent entrepreneurship on and off the farm as detours for immediate connection between the marginal productivity of individuals' property and skills and the distribution of income between their families.

Clark's theory, and also other contemporary versions of marginal-productivity analysis, had been aspects of the so-called marginalist revolt against cost or supply theories of value — against any form of the labour theory of value in particular. This group of theories, propounded between the 1870s and the First World War, generally stressed demand, which they traced to cardinal utility; they reduced cost to demand for alternative goods — derived demand, in the case of inputs — leaving the demand for and utility of 'leisure' out of account. True, Alfred Marshall's *Principles of Economics* (first edition 1890) had gone a long way towards redressing the balance before Clark wrote. Most of Clark's message, nevertheless, could be accepted only against a backdrop of completely inelastic input supplies — which is to say, in the case of a labour input, a fixed number of days and hours of that type of labour supplied per period, regardless of the wage offered. (This amount, a vertical line on the conventional textbook diagram, could of course shift over time, but probably not with wage rates for other types of labour skills.) Anything less — any acknowledgement of elasticity in input supplies — reduces marginal productivity from a theory of input pricing to a theory of input demand alone. A theory of input demand alone requires, no doubt, a concomitant theory of input supply for legitimate expansion into a theory of input prices. But if marginal productivity be attenuated from a theory of input price to one of input demand solely, 'what good is it?' (I have myself been asked this question many times — usually by people who willingly proceed from demand *and supply* explanations of *output* prices!)

In later years, the adequacy of marginal-productivity explanations even when restricted to the demand side of input markets, has been questioned repeatedly. It can in fact no longer be regarded as a general explanation of input demand — at least, not in the form presented by Clark in 1899. Let us consider the sceptical doubts about marginal productivity as an explanation of input demand under six heads: imperfect competition; the multiple-goal firm; the cost and inadequacy of information on marginal productivity; the inelasticity of input demand; all-or-none bargaining and approaches thereto; the technical links between marginal-productivity and input-demand functions. We shall spend little time on each one, since most if not all are well and widely known.

(1) In the presence of either monopoly–oligopoly on the employer's

output markets or monopsony–oligopsony on his input markets, the basic equilibrium equality is no longer between input prices and the value of marginal physical products, but between marginal input costs and marginal revenue products. (Marginal input costs exceed input prices, and marginal revenue products fall short of the value of marginal physical products.[2])

(2) The Clarkian equality between input prices and the values of marginal products requires not only purity of competition but a single-minded pursuit by the employer in successive periods. Such conflicting considerations as growth, market share, 'modernity', 'the good life', social repute, and the general tenor of employer–employee or employer–supplier relations often enter in as well. The distortions they produce may of course cancel each other out or be otherwise confined to the second order of residuals. But then again they may not.

(3) Marginal productivity is in fact difficult and expensive to estimate when inputs cannot practically be varied one at a time, when the output is itself a changing mix, and in the presence of lags between inputs and outputs when these lags are at all variable.

(4) When a 'technique' in the sense of Joan Robinson (1956, ch. 7) and Piero Sraffa (1960) rules out input substitution (unless, of course, one shifts from 'technique Alpha' to 'technique Beta'), input demand becomes completely inelastic with respect to input prices. This means that input prices themselves are determined entirely by considerations on the supply side.

(5) All-or-none bargaining is a frequent technique, particularly in labour negotiations. Under such a system a trade union (or other supplier) bargains both for input prices (wage rates) and for the quantity of employment thereunder (job security). More commonly, the bargaining is for a set of working rules that, while less extreme than all-or-none-bargaining, also require provision of more employment than 'economic' demand would otherwise require, presumably on marginal-productivity grounds.

(6) Two problems enter into the relationship between marginal-productivity and input-demand functions, which are generally related but seldom identical. The better-known problem, which we may call (6-a), relates to Euler's theorem on homogeneous functions, the 'adding up theorem' of input demand.[3] When this theorem does not hold – it *does* hold, for example, for production at minimum average cost – there remains a residual (positive or negative) when each input price equals the value of its marginal physical product; this residual must be allocated on other grounds than marginal productivity. A lesser-known problem (which we call 6-b) is: whereas marginal-product computations assume the *quantities* of related inputs are being held constant, input demand curves assume no

changes in the *prices* of these related inputs. (For an explanation of what differences this may make, see Bronfenbrenner, 1971, p. 136f.)

Our discussion thus far has assumed implicitly the existence, at least for the individual firm if not for the macroeconomy, of a purely physical production function $x = f(a)$, where x is a vector of output x_i and a a vector of inputs a_j. (The number of inputs need not equal the number of outputs; it may be either more or less.) The 'X-efficiency' studies of Harvey Leibenstein, among others, have however called into question the existence, or more accurately the uniqueness, of any such function. If workers, for example, are chosen with more care, given higher pay, and employed under conditions less 'degrading' or 'dehumanizing', the entire production function can be shifted upward as morale improves. Most or all of the marginal physical productivities $(\partial f/\partial a_1, \partial f/\partial a_2, \ldots)$ are increased. The improvements may then sometimes, but by no means always, pay for themselves after a longer or shorter time lag.

The true believer in marginal productivity should however maintain, as I do myself, that even after all these erosions and concessions, a sizeable area remains within which marginal productivity governs at least input demand (though usually not input price) and with the remaining impediments of minor quantitative importance, at least to a first approximation. Common-sensical marginal-productivity analysis retains, it seems to me, the appeal it had for Ricardo in his original treatment of extensive and intensive margins of cultivation.

Among recent developments or improvements in marginal-productivity analysis, the general-equilibrium extension in Harry Johnson's *Theory of Income Distribution* (1973, chs 7–8) stands out. Johnson works with two outputs and two inputs simultaneously, as we shall see, somewhat after the manner of his previous two-country, two-factor, two-output models in international economics. The relationship between production functions and relative shares has also been explored further, with results disappointing to those believing, as I formerly did, that the Cobb–Douglas function in particular might be used for empirical verification of marginal-productivity analysis. (It cannot, for certain mathematical reasons we shall also explore.) But the main thrust of distribution theory since, say, the mid-1960s, has been diverted at least temporarily to the measurement and exploration of inequality of the personal income distribution and to the so-called 'Two Cambridges' controversies in the 'neo-Cambridge' theory of capital.

Johnson's argument is compressible into a four-quadrant diagram in as many compound variables: relative input quantities (a/b), relative output quantities (x/y), relative input prices (p_a/p_b) and relative output prices

(p_x/p_y) (Figure 16.1). As our figure is drawn, output x is more a-intensive and less b-intensive than output y at all input price ratios. This may be seen in the first (north-east) quadrant of the figure, where D_x and D_y are separate demands from the x and y industries respectively, although the supply function S is to both industries at once. The greater a-intensity of

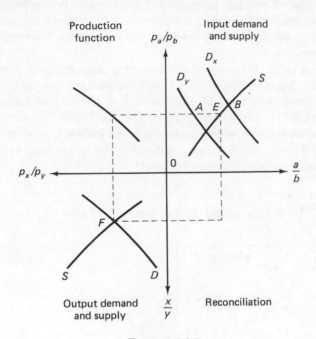

FIGURE 16.1

the x industry is indicated by D_x lying to the right of D_y at all (p_a/p_b) values. The fourth (north-west) quadrant also indicates x to be the more a-intensive output, since its relative price moves directly with that of input a.

The third (south-west) quadrant of the figure shows relative output supply and demand, with equilibrium at the focal point F. This construction assumes that relative demand D (for outputs) is independent of input prices, and hence of distributional considerations generally. This is indeed a departure from complete generality. For some choices of $(a, b; x, y)$ the departure may be important.

Drawing dashed lines from point F, both vertically upward and horizontally rightward, and using the second (south-east) quadrant as a pivot for reconciliation purposes only, we find the equilibrium relative to input quantity and price to be at point E. Note that point E, on the first quadrant, lies within the range AB. This is no accident. Were it not so, there would be unemployment of either input a (to the right of point B) or of input b (to the left of point A). Also, positioning E within the range AB implies that both the a-intensive industry x and the b-intensive industry y can continue to operate. Interesting exercises might involve working out the consequences of reversing the positions of the partial demand curves D_x and D_y, or of permitting them to cross; we cannot, however, explore these consequences here.

I do not know the history of the interesting theorem that any two-input production function that satisfies Euler's theorem and also yields constant income shares must be Cobb–Douglas as a matter of pure mathematics. Anwar Shaikh in his 'humbug' paper (Shaikh, 1980) apparently takes credit for the theorem, which is indeed not well known. I, however, learned it from William McElroy, who did not claim originality, well before Shaikh's essay appeared. A proof follows:
Assume:

$$\frac{ap_a}{x} = s \quad \text{(the relative share of input } a \text{, and also}$$

$$\left(p_a = \frac{\partial f}{\partial a}, \text{ where } p_x = 1 \right)$$

and $x = f(a, b)$, satisfying Euler's theorem. We then have:

$$\frac{a}{x} \frac{\partial x}{\partial a} = a \frac{\partial \log x}{\partial a} = s \quad \text{and} \quad \frac{\partial \log x}{\partial a} = \frac{s}{a}$$

Integrate the last (partial) differential equation:

$$\log x = s \log a + \log g(b) = \log a^s g(b)$$

where g is an arbitrary function of input b (which will be investigated further) and $\log g(b)$ is a constant of integration. Taking anti-logs, we get:

$$x = f(a, b) = a^s g(b) \tag{16.1}$$

Since Euler's theorem applies:

$$x = a \frac{\partial x}{\partial a} + b \frac{\partial x}{\partial a}$$

or, using equation (16.1):

$$a^s g(b) = a [sa^{s-1} g(b)] + b [a^s g'(b)]$$

so that:

$$\frac{1-s}{b} = \frac{g'(b)}{g(b)} \tag{16.2}$$

The left and right sides of equation (16.2) are, respectively:

$$(1-s)\,\frac{d \log b}{db} \quad \text{and} \quad \frac{d \log g(b)}{db}$$

Equate these expressions and integrate again:

$$\log g(b) = (1-s) \log b + \log x_o$$

where x_o is another arbitrary constant and $\log x_o$ a constant of integration. Taking anti-logs:

$$g(b) = x_o b^{1-s}$$

Inserting this expression into (16.1), we get at once:

$$x = x_o a^s b^{1-s}$$

which is a simple form of the Cobb–Douglas function. It is therefore not legitimate to consider the goodness of fit of a Cobb–Douglas function an empirical verification of marginal-productivity analysis when the functional distribution of income is approximately constant, since the conclusion is to some extent embodied in the mathematics as distinguished from the statistical observations.

The 'Two Cambridges' controversy has gone into remission with each Cambridge claiming victory, and with economics as a whole suffering a setback to its scientific pretensions and aspirations. In this situations we too are content to let sleeping dogs lie and lying dogs sleep, while agreeing with the heretics that:

(1) Distribution is economically indeterminate in the non-substitution models of Mrs Robinson (1956), Sraffa (1960), and likewise of Wassily Leontief (1951) if we take the national income and its composition as given.

(2) Double-switching and reswitching between capital and labour inputs cannot be ruled out reasonably *a priori*. Changes in a wage–rental ratio may cause changes of capital–labour ratios in the 'wrong' direction along part of the so-called 'factor-price frontier'. Such cases, however, seem to be pathological and occur very seldom — like the 'Giffen paradox' in demand, perhaps.

(3) If we identify marginal productivity $\partial x/\partial a$, a partial derivative, with

corresponding total derivative dx/da, as is done, for example, by Edward Nell (Nell, 1973, pp. 108–10) one obtains a 'contradiction of capitalism' comparable to the alleged 'great contradiction' of Karl Marx's *Capital*. But the two are in general difference since, if $x = f(a, b)$, we have by Young's Theorem:

$$\frac{\partial x}{\partial a} = \frac{dx}{da} - \frac{\partial x}{\partial b}\frac{db}{da}$$

(4) Capital is malleable only in the very long run, and individual goods are not malleable at all. On this point it is difficult to improve upon a well-known passage by J. B. Clark himself about the economic evolution of New England (Clark, 1899, p. 118):

> Again, capital is perfectly mobile; but capital-goods are far from being so. It is possible to take a million dollars out of one industry and put them into another. Under favorable conditions, it is possible to do this without waste. It is, however, quite impossible to take bodily out of one industry the tools that belong to it and to put them into another. The capital that was once invested in the whale fishery of New England is now, to some extent, employed in manufacturing; but the ships have not been used as cotton mills. As the vessels were worn out, the part of their earnings that might have been used to build more vessels was actually used to build mills. The nautical *form* of the capital perished; but the capital survived and, as it were, migrated from one set of material bodies to the other. There is, indeed, no limit to the ultimate power of capital, by changing its forms of embodiment, thus to change its place in the group-system of industry.

But Mrs Robinson also raises the basic question: what *is* this 'capital' that is supposed, along with labour and perhaps also land, to be an independent variable in production functions, and to have a marginal product additional to that of the other inputs embodied in it (and in which it is embodied)?[4] In what units is it measured? Is it a disparate mass of capital goods somehow evaluated at some set of base-period prices (and interest rates, and wages)? Such is the 'materialist' view. Or is capital rather a sum of money or liquid assets, the 'fundist' view? If the materialists are right, why is interest paid on unproductive money balances? If the fundists are right, how can capital be called productive at all, rather than exploitative as Marxists would have it? And if these sceptical doubts do not suffice, how can we separate the marginal product of capital accumulation from that of technical change in the forms of existing capital stock as it depreciates and obsolesces? Is it capital as such or the innovative process that is productive? If it is both, how is the increment divided?

These are difficult and legitimate questions. Mrs Robinson does not go out of her way to make them easier to answer, since she regards the entire notion of capital productivity as apologetic for capitalism. We repeat one of her better-known statements (Robinson, 1962, p. 68):

> it is still common to set up models in which quantities of 'capital' appear, without any indication of what it is supposed to be a quantity of. . . [The] problem of giving a meaning to the quantity of 'capital' is avoided by putting it into algebra. K is capital, ΔK is investment. Then what is K? Why, capital, of course. It must mean something, so let us get on with the analysis, and do not bother about these officious prigs who ask us to say what it means.

The present writer claims to be a materialist rather than a fundist, but recognizes 'Wicksell effects' (changes in capital values) as wedges between changes in quasi-rents on capital instruments and changes in interest rates. This implies that real capital values should be estimated by deflating nominal prices not only for price-level changes but also for changes in the wage–rental ratios for different types of capital goods. Interest on money balances may be explained as reflecting the productivity of the capital goods obtainable by the borrower from his loan – or by time- and liquidity-preference in case the loan is for public or private consumption, whose productivity is at most indirect.

The disentangling of innovation from accumulation in raising the productivity of the capital stock is a harder nut to crack. But consider a neoclassical production function of a modified Solow type:

$$Y = e^{gt} f[\alpha(t) K, \beta(t) N]$$

where (α, β) are improvement factors, functions of time, for capital and labour respectively. The computed capital statistics represent not K itself but $\alpha(t) K$. Improvement factors are, however, estimated regularly by experts and specialists like Dr Edward Denison of the United States Department of Commerce. They represent technical change embodied in capital instruments, usually new ones, and they can be separated out for an estimate of K itself. The exponential e^{gt} represents disembodied technical change which also affects 'old' capital and labour, as in the Solow model (Solow, 1958).

We cannot be sure that this combination, or any other combination of improvement factors and disembodied changes, will in practice produce estimates sufficiently plausible to meet Mrs Robinson's criticisms. There is disconcerting variability between the estimates of the importance of innovation as made by Robert Solow (Solow, 1958) and by Zvi Griliches (Griliches, 1967). Neither can one be sure that any massaging of the data would produce any results to justify the necessary labour and computer time on a cost–benefit basis. The writer's only objection is to the *ex ante* assumption that such devices cannot help us, or that capital-stock variables are intrinsically unmeasurable rather than being merely difficult to estimate.

NOTES

1. Charles Ferguson's *Neoclassical Theory of Production and Distribution* (1969) is both earlier and technically more advanced than my 1971 volume, but pays less attention to issues on the 'fuzzy borderland' between economics and other social sciences. Another approximate contemporary, Jan Pen's *Income Distribution* (1971), tends rather to neglect the former theory as unhelpful in the extreme.

2. Technically speaking, the relationships are:

$$(mic)_a = p_a \left(1 + \frac{1}{e_a}\right) \quad \text{and} \quad (mrp)_a = p \left(1 - \frac{1}{\eta_a}\right) \frac{\partial x}{\partial a}$$

Here x is the physical quantity of an output and a of an input; the corresponding prices are p and p_a; (mic) refers to marginal input cost and (mrp) to marginal revenue product; e_a and η_a are elasticities of input supply and output demand, respectively, to the employing firm, not to its industry. The basic source here is Joan Robinson, *Economics of Imperfect Competition*, Books 7–9.

3. This theorem as applied to economics, says that if x is an output and (a, b, c) are three inputs, with production following the function $x = f(a, b, c)$, and if the function f is linear-homogeneous with $kx = f(ka, kb, kc)$ for all positive values of k, then:

$$x = a \frac{\partial f}{\partial a} + b \frac{\partial f}{\partial b} + c \frac{\partial f}{\partial c}$$

As a corollary:

$$pc = ap_a + bp_b + cp_c$$

when, as under marginal productivity analysis:

$$p_a = p \frac{\partial f}{\partial a} \quad \text{and so on for the other inputs.}$$

4. I owe to my teacher Frank H. Knight the persistent insistence that there are no 'original' factors of production, that all inputs are on the same footing, and that 'land, labour, and capital make land, labour, and capital'.

REFERENCES

Bronfenbrenner, M. (1971) *Income Distribution Theory*, Chicago: Aldine.

Bronfenbrenner, M. (1977) 'Ten Issues in Distribution Theory', in S. Weintraub, *Modern Economic Thought*, Philadelphia: University of Pennsylvania Press.

Clark, J. B. (1899) *The Distribution of Wealth*, New York: Macmillan.

Ferguson, C. E. (1969) *Neoclassical Theory of Production and Distribution*, Cambridge: Cambridge University Press.

Griliches, Z. (1967) 'Production Functions in Manufacturing: Some Preliminary Results', in *Theory and Empirical Analysis of Production*, Studies in Income and Wealth, vol. 31, New York: Columbia University Press.

Johnson, H. G. (1973) *Theory of Income Distribution*, London: Gray-Mills.

Leontief, W. (1951) *Structure of the American Economy*, revised edn, Cambridge, Mass.: Harvard University Press.

Marshall, A. (1890) *Principles of Economics*, vol. 1, London: Macmillan.

Nell, E. J. (1973) 'The Fall of the House of Efficiency', *Annals of the American Academy* (September).

Robinson, J. (1933) *Economics of Imperfect Competition*, London: Macmillan.

Robinson, J. (1956) *The Accumulation of Capital*, London: Macmillan.

Robinson, J. (1962) *Economic Philosophy*, London: Watts.

Shaikh, A. (1980) 'Laws of Production and Laws of Algebra: Humbug II', in E. J. Nell (ed.), *Growth, Profits, and Property*, Cambridge: Cambridge University Press.

Solow, R. M. (1958) 'Technical Change and the Aggregate Production Function', *Review of Economics and Statistics* (August).

Sraffa, P. (1960) *Production of Commodities by Means of Commodities*, Cambridge: Cambridge University Press.

17 The Theory of Economic Growth: From Steady States to Uneven Development

DONALD J. HARRIS

INTRODUCTION

In considering the general character of the process of capitalist development as it has appeared historically across many different countries over a long period of time, one of its most striking characteristics is the phenomenon of uneven development. By this I mean specifically that the process is marked by persistent differences in levels and rates of economic development between different sectors of the economy.

This differentiation appears at many levels and in terms of a multiplicity of quantitative and qualitative indices. Relevant measures that sharply identify the pattern of differentiation would include, for instance, the level of labour productivity in different sectors, the level of wages, occupational and skill composition of the labour force, the degree of mechanization of production techniques, the level of profitability as measured by sectoral rates of profit, the size structure of firms, and rates of growth at the sectoral level. This phenomenon appears regardless of the level of aggregation/disaggregation of the economy, except for the extreme case of complete aggregation — in which case, of course, one cannot say anything about the structural properties of the economy. For example, it appears at the level of comparing the broad aggregates of manufacturing industry and agriculture. It appears also at the level of individual industries within the manufacturing sector. It appears on a regional level as well as on a global scale within the international economy. In this latter context, one form that it takes is the continued differentiation between underdeveloped and advanced economies, usually identified as the problem of underdevelopment.

These disparities appear from observing the economy as a whole at any given moment and over long periods of time. And while the relative position of particular sectors may change from one period to another, nevertheless, there is always a definite pattern of such differentiation. We might say, therefore, and certainly it is an implication of these observations, that these disparities are continually reproduced by the process of development of the economy. Uneven development, in this sense, is an intrinsic or inherent property of the economic process. Far from being merely transitory, it seems to be a pervasive and permanent condition.

Now, it is an equally striking fact that, when we come to examine the theoretical literature on economic growth, we find the completely opposite picture. In particular, the dominant conception of the growth process that has motivated the post-Second World War literature is one that is constructed in terms of uniform rates of expansion in output, productivity and employment in all sectors of the economy. It is largely a literature of steady-state growth.[1] Furthermore, much of existing economic theory predicts that, given enough time, many of the features of differentiation that we observe empirically would tend to wash out as a result of the operation of competitive market forces. Such differentiation should therefore be viewed only as a transitory feature of the economic process. But, in fact, we observe the opposite.

Thus, on the one side, we find a historical picture of uneven development as a persistent phenomenon. On the other side, we find a theory that essentially negates and denies this fact. It is as if the theory existed on one side and the historical reality on the other, and never the twain shall meet.

There is an obvious problematic here, which requires deep investigation. It is also necessary to try to bridge the gap. Within the brief confines of this chapter, I seek only to present an overview of some of the theoretical issues involved and, in addition, to propose an alternative path for dealing with analysis of the problem.

STEADY-STATE GROWTH

It is useful to consider, first of all, what if any is the real achievement of the work that has been done on steady-state growth. I wish to propose that there is a real analytical significance to be attached to that series of exercises despite the fact that they may seem, on the face of it, to negate interesting and important historical questions, and despite the fact that it now appears fashionable to dismiss that work. In seeking to go beyond that work it is important to be able to recognize its achievement and its failures in order the better to negotiate the transition to a more adequate analysis.

The significance of the work on models of steady-state growth is that it was a necessary first step in developing a full-fledged theoretical analysis of the process of economic growth. It provides a logical starting point by considering, as a first approximation, so to speak, the simplest possible case of growth, that is, a case of simple quantitative expansion with all proportions remaining the same or expansion by quantitative replication. The analysis then examines the consistency conditions that are required, under this simplifying assumption, for the sustaining of the expansionary process.

Evidently, this analysis focuses upon the idea of aggregate expansion or of *growth as a process pertaining to the economy as a whole*, where the individual component parts are, for the purpose of simplification, assumed to grow in proportion to one another. In this respect the analysis abstracts from the process of uneven growth. It simplifies or abstracts in order to deal with certain elementary interrelationships and essential properties of an expanding economy that have to be understood for adequately characterizing the process of expansion in its full complexity. This in itself is a defensible methodological procedure. It conforms to a process of scientific analysis through successive approximation, by which one starts off with simple cases, examines them in depth, and then, through a subsequent development, incorporates the complexities that need to be understood in moving to a more concrete level.

Moreover, there are genuine theoretical insights that were gained from this analysis. The chief such insight was the identification of the necessary macroeconomic balancing conditions that must hold in an expanding economy if the economy is to sustain its overall rate of expansion. By considering the simple models, it was possible to isolate and identify exactly the quantitative form of those balancing conditions and to analyse their implications for the concrete workings of the economy.

In general it was shown that there is a definite condition of macroeconomic balance in the economy that derives from the requirement of balance in the flow of investment and saving (or of total expenditure and income). It is a condition that, furthermore, may be considered to impose itself on the workings of the economy independently of the underlying microeconomic structure. This idea was central to the argument developed by both Keynes (1936) and Kalecki (1971) concerning the forces that govern the operation of the capitalist economy. A similar idea is also to be found in Marx's analysis. The work on models of steady-state growth extended and generalized this idea to the context of growth and through disaggregation of the economic structure. It is useful to examine in some detail the main line of development of the idea in order to specify more sharply its theoretical content.

In its most elementary form, the macroeconomic balancing condition is simply that:

$$I = S \tag{17.1}$$

or the total value of planned spending on investment I is equal to the value of planned saving S. Now, assume that there is a constant average propensity to save out of income, $S = sY$, and that the level of aggregate investment is given at I^*. Then it follows immediately that:

$$Y = \frac{1}{s} I^* \tag{17.2}$$

Thus, there is a necessary level of income that will insure that enough saving is forthcoming out of that income to match the investment that is taking place. That level of income is given by the size of the multiplier $1/s$ and by the level of investment. The actual level of income must adjust to that level for balance in the flow of income and expenditure to be achieved. This is so, no matter what the intentions of the individual agents in the economy might be. If, for instance, they sought by individual action to increase their wealth and income by increasing their rate of saving, the overall effect would be to reduce aggregate income. This is to say that there is an aggregate condition that dictates the possible outcomes in the economy at any given moment and to which the economy will adjust, given certain underlying behavioural properties. That condition would be enforced by the movement in employment and income which would come about if it were not satisfied. It is therefore a condition that dominates, or even contradicts, the intentions of the individual actors. In this respect it is a macroeconomic condition that itself exerts a powerful influence on the microeconomic actions taking place in the economy and is not merely an aggregation of those microeconomic actions. This argument presupposes a necessary role for the relations of money and credit in the economy which, for completeness, would need to be made explicit but is left aside here.

This is a result that comes from the simplest Keynesian model. It is this insight, stated starkly and simply here, which became incorporated into the literature on steady-state growth.

Consider the extension of this idea in the form of the argument developed by Harrod (1948) and Domar (1957). In particular assume as before a uniform saving rate and, in addition, that there is a given ratio of capital to income $K/Y = v$. Then, from equation (17.1), it follows that

$$g = \frac{I}{K} = \frac{s}{v}$$

Here it is recognized that investment both adds to productive capacity in the amount specified by the proportion v and generates the effective demand (through the multiplier) that allows utilization of that productive capacity. In this context, the requirement of balance between investment and saving now entails that there is a necessary rate of growth (of both capital and income) at which the economy must expand if the capitalists' expectations about profitability of their investment are to be justified through generation of demand sufficient to ensure that productive capacity is fully utilized. This is to say that, under the given conditions, there is one and only one growth rate at which the economy could settle if effective demand is to be forthcoming to match the growing productive capacity and if, consequently, capitalists' investment plans are to be justified. Harrod called this the 'warranted rate of growth'.

This is a statement of a macroeconomic balancing condition that must hold, in this case, if the economy is to undergo a smooth process of sustained expansion. It is a result that gives rise to a definite understanding of the dynamic motion of the economy. The argument is that, if this condition is not satisfied, then there are certain necessary adjustments, given the underlying behavioural properties of the economy, that the economy must undergo. In particular, it was Harrod's view that the economy would tend to diverge from this path and to undergo various forms of crises as it fluctuates through booms and recessions.

A large part of the subsequent development of growth theory centred around the further analysis of this basic point. In this process, modifications, qualifications and extensions were made to the specific results of the Harrod–Domar analysis. Still, the basic thrust of the analysis remained the same. The macroeconomic balancing condition continued to serve as the basis from which was derived the form of motion of the economy and the associated adjustments that the economy undergoes in the course of its expansion. Two such modifications are worth considering here, both of which involve a degree of disaggregation of the economic structure.

One modification was made by some of the post-Keynesian authors, following earlier contributions by Kalecki.[2] It was argued that the aggregate saving in the economy is actually a composite of the saving out of profits and the saving out of wages. Thus instead of the idea of a uniform average propensity to save, one must recognize that it is the distribution of income that governs saving, given the different saving propensities of wage-earners and profit recipients. In that case it follows that the appropriate macroeconomic condition is now:

$$g = \frac{s_r R + s_w W}{K} = (s_r - s_w)r + \frac{s_w}{v}, \ s_r > s_w \qquad (17.4)$$

where total income is divided into profits R and wages W, the overall rate of profit is r, and the capital–income ratio v is assumed to be given. Here the warranted growth rate is uniquely related to the rate of profit, given the saving propensities out of profits and wages and the capital–income ratio.

Thus, a new implication of the macroeconomic balancing condition emerges when saving is disaggregated into its major components, recognizing that there is a difference in economic behaviour governing each of the components. A different requirement must now be satisfied in order for the economy to sustain its overall rate of expansion. In particular, the overall profit rate, as an average of the rate that individual firms earn through their mark-ups, must be at a certain level, given the other magnitudes in equation (17.4), in order that the balancing condition can be satisfied. A necessary structural connection is thereby established between the overall rate of expansion of the economy and the average profitability of firms. This connection must hold because it is the condition that ensures that there is just enough saving forthcoming out of the total pool of profits and wages, given the saving rates out of profits and wages respectively, to match the investment that is occurring when the economy as a whole is expanding at a certain rate. This condition is independent of the underlying microeconomic relationships. Specifically, it is independent of the individual pattern of pricing by firms, hence of their respective market positions. But those microeconomic relationships must be consistent with it in order for the process of expanded reproduction to be smoothly carried out. If they are not consistent, complex adjustments would have to take place in order to bring them into line. The literature is, however, seriously deficient in its analysis of the process by which these adjustments are supposed to occur.

So, here again we have a rather striking result, a result that says that macroeconomic forces, associated with the balancing condition for investment and saving, exert a powerful influence on the underlying micro-

economic relationships to bring them into line with requirements of the
accumulation process as a whole. That is a result that comes, in this case,
from disaggregation of saving into its components. It is reinforced when a
second modification is introduced so as to take explicit account of the
structure of the economy through disaggregation by individual commodity-
producing sectors.

To illustrate the argument, let production activities be represented in
terms of the familiar linear model of production.[3] Competitive conditions
are assumed so that the rate of profit is uniform and the wage rate is the
same for homogeneous labour. The prices of production that would prevail
under those conditions are given by the vector P, where:

$$P = a'_O w (1 + r) + (\delta + rI) A' P \qquad (17.5)$$

These prices cover costs of production consisting of wages, plus depreciation, plus profits calculated on the total capital advanced in the form of
wages and capital-good inputs. This condition entails a definite set of
prices consistent with the going rate of profit and technical conditions of
production. Accordingly, we can derive a functional relationship such that:

$$\frac{P}{w} = [I - A'(\delta + rI)]^{-1} a'_O (1 + r) = A_O(r) \qquad (17.6)$$

In such an economy, output is disaggregated into a vector X of specified
commodities and the capital stock is disaggregated into the component
elements required to produce those commodities, AX. The output–capital
ratio for the economy as a whole can be found by aggregating those outputs
and capital stocks evaluated at the prevailing prices to get $Y/K = P'X/P'AX$.
With this specification of the economic structure, the macroeconomic
balancing condition now becomes:

$$g = (s_r - s_w)r + s_w \frac{A'_0(r) X}{A'_0(r) AX} \qquad (17.7)$$

Evidently, a further requirement is established by this new condition. Not
only must there be a definite level of the rate of profit (here, the uniform
rate that is earned in the individual sectors and enforced by competition)
but in addition, there must be simultaneously a definite pattern of prices
at that rate of profit so as to ensure that the associated capital–output
ratio is exactly such as to be consistent with macroeconomic balance. A
direct connection is thereby established between the overall rate of expansion of the economy and the underlying microeconomic relationships
through the price system necessary to support the balancing condition.[4]

This connection was, in a sense, disguised in the previous analysis because of the aggregation which that analysis entailed. Once the microeconomic relationships out of which those aggregates emerge is specified then that connection appears with full force. The fact is, also, that the macroeconomic condition continues to hold even after all the relevant microeconomic relationships are introduced. It would continue to hold no matter what the degree of disaggregation of such relationships. In this respect, the macroeconomic condition is independent of the degree of disaggregation of the economic structure. It is a condition that the microeconomic relationships themselves must satisfy. This necessity, in turn, derives from the requirement of balance in the accumulation process as a whole. Thus, the original insight that macroeconomic forces influence the microeconomic relationships in the economy continues to be preserved.

These relations emerge most clearly in the context of steady-state growth because it is in that context that they can be most readily defined and quantitatively specified. By virtue of the conditions assumed to characterize the steady state, concepts like the rate of growth, the rate of profit, the value of capital and of income, net saving and net investment, have a clear and unambiguous meaning. Outside of the steady state they are more difficult to grasp. It is therefore a matter of great analytical convenience to be able to work out the analysis in this context.

However, this advantage is gained at considerable cost. The cost is that, for the purpose of constructing the simplified conception of a steady state, the analysis takes as given much that is of crucial interest from the standpoint of a theory of economic growth. Most striking in this regard is the assumption that the overall growth rate itself is given by factors that are themselves exogenous to the growth process, in particular by the exogenous growth rates of labour supply and of productivity due to technical change. Even the form of technical change, in the particular sense of its factor saving bias, is arbitrarily specified to fit the preconceived requirements of steady-state growth. Similarly, saving rates, though recognized to be dependent on behavioural factors associated with the distribution of income, are taken as given for each category of distribution. The sectoral composition of output is also given and unchanging, both because of a fixed and uniform growth rate and because implicitly or explicitly income elasticities of demand are fixed and equal to unity. Furthermore, since the rate of technical change is uniform across all sectors, the relative conditions of productivity as between different sectors remain the same. Consequently, the whole structure of the economy remains fixed. Steady-state growth is, thus, growth within a fixed economic structure. It is growth without structural change. The deficiency of this analysis is, therefore, that it ignores altogether the necessity of structural change and hence fails to give an account for the process that generates the observed and continuing pattern of uneven development.

As a qualification to these remarks, it must be added that the existing literature is not lacking in exceptions to the general rule, at least with respect to treatment of one or another component of the analysis. One such exception, for instance, to the general idea of an exogenous growth rate directly limited by labour supply, is the well-known model of von Neumann (1945). In this model the overall growth rate is endogenously determined as a matter of a maximization decision subject to a given real wage and the available methods of production. But, even here, once the maximal path has been chosen, the economy grows along it within a fixed structure. Moreover, the condition of a fixed wage, in-so-far as it is taken to represent the requirements of a labour-feeding process with labour as its output, may be considered tantamount to labour-supply limited growth.

Another exception is the recent work of Pasinetti (1981) which makes a significant advance in the direction of formalizing a conception of uneven growth. This is achieved through adaptation of the linear model of production so as to allow for unequal rates of growth in the production coefficients of different sectors and in the coefficients of final demand. It is shown that the growth process under these conditions systematically generates a chronic tendency to disproportionality among sectors and generalized unemployment. In many ways the analysis successfully reproduces observable features of the historical process of growth and provides an interesting taxonomic scheme for representing patterns of uneven growth. But it does not give an account of what internal mechanism drives the process and makes it intrinsically a process of uneven growth. Though recognized to be uneven at the sectoral level, growth is again a matter of the exogenous growth of demand, productivity and labour supply.[5]

If we consider for a moment the recurrent idea that the growth rate of labour supply is exogenously given, this idea evidently does violence to historically observed experience. As shown for instance in the study by Kindleberger (1967) of post-Second World War growth in Western Europe, there is no strict sense in which the labour supply is exogenously fixed or bounded even for the most rapidly expanding advanced capitalist economies.[6] This is because they are able to draw upon a large inflow of labour from other capitalist economies, and in particular from the relatively underdeveloped economies. One might say, then, that the process of uneven development generates its own labour supply. This is so in-so-far as the rapidly growing sectors are able to draw upon the labour supply available in the backward sectors. The process of displacement of labour in those sectors may itself be a consequence of the expansion of capital into the backward sectors. There is, then, one may hypothesize, a two-sided process by which uneven development allows expansion to feed on itself. This alternative conception makes it possible to free the growth rate from its moorings in the exogenous growth of labour supply and, instead, to root it in the accumulation process itself conceived as being intrinsically a process of uneven development.

THE ANALYSIS OF UNEVEN DEVELOPMENT

In order to go beyond the analysis of steady-state growth, it is necessary to start by recognizing the intrinsic character of the individual firm as an expansionary unit of capital.[7] Growth is the strategic objective on the part of the firm. This urge to expand is not a matter of choice. Rather, it is a necessity enforced upon the firm by its market position and by its existence within a world of firms where each must grow in order to survive. It is reinforced also by sociological factors, such as the social status and power associated with being the owner, director, or manager of an expanding enterprise. It is this character of the firm that constitutes the driving force behind the process of expansion of the economy.[8]

This is a crucial starting point because it establishes the idea of growth as the outcome of a process that is driven by active agents and not by exogenous factors. In particular, in the context of the capitalist economy, growth is the outcome of the self-directed and self-organizing activity of firms, each seeking to expand and to improve its competitive position in relation to the rest. Once this principle is recognized it becomes possible to move towards an understanding of the problem of uneven development.

The imperative of growth impels the firm constantly to seek out new investment opportunities wherever they are to be found. Such investment may occur in existing product lines, in new products and processes, or in the takeover of existing firms. The emergence of growth centres or leading sectors is a reflection of this underlying process. It is a consequence of the effort on the part of many firms to rush into those spheres in which a margin of profitability in excess of the average exists in order to capture new investment opportunities.[9] Such new spheres are always being opened up as a consequence of the ongoing innovative activity of firms and the competitive interactions among them. It is this constant flux, consisting of the emergence of new growth centres, their rapid expansion relative to existing sectors, and the relative decline of other sectors, that shows up in the economy as a whole as uneven development.

The form that this process takes, as it appears at the level of particular industries and product lines, has been well documented through empirical research. These studies show that the growth of many new industries and products follows a life-cycle pattern that may be represented by an S-shaped curve as in Figure 17.1. There are correspondingly three phases of

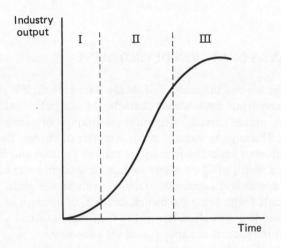

FIGURE 17.1 *Life-cycle of an industry*

expansion. In the initial phase, total output of the new industry is a minute share of the overall aggregate output in the economy and the rate of growth of output is low. This is followed by a phase of rapid growth in which this sector's output expands rapidly relative to overall output and its share of aggregate output grows. Then there is a third phase in which the sector reaches a threshold beyond which the growth rate tends to level off and perhaps to decline.

Of course the process does not come to an end at that point. We must understand this sequence, schematically described here, as but a small segment of the time sequence characterizing the historical evolution of the economy. Given that firms are growing, making profits, and seeking to continue to grow, it would be necessary for them, having entered into phase III, to launch out into new sectors. They will therefore actively seek to find new products that will initiate a corresponding new sequence.

It follows that we can map out the dynamic evolution of the economy in terms of *a sequential process*, where the overall growth is accountable for on the basis of (i) the individual growth of particular new sectors, (ii) the growth of pre-existing sectors each of which is growing at a different rate depending on the particular phase reached in its life-cycle, and (iii) the constant accretion of new sectors into the economy owing to the introduction of new products.

The existence of a life-cycle pattern of industrial growth is a significant stylized fact for the purpose of constructing a theory of uneven development. But the question remains as to how this particular pattern is itself to be explained.

We can go part of the way to understanding the anatomy of the process if we take account of the technological innovation process tied up with it. In this connection it is helpful to draw upon Kuznets's suggestive characterization of general features of the innovation process for 'major' innovations. Specifically, Kuznets (1979) identifies a sequence of four distinct phases as constituting the life-cycle of an innovation. It begins with a *preconception* phase in which necessary scientific and technological preconditions are laid. This is followed by a phase of *initial application* involving the first successful commercial application of the innovation. Then comes the *diffusion* phase marked by spread in adoption and use of the innovation throughout the economy along with continued improvements in quality and cost. Finally, there is a phase of *slowdown* and *obsolescence* in which further potential of the innovation is more or less exhausted and even some contraction may occur. This taxonomy is restricted by Kuznets to the case of 'major' innovations. For our purposes, that restriction could be regarded as appropriate from the standpoint of relevance of an innovation to the overall process of growth. The taxonomy itself is useful and suggestive in pointing to a certain internal logic of the innovation process related to 'the purely technological problems in breaking through to an effective invention and resolving the difficulties in development, prototype production, etc, . . . [and] . . . the complementary and other organizational and social adjustments that would assure adequate diffusion and economic success' (pp. 64-5). These factors determine the time duration of the process and the magnitude of its impact, especially in the second and third phase, through the evolution of costs and profitability of the innovation.

The anatomy of this process can be further understood by taking account of its connection with the changing firm-structure of the industry. In particular, it has been observed that, for many industries, there is a proliferation of small firms in phase I of the industry's life-cycle. But as the diffusion of the product occurs and growth speeds up, there is a 'shaking out' process by which many of the smaller firms disappear and the available market is concentrated in the remaining firms. When the industry reaches 'maturity', in phase III, there is a high degree of concentration.

This association between industry life-cycle and firm-structure of the industry suggests that the dynamic of expansion through innovation is simultaneously a process of the concentration of capital. Further investigation of this link may provide a key to understanding the internal mechanisms and forces that feed the expansion process and account for its character as a process of uneven development. Without going into these in depth, it may be suggested here that there are a number of factors at work.

One is the phenomenon of economies of scale in production and marketing. Such economies give to the larger firms a decisive advantage in exploiting an innovation. Small firms may well have unique advantages in the research and development phase of innovation and, in many cases, are observed to lead the process in that phase. But they often lose out to the larger firms at the stage of standardization, mass production and mass marketing of the product. The larger firms, on their part, may gain from foregoing the risks associated with the first phase and choosing to enter at a later stage through adoption of a proven innovation or takeover of a successful firm.

Another factor is the power of finance. The capacity to command finance is a powerful lever in the expansion process, deriving its significance from the substantial financial outlays involved in product development, production, and marketing that have to be made well in advance of sales. This capacity depends both on the generation of internal funds and on access to external funds. Large firms have an advantage here because of their larger profits, to begin with, and because of their superior ability to borrow.

Because of these complementary relationships one might say that it is the large firms that drive the process, at least within certain phases of it. It is still a process that is driven by the expansion of firms, but it turns out that some firms are more equal than others in this process.

What role is to be assigned to demand as a factor in this process? At the level of individual consumer products or industries, a common conception is that demand acts as an autonomous factor with a direct influence on the life-cycle pattern of evolution of the product. That influence is exerted in the early phase of introduction of a new product because of an element of resistance due to 'habit' formed in a customary pattern of consumption. It is exerted also in the maturity phase because of the operation of 'saturation effects' in consumption. But there are reasons to doubt the strength and effectiveness of such factors, as well as their supposed autonomy.

First of all, in an economy undergoing regular and rapid change, it is not evident what role there is for habit except for the habit of change itself. The experience of and adaptation to change may create a high degree of receptivity to change. What then becomes decisive in the evolution of demand for consumer goods is the growth of income, and the changing relative prices and quality of products.

Second, in-so-far as these latter factors are crucial to the formation of demand, it may be argued that there is a certain self-fulfilling aspect of the expansionary process at the level of industry demand. In particular investment generates the demand that provides the market for the new products that investment creates. This occurs in two ways. First, investment generates income both directly in the sector undergoing rapid expansion and indirectly, via backward and forward linkages, through the stimulation of demand and investment in other sectors. In this respect, structural interdependence in the economy at the level of both production and expenditure patterns allows for the possibility of a certain mutual provisioning of markets when expansion takes place on a broad front. Second, as a new product unfolds through the stages of the innovation process, it undergoes both improvements in quality and a decline in price relative to other products. This development provides a substantive basis for making inroads into the market for existing closely related products and hence promotes demand through a shift from 'old' to 'new' products. It is perhaps this *shift effect* that is mistakenly identified as a *saturation effect* by adopting a one-sided and static view of a dynamic and interdependent process.

Of course, though investment generates demand in these two ways, there is no guarantee here that in the aggregate there is always sufficient demand for all products. In determining the overall expansion, the macroeconomic balancing condition would continue to play a definite role, albeit in a modified form. This brings us, now, to a crucial point.

All of the preceding argument concerns the pattern of sectoral growth viewed at the level of individual industries, products, and firms. There is nothing in that argument to indicate how the pattern of sectoral growth translates into aggregate expansion at the level of the economy as a whole, or how the various sectoral patterns fit together to form a complete whole. This is a substantive problem requiring further analytical treatment on its own terms. Its significance derives from the recognition that the economy as a whole is not just the sum of its parts. Hence, the motion of the economy cannot simply be deduced from the movement of its parts.

One aspect of this problem is associated with the macroeconomic balancing condition. It is here that the argument comes full circle, so to speak, back to the problem of macroeconomic balance. This problem, as we have seen, was a central focus of the analysis of steady-state growth. It appears, now, that it cannot be escaped in making the transition to the analysis of uneven development. This must be so in-so-far as this problem has the significance that was claimed for it in the previous discussion. Of course, the particular form and meaning of the macroeconomic balancing condition now has to be made specific to the changed context of the analysis.

Another aspect of the problem is associated with the manifold and complex ways in which growth in one sector mutually conditions and is conditioned by growth in all other sectors. Such mutual interaction is a necessary consequence of economic interdependence. The existence of such interactions implies that there is a certain cumulative effect intrinsic in the growth process. Understanding the exact mechanisms through which this effect operates is one of the central analytical problems for the analysis of uneven development.

CONCLUSION

The preceding discussion seeks to propose the analysis of uneven development as an alternative path that offers a significant potential for breaking through the narrow limits of the existing theory of steady-state growth and advancing towards a historically and empirically relevant theory. Various components of the analysis have been identified which point the directions for further work. Much remains to be done in fleshing out the general conception and setting it on a firmer theoretical and empirical footing. Some results of this effort by the present author are to be reported in a forthcoming volume (*The Theory of Uneven Development*, in preparation).

NOTES

1. A detailed review and critique of the analytic foundations of this work is presented in Harris, 1978, the general thrust of which is to point to the need for a *theory of uneven development* in order to transcend the conception of steady-state growth.
2. On this see, in particular, Kaldor, 1960; Pasinetti, 1974; and Robinson, 1962.
3. Production is represented by the $(n \times n)$ matrix A of capital good requirements, the vector a_O of direct labour requirements, and the diagonal matrix δ of depreciation rates. The details of the analysis are worked out in Harris, 1978.

4. Allowance may be made for a 'choice of technique' if it is assumed that there are alternative methods of production. In that case, the choice of technique would also have to be consistent with the macroeconomic balancing conditions. This feature of the problem is the primary focus of neoclassical growth theory. But uniqueness and stability of the neoclassical solution are not guaranteed, once heterogeneity of the production structure is recognized.
5. For a further elaboration of these remarks, see Harris, 1982.
6. On this, see also Cornwall, 1977.
7. Various efforts have been made to develop a theory of the firm on this basis. See, for instance, Penrose, 1959; Baumol, 1959; and Marris, 1967.
8. This is a fundamental insight expressed in Marx's conception of the general circuit of capital, as is also the idea that there are contradictory relations entailed in the reproduction process of the system of individual circuits. For an elaboration of these ideas, see Harris, 1979.
9. This idea is an essential feature of the Schumpeterian conception of the development process. See Schumpeter, 1934, and the important new contribution of Nelson and Winter, 1982.

REFERENCES

Baumol, W. J. (1959) *Business Behavior, Value and Growth*, New York; Harcourt, Brace & World.

Cornwall, J. (1977) *Modern Capitalism, Its Growth and Transformation*, New York: St Martin's Press.

Domar, E. D. (1957) *Essays in the Theory of Economic Growth*, New York: Oxford University Press.

Harris, D. J. (1978) *Capital Accumulation and Income Distribution*, Stanford: Stanford University Press.

Harris, D. J. (1979) 'Value, Exchange, and Capital', unpublished manuscript, Department of Economics, Stanford University.

Harris, D. J. (1982) 'Structural Change and Economic Growth, A Review Article', *Contributions to Political Economy*, 1: 25–45.

Harrod, R. F. (1948) *Towards a Dynamic Economics*, London: Macmillan.

Kaldor, N. (1960) *Essays on Economic Stability and Growth*, Glencoe, Ill.: Free Press.

Kalecki, M. (1971) *Selected Essays on the Dynamics of the Capitalist Economy, 1933–1970*, New York: Cambridge University Press.

Keynes, J. M. (1936) *The General Theory of Employment, Interest, and Money*, London: Macmillan.

Kindleberger, C. P. (1967) *Europe's Postwar Growth: The Role of Labor Supply*, Cambridge, Mass.: Harvard University Press.

Kuznets, S. (1979) *Growth, Population, and Income Distribution, Selected Essays*, New York: Norton.

Marris, R. (1967) *The Economic Theory of 'Managerial' Capitalism*, London: Macmillan.

Nelson, R. R. and Winter, S. G. (1982) *An Evolutionary Theory of Economic Change*, Cambridge, Mass.: Harvard University Press.
Neumann, J. von (1945) 'A Model of General Economic Equilibrium', *Review of Economic Studies*, 13: 1–9.
Pasinetti, L. L. (1974) *Growth and Income Distribution*, New York: Cambridge University Press.
Pasinetti, L. L. (1981) *Structural Change and Economic Growth*, New York: Cambridge University Press.
Penrose, E. T. (1959) *The Theory of the Growth of the Firm*, Oxford: Blackwell.
Robinson, Joan (1962) *Essays in the Theory of Economic Growth*, London: Macmillan.
Schumpeter, J. (1934) *The Theory of Economic Development*, Cambridge, Mass.: Harvard University Press.

18 Some Observations on the Engine and Fuel of Economic Growth

G. R. FEIWEL

The economic merit of a system depends on the valuation scale and the time-frame adopted. An economy's resources could be used for various ends, for good or evil, fully or partly, more or less efficiently at a point of time or in the long run, with greater or smaller capacity to create new and destroy the old, with varied arrangements for resource allocation, with varied institutional and ideological adjustments to change, and with divergent consequences for the quality of life. The kind of society we want and the ends of economic activity we must choose ourselves; our function as economists is to enlighten our fellow citizens about what can and cannot be done. Regretfully in matters of economic policy the don'ts are often much clearer than the do's.

Clearly people do not live by economics alone, but the ends to which resources are deployed and the technical and social arrangements for production, exchange and distribution are weighty components affecting the population's well-being, social consciousness and quality of performance. In final analysis how to enhance the real progress of society is what economics is (or should be) all about. But there is a wide spectrum of perceptions about real progress and how, if at all, it is to be promoted.

The scope and character of intervention (the extent to which the *laissez-faire* system is to be redesigned) depends, *inter alia*, on the aims of the economy and on the political feasibility constraints. To be sure the character and intensity of 'correctives' (deliberate design or planning) depends not only on the postulated aims; economic actors evince specific preferences for given policy instruments and institutions. Thus, whereas we tend to treat institutions and instruments as variables in the search for optimal solutions, the degree of freedom in changing existing arrangements is much narrower than is commonly assumed. Often particular institutions are components of the preference function itself, thus more or less predetermining particular solutions. Economists tend to exaggerate the scope for choice in designing and executing policy.

Growth, efficiency, avoidance of inflation, external balance, etc. are not ultimate ends of economic activity, but merely means for accomplishing the end(s), however determined. The ultimate question is: growth (efficiency) for what and for whom? (Growth and efficiency do matter if only because a more efficacious husbandry of resources enables the economy to achieve a higher realization of the ends of economic activity). Thus economic growth should be viewed as the consequence rather than the end of a prudent economic strategy that takes both the long and short views.

The aim of economic activity *ought* to be to deploy economic resources to ensure and sustain meaningful full employment and to enhance over time the living standard and quality of life of the population as a whole. This is not tantamount to maximization of immediate consumption and pleasures, mainly because without a prudent accumulation of capital, no sustained improvement in living standards and working conditions could take place. The intertemporal allocation of resources between present needs and pleasures and those of the future is one of those formidable, largely unsolved, questions of political economy. One of the perennial issues is what determines the economic actors' willingness to produce and trade and how they react to economic stimuli and conditions – the forces that determine distributive shares (in the form of wages, interest, and profits) and their effects on the temporal and intertemporal allocation and utilization of resources.

Technically the growth of the economy's capacity to produce is limited by the growth of the labour force (resource constraints) and productivity. The latter is considered to be determined by trends in technical and organizational progress – a function of the allocation of resources to those activities and factors facilitating diffusion of knowledge, mobility of resources, and international flows – factor substitution, economies of scale, labour skills, education and motivation, quantity and quality of capital, and supplies and quality of natural resources. The analysis tends to concentrate on the technical aspects of production and to underrate the social relations in the process of production, exchange, and distribution, and also to slight the issue of effective demand over time as a factor limiting production. There seems to be an overemphasis on the quantitative, at the expense of the qualitative, aspects of growth of production.

For a variety of reasons after the Second World War a high premium was placed on the rate of economic growth. But the highest attainable growth rate cannot be identified as the touchstone of economic progress. The growth rate as such is essentially a quantitative measure of economic change that understates the critical and refractory qualitative dimensions. A high growth rate of output (aggregate or per capita) can hardly be the sole desideratum; nor is maximization of the growth rate a sensible aim of economic policy.

Conventional GNP (or its variants) is a measure of production and not one of consumption or of economic welfare. Nor is welfare yielded only by produced goods and services. Centring on the growth rate as a criterion of progress detracts attention from the following: composition of production, consumption, utilization of labour and other resources, the quality of life, income distribution, and costs (including the non-material costs) of achieving output. A significant share of production may well be illusory from the standpoint of enhancing welfare; some of it may even be deleterious or perilous.

There are different ways of achieving identical growth rates. These ways are important for society not only because they bear on working and living conditions at a given time; but in-so-far as they affect the will to produce, creativity, and future knowledge and skills, these ways also influence future growth rates and living standards. Certain ways may tend to produce transitory high growth rates, but they may be particularly destructive to the human element − an indictment against them not only on moral grounds but also on economic ones.

All this is not an accolade to those who argue that higher growth rates of GNP result in 'gross national pollution'; that they are achieved at the price of irreparable decay of environment and welfare, and that *ipso facto* a smaller GNP would result in 'greater national pleasure'. This is not the place to resolve the controversy about the possibility, desirability, and necessity of economic growth. Whatever the pros and cons are, growth does matter, particularly to those who have not yet experienced its delights and banes. Moreover, in practice it is difficult to make sweeping changes in allocation of resources and distribution of income. Such allocations are more feasible from the increment of GNP. Indeed, a smaller GNP will only aggravate the social demerits of a system.

Classical economics was largely about economic growth, its determinants and mechanism. The perceptions of the propellers of economic growth and the benefits derived therefrom have shifted over time. Nowadays we pay much less attention to accumulation of physical capital and more to technical dynamism, to investment in human capital, and to the non-investment sources of growth. The economy's *modus operandi* plays a significant role in affecting the willingness to produce, work performance, and the innovative and entrepreneurial activity of economic actors. Thus the powerful classical approach that assigned the key role to accumulation is extended by attributing varied strengths to such factors as scientific and engineering progress, investment in human beings, motivation of economic actors, system of rewards and incentives, income distribution, resource allocation policies, macroeconomic conditions, and the entire framework of the economy's working arrangements.

A historian of contemporary economic thought will observe that in the main economists' preoccupation with business cycles before the Second World War shifted to problems of economic growth in the postwar years, without sufficient attempt at integrating these two approaches. Technically very refined theories of growth were constructed that were quite remote from the world we live in. At this juncture, it is essential again to underline the fundamental point that institutional arrangements are an intrinsic component of economic dynamics. There is a definite need to restructure economic theory so as to integrate macro and micro; to relate growth theory to business-cycle theory; and to give up the concept of a universal growth theory; rather, to develop theories that would take into account institutional arrangements that derive from the social and political systems.

To accentuate the divergence of views regarding the engine of economic growth and the fuel that may be used to propel it, this chapter reviews some of the important classical and modern analyses of growth propellers and constraints; it focuses on the economic and institutional factors promoting dynamic efficiency; and it briefly outlines two basic approaches to stimulate growth; one that concentrates exclusively on supply and the other that integrates supply and demand. Or, from a somewhat different vantage point, one that uses a microeconomic approach to macroeconomic problems and the other that integrates both macro and micro approaches. Basically, the approaches differ in their perceptions of the dynamics and *modus operandi* of a modern economy, the range and effectiveness of policy options, and the elasticity of response of agents to economic stimuli. Economic models of the first approach essentially distort reality if they do not perceive the economy as subject to trend, fluctuations, stochastic disturbances, and major market failures, in contrast to the second approach that does attempt to incorporate these factors in its models.

DRIVING FORCES AND ENVIRONMENT OF ECONOMIC GROWTH

To a student of economic theory and policy the concern with the economy's productive capacity, and hence with the factors that promote or inhibit its expansion and utilization, is an economic problem *par excellence* that has a long and distinguished history. Review of the literature exceeds the scope of this chapter, but a certain retrospect is necessary.

Classical economics stressed production, productivity growth and expansion of the economy's productive potential. To point out just a few strands: the full title of Adam Smith's classic is *An Inquiry into the Nature and Causes of the Wealth of Nations*. By 'wealth of nations' Smith meant flow of production. He accentuated capital accumulation as the mainspring of economic growth under the institutional arrangements of a competitive private enterprise market economy. He perceived competition as part of the growth process and conceived the allocation problem within the context of a dynamic economy, with changing endowments of resources, techniques and tastes. Ricardo shifted the focus to the problem of partition of national product among social classes. But it was not so much the question of income distribution that preoccupied him as the consequences of shifts in distribution on the accumulation of capital. In contrast with Ricardo, Malthus was concerned with the accumulation-consumption dilemma: the detrimental effects of excessive accumulation on labour's will to produce and of excessive consumption on the economy's growth potential:

> No considerable and continued increase in wealth could possibly take place without that degree of frugality which occasions capital formation. . . and creates a balance of produce over consumption; but it is quite obvious. . . that the principle of saving, pushed to excess, would destroy the motive to production. . . If consumption exceeds production, the capital of the country must be gradually destroyed from its want of power to produce; if production be in great excess above consumption, the motive to accumulate and produce must cease from want of will to consume. The two extremes are obvious: and it follows that there must be some intermediate point, though the resources of political economy may not be able to ascertain it, where taking into consideration both the power to produce and the will to consume, the encouragement to the increase of wealth is greatest (Malthus, 1936 [1820], pp. 6-7):

John Stuart Mill argued that separate laws govern production and distribution in contrast to the long-standing and perenially revived argument that inequality of income distribution (in favour of capital) is a necessary component of rapid growth.

Marx provided us with the enthralling vision of the complex capitalist system in motion, under its own steam and in historical time, increasingly hampered by class conflict. He treated the institutional arrangements and social relations as key determinants of the system's dynamics and as 'variables' in the problem of resource utilization. He also pointed to the difficulties of sustaining technical progress that would entail raising the capital–output ratio and a falling rate of profit.

The rationale and *raison d'être* of capitalist accumulation before the First World War was insightfully articulated by Keynes (1919, pp. 16–17):

> Society was so framed as to throw a great part of the increased income into the control of the class least likely to consume it. The new rich of the nineteenth century were not brought up to large expenditures, and preferred the power which investment gave them to the pleasures of immediate consumption. In fact, it was precisely the inequality of the distribution of wealth which made possible those vast accumulations of fixed wealth and of capital improvements which distinguished that age from all others. Herein lay, in fact, the main justification of the Capitalist System. If the rich had spent their new wealth on their own enjoyments, the world would long ago have found such a regime intolerable. But like bees they saved and accumulated, not less to the advantage of the whole community because they themselves held narrower ends in prospect.
>
> The immense accumulations of fixed capital which, to the great benefit of mankind, were built up during the half century before the war, could never have come about in a Society where wealth was divided equitably. The railways of the world, which that age built as a monument to posterity, were, not less than the Pyramids of Egypt, the work of labour which was not free to consume in immediate enjoyment the full equivalent of its efforts.
>
> Thus this remarkable system depended for its growth on a double bluff or deception. On the one hand the labouring classes accepted from ignorance or powerlessness, or were compelled, persuaded, or cajoled by custom, convention, authority and the well-established order of Society into accepting, a situation in which they could call their own very little of the cake, that they and Nature and the capitalists were co-operating to produce. And on the other hand the capitalist classes were allowed to call the best part of the cake theirs and were theoretically free to consume it, on the tacit underlying condition that they

consumed very little of it in practice. The duty of 'saving' became nine-tenths of virtue and the growth of the cake the object of true religion. There grew around the non-consumption of the cake all those instincts of puritanism which in other ages has withdrawn itself from the world and has neglected the arts of production as well as those of enjoyment. And so the cake increased; but to what end was not clearly contemplated.

Schumpeter (1970) provided a remarkable, insightful, provocative, and controversial grand vision of capitalism in motion and of its powerful propelling engine, as well as a diagnosis of the manner in which capitalist society would eventually break down. As he himself warned, his generalized picture of the essential features of earlier capitalist reality was 'historically bounded' and at least partly obsolete if applied to later stages of development:

> Capitalism does not merely mean that the housewife may influence production by her choice between peas and beans; or that the youngster may choose whether he wants to work in a factory or on a farm; or that plant managers have some voice in deciding what and how to produce: it means a scheme of values, an attitude toward life, a civilization — the civilization of inequality and of the family fortune. This civilization is rapidly passing away, however. Let us rejoice or else lament the fact as much as every one of us likes; but do not let us shut our eyes to it (Schumpeter, 1950, p. 419).

Schumpeter's vision of the capitalist economy is not merely of a system expanding in a steady manner, but of one revolutionized endogenously by the intrusion of 'new enterprise' with existing structure and all conditions of doing business constantly undergoing change and in a process of turmoil. He sees every situation as being upset before it has even had time to work itself out.

Schumpeter's (1950, pp. 73-4) vision is intrinsically of interest as a grand scheme, both when it is right and when it is wrong, and because it is in modern times being resurrected and, as Schumpeter himself might say, at the wrong time and the wrong place (with altered institutions, a transformed society, revolutionized communications, etc.):

> Unlike the class of feudal lords, the commercial and industrial bourgeoisie rose by business success. Bourgeois society has been cast in a purely economic mold: its foundations, beams and beacons are all made of economic material. The building faces toward the economic side of life. Prizes and penalties are measured in pecuniary terms.

Going up and going down means making and losing money. . . within its own frame, that social arrangement is, or at all events was, singularly effective. In part it appeals to, and in part it creates, a schema of motives that is unsurpassed in simplicity and force. The promises of wealth and the threats of destitution that it holds out, it redeems with ruthless promptitude. Wherever the bourgeois way of life asserts itself sufficiently to dim the beacons of other social worlds, these promises are strong enough to attract the large majority of super-normal brains and to identify success with business success.

Schumpeter (1950, p. 75) contends that the British classical economists 'were quite convinced that within the institutional framework of capitalism, the manufacturer's and the trader's self-interest made for maximum performance in the interest of all. Confronted with the problem we are discussing, they would have had little hesitation in attributing the observed rate of increase in total output to relative unfettered enterprise and the profit motive'. However, he (1950, p. 75) reminds us that these:

were of course the typical views of the English bourgeois class, and bourgeois blinkers are in evidence on almost every page the classical authors wrote. No less in evidence are blinkers of another kind: the classics reasoned in terms of a particular historical situation which they uncritically idealized and from which they uncritically generalized. Most of them, moreover, seem to have argued exclusively in terms of the English interests and problems of their time. This is the reason why, in other lands and at other times, people disliked their economics, frequently to the point of not even caring to understand it.

Schumpeter (1950, p. 77) stresses that 'capitalist reality is first and last a process of change'. Thus in analysing capitalism, the essential point is to perceive it as an evolutionary process — a fact that was long ago perceived by Marx:

Capitalism, then, is by nature a form or method of economic change and not only never is but never can be stationary. And this revolutionary character of the capitalist process is not merely due to the fact that economic life goes on in a social and natural environment which changes and by its change alters the data of economic action. . . Nor is this evolutionary character due to a quasi-automatic increase in population and capital or to the vagaries of monetary systems. . . The fundamental impulse that sets and keeps the capital engine in motion comes from the new consumers' goods, the new methods of production or transportation, the new markets, the new forms of industrial organization that capitalist enterprise creates (Schumpter, 1950, pp. 82–3).

Schumpeter (1950, p. 83) emphasizes the capitalist perennial 'gale of destruction':

> The opening up of new markets, foreign or domestic, and the organizational development from the craft shop and factory to such concerns as U.S. Steel illustrate the same process of industrial mutation — if I may use that biological term — that incessantly revolutionizes the economic structure *from within*, incessantly destroying the old one, incessantly creating the new one. This process of Creative Destruction is the essential fact about capitalism. It is what capitalism consists in and what every capitalist concern has got to live in.

Schumpeter (1950, p. 84) makes the controversial point that the problem usually perceived is 'how capitalism administers existing structures, whereas the relevant problem is how it creates and destroys them'.

Since the dimensions of the economic process are not easily and rapidly perceivable, it is pointless to evaluate the performance of the dynamic process at any particular point of time, rather a longer time-frame is required. Hence Schumpeter's (1950, p. 83) important statement about dynamic efficiency:

> A system. . . that at *every* given point of time fully utilizes its possibilities to the best advantage may yet in the long run be inferior to a system that does so at *no* given point of time, because the latter's failure to do so may be a condition for the level of speed of long-run performance.

Schumpeter (1950, p. 82) stresses the fact that technical progress most conspicuously originated in industrial giants. 'As soon as we go into details and inquire into the individual items in which progress was most conspicuous, the trail leads not to the doors of those firms that work under conditions of comparatively free competition but precisely to the doors of the large concerns.'

> Thus it is not sufficient to argue that. . . the large-scale establishment or unit of control must be accepted as a necessary evil inseparable from the economic progress which it is prevented from sabotaging by the forces inherent in its productive apparatus. What we have got to accept is that it has come to be the most powerful engine of that progress and in particular of the long-run expansion of total output. . . (Schumpeter, 1950, p. 106).

All this, of course, depends very much on the evolution and type of technical advance. For example, at this juncture, much of the advance made in high technology comes from relatively small firms (see Nelson, 1981, p. 1051).

Schumpeter (1950, pp. 84-5) has an interesting view of competition in the modern world that centres on technology. He speaks of the:

> competition from the new commodity, the new technology, the new source of supply, the new type of organization (the largest-scale unit of control for instance) — competition which commands a decisive cost or quality advantage and which strikes not at the margins of the profits and the outputs of the existing firms but at their foundations and their very lives. This kind of competition is much more effective than the other as a bombardment is in comparison with forcing a door, and so much more important that it becomes a matter of comparative indiffer-
> ence whether competition in the ordinary sense functions more or less promptly; the powerful lever that in the long run expands output and brings down prices is in any case made of other stuff.

In his scheme of things, Schumpeter emphasizes the driving force of the entrepreneur in the process of technological innovation. To him (1950, p. 132):

> the function of entrepreneurs is to reform or revolutionize the pattern of production by exploiting an invention or, more generally, an untried technological possibility for producing a new commodity or producing an old one in a new way, by opening up a new source of supply of materials or a new outlet for products, by reorganizing an industry and so on. . . To undertake such new things is difficult and constitutes a distinct economic function, first, because they lie outside the routine tasks which everybody understands and, secondly, because the environment resists in many ways that vary, according to social conditions, from simple refusal either to finance or to buy a new thing, to physical attack on the man who tries to produce it. To act with confidence beyond the range of familiar beacons and to overcome that resistance requires aptitudes that are present in only a small fraction of the population and that define the entrepreneurial type as well as the entrepreneurial function. This function does not essentially consist in either inventing anything or otherwise creating the conditions which the enterprise exploits. It consists in getting things done.

However, he was prompt to notice that by the mid-1900s the entrepreneur's social and economic functions were already on the wane, primarily because innovation had become institutionalized, so to speak, and resistance to innovation was fading away, especially where new goods were concerned. However, it still persisted where personal or group interests were threatened. The future would be characterized by economic progress that 'tends to become depersonalized and automatized. Bureau and committee work tends to replace individual action' (Schumpeter, 1950, p. 133). In Schumpeter's vision (p. 134) this process would not only render the entrepreneur obsolete, but it would also sound the death knoll of the capitalist class:

> The perfectly bureaucratized giant industrial unit not only ousts the small and medium-sized firm and 'expropriates' its owners, but in the end it also ousts the entrepreneur and expropriates the bourgeoisie as a class which in the process stands to lose not only its income but also what is infinitely more important, its function.

Thus he (1950, p. 156) concludes:

> Faced by the increasing hostility of the environment and by the legislative, administrative and judicial practice born of that hostility, entrepreneurs and capitalists. . . will eventually cease to function. Their standard aims are rapidly becoming unattainable, their efforts futile. The most glamorous of these bourgeois aims, the foundation of an industrial dynasty, has in most countries become unattainable already, and even more modest ones are so difficult to attain that they may cease to be thought worth the struggle as the permanence of these conditions is being increasingly realized.

Schumpeter's vision of the future of capitalism is relatively gloomy. He (1950, p. 111) sees 'symptoms of a permanent loss of vitality which must be expected to go on and to supply the dominating theme for the remaining movements of the capitalist symphony; hence no inference as to the future can be drawn from the functioning of the capitalist engine and of its performance in the past'.

Generalizing on a lifetime of quantitative research, Kuznets (1981, p. 410) singles out three main driving forces behind modern economic growth in developed market economies: (i) a high rate of accretion of useful knowledge and the technological innovations derived therefrom, (ii) the associated process of shifts in the economy's production structure as regards output, labour and capital, with a close link between the high growth rate of per capita product and a high rate of shift among the different production sectors, and (iii) the complex and interdependent functions and influences of the national sovereign state. However, Kuznets

(1981, p. 247) concludes that an overriding force propelling economic growth must have been:

> the desire of man for greater supply of economic goods — for welfare or for power. But in absence of socially acceptable means to satisfy this desire, it could hardly be a driving force of consequence. Hence, the availability of such means, their characteristics, their capacity to enhance productivity and thus to stimulate economic growth become crucial — as permissive yet in themselves not compelling, as necessary yet not sufficient, factors.

He (1981, p. 427) asks the pertinent, yet not fully answerable question, whether this desire was stronger in the modern market economies in the last two centuries than in the preceding ones. 'But as long as this basic desire remained in some strength, rather than be replaced by rigid asceticism, the immensely greater power to implement it because of the contributions of new knowledge and technology, is what counted.'

Elaborating further on these points, Kuznets (1981, pp. 410-11) writes:

> In the present connection, the high rate of technological innovations and their large cumulative impact on economic growth is reflected in the known succession of major innovations in a variety of fields; in the pervasiveness of new technology in extending to even the oldest production sectors (like agriculture); and in the large proportion of goods, and of old goods produced by new methods, in the total product of developed countries.

The unpredictability of long-term consequences of technological innovation is one of its key features. This is particularly true of a cluster of related innovations. 'But when we consider the long-term cumulative consequences of the unfolding of such a cluster, we find a long, interrelated chain of changes in technology and changes in institutional and social adjustments, spread over decades and occurring in a complex and changing national and international environment' (Kuznets, 1981, p. 414). What Kuznets (p. 415) emphasizes is 'that predicatability of the more sober type, one that would yield acceptably firm expectations of direction and magnitude, was not possible, because the chain of connections began with technological innovation that contained a substantial component of unknown and hence of ignorance, to be overcome only with extended application and continued to generate a long chain of interweaving links of technological and social change in a sequence of uncertain speed and mixture of successes and temporary failures'. And, in the face of such unpredictability, it was very difficult to take remedial action to either counteract obstacles or to promote the positive aspects. Thus the ensuring discontinuities, bottlenecks and pressures.

Kuznets (1981, p. 412) cautions that because of the innovation's novelty, we are ignorant and not sufficiently far-sighted to envision all its implications. Thus a high rate of technical innovation requires a society:

> that encourages the continuous production of a variety of new know-ledge relevant, directly or indirectly, to problems of economic production; that contains an entrepreneurial group perceptive of such new knowledge, and capable of venturing attempts to apply it on a scale sufficient to reveal its potentials; and a capacity to generate, without costly breakdowns, institutional changes and group adjustments that may be needed to channel efficiently the new technology — with its distinctive constraints. The driving forces or permissive factors are those involved in man's search for new knowledge of nature and of the universe within which we live, including the inventive links between it and production; and the capacity of societies both to encourage technological innovations, and to accommodate them, despite the disruptive unevenness of their impact on different social groups.

The technological innovations that have been part of modern growth have been primarily capital-intensive, necessitating vast outlays of capital for mechanization and saving on labour inputs. Kuznets (1981, p. 413) suggests that 'large amounts of fixed capital meant a large scale of plant and economic enterprise, with increasing economies of scale continuously pushing upwards the optimum scale involved. There was thus a direct line of connection between the greater productivity available in the new technology, the greater volume of physical non-human power that the latter employed in the mechanization of a variety of productive processes, the increasing demand for fixed capital that embodied and controlled the new power, and the rising scale of plant and of the economic firm unit.'

Reviewing the obstacles to the development of new technology, Kuznets (1981, p. 413) singles out the large requirements for fixed capital and the limited supply of both innovative and technical talents. These may have been responsible for the observed lags in the stream of new technology and for its selective penetration into various sectors — a selectivity that varied from period to period.

A very important aspect was the progressive alteration of institutions, for example, those for mobilizing savings and financing the large capital investments (Kuznets, 1981, p. 414).

Kuznets (p. 416) vividly illustrates the influence of the structural shifts on the fabric of society:

The high rate of increase of product per worker or per capita, characteristic of modern economic growth, was inevitably associated with a high rate of structural shifts. These were changes in the shares of production sectors in the country's output, capital, and labor force, with implicit changes in shares of various labor-status groups among the gainfully engaged and in the conditions of their work and life; of different types of capital and forms of economic enterprise; and in the structure of the country's trade and other economic interchanges with the rest of the world. The implications of such structural shifts for the changing position of the several socio-economic groups were particularly important, because the responses of these groups to the impacts of advancing technology shaped modern society.

However, in this connection, as in many others, one has to distinguish between the type of new technology developed in the past and the kind that may develop in the future. Thus the future may not be characterized by either the types of institutions developed in the past nor by the past constraints on innovations.

FROM DEMAND TO SUPPLY AND DEMAND-CONSTRAINED PRODUCTION

The trauma of the worst depression in the history of the capitalist economy gave impetus to revolutionizing macroeconomic theory and policy. With enormous unemployment and idle capacity, output was obviously not limited by the availability of resources, but primarily by the deficiency of aggregate demand. The major problem was one of finding markets for the output that could or would have been produced had the productive potential been fully utilized. The Second World War was an exogenous shock: one that shifted the problems of effective demand to those of a supply-constrained economy. The postwar relative and fairly continuous success story (at least until the late 1960s) was an admixture of old and new elements and forces.

This was the era of economic growth, prosperity and progress, high employment, with only moderate macroeconomic instabilities, and advance of the welfare state. The government and public institutions performed a major role in modifying the function of the market mechanism and exercised limited economic control. Individual and public consumption rose for almost the whole population in the industrialized countries of the world. Although the upsurge in per capita material consumption might not be tantamount to a rise in the standard of living and human welfare, there was an astonishing contrast with the prewar stagnation and deep depression, at least by the traditional success criteria. Business cycles did not fade away, but their amplitudes did moderate substantially; sharp depressions of the prewar variety were avoided.

Until the mid-1960s the postwar capitalist economies had relatively remarkable employment and growth rates and avoided high inflation. The standard of living was much higher than that which would have been achieved under *laissez-faire*. Profound economic and social transformations took place.

Government assumed the responsibility of stabilizing acute output, employment and price fluctuations. It tried more haphazardly and with less success to promote and maintain economic growth. In the process the government's economic functions and discretionary interference increased. High taxation was to give governments command over resources for financing welfare transfers that redistributed income and for the military build up. The policies pursued improved conditions from what they would have been under *laissez-faire*, but they were accompanied by adverse effects such as production of means of destruction and in the 1970s a growing inflation that aroused public ire.

The last fifteen years have witnessed growing instabilities and a sequence of extraordinarily unfavourable exogenous shocks, manifested in simultaneously rapidly rising prices, high or rising unemployment, and stagnating or declining growth of output and productivity – stagflation. And, importantly, at this juncture it is still difficult to distinguish to what extent we are witnessing a long-term deteriorating trend or the interaction of cyclical, transitory and random forces.

For a variety of reasons, among which stagflation plays a major role, the 1970s have witnessed increasing questioning of and disaffection from what rightly or wrongly came to be identified with Keynesian economics. The phenomenon is a complex one for it involves interaction of science, ideology and politics. The Keynesian revolution has always been under attack from various quarters, primarily the radical left and radical right. The former objected to the attempt to save capitalism and the latter to the redistributive effects, the shifting economic power in favour of trade unions and the government, the resultant erosion of the Protestant ethic and compliance of labour, and the dangers of inflation. From Hayek, through Knight and Friedman, to the present conservative offensive there runs a stream of questioning not only of the so-called Keynesian techniques, but fundamentally of the ends to which they were employed and of the changes in the fabric of society to which they gave rise.

We have elaborated on Keynes and the Keynesian revolution in Chapters 1 and 2. Here we would simply like to note that he understandably focused on the effective demand rather than the supply constraints of production. He focused on the short-term view and was not primarily preoccupied with long-term forces and tendencies. His main concern was about the income-generating effects of investments and not with their capacity-creating effects. He had little to say about growth. In the postwar period growth model building became a flourishing industry (see Chapter 1 in the companion volume and Chapters 1, 2 and 4 in this volume). However, on the plane of theory one of the major flaws was a lack of integration between growth and business-cycle theories and, on the policy plane stabilization policies concentrated on the short-term effects and lacked cohesive growth policy foundations. Regretfully some of the well-propagandized supply-side approaches have inherited both defects in that they view the economy as if it were not subject to business cycles and trend.

There are inherent dangers in any approach that inordinately concentrates either on demand or supply or almost solely on short- or long-run tendencies, for it loses perspective on the totality of the economic process. Whatever else needs to be said about neoclassical economics, one of its great achievements was its stress on both the demand and supply sides of the economic process and the mechanism of eradication of imbalances. *Mutatis mutandis* Marshall's famous focus on the determination of price by mutual interaction of demand and supply (both blades of the Marshallian scissors are needed to perform the cutting) is as ever.

In broad contours two distinct approaches to the supply side emerge (i) exclusive concentration on supply, and (ii) integration of supply and demand. From a somewhat different vantage point, one could distinguish between (i) those that use primarily a microeconomic approach to macroeconomic problems, and (ii) those that integrate both macro and microeconomic approaches. Fundamentally the approaches differ in their perceptions of how a modern economy works and of world economic interdependencies. Here I mean not only different perceptions of the strategic growth factors and constraints, but also macroeconomic instabilities and their sources, of aggregate supply demand functions, of the range and effectiveness of policy options and of the cumulative effects of 'short-view' policies, of the way markets operate and of the transmission of disturbances or impulses throughout the system, and of the magnitudes of coefficients of response of economic actors to economic stimuli.

Expansion of the economy's capacity to produce is clearly constrained by the rate of growth of resources, the efficiency with which they are combined and utilized, and the improvements in techniques. The economy's secular production possibilities are determined by the economic actors' willingness to work and propensities to save, by productivity, and by the system's dynamic efficiency. However, the contention that the long-term rate of growth of real output is determined solely on the supply side is a questionable one (see Kalecki, 1970; Matthews, 1976; Rosenberg, 1982). Be that as it may, the questions here are: what are the determinants of the determinants? Can they be influenced at all and, if so, how and by what policies?

THE TAX-BASED MICRO APPROACH TO THE SUPPLY SIDE

The first approach concentrates on incentives to work and save and on the tax system and removal of other government-created disincentives to work, entrepreneurship, and productivity. The second approach is broader than the stress on saving and the incentive effect of taxation. It combines the theoretical aggregative system of final demand and income determination with a generalized Leontief-type model of inter-industrial flows. It concentrates on more direct measures or more specific microeconomic interventions to stimulate private capital formation, technical dynamism, 'learning by doing', on widening specific bottleneck areas of production, on promoting strategic sectors or activities, on encouraging 'winners' in international competition, and on promoting fuller utilization of resources.

The adverse effects of taxation on the performance of economic actors has a long literature. (The opposite view was taken by the mercantilists who believed in the 'backward sloping' supply curve.) The first approach stresses that high and particularly steeply graduated tax rates and inflationary bracket-creep discourage production, weaken the incentives to work, produce and save, and inhibit growth. It also advocates lower taxes to cut government spending which it considers largely wasteful and an incursion into the private sector.[1]

The first approach focuses attention on the effects of alternative tax structures on the level and pattern of economic activity and the total amounts of government revenue generated by these alternatives. There is much more to this approach than the famous (or infamous) Laffer curve and the questionable proposition that the 'tax reductions will pay for themselves' (Laffer and Seymour, 1979, pp. 5–43). Here the critical empirical issue is whether the US tax system is on the downslope of the Laffer curve (see Blinder, 1981; Pechman, 1981).

If, in the USA taxes did not approach or transgress the critical revenue collecting level, this does not mean that they should not be lowered, but merely that other effects need to be taken into account, that is, they should be subject to a cost–benefit calculus. This, in turn, implies explicit criteria function and reliable or reasonable evidence as to the probable order of magnitudes involved.

Whatever the absurdities and inequities of the tax structure and however serious or minor its impact on distorting *relative* prices and decisions based on wrong coefficients of economic choice, it is not certain, or even probable, that the overall level of taxation in the USA is already so prohibitively high as to seriously damage economic activity. Even if it were so, the pragmatic questions would be whether and to what extent reduction of the effective tax burden would elicit extra effort and palpably improve productivity. In some cases palpable incentives are already built into the tax structure (e.g. investment tax credit) and only the marginal pay-off that such a change would elicit is at issue.

There appears to be a widespread popular belief that high and progressive taxes, together with transfer payments and other benefits of the welfare state, have a stifling effect on the performance of economic actors and contribute to the erosion of the work ethic and retardation in productivity growth. *Ipso facto*, the first approach considers that cuts in social outlays and transfer payments would substantially strengthen work incentives and force 'work evaders' to engage in productive activities. Hard evidence does not seem to bear them out (see Maital and Meltz, 1980). In a broader sense this attitude reflects on the nature of unemployment — voluntary versus involuntary: whether the problem is fundamentally one of lack of opportunities for finding employment owing to insufficiency of effective demand or whether it is one of idleness and insufficient incentives to work. If the latter were to hold, as the first approach would have us believe, the analysis of the Great Depression (or for that matter of the situation among US car workers in the early 1980s) could be reduced to a chronic attack of severe laziness.

The potential stimulative effect of tax reduction on economic actors is an intensely controversial issue. Not surprisingly there is not even unanimity on the direction of change, not to speak of the quantitative effect (see Aaron and Pechman, 1981; *Tax Aspects*, 1981; Penner, 1981). Clearly the answer to this thorny question depends, *inter alia*, on the type and size of cuts and a host of supporting or contradictory measures. And, as nearly always, the time dimension is critical.[2] Even if we confine ourselves to the federal budget in considering the incentive effects of taxation, it is faulty to limit the investigation merely to the revenue side, for measures on both sides constitute alternatives to elicit the desired response or resource allocation between the private and the public sector.[3]

The first approach tends to grossly oversimplify the multivariable and controversial labour supply function. To recall, the typical neoclassical labour supply function is upward sloping, which is not always true of the classical one. If we postulate a positive relation between real after-tax wage and the quantity of labour supplied, then, *ceteris paribus*, a tax reduction increases the relative attractiveness or reward of work. The presumption is that labour supply will be positively affected. There are many problems with the function, including the interdependence of preferences, the effect of affluence or of the welfare state on performance, etc. (Lindbeck, 1982; Schumpeter, 1950, pp. 409–25; Kaldor, 1983). But even on the grounds of neoclassical theory, one cannot predetermine what the likely effect is going to be. For, as every student of price theory knows, there is a distinction between the substitution and income effects of price change. Thus tax cuts tend to (i) have a positive effort-releasing effect by raising the rewards from work, and (ii) discourage work by the income effect. The final outcome depends on the relative strengths of (i) and (ii).

The evidence of the effects of the tax system on labour supply appears to be most unsatisfactory (Brown, 1980, p. 108; Hausman, 1981a, pp. 173ff.). At best it indicates that the net effect is positive but fairly weak for primary breadwinners and somewhat stronger for the secondary ones, but there seems to be no support for the outlandish claims by some of the supply-side enthusiasts.[4]

Taxes may affect the work–leisure decision in a number of ways. This fact is not always clearly kept in mind even in sophisticated econometric estimates (see Hausman, 1981b). We often tend to stress one dimension of the (short-term) labour supply function such as the impact of taxes on the number of hours worked per annum. Taxes may be one of the factors in the work–leisure decision in terms of the duration of the working life, the acquisition of education and experience, the choice of career, and the diligence and quality of performance. And such a decision depends not only on other stimuli, opportunities, and constraints facing the individual, but on the diversity of preferences – an often underestimated factor. Furthermore, many people of superior abilities will not let them lie fallow because of taxation or inadequate financial rewards, for they reap a great benefit from the satisfaction derived from exercising those abilities (see Chapter 3 this volume).

Any changes in the tax structure tend to have not only incentive, efficiency, or stabilization effects, but also redistributive effects. Here the pregnant question of trade-off between equity and efficiency and the delicate and sensitive question of reconciling sometimes conflicting aims of the tax system (e.g. high employment, non-inflationary growth, and the income distribution that the community desires) come to the fore. Here, as always, one should distinguish between the normative and positive aspects of economics.

The first approach also considers the taxation burden as one of the prime deterrents to saving and capital formation. *Ipso facto*, relief of that burden should boost saving. The behaviour of households depends, *inter alia*, on the size, type, and effective graduation of taxes and their expected 'life-long' income and on how they perceive (fiscal surprises versus steady course) the government spending and taxing policies. Clearly, personal income tax cuts increase disposable income. The answer to the question by how much saving will rise depends on income distribution, the various income groups' propensities to save, and the expected government policies. Saving can be increased by income redistribution from the poor to the rich, by the 'Keynesian route' of increased income, by reducing government dissaving, and by improving the after-tax pay-off on saving. Measures to foster saving also include substitution of one tax for another, of which a shift from income to expenditure taxes is the prime example (see Pechman, 1980).

The evidence seems to suggest that there is little or weak response of saving to the variations of the rate of interest. Despite major changes in rates of inflation, interest rates, per capita income, welfare programmes and the economic environment, in the USA the private saving ratios have been remarkably stable since 1929. Thus, as Denison (1976) argued, great circumspection should be exercised in claiming that public policy can significantly modify saving behaviour. In a recent study von Furstenberg (1981) found statistically insignificant relations between the rates of return and saving. In common with the fashionable distinction between the effects of anticipated and surprise government actions, he found that unanticipated taxes or transfers have only a minor effect on saving, for households expect that the deviations from the government's normal policies would soon be reversed. Empirical estimates by Charles Steindel (1981) of the determinants of private saving in the USA suggest that the saving function can be shifted outward by shifting taxes from capital to labour, but such redistributive policy could adversely affect work incentives. Moreover, in the USA the bulk of income from capital escapes taxation.

One of the achievements of mainstream macroeconomics has been the cogent distinction between the acts of saving and investment. Larger saving may or may not transform itself into larger investment. Hence even if the policy is successful in eliciting increased saving this cannot be equated with increased capital formation.

In an economy where resources are underutilized, successful measures to encourage saving, leading to a fall in effective demand, will have a perverse effect on 'animal spirits' and will not result in increased investment. If it is not offset by demand-increasing policies, such a slowdown might reduce the volume of saving as the 'paradox of thrift' analysis suggests. Moreover, as is well known, saving takes many forms (such as real estate, antiques, fine art, jewellery, and foreign holdings) and capacity-augmenting investment is only one (and in stagflation not necessarily the favourite one) of its many uses. And, as Denison's (1976) painstaking research indicates, significant alterations in the US growth rate cannot be ascribed to modifications in the private propensity to save.

Whatever its other shortcomings that we have outlined, the first approach suffers from exaggerated claims for the effectiveness of its remedies. Indeed, it appears that most expected quantitative results of the first approach are based on bold assertions that were not extrapolated from convincing statistical evidence. Michael Evans's (1981) major attempt to build a new macroeconomic supply-side model of the US economy appears to be so riddled with errors and bad judgement as to make it practically useless (Ando, 1981; see Eckstein, 1980; Klein, 1980a).

SUPPLY CUM DEMAND

The second approach concentrates on policies to maintain high utilization of resources over time and to promote prudent capital formation that enhances productivity and increases the long-term flow of output as a part of the plethora of measures to relieve stagflation. Such measures are particularly strong if they detect and widen bottlenecks, remove growth barriers, and combat shortages in sensitive activities, improve acquisition of knowledge and enrich work experience, and reduce labour costs per unit of output, thus allowing the economy to keep the upward movement closer to the non-inflationary wage path. The higher the gains in productivity, the lesser the danger of inflationary content of expansionary policy. But there is a considerable lag before productivity gains from capital accumulation become visible and are reflected in economic statistics. Thus investment is not only needed for creating a firmer and more sustained basis for longer prosperity, but also as an instrument in an anti-inflationary programme. Whether such a policy can do without some form of incomes policy is an open and controversial question.

The sharp disagreements about the effects of tax policy on capital formation partly reflect the differences in approaches to the thorny question of the determinants of investment behaviour. Business-cycle theory stresses that to understand the investment process it is necesary to take into account the time lag structure and the dynamics of the adjustment process (see Feiwel, 1975, p. 139; Fisher, 1971, pp. 250ff.). Investment depends on the variance between the actual and desired stock of capital which, in turn, depends on the expected future 'permanent' sales and the user costs of capital (including interest rate, inflationary expectations, depreciation, taxes, and subsidies).

For a number of reasons, it is preferable to use more direct investment incentives, that is, specifically tailored measures influencing investment decisions directly through the strategic variables that affect the after-tax rate of return on investment and rental cost of capital. The standard and proven tools of tax policy to stimulate investment in and modernization of fixed capital include (i) investment tax credits, including such options as augmenting them and extending their coverage or differentiating rates favouring, for example, introduction of more fuel-efficient capital (ii) liberalization of depreciation and (iii) credit for research and development.

A vigorous expanding economy not only generates high and growing entrepreneurial and labour incomes, an enlarged tax base, etc., but power-fully strengthens the inducements to invest. While some economists concentrate on the interaction of inflation and taxation as the strategic factors in the decline in corporate capital accumulation in the 1970s, others have argued that the strategic factor was a failure to stimulate prosperity or the fighting of inflation with unemployment (see Feldstein and Summers, 1978; Summers, 1981; Pechman, 1981). The fiscal policy to encourage investment needs to be dovetailed with an appropriate accommodating monetary policy. The prescription of the neoclassical synthesis for augmenting capital formation is the very opposite of the recent US policy where the investment incentives were undermined by an overly restrictive monetary deflationary policy. Thus the disappointment with the response of investment to recent investment stimuli, operating via tax options for reducing the user cost of capital, suggests that investment can be more effectively stimulated by fostering high and sustained rates of output expansion and capacity utilization (see Hendershott and Hu, 1981; Fralick, 1981; Kopcke, 1981; Moore, 1981; Penner, 1981; Nordhause, 1983).

One of the problems in activating investment incentives is not to provide incentives for investments that would have been undertaken anyway. Nor is more investment always and necessarily beneficial. In the past investment stimuli were often dictated by the exigencies of the stabilization policy rather than by a coherent growth policy (see Klein, 1981b; Garison, 1983;

Kaldor, 1983). Moreover, there is the possibility of public investment to be directed into areas that will not attract private investment.

To the extent that encouragement of investment is successful, it follows from the logic of the investment process that the effects on improvement in productivity materialize only in the future and the time path is hardly favourable. Research seems to indicate that the quantitative results are likely to be modest (Pechman, 1981; see Summers, 1981; Denison, 1976). Still many economists believe that there is no other route to follow, for improvement in productivity (Klein, 1981a; see also Nordhaus, 1983; *The Decline*, 1980; and Boskin, ch. 20 of this volume) is essential for mitigating both interdependent components of stagflation. As we have seen, (Kuznets 1966), a distinctive characteristic of modern economic growth in industrialized capitalist economies is that the high growth rates of per capita national output were accomplished primarily by improvement in quality – and, to a much lesser extent, by increased quantity – of inputs; that is, essentially by a rise in productivity traceable to rapid advances in technical, organizational, and managerial know-how. Thus the high rates of technical advance and efficiency have been partly instrumental in maintaining relatively modest shares of capital formation and high shares of consumption in national income.

This raises the vexed quation of the determinants of growth and productivity and what can be done to foster them.[5] The evidence relating to the various factors promoting productivity and their relative weight is tenuous.[6] Our knowledge how to affect these factors is also limited (see *The Decline*, 1980, pp. 57, 155-77 and *passim*).[7] Some of these often strongly interacting factors are: investment in fixed and human capital; generation and diffusion of technical and organizational advance; acquisition of experience; shifts of resources from lower to higher productivity activities; reaping economies of scale; improved international flows of goods, capital and know-how; appropriate working arrangements for resource mobilization, allocation and utilization as well as motivation for economic actors to engage in the process of 'creative destruction'; *avoidance* of slumps and major declines in rates of aggregate economic activity.[8]

Thus, clearly the point is not one of encouraging investment as such, but of stimulating certain types of investment and fostering dynamic efficiency. It is not only the fixed capital, but increasingly investment in human capital that matters (Schultz, 1981). For many purposes gross investment is a better measure than net investment for in a dynamic economy replacements are not merely replicas of old technologies, but incorporate capital of latest vintage. While in the real world the distinction does not hold in pure form, it is useful to decompose investment into

(i) extensive type or capital-widening where merely more of the same quality is used to produce more output, (ii) substitution of capital for labour or capital-deepening, or substitution of capital and labour for energy due to changes in relative prices (so-called movement along the isoquant), and (iii) innovative and entrepreneurial investments that shift the parameters of the production function (isoquants towards origin or expand the production possibility frontier) (Solow, 1956; Hendershott and Hu, 1981). It is the third type that is the most promising and indeed the most difficult to accomplish and raises the fundamental question about the kind of environment conducive to it. Put somewhat differently, it is not only the share of national income that is saved and invested, but the composition and quality of investment and the returns derived therefrom that really matter. (The overall rate of capital formation in the USA is probably inadequate, by at least two percentage points and the existing capital stock is seriously misallocated among the sectors of the economy and types of capital (Klein, 1981b; and *Public Policy*, 1981).)

Without addressing ourselves to the formidable question of the optimal rate of capital formation for the USA, one could argue that a most important aspect of a viable supply-side approach is a set of measures to improve the composition of investment, to channel physical investment into more productive uses, to shift more resources to activities that promote investment in human capital and research and development, and to spur innovative and truly entrepreneurial activities, and last, but not least, to create propitious macroeconomic conditions, including the stimulating of demand, the opening up of new markets, and appropriately redesigning institutions.

A major contribution in the second approach is the generalized model of both the supply and demand sides by Lawrence Klein (1978, 1980b, 1981a, 1981b, 1982). It combines a generalized (with coefficients varying with variations in relative prices) Leontief-type input–output model with a macro model of final demand, income generation, and market pricing. The generalized model is an interactive feedback system. The input–output system of inter-industry flows is driven by the final demand and income-generation macro model, but the latter cannot be solved without knowing the sectoral composition of output and pricing. In fact, the system is not decomposable and does not generally admit a solution to either the supply or demand sides separately. Both must be solved simultaneously in joint dependency.

Some important microeconomic activities are perforce outside the purview of econometric models. The trend is to enlarge the set of endogenous variables which, in a sense, makes the model more cumbersome but more realistic. One aspect of the model is to approximate in empirical work Walrasian general equilibrium. This is an almost unattainable task. But a continuous attempt is being made to achieve a better approximation, incorporating an increasing number of intricate microeconomic specifications without sacrificing the ability to add the micro components into the principal macro variables that constitute standard aggregative magnitudes of a mainstream (Wharton) econometric model.

Much, but by no means all, of supply-side analytical modelling and policy prescriptions is microeconomic. Hence the need to rely heavily on solid microeconomic theory, for clearly a spurious policy might be generated by a false or incomplete theoretical base. This raises the fundamental and formidable question of microfoundations for macroeconomics (see Part II of this volume.)

In this model the supply side does not supplant the demand side; rather it complements it and makes the system more coherent with both sides modelled together. Thus the supply side is a necessary but not sufficient component of a comprehensive and internally consistent economic policy. To deal successfully with stagflation macro policy has to be complemented by a structural policy aimed at specific economic problems, activities, processes, bottlenecks, and groups or agents. Given adequate time, an appropriate combination of macro and structural policies can promote non-inflationary growth, according to the underlying model that is long-term in concept.

As we have seen, supply-side economics that is concerned primarily with reactions to the tax system (the first approach) is quite superficial and lacks scientific credibility. Nor does it explore sufficiently the range of opportunities for the tax system to foster capital formation and productivity growth. Nor do the tax policies provide a sufficiently broad range of policy instruments for reaching simultaneously the usually postulated laudable objectives of vigorous output and productivity growth, tolerable inflation and external balance. And, no matter what its intrinsic weaknesses are, the first approach cannot succeed when combined with central-bank monetarist policies that fight inflation with higher unemployment and reduced capacity utilization in the economy.

By contrast, the second approach, resting on a more solid theoretical and empirical base, tackles the problems of stagflation with a wide range of instruments. Rather than using the indirect route of general tax reduction, it favours more frontal attacks on declining productivity growth and inflation and forceful, specific and direct policies and straightforward methods aimed at the size and composition of capital formation (including non-uniform, selective, discriminatory concessions), fuller utilization of resources, reduction of the cyclical component of stagflation, setting an accommodative monetary policy, and improving the intermediate flows. Thus, there is a whole matter of inter-industry relationships, anticipating and remedying emerging bottlenecks, facing up to such pervasive new or intensified problems as supply shocks, shortages of materials and energy, speculative waves, cartel pricing, harvest failures, environmental problems, population growth, structural unemployment and manpower training, the degree of modernization of capital, promotion of exports, the flow of research and development, the amount of basic research, and the like.

In contrasting the two approaches, it is imperative to distinguish between the more fundamental philosophical questions about the kind of society that we want (including such economic value-judgement questions as composition and distribution of output, reordering of priorities for defence, growth, or welfare, private versus public sector, and types of institutions and instruments) and the purely technical–economic questions of opportunities, constraints, and effectiveness of alternative policies.

As Tinbergen (1956) emphasized, welfare is not indifferent to the types of instruments of economic policy used, for their application entails both certain material (alternative uses forgone) and non-material (such as economic actors' aversion to certain restrictions on their freedom of choice or the frictions arising out of them) costs. Economic actors and political parties have preconceived notions about the desired and appropriate range of instruments to be used. Thus, particular ideologies strongly favour or reject use of certain instruments or restrict and impose side conditions on the use of others.

One of the fundamental philosophical questions that contrasts the two approaches is their respective perceptions of the potentials, limitations and operation of the market. The first favours working through the market and the creation of overall conditions and general environment conducive to business expansion and growth. It favours aggregative 'gentle', indirect measures that interfere least with the operation of market, microeconomic choices, and adjustments. Of course, the results and distributional implications are quite harsh especially as regards welfare benefits, the infrastructure, protection of the environment, and public investment in human capital. Whatever objections one may have against the distributional and priority implications, prima facie, one would expect the measures to foster economic efficiency. But even here they are bound to falter for the erosion of public support for investment in the infrastructure and in human capital and research and development will have adverse long-term effects on dynamic efficiency.

By contrast, the second approach favours a market economy corrected for market failures and guided by an activist policy and more specific interventions into many areas as previously described. Briefly, it favours an aggressive industrial policy that attempts to outguess and be a step ahead of the market, similar to the experience of other Western industrialized countries. The 'picking of winners' and 'dealing with losers' both for the domestic and foreign markets is a most arduous and controversial component of industrial policy. The winners are promoted beyond the scope of free market choices by targeting specific industries for exceptional support and encouragement. One of the important unresolved problems is how to sort out successfully the winners from the losers. Another is how to avoid backing the losers despite powerful pressures to rescue troubled industries.

Economic models can never fully capture the richness and complexity of economic reality, but it is an essential distortion if they do not perceive our economy as subject to trend, cyclical fluctuations, stochastic disturbances, major market failures and institutional imperfections, as *inter alia*, does the first approach or its practitioners, as contrasted with the second approach that does make an attempt to incorporate those factors in its modelling.

Any constructive and sensible model has to have both supply and demand components and has to capture the essence of the dynamics of economic processes and the way that intermediate goods flow through the system. As is well known, we cannot have scissors with one blade or, as Samuelson quipped, God gave economists two eyes; one to watch supply and the other to watch demand. And, any one-sided, unidirectional and relatively simple solution (such as, *inter alia*, the first approach) has popular appeal but is usually wrong. Indeed, empircal research shows that there is a vast plethora of factors affecting growth, productivity and inflation which suggests the use of a wide gamut of instruments on a broad variety of fronts as advocated by the second approach. As Klein (1978, p. 5) put it:

In terms of the history of economic thought, the above approach means thinking in terms of the empirical implementation of the Walrasian system. Essentially, Tinbergen implemented the Keynesian system and Leontief implemented a part of the Walrasian system. By putting the two together, with due allowance to Kuznets for making the data bases of final demand and national income available, a complete synthesis of supply and demand in the economy as a whole can be put together. This gives the antecedents of what is meant by modeling supply, taking into account what is needed from demand models at the same time.

It is a legitimate task and duty of democratic governments to design and implement an appropriate economic policy to ensure sustained long-term expansion and full utilization of economic potential and to raise the standard of living of the entire population over time. *Ipso facto*, this calls for a unified theory of growth, fluctuations, price and distribution and for an innovative mix of compatible macroeconomic and microeconomic policies directed at both short-term fluctuations and long-term growth and at overall composition of output and income, employment, capital accumulation, choice of techniques, productivity and structural imbalances. By implication, under the present circumstances, the conventional fiscal and monetary policies are inadequate; at the very least they need to be reconstructed and dovetailed with prudent supply management and incomes policies. To be effective such policies have to recognize political and institutional realities and account for the fact that political interventions having a timing of their own, while many of our problems require a long-term approach.

This is a tall order and a challenge. But to those of us who perceive the inherent instabilities and failures of the market and see both opportunities and limitations in private and government actions there hardly seems to be a period in postwar history when active and innovative policy is more imperative.

NOTES

1. For statements of the position of the populist supply-side economists see Laffer, 1981; Laffer and Seymour, 1979; Cantor, Joines, and Laffer, 1981; Rutledge, 1981; Ture, 1981; Penner, 1981; 'Supply Side Symposium', 1981.
2. Specifically targeted tax incentives tend to be more effective than those of the same magnitude across the board. It is often held that tax increases are deflationary whereas increases in public expenditures are inflationary. But again the effect depends on the size and kind of fiscal measures. For instance, payroll or excise taxes are price determining and some subsidies dampen cost and price increases (see Eisner, 1981, p. 33). Strong short-run effects of a tax cut may differ substantially from or outweigh the long-term supply effects of increases in output and productivity that materialize only with a long and variable time lag.
3. The advantages of linking the tax and expenditure sides of budget policy and of viewing public services at all times as vying with each other as well as with private demand for consumption and investment

for the limited resources available have been persuasively articulated in the literature on public finance (see Samuelson, 1966, pp. 1223ff; Musgrave and Musgrave, 1980).

4. Ingenious and controversial econometric investigations by Jerry Hausman (1981b) suggest that a combination of federal and state income and payroll taxes reduced the labour supply of husbands by a (still relatively modest) 8 per cent which is higher than the results of earlier research. Hausman argues that it is a common misconception to postulate that tax is not distortionary if it has a minor or no effect on market behaviour. Economists should focus on the economic cost of taxation rather than on the labour supply effects. He contends that the economic cost of a progressive income tax is higher than most previous studies have suggested. His findings are questionable on several grounds, including the fact that some agents derive satisfaction from the more egalitarian tendencies of a progressive tax system (see Burtless, 1981; and Chapter 3 of this volume).

5. For the heated Denison–Jorgenson–Griliches controversy on issues in growth accounting and the explanation and measurement of productivity change see, *Survey*, 1972. For a general survey of issues in growth accounting and eclectic research on productivity growth see Nelson, 1981, pp. 1032–54. For a survey of factors contributing to the decline in US productivity growth, see *The Decline*, 1980; and Nordhaus, 1983. For some international comparisons, see Lindbeck, 1982; Maddison, 1982; and Maital and Meltz, 1980.

6. Inflation does not necessarily and always cause unemployment. Contrary to popular beliefs there is no well-defined and fixed relationship between inflation and unemployment. Economics has not provided any conclusive, or even tentative, answers to a trade-off between growth of output (employment) and inflation. Empirical research on the worldwide relations between inflation and unemployment provides quite a mixed evidence. Both cases of a positive and inverse association between inflation and unemployment are encountered. If any empirical generalization can be made at this state, it is that there is no significant correlation between inflation and unemployment. Some countries have experienced rapid growth with low and others with high rates of inflation. Similarly, low-growth countries exhibited both high and low rates of inflation.

7. 'Economists clearly are not in agreement about how much of the current productivity growth slowdown stems from the higher unemployment and inflation rates, and from the wide fluctuations that have been experienced, and it can be argued that slow productivity growth is itself one of the causes of the poor employment and price performance of the economies. In my eyes at least, research on the connections among long-run growth of economic potential and shorter-run macroeconomic performance still has not yet clearly identified, much less quantified, the key mechanisms involved. In part this is because there are so many different and interconnected mechanisms. From an orthodox point of view, the macroeconomic climate has a direct effect on productivity growth through its influence on investment. To the extent that econ-

omic slack involves excess capacity, investment is deterred, the growth of the capital–labour ratio is slowed, and so is the introduction of best practice. A decline in investment may also slow down the pace of advance of technological knowledge, and not merely the rate of which best practice is absorbed into use' (Nelson, 1981, p. 1056).

8. The extent to which investment should be stimulated should be judged not only in the light of the exigencies of effective demand, but of the requirements of growth of output, employment, consumption, and reducing inflation over time. Deficiency of effective demand is not a sufficient rationale for stimulating investment nor should long-run growth of supply and productive capacity be dictated by short-run vagaries of effective demand.

Business investment is often conceived to depend on the discrepancy between the existing stock of capital and what is considered the desirable stock needed to support future growth or to adjust itself to new factor price relationships. Since the desired capital stock depends on businesses balancing the expected after-risk and after-tax revenue with the costs of securing the real capital and producing the expected flow of output, fiscal and monetary policies affect significantly the expected return on investment through investment tax credit (what some consider 'give-aways', accelerated depreciation, corporate profit tax, nominal interest rates, and expected rate of inflation. *Ceteris paribus*, investment demand increases with the after-tax expected sales value of output and falls with the expected real cost of securing the required capital and other inputs. But, whatever else needs to be said about the formidable problem of investment decision, one cannot overstate that expanding markets, confidence in sustained rise of sales, the existing stock of capital, and the rate of utilization are all of fundamental importance in affecting business decisions.

Investment tends to be strong if business operates and expects to operate near full capacity and weak if there is large spare capacity. As long as expected output can be produced by employing the existing spare stock of capital there is little inducement to expand the latter. If business experiences prosperity, whether brought about by endogenous forces or promoted by public policy, without stop–go spurts of contraction and expansion, it will undertake investment and thus reduce cyclical instability. Contrariwise, protracted experience with vastly underutilized capacity owing to insufficiency of effective demand can transform contraction into a long-term underemployed economy.

REFERENCES

Aaron, H. J., and J. A. Pechman (eds) (1981) *How Taxes Affect Economic Behavior*, Washington: Brookings.

Ando, A. (1981) 'Discussion of the Evans Paper', in L. H. Meyer (ed.), *The Supply-Side Effects of Economic Policy*, St Louis: Center for the Study of American Business, pp. 103–11.

Blinder, A. S. (1981) 'Thoughts on the Laffer Curve', in L. H. Meyer (ed.), *The Supply-Side Effects of Economic Policy*, St Louis: Center for the Study of American Business, pp. 81–92.

Brown, C. V. (1980) *Taxation and the Incentive to Work*, Oxford: Oxford University Press.

Burtless, G. (1981) in H. J. Aaron and J. A. Pechman (eds), *How Taxes Affect Economic Behavior*, Washington: Brookings, pp. 76–83.

Cantor, V. A., D. H. Joines, and A. B. Laffer (1981) 'Tax Rates, Factor Employment, and Market Production', in L. H. Meyer (ed.) *The Supply-Side Effects of Economic Policy*, St Louis: Center for the Study of American Business, pp. 3–32.

Denison, E. F. (1976) 'The Contribution of Capital to the Postwar Growth of Industrial Countries', in US Congress, Joint Economic Committee, *US Economic Growth from 1976 to 1986*, vol. 3, Washington: GPO, pp. 45–83.

Eckstein, O. (1980) in US Congress, Joint Economic Committee, *Forecasting the Supply Side of the Economy*, Washington: GPO, pp. 24–39.

Eisner, R. (1981) in *Colloquium on Alternatives for Economic Policy*, New York: The Conference Board, pp. 28–35.

Evans, M. (1981) 'An Econometric Model Incorporating the Supply-Side Effects of Economic Policy', in L. H. Meyer (ed.) *The Supply-Side Effects of Economic Policy*, St. Louis: Center for the Study of American Business, pp. 33–80.

Feiwel, G. R. (1975) *The Intellectual Capital of Michal Kalecki*, Knoxville: University of Tennessee Press.

Feiwel, G. R. (1982) 'Samuelson and the Age After Keynes', in G. R. Feiwel (ed.) *Samuelson and Neoclassical Economics*, Boston: Kluwer-Nijhoff, pp. 202–43.

Feldstein, M., and L. H. Summers (1978) 'Inflation, Tax Rules, and the Long-Term Interest Rate', *Brookings Papers on Economic Activity*, 1.

Fisher, F. M. (1971) 'Discussion', in G. Fromm (ed.) *Tax Incentives and Capital Spending*, Washington: Brookings, pp. 243–55.

Fralick, J. S. (1981) 'Tax Policy and the Demand for Real Capital', in *Public Policy and Capital Formation*, Washington: Federal Reserve System, pp. 177–90.

Garison, C. (1983) 'The 1964 Tax Cut: Supply-Side Economics or Demand Stimulus?' (mimeo).

Hausman, J. (1981a) 'Income and Payroll Tax Policy and Labor Supply', in L. H. Meyer (ed.) *The Supply-Side Effects of Economic Policy*, St Louis: Center for the Study of American Business, pp. 173–202.

Hausman, J. (1981b) 'Labor Supply', in H. J. Aaron and J. A. Pechman (eds), *How Taxes Affect Economic Behavior*, Washington: Brookings, pp. 27–72.

Hendershott, P. H., and S.-C. Hu (1981) 'Investment in Producers' Equipment', in H. J. Aaron and J. A. Pechman (eds), *How Taxes Affect Economic Behavior*, Washington: Brookings, pp. 85–126.

Kaldor, N. (1983) *The Economic Consequences of Mrs Thatcher*, London: Duckworth.

Kalecki, M. (1935) 'A Macrodynamic Theory of Business Cycles', *Econometrica*, 3 (July): 327–44.

Kalecki, M. (1970) 'Theories of Growth in Different Social Systems', *Scientia* (May–June): 311–16.

Keynes, J. M. (1919) *The Economic Consequences of the Peace*, London: Harcourt Brace.

Klein, L. R. (1978) 'The Supply Side', *American Economic Review*, 68 (1) (March): 1–7.

Klein, L. R. (1980a) in US Congress, Joint Economic Committee, *Forecasting the Supply Side of the Economy*, Washington: GPO, pp. 53–7.

Klein, L. R. (1980b) 'Some Economic Scenarios for the 1980s', Stockholm: The Nobel Foundation (mimeo).

Klein, L. R. (1981a) 'Industrial Policy', Stockholm: Federation of Swedish Industries (mimeo).

Klein, L. R. (1981b) 'Tax Policies and Economic Expansion in the US', *Technology in Society*, 3: 205–12.

Klein, L. R. (1982) 'The Neoclassical Tradition of Keynesian Economics and the Generalized Model', in G. R. Feiwel (ed.) *Samuelson and Neoclassical Economics*, Boston: Kluwer-Nijhoff, pp. 244–62.

Kopcke, R. W. (1981) 'The Efficiency of Traditional Investment Tax Incentives', in *Public Policy and Capital Formation*, Washington: Federal Reserve System, pp. 163–75.

Kuznets, S. (1966) *Modern Economic Growth*, New Haven: Yale University Press.

Kuznets, S. (1981) 'Driving Forces of Economic Growth: What Can We Learn from History?' *Weltwirtschaftliches Archiv*, 116: 409–31.

Laffer, A. B. (1981) in House of Representatives, Ninety-Seventh Congress, *Tax Aspects of the President's Economic Program*, Washington: GPO, pp. 396–429.

Laffer, A. B., and J. P. Seymour (eds) (1979) *The Economics of the Tax Revolt*, New York: Harcourt Brace Jovanovich.

Lindbeck, A. (1982) 'The Recent Slowdown of Productivity Growth', Stockholm Institute for International Economic Studies, Seminar Paper no. 222 (October).

Lucas, R. E. (1981) *Studies in Business Cycle Theory*, Cambridge, Mass.: MIT Press.

Maddison, A. (1982) *Phases of Capitalist Development*, Oxford: Oxford University Press.

Maital, S., and N. M. Meltz (eds) (1980) *Lagging Productivity Growth*, Cambridge, Mass.: Ballinger.

Malthus, T. R. (1936) *Principles of Political Economy*, London: 1820.

Matthews, R. C. O. (1976) 'Public Policy and Monetary Expenditure', in T. Wilson and A. S. Skinner (eds), *The Market and the State*, Oxford: Clarendon Press, pp. 330–45.

Nelson, R. R. (1981) 'Research on Productivity Growth and Productivity Differences: Dead Ends and New Departures', *Journal of Economic Literature*, 19 (September): 1029–64.

Nordhaus, W. D. (1983) 'Macroeconfusion: The Dilemmas of Economic

Policy', in J. Tobin (ed.), *Macroeconomics Prices and Quantities*, Washington: Brookings, pp. 247–67.

Moore, G. R. (1981) 'Taxes, Inflation, and Capital Formation', in *Public Policy and Capital Formation*, Washington: Federal Reserve System, pp. 303–26.

Musgrave, R. A., and P. B. Musgrave (1980) *Public Finance in Theory and Practice*, New York: McGraw-Hill.

Pechman, J. A. (ed.) (1980) *What Should be Taxed: Income or Expenditure?* Washington: Brookings.

Pechman, J. A. (1981) in House of Representatives, Ninety-Seventh Congress, *Tax Aspects of the President's Economic Program*, Washington: Brookings.

Penner, R. G. (1981) in *Colloquium on Alternatives for Economic Policy*, New York: The Conference Board, pp. 72–9.

Public Policy and Capital Formation (1981) Washington: Federal Reserve System.

Rosenberg, N. (1982) *Inside the Black Box: Technology and Economics*, Cambridge: Cambridge University Press.

Rutledge, J. (1981) in House of Representatives, Ninety-Seventh Congress, *Tax Aspects of the President's Economic Program*, Washington: GPO, pp. 437–8.

Samuelson, P. A. (1966) *The Collected Scientific Papers of Paul A. Samuelson*, J. E. Stiglitz (ed.), 2 vols, Cambridge, Mass.: MIT Press.

Schultz, T. W. (1981) in *Colloquium on Alternatives for Economic Policy*, New York: The Conference Board, pp. 86–93.

Schumpeter, J. A. (1950) *Capitalism, Socialism and Democracy*, New York: Harper & Row.

Solow, R. M. (1956) 'A Contribution to the Theory of Economic Growth', *Quarterly Journal of Economics*, LXX (February): 65–94.

Steindel, C. (1981) 'The Determinants of Private Saving', in *Public Policy and Capital Formation*, Washington: Federal Reserve System, pp. 101–14.

Summers, L. H. (1981) 'The Effect of Economic Policy on Investment', in L. H. Meyer (ed.), *The Supply-Side Effects of Economic Policy*, St Louis: Center for the Study of American Business, pp. 115–48.

'Supply-Side Symposium' (1981) *Morgan Guaranty Survey* (August): 3–9.

Survey of Current Business (1972) 52 (May): pt II.

Tax Aspects of the President's Economic Program (1981) House of Representatives, Ninety-Seventh Congress, Washington: GPO.

The Decline in Productivity Growth (1980) Conference Series no. 22, Boston: Federal Reserve Bank of Boston.

Tinbergen, J. (1956) *Economic Policy*, Amsterdam: North-Holland.

Tobin, J. (1981) 'The Reagan Economic Plan–Supply-side, Budget and Inflation', in *The Reagan Economic Program*, San Francisco: Federal Reserve Bank (1 May): 5–14.

Ture, N. B. (1980) in US Congress, Joint Economic Committee, *Forecasting the Supply Side of the Economy*, Washington: GPO, pp. 61–74.

Ture, N. B. (1981) 'Discussion of the Summers Paper', in L. H. Meyer (ed.), *The Supply-Side Effects of Economic Policy*, St Louis: Center for the Study of American Business, pp. 165–70.

von Furstenberg, G. M. (1981) 'Saving', in H. J. Aaron and J. A. Pechman (eds), *How Taxes Affect Economic Behavior*, Washington: Brookings, pp. 327–402.

19 The Asset Price Approach to the Analysis of Capital Income Taxation*

LAWRENCE H. SUMMERS

This chapter summarizes and attempts to place in a broader context my recent research directed at developing an asset price approach to the analysis of the effects of capital income taxation. The link between asset markets and real investment decisions has been an important theme of much recent research in macroeconomics dating at least from Tobin's seminal q theory of investment. However, asset markets have been subordinate in most previous theoretical and empirical efforts to model the effects of capital income taxation on economic behaviour. Although changes in asset prices are the proximate determinants of who gains and loses following tax reforms, asset markets are suppressed in standard models used to study tax incidence.

A recurring theme in much of the empirical work described here is the effect of inflation on the tax system. Empirical work on the macroeconomic effects of tax reforms has always been difficult because of the paucity of statutory changes. In this limited respect, inflation has been salutary, because its frequent increases during the 1970s and recent sharp decreases have significantly altered the effective taxation of real income because of

*Much of the research summarized in this chapter was contained in my doctoral thesis. I am indebted to the many people thanked in my thesis for a variety of types of assistance in connection with the research reported here. Financial support was provided by the National Bureau of Economic Research. Computational assistance was provided by Data Resources Incorporated.

nominal accounting practices. Indeed, it is fair to say that most of the variation in tax rates on corporate capital over the last two decades can be traced to the effects of inflation.

Beyond its scientific interest, an analysis of capital income taxation and particularly its interactions with inflation is highly pertinent in the light of recent economic events. The inflationary decade of the 1970s witnessed important changes in traditional patterns of capital accumulation and valuation in the US economy. The real price of corporate capital relative to consumption goods declined by almost 50 per cent. Almost as dramatic was the real appreciation in the relative price of owner-occupied housing and land. As a consequence of these changes, the relative value of the two principal forms of wealth in the economy changed by a factor of more than two. During late 1982, the rate of expected inflation fell very sharply, and the stock market rose very dramatically, while real housing prices remained relatively stable. These large changes in relative prices were reflected in movements in rates of investment. The growth rate of non-residential business capital employed per man-hour declined from 3.4 per cent in the 1949-74 period to 0.2 per cent in the 1976–80 interval, while the share of net investment devoted to residential capital rose significantly.

The first section of this chapter describes in more detail what is meant by the asset price approach to capital income taxation and discusses its advantages for studying certain public finance questions. The second section illustrates how the effects of tax reforms on both asset prices and investment can be estimated in a simple partial equilibrium setting. The third and final section of the chapter summarizes research on the relationship between taxes and the pricing of capital assets and suggests directions for future research.

THE ASSET PRICE APPROACH

The asset price approach to capital income taxation provides a unified framework in which three traditional issues in the analysis of capital income taxation can be addressed. These issues include the short-run effects of tax reforms on investment, their long-run effects on capital accumulation and growth and their effects on horizontal and vertical equity. The relationship between the asset price and traditional approaches to each of these issues is discussed below.

Taxation and Investment

Before discussing the advantages of focusing on asset prices in analysing the effects of capital income taxes on investment, it is useful to review briefly more standard approaches to the problem. There exists a large literature attempting econometric evaluation of the effects of investment incentives. This literature, which is extensively summarized in Eisner and Chirinko (1980), is based on extensions of the flexible accelerator approach to investment developed in the seminal work of Hall and Jorgenson (1967). These studies all model investment as an adjustment process to a desired capital stock. The desired capital stock is postulated to be a function of the past levels of real output and the cost of capital. Often, as in Jorgenson's work, theory is used to tightly constrain this function. As Eisner and Chirinko illustrate, there is room for substantial disagreement about these constraints and the specification of the cost of capital. Here I leave these issues aside, and consider two more fundamental problems with the use of flexible accelerator-type econometric investment equations to model the effects of investment incentives.

The major conceptual difficulty with flexible accelerator approaches is that they treat output as predetermined from the point of view of the firm's investment decision. The desired capital stock is chosen conditional on output rather than being simultaneously determined. This is an important problem. Presumably, government's reason for offering investment tax incentives is the belief that reductions in the cost of capital will raise the level of output firms desire to supply. This in turn leads to increased invest-investment. It is difficult to imagine how investment incentives could be beneficial, if they have no impact on the level of output firms expect to produce. Yet this constraint is imposed *a priori* in studies using flexible accelerator approaches to model investment.

This objection is sometimes met by embedding equations of this type in large-scale Keynesian models, and simulating the path of the economy, under alternative assumptions about tax policy. This approach brings with it all the well-known problems of such models. More importantly, it does not really meet the objection that meaningful evaluation of the effects of investment incentives requires analysis of their effects on the desired supply of output. In standard Keynesian models, output is demand-determined with essentially no role left for the effects of policies on aggregate supply.

A second problem with flexible accelerator models is the treatment of expectations. Presumably the desired capital stock should be a 'forward looking variable' depending on expectations about the future marginal product and cost of capital. Standard approaches assume that these variables can be adequately proxied by lagged values of output and the cost of capital. This seems implausible. Announced but not yet implemented tax policies will clearly have effects on the level of investment, but this possibility is precluded in standard investment equations. A second example is provided by changes in the production function through time. Flexible accelerator approaches typically assume that the marginal product of capital is a stable function of the capital–output ratio. The substantial variation in observed rates of profit suggests that this assumption is unwarranted. These examples are merely illustrations of Robert Lucas's (1976) famous critique of standard large-scale econometric models. In general, the estimated parameter will be complex combinations of underlying structural parameters, and the stochastic processes followed by policy and other exogenous variables. It is unlikely that the estimates will be stable from period to period, especially when policy rules are altered.

The asset price approach to analysing the effects of capital taxation relied on here takes as its point of departure a different strand of the literature on investment. A number of authors including Eisner and Strotz (1963), Lucas (1967), Treadway (1969), and Abel (1980) have recognized the *ad hoc* character of the delivery lags introduced in many models of investment, and developed models of investment in which costs of adjustment enter explicitly. In these models, the level of investment depends on the shadow price associated with the capital accumulation constraint. When the value of capital rises, firms are willing to incur more adjustment costs in order to rapidly increase their capital stock. As Hayashi's (1982) important paper demonstrates, these models of competitive firms facing adjustment costs are under constant returns to scale assumptions, closely related to q investment models of the type pioneered by Tobin (1969). In models the rate of investment is a function of q, the ratio of the market value of the capital stock to its replacement cost. In fact, the observed q ratio can be used to infer the shadow price of capital goods in the model of a firm facing costs of adjustment.

These linkages are important because they imply that an asset price approach can avoid the difficulties with standard econometric evaluations of investment incentives that were considered above. When adjustment costs are introduced, it is possible to develop a meaningful theory of supply even for firms with constant returns to scale. In any given period, the firm will choose its desired level of output depending on its previous capital stock. The growth rate of the capital stock will depend on the return on capital investment. Thus the asset price approach is supply based and so can be used to evaluate the effects of investment incentives.

The link between the observable q ratio and the shadow price of capital in the firm's dynamic optimization problem also solves the problem of modelling expectations. The q ratio will summarize the expectations of future profitability and costs of capital on which investment depends. Thus it obviates the need to adopt complex procedures for estimating expectations about these future variables. The relationship between investment and q is structural in the sense that it should be invariant with respect to changes in policy rules and should depend only on technology. Therefore the asset price approach can be used to estimate the effects of policy announcement and temporary measures, which are not susceptible to analysis using alternative econometric approaches.

Taxation and Capital Accumulation

The asset price approach also bears on the literature in public finance examining the long-run effects of capital income taxation on both the accumulation and allocation of capital, and the long-run efficiency and incidence implications of capital income taxation. This literature originating in Harberger's (1962) seminal paper on the corporate income tax has largely ignored the process of investment. The models employed are not well suited to analysing the short- and intermediate-run response of the economy to changes in tax policy since they assume that there are no costs of adjustment impeding the accumulation or reallocation of capital. As a consequence, sectoral marginal products of capital are always equated. This means that there is essentially no scope for variation in the asset price of existing capital goods.

The evident volatility of observed asset prices demonstrates the unrealism of the maintained assumption of instantaneous adjustment. In order for large relative price changes to occur, it is necessary that adjustment be slow so that divergences of the marginal product of capital and its cost endure. The asset price approach developed here provides a basis for explicitly estimating the extent of these adjustment costs and modelling more realistically the transition of the economy following tax changes.

Tax Incidence

The presence of large adjustment costs also has important implications for the analysis of the incidence of capital income taxation. The implausibility of standard models without adjustment costs may be seen by noting that they imply that corporate share-owners would not gain relative to home-owners from an equalization of the tax rates on residential and corporate capital. This is because the standard approach to tax incidence ignores an important aspect of the actual economy's response to such a tax change. In the short run, the price of existing corporate capital would rise, and of existing homes would fall, as investors adjusted their portfolios. The price changes would capitalize the expected present value of the effects of the tax reform on future returns, conferring windfall gains on the owners of corporate capital, and losses on home-owners. These price changes would act as signals to the suppliers of new capital, calling forth more plant and equipment and fewer homes, until their relative prices were again equated to their relative long-run marginal costs of production.

Because an essential step in the asset price approach is the estimation of the effects of tax reforms on the market valuation of existing assets, it is ideally suited for evaluating the short-run incidence of tax policy changes. Such an analysis is important to evaluating the effects of tax reforms on both vertical and horizontal equity. Given information on the effects of tax reforms on asset prices, and the distribution of wealth holding, it is possible to evaluate the vertical equity effects of tax reforms. As Feldstein (1976) pointed out, horizontal equity is best achieved by avoiding reforms that give rise to windfall gains and losses.

The asset price approach also highlights the very different incidence of reforms that reduce taxes on all capital income and those that benefit only new investments. While appropriately chosen reforms of these two types may have an equal impact on investment, they are likely to have very different effects on existing wealth-holders. Measures that reduce the tax burden on all capital are likely to substantially raise the market value of existing assets, conferring a windfall gain on the holders of existing assets. On the other hand, measures that subsidize only new capital may well actually reduce the wealth of owners of the existing capital which must compete with newly subsidized capital. These distinctions are not recognized within standard analyses that focus on the effects of tax policy changes on after-tax rates of return but not on the value of existing assets.

THE DYNAMICS OF INVESTMENT AND MARKET VALUATION

The asset price approach to public finance and its implications for investment and market valuation can be illustrated in the context of a simple stylized model. A more complex version of this framework is used in much of the research described in the next section.

The dynamics of investment and market valuation are considered in a model in which there is no inflation, capital does not depreciate, investment is financed through retained earnings, and the only tax is a proportional levy on corporate income. In this setting it is reasonable to assume that investment depends on the ratio of the market value of existing capital to its replacement cost. Unless an investment of one dollar increases the market value of the firm by more than one dollar, there is no reason to invest. Given the costs of adjustments and lags in recognition and implementation, there is no reason to expect that all investments that increase market value by more than their cost will be made immediately. As Tobin argued, these considerations lead to an investment equation of the form:

$$I = I\left(\frac{V}{K}\right) K \tag{19.1}$$

$$I(1) = 0 \quad I' > 0$$

where I represents gross investment and V/K is the q ratio of market value to replacement cost. Since inflation is assumed to be zero, the price of capital can be taken to be 1. The assumption that the ratio of I/K depends on q ensures that the growth rate of the capital stock is independent of the scale of the economy. It is important to recognize that the investment schedule given by equation (19.1) is a technological relation that depends only on the adjustment cost function.

It is assumed that equity owners require a fixed real rate of return to induce them to hold the existing stock of equity. This return comes in the form of dividends – equal to after-tax profits minus retained earnings for new investment – and capital gains. Hence the condition:

$$\rho = \frac{Div}{V} + \frac{\dot{V}}{V} \tag{19.2}$$

which implies:

$$\dot{V} = \rho V - (1 - \tau) F'(K)K + I\left(\frac{V}{K}\right) K \tag{19.3}$$

where τ- is the corporate tax rate, and the production function, with labour input fixed, is given by $F(K)$. Because it is assumed that the economy's fixed labour force is fully employed, the rate of profit, $F'(K)$, declines as the capital stock increases. It will be convenient to examine the dynamics in terms of K and q. Equations (19.2) and (19.3) imply that the system's equations of motion are:

$$\dot{K} = I(q) K \tag{19.4}$$

$$\dot{q} = [\rho - I(q)] q + I(q) - (1 - \tau)F'(K) \qquad (19.5)$$

The steady state properties of the model are easily found by imposing the conditions $K = 0$ and $q = 0$. These imply:

$$q = I^{-1}(0) = 1 \qquad (19.6)$$

$$\rho = (1 - \tau)F'(K) \qquad (19.7)$$

Equation (19.6) indicates that in the steady state, the value of q must equal 1 so that the market value of capital goods equals their replacement cost. Equation (19.7) indicates that, in equilibrium, firms equate their net marginal product of capital to the cost of capital. Inspection of (19.6) and (19.7) makes clear that a change in the corporate tax rate affects the steady-state capital stock but has no effect on steady-state q because the change does not influence the cost to the firm of acquiring new capital goods.

The dynamics of adjustment following a tax change are illustrated in figure 19.1, a phase diagram representing equations (19.4) and (19.5). In

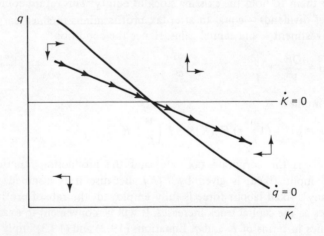

FIGURE 19.1

the figure, the arrows depict the equations of motion of the system when it is not in equilibrium. The dark line represents the saddle-point path along which the system will converge to a steady state. A reduction in the corporate tax rate does not immediately affect the capital stock. The value of q jumps from E_1 to B, as shown in Figure 19.2. As capital is accumu-

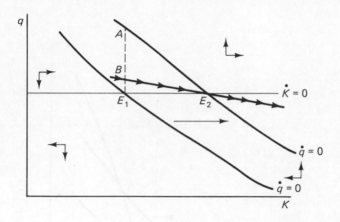

FIGURE 19.2

lated, the marginal product of capital falls and the system converges to E_2, where q is again equal to its equilibrium value. This path assumes that investors have perfect foresight and take account of the capital losses that occur as capital is accumulated. An alternative assumption is that the investors have myopic expectations and fail to foresee the effects of capital accumulation. In this case, the system jumps from E_1 to A and then converges to E_2 along the $q = 0$ schedule; along this transition path investors consistently earn less than their required rate of return.

An alternative type of tax reform benefits only new investment. Consider the introduction of a subsidy at rate s, a new investment. This reduces the effective purchase price of capital goods to firms. It also reduces corporate tax payments for any firm that invests. The effects of such a subsidy are displayed in Figure 19.3. Unambiguously, the steady-state level of capital-intensity increases. However, the short-run effect of the tax change on the market valuation of existing capital is unclear, as illustrated in Figure 19.3. There are two offsetting effects. The investment subsidy reduces tax payments tending to increase market valuation, but it also increases the competition for old capital tending to reduce the value of existing capital. The crucial distinction between tax reforms that benefit

438

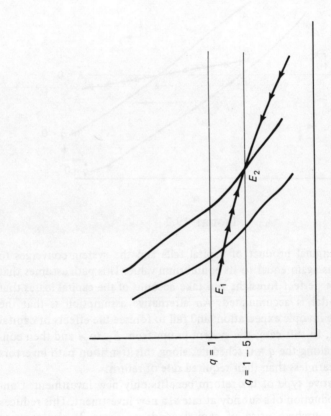

FIGURE 19.3

all capital, and those that benefit only new capital (discussed in the previous section) can be readily observed by comparing Figures 19.2 and 19.3).

This discussion illustrates the asset price approach to the analysis of tax policy in a particular simple context. Note that all that is necessary to evaluate the effects of implementing any given tax policy path is knowledge of the profit function $F(k)$ and the investment schedule $I(q)$. Both are estimable from observable data and do not depend on commeasurable expectations. Given knowledge of these functions, equations (19.3) and (19.4), together with an initial condition on the capital stock and the terminal condition (19.6) can be used to calculate the evolution of V, K, and I. Formally, a solution of a two-point boundary value problem is involved. While this can be difficult in models with multiple assets, Lipton, Poterba, Sachs, and Summers (1982) have developed an algorithm that can be used to solve problems of moderate size.

SUMMARY OF RESEARCH ON TAXATION AND ASSET PRICES

In an earlier work (Summers, 1981), I developed a q theory of investment where the linkage between the 'average q' as measured on financial markets, and marginal q, the shadow price of investment in a dynamic model of firm investment decisions when adjustment is costly is established. The model considered is stochastic and includes a fairly detailed tax structure. The performance of standard q investment equations, and equations using a q variable that is adjusted for the effect of taxation, in explaining fluctuations in investment at both the firm and the aggregate level are then contrasted. The econometric results support the theory as the tax adjusted q variable outperforms the standard variable in explaining both aggregate and firm investment. These results are confirmed using data on individual firms in Salinger and Summers (1983).

The next stage in this research, also described in Summers (1981), involves using these econometric results to calibrate a partial equilibrium simulation model capable of examining the effects of alternative tax reforms on investment and stock market valuation. the model used is partial equilibrium in the sense that it takes as exogenously fixed the real after-tax rate of return required by equity investors. Results of simulations suggest that the interaction of inflation and the tax system can significantly reduce investment and the level of the stock market. The estimates suggest that indexation of the tax system would raise the stock market by about 20 per cent and investment by about 15 per cent. Various statutory tax reforms are then considered. The results suggest that measures directed at reducing capital gains taxes and accelerating depreciation have the largest impact on investment per dollar of revenue foregone.

Summers (1982) takes a first step towards the construction of a general equilibrium model in which the effect of taxation on asset prices and investment can be studied. The model incorporates owner-occupied housing and land as well as corporate capital. In the model, consumption is determined by intertemporal optimization. The model is designed to capture the wealth effects of fiscal policies that are ignored in standard models used in public finance. Three substantive conclusions emerge from the analysis. First, the supply of funds to the non-financial corporate sector is likely to be highly elastic so that tax policies will have relatively little impact on the required rate of return. Second, indexation of the tax system would generate significant windfall gains for equity owners and stimulate corporate investment. Large losses would be suffered by bond owners. Home-owners and landowners would also lose as portfolio reallocations towards corporate capital reduced the value of their investment. Third, the form of tax incentives has a major impact. The elimination of the corporate income tax, and the implementation of an accelerated depreciation programme like that recently enacted, have similar effects on long-run corporate capital-intensity. However, they have very different effects on the stock market in the short run. The former measure raises the value of the market by about 80 per cent relative to the latter. The consumption caused by the greater increase in wealth leads to higher interest rates, so the crowding out effects of eliminating corporate taxes are much greater than those of instituting accelerated depreciation.

The research described so far is directed at developing estimates of the effects of tax reforms, assuming the validity of the assumption underlying the asset price approach. A major virtue of working with asset price information is that it can be used to provide tests of alternative models of the effects of tax changes.

Microeconomic tests of the asset price model are presented in Summers (1981). The tests rely on differences between the firms in the tax effects on inflation. The 'tax effects' hypothesis predicts that high leverage firms, using LIFO inventory accounting, for which depreciation is a small part of cash flow, should benefit from increases in inflation relative to firms with opposing characteristics. The 'inflation illusion' view of Modigliani and Cohn has the opposite implications. These hypotheses are tested using a sample of 1200 firms drawn from the *compustat* tapes. The econometric results are generally favourable to the tax effects hypothesis. The data suggest that FIFO firms lose substantially from inflation, relative to others. Highly levered firms appear to benefit from inflation. The evidence on depreciation is more mixed, with the results suggesting that inflation illusion was present in the 1960s but had almost vanished by the late 1970s. The cross-section results are then used to try to explain the disastrous performance of the market during the 1970s. I conclude that tax effects can explain about a 15 per cent decline, with another 25 per cent potentially attributable to increasing awareness of the need to adjust reported historic cost depreciation.

The adjustment of nominal interest rates to changes in expected inflation plays a critical role in any analysis of inflation–tax interactions. This issue is taken up in Summers (1982). A simple general equilibrium model in which the effects of taxation on the Fisher relationship can be studied is developed. Theoretical analysis with almost any plausible parameter values suggests that in the presence of taxes, steady inflation should raise nominal interest rates by more than point for point. Theoretical analysis does not identify the short-run relationship between interest rates and inflation, which depends on the source of stochastic shocks. Standard econometric procedures are therefore not well suited to testing the predictions of the model. Tests of the Fisher relationship are presented which use band-spectrum regression to filter out high-frequency movements in the variables. The results are disappointing in suggesting the failure of nominal interest rates to adjust for inflation as fully as theory would predict. This conclusion is robust, holding over 120 years of US data. The possibility that the failure of interest rates to rise with inflation is the result of correlation between inflation and measures of either the marginal product of capital or the measures of risk is considered and rejected. The possibility that financial markets exhibit inflation illusion is entertained tentatively.

Recognition of the importance of changes in asset prices has crucial implications for the analysis of the effects of taxation of risky assets. Bulow and Summers (1982) demonstrate that previous analyses that have typically assumed that depreciation rates are constant and that the future price of capital goods is known with certainty are very misleading as guides to the effects of corporate taxes. In an environment where asset prices are variable, the concept of economic depreciation requires careful definition. We show that an appropriate *ex ante* depreciation schedule depends on future asset price risk. Some empirical calculations suggest that the appropriate adjustments for risk are large and greatly affect the estimated burden of the corporate income tax.

Data on asset prices can also be used to test alternative hypotheses regarding corporate financial policy. Poterba and Summers (1983) exploit the substantial variations in UK dividend taxation that have occurred over the last thirty years, to contract the 'tax capitalization' and 'traditional' models of the effects of dividend taxation. The tests rely on the specification of investment equations based on alternative specification of 'tax adjusted q' variables.

Asset prices can also be used to study questions in other areas of public finance. Rosen (1982) uses information on housing prices to assess the effects of California's Proposition 13 on individual localities. Potentially this approach could be extended to consider other types of governmental spending programmes. These might include agricultural measures whose incidence is reflected in changes in the price of farm land, and direct or indirect subsidies to industries that affect stock prices. The research described here illustrates two propositions. First, the effect of tax policies on asset prices can be estimated and used to measure their incidence. Second, asset price data can be used to answer otherwise very difficult empirical questions in public finance. Future research on the issues mentioned here and others will contribute to our understanding of the effects of the functioning of taxation on our economy.

REFERENCES

Abel, A. B. (1980), 'Empirical Investment Equations: An Integrative Framework', in K. Brunner and A. H. Metzler (eds), *On the State of Macro-Economics*, Carnegie-Rochester Conference Series on Public Policy, 12, Amsterdam: North-Holland, 39–91.
Bulow, J. I., and L. Summers (1982) 'Risk and Taxes Reconsidered' (mimeo).
Eisner, R., and R. Chirinko (1980) 'Tax Policy and Business Investment, unpublished.
Eisner, R., and R. H. Strotz (1963) 'Determinants of Business Investment', in Commission on Money and Credit, *Impacts of Monetary Policy*, Englewood Cliffs, N.J.: Prentice-Hall, pp. 59–337.
Feldstein, M. (1976) 'Toward a Theory of Tax Reform', *Journal of Public Economics*, 6 (July–August): 77–104.
Hall, R. E., and D. W. Jorgenson (1967) 'Tax Policy and Investment Behavior', *American Economic Review*, 57 (June): 391–414.
Harberger, A. (1962) 'The Incidence of the Corporation Income Tax', *Journal of Political Economy*, 70(3): 215–40.
Hayashi, F. (1982) 'Tobin's Marginal q and Average q: A Neoclassical Interpretation', *Econometrica*, 50 (January): 213–24.
Lipton, D., J. Poterba, J. Sachs and L. Summers (1982) 'Multiple Shooting in Rational Expectations Models'. *Econometrica*, 50 (September): 1329–33.

Lucas, R. E. Jr (1967) 'Adjustment Costs and the Theory of Supply', *Journal of Political Economy*, 75 (August): 321-34.

Lucas, R. E. Jr (1976) 'Econometric Policy Evaluation: A Critique', in *The Phillips Curve and Labor Markets*, Carnegie-Rochester Conference Series on Public Policy, 1, Amsterdam: North-Holland, 19-46.

Poterba, J., and L. Summers (1983) 'Dividend Taxes, Corporate Investment and *q?' Journal of Public Economics* 22 (November): 135-67.

Rosen, K. T. (1982) 'The Impact of Proposition 13 on House Prices in Northern California', *Journal of Political Economy*, 90 (February) 90: 191-200.

Salinger, M., and L. Summers (1983) 'Corporate Tax Reform and Securities Prices; A Simulation Approach', forthcoming in National Bureau of Economic Research Conference Volume on *Tax Simulation Analysis*.

Summers, L. (1981) 'Taxation and Corporate Investment: A *q* Theory Approach', *Brookings Papers on Economic Activity* (January): 67-127.

Summers, L. (1982) 'Inflation and the Valuation of Corporate Equities', National Bureau of Economic Research, Working Paper.

Summers, L. (1983a) 'Taxation and Asset Prices in a General Equilibrium Model', unpublished.

Summers, L. (1983b) 'The Non-adjustment of Nominal Interest Rates: A Study of the Fisher Effect', in J. Tobin (ed.), *Macroeconomics: Prices and Quantities*, Brookings, pp. 201-47.

Tobin, J. (1969) 'A General Equilibrium Approach to Monetary Theory', *Journal of Money, Credit and Banking*, 1 (February): 15-29.

Treadway, A. B. (1969) 'On Rational Entrepreneurial Behavior and the Demand for Investment', *Review of Economic Studies*, 36: 227-39.

20 A Longer-term Perspective on Macroeconomics and Distribution: Time, Expectations, and Incentives*

MICHAEL J. BOSKIN

INTRODUCTION

Many of the most important modelling and policy issues in both macro-economics and income distribution revolve around the emphasis placed on the length of the time horizon, the role of expectations, and the responsive-ness of behaviour to incentives.[1] These three concerns continually arise in various theoretical models and empirical studies addressing the most fundamental concerns of economists. Debates over the potential efficacy of activist monetary (and indeed, fiscal) policy in stabilizing the economy; the optimal redistributive tax/transfer system; and the determinants of long-term growth all must come to grips with these central issues. While

*This brief chapter is designed to be impressionistic, not encyclopedic. All references are to examples, not to prioritise contributions. Also, I have deliberately refrained from using labels such as 'monetarist', 'rational expectations', 'supply-side', or 'Keynesian'.

debates currently rage on the appropriateness of the 'new classical macro-economics', 'optimal tax theory', etc., as bases both for descriptions of economic performance and prescriptions for economic policy, the three elements mentioned above that these and other recent advances have brought to the forefront of economic analysis are likely to remain key elements of the economist's tool kit well beyond the life-cycle of any particular model or school of thought. In fact, future historians of econ-omic thought may well view these as the most enduring components of economic research in recent years. The focus on time horizon, incentives, and expectations permeates much day-to-day economics, for example, the type of information used for evaluation of government policy proposals.

It is quite remarkable that sets of scholars working on very different issues in economics have found it necessary to incorporate these three concerns in their analyses. From the attempt to explain the apparent oddity of monetary policy being powerful in the short run while neutral in the long run in the context of fluctuations in real output and employment to understanding the personal distribution of income to the welfare economics of evaluating alternative tax/transfer programmes, many of the same issues arise.

It is also clear that many of these issues arise in debating the historical, and/or possible future, efficacy of government policy in achieving various desirable economic outcomes.

This brief chapter is designed to highlight the importance of time horizon, incentives, and expectations through the vehicle of several import-ant examples relating to macroeconomics and distribution. It is offered as a conjectural history of economic thought. The emphasis of modelling and empirical work has shifted to a concern for larger time horizons, incentives and expectations in marked contrast to work that was the norm only a few years ago. While the ultimate place of such work in the daily tool kit of the future working economist remains to be seen, it seems clear that we shall not return to a virtually exclusive focus on the world of the short-run and totally inelastic behaviour. Towards this end, the next section discusses some examples of recent work in what is sometimes called the 'new public finance' in comparing typical studies of the distributive effects of taxes and transfers and the welfare economics thereof with more recent approaches to highlight the key role played by time horizon, expectations, and incentives. The third section deals with the timely and timeless prob-lem of the efficacy of fiscal policy and the role of government debt in macroeconomics and the role that these three concerns play in various models of the efficacy of fiscal policy. The fourth section offers a brief conclusion.

DISTRIBUTION AND TAX INCIDENCE

Perhaps nowhere is the emphasis on time horizon and incentives more widely disseminated among academic economists than in the field of the analysis of the distributive impact of taxation and transfer payment schemes. The bulk of public discussion of various tax and transfer devices (for example, the Reagan tax cuts, or more subtlty, the reductions in means-tested benefit programmes, eligibility standards) is still in terms of their 'initial impact'. Such studies take the existing tax laws and apply the change to estimate changes in disposable income; they have been sharply discredited in professional research. While this simple short-run cross-tabulation view of the incidence and effects of various tax devices may provide some potential insight for analysing the transition problems, it would be fair to say that much of the discussion in public finance has shifted to a much longer time horizon, indeed, the entire lifetime. This occurs for at least three reasons.

First, the development of life-cycle models of earnings and capital formation has provided an analytical basis for making such calculations.[1]

Second, various bodies of data have beome available in the last decade, which follow people over a substantial length of time and enable at least the beginnings of a serious econometric attempt to estimate lifetime income or the present value of expected future earnings conditional on various characteristics.[2]

Third, theoretical models of incidence have now begun to incorporate intertemporal human investment and capital formation decisions, and therefore, the behavioural assumptions underlying the theory of tax shifting and our views of incidence have undergone something of a revolution in the last dozen years.[3]

All this combines with the substantial growth in various fiscal institutions whose explicit purpose is to transfer resources across lifetimes and between generations. The enormous growth of social insurance programmes in the advanced economies of Western Europe and the USA is perhaps the most important of these. The archetypal social insurance programme is financed on a pay-as-you-go basis, where the current tax payments are used to finance current benefit payments. Thus, if nothing else occurred, the current generation of taxpayers would be transferring income to the current generation of retirees. Of course, this is only the beginning of the story, similar to the simple cross-tabulation of incidence by income class that used to be the *sine qua non* of tax policy discussions. However, it is clear that a variety of potential adjustments may be triggered by the growth of social security and that the tax and benefits themselves may have explicit behavioural implications. While it is not our purpose here to review the state of knowledge on such subjects, it is clear that social security may well affect retirement behaviour, pre-retirement labour supply, and saving behaviour. It also may substantially affect the demand for various types of private insurance. Further, taken directly, social security has an 'unfunded' present value of expected future debt which is many times the regular national debt in most countries, for example, something on the order of four or five times the regular national debt of the USA.[4] This occurs because the present value of expected benefits substantially exceeds the present value of expected future taxes over any particular time horizon chosen (usually the next seventy-five years for simulation studies). Thus, some combination of future tax increases and reductions in expected future benefits totalling about $5 trillion in discounted 1983 dollars must occur in social security to insure its solvency.

What of this implicit debt? Barro (1974) has argued that it is exactly offset by private intra-family intergenerational transfers of resources. The argument, which is discussed in more detail in the next section in discussing the fiscal impotence doctrine, is simply that in response to the growth of social security, the older generation will adjust its bequests in order to leave its heirs no worse off than before the advent of social security. Thus, the reduction in private saving predicted by Feldstein (1979), is absorbed by private behaviour, and there will be no long-run effects on capital formation and future standards of living. While I believe that there is much to this point of view, in the extreme form, it is substantially overstated in my opinion, a point I will return to below. In this section, the key issue is the enormous change in the *lifetime* resources of different individuals and groups in the population that occur from changes in social security legislation which are hardly even mentioned in the popular press compared to relatively minor changes in current (or lifetime) resources caused by tax changes. For example, the Reagan tax cut of 1983, even if it is a permanent one, will result in a much smaller change in lifetime private resources available to younger workers than will the provision of the social security amendments passed just prior to this tax cut, which gradually raises the age for eligibility for full retirement benefits to 67 years of age. Thus, in writing down the lifetime resource constraint of an individual or family, this more subtle fiscal policy change, in a world where we focus on lifetime resources, has enormous consequences.

No doubt the analyses in public finance were made possible by the development of the theory (and corresponding empirical work) of human capital and of life-cycle accumulation.[5] While the latter was primarily developed to explain macroeconomic phenomena, these twin pillars have enabled us to reinterpret annual data as conditional on age. The usual estimates of the distribution of income taken for a given year, for example, in a census survey, apparently overstate the degree of inequality in our society. While substantial inequality exists, a large part of it is due to differences in age, experience, and the corresponding accumulation of human and non-human capital. Put simply, at a given point in time, we are lumping together, in analysing distribution, people at different points of their lifetime income profile, and this can be exceptionally misleading. Thus, recent attempts to estimate the degree of inequality using even simplistic and flawed measures such as Gini-coefficients conclude that the degree of inequality is somewhat less when attention is paid to making even simple corrections for age.

All this has had a tremendous impact on the thinking of economists on a variety of other tax issues. An important case in point is in the debate over the appropriate base for taxation.

Economists have long favoured taxing consumption rather than income on efficiency grounds. More recently, it has become clear that in a second-best world, that case is no longer analytically determinate, although empirical and simulation studies still suggest consumption would be a much more efficient tax base than would income.[6] The important point here is that changing to a somewhat longer time horizon, as suggested by life-cycle and human capital considerations, drastically changes the perception of income taxes as somehow more equitable than consumption taxes. That case was primarily made by an appeal to data for a single year which shows the ratio of consumption to income declining as we move up the income scale, and therefore the argument is that a (flat rate) consumption tax would be regressive relative to a (flat rate) income tax. Not only does this ignore the issues of the potential capital formation such an equal tax yield shift from an income to a consumption tax would cause and therefore, the increase in future wages, but it also ignores the fact that much of this variation in the consumption–income ratio is due to systematic age-income relationships. Harking back to the permanent income notion of Friedman, it is clear that persons with the same amount of wealth may have different incomes, depending on their attitudes towards risk and the different yields on different types of assets. Current income may be a poor measure of a person's permanent income. On the other hand, consumption may be closely related to permanent income. Consider the simplest possible life-cycle model. Everyone enters the labour force at some specified age with an endowment of skills and training, no future human investment occurs, and the wage rate is constant throughout the life of the individual. There is a perfect capital market, and interest rates are assumed to remain constant. Thus, the present value of future wages is the wealth of each individual. Ignoring bequests and inheritances for simplicity, this individual's consumption must equal the present value of his or her wages over the lifetime. That is, a consumption tax, in this rarefied model, amounts to a tax on the individual's wealth or endowment.

Thus, this longer time horizon has made the younger generation of public finance economists much more vehement proponents of consumption taxation and opponents of income taxation than the generation that preceded them. This is not surprising since that generation, having lived through the Depression, was all too aware of the fragility of capital markets.

Sometimes, I believe, it is possible to go too far and to evaluate such arguments *exclusively* on the basis of the expected lifetime impact of the programme. First, there is considerable heterogeneity in the population, and different individuals will fare differently over their lifetimes. Second, clearly the assumption of perfect capital markets is quite extreme, not the least of the imperfections reflecting the tax system, the absence of a full set of futures markets and the inability to borrow fully against one's expected future earnings for well-known reasons. Thus, it has become clear that while most of the basic questions in public finance are beginning to be re-evaluated on a lifetime or at least longer-term horizon basis, I believe that we will ultimately attempt to make the day-to-day input to public policy-making reflect some convex combination of these two types of information. I do not believe that we will ever go back exclusively to a focus on short-run current changes in disposable income, assuming all behavioural responses are zero. On the other hand, I do believe that some of the short-term transition issues are important enough that we will have to include such analyses side by side with estimates of longer-term impacts of various policies.

Expectations and incentives also play a role in discussions of income distribution and tax/transfer incidence. Obviously, in any model of capital formation (human and non-human), intertemporal elasticities of substitution will be important in determining ultimate tax incidence. For example, in my analysis of taxation, saving, and the real net return,[7] I concluded that the estimates imply that about half of *capital* income taxes are *shifted on to labour*. In their otherwise excellent study, Pechman and Okner (1972) provide careful estimates of the incidence of various taxes based on a variety of incidence assumptions. However, they ignore these long-run capital formation effects, and assume capital income taxes are generally borne by capital and income taxes in proportion to income.

While such incentive effects are basically empirical propositions, and the econometric study of them has perhaps raised more questions than it has answered, this longer-run way of thinking is becoming the basis for a much larger fraction of the work being done in public finance today. Further, various assumptions about expectations and foresight of consumers are being built into various analytical and, in particular, simulation models. The recent interesting general equilibrium simulation models of Auerbach, Kotlikoff and Skinner,[8] and Shoven *et al.*,[9] analyse explicitly the impact on the economy of different perceptions of expected future taxes. Indeed, for the moment, the primary focus of research currently has shifted not only from the immediate short-run to longer-run lifetime but actually to debates concerning the nature and importance of the bequest motive. This turns out to be quite crucial, as will be documented below in the discussion of fiscal policy, but it highlights the evolution of research on distributional issues in public finance.

It seems safe to conclude that we will never go back to the world of simple cross-tabulations of current income by current income class, assignment of tax burdens thereby, and assumptions that supplies and demands are perfectly inelastic. While I believe that such information will continue to be used, it will undoubtedly progressively be supplemented by, and perhaps even eventually be eclipsed by, estimates of these longer-term impacts. Of course, since people respond to expected future outcomes, these longer-term impacts may indeed be felt quite quickly.

Whether one believes the theory (and the empirical work based on it) of human capital, life-cycle accumulation, bequests, etc. is sufficiently advanced to provide some reasonably accurate information for the analysis of tax and spending policy is an issue upon which reasonable people can disagree. However, an historian of economic thought writing two or three decades from now will undoubtedly argue that there was something of a turning point in analyses of public finance in the 1970s and 1980s away from the shorter time horizons to longer ones; away from assumptions of substantial inelasticities to attempts to estimate the behavioural parameters with improved econometric techniques and data; and to the incorporation of the notion of expected future values and occurrences in fiscal policy into the behavioural responses of consumers and investors. This much is certain to survive; which particular models and estimates will prove robust remain to be seen. Further, it seems certain that the notion of a heterogeneous population not only in their endowments, but in their tastes, and other attributes will become more and more important in such analyses in the future.

MACROECONOMICS

In the decade and a half since I have left graduate school, the burst of intellectual activity in macroeconomics has been spectacular. While clearly there is no consensus among macroeconomists today about an 'appropriate' model to describe macroeconomic performance, in either closed or open economies, I believe much progress has been made, even though the naïve and simplistic early post-Second World War Keynesian models have had to be abandoned in the process. Life has become more difficult, but this is merely because some excellent research has raised more questions than it has yet been able to answer definitively. Indeed, when I was a graduate student in the late 1960s and early 1970s, so sure were the post-Keynesians of their analyses, forecasting ability, and the ability of demand management to fine-tune the economy that papers were written entitled, 'Is the Business Cycle Obsolete?' Clearly, this was presumptuous.

The re-emphasis of the role of expectations, incentives, and time horizons has been among the most interesting developments in macroeconomics, and in public finance.[10] Much emphasis has been given to attempting to reconcile short-run and long-run behaviour. While I think it would be going overboard to suggest that these important analytical developments, combined with mixed empirical results, should lead us to abandon the view that fiscal policy can have any stabilizing influence on the economy, it surely has given us pause to re-evaluate the extravagant claims made for the efficacy of such policies. Too often, in the economics profession, there seems to be a bifurcation into those who are looking at 'short-run' phenomena and those who are looking at 'long-run' phenomena. Often developments go merrily along their way within each of these two groups of researchers, and the harder work of reconciling the two is left unattended. This left some curious intellectual gaps, and while no definitive answers have been provided, those seeking to analyse, forecast, or prescribe policy based on the short run have had to re-evaluate their positions. Probably the most obvious of these concerns the 'natural rate' hypothesis of Friedman[11] and Phelps.[12] They have argued that anticipated inflation would be neutral in its effect on employment, and only unanticipated inflation could be expected to stimulate employment. Many macroeconomists today still claim that the short run is at least a partially Keynesian world (perhaps due to liquidity constrained consumers), while conceding the long run to the natural rate hypothesis. Lucas,[13] as so often, has provided a simple insight into this irreconcilability. As an activist demand manager, consider using a particular short-run macroeconometric model to guide the choice of money growth year by year, based on conditions in that year. Conceding the long run to the natural rate hypothesis, use it to guide the average rate of money growth over, say, a decade. As Lucas notes:

> Too late! This decision has already been made. . . If we concede that Model A gives us an inaccurate view of the 'long-run' than we have conceded that it leads us to bad short-run decisions because these decisions are sufficient to dictate our long-run situation as well. (This is not a hypothetical story of the 1980s, is it? It is a history of the 1970s.)

Thus, inflationary expectations play a central role in the efficacy of short-run monetary policy, even though it is the _long-run_ neutrality of money that is emphasized. As with monetary policy, so with fiscal policy in recent analytical developments.

The most important attack on the efficacy of fiscal policy (in the sense of deficit financed tax reductions, given government spending) is that of Barro,[14] building on work that dates from Ricardo. Barro develops a model of overlapping generations, where the well-being of a representative individual in each generation depends not only on his own lifetime consumption, but also upon the consumption preferences of his heirs. Thus, _all_ generations are linked because the parents are concerned about the well-being of their children, but their children's well-being depends upon the well-being of _their_ children. In such a model, the observation of substantial positive bequests of the older to the younger generations, as is the case in the USA, has striking implications for interpreting the potential efficacy of fiscal policy. Substitution of debt for tax finance may alter, in the first instance, the pattern of debt burdens by age; apparently, older workers and retirees will be getting a break, shifting the burden on to younger workers. Note, however, that the debt finance commits the government to a stream of future interest payments and possible repayments of principal. These must be financed by future taxes whose present value approximate the value of the debt. Since those who are paying taxes currently shift the liability to future generations, they can undo this shift in tax burdens to future generations themselves by adjusting their bequests. Since they are already at an interior solution, so long as we do not move to a corner, changes in private intra-family intergenerational transfers of income will offset the government's fiscal policy, thereby leading to no perceived changes in wealth for consumers. Thus, there will be no change in spending, and therefore, no stimulative effect from the fiscal policy.

Many caveats have been raised to the Barro proposition,[15] ranging from the fact that only a small fraction of decedents leave direct bequests to their heirs to the argument that many who would like to leave negative bequests, because they are not enforceable, leave nothing. *Inter vivos* gifts are difficult to measure; parental support of education and child-rearing may have to be included as well. Barro argues that this argument is of an order of magnitude more important than the shapes of IS-LM curves in determining the efficacy of fiscal policy.

Note the key role that expectations, incentives, and time horizons play in this argument.[16] The time horizon has been extended from that of a single short period, say, a year (the traditional focus on current disposable income in Keynesian analyses), beyond the life-cycle considerations of Modigliani (the inclusion of a lagged wealth term in the consumption function implying an average propensity to consume over the life-cycle of one) to intergenerational issues. Further, the concern of parents for their children leads to a consideration whereby all future generations are linked, thus the time horizon is approaching infinity. The assumption is that individuals are willing and able to alter their saving/bequest behaviour in order to adjust to their optimal intertemporal (including across generations) consumption preferences, given their resource constraint. It is the *expectation* of future taxes that produces the result that there is no perceived change in wealth for *current* consumers, and hence no impact on aggregate demand. Each of these assumptions has been attacked as oversimplified. For example, as mentioned above, the population is quite heterogeneous with respect to their actual bequests; the majority leave virtually nothing. Substantial uncertainty may exist about future taxes, and hence, they may be heavily discounted, and on and on. While these are all interesting and important empirical matters, my major point is not that this analysis has, should, or would completely replace older notions of the stimulative effects of deficit finance versus tax finance, but these insights arc likely to leave a mark on all future research on fiscal policy, and that their underpinnings are a re-examination of time horizon, incentives, and expectations.

An important distinction must be made between the inability of any particular model to describe saving behaviour accurately at any particular point in time, and who is affecting what at the margin. Perhaps only a fraction of the population may genuinely behave in a Barro-fashion, and upon examining actual data on savings and/or bequests, one might deduce some mixture of short-run, life-cycle and intergenerational motives operating, but this would not necessarily imply that Barro's conclusions do not hold. If there is enough of such intergenerational behaviour at the margin, it will be driving the final results in equilibrium, even though there may be many inframarginal adjustments and events it does not explain well.

Even those concerned with long-run aspects of fiscal policy have begun

to see differences in implications for both growth policy and public investment criteria of longer time horizons and expectations and assumptions
about incentives. The long debate over the social rate of discount and the
appropriate shadow price or opportunity cost of public funds has led back
to estimates of the interest elasticity of saving and investment. Some of
the early work on the social rate of discount built arguments based on
assumptions of saving being a simple function of disposable income; later
work argued that individuals or the government operating paternalistically
could be modelled as maximizing the infinite sum of discounted utility.
This latter assumption has a striking implication, namely that in the long
run consumer equilibrium implies that the net of tax rate of interest is a
constant equal to the pure rate of time preference plus the elasticity of
marginal utility times the Harrod neutral rate of labour augmenting
technical change. Thus, the supply of capital is perfectly elastic in the long
run. Think of what this simple assumption, which may not be all that
unreasonable, does to a host of policy prescriptions!

As with my conclusion for distribution and incidence analysis in public
finance, my conclusion as a conjectural historian of economic thought is
that the macroeconomics of the last fifteen years will be viewed primarily
as having brought the issues of time horizon, incentives, and expectations
to the fore. Probably no particular model currently used will survive. This
is because the difficult task of reconciling short-run observed phenomena
with long-run analytical implications has been done primarily via a series
of parables and examples. I think these have taught us much, but they
obviously have a long way to go as complete descriptions and empirically
implementable models.

CONCLUSION

The renewed emphasis on time horizons, incentives, and expectations is a
healthy development for both micro- and macroeconomics, and for my
own particular field, public finance, and all that it implies for the analysis
of public policy. While most of the analytical results suggest that the hard
work of producing improved and reliable statistical estimates of these
incentive effects, empirical models of the formation of expectations, etc. is
still to be done, I do not think that we should view the last fifteen years in
the nihilistic way that some commentators do. Because we have had
revealed to us that the world was somewhat more complicated than the
simple models used day to day in the 1960s in analysing distribution and
macroeconomic, especially policy, issues, and because we do not yet have

very accurate answers to such perplexing questions as to how to combine the assumptions of various models in a way that provides the most predictive power under more general conditions, I believe that enormous progress has been made.

In addition to the important analytical work to be done, the paucity of our empirical knowledge must also be emphasized. While I believe that we will never return to the assumption that everything is inelastic or that this is sufficient for policy prescription purposes, our priorities on the relevant elasticities (despite substantial and improved empirical work in the last decade) are still quite diffuse. For example, effective labour supply reflects decisions on hours of work, human investment and effort, as well as individual ability. Little is known empirically about the determinants of how hard people work. Nor do we have much agreement on the determinants of human investment, other than the general supposition that they respond to costs and returns. Most of the progress made in analysing labour supply incentives has been on those reflected in labour force participation and hours of work.[17] While it is beyond the scope of this chapter to give a substantive review of this literature here, I have elsewhere argued that a reasonable summary would be that such labour supply elasticities are quite small (perhaps one-half or less) for the largest group in the labour force — prime-age husbands. For secondary workers — particularly second earners in the family and elderly persons — the wage elasticity of labour supply so measured may exceed unity.

From the detailed econometric studies of labour supply, it would be hard to gleam the very large intertemporal substitution elasticities necessary to form the lynchpin of recent business-cycle theories. But these data and analyses are primarily addressed to longer-term issues; the central focus of Lucas-type models of business cycles revolves around the fact that very short-term elasticities may be quite large as people see and take advantage of temporary opportunities. On this point, I remain agnostic. It is an interesting conjecture, but one that is difficult to evaluate empirically.

What about the interest elasticity of saving? Once again, the relevant time horizon, assumptions about the appropriate experiment being performed (what is being held constant, what varied), etc. must be answered even to interpret the consumption function estimates that I and others have estimated. Given this caveat, what appeared revolutionary as little as five years ago, namely that the interest elasticity of saving may be a small positive number, does not appear so revolutionary today. Indeed, there seems to be a time trend in the estimated elasticities drifting them upward. Once again, the issue of the appropriate time horizon under consideration is quite important. For example, my estimate of 0.4, when interpreted in a lifetime context, should be about doubled in moving from an annual rate to the lifetime saving/dissaving profile change.

What is important is that even elasticities of this order of magnitude (perhaps one-half for labour supply or slightly less; modest, but positive for private saving) have striking implications for a variety of analyses. As noted above, such an interest rate elasticity implies that a substantial fraction of taxes on capital is *ultimately* shifted on to labour; that the shadow price or social opportunity cost of public funds is somewhat below the private marginal product of capital, since some of the funds come from increased private saving, as opposed just to forgone private investment; etc.

It is also clear that the beginnings of the empirical research and the extent to which consumers anticipate future taxes should at the very least lead us to question the simple specification of a consumption function, ignoring the potentially expected future changes in private resources. Much remains to be done on this score, including the fact that typical budget documents, especially those for the USA, drastically misstate the relevant fiscal policy numbers (expenditures, taxes, deficits, and debt).

Perhaps it is a reflection of my age that I am excited about the prospects for learning more about the operation of the macroeconomy, the distribution of income, and the incidence of taxes and transfers. Economists of my generation apparently will have much to keep them busy for years ahead. Those who look back on the last fifteen years as only having undermined particular models, policy prescriptions, etc., are missing the point. Einstein once said that it is the ultimate honour of all analysis to be replaced by more general analysis. It would be misleading to describe recent trends in macroeconomics and in public finance as having replaced earlier models and estimates in anywhere near the same way that relativity supplanted Newtonian physics. Future historians of economic thought, however, may well look back on this last decade and a half as having been the era in which economic events, economic analysis, data and techniques led to the widespread belief that the earlier analyses, models, and data were incomplete and, in some cases, inaccurate and misleading. And that by a renewed focus on a longer time horizon, the relative importance of various incentives, and of expectations, improved understanding of economic phenomena may ultimately result.

NOTES

1. While we cannot review the literature here, the seminal work of

Schultz, Becker, Mincer, Modigliani, and others have now become part of the tool kit of practitioners in public finance, although these models were mostly developed for application in labour economics and macroeconomics respectively.
2. See, Jorgenson and Pachon, 1981.
3. See, among others, Feldstein, 1974.
4. See US Senate, Committee on Finance, 1982.
5. This is not the appropriate place to review the development of human capital theory or of life-cycle saving theory. However, this seminal work, originally developed for analyses in labour economics and macroeconomics respectively, has become quite important in public finance. Today's public financiers owe much to Schultz, Becker, Modigliani *et al.*
6. See Boskin and Shoven, 1980.
7. See Boskin, 1978.
8. See Auerbach, Kotlikoff and Skinner, 1983.
9. See Shoven *et al.*, 1982.
10. Some observers may argue that the key issue in macroeconomics is whether one insists on an equilibrium model of business cycles. Clearly the fixprice equilibria systems are important contributors to understanding short-run performance, but mostly they leave the question of why these price rigidities persist unanswered. Transaction costs, information issues, etc., are the usual culprits. For example, the tendency for union contracts to extend over three years is often mentioned. However, clearly such contractual arrangements must eventually be taken as endogenous. Thus, the time-frame over which fixprice models may be expected to apply is limited, but not necessarily unimportant. In any event, I believe this issue is really a component of the broader concern with time-horizons, expectations and incentives, and hence I do not stress it here.
11. See Friedman, 1968.
12. See Phelps, 1968.
13. See Lucas, 1981.
14. See Barro, 1974.
15. See Feldstein, 1979.
16. They are also important in other contributions to macroeconomics. For example, Feldstein (1983) correctly points to the nature of the tax structure influencing investment incentives and the *interpretation* of monetary policy in an inflationary economy without perfectly indexed taxes.
17. These are discussed in more detail in Boskin, 1981.

REFERENCES

Auerbach, A., Kotlikoff, L., and J. Skinner (1983) 'The Efficiency Gains from Dynamic Tax Reform', *International Economic Review* (February). 24 (1): 81–100.

Barro, R. (1974) 'Are Government Bonds Net Wealth?' *Journal of Political Economy* 82 (November/December). 1095-1117.

Boskin, M. (1978) 'Taxation, Saving and the Rate of Interest', *Journal of Political Economy* 86 (April). Part II 5-3-5-27.

Boskin, M. (1981) 'Some Issues in "Supply-side" Economics' in K. Brunner and A. H. Meltzer (eds), *Supply Shocks, Incentives and National Wealth*, Carnegie-Rochester Conference Series on Public Policy. Vol. 14. Amsterdam: North-Holland, pp. 201-20.

Boskin, M., and J. Shoven (1980) 'Issues in the Taxation of Capital Income in the US', *American Economic Review* 70 (May). 164-70.

Feldstein, M. (1974) 'Tax Incidence In a Growing Economy with Variable Factor Supply', *Quarterly Journal of Economics* 88 (November). 551-73.

Feldstein, M. (1979) 'The Effect of Social Security on Private Saving: The Time Series Evidence', NBER Working Paper no. 314 (February).

Feldstein, M. (1983) 'The Fiscal Framework of Monetary Policy', *Economic Inquiry* 21 (January). 11-23.

Friedman, M. (1968) 'The Role of Monetary Policy', *American Economic Review* 58 (March). pp. 1-17.

Jorgenson, D., and A. Pachon 'Lifetime Income and Human Capital', Harvard Discussion Paper no. 781 (February).

Lucas, R. (1981) 'Tobin and Monetarism: A Review Article', *Journal of Economic Literature* 19 (June). 558-67.

Pechman, J., and B. Okner (1972) 'Individual Income Tax Erosion by Income Class', in US Congress, Joint Economic Committee, *General Study Papers*, Part I. Washington: GPO, 13-40.

Phelps, E. (1968) 'Money–Wage Dynamics and Labor Market Equilibrium', *Journal of Political Economy* 76 (July/August). 678-711.

Shoven, J., J. Whalley, C. Ballard, and L. Goulder (1982) 'General Equilibrium Simulation of Tax Reform' (mimeo).

US Senate, Committee on Finance (1982) 'Long-Range Status of Social Security Trust Funds', (December). Washington: GPO.

Index*

*See also the index to *Issues in Contemporary Microeconomics and Welfare*.